ENTANGLING ALLIANCE

There is nothing which will have a greater effect to overawe the English, and induce them to respect us and our rights, than the Reputation of a good understnading with the French. My voice and advice will, therefore, always be for discharging, with the utmost fidelity, gratitude, and exactness, every obligation we are under to France, and for cultivating her friendship and alliance by all sorts of good offices.

John Adams to Robert R. Livingston,
Paris, July 11, 1783

For unless treaties are mutually beneficial to the Parties, it is in vain to hope for a continuance of them beyond the moment when the one which conceives itself to be overreached is in a situation to break off the connexion. And I believe it is among nations as with individuals, the party taking advantage of the distresses of another will lose infinitely more in the opinion of mankind and in subsequent events than he will gain by the stroke of the moment.

George Washington to Gouverneur Morris,
Philadelphia, July 28, 1791

The Jacobin's Creed

I believe there is no God but nature; no religion but revolution (alias regeneration;) no just government but anarchy; and no civil liberty where the guillotine is not erected.

I believe that Roberspierre [sic] was the great apostle of liberty, and that he would have emancipated the whole world from the shackles of laws, had not death cut short his glorious career.

I believe Genet is a prodigy of wisdom, and that his ipse dixit is better authority than Montesquieu, Pufferdorf [sic], and Vattel, those musty, antiquated aristocrats.

I believe that war is better than peace, confusion than order, terror than mildness, and the guillotine than all the courts of justice extant.

I believe that the United States of America ought to be under the direction of my brothers in France, and that George Washington, commonly called President Washington, is an impertinent jackanapes for counteracting our noble designs.

I believe the terrorists were a band of consummate statesmen, genuine patriots, great benefactors, and virtuous representatives.

I believe that no person who dissents from our fraternity, ought to be permitted to speak, write or communicate his sentiments.

*The New Hampshire and Vermont Journal:
Or, The Farmer's Weekly Museum*
(Walpole, N. H.), July 12, 1796.

ENTANGLING ALLIANCE

Politics & Diplomacy under George Washington

by

Alexander DeConde

DUKE UNIVERSITY PRESS   *Durham, N. C.*   1958

PRINTED IN THE UNITED STATES OF AMERICA
BY THE SEEMAN PRINTERY, INC., DURHAM, N. C.

To Thomas A. Bailey

TEACHER AND FRIEND

PREFACE

THIS IS the first book to deal with the interaction of politics and diplomacy centering on the French alliance of 1778 in the Washington years, and the second book to treat the alliance as a central theme. The first, Edward S. Corwin's *French Policy and the American Alliance of 1778* (Princeton, 1916), covered the period of the alliance's origins to the Treaty of Paris of September 3, 1783. Based primarily on French archival sources, written from the viewpoint of European diplomacy, and concentrating on diplomatic history almost exclusively, it concluded that even though by treaty the alliance remained in force it really ended with the peace of 1783. The alliance had done its work. The United States were free and independent and France had deprived Great Britain of a vast continent.

While stressing the Washington years, this book takes up where Professor Corwin ended, touching on the period of the Confederation, taking into account changes in points of view toward the alliance by both France and America, and showing that for over a decade the alliance still lived. Although this book covers basically the presidency of George Washington from 1789 to 1797 and assesses the period as diplomatic history, it is not a diplomatic history in the traditional sense; it is a synthesis of domestic political history and diplomatic history. Its main theme is the interaction of foreign policy and domestic politics centering on the French alliance. Although I hope it will contribute to a better understanding of Washington's presidency, it does not attempt to fill the need for a full and satisfactory account of Washington as President.[1]

[1] After the type for this book had been set, Charles Scribner's Sons published *George Washington: First in Peace* (New York, 1957). This volume, which concludes Douglas Southall Freeman's biography of Washington (six volumes of which had been completed before Freeman's death), was written by John Alexander Carroll and Mary Ashworth Wells, Freeman's former

At the beginning of the federal government, as George Washington took office, the French alliance was the cornerstone of American foreign policy; it had contributed immeasurably to American independence and had established American foreign policy orientation. At the end of Washington's second term, in fact as he prepared his farewell to public life, the life-giving alliance was dead and the United States were virtually at war with France. The main problem dealt with in this book is how and why in eight formative years such a drastic reversal in foreign policy took place.

In probing the problem I have attempted, wherever possible, to analyze the role of ideas and attitudes in the evolving Franco-American rupture. This approach, within the context of the main theme, led to an analysis of the origins of national political parties as well as of the origins of foreign policy, for from the beginning foreign policy mixed with domestic politics; it was an intrinsic part of party origins.

In dealing with conflicting ideas, I have tried, wherever appropriate, to show the relationship between domestic political developments and foreign policy and also the political basis for foreign-policy decisions. In stressing the relations of domestic politics and diplomacy, I encountered the usual difficult questions: What influenced foreign policy and how? Was determination of foreign policy in these formative years governed by the idea? Did foreign policy in practice conform to principle or was it *ad hoc?*

If one were to view history in its broad sweep where the human actors, like figures in a Chinese landscape painting, are dwarfed and appear insignificant in comparison to impersonal forces overshadowing them, the answers to such questions might not appear perplexing. In a detailed study of this kind, however, big questions cannot be satisfactorily answered with broad generalizations. The more we concentrate on individual men, on their special ideas, and on the events they influenced, perhaps decisively, the more important the role of the individual, of the individual idea, and of the specific event seems. While each piece of the pattern may conform to a general idea, each fitting of the piece appears *ad hoc,* a unique approach, at a unique time, to a unique problem.

assistants. It covers the last seven years of Washington's life, including his second term as President.

Whether the decisive factor in determining foreign policy was the *ad hoc* response to the special situation or the over-all idea or principle apparently was not preordained by circumstances, but depended upon the particular situation. In sum, the application of the principle, if principle appears the determining factor, was *ad hoc*.

While dealing primarily with men and events, I have emphasized analysis, interpretation, and ideas, trying to weave these into the narrative. This kind of problem-analysis cannot be confined easily to straight chronological treatment. The same problems, the same policies, the same developments, to be understood, often have to be approached from different angles and perspectives; hence there is bound to be some repetition. The Jay treaty, for example, had to be approached from three different avenues: I had to take into consideration the British position, the French position, and the role of American politics and diplomacy. I endeavored to keep repetition to a minimum, using it only for clarity and emphasis.

In dealing with ideas, I have tried not to isolate them but to relate thought to action. Wherever possible I sought to pin down ideas to specific events, hoping to avoid the pitfall of supporting an idea of one year with the events of other years. Men and ideas change; out-of-context ideas tend to give a distorted view of history. This is one reason why I tried to support most citations with place and date. Except for illustrative purposes, I have cast a wary eye on official documents, particularly party pronouncements, official defenses, and personal apologies. Policy, even though embedded in ideas, is the unfolding of events, not the uttering of pious words.

* * * * *

While my sources are varied the book is based primarily on a re-examination of original sources. I relied often on the invaluable contributions of other scholars, but usually I traced their work to the sources. In many instances ideas were original with the men who wrote on the period. To them I am most grateful and acknowledge a great debt, and I hope that in the text I have given adequate recognition to the sources of ideas and interpretations.

From the three major countries in this study, France, Great Britain, and the United States, I have used archival material, manuscript and printed, without, I hope, giving an official cast to my findings. Some of the most illuminating sources proved to be the writings of partisan observers, secondary statesmen, and men of ideas and discernment contemporary with the events studied. Personal dispatches, letters, diaries, and newspapers proved, in most cases, more enlightening than official documents. I hope that in their presentation and refinement they prove as much a challenge and a stimulus to the reader as they did to the writer.

Like all who have attempted works of historical synthesis I am indebted to many for help. To those who have aided directly and indirectly I am deeply grateful. The following merit my special appreciation. Professor Thomas A. Bailey of Stanford University provided encouragement from beginning to end. My colleagues in the Duke University Department of History took time from their own pressing obligations to aid me when needed. Professor Paul H. Clyde gave portions of the manuscript exacting textual criticisms and offered sound counsel; Professor William T. Laprade read the entire manuscript and saved me from grievous errors; Professor John R. Alden also read the entire manuscript; contributed valuable suggestions, and gave personal guidance; Professor John Tate Lanning gave help when sorely needed. Professor Russell A. Fraser of the Princeton University Department of English read parts of the manuscript and uncovered flaws in English usage and style. Ashbel G. Brice, Director of Duke University Press, gave courteous and needed assistance and John Menapace, also of Duke University Press, contributed long hours of invaluable editorial help. All share in whatever merits the book may have, but the shortcomings, of course, are mine.

I am also indebted to several foundations which have contributed generously to the improvement of American historical scholarship. In particular I owe thanks to the Social Science Research Council for a grant-in-aid-of-research for 1951 and to the Duke University Council on Research for financial support in research and publication. Without their assistance I could not have completed the research on which this book is based.

The staffs of libraries and historical societies without exception provided courteous and generous help. In particular I thank the staff of Duke University Library for assistance beyond the requirements of duty. Mr. Benjamin E. Powell, Mr. John P. Waggoner, Mr. Elvin Strowd, Miss Gertrude Merritt, Miss Wilhelmina Leman,

Miss Shirley Stevens, Mrs. Catharine J. Pierce, Miss Florence E.
Blakely, Mrs. Margaret Thomson, Miss Mattie Russell, and Mr.
Emerson Ford merit personal appreciation. In my earlier researches
the staff of the Huntington Library made the life of scholarship
notably pleasant. Miss Norma B. Cuthbert and Miss Mary Isabel
Fry showed an unusual consideration for my problems. In the
Manuscripts Division of the Library of Congress Mr. Robert H.
Land, Mr. Percy C. Powell, and Mr. John J. de Porry, not only were
gracious in their help, but also made my research trips to Washington pleasant personal experiences. I owe Mrs. Frank A. Hanna
more than the usual thanks for typing the final draft of my manuscript. My wife, Jeanne Seeger DeConde, gave encouragement and
assumed more than her share of family obligations while this book
was in progress.

ALEXANDER DeCONDE

Durham, North Carolina
July 1, 1956

BIBLIOGRAPHICAL NOTE

SINCE THE FOOTNOTES are unusually full and should serve as satisfactory guides for those who may wish to trace through the sources, this book does not have a formal bibliography. The first entry of any item is listed by author in the index so that the interested reader may easily obtain the full title by turning to the page where it is cited. Most of the printed materials used in this study may be obtained in any of a number of major research libraries in the United States. Most of the newspapers cited are in the Duke University Library, the Huntington Library, San Marino, California, and the Library of Congress. The manuscript sources are in a number of scattered depositories; the place of each depository is mentioned with the first entry of each manuscript citation.

Below are a number of journal titles most frequently cited and their abbreviations as used in this book.

Alumni Bulletin of the University of Virginia   ABUV
American Historical Association Annual Report   AHA Ann Rep (year)
American Historical Review   AHR
American Journal of International Law   AJIL
Columbia University Quarterly   CUQ
French-American Review   FAR
Historical Magazine   HM
Journal of Economic and Business History   JEBH
Journal of Modern History   JMH
Journal of Race Development   JRD
Journal of Southern History   JSH
Mississippi Valley Historical Review   MVHR
New England Quarterly   NEQ
Pennsylvania Magazine of History and Biography   PMHB
Political Science Quarterly   PSQ

Proceedings of the American Antiquarian Society PAAS
Quarterly Journal of the University of North Dakota QJUND
Revue des deux mondes RDM
Revue d'histoire diplomatique RHD
Review of Politics RP
South Atlantic Quarterly SAQ
Southwestern Social Science Quarterly SSSQ
Virginia Magazine of History and Biography VMHB
William and Mary Quarterly WMQ
World Politics WP

CONTENTS

ENTANGLING ALLIANCE

CHAPTER ONE

BASIS FOR ACCORD AND
SEEDS OF DISCORD

They [the French] are interested in separating us from Great Britain, and on that point we may, I believe, depend upon them; but it is not their interest that we should become a great and formidable people, and therefore they will not help us to become so.—John Jay to Robert R. Livingston, Paris, November 17, 1782.

It is our firm connexion with France that gives us weight with England and respect throughout Europe. If we were to break our faith with this nation, on whatever pretense, *England would again trample on us and every other nation despise us. . . .*

In my opinion, the true political interest of America consists in obsering and fulfilling, with greatest exactitude, the engagements of our alliance with France, and behaving at the same time towards England so as not entirely to extinguish her hopes of a reconciliation.—Benjamin Franklin to Samuel Cooper, Passy, France, December 26, 1782.

*   *   *   *   *

T HE DAY [March 4, 1797] ought to be a JUBILEE in the United States," exulted the Republican press.[1] Why? Was it because austere John Adams had just become President? Actually, the cause for jubilation was the end of the second administration of President George Washington. On this day he ceased to guide the new nation he had fathered. The attacks of his political opponents and their

[1] *Aurora* (Philadelphia), March 6, 1797, quoted in John B. McMaster, *A History of the People of the United States from the Revolution to the Civil War* (8 vols., New York, 1886-1926), II, 306 n.

unconcealed joy over his departure marked the failure of an ideal. Washington had hoped to establish a nation without political parties, a land freed from the woes and jealousies of Europe.

According to his enemies, "after bringing the country to the very brink of ruin, Washington had fled from the gathering storm. Having run the ship [of state] between rocks and shoals, he had abandoned the helm and left the vessel to her fate." When he became President, "America was indeed a happy land; now by his means she has become most miserable. Then every Frenchman was her friend; now every Frenchman is her foe."[2] The criticism, however unjust, penetrated to the core of the dominant problem of Washington's last years in office. From friend to foe in eight years, this was indeed a turnabout in Franco-American relations.

Why and how did such a drastic reversal take place? What were the causes and what were the forces involved? What happened to the life-giving Franco-American alliance of 1778 which was to endure "forever"? What were the politics of these years and how did they affect American foreign policy? For answers to these questions and to others equally significant we shall have to go back to the beginning of George Washington's first term and also glance briefly at the earlier background of American foreign relations.

*   *   *   *   *

Ever since France had aided Americans in their revolution against England she had occupied a special place in American hearts. Regardless of the motives behind French help, most Americans believed that without France there probably would have been no United States of America.[3] The bonds between the United

---

[2] *Aurora* (Philadelphia), March 13, 14, 1797, cited in *ibid*.

[3] For differing views on why France aided the colonies, see Edward S. Corwin, *French Policy and the American Alliance of 1778* (Princeton, 1916), pp. 1-22 (this is the standard study of the French alliance through 1783); Claude H. Van Tyne, "Influences Which Determined the French Government to Make the Treaty with America, 1778," *American Historical Review*, XXI (April, 1916), 528-541; see also Samuel F. Bemis, *The Diplomacy of the American Revolution* (New York, 1935), pp. 41-69 (this is the basic study for the diplomacy of the period and is based on wide knowledge of the sources). For basic French documents on the alliance, see Henri Doniol, ed., *Histoire de la participation de la France à l'établissement des États-Unis d'Amérique* (5 vols., Paris, 1886-92), V, 610 ff. See also the historical introduction in John J. Meng, ed., *Despatches and Instructions of Conrad Alex-*

States and France were wrought in the American Revolution and
went beyond formal agreements of friendship. Yet there were
formal agreements, two treaties signed at Paris on February 6,
1778.[4] The first, a "Treaty of Amity and Commerce," constituted
the first official recognition of the United States by a major power.
It brought France into the struggle against Great Britain. By its
terms both countries granted each other most-favored-nation treatment and other liberal trading privileges.

The second agreement was a "Treaty of Alliance." If war
should break out between France and Great Britain—a war which
was almost certain to follow—as a result of the first treaty, the
"defensive alliance" provided that France and the United States
would fight together until American independence was assured.
Neither party was to "conclude either Truce or Peace with Great
Britain, without the formal consent of the other first obtain'd."
France guaranteed American independence and territory "forever"
and renounced possession of any portion of the North American
mainland held by Great Britain in 1763. In return the United
States pledged to guarantee French possessions in America against
all powers "forever."[5]

Although partnership with France had been eagerly sought, some
Americans were reluctant to make a military alliance.[6] Men such
as John Adams, whose labors earned him the title "Atlas of Independence," did not like becoming embroiled in European conflicts,

---

*andre Gérard 1778-1780: Correspondence of the First French Minister to the
United States with the Comte de Vergennes* (Baltimore, 1939). Various
theories which attempt to explain the "why" of French aid to the American
cause are summarized in Arthur B. Darling, *Our Rising Empire 1763-1803*
(New Haven, 1940), pp. 22-26.

[4] For the texts of the treaties see David Hunter Miller, ed., *Treaties and
Other International Acts of the United States of America* (7 vols., Washington, 1931-), II, 3-41.

[5] Great Britain, through a spy, Dr. Edward Bancroft of Westfield, Massachusetts, knew of the terms of the alliance and of the commercial treaty long
before they were known in America. Samuel F. Bemis, "British Secret
Service and the French-American Alliance," *AHR*, XXIX (April, 1924), 490-
91.

[6] Dr. Benjamin Rush, for example, wrote to John Adams, Yorktown,
January 22, 1778, "Our people here pant for a French war," they wish and
pray for it. Lyman Butterfield, ed., *Letters of Benjamin Rush* (2 vols.,
Princeton, 1951), I, 190-191.

or having Europe become involved in American affairs.[7] Memories of past wars were too fresh.

As a member of the Continental Congress, Adams had opposed an alliance with France "which should entangle us in any future wars in Europe." Uncannily he had touched on the very problem which was to plague Washington, the question of foreign meddling in America's internal affairs. He stressed neutrality and warned against attachment to either England or France. He predicted that "in any future war, we must become too subordinate and dependent on that nation, and should be involved in all European wars, as we had been hitherto; that foreign powers would find means to corrupt our people, to influence our councils, and, in fine, we should be little better than puppets, danced on the wires of the cabinets of Europe. We should be the sport of European intrigues and politics."[8]

A few months later (March, 1776) Adams expressed his conception of an acceptable treaty with France. He wanted "only a commercial connection" and stressed the principle of no political and military connection.[9] Embodying a typically eighteenth-century idea, his concept of alliance did not imply a political bond. It

[7] For evidence of early isolationist sentiment in America, particularly as expressed by John Adams, see J. Fred Rippy and Angie Debo, "The Historical Background of the American Policy of Isolation," Smith College Studies in History, IX (April-July, 1924), 71-94; Gerald Stourzh, Benjamin Franklin and American Foreign Policy (Chicago, 1954), pp. 116-123. Professor Felix Gilbert, in a stimulating article, "The 'New Diplomacy' of the Eighteenth Century," World Politics, IV (Oct., 1951), 28 n., maintains "that the isolationist features of early American foreign policy have been overemphasized, and that, in the years of the beginnings of American independence, isolationist and internationalist elements are by no means clearly separated, but are mixed, and the course which American foreign policy would take was by no means fixed. These two contradictory trends could go hand in hand because both placed decisive importance on commerce." See also Gilbert, "The English Background of American Isolationism in the Eighteenth Century," William and Mary Quarterly, 3rd Series, I (April, 1944), 138-160.

[8] "Autobiography," 1775, in Charles F. Adams, ed., The Works of John Adams (10 vols., Boston, 1850-1856), II, 505. Hereinafter cited as Adams, Works.

[9] "Notes of Debates in the Continental Congress," March 4, 1776, in Adams, Works, II, 488-489. Adams frequently emphasized this idea. To John Winthrop, for example, he declared that "I am not for soliciting any political connection, or military assistance, or indeed naval, from France. I wish for nothing but commerce, a mere marine treaty with them." Philadelphia, June 23, 1776, ibid., IX, 409.

called for political co-operation by the contracting parties without necessarily creating a binding political connection. So, even though the United States did ally itself to France, Adams believed that America's contacts with her, as with other nations, should be limited to trade. Avoid dependence upon any one power of Europe and shun all obligations and temptations to take part in European wars, he warned; "the business of America with Europe was commerce, not politics or war."[10]

Adams's reasoning developed logically from his eighteenth-century concept of alliance, a concept shared by other Americans. This reasoning discerned little difference between the two French treaties of 1778. In fact, the separation of political treaties from those of commerce marked a new departure in diplomacy.[11]

When the United States negotiated the French treaties the concept of alliance was in transition; it did not yet definitely carry the modern connotation of a military-political commitment. At the time, in keeping with past usage, many American statesmen saw little distinction between the treaty of alliance and that of commerce. Oftentimes they referred to both collectively as either the treaty of alliance or the treaty of commerce. Even though France entered the Revolutionary War against England under the terms of the alliance, Congress held to the doctrine that America's future relations with other nations—France included—should be restricted to trade and commerce. In this, American statesmen acted in accord with radical eighteenth-century thought.[12]

Regardless of the background of ideas, contradictory or otherwise, American policy was governed by existing conditions. Despite what seemed obvious dangers, in times of distress a weak power groping for aid had no choice. It had to risk even puppetry and grasp the hand of the devil if proffered, well-reasoned theories and fears notwithstanding. At Valley Forge General George Washington greeted the news of the French alliance with "heartfelt joy," recognizing that it was "big with important events," and that it must

[10] Adams to Secretary Robert R. Livingston, Paris, February 5, 1783, in Adams, *Works*, VIII, 35.

[11] For a discussion of these ideas on alliance and isolation, see Gilbert, "The 'New Diplomacy' of the Eighteenth Century," *WP*, IV, 19-20.

[12] *Ibid.*, pp. 27-28.

"chalk out a plain and easy road to independence."[13] Franco-American friendship thus was tempered in war—purportedly "forever."

* * * * *

As a result of the French alliance, the revolt of a few American colonists touched off a world war, a war in which the major antagonists were France and Great Britain. On the allied side the role of the American states was relatively minor. Beset on all sides by enemies, Great Britain finally acquiesced in independence for her thirteen rebelling colonies. Independence followed the surrender on October 19, 1781, at Yorktown, Virginia, where France's temporary command of the sea, combined with George Washington's land armies—composed by almost half of Frenchmen—brought victory. But military victory did not bind the French and American allies any closer; instead, it disclosed the flaws in their alliance.

During the period of the war partnership the aim of the French government had been independence for the United States and destruction of English power, with the latter objective foremost. Frenchmen rejoiced over victory in America not because Americans had won independence, but primarily because it dealt England— her trade and her empire—a severe blow.[14] The French government, with these objectives foremost, had tried to direct American policy and government to the ends of its foreign policy. If France did not expect Americans to dance like "puppets" on the wire, she did expect them to take their cue from her and to subordinate themselves to her in many matters of policy.[15]

[13] Washington to Richard Henry Lee, Valley Forge, May 25, 1778, in John C. Fitzpatrick, ed., *The Writings of George Washington from the Original Manuscript Sources, 1745-1799* (39 vols., Washington, 1931-44), XI, 450. Hereinafter cited as Fitzpatrick, *Washington's Writings.*

[14] Louis R. Gottschalk, *The Place of the American Revolution in the Causal Pattern of the French Revolution* (Easton, Penn., 1948), p. 8; Corwin, *French Policy and the American Alliance . . . ,* pp. 1-22; Carl L. Lokke, *France and the Colonial Question: A Study of Contemporary French Opinion, 1763-1801* (New York, 1932), pp. 62-64.

[15] Years later Federalist politicians, intent on counteracting pro-French sentiment in the United States, claimed that from the beginning of the French alliance the French court "did not wish to see us absolutely independent." It wished for an immortal hatred between the United States and Great Britain. William Vans Murray Papers, Commonplace Book, October [?], 1796, Princeton University Library (microfilm copies in the Huntington

With the coming of peace, on the other hand, British foreign policy strove to destroy the close friendship between France and her American ally. In keeping with this objective Great Britain granted liberal terms—out of proportion to the actual military situation— to the United States in the Treaty of Paris signed on September 3, 1783.[16] So generous was the definitive peace treaty that in England patriots condemned it. Regardless of impassioned public feelings in England, the treaty fitted well the policy of weaning the United States from postwar French influence. Where English force had failed, English diplomacy might succeed.

Contrary to the spirit if not the strict letter of the French alliance, the American peace commissioners had conducted separate peace negotiations with Great Britain. When France learned of the negotiations she naturally resented being by-passed. The French government had expected, as an ally, to be informed of all stages of any negotiations. Congress had so instructed the American commissioners. As things turned out, however, the American commissioners did not consult France on the terms of the preliminary treaty; they laid the foundation for the final Anglo-American peace settlement without French participation.

One reason for this independent American diplomacy was that some highly placed Americans distrusted the French alliance. Now that peace was theirs certain influential American statesmen looked upon the alliance as a nuisance, as something to jettison as soon as possible. John Jay, who was instrumental, with Benjamin Franklin, in bypassing the French in the peace negotiations, supported this view. At this time Jay did not mean "that we should deviate in

Library, San Marino, California). Some Americans had feared just such a consequence flowing from the French alliance, that it would lead them into having their allies at last as their masters. See "To The People of Pennsylvania.—Letter V," signed Cato, March 1776, in Peter Force, comp., *American Archives,* 4th Series (9 vols., Washington, 1837-53), V, 542-543.

[16] For the text of the treaty, see Miller, *Treaties* . . . , II, 151-156; for Britain's reasons in granting generous peace terms, see A. L. Burt, *The United States and Great Britain and British North America from the Revolution to the Establishment of Peace after the War of 1812* (New Haven, 1940), pp. 33-34; Bemis, *Diplomacy of the American Revolution,* pp. 248-249; Vincent T. Harlow, *The Founding of the Second British Empire, 1763-1793* (London, 1952), pp. 232-34, 299-300; Edmond G. P. Fitzmaurice, *Life of William, Earl of Shelburne* . . . (2nd and rev. ed.; 2 vols., London, 1912), II, 187.

the least from our treaty with France; our honour and our interest
are concerned in inviolably adhering to it. I mean only to say that
if we lean on her love of liberty, her affection for America, or
her disinterested magnanimity, we shall lean on a broken reed,
that will sooner or later pierce our hands. . . ."[17]

In their disenchantment with the French alliance, Americans
believed that with independence they no longer needed foreign
aid. The alliance, consequently, lost much of the attractiveness it
may have possessed. The French knew that leading American
statesmen disliked the alliance. They were aware that men like
John Adams believed that with the peace Americans were "independent of France, in point of moral and political obligation."[18]

Before the definitive treaty was signed, however, the United
States informed France of the peace terms, and France gave her consent to the final terms without much protest. Thus America's ally
bowed before what was almost a *fait accompli*. She did this because
more important European problems harassed her statesmen and because the Anglo-American treaty was only one part, a lesser part,
of the general European peace settlement. If France had not been
embarrassed by demands of her other ally, Spain, and had not been
anxious to extricate herself from conflicting commitments she had
made to Spain and to the United States, her reaction to the independent negotiations might have been different. As it was, and as it was
to be again and again in American history, the American nation at
its birth profited from the complications of European diplomacy.[19]

[17] Jay to Robert R. Livingston, Paris, Nov. 17, 1782, in Henry P. Johnston,
ed., *The Correspondence and Public Papers of John Jay* (4 vols., New York,
1890-93), II, 451-452. Jay explained to Livingston, Passy, July 19, 1783, why
the provisional articles, contrary to congressional instructions, were signed
without consulting the French, *ibid.*, III, 56-64. He insisted that the unilateral
action of the American commissioners "was no violation of our treaty with
France, and therefore she has no room for complaint, on that principle against
the United States."

[18] Comte de Vergennes to Chevalier de la Luzerne, Versailles, Sept. 7,
1783, Archives des Affaires Étrangères, Correspondance Politique, États-
Unis, Vol. XXV, ff. 261-265 (reproductions in the Library of Congress).
Hereinafter cited as AAE CP EU. For quotation, see Adams to John Jay,
Auteuil, April 13, 1785, in Adams, *Works*, VIII, 235.

[19] Vergennes, who was instrumental in creating American independence,
afterward feared that independence would be a bad example for other colonies,
particularly the Spanish colonies in the Americas. [François] Barbé-Marbois,
Histoire de la Louisiane . . . (Paris, 1829), pp. 163-164.

Before independence the French alliance entangled the United States in European diplomacy and politics, and before independence the alliance was under strain. American independence resulted from a major readjustment in the European balance of power. A loosely united nation was born by playing off Britain and France against each other, by accepting the risks of allying itself to a world power. The American diplomatists of the day who negotiated the peace, Benjamin Franklin, John Adams, and John Jay, knew well and used brilliantly the diplomatic arts of the small power against the large ones. Skilful American diplomacy alone could not maintain an independent foreign policy. The new nation could not extricate itself from European politics. Relations with France and Great Britain in time dominated not only American foreign relations but domestic politics as well. Upon these relations with the world's two most powerful states in the first two decades of independence rested America's destiny. Let us, therefore, turn to these relations.

* * * * *

Following independence the United States, joined loosely by the Articles of Confederation, sought to enter normal international life and commerce. But its government was limited in domestic powers and impotent to act for the nation as a whole in many areas of foreign affairs. It was not surprising, therefore, that European nations, particularly France and England, tried to control American affairs; control of American affairs, it seemed obvious to foreign observers, was beyond the power of the central government. The French minister in New York in 1788, in fact, believed that the American government's control over foreign policy was so weak that in a war against England the United States would be useless as an ally.[20]

This state of affairs embarrassed leading American merchants, who lamented that "no commercial nation will regret our disjointed condition or wish the States to unite in any system of commerce.

[20] These views are reflected in the despatches of Le Comte de Moustier. See Moustier to Le Comte de Montmorin, New York, Feb. 8, 1788, AAE CP EU, Vol. XXXIII, ff. 16-21; also Renaud de Moustier, "Les États-Unis au lendemain de la guerre de l'indépendance d'après la correspondance diplomatique inédite du Comte de Moustier," *Revue d'histoire diplomatique,* VI (1892), 521.

Every partizan of France or England residing among us, uses his utmost exertions to inspire the People of the different states with jealousies of each other."[21] Americans, with the assistance of foreign agents or without, began to divide on many issues of both domestic politics and foreign policy according to their predilection for France or Great Britain.

With Great Britain during the period of the Confederation the United States faced difficulties over various violations of the Treaty of Paris of 1783, particularly over the section dealing with the frontier posts in the Northwest. Britain refused to enter normal diplomatic relations; aware that Congress was powerless to retaliate, she actually levied commercial war against the United States. Lamenting the status of Anglo-American commercial relations soon after independence, some Americans complained that Britain was apparently "aiming to bring about a general bankruptcy in America after finding our trade had returned to its former channel, and that our importations were as great as formerly. . . ."[22]

The United States differed with Spain over the Southwest boundary and the right of navigation down the Mississippi River to its mouth. And with almost all the European powers the United States ran into problems concerning trade and commerce. John Jay, Secretary for Foreign Affairs during most of the Confederation, summed up the problem of foreign relations in these years: "To be respectable abroad, it is necessary to be so at home; and that will not be the case until our public faith acquires more confidence and our government more strength."[23]

    [21] Rufus King to Jonathan Jackson, New York, June 11, 1786, in "Letters of Rufus King 1784-1786," *Massachusetts Historical Society Proceedings,* XLIX (Oct., 1915–June, 1916), 85-86.
    [22] "A Friend to Commerce" in *Independent Chronicle and the Universal Advertiser* (Boston) reprinted in *Connecticut Gazette and the Universal Intelligencer* (New London), Aug. 13, 1784. In the British West Indies American shippers built up an illicit trade in this period which in part overcame British restrictions. Alice B. Keith, "Relaxations in the British Restrictions on the American Trade with the British West Indies, 1783-1802," *Journal of Modern History,* XX (March, 1948), 2.
    [23] Jay to Thomas Jefferson, New York, July 14, 1786, Johnston, *Correspondence of John Jay,* III, 206. Quoting a staunch advocate of strong government is not intended to imply that the period of the Confederation was "one of stagnation, ineptitude, bankruptcy, corruption, and disintegration." Evidence to the contrary is presented by Merrill Jensen, *The New Nation: A History*

From France, ally and war-comrade, the United States had expected better treatment than from Great Britain and other European powers. "Commercial privileges, granted to us by France, at this season of British ill-humour," said John Jay, "would be particularly grateful."[24] Americans received better treatment. France at the outset relaxed her mercantilist restrictions and granted American ships a limited right to trade with certain ports in the Caribbean, whereas other countries kept their ports closed in accordance with mercantilist doctrine. But this was not enough. Americans were disappointed in the French concessions; they had expected more.

In the alliance of 1778 France guaranteed American independence and also American territory as fixed by the peace with England. After the peace British garrisons continued to occupy frontier posts in the Northwest—in territory belonging to the United States. Thomas Jefferson, then American minister in Paris, sounded the French government for its views on the British-occupied posts. He received a noncommittal answer. The Continental Congress, however, did not ask France to enforce her guarantee; the alliance was not invoked.

France's actions were consistent with her American policy. Throughout the period of the Confederation the French government adhered to its purpose of retaining its war-won friendship but at the same time of trying to keep the United States relatively weak. According to certain Anglophiles of the time, France "used every possible means to divide Us, to excite Jealousies and Animosities between the States and different parts of the same State, to draw off our attention from those arrangements which would give us stability and lead to an extension of our Commerce with Britain." They discerned that France wished "by divisions &c to bring on us general confusion and convulsions, expecting that this may issue, in a form of Government much more favourable to her Views."

---

of the United States During the Confederation, 1781-1789 (New York, 1950). For a concise summary of revised historical interpretation of the Confederation period, see Max Beloff, *Thomas Jefferson and American Democracy* (London, 1948), pp. 119-121. Nonetheless, the inadequacy or apparent inadequacy of the Confederation government influenced the foreign relations of the time.

[24] Jay to Lafayette, New York, Jan. 19, 1785, in Johnston, *Correspondence of John Jay*, III, 138.

Already, at this early date (1784), French policy was obnoxious to pro-British Americans who believed that "we must have the assistance of Britain to enable us to withstand the Wiles of [France]."[25] Regardless of the exaggerated fears of Francophobes, American statesman realized that an America without strength, dependent upon the protection of her French ally, would be easier for French statesmen to control than would a comparatively powerful and stable United States.

Even though French statesmen could plan their American policy, they could not control the future in which their policy must function. As war threatened in Europe and as the French future appeared increasingly uncertain, Americans spun ideas of their own as to future relations with France. Some of them saw opportunities to profit once more from Europe's distresses. William Vans Murray, an American writing from London in the summer of 1785, foresaw that "should the Cock [France] and the Lion [England] go to blows the United States may profit by it—Its ports will abound in all the splendor of neutrality—." Continuing, he prophesied lucrative rewards for Americans. "Should a war come on American bottoms will be the only safe vehicles." Let them war, he said; "I should like the rocking of the battlements."[26]

France as well as England meddled in American affairs and did what she could to direct American government to her own interests.[27] John Adams had predicted that Americans would be subjected to such usage—a tug of war between France and England with the United States in the middle. He had warned "that France and England both would endeavor to involve us in their future

[25] Stephen Higginson to ———, April, 1784, in J. Franklin Jameson, ed., "Letters of Stephen Higginson, 1783-1804," *Annual Report of the American Historical Association for the Year 1896,* I (Washington, 1897), 715-716.

[26] Murray to his parents, Aug. 6, 1785, William Vans Murray Papers, Library of Congress (microfilm copies in the Huntington Library, San Marino, California).

[27] The French government, in many ways, carefully avoided any outward appearance of interfering in American domestic affairs. Certain elements in the French government, moreover, wished the American government well and were not entirely motivated by selfish desires. For example, France did not attempt to block the adoption of the Federal Constitution even though the end result was a stronger, more independent United States. See Clyde A. Duniway, "French Influence on the Adoption of the Federal Constitution," *AHR,* IX (Jan., 1904), 304-309.

wars." From the beginning America "had been a foot-ball between contending nations." Fearing "that all the powers of Europe will be continually manoeuvring with us, to work us into their real or imaginary balances of power," Adams sounded the alarm that "they will all wish to make of us a makeweight candle."[28] Except "in commerce," he advised on his oft-repeated theme, the United States sould be completely independent and should have nothing to do with either England or France.

Almost as if the government had accepted the reasoning of John Adams as an unofficial framework for American foreign policy, important statesmen of the Confederation, consciously or unconsciously, worked within it. They regarded the Franco-American alliance as terminated by the Treaty of Paris and the United States as freed of European attachments. "Forever" was not to be measured by the glass of time, but by convenience and necessity. With independence a fact, the French alliance was no longer needed; it was an embarrassing nuisance.[29] The British, in fact, through American sources, believed that the alliance had ended in 1783.

France would not accept such effrontery. She wanted to keep the United States from being pulled back under British hegemony of any kind; she insisted as a matter of policy that the alliance was still in effect. "Those who have once been the allies of France," according to the Comte de Vergennes, the French foreign minister, when confronted with the questioned status of the American alliance, "are her allies always."[30]

But this was not enough. To the end of the Confederation period prominent Americans persisted in believing the alliance dead. When the Comte de Moustier, French minister to the United States, had his first audience with John Jay in 1788, the American Secretary for Foreign Affairs expressed doubt that the alliance was still in effect. When relayed to France this contention shocked the then French Minister of Foreign Affairs, the Comte de Montmorin,

---

[28] Adams, *Works*, III, 308, 316, Diary, entries of Nov. 11, 18, 1782.

[29] See Gilbert, "The 'New Diplomacy' of the Eighteenth Century," *WP*, IV, 30-31.

[30] Quoted in George H. Guttridge, *David Hartley, M.P., An Advocate of Conciliation, 1774-1783*, University of California Publications in History, Vol. XIV, No. 3 (Berkeley, Cal., 1926), p. 319.

who vigorously denied Jay's assumption.[31]   The alliance could not be dropped so easily; domestic strife and foreign hostilities were to be the price of freedom from the alliance.

* * * * *

Another complication in Franco-American relations in the years of the Confederation was American default on repayment of money France had loaned the United States during the Revolutionary War.[32]   France was not the only creditor to suffer.   The Congress of the Confederation was powerless to pay instalments on the principal or to keep up the interest payments on any foreign loans. Being the major creditor, however, France was the main sufferer. Only by levying import duties or by requisitioning the states could Congress raise money.

No longer faced with an immediate foreign danger, the states were deaf to congressional demands.   Congress, however, could not ignore the vexing solicitations of French agents on the subject of debt payment, nor could Thomas Jefferson, American minister to France. He reported that the question of debts "draws on us a great deal of censure, & occasioned a language in the Assemblée des Notables very likely to produce dissatisfaction between us."[33]   Yet the French government applied no pressure, even when faced with bankruptcy, to force payment; it was reconciled, by 1789, to never being paid.[34]

[31] See H. E. Bourne, ed., "Correspondence of the Comte de Moustier with the Comte de Montmorin, 1787-1789," *AHR,* VIII (July, 1903). Moustier to Montmorin, New York, Feb. 12, 1788, p. 723, and Montmorin to Moustier, Versailles, June 23, 1788, p. 728.

[32] For a discussion of the debt, see A. Aulard, "La Dette Américaine envers la France, sous Louis XVI et sous la révolution," *La Revue de Paris,* XXXII (Mai-Juin, 1925), 319-338; Samuel F. Bemis, "Payment of the French Loans to the United States, 1777-1795," *Current History,* XXIII (March, 1926), 824-831; Henri L. Bourdin, "How French Envoys Sought Payment of America," *ibid.,* XXIII, 832-836.

[33] For solicitations of French agents, see U. S. Continental Congress, *Journals of the Continental Congress, 1774-1789* (34 vols., Washington, 1904-1937), XXIX, 595 n., 599 ff.; XXX, 54-59; Jefferson to John Adams, Paris, July 1, 1787, Paul L. Ford, ed., *The Writings of Thomas Jefferson* (10 vols., New York, 1892-99), IV, 398. Cited hereinafter as Ford, *Writings of Jefferson.*

[34] In the French National Assembly on Nov. 5, 1789, an effort was made to salvage the American debt.   Mirabeau moved that payment in flour be negotiated.   In the course of debate some members stated that the debt

This state of affairs, for good reason, had not entirely displeased the French government. Even though France had not been able to collect her just debts, her statesmen were content with a United States unable to raise money enough to maintain a strong government. A government politically weak and financially unstable, they realized, would be much more amenable to French control than would a strong and financially sound government.

To depict French policy of this period as all selfishness and American policy toward France as all suspicion would be wrong. A warm bond still existed between Americans and the people of France.[35] Franco-American relations throughout the period of the Confederation were friendly, unmarred by serious dissension. George Washington, for example, when questioned on the state of Franco-American amity told the French minister: "I am egregiously deceived if the people of this Country are not in general extremely well affected to France . . . no prejudice has been revived, no jealousy excited, no interest adduced, and, in short, no cause has existed (to my knowledge) which could have wrought a revolution unfriendly to your nation."[36] French opinion, according to contemporary estimates, favored the United States more than any other foreign country.

Relations between government and government had cooled since the American Revolutionary struggle, but they too were still cordial.[37] The French court had become hostile to Americans; but at best the King and most of his ministers had shown little enthusiasm for Americans, who were republicans, hence antimonarchical. Queen Marie Antoinette, who earlier had made America's Revolutionary cause fashionable at the French court, in 1788 refused to receive the Comte de Moustier, who was to sail as minister to the

---

must be written off as a bad one. William Short to Secretary of State, Paris, Nov. 7, 1789, National Archives, State Dept. Diplomatic Despatches, France (microfilm copies).

[35] For expressions of Franco-American friendship, see Howard Mumford Jones, *America and French Culture, 1750-1848* (Chapel Hill, 1927), pp. 525-526; for anti-British sentiment see pp. 527-530.

[36] Washington to Comte de Moustier, Mount Vernon, March 26, 1788, in Fitzpatrick, *Washington's Writings,* XXIX, 447-448.

[37] For evidences of French sentiment based on contemporary sources, see Lewis Rosenthal, *America and France: The Influence of the United States on France in the XVIIIth Century* (New York, 1882), pp. 97 ff., 138 ff.

United States. "She had nothing to say to a people among whom the name of King and that of Queen must be hated."[38] Royal disfavor was not a true reflection of French sentiment. As Thomas Jefferson had observed in France, "It is very much our interest to keep up the affection of this country for us, which is considerable. A court has no affections, but those of the people whom they govern influence their decisions even in the most arbitrary governments."[39]

Much of the information reaching France and the United States about each other apparently was blackened or otherwise colored by the English. England was the great information clearinghouse for Americans; most of the English translations of contemporary French works read in the United States were made, edited, and published in Great Britain. Even war could not permanently break the bond of culture, of blood, and of a common tongue.[40] Most of the intercourse and exchange of information between France and the United States went through England, in large part because of British control of the seas; there was seldom direct mail between France and the United States.[41] French officials de-

[38] Quoted in Bernard Faÿ, *The Revolutionary Spirit in France and America*, trans. Ramon Guthrie (London, 1928), p. 172.

[39] Jefferson to James Monroe, Paris, June 17, 1785, in Ford, *Writings of Jefferson*, IV, 50-51.

[40] See Faÿ, *Revolutionary Spirit . . .* , pp. 172-173. Jefferson, writing from Paris to Richard Henry Lee, July 12, 1785, commented: "You are right in supposing all letters opened which come either thro' the French or English channel, unless trusted to a passenger. . . . I think I never received one through the post office which had not been. . . . I should be happy to hear that Congress thought of establishing packets of their own between N. York and Havre." Ford, *Writings of Jefferson*, IV, 69. Jefferson also regarded English papers "as a prejudiced and impure source" when dealing with French or American affairs. Dumas Malone, *Jefferson and the Rights of Man* (Boston, 1951), p. 92.

[41] During the American Revolution and in the period of the Confederation the French launched a program designed to influence American public opinion, especially to counteract British influence in the United States. Although the program was in accord with expressed ideas of Franco-American friendship of the time, most of the effort came from one side, the French side. Hence the movement failed. Fundamentally, the French could not overcome deep-seated connections of culture, tongue, and blood shared in common by Americans and Englishmen. See Allen J. Barthold, "French Journalists in the United States, 1780-1800," *Franco-American Review*, I (Winter, 1937), 221.

plored the weaknesses in direct Franco-American communication and tried to overcome them.[42]

Recognizing their advantages over the French, Englishmen grasped every opportunity to place themselves and their country in a favorable light and to debase their rivals. Was it not the policy of the British government to break the Franco-American partnership? Nevertheless, in so far as it has been possible to gauge public opinion of the times, it seems apparent that most of the literate populace of France and America shared a common sympathy. Good will between Americans and Frenchmen may even have increased in the years following the American Revolution. The middle classes were not aware of, or were not concerned with, the matters of difference between governments; it took more than defaults and difficulties over the interpretation of a treaty to affect their feelings.[43]

Although French policy sought to keep the United States friendly but weak, it also tried to profit from American friendship and to build up Franco-American commercial relations.[44] In fact, the breaking of America's commercial dependence on England had been a foremost objective of French aid during the American Revolution; to it "the severance of the political bond stood somewhat in the relation of means to end."[45] To implement its commercial program the French government cut away certain barriers in its exclusive mercantilist empire in order to attract American trade.[46]

[42] The French minister of marine, for example, on Dec. 9, 1792, proposed to the President of the National Convention that more packet boats be placed into direct service between France and America. He wanted to improve communications and to strengthen Franco-American relations. Aware that England had taken advantage of French weakness in America by maintaining ample connections with the United States, the French government, with high hopes for improving American relations, authorized an increase in packet-boat service. AAE CP EU, Vol. XXXVI, ff. 209-210, and "Memoire sur les Paquebots," no date but *ca.* Dec., 1792, *ibid.,* ff. 460-62.

[43] See Faÿ, *Revolutionary Spirit . . . ,* p. 175; Rosenthal, *America and France . . . ,* p. 113, *et passim.*

[44] Frederick L. Nussbaum, "The French Colonial Arrêt of 1784," *South Atlantic Quarterly,* XXVII (Jan., 1928), 62-82; Jensen, *The New Nation,* pp. 166-168.

[45] Corwin, *French Policy and the American Alliance . . . ,* p. 369.

[46] Edmund Buron, "Statistics on Franco-American Trade, 1778-1806," *Journal of Economic and Business History,* IV (May, 1932), 571-580.

In this manner France hoped to develop a thriving commerce, not merely between French colonies and the American states, but between the United States and the homeland as well. British influence and the British share of American commerce would, she believed, decrease while hers might increase.[47] This was an audacious policy on the part of the French government—a policy unpopular with French merchants, who objected vehemently to liberties granted American commerce in French ports. What is more, such a policy constituted a revolution in the nation's long-standing economic principles.[48]

To carry out its American economic program the French government sent to the American states consuls or vice-consuls, such as G. J. A. Ducher, who gathered information on American conditions, particularly on matters which might benefit French commerce. Frenchmen who knew America and were known by Americans, such as Pierre François de Barbé-Marbois, who had fought in the American Revolution, and Hector Saint-Jean de Crèvecoeur, popular for his idyllic representation of American life in a widely read book, were prominent appointees.[49]

More than did the French, Americans profited from the newly opened channels of Franco-American trade. French merchants in many instances resented American competition and the concessions granted to Americans.[50] They had no desire to see the Franco-

[47] Vernon G. Setser, *The Commercial Reciprocity Policy of the United States, 1774-1829* (Philadelphia, 1937), p. 80. Lafayette was a leading advocate of improved commercial relations between the United States and France in the 1780's. See Louis R. Gottschalk, "Lafayette as Commercial Expert," *AHR*, XXXVI (April, 1931), 561.

[48] Buron, "Statistics on Franco-American Trade. . . ," p. 574. An example of a merchant protest is that of a certain Pierre Texier to the Comte de Vergennes, Bordeaux, July 29, 1783, AAE CP EU, Vol. XXV, ff. 10f-10g.

[49] Frederick L. Nussbaum, *Commercial Policy in the French Revolution: A Study of the Career of G. J. A. Ducher* (Washington, 1923), pp. 11-36; E. Wilson Lyon, *The Man Who Sold Louisiana: The Career of Francois Barbe-Marbois* (Norman, Oklahoma, 1942), pp. 31-32; and Robert de Crèvecoeur, *Saint John de Crèvecoeur, sa vie et ses ouvrages* (Paris, 1883), pp. 89-115.

[50] For example, the merchants of Nantes cared more for the loss of a trade monopoly as a consequence of concessions to Americans than they did for the increased trade opportunities in the new American market opened to them. Henri Sée, "Commerce between France and the United States, 1783-1784," *AHR*, XXXI (July, 1926), 737; see also the grievances of the

American political bond become economic; they did not want Americans—former British subjects—trading freely in the French Caribbean islands. Their protests caused minor trade readjustments in their favor, but the basic trade policy toward the United States continued.

Despite good intentions and unusual exertions French commercial policy failed. It failed in France and in the United States, even though Americans gained more than did France from the increased trade; it failed because France purchased more from the United States than the American states did from her.[51] In spite of artificial pro-French stimuli, Americans preferred British goods. The French could not overcome habit, common language, custom, law, and the availability of long-term credits in England. By 1789 American trade was once more overwhelmingly in the hands of English merchants; in volume it exceeded that preceding the Revolutionary War.[52] Failure of French commercial policy and the triumph of English manufactures did not contribute to Franco-American harmony.

* * * * *

France and the United States had hoped that a prosperous commerce between the two countries would replace the prewar Ameri-

merchants of Le Havre in Nussbaum, "The French Colonial Arrêt of 1784," *SAQ*, XXVII, 71; for the Caribbean, see Lokke, *France and the Colonial Question* . . . , pp. 63-64.

[51] See Jefferson's report to Congress of his conversations with Vergennes over why "the trade of the United States had not yet learned the way to France, but continued to centre in England, though no longer obliged by law to go there," in Ford, *Writings of Jefferson*, IV, 117-130. For Washington's views on British commercial success, see Washington to Moustier, Mount Vernon, March 26, 1788, in Fitzpatrick, *Washington's Writings*, XXIX, 448. In 1788-89 American tonnage in Franco-American trade was approximately ten times that of France. William K. Woolery, *The Relation of Thomas Jefferson to American Foreign Policy, 1783-1793* (Baltimore, 1927), p. 57.

[52] To all practical purposes the United States "remained an English colony in economic status." Setser, *Commercial Reciprocity* . . . , p. 52. For statistics on Anglo-American trade, see Samuel F. Bemis, *Jay's Treaty, A Study in Commerce and Diplomacy* (New York, 1923), pp. 33-34; Anna C. Clauder, *American Commerce as Affected by the Wars of the French Revolution and Napoleon, 1793-1812* (Philadelphia, 1932), pp. 22-25; Timothy Pitkin, *A Statistical View of the Commerce of the United States of America* (2nd ed., Hartford, 1817), pp. 30, 167.

can trade with England. Statesmen of the two countries had attempted to place the development of commerce on a solid basis by a treaty. This had seemed desirable to both nations. American commerce did well under liberal French decrees, but the French concessions were gratuitous; they were subject to local exceptions, and they could be withdrawn at any time. On the other hand, the thirteen states vied with each other for foreign trade; they violated the most-favored-nation clause of the Treaty of Amity and Commerce of 1778, and they manipulated tariff and tonnage duties to the annoyance of French merchants. Under the Articles of Confederation, John Jay, the Secretary for Foreign Affairs, could do little to enforce uniform treatment of French commerce. This provoked French retaliation. The commercial treaty of 1778, moreover, while providing for establishment of consuls, said nothing about their obligations, functions, privileges, and immunities.

As far back as 1781 the United States and France had negotiated over consular matters, and from early 1782 to the middle of summer 1784, Vergennes and Benjamin Franklin, American minister in Paris, had discussed and finally agreed to a consular convention which was technically and legally reciprocal.[53] Actually and practically it was not. The privileges and immunities granted to French consuls impinged on American sovereignty. Also the treaty stressed the sovereign qualities of the thirteen separate states rather than the undivided sovereignty of United States. The French consuls were to deliver their credentials to state authorities rather than to the Congress of the Confederation.

In providing for consular jurisdiction—in case of disputes—over the nationals of one country residing in the territory of the other, the convention might have clashed with domestic law and custom in the United States. Such procedure was a form of extraterritoriality. This in itself was not shocking; the United States was then a weak

[53] The memorial and draft consular convention submitted to the Congress, July 27, 1781, by Le Chevalier de la Luzerne, French Minister to the United States, is in U. S. Continental Congress, *Secret Journal of the Acts and Proceedings of Congress* (4 vols., Boston, 1820-21), III, 5-19; for the amended draft convention with the report of the Congressional Committee which had considered it, see U. S. Continental Congress, *Journals of the Continental Congress . . . ,* XXII, 17-28; for the convention as finally signed by Franklin, see U. S. Dept. of State, *The Diplomatic Correspondence of the United States of America* (3 vols., Washington, 1837), I, 211-218.

nation without uniform laws for the whole country. France, on the other hand, prided herself as being the most advanced country in the Western World. As Jefferson observed, Europe regarded American diplomats in Europe as "the lowest and most obscure of the whole diplomatic tribe."

Another provision which gave unusual immunities to consuls and their "agents" also upset Americans. This provision undoubtedly would have subjected the internal affairs of the weaker state to unnecessary scrutiny and interference by the stronger power. French consuls and their "agents" would not have been subject to American law and would have been free to do practically what they would. They could build up a dangerous political machine, and they could through propaganda and politics meddle in and perhaps even dominate America's domestic politics. The United States was allowed the same privileges in France, but, because of varying conditions in the two countries, the agreement favored France. It fitted French desires to subordinate American freedom of action to French foreign policy.

The convention was not concluded until July, 1784, and did not reach the United States until summer of the following year. In December, 1784, John Jay became Secretary for Foreign Affairs; consequently he had to deal with it. Ironically, a week before he assumed his post Jay had presented a motion to Congress calling for suspension or delay of negotiations. Even though Congress adopted the motion, it was five months too late. The treaty had been completed. France considered it an accomplished fact.[54]

After the French pressed for action on ratification, Jay studied the signed convention and submitted an exhaustive report to Congress urging it not to ratify.[55] He recommended that Jefferson be instructed to negotiate a new agreement which did not include as many undesirable features and which took cognizance of the national sovereignty of "The United States of America." Congress, no longer impelled by urgent need to co-operate closely with its war-

[54] Congress was unaware that the Convention had already been signed in Paris. See R. L. Jones, "America's First Consular Convention," *Southwestern Social Science Quarterly,* XIII (Dec., 1932), 256.

[55] Jay's report of July 4, 1786, to Congress on the Convention and his recommendations of August 18, 1786, in U.S. Dept. of State, *Diplomatic Correspondence . . . ,* I, 218-234.

time ally, could now insist upon absolute equality and real reciprocity. Jay did not want any consular convention, and in particular he did not want one with France.[56]   Besides, American policy at this time opposed treaties of this kind; Franklin had gone beyond his instructions, and circumstances had changed considerably since the negotiations had started.

Following Jay's advice, Congress did not ratify the convention; it instructed Jefferson to obtain basic changes in the agreement. Such delaying tactics disturbed the French government and upset the hoped-for intimate-subordinate relationship of the United States to France.[57]

Finally, to keep faith with an agreement once assented to, Jefferson signed a revised consular convention in November, 1788, in which France recognized the sovereignty of "The United States of America." Many of the objectionable features of the original draft and of the convention signed in 1784 had been removed, but the new agreement still provided for the exercise of civil jurisdiction by consular courts over their own nationals. This was the best Jefferson felt he could do. Only with growth and increased strength could the United States erase the stigma of extraterritoriality under any guise.

The convention established the normal functions of consular jurisdiction and was limited to twelve years. When ratified by President Washington in 1789, this treaty became the first (other than Indian treaties) to be approved by the Senate under the new federal Constitution.[58]   Again, American desires for complete independence and French plans for American subordination clashed. Although the result was a compromise, it did not strengthen Franco-American friendship.   *   *   *   *   *

[56] Jones, "America's First Consular Convention," *SSSQ*, XIII, 258. Vergennes regarded Jay as unfriendly to France. See Frank Monaghan, *John Jay* (New York, 1935), p. 261.

[57] The Comte de Moustier, French minister in the United States, wrote a memoir explaining the American delay in signing the convention. New York, March 5, 1788, AAE CP EU, Vol. XXXIII, ff. 132-142; French concern was also expressed in Moustier to Montmorin, New York, May 28, *ibid.*, ff. 170-72.

[58] For the final text of the Convention, see Miller, *Treaties . . .* , II, 228-244; for Jefferson's contributions, see Woolery, *The Relation of Thomas Jefferson to American Foreign Policy . . .* , pp. 58-65.

Louisiana was, during the period of the Confederation, essentially a problem in Spanish-American relations. Yet French interest in the region was not dead, and this interest touched on Franco-American relations.[59] Frenchmen in Louisiana had never reconciled themselves to Spanish rule, and as early as 1779 they had sent agents to Philadelphia who urged secretly that France recover the province. Tempting though the entreaties might be, the French government paid little attention to them. At this time French interest in Louisiana was primarily commercial. In fact, with Spanish permission, France carried on a profitable trade with her former subjects in Louisiana. Her policy was to advance her own interests by ostensibly advancing those of Spain.

Spanish policy tried to build a dike against American westward and southward expansion. Vergennes supported this Spanish policy. To achieve her objective Spain engaged in intrigues along the American frontier and at the same time denied Western Americans access to the sea via the Mississippi River.[60] In this frontier diplomacy France (according to available evidence) maintained a correct position *vis-à-vis* the United States. Rumors spread, nonetheless, that France sought to recover her former continental domain and that French agents on the frontier conspired to this end.[61] Persistence of these rumors led Jay to ask the French government if they were true. Vergennes denied that they were and said that

[59] For fuller discussions of Franco-American relations in the diplomacy of Louisiana during the Confederation, see E. Wilson Lyon, *Louisiana in French Diplomacy, 1759-1804* (Norman, Oklahoma, 1934), pp. 58-66 and Darling, *Our Rising Empire . . . ,* pp. 115-122.

[60] Frederick J. Turner, "The Policy of France Toward the Mississippi Valley in the Period of Washington and Adams," *AHR,* X (Jan., 1905), 256; William R. Shephard, "Wilkinson and the Beginnings of the Spanish Conspiracy," *ibid.,* IX (April, 1904), 490-506. England, too, was involved in the intrigues of the Southwest frontier.

[61] L. G. Otto to Vergennes, New York, April 23, 1786, in George Bancroft, *History of the Formation of the Constitution of the United States of America* (2nd ed.; 2 vols., New York, 1882) (hereinafter referred to as Bancroft, *History of the Constitution*), I, 498. Alexander McGillivray in a letter to Arturo O'Neill, April 18, 1787, reported an Indian as saying the Spaniards "were preparing to evacuate Pensacola to the French who were Soon expected there. . . . The News papers give an account that an exchange was likely to take place with France," in John W. Caughey, *McGillivray of the Creeks* (Norman, Oklahoma, 1938), p. 51.

"there has never been a question of an exchange of Louisiana for a French possession in the West Indies."[62]

Not until the closing years of the Confederation did certain French statesmen actually propose recovery of Louisiana and re-establishment of a French empire on the American continent. At that time, in a memoir presented to the French Foreign Office (March, 1789), the Comte de Moustier advocated recovery of Louisiana and even alluded to the possibility of separating the Western territories from the American states and attaching them to Louisiana. Among other things, he argued that France would actually strengthen her friendship with the United States by the acquisition and by opening the Mississippi to American commerce. Such action would give France great commercial advantage, and, paradoxically, it would also preserve the union between the American West and East. This was the first serious suggestion backed by a responsible official that France re-establish herself on the American mainland.[63]

Moustier's memoir coincided with a new interest in colonies inspired by the French Revolution. Patriots of the Revolution never reconciled themselves to the loss of Louisiana. But to recover Louisiana, France had to move before American frontiersmen overwhelmed the Spanish dike confining them east of the Mississippi. This interest in Louisiana portended Franco-American enmity.

* * * * *

During the years of the Confederation Benjamin Franklin and Thomas Jefferson represented the United States at the French

[62] Vergennes to Otto, Versailles, Aug. 25, 1786, in Bancroft, *History of the Constitution*, II, 387.

[63] Lyon, *Louisiana in French Diplomacy . . .* , p. 65. Jefferson apparently had heard of Moustier's Louisiana project. Jefferson to William Short, New York, Aug. 10, 1790, in Ford, *Writings of Jefferson*, V, 220; Turner, "Policy of France Toward the Mississippi Valley . . . ," *AHR*, X, 257; Moustier, "Les États Unis . . . ," *RHD*, VI, 528; Mildred S. Fletcher, "Louisiana as a Factor in French Diplomacy from 1763 to 1800," *Mississippi Valley Historical Review*, XVII (Dec., 1930), 367. Moustier apparently obtained much of his information on Louisiana from a memorial by Barthélemi Tardiveau, a French trader, who for economic reasons advocated that France regain Louisiana. Tardiveau's *Mémoire sur le Mississippi* was prepared in 1787 and later presented to Moustier. Howard C. Rice, *Barthélemi Tardiveau: A French Trader in the West* (Baltimore, 1938), pp. 13-15.

court. Few men have succeeded in capturing a people in a foreign land as did Franklin.[64] The French considered him one of the great men of the world. So deeply did they venerate him that they reproduced his likeness in a thousand ways; in Paris virtually everyone knew the well-loved American minister. Of greater significance, his influence went beyond the existing friendly relations of his own country with France.

During the American Revolution Franklin's diplomacy helped win France to the American cause; his skilful services helped to create America's first diplomatic triumph—the French alliance. He did not escape criticism from home; critics accused him of having "lost in France the cause of America." Moreover, he disagreed seriously with John Adams over the course of Franco-American diplomacy, particularly on the significance of the French alliance.[65] While he did his most important work in these years, his services continued into the period of the Confederation; he represented the United States in France for approximately eight and a half critical years.

Even though Franklin continued a beloved figure in France and an asset in Franco-American amity, by 1784, because of old age and illness, he was ready to return to America to spend his last days. When he left Passy, the Queen placed her litter at his disposal and, though the offer came too late, the French also tendered use of a royal frigate for the voyage home.[66] He had won royal favor, but more important, he left behind him an enduring legacy of good will among the French people.[67]

[64] Franklin's diplomatic activities are discussed in detail in Elizabeth S. Kite, "Benjamin Franklin—Diplomat," *Catholic World*, CXLII (Oct., 1935), 28-37; Stourzh, *Benjamin Franklin and American Foreign Policy*, pp. 113 ff.; Verner W. Crane, *Benjamin Franklin and a Rising People* (Boston, 1954), pp. 172-191; Bernard Faÿ, *Franklin, The Apostle of Modern Times* (New York, 1929), pp. 261 ff.; Carl Van Doren, *Benjamin Franklin* (New York, 1938), pp. 527 ff.; Edward E. Hale and Edward E. Hale, Jr., *Franklin and France* (2 vols., Boston, 1887-88); David J. Hill, "Franklin and the French Alliance of 1778," *Records of the Columbia Historical Society*, XXXI-XXXII (Washington, D. C., 1930), 151-173.

[65] See Stourzh, *Benjamin Franklin and American Foreign Policy*, pp. 150-160; Crane, *Benjamin Franklin and a Rising People*, p. 185. Adams actually believed Franklin to be a dupe of Vergennes.

[66] Van Doren, *Franklin*, pp. 722-23.

[67] At Passy Franklin had set up a private press where he printed for

His successor recognized Franklin's unique position among the French. No one could replace him, Jefferson remarked, one could only succeed him.[68] Yet Jefferson also exerted considerable personal influence in France and earned a special place for himself as America's representative. From the beginning the French received him kindly, and he found the government to be "entirely disposed" to be friendly to the United States. While he did not like French weather, missed his Virginia sunshine, and felt that Europe and European institutions had little to offer Americans, he liked the French and they liked him.[69] He enjoyed the urbanities of the salons and the gaiety of French life. As a cultured gentleman, he, like Franklin before him, charmed the ladies with his conversation and wit and made his house a center for the diplomatic set.

While enjoying life in France he never let up in his task of cultivating French friendship and of removing "from between us every subject of misunderstanding or irritation."[70] To this end he devoted his personal influence; he believed in regard to France that "nothing should be spared, on our part, to attach this country to us. It is the only one on which we can rely for support, under every event. Its inhabitants love us more, I think, than they do any other nation on earth."[71]

Friendship with France, according to Jefferson, benefited America because the two countries were complementary to one another. Despite the opposites represented by their institutions, he felt there

---

private circulation essays covering various subjects. Like his other activities, his printings had the practical effect of enhancing his usefulness as a diplomat and of informing the French about America. See Richard E. Amacher, *Franklin's Wit & Folly: The Bagatelles* (New Brunswick, 1953), pp. 20-21.

[68] Hale and Hale, *Franklin in France*, II, 332.

[69] For information on Jefferson as minister to France, see Malone, *Jefferson and the Rights of Man*, pp. 3 ff.; Marie Kimball, *Jefferson and the Scene of Europe, 1784-1789* (New York, 1950); Gilbert Chinard, *Thomas Jefferson, The Apostle of Americanism* (2nd ed., rev.; Boston, 1939), pp. 159 ff.; Chinard, *Trois amitiés françaises de Jefferson* (Paris, 1927), pp. 3-10; François Alexandre Frédéric, duc de la Rochefoucauld-Liancourt, *Travels Through the United States of North America . . . in the Years 1795, 1796, and 1797 . . .* (2 vols., London, 1799), II, 78.

[70] Jefferson to John Adams, Paris, July 1, 1787, in Ford, *Writings of Jefferson*, IV, 398; see also Rosenthal, *America and France . . .* , pp. 128-130.

[71] Jefferson to James Madison, Paris, Jan. 30, 1787, in Ford, *Writings of Jefferson*, IV, 367.

was no real political rivalry between them and that their commerce was for the most part supplementary, not competitive.[72] His partiality for France, however, was not blind. He was aware of his own insignificant position among the diplomats at the French court; he was not often given the opportunity to forget it.

As the representative of a new nation, a republic in the day of monarchy, Jefferson had many uncomfortable moments in France; his post in many ways "was an excellent school of humility." He remained firm, nevertheless, in the idea that there were many motives, both moral and political, which bound "the two countries together by as many ties as possible of interest and affection." He realized that self-interest, not altruism, governed French policy, as it did that of all nations. "I cannot," he declared while referring to America's attachment to France, "pretend to affirm that this country [France] will stand by us on every just occasion, but I am sure, if this will not, there is no other that will."[73]

Before he left France, Jefferson witnessed the beginning of the French Revolution, a revolution with which he sympathized and in which he acted as something of an outside expert on the making of revolution.[74] Through the years, although national self-interest and immediate circumstances modified his views, Jefferson retained his enthusiasm for the French and their Revolution.[75] This partiality in later years affected his view of American foreign policy and influenced the domestic development of the United States. Events in France were not the only ones of ramifying consequence in 1789 as Jefferson brought his diplomatic activities in France to a close. His countrymen had adopted a new constitution and a

[72] Malone, *Jefferson and the Rights of Man*, p. 48.

[73] Jefferson to Dr. Ramsay, Paris, Oct. 27, 1786, in H. A. Washington, ed., *The Writings of Thomas Jefferson* (9 vols., Washington, 1853-54), II, 49.

[74] John H. Latané, "Jefferson's Influence on American Foreign Policy," *Alumni Bulletin of the University of Virginia*, XVII (Third series, July-Aug., 1924), 253-254.

[75] Otto Vossler, *Die amerikanischen Revolutionsideale in ihrem verhältnis zu den europäischen: Untersucht an Thomas Jefferson* (Munchen, 1929), maintained that Jefferson's years in France had a profound influence on his thinking; that Jefferson returned to America wishing "to make his country come up to the ideals of the French revolutionary ideology," p. 127. For a digest of Vossler's book, see R. R. Palmer, "A Neglected Work: Otto Vossler on Jefferson and the Revolutionary Era," *WMQ*, 3rd Series, XII (July, 1955), 462-471.

new government had succeeded the Confederation—peacefully. The two contemporary revolutions in government, in France and in the United States—one characterized in relative terms by peaceful change to the right and the other by violent upheaval to the left— were to influence the course of Franco-American relations and the political development of the American nation.

CHAPTER TWO

POLITICS

THE HAMILTONIAN SYSTEM

To make us one nation as to foreign concerns, and keep us distinct in Domestic ones, gives the outline of the proper division of powers between the general and particular governments.—Thomas Jefferson to James Madison, Paris, December 16, 1786.

A ruler must be a MAN, *a man of feeling, who can make allowances for the frailties of human nature. He must be of no party, for the moment he espouses the side of a party he becomes prejudiced, and sees everything by halves.*—Georgia Gazette (Savannah), June 9, 1794, reprinted from the Hartford Gazette.

* * * * *

Under the Articles of Confederation the weakness or apparent weakness of the national government deprived American diplomacy of effectiveness. Keenly aware of American impotence when contrasted to European might, the founding fathers argued that a vigorous and respected foreign policy could be based only on a stronger national government, such as the new federal Constitution would provide.[1] Foreign affairs were at the heart of the politics of ratifica-

[1] Evidence of this argument can be found in the *Federalist* in the words of all three authors. Note, for example, *Federalists* Nos. 2-5, any edition. See the argument of Thomas Dawes of Boston in support of the Constitution in Bancroft, *History of the Constitution,* pp. 399-400. Men like Washington, who were impressed with the international weakness of America's position, supported the change to the new Constitution to strengthen that position. See Washington to Thomas Jefferson, Mount Vernon, Jan. 1, 1788, and to Henry Knox, Mount Vernon, March 3, 1788, in Fitzpatrick, *Washington's Writings,* XXIX, 350-351 and 435; Beloff, *Thomas Jefferson and American Democracy,* p. 121. Jefferson's experience as minister to France had con-

tion, politics which divided the country into factions favoring or opposing the adoption of the Constitution of 1789. At the same time, just as the French Revolution and events abroad influenced American foreign relations and domestic politics, the political differences at home, often originating with or dominated by local issues, gave direction to foreign policy. To place basic developments in foreign affairs in the George Washington administrations in proper perspective, therefore, we shall probe the beginnings of national political parties.

During these embryo-years politics on a national level and foreign policy—as they touch directly on the scope of this study—revolved broadly around two major issues. The first was the economic-political system of Alexander Hamilton; the second consisted of problems arising from the wars of the French Revolution. Within both issues domestic politics and foreign affairs were intertwined. Foreign policy, in fact, became the outstanding issue between the two national political parties which sprang into existence in these years.[2] Before Washington completed his first term so obvious was the interconnection between domestic politics and foreign affairs that most people recognized them as two sides of the same coin.

*　*　*　*　*

vinced him that the Confederation government needed strength in foreign affairs; see Caleb P. Patterson, *The Constitutional Principles of Thomas Jefferson* (Austin, Texas, 1953), p. 33. See also Jefferson's criticism of the Confederation Congress's treaty-making power in letters to James Monroe (Paris, June 17, 1785) and to John Adams (Paris, July 7, 1785) in Ford, *Writings of Jefferson*, IV, 54-55, and in Andrew S. Lipscomb and Albert E. Bergh, eds., *The Writings of Thomas Jefferson* (20 vols., Washington, 1903-4), V, 32; hereinafter cited as Lipscomb, *Jefferson's Works*. For the general reaction in the states, see Allan Nevins, *The American States during and after the Revolution, 1775-1789* (New York, 1924), pp. 599-601.

[2] In the Washington administrations foreign events and foreign issues dominated American politics; Americans along the coast, in thought and ideals, were closer oftentimes to Europe than to their own hinterland. They believed that the fate of their country depended upon the outcome of events in Europe. American newspapers therefore devoted most of their news columns to European news. Politically, intellectually, and diplomatically Americans in these years were tied closely to Europe. See Samuel Eliot Morison, *The Life and Letters of Harrison Gray Otis, 1765-1884* (2 vols., Boston, 1913), II, 51-52; W. Stull Holt, *Treaties Defeated by the Senate: A Study of the Struggle Between President and Senate Over the Conduct of Foreign Relations* (Baltimore, 1933), pp. 14-15.

When George Washington launched the new government under the federal Constitution in 1789 there were no national political parties. Political groupings had long existed in the colonies and then in the states, and group-political action led to adoption of the new Constitution. Some historians have seen in the contest over ratification of the federal Constitution the basis for the formation of American political parties.[3] In principle, theory, and composition they saw in the federalists, who supported ratification, and in the antifederalists, who opposed it, the fundamental division followed by national political parties when they developed in the 1790's. While there was much in common between the forces which fought the battle of ratification and those which sought to control the machinery of government after ratification, the special state and local political groups, federalist and antifederalist, did not blossom into national political parties. They broke up after the Constitution was adopted and were never reconstituted on their old foundations.[4]

[3] For example, see Wilfred E. Binkley, *American Political Parties: Their Natural History* (2nd ed., New York, 1945), pp. 26-28, and Charles A. Beard, *Economic Origins of Jeffersonian Democracy* (New York, 1915), pp. 9-33; Manning J. Dauer, *The Adams Federalists* (Baltimore, 1953), pp. 3 ff. Dauer discusses the basis of early political groupings. For a contemporary rejection of pre-1778 political alignment as the origin of political parties, see James Madison's "A Candid State of Parties," Sept. 26, 1792, reprinted from the *National Gazette* in Gaillard Hunt, ed., *The Writings of James Madison* (9 vols., New York, 1900-1910), VI, 106-119. For a contemporary account of political parties in this period by a keen foreign observer, see La Rochefoucauld-Liancourt, *Travels . . .* , II, 511-520. The whole design of the federalists, he asserts, was to detach the United States from England, to destroy the French alliance.

[4] The literature on the origin of political parties is voluminous and confusing. Much of it is based on mere conjecture. Some of the most enlightening information on party origins is to be found in special studies dealing with local political situations. The bulk of recent scholarship supports the view expressed herein. For general treatments of party origins, see Binkley, *American Political Parties . . .* ; Edgar E. Robinson, *The Evolution of American Political Parties* (New York, 1924); James A. Woodburn, *Political Parties and Party Problems in the United States* (3rd ed., New York, 1924). For specialized studies, see George D. Luetscher, *Early Political Machinery in the United States* (Philadelphia, 1903); O. G. Libby, "Political Factions in Washington's Administrations," *Quarterly Journal of the University of North Dakota,* III (July, 1913), 239-318; Walter R. Fee, *The Transition from Aristocracy to Democracy in New Jersey, 1789-1829* (Somerville, New Jersey, 1933); David K. McCarrell, "The Formation of the Jeffersonian Party in Virginia" (Unpublished Ph.D. dissertation, Dept. of History, Duke University, 1937); William A. Robinson, *Jeffersonian Democracy in New England* (New Haven, 1916); Bernard Faÿ,

Regardless of the precise origin of political parties, the men who controlled the new government came mainly from among those who fought for ratification of the Constitution—the federalists. They chose the most illustrious of their number for the nation's first president. From the beginning George Washington identified himself with one of the early special political alliances and was its most prominent figure. Yet he was not a candidate of that or any other political group. For President he was the choice of almost all men. His Revolutionary exploits won the unanimous support of the electoral college; his reputation united Americans behind the new government he was drafted to lead. But for his support, furthermore, the new Constitution might never have been adopted.[5]

Despite pleas of Hamilton and others that he was an "indispensable" man and that upon his acceptance of the Presidency "the success of the new government in its commencement may materially depend," Washington was reluctant to embrace the high office; he wished to be saved "from the dreaded Dilemma of being forced to accept or refuse." Unwilling to enter an unexplored field, "enveloped on every side with clouds of darkness," the hero of the Revolution had but one thing more he desired of life—to live "in *peace* and *retirement.*"[6] That his friends should ignore his deep-felt desires was logical. They needed his services and enormous prestige to pilot the government.

"Early Party Machinery in the United States: Pennsylvania in the Election of 1796," *Pennsylvania Magazine of History and Biography,* LX (Oct., 1936), 375-390. One of the recent studies incorporating previous scholarship on the subject is an unpublished doctoral dissertation in the Duke University Library by Noble E. Cunningham, Jr., "The Jeffersonian Party to 1801: A Study of the Formation of a Party Organization" (Dept. of History, 1952); another recent study which breaks new ground is Harry Ammon, "The Formation of the Republican Party in Virginia, 1789-1796," *Journal of Southern History,* XIX (Aug., 1953), 283-310.

[5] Douglas Southall Freeman, *George Washington: A Biography* (6 vols., New York, 1948-1954), VI, 140 (hereinafter cited as Freeman, *Washington*).

[6] Washington to Thomas Johnson, Mount Vernon, April 20, 1788, in Fitzpatrick, *Washington's Writings,* XXIX, 463; to Alexander Hamilton, Mount Vernon, Oct. 3, 1788, XXX, 110; to Benjamin Lincoln, Mount Vernon, Oct. 26, 1788, XXX, 119; Nathaniel W. Stephenson and Waldo H. Dunn, *George Washington* (2 vols., New York, 1940), II, 250. For an interesting brief commentary on Washington's acceptance of the Presidency, see Douglas S. Freeman, "Washington's Hardest Decision," *Atlantic,* CXC (Oct., 1952), 45-51.

Washington took office as, theoretically, a nonpolitical president. During his eight years in office he did not consider himself a party man. In a sense he was not a political president and many contemporaries did not consider him such. In him was centered the unity of the government. Abhorring politics and parties, he identified political opposition as "faction," something disloyal, something to be distrusted. He often referred to himself as "one, who is of no party," and urged his countrymen to "drive far away the demon of party spirit."[7]

His thinking reflected political ideas of the times. The Constitution had no provision for political parties, and a government above party was Washington's ideal.[8] In his first inaugural address he spoke out against "party animosities." Almost eight years later as he looked forward to retirement he defended his ostensibly nonpolitical administration. "I was no party man myself," he declared, "and the first wish of my heart was, if parties did exist, to reconcile them."[9]

On the basis of a nonpolitical administration and of using the best talents regardless of differing political outlook Washington chose Alexander Hamilton and Thomas Jefferson to fill his two most important departmental posts, the Treasury and State departments. Ironically, these two men of divergent political and social philosophies within his government rendered Washington's governmental ideal unworkable. They became the principal architects of America's first national political coalitions.

In practice, Washington's was a conservative-aristocratic government dominated, for the most part, by the same group of men who

[7] Stephenson and Dunn, George Washington, II, 275-276; Louis M. Sears, George Washington (New York, 1932), pp. 368-370; Libby, "Political Factions in Washington's Administrations," QJUND, III, 299.

[8] For a concise summary of Washington's political views, see Harold W. Bradley, "The Political Thinking of George Washington," JSH, XI (Nov., 1945), 469-486; also Norman J. Small, Some Presidential Interpretations of the Presidency (Baltimore, 1932), p. 16. Washington's contemporaries were also perplexed as to the place of political parties in government; see Leonard D. White, The Federalists: A Study in Administrative History (New York, 1948), p. 92 n.; and Stuart G. Brown, The First Republicans: Political Philosophy and Public Policy in the Party of Jefferson and Madison (Syracuse University Press, 1954), p. 49.

[9] Washington to Thomas Jefferson, Mount Vernon, July 6, 1796, in Fitzpatrick, Washington's Writings, XXXV, 119.

had been responsible for the drafting and the adoption of the federal Constitution.[10] Theoretically nonpolitical at its inception, the administration, as it established itself, became increasingly political.

By the end of his first term, although he did not realize it, or at least would not admit it, Washington had become essentially a political president,[11] and his government, as he came more and more under the influence of Alexander Hamilton, a one-party government. Political parties had, by this time, become a part of American society.[12]

* * * * *

The political foundations of Washington's government were, for the most part, anchored in the philosophy, ideas, and governmental program of Alexander Hamilton.[13] A brilliant young man of thirty-four when he became Secretary of the Treasury, Hamilton had already acquired a taste for high office and a thirst for power. He had already formed his ideas on politics and foreign policy,

[10] Sears, *George Washington,* pp. 414, 445. Washington, even though influenced by his advisers, was fully responsible for his administration. See White, *The Federalists . . . ,* pp. 7, 27; Robinson, *The Evolution of American Political Parties,* p. 59. No man who had opposed ratification of the Constitution was in Washington's official family.

[11] "To the end of his life Washington failed to recognize the close relationship between partisan politics and the practical views of the majority." Bradley, "Political Thinking of George Washington," *JSH,* XI, 480; see also James Hart, *The American Presidency in Action, 1789: A Study in Constitutional History* (New York, 1948), p. 2.

[12] Cunningham, "The Jeffersonian Party to 1801 . . . ," pp. 107, 175, 183-184.

[13] For a concise appraisal of Alexander Hamilton and his policies, see Rexford Guy Tugwell and Joseph Dorfman, "Alexander Hamilton: Nation Maker," *Columbia University Quarterly,* XXIX and XXX (Dec., 1937, and March, 1938), 209-226 and 59-72; Vernon L. Parrington, *Main Currents in American Thought . . .* (3 vols., New York, 1927-30), I, 292-306; for a precise outline of his life, see Allan Nevins in the *Dictionary of American Biography;* for a readable one-volume biography, see Nathan Schachner, *Alexander Hamilton* (New York, 1946); for an over-all view of the Hamilton-Jefferson clash, see Claude Bowers, *Jefferson and Hamilton, The Struggle for Democracy in America* (Boston, 1925); for a contemporary appraisal see La Rochefoucauld-Liancourt, *Travels . . . ,* II, 466-467. Even those who were opposed to Hamilton's policies recognized his great talent. Contemporaries believed that Hamilton directed the conduct of the Washington government, particularly in the latter years.

and he had formulated plans for putting those ideas into practice. To understand these ideas and plans a brief survey of his background should prove useful.

In the British West Indies where he had been born, the illegitimate son of Scottish and French parents, Hamilton had lived his first seventeen years.[14] In 1772, just before he reached eighteen, he went to New York at the expense of relatives and there entered King's College (later Columbia University) to complete his education. He quickly distinguished himself, revealing a remarkable mental maturity, and, espousing the colonial cause in opposition to British policies, he engaged actively in New York politics.

When hostilities broke out Hamilton took up arms under American colors, and at twenty-two became one of General Washington's aides-de-camp with the rank of lieutenant-colonel. In this strategic, if relatively unglamorous job, he came to know Washington; he learned much of the army; and more important, he learned much of the nation in the making.[15] Never reconciling himself to irksome clerical duties, he chafed impatiently under the conviction which he was to carry to his grave—that he was capable of and destined for a brilliant military career.[16]

Hamilton, not fortunate enough to have been born into the ruling landed aristocracy he admired, married into that society. At twenty-five, approximately a year before the surrender at Yorktown, he wed the second daughter of General Philip Schuyler, one of Washington's four major-generals and one of the wealthiest of the New York land barons.[17] In political, social, and financial

[14] Hamilton has generally been considered to have been two years younger than he was in fact. This in part explains his reputation for extraordinary precociousness. See Harold Larson, "Alexander Hamilton: The Fact and Fiction of His Early Years," *William and Mary Quarterly,* 3rd Series, IX (April, 1952), 145-146, and Broadus Mitchell, "The Secret of Alexander Hamilton," *Virginia Quarterly Review,* XXIX (Autumn, 1953), 595-609.

[15] How warm or how cordial was the friendship between Hamilton and Washington is a moot question. See Bowers, *Jefferson and Hamilton . . . ,* p. 41; John C. Hamilton, *History of the Republic of the United States of America, as Traced in the Writings of Alexander Hamilton and His Contemporaries* (7 vols., New York, 1857-64), II, 172-177.

[16] This is stressed in Adrienne Koch, "Hamilton, Adams and the Pursuit of Power," *Review of Politics,* XVI (Jan., 1954), 48; see also Bowers, *Jefferson and Hamilton . . . ,* p. 27.

[17] Moreau de Saint-Méry in his *Voyage aux États-Unis de l'Amérique,*

outlook, Hamilton found himself at home in his father-in-law's aristocratic circle. With the zeal and conviction often evident in the newly converted, he became an apostle of wealth, status, and stability.[18]

After the end of the war and with establishment of the government under the Articles of Confederation, Hamilton practiced law, served a term in Congress, and threw himself into the movement for a stronger central government. His contributions in support of the federal Constitution were major. In collaboration with James Madison and John Jay he defended the Constitution in *The Federalist*. He alone wrote over half the papers in this brilliant commentary on republican government.

Even though he had early fought the British in defense of the American cause, Hamilton admired the British constitution and system of government, which he maintained were the best in the world. At the Constitutional Convention he asserted, for example, that Americans could do no better than to model their new government after the British constitution.[19] Having no faith in the people, he distrusted the common man. To him the man-in-the-street was ignorant, irresponsible, lacking in control, completely incapable of wise government, and dominated by "selfish passions." Power in government should be entrusted to men of intelligence, educa-

---

1793-1798, ed. Stewart L. Mims (New Haven, 1913), p. 147, maintained that by his marriage Hamilton also acquired powerful connections in English political circles. For the English translation see Kenneth and Anna M. Roberts, eds. and translators, *Moreau de St. Méry's American Journey, 1793-1798* (Garden City, 1947), pp. 137 and 154 n. Such connections undoubtedly did not detract from Hamilton's pro-English leanings.

[18] For an instructive commentary on Hamilton's position in regard to government and the "protection of wealth," see Thomas P. Govan, "The Rich, the Well-born, and Alexander Hamilton," *Mississippi Valley Historical Review*, XXXVI (March, 1950), 675-680.

[19] See Hamilton's comments in the Committee of the Whole as reported by James Madison, June 18, 1787, in Charles C. Tansill, ed., . . . *Documents Illustrative of the Formation of the Union of the American States* (Washington, 1927), p. 220; also Frederick S. Oliver, *Alexander Hamilton: An Essay on American Union* (New York, 1907), p. 155; Lynton K. Caldwell, *The Administrative Theories of Hamilton and Jefferson: Their Contribution to Thought on Public Administration* (Chicago, 1944), p. 2 (hereinafter cited as Caldwell, *Hamilton and Jefferson*); James Bryce, *The Predictions of Hamilton and De Tocqueville* (Baltimore, 1887), p. 13.

tion, and wealth—an elite of superior individuals.[20] As men with property interests for the government to protect, they would have a selfish stake in that government, a stake they would defend.

Men, according to Hamilton, were not to be trusted on their own—*"every man must be supposed a knave."*[21] Even those whom he would have govern others were essentially untrustworthy, as they too placed "selfish passions" above principle. But Hamilton used those "selfish passions" to build the kind of strong central government he desired.[22]

* * * * *

Envisaging himself as something of a prime minister in Washington's official family, Hamilton developed and carried out a bold program designed to place the country on respectable footing in the world community of nations and to give it financial stability. At the same time he tried to weave his political philosophy into the nation's government in its formative years. His immediate objectives were to establish the nation's credit at home and abroad and to strengthen the national government at the expense of the states. To do this he launched a program which may be considered under four categories: economic, political, diplomatic, and constitutional. Using economics as his blueprint, Hamilton undertook to construct a governmental foundation on which to build a nation. Whatever contributed to a strong union, hence to his system, he believed was good policy.[23]

Actually, Americans took the first step in this program before Hamilton assumed office. Even so, he apparently had a hand in its formulation and it represented his views.[24] In essence it con-

[20] Govan, "The Rich, the Well-born, and Alexander Hamilton," *MVHR*, XXXVI, 675-680; Tansill, ed., . . . *Formation of the Union* . . . , p. 221; Caldwell, *Hamilton and Jefferson*, p. 10.

[21] Hamilton in "The Farmer Refuted," Feb. 5, 1775, citing David Hume, in John C. Hamilton, ed., *The Works of Alexander Hamilton* (7 vols., New York, 1850-51), II, 51 (hereinafter cited as Hamilton, ed., *Hamiltons' Works*).

[22] At the Constitutional Convention Hamilton urged strengthening the national government at the expense of the states. See his remarks, June 19, 1787, in Tansill, ed., . . . *Formation of the Union* . . . , pp. 786-787.

[23] For a variation of this interpretation, see Caldwell, *Hamilton and Jefferson*, p. 51; Joseph Charles, "Hamilton and Washington: The Origins of the American Party System," *WMQ*, 3rd Series, XII (April, 1955), 245.

[24] Edward Channing, *A History of the United States* (6 vols., New York, 1905-1925), IV, 64; Hamilton, *History of the Republic* . . . , IV, 4-7.

sisted of a series of laws passed by Congress in the summer of 1789:
the tariff act, the tonnage act, the act to regulate the collection of
duties, and the act for the registering and clearing of vessels.[25]
This commercial system produced needed revenue and laid down
a policy of limited protection for American industrial and commercial interests, and, through discriminatory imposts, could be
an effective instrument in foreign policy. As finally passed, the laws
favored Great Britain to the disadvantage of France and so laid the
foundation for Hamilton's system.[26]

Hamilton himself proposed the next step. In January, 1790,
he laid before Congress his plans for funding the national debt at
face value and for assumption in full by the national government
of debts incurred by the states during the Revolutionary War.[27]
So that American credit and status abroad might rise from their
low state, most congressmen felt that the nation's foreign debt—

[25] See *Annals of the Congress . . . ,* I, 46 (June 11 and 17, 1789); 53
(July 27, 1789); 73 (Aug. 25, 1789); U. S. Congress, Senate, *Tariff Acts
Passed by the Congress of the United States from 1789 to 1895 . . . ,* 54th
Cong., 1st Sess., Senate Document No. 219 (Washington, 1935), pp. 9-11;
William Hill, *The First Stages of the Tariff Policy of the United States,*
Publications of the American Economic Association, VIII (Baltimore, 1893),
107-130. Nathan Schachner in *Thomas Jefferson: A Biography* (2 vols.,
New York, 1951), I, 479, maintained that "every governmental policy—
foreign as well as domestic—hinged on the financial structure of the United
States." See also Beloff, *Thomas Jefferson and American Democracy,* pp.
113-115; also Nathan Schachner, *The Founding Fathers* (New York, 1954),
pp. 36-46. In later years an ardent Republican in attacking Hamilton's
commercial system, which he characterized as the "war system," declared that
it was like a "common hall" in a structure which "gives you access to all
the rooms of the federal building," Abraham Bishop, *Connecticut Republicanism : An Oration on the Extent and Power of Political Delusion . . .*
[delivered Sept., 1800] (Philadelphia, 1800), pp. 3, 10.

[26] The motives behind the tariff and tonnage laws have been the subject
of much controversy as to whether they were essentially protective or revenue-
producing. See Thomas W. Page, "The Earlier Commercial Policy of the
United States," *Journal of Political Economy,* X (March, 1902), 178; David
W. Brown, *The Commercial Power of Congress Considered in the Light
of Its Origin* (New York, 1910), pp. 154-155; Davis R. Dewey, *Financial
History of the United States* (12th ed.; New York, 1934), pp. 80-85.

[27] Hamilton spelled out his program in four notable reports which he submitted to Congress: (1) the First Report on the Public Credit, Jan. 14, 1790,
(2) the Second Report on the Public Credit, Dec. 13, 1790, (3) the Report on
the National Bank, Dec. 14, 1790, and (4) the Report on Manufactures,
Dec. 5, 1791. The reports are in Henry Cabot Lodge, ed., *The Works of
Alexander Hamilton* (9 vols., New York, 1885-86), Vols. II and III.

owed chiefly to French and Dutch creditors—should be paid in full.[28] But the proposed face-value payment of the domestic debt held by American bondholders—rascals and speculators as well as the original creditors—aroused opposition in Congress.

Hamilton and his followers insisted that the entire national debt, domestic and foreign, which they felt could not rightfully be divided, should be paid at face value. The opposition, led by James Madison in the House of Representatives, fought such payment on the ground that government bonds had depreciated to about twenty to fifteen cents and even as low as seven cents on the dollar and at those low figures had been bought by speculators who could afford to hold them and who anticipated a financial killing under Hamilton's scheme.[29] To allow such men to capitalize on their greed, the opposition maintained, would be to reward government-sponsored speculation and to discriminate against patriotic original holders. The contention was sound. Many of Hamilton's friends and others privy to the proposed funding had precipitated a scramble of speculation in an effort to buy the seemingly worthless bonds at low prices from unsuspecting holders, particularly from those in the South.[30]

Hamilton's motives in proposing funding were as much political and diplomatic as they were economic. By paying the debt he

[28] Jefferson also favored paying the foreign debt. He believed that "the existence of a nation having no credit is always precarious." Jefferson to James Madison, Paris, May 3, 1788, in Lipscomb, *Jefferson's Works*, VI, 455, and Malone, *Jefferson and the Rights of Man*, p. 289.

[29] For Madison's role in the battle over assumption, see Irving Brant, *James Madison: Father of the Constitution, 1787-1800* (Indianapolis, 1950), pp. 290-305. According to Brant, Madison by fighting Hamilton's assumption scheme "split the original Federalists asunder, fused one part of them with the radical wing of the vanishing Anti-federalists and gave direction to the political cleavage which swiftly divided the American public into Federalists and Republicans." Moreover, Madison "planted the seed and started the growth of the party which received the Jeffersonian label. He did this before Jefferson re-entered the national scene from his diplomatic exile." In Virginia Hamilton's assumption proposals created a political opposition to the government; in fact, Hamilton's fiscal program may have produced the first real antagonism against the Washington administration. See Ammon, "The Formation of the Republican Party in Virginia," *JSH*, XIX, 289, 297.

[30] Remarked anti-Hamilton William Maclay, "The great object is, by funding and so forth, to raise the certificates to par; thus the speculators, who now have them nearly all engrossed, will clear above three hundred per cent." William Maclay, *The Journal of William Maclay, United States Senator from Pennsylvania, 1789-1791* (New York, 1927), p. 195, entry of Feb. 19, 1790.

would establish American credit abroad and would bind the men of wealth and status, who had come to acquire most of the domestically held bonds, to the new national government. Through exchange of their bonds at face-value for interest-bearing certificates, Hamilton would reward them handsomely and at the same time place the government in their debt. America's wealthy citizens would acquire a vested interest in, and, to protect their own interests, would support, the government. Hamiltonians pushed the funding plan through Congress.

Similar motives impelled Hamilton to propose, and the Congress to adopt, assumption of state debts by the federal government. Regarding the Constitution as weak cement for union—"a frail and worthless fabric"—and sectionalism as an ever-present danger, he hoped through assumption to add strength to the central government by making the states financially dependent.[31] The French *chargé d'affaires* understood Hamilton's objective. He observed that funding the state debts would help to consolidate the United States and believed that Hamilton's system would make a nation of a dozen republics.[32] Another foreign diplomat, however, noted general dissatisfaction with Hamilton's measures and increasing distrust between Northern and Southern states.[33]

* * * * *

Another step in the program was creation of the first Bank of the United States, modeled after the Bank of England. Four-fifths of the bank's capital stock was to be subscribed by private individuals; the remaining fifth was to be held by the federal government. While remaining a privately controlled bank, it would serve as a depository for federal funds and would be authorized to issue paper money on the basis of securities it held.

Again in this proposal Hamilton went beyond the realm of

[31] For a fuller discussion of the funding and assumption schemes, see John S. Bassett, *The Federalist System, 1789-1801* (New York, 1906), pp. 30-38; Schachner, *The Founding Fathers,* pp. 83-121.

[32] Louis-Guillaume Otto to [Minister of Foreign Affairs], New York, Jan. 19, 1790, Edmond C. Genet Papers, Library of Congress, VII, 2176-2177.

[33] John Hamilton, British Consul at Norfolk, to Duke of Leeds, Norfolk, Va., April 10, 1791, British Foreign Correspondence: America, Henry Adams Transcripts, Library of Congress. Hereinafter cited as the Henry Adams Transcripts.

finance, and the measure, in the long run, proved more important for its political and constitutional implications. His reasons for wanting the bank may be reduced to three: first, by benefiting the business classes, which would largely control it, the bank would serve as another tie between that group and the central government; second, by chartering the bank Congress would at the same time add strength to the federal government—by accepting the principle of implied powers; and, third, by enlarging the powers of the national legislature the federal government would increase in power while the sovereignty of state governments would decline.

There was nothing in the Constitution which authorized Congress to create a bank. Basis might be found only in the clause of Article I of the Constitution which gave Congress power to enact laws which were "necessary and proper" for carrying out the powers of government as laid down by the Constitution.[34] When confronted with the bank charter after it had passed Congress, Washington asked his department heads, as came to be his practice, to submit their written opinions on the question before signing it. He was puzzled as to its constitutionality.[35]

Declaring that Congress had no powers not granted it specifically by the Constitution, Jefferson maintained the bank measure was unconstitutional. In referring to the "necessary and proper" clause, he made the word "necessary" the foundation for his contention that, while the bank might be a useful instrument for regulating the currency, it certainly was not indispensable or "necessary" for the task.[36]

Hamilton, on the other hand, advanced the doctrine of implied powers by asserting that the federal government, within the limits of its delegated powers, could determine necessary methods for executing its functions. In referring to the "necessary and proper"

[34] For details on the bank, see John T. Holdsworth and Davis R. Dewey, *The First and Second Banks of the United States* (National Monetary Commission, 61st Cong., 2nd Sess., Senate Document No. 571, Washington, 1910), pp. 9-144, and Joseph S. Davis, *Essays in the Earlier History of American Corporations,* Harvard Economic Studies, XVI (2 vols., Cambridge, 1917), pp. 50-54; James O. Wettereau, "New Light on the First Bank of the United States," *PMBH,* LXI (July, 1937), 263-285.

[35] Freeman, *Washington,* VI, 291-293.

[36] Jefferson's "Opinion on the Constitutionality of a National Bank," Feb. 15, 1791, in Ford, *Writings of Jefferson,* V, 284-289.

clause, he, in turn, emphasized the word "proper" as the basis for his argument. Since Congress had the right to regulate the currency, it had the power to charter a national bank as a "proper" and advantageous means for regulating the currency.[37] Washington accepted Hamilton's views and in February, 1791, signed the bank bill into law.

In carrying out his program Hamilton was defeated in only one sweeping measure. This was in his proposal, embodied in the Report on Manufactures of December 5, 1791, to aid the growth of infant American industries through various protective laws. Behind the report lay the basic idea that the general welfare required encouragement of manufactures and that the federal government was obligated to direct the national economy to that end.

Previously Madison and others had urged a protectionist tariff policy, which at the time was a special policy of expediency designed to strike at England. In his report Hamilton, too, urged a protectionist commercial policy, but not a policy of immediate expediency. It was, instead, a broad theoretical policy fitting his over-all system, a policy based not on antagonism toward England but on admiration of England's commercial society, which Hamilton would have America emulate.[38] Instrumental in this first important Hamiltonian defeat was the opposition of Jefferson and Madison.[39]

* * * * *

[37] See Hamilton's "Opinion as to the Constitutionality of the Bank of the United States," Feb. 23, 1791, Hamilton, ed., *Hamilton's Works*, IV, 104-138. For accounts involving the principals of the bank issue, see Malone, *Jefferson and the Rights of Man*, 337-350; Schachner, *Alexander Hamilton*, 268-273; Freeman, *Washington*, VI, 289-293.

[38] The report is in Lodge, *The Works of Alexander Hamilton*, III, 294-416; for a discussion of the theory of the report see Caldwell, *Hamilton and Jefferson*, pp. 63-68; Arthur H. Cole, *Industrial and Commercial Correspondence of Alexander Hamilton Anticipating His Report on Manufactures* (Chicago, 1928), p. 234; see also Schachner, *The Founding Fathers*, pp. 185-188.

[39] The ideological basis for the defeat is stated succinctly in Adrienne Koch, *Jefferson and Madison: The Great Collaboration* (New York, 1950), pp. 127-131. Despite the defeat, Hamilton's ideas expressed in the Report influenced Federalist thought and deed. In later years, for example, William Vans Murray, Federalist congressman from Maryland, in analyzing the program he had supported in Congress, placed at the head of his list manufactures—"agreeable to Mr. Hamilton's excellent Report (and indeed of A. Smith & others) of 1791." See William Vans Murray Papers, Commonplace Book, July 28, 1795 (Princeton).

Two more major steps completed Hamilton's policy structure. One was an excise tax placed on whiskey; the other was the Proclamation of Neutrality of 1793. To pay for funding and assumption the government needed money. To raise money and to assert the power of the federal government Hamilton proposed an excise tax on distilled liquors.[40] For various reasons this tax, when adopted, hit hardest the small farmers of the interior, West and South, who commonly converted their corn into easily transported, easily sold, and easily consumed whiskey. While designed to raise money, the excise tax was also a political device. This internal tax, imposed by the central government in a domain considered by the states to be theirs exclusively, would serve to impress the anti-Hamiltonian rural folk with the power of the central government. At the same time, through federal enforcement, the tax would serve to combat sectionalism. Heartily opposed by Westerners from the day it first became law in March, 1791, the excise tax finally, in 1794, led to an uprising of farmers in western Pennsylvania known as "The Whiskey Rebellion."[41]

To Hamilton the rebellion presented an opportunity he had long coveted. Some Hamiltonians, however, were frightened; they believed that the "insurrection" was part of a plot to destroy the federal government.[42] Under the Constitution Congress had power to use the militia "to execute the laws of the union" and to "suppress insurrections." Congress, in turn, had authorized the President to call out state militia for such enforcement. With Western farmers openly defying national law, the issue was clear. The strength of the federal government, as opposed to local defiance, was for the first

[40] See Hamilton's First Report on the Public Credit, Jan. 14, 1790, in Lodge, *The Works of Alexander Hamilton*, II, 90-92; Hamilton's theory of collateral taxation is discussed in Caldwell, *Hamilton and Jefferson*, pp. 57-61.

[41] For accounts of the Whiskey Rebellion, see *American State Papers, Miscellaneous*, I, 83-113; Leland D. Baldwin, *Whiskey Rebels: The Story of a Frontier Uprising* (Pittsburgh, 1939); Bennett M. Rich, *The Presidents and Civil Disorder* (Washington, 1941), pp. 2-20; Russell J. Ferguson, *Early Western Pennsylvania Politics* (Pittsburgh, 1938), pp. 126-129; Raymond Walters, Jr., *Alexander James Dallas: Lawyer-Politician-Financier* (Philadelphia, 1943), pp. 52-64; Harry M. Tinkcom, *The Republicans and Federalists in Pennsylvania, 1790-1801: A Study in National Stimulus and Local Response* (Harrisburg, Pa., 1950), pp. 91-112.

[42] William Vans Murray Papers, Commonplace Book, Dec. 11, 1795 (Princeton).

time to be tested on the field of battle. Would the states remain loyal to the Union? Would they respond to a call to use force on behalf of the central government against a sister state? The crisis was met. Four states, including Pennsylvania, answered Washington's call for troops.

At the head of federal troops, 9000 foot and 3000 horse, Hamilton put on a show of force and marched on Pennsylvania's western counties. Opposition melted away and no battle ensued. A few rebel leaders were apprehended and in time pardoned. Their detention was not important. What did matter was that federal authority had triumphed against its first rebellious adversary and that in the crisis it had won support of state governments.[43]

Expressing well the Hamiltonian attitude, a congressman rejoiced that "the insurrection in Pennsylvania is the happiest event that ever happened to the United States. It has exhibited Democracy in practice and even Democrats are frightened with the horrid monster ... the suppression of this insurrection will give the Government of the United States a tone, an energy, and dignity, which will defy all the efforts of Anarchy and Jacobinism."[44]

But Hamilton's policies needed more than domestic success. They were predicated upon peace and friendship with Great Britain. Without a sympathetic and co-ordinated foreign policy Hamilton's elaborate blueprint for the making of a nation could not be translated into a functioning system of government. In Hamilton's view, moreover, the attitude of foreign powers was the determining force in measuring the prestige of a government.[45]

When news of war between France and England reached the United States in April, 1793, Hamilton, in opposition to Secretary of State Jefferson, urged President Washington to announce America's determination to remain neutral. In addition to harboring a personal partiality for England he saw that if the United

[43] Adrienne Koch in "Hamilton, Adams and the Pursuit of Power," *RP*, XVI, 49 stresses Hamilton's role in the Whiskey Rebellion as evidence of Hamilton's influence over Washington and that the government was functioning according to his views.
[44] Zephaniah Swift to David Daggett, Philadelphia, Nov. 11, 1794, in Franklin B. Dexter, ed., "Selections from Letters Received by David Daggett, 1786-1802," *Proceedings of the American Antiquarian Society*, New Series, IV (1885-87), 373.
[45] See Caldwell, *Hamilton and Jefferson*, p. 11.

States did not remain at peace with and friendly to Great Britain—despite the alliance with France—his entire program would collapse.

Most of America's trade was with Great Britain; the Hamiltonian program was financed by the income from import duties; war against Great Britain would destroy the program.[46] Without British trade the new nation's efforts to establish a respectable credit standing abroad would fail. The very existence of the country, the Secretary of the Treasury feared, would be jeopardized. Great Britain, with her powerful navy, was then the only power capable of mounting a transatlantic attack against the United States. She must not be antagonized. Shunting aside obligations under the French alliance and gratitude for French help in the Revolution, Hamilton was convinced that England was the nation whose interests were most compatible with those of the United States.[47]

While more will be said about the neutrality legislation, it is sufficient at this point to indicate that Washington followed Hamilton's advice and issued the Proclamation of Neutrality on April 22, 1793. Thus in its major aspects Hamilton completed his program.

* * * * *

By the end of 1790 and the beginning of 1791 Hamilton's contemporaries realized that his economic-political-constitutional-diplomatic measures were dividing the country. In government and out men were coalescing into two political factions. Precisely when this division took place is not known. Historians and students of politics have advanced varying interpretations as to when the split occurred and what produced it. Despite blurred details of party origin, scholars generally agree that the first national political parties were spawned by the Hamiltonian system and solidified by foreign-policy problems arising out of relations with France and England. By 1792, the close of Washington's first term, the United States had two clearly discernible national political groupings. One of these looked to Hamilton and Washington for leadership.

[46] For significance of Anglo-American trade, see Bemis, *Jay's Treaty . . . ,* pp. 33-36. In 1790 nearly two-thirds of America's foreign trade was with countries under the British flag; see Emory R. Johnson and others, *History of Domestic and Foreign Commerce of the United States* (2 vols., Washington, 1915), II, 6-7.

[47] For a discussion of Hamilton's ideas on foreign policy bearing on a similar theme, see Caldwell, *Hamilton and Jefferson,* pp. 74-75.

Successful though he was in gaining support of Washington and of other prominent conservatives for his program, Hamilton was never able to win any appreciable popular support for it. His plans, however, were not predicated on the assumption of popular support, which he held in contempt.[48] With each new success Hamilton's policies aroused greater and more effective opposition, so much so that Thomas Jefferson, alarmed by various aspects of the Hamiltonian "system," undertook, with James Madison, the task of organizing a political opposition to contest the control of government by Hamilton and his followers.[49]

Even though he may have deplored "faction" and party strife, Washington was not above partisan politics, particularly in his second administration. While Hamilton designed the economic-political program, Washington made it the basis of his government. Although he relied heavily on department heads and deferred to their views, all decisions were his; responsibility for policies followed rested ultimately with Washington.[50]

The President accepted Hamilton's policies because he was under the influence of his Secretary of the Treasury, and because he too believed that only a strong central government could secure a respected place in the world community of nations. Washington's method of conducting government aided implementation of Hamilton's ideas. Foreign policy, a main source of conflict between Jefferson and Hamilton, was generally the major subject for discussion in Cabinet meetings. In these meetings Hamilton, backed by his personal partisans, almost always won acceptance for his ideas on foreign policy.[51]

[48] Many Federalists shared Hamilton's contempt for "popularity," which was believed to be "an evil most felt in a free govt. . . . a vice without limits." William Vans Murray Papers, Commonplace Book, July 23, 1795 (Princeton). See also Bowers, *Jefferson and Hamilton* . . . , pp. 29, 266; Schachner, *Alexander Hamilton*, p. 339; Caldwell, *Hamilton and Jefferson*, pp. 7, 11-12. Hamilton apparently never fully understood the necessity of popular leadership for the kind of "system" he wanted.

[49] See Malone, *Jefferson and the Rights of Man*, p. 350; Brant, *Madison: Father of the Constitution* . . . , pp. 332-333.

[50] See Bradley, "The Political Thinking of George Washington," *JSH*, XI, 486; White, *The Federalists* . . . , p. 27; Herbert Agar, *The Price of Union* (Boston, 1950), p. 74.

[51] Freeman, in *Washington*, VI, 293, maintained that Washington believed in a strong central government because only thus could the United States

The men who accepted the political leadership of Hamilton
and Washington—in the main they were merchants, bankers, and
professional men of New England and the Eastern Seaboard—
formed the core of America's first national political coalition, the
Federalist party.[52] They emphasized efficient government and stable
social and economic conditions, as opposed to uncontrolled freedom,
which they saw as anarchy. The party dedicated itself to securing a government under the tutelage of the rich and well-born;
indeed, many of the Federalists favored a monarchy.[53]

Financially and politically, Federalist leaders were bound together by common interests.[54] Their organization had more the
cohesiveness of a closed corporate body than of a political organization, which by its very nature must cater to diverse interests. The
interlocking lines of connections among Federalist leaders crossed
the Atlantic and extended to England. By marriage, blood relation-
ships, and common financial interests, Federalist leaders were
tied to persons of high finance and politics in Great Britain, the
ruling element in Parliament.[55] British influence with them was

---

remain free. See also Bradley, "The Political Thinking of George Washington," *JSH*, XI, 472; Caldwell, *Hamilton and Jefferson*, p. 228; White, *The
Federalists* . . . , p. 217; Charles, "Hamilton and Washington . . . ," *WMQ*,
3rd Series, XII, 255-256.

[52] Not the same federalists who had fought for ratification of the Constitution.

[53] No evidence has been unearthed to reveal that the Federalists in power
ever set on foot "definite projects" for establishing a monarchy; see Louise
B. Dunbar, *A Study of "Monarchical" Tendencies in the United States, from
1776-1801,* "University of Illinois Studies in the Social Sciences," X, No. I
(Urbana, Ill., 1923), 115. Nonetheless, Republicans believed that Hamiltonians
saw "no stability, no security in any kind of government but a monarchy."
Jefferson, The Anas, Nov. 21, 1792, in Ford, *Writings of Jefferson,* I, 209.

[54] Federalists never did form a truly national political party in the same
sense that their opponents did; they never did believe in political parties; see
Binkley, *American Political Parties* . . . , p. 49; Marshall Smelser, "The Jacobin
Phrenzy: Federalism and the Menace of Liberty, Equality, and Fraternity,"
Review of Politics, XIII (Oct., 1951), 458. In New Jersey, for example, al-
though Federalists were dominant until 1800 they never organized a highly
developed state machine. Richard P. McCormick, *The History of Voting in
New Jersey: A Study of the Development of Election Machinery, 1664-1911*
(New Brunswick, 1953), pp. 87-88.

[55] Channing, *A History of the United States,* IV, 167-168; Samuel E.
Morison, *The Maritime History of Massachusetts, 1783 to 1860* (Boston, 1921),
pp. 168-69.

not based on mere theorizing or intellectual predilection; it was in the air they breathed.

In spite of Washington's Federalist views, in the beginning of the national government whatever political "opposition" existed directed itself not against him but against Hamilton.[56]   As the government sank roots, those who opposed the Federalists were at first known simply as antifederalists.   Later, as they coalesced and formed a political organization, they were distinguished as Republicans, and their organization became the Republican party.

*   *   *   *   *

Differing with Federalists in fundamental issues, Republicans favored a comparatively weak national government under popular control, a government whose primary foundation was to be the small farmer of the interior.   In foreign policy Republicans supported the French alliance, whereas Federalists would scuttle the alliance and favored close ties with England.   The Republicans, opposed to a governmental elite of intellect and wealth, believed that the common people, the small farmer folk, were capable of governing themselves.

In general, they espoused local political autonomy as against centralized political control, and fought the fourfold Hamiltonian program.   Governments were not ends in themselves, Republicans contended; governments existed to promote the individual happiness and well-being of all men, not to enrich the special few. With their main concentrations in the back-country settlements and in the rural-planter South, Republicans had in Thomas Jefferson the leader who met their needs.[57]

[56] Malone, *Jefferson and the Rights of Man,* p. 421; Brant, *James Madison: Father of the Constitution* . . . , pp. 351-370; for Washington's popularity, see Freeman, *Washington,* VI, 322, 353-354.

[57] Joseph Charles in "Adams and Jefferson: The Origins of the American Party System," *WMQ,* 3rd series, XII (July, 1955), 446, concluded that "Jefferson did not create a party; a widespread popular movement recognized and claimed him as its leader."   For a succinct statement of the Jeffersonian view of government and how it differed from the Hamiltonian position, see Beloff, *Thomas Jefferson and American Democracy,* pp. 127-139; see also Carl L. Becker, "What Is Still Living in the Political Philosophy of Thomas Jefferson," *American Historical Review,* XLVIII (July, 1943), 691-706; Charles M. Wiltse, *The Jeffersonian Tradition in American Democracy* (Chapel Hill, 1935).

Unlike Hamilton, Jefferson was a great planter and aristocrat in his own right, being during most of his life the master of some 10,000 Virginia acres and from 100 to 200 slaves. Yet he was the champion of the small farmer, a liberal by intellectual conviction.[58] Again unlike Hamilton, he knew the back country, its people, and its problems. Born the son of a pioneer gentleman-settler in one of Virginia's western counties, he grew to manhood among frontiersmen and small farmers of the interior.

After being educated in his early years by a tutor, Jefferson at seventeen went to Williamsburg, where he entered the College of William and Mary. There for the first time he saw town life; for the first time he saw "culture." Leaving William and Mary he turned to law, which in turn led to politics and public office. In or out of office he was active in the events which led to the American Revolution, making notable contributions with his writing. From his pen flowed the words of the Declaration of Independence.

Following terms in the Virginia House of Burgesses and in the Continental Congress in the summer and autumn of 1775, Jefferson served as war-governor of Virginia. Elected governor in 1779, he served a term of office which was not particularly noteworthy and which ended ingloriously. Once again, in 1783, he served in Congress, this time for six months. Being a poor public speaker, Jefferson was never able to sway men in large groups. Like Hamilton, he did his most effective work in public office with his pen.

Leaving behind him domestic tribulations of a raw government, Jefferson in 1784 sailed for France to assist John Adams and Benjamin Franklin in obtaining commercial treaties for the new United States. In the following year Congress appointed him Franklin's successor as minister to France, a post he held until October, 1789. Jefferson was convinced that America's welfare depended on continued close relationship with France, a doctrine he called the "polar star" of his policy.[59] Although he placed his country's welfare above the French alliance, he believed that his country owed to France a debt of gratitude and thought that

[58] Becker, ". . . Political Philosophy of Thomas Jefferson," *AHR*, XLVIII, 700.

[59] Jefferson, "The Anas," Dec. 27, 1792, in Ford, *Writings of Jefferson*, I, 212.

France would serve as a valuable counterpoise against England. Regarding England as selfish, commercially arrogant, and hostile to the United States, he feared her as a country not to be trusted.[60]

With France in revolution Jefferson ended his duties abroad and in November, 1789, returned to the United States. Soon after his return President Washington offered him the post of Secretary of State. Always shy and somewhat fearful of publicity, Jefferson was at first reluctant to accept the office, but finally, for patriotic reasons, he consented. He began his new duties in March, 1790.

While Jefferson had not personally taken part in establishing the new government and had considered the Articles of Confederation as forming an excellent framework for a democratic society, he nonetheless had favored a stronger national government and in general approved of the federal Constitution. In particular he approved of placing foreign affairs under exclusive federal control.[61] From firsthand experience he had seen the flaws in a diplomacy lacking the support of a national government.

Unaware of the conservative reaction in government during the years he was in France, the new Secretary of State applied himself to his job and soon grasped the significance of the power wielded in the new order of affairs by Hamilton. What particularly shocked Jefferson was that the nation's former enemy and his own object of distrust—England—was emulated and held in high esteem by those in power while France, ally and proven friend, was scorned and hated.[62] When Jefferson came into Washington's official family Hamilton had already launched his fourfold program. The rich,

[60] The literature on Jefferson is enormous. For reliable short biographies, see Gilbert Chinard, *Thomas Jefferson: The Apostle of Americanism* (2nd rev. ed.; Boston, 1939); Saul K. Padover, *Jefferson* (New York, 1932); Nathan Schachner, *Thomas Jefferson: A Biography* (2 vols., New York, 1951); the most recent and best multivolume biography, of which two volumes have been published, is Dumas Malone, *Jefferson and His Time* (Boston, 1948—); for a discerning French appraisal of Jefferson, see La Rochefoucauld-Liancourt, *Travels . . . ,* II, 77-80; for Jefferson's ideas, see Adrienne Koch, *The Philosophy of Thomas Jefferson* (New York, 1943).

[61] Malone, *Jefferson and the Rights of Man,* p. 174; Jefferson believed that the primary function of the government of the Confederation was management of foreign affairs; the state governments were responsible for domestic affairs; see Patterson, *The Constitutional Principles of Thomas Jefferson,* p. 77.

[62] See Schachner, *Thomas Jefferson . . . ,* I, 406-407.

and those who aspired to be rich, were praising it, and the debate over assumption and funding was reaching a climax.[63]

At the outset Jefferson and Hamilton showed no hostility; they had not met until they became colleagues in the spring of 1790. Despite his concern over things he heard and saw in the government, Jefferson at first appeared determined to co-operate with Hamilton. He even expressed approval of part of the Hamiltonian program, as for example the payment of the foreign and domestic debt at face value. Active and organized political activity was far from his mind. As the Hamiltonian program developed and as Hamilton's ideas came to dominate government, early making themselves felt in foreign affairs, the Secretary of State found himself increasingly at odds with the Secretary of the Treasury.[64]

Jefferson in principle opposed assumption of state debts, but he yielded to Hamilton on this issue to avoid an apparent sectional split in the Union. He made a "bargain" with Hamilton over the location of the national capital. The South got the nation's capital city and Hamilton and the Northern financiers received in return "assumption" of the state debts by the federal government.[65]

On the question of the national bank the two men were far apart. After Washington, in February, 1791, signed the bank bill into law, Jefferson turned from private appeals to the President to open political opposition to advance his own ideas and governmental program. The unity Washington cherished had not lasted through his first term in office.[66]

[63] Hamilton had also already started to implement his concept of administrative responsibility, that is, his role in government; see Caldwell, *Hamilton and Jefferson*, p. 218.

[64] Hamilton, for example, corresponded directly with American ministers abroad and directly with foreign diplomatic representatives in the United States; see Caldwell, *Hamilton and Jefferson*, p. 228.

[65] For a detailed account of the "bargain," see Malone, *Jefferson and the Rights of Man*, pp. 298-303, 506. For newspaper debate over the seat of government, see Margaret Woodbury, *Public Opinion in Philadelphia, 1789-1801*, "Smith College Studies in History," V, Nos. 1-2 (Northampton, Mass., 1919-1920), 106.

[66] One of Jefferson's recent biographers believes that the bank issue marked the "definitive break" between Hamilton and Jefferson and that more than any other cause it hastened formation of the Federalist and Republican parties. See Schachner, *Thomas Jefferson . . .*, I, 416, 422; also Malone, *Jefferson and the Rights of Man*, pp. 349-350.

Differences between Hamilton and Jefferson were not merely personal, nor were the political parties they came to head based upon personalism. They, as individuals, symbolized issues larger than personal quarrels. Their ideological differences represented the political division between two segments of American society.[67] Jefferson feared concentrated power most; his ideal was as little government as possible. Foreign affairs, not the everyday affairs of the people, were the major concerns of the federal government. Local and domestic problems were, he felt, the exclusive concern of the state governments. In this way American soil would breed no tyranny; its fertility would be for liberty only.[68] To Hamilton, on the other hand, this would lead to hateful anarchy. Hamilton wanted to build a nation based on industry and commerce, a nation with a balanced economy. Jefferson, in contrast, would build his America on the small farmer and the artisan. Being something of a pacifist, Jefferson saw commerce as a weapon of coercion with which to avoid war; Hamilton would, and did, use commerce to support a stratified society modeled on that of England.

In their ideas on society, on the kind of nation they envisioned the America of the future to be, can be found an important link to the foreign-policy concepts of Jefferson and Hamilton. Although Jefferson accepted commerce and industry as necessary adjuncts to agriculture, he was wedded to the idea of an agrarian America, and detested commercial, industrial society. England to him was an example of what the United States should not be; he was convinced that it would be fatal for the United States "to become a mere city of London, to carry on the commerce of half the world

[67] For covenient summary of "The Hamilton-Jefferson Feud," see White, *The Federalists* . . . , pp. 222-236; also Malone, *Jefferson and the Rights of Man*, p. 421; Beloff, *Thomas Jefferson and American Democracy*, p. 132. The "root" of Jefferson's opposition to Hamilton's program seems to have been essentially political rather than economic: Hamilton was likewise politically motivated. At times he opposed measures or reversed himself primarily to be on the side opposite Jefferson. See Tugwell and Dorfman, "Alexander Hamilton . . . ," *CUQ*, XXX, 66 n.; for economic emphasis, see Beard, *Economic Origins of Jeffersonian Democracy*, p. 216; for future implications of the Jefferson-Hamilton clash, see James Truslow Adams, "Jefferson and Hamilton Today: The Dichotomy in American Thought," *Atlantic Monthly*, CXLI (April, 1928), 443-450.

[68] Jefferson's concepts of government are discussed in Caldwell, *Hamilton and Jefferson*, pp. 112-117.

at the expense of waging eternal war with the other half." That through commerce, banking, industry, and other allied evils, England was losing her freedom—the most striking example of such a country in the world—he never wearied to point out. If Americans did not profit by the example, he feared they would suffer the same loss.[69] This concept, in part, explains Jefferson's foreign-policy orientation toward France and his antipathy toward England.

Hamilton, on the other hand, saw no future in an essentially agrarian economy. Everything in society he admired and would seek to reproduce—commerce, industry, banking, a stable social stratification in which the wealthy ruled—could be found in England. England was an island; Hamilton would make a continent in her image.[70] In France he saw an agrarian economy racked by anarchy, instability, and, as a result of revolution, by the excesses of democracy.

In the French Revolution and ideas of French philosophers, Jefferson saw the kind of liberty he wanted for the United States. The evolving French Revolution, in fact, strengthened his conviction that France and America were bound together not merely by political alliance but also by ideology, by strength of ideas.[71] With

[69] See Becker, ". . . Political Philosophy of Thomas Jefferson," *AHR,* XLVIII, 700; for Jefferson's enmity toward England, see Woolery, *The Relation of Thomas Jefferson to American Foreign Policy,* pp. 85-86.

[70] For evidences of Hamilton's use of England as a model, see the comparative statements in Govan, "The Rich, the Well-born, and Alexander Hamilton," *MVHR,* XXXVI, 675-680. "Hamilton," noted a contemporary as to his system, "seems to have profited by the practice of the wisest European nations, England especially." See Peter Van Schaack to Henry Van Schaack, Kinderhook, Feb. 7, 1790, in Henry C. Van Schaack, *The Life of Peter Van Schaack, LL.D.* (New York, 1842), p. 434.

[71] To Brissot de Warville Jefferson declared that he was "eternally attached to the principles" of the French Revolution, Philadelphia, May 8, 1793, in Ford, *Writings of Jefferson,* VI, 249. In general, however, Jefferson is considered to have been slightly influenced by French thought; see Wiltse, *The Jeffersonian Tradition . . . ,* pp. 49-52. Yet such a conclusion is difficult to reconcile with his admiration of France and the principles of the French Revolution. Certain French thinkers, probably the Physiocrats, undoubtedly had an influence on Jefferson as did certain aspects of French society; see Joseph Dorfman, "The Economic Philosophy of Thomas Jefferson," *Political Science Quarterly,* LV (March, 1940), 106. Hamilton, for example, believed that Jefferson "drank freely of the French philosophy, in religion, in science, in politics." Hamilton to Col. Edward Carrington, Philadelphia, May 26, 1792, in Lodge, *The Works of Alexander Hamilton,* VIII, 259; see also Vossler,

Hamilton and his followers constantly avowing their admiration for the English constitution, English finance, and English society, Jeffersonians concluded that "the zealous apostles of English despotism" were working to establish a monarchy in North America in the image of the mother country. That Americans could countenance such an idea distressed Jefferson, who saw America's national welfare threatened by France's monarchical enemies, "the confederacy of princes against human liberty."[72]   Hamilton was convinced that the everlasting tie with England could not be escaped. "We think in English," he said.

Even though the national political struggle that was in the making from 1791 to 1793 was the product, in many respects, of domestic differences, the question of foreign policy was always present. / Control over foreign policy was inherent in the struggle; it sparked organized political activity.   The future and immediate welfare of the American democratic experiment was harnessed to relations with France and England.   And it was precisely in the critical area of foreign affairs that Hamilton and Jefferson first clashed.[73]

Die amerikanischen Revolutionsideale in ihrem verhältnis zu den europaischen: Untersucht en Thomas Jefferson (Munich, 1929), p. 127; Palmer "A Neglected Work . . .," *WMQ,* 3rd Series, XII, 466-467.   Vossler maintains that Jefferson turned from Locke to Rousseau.   Woodrow Wilson believed that Jefferson's ideas were "un-American" because "of the strain of French philosophy that permeated and weakened all his thought . . . ," quoted in Latané, "Jefferson's Influence on American Foreign Policy," *Alumni Bulletin of the University of Virginia,* XVII, 245-246.

[72] The quotations are from Jefferson to Brissot de Warville, Philadelphia, May 8, 1793, and Jefferson to James Madison, Philadelphia, May 19, 1793, in Ford, *Writings of Jefferson,* VI, 249, 261; see also Jefferson to Harry Innes, Philadelphia, May 23, 1793, pp. 265-266.   Jefferson's "rooted aversion to Great Britain," contended the British minister in Philadelphia, stemmed from being a British debtor.   This united him in sympathy with other debtors, "the great mass of individuals who were in a similar situation"; see George Hammond to Grenville, Philadelphia, March 7, 1793, Henry Adams Transcripts.

[73] The greatest personal grievance which Jefferson held against Hamilton was his interference in foreign affairs.   Malone, *Jefferson and the Rights of Man,* p. 452; also pp. xx, 304, 328; White, *The Federalists . . . ,* p. 224; Caldwell, *Hamilton and Jefferson,* p. 228.   In Connecticut, as elsewhere, for example, differing views on foreign policy provided the issue which split the people into two political groups or parties.   Richard J. Purcell, *Connecticut in Transition, 1775-1818* (Washington, 1918), p. 288.   To Jefferson and other Republican leaders the unanimity of sentimental appeal offered by the French

The Hamiltonian program conflicted with the foreign policy which Jefferson as Secretary of State wanted. Anglo-American and Franco-American relations, in their political implications, were inseparable. Foreign policy, therefore, dominated domestic politics and American life as it has at virtually no time since.

* * * * *

By the spring of 1791 Jefferson and Hamilton were committed to political war. Hamilton's victory in the bank issue had been but one of many factors hastening the formation of national political alignments. Jefferson, Madison, and their cohorts launched an offensive against Hamilton. With widespread disapproval of Washington's policy toward France as a rallying point, they organized popular opposition to Washington's policies, an opposition which had existed but which had not before been exploited.[74] Even though Jeffersonians made policy toward France a central issue the Jeffersonian objective remained constant—destruction of Hamiltonianism and capture of the government.

Jefferson tried to sabotage Hamilton's status with the President, to emasculate his Treasury Department, to destroy him through attacks in the House of Representatives, and in all ways to demolish his power. Though often driven to the defensive, Hamilton fought back, counterattacked, and continued to press forward his program. On one occasion, when he opposed placing the Secretary of State second in line for the Presidency, Hamilton said that he "ran counter to Mr. Jefferson's wishes; but if I had no other reason for it, I had already experienced opposition from him which rendered it a measure of self-defence."[75]

Revolution, which they favored, presented political opportunities which they did not fail to utilize for party purposes. McCarrell, "Formation of the Jeffersonian Party in Virginia," pp. 100-101. In Pennsylvania, too, foreign policy split the people politically; year after year the governor referred to foreign policy in his message to the state legislature. Kenneth R. Rossman, *Thomas Mifflin and the Politics of the American Revolution* (Chapel Hill, 1952), p. 290.

[74] Ammon, "The Formation of the Republican Party in Virginia . . . ," *JSH*, XIX, 300.

[75] By May, 1792, Hamilton was convinced that Jefferson "aims with ardent desire at the Presidential chair," and that such desire was a source of Jeffersonian party politics. Hamilton to Colonel Edward Carrington, Philadelphia, May 26, 1792, in Lodge, *The Works of Alexander Hamilton,* VIII, 261. The

As for the assaults on the administration's policy toward France, Hamilton believed that Jefferson and Madison in foreign policy were "unsound and dangerous," that they had "a womanish attachment to France and a womanish resentment against Great Britain." If they were left to pursue their own course in foreign policy he was convinced that in less than six months they would have the country at war with England. Jefferson, he concluded, had come back to the United States "electrified with attachment to France, and with the project of knitting together the two countries, in the closest political bands [sic]."[76] This Hamilton was determined to thwart. For two years, 1791 to 1793, the feud raged; for two years the two antagonists remained in Washington's "non-partisan" government; and for two years the President usually sided with Hamilton.[77]

So critical a struggle could not be restricted to those in government. Partisans of the press enlivened the feud. At the urging of Madison, in October, 1791, Philip Freneau founded a weekly newspaper, the *National Gazette,* in Philadelphia. Poet, experienced newspaperman, and politician, Freneau was more Jeffersonian than Jefferson. While editor of the *National Gazette* he held an official government position given him by Jefferson—that of translating clerk in the Department of State at $250 per year. His official duties were not to interfere with his newspaper work; they did not.[78]

---

entire letter should be read for insight into the Hamilton-Jefferson feud. Carrington was an old and trusted friend to whom Hamilton in confidence unburdened his woes.

[76] *Ibid.,* pp. 259-260.

[77] Hamilton's concept of governmental responsibility was broad. In his view a cabinet or administrative officer, in order to carry out his responsibilities, could undertake more than his specific duties required; he was not restricted to the limits of his office. Under such an idea it was logical for Hamilton to attempt to control all aspects of government to implement his system and for him to interfere in the functions of Jefferson's Department of State. See Caldwell, *Hamilton and Jefferson,* pp. 29, 220-221.

[78] Freneau denied, as did Jefferson, that he was controlled by Jefferson in his newspaper activity. Philip M. Marsh, "Freneau and Jefferson: The Poet-Editor Speaks for Himself About the National Gazette Episode," *American Literature,* VIII (May, 1936), 187. John Ward Fenno, however, "proved," so he declared, "to every impartial mind, that Mr. Jefferson is the Institutor and Patron of the National Gazette," *Gazette of the United States* (Philadelphia), Sept. 15, 1792. William Loughton Smith, in his pamphlet, *The Politicks and Views of a Certain Party Displayed* (n. p., 1792), p. 27, accused Jefferson

In virulent prose and poetry, Freneau each week attacked Hamilton, Washington, and even Mrs. Washington.

Freneau's tirades were not unchallenged. In vituperation they were matched, if not exceeded, by John Ward Fenno in the *Gazette of the United States*. Founded in 1789 in New York and transplanted to Philadelphia in 1790 when that city became the national capital, the *Gazette of the United States* had the trappings of a semi-official newspaper—government printing contracts, especially from the Treasury Department, subsidies and editorial contributions from prominent Hamiltonians, and a policy in complete accord with the Hamiltonian program.[79]

Washington could no longer ignore the bitter intra-administration strife. In August, 1792, he took notice of the "internal dissensions . . . harrowing and tearing our vitals." To both Jefferson and Hamilton he sent pleas for "mutual forbearances, and temporising yieldings on *all sides*." But the tear in the "goodly fabric" of government could not be repaired with soft words; Jefferson and Hamilton could not be reconciled.[80]

Admitting his aversion to Hamilton's system, which "flowed from principles adverse to liberty," Jefferson in his response complained of Hamilton's dominance in the government, of his tampering with Jefferson's domain of foreign policy, particularly "in the case of the two nations with which we have the most intimate connections, France and England." Despite this aversion to Hamilton's

---

of setting up Freneau with the express purpose of ruining Hamilton. For further information on the Jefferson-Freneau relationship, see Lewis Leary, *That Rascal Freneau: A Study in Literary Failure* (New Brunswick, 1941), pp. 193-246; Philip M. Marsh, "Jefferson and Freneau," *American Scholar,* XVI (Spring, 1947), 201-210; Samuel E. Forman, *The Political Activities of Philip Freneau,* "Johns Hopkins Studies in Historical and Political Science," XX, Nos. 9-10 (Baltimore, 1902); Philip M. Marsh, ed., *Monroe's Defense of Jefferson and Freneau Against Hamilton* (Oxford, Ohio, 1948).

[79] For Fenno's activities, see Frank L. Mott, *American Journalism: A History of Newspapers in the United States Through 260 Years: 1690-1950* (rev. ed.; New York, 1950), pp. 122-123.

[80] See Washington to Jefferson, Mount Vernon, Aug. 23, 1792, and to Hamilton, Mount Vernon, Aug. 26, 1792, in Fitzpatrick, *Washington's Writings,* XXXII, 128-134; Freeman, *Washington,* VI, 368-371. The British minister recognized that open hostilities within the administration could not continue, and that reconciliation was hopeless, Hammond to ———, Philadelphia, Nov., 6, 1792, Henry Adams Transcripts.

foreign policy, which "was exactly the reverse" of his own and
which he considered to be "inconsistent with the honor and interest of our country," Jefferson maintained that he had executed
the administration's foreign policy faithfully. Without retreating
from his position he then made clear his intention to resign.

Considering himself "as the deeply injured party," Hamilton,
too, refused to retreat. He said that Jeffersonian "machinations,"
designed to subvert his system, were a danger to the government
and he "considered it as a duty to endeavor to resist the torrent."
To restore tranquillity within the government he suggested that
both he and Jefferson resign.[81] This was precisely what the President did not want—"faction" destroying the unity of his government. For a while longer he managed to keep both advisers in his
official family.

About the same time Washington had reached another important
decision in the cause of governmental "unity." Weary of public
life, bitterly resentful of press attacks, and disgusted by the prolifera-
tion of "party spirit," he had planned to retire to Mount Vernon
at the end of his first term.[82] With his official family split, however,
and with the political struggle increasing in tempo, he was the
only man available who Americans generally still considered to be
above party. Fearing collapse of his yet-to-be-completed system,
which was dependent on Washington's continued support, Hamilton implored the President to reconsider. Washington's refusal
to take a second term, he said, would be "the greatest evil that
could befall the country at the present juncture." Bluntly, he added,
"if you quit, much is to be dreaded." Jefferson too saw danger. He
wanted Washington to continue because "Monarchical federalists,"
who were using "the new government merely as a stepping stone
to monarchy," might take over completely. Touching on widespread
fears that as one consequence the nation might split, he told the
President that "North & South will hang together, if they have you

[81] Jefferson to Washington, Monticello, Sept. 9, 1792, and Hamilton to
Washington, Philadelphia, Sept. 9, 1792, in Hamilton, ed., *Hamilton's Works,*
IV, 293-305.

[82] "During the last six months," reported the British minister, "the Press,
which in this country, perhaps more than in any other, is the clearest indication of the public mind, has teemed with the most virulent abuse of the
President." Hammond to Grenville, Philadelphia, March 7, 1793, Henry
Adams Transcripts.

to hang on."[83] Others added their pleas, and Washington consented to stand for re-election.

Washington's decision eliminated the possibility of party strife over the Presidency and perhaps of disunion; the public was still wedded to the concept of a President above partisan politics. Once again his people chose Washington unanimously. His decision did not, however, eliminate political rivalry. Although party lines were not clearly drawn and men did not wear official party labels, partisans in the states fought bitterly in the 1792 elections for congressional seats.[84]

On the national level, election of the Vice-President developed into a political battle between hardening Federalist and Republican party alliances, between monarchically inclined "monocrats" and "the Jackalls of Mobocracy." Republicans trained their political artillery on Vice-President John Adams and concentrated their principal support behind George Clinton of New York. Adams, who had offended some Federalists as well as Republicans, won easily, but Clinton received a heavy vote. In the face of determined Republican opposition, Federalists regarded Adams's re-election as a triumph.[85]

While not yet a political party in the sense of a national organization with a center of operations, the Republican "interest" had done well in its first challenge to Federalist dominance. The Executive Branch remained in Federalist hands, as did the Senate, but in the House of Representatives for the first time the Republicans held

[83] Hamilton to Washington, Philadelphia, July 30, 1792, *ibid.*, pp. 235-236; Jefferson to Washington, Philadelphia, May 23, 1792, in Ford, *Writings of Jefferson*, VI, 5; Freeman, *Washington*, VI, 355-384.

[84] The role of political organization on a party basis in the 1792 elections is discussed in Cunningham, "The Jeffersonian Party to 1801 . . . ," pp. 48, 77-78. To some Jeffersonians the elections were "a contest between the Treasury Department and the people." Schachner, *Thomas Jefferson . . . ,* I, 473; see also Malone, *Jefferson and the Rights of Man*, pp. 478-484.

[85] Hammond to Grenville, Philadelphia, Jan. 1, 1793, Henry Adams Transcripts; Gilbert Chinard, *Honest John Adams* (Boston, 1933), p. 242; Dauer, *The Adams Federalists,* pp. 85-86; Oliver Wolcott, Jr., to Oliver Wolcott, Sr., Philadelphia, Nov. 21, 1792, and Wolcott, Sr., to Wolcott, Jr., Middletown, Conn., Dec. 5, 1792, in George Gibbs, ed., *Memoirs of the Administrations of Washington and John Adams, Edited From the Papers of Oliver Wolcott, Secretary of the Treasury* (2 vols., New York, 1846), I, 83-84. Hereinafter cited as Gibbs, *Wolcott Papers.*

a majority. To Jefferson the tide of the Federalist regime was at its "fullest"; soon, he felt, it would "retire and subside."[86]

Varied factors contributed to the growing strength of the Republicans. Before the 1792 elections the economic prosperity which had come in with the new federal government had crumbled. Hamilton's system had been rocked by a financial crisis and by public criticism—not necessarily inspired by Jeffersonians.[87] Added to this, American arms late in 1791 suffered a humiliating defeat at the hands of Indians on the Northwest frontier. General Arthur St. Clair's rout alarmed the frontier, aroused indignation throughout the country, and created political fodder for the Republicans. While Washington nonetheless continued to remain above party warfare, the bursting of the speculative bubble brought on, it appeared, by Hamilton's policies, and the revelations of a Republican-inspired congressional investigation of the St. Clair disaster, reacted against Federalists.[88]

* * * * *

With each house of Congress controlled by a different party, politics became increasingly bitter. Party lines on a national basis emerged strong and distinct. "The spirit of party," Hamilton complained, "has grown to maturity sooner in this country than perhaps was to have been counted upon."[89] By its close Washington's administration had lost the nonpartisan flavor it had once possessed. "Party-spirit," it was clear to most observers, "infects the most respectable, as well as the meanest of men."[90]

[86] Jefferson to Thomas Pinckney, Philadelphia, Dec. 3, 1792, in Ford, *Writings of Jefferson*, VI, 143-144; Bassett, *Federalist System . . .* , pp. 54-55.

[87] See Bassett, *Federalist System*, pp. 52-53; McMaster, *History of the People of the United States . . .* , II, 38-41; Schachner, *The Founding Fathers*, pp. 214-217.

[88] The investigation, in fact, was the first instance of congressional probing of an executive activity; see Wilfred E. Binkley, *President and Congress* (New York, 1947), p. 46. For the investigation, see *American State Papers, Military Affairs*, I, 36-39; see also Beverly W. Bond, Jr., *The Civilization of the Old Northwest* (New York, 1934), pp. 250-252; Bassett, *The Federalist System . . .* , pp. 53-54.

[89] Hamilton to William Short, Philadelphia, Feb. 5, 1793, in Lodge, *The Works of Alexander Hamilton*, VIII, 292.

[90] La Rochefoucauld-Liancourt, *Travels . . .* , I, 545. Another foreigner saw in the rise of parties a disease fatal to the peace and existence of the Constitution. Hammond to Grenville, Philadelphia, March 7, 1793, Henry Adams Transcripts.

In other ways, too, the complexion of the government changed. More than once Washington had persuaded his Secretary of State to remain when he seemed determined to leave, but finally, despite Presidential entreaties, on the last day of December, 1793, Jefferson resigned. The breach with Hamilton had become too great for both to remain in the same Cabinet.[91]

Jefferson's resignation caused repercussions in foreign relations, particularly in those with France. Upset by persistent rumors of Jefferson's resignation, the French had long feared that his successor would be less attached to the Franco-American alliance and less opposed to English influence in government.[92] French hopes for strengthening the alliance had rested on Jefferson. No other influential person who had the ear of Washington could be classed pro-French; with the exception of Attorney General Edmund Randolph, almost all could be considered pro-English. With Jefferson gone, the French alliance had no defenders in government.

Lashed by criticism, tired, and anxious to provide for his family, Hamilton left the Cabinet on January 31, 1795, a year after Jefferson's resignation. Although reluctant to see him go, Washington finally accepted his resignation. Hamilton's departure did not sever his connection with the government; his influence as an unofficial adviser became stronger than ever.[93] Washington and his Cabinet members consulted him on almost all policy matters.

[91] The term "cabinet," used to describe Washington's principal officers as a body of advisers, did not come into general use until 1793. See Henry B. Learned, *The President's Cabinet: Studies in the Origin, Formation and Structure of An American Institution* (New Haven, 1912), pp. 135-36; Mary L. Hinsdale, *A History of the President's Cabinet,* "University of Michigan Historical Studies," I (Ann Arbor, 1911), 15.

[92] [Minister of Foreign Affairs] to Edmond Genet, Paris, April 10, 1793, AAE CP EU, Vol. XXXVII, ff. 208. After leaving, Jefferson did not let up on his attacks; he redoubled his efforts to discredit the Hamiltonians, stressing time and again that Federalists were British-dominated. Channing, *History of the United States,* IV, 166-167.

[93] Just as the French lamented Jefferson's leaving, so did the English bemoan Hamilton's departure; they feared mistakenly that with the departure of the most influential member of the administration, they would lose a decisive diplomatic advantage. Hammond to Grenville, Philadelphia, Jan. 5, 1795, Henry Adams Transcripts; see also Sears, *George Washington,* p. 453; Washington to Hamilton, Philadelphia, Feb. 2, 1795, in Fitzpatrick, *Washington's Writings,* XXXIV, 109-110.

While Hamilton, the private citizen, continued to mold government policy, the character and the caliber of the President's official family changed. After several reshufflings, by August, 1795, the Cabinet had not one of its original members remaining. It had deteriorated in quality and its policy functions devolved on Hamilton. In the face of rising militant Republican opposition, Washington reorganized the Cabinet on a strictly party basis. "I shall not," he said, "whilst I have the honor to Administer the government, bring a man into any office, of consequence knowingly whose political tenets are adverse to the measures, which the *general* government are pursuing; for this, in my opinion, would be a sort of political Suicide."[94]

To find outstanding men for Cabinet positions was difficult. After Jefferson's successor as Secretary of State, Edmund Randolph of Virginia, was forced to resign under a cloud, Washington offered the post to five men, all of whom refused. By the end of January, 1796, the President once more had a complete Cabinet: a party Cabinet, a unified Cabinet, a second-rate Cabinet. Timothy Pickering headed the Department of State, Oliver Wolcott, Jr., took over the Treasury Department, Charles Lee became Attorney General, and James McHenry became Secretary of War. Although weak, this Cabinet was not rent by an internal feud; it had unity and a common purpose—supplied by Hamilton.[95]

At the same time Republicans closed ranks and aimed telling blows at Hamilton, at his fourfold "system," and at the Washington administration. Even Washington could not escape political assaults and character assassination. Charges of corruption and malfeasance in office were bruited about. Under leadership of Albert Gallatin,

[94] Washington to Timothy Pickering, Mount Vernon, September 27, 1795, in Fitzpatrick, *Washington's Writings,* XXXIV, 315; Stephenson and Dunn, *George Washington,* II, 395; Bassett, *Federalist System* . . . , pp. 136-137. With Hamilton out even Federalists saw that "the government does not seem to grow better, as to its agents. In every part of it—instead of growing more mellow—it seems more crude & green"; they admitted that "we certainly are retrograding as to characters." William Vans Murray to James McHenry, Philadelphia, Dec. 16, 1794, and Jan. 1, 1795, in Bernard C. Steiner, *The Life and Correspondence of James McHenry* (Cleveland, 1907), pp. 156, 158.
[95] Schachner, *Alexander Hamilton,* p. 353.

the Republican-controlled House of Representatives in 1795 and 1796 attacked Hamilton's financial structure.[96]

To escape political abuse Washington retreated from the Presidency. Extremely sensitive and still clinging to the shattered ideal of a government above party, Washington in his old age could not stand a political campaign for office.[97] His decision not to run removed the last obstacle to a party battle—America's first—for the Presidency in 1796. With the Hamiltonian system and relations with France main issues, Washington's tenure of office, which had opened theoretically on a nonpolitical basis, closed in the midst of political warfare.

[96] Bassett, *The Federalist System* . . . , p. 139; Henry Adams, *The Life of Albert Gallatin* (Philadelphia, 1879), p. 157.

[97] John C. Fitzpatrick, *George Washington Himself* (Indianapolis, 1933), p. 495; Stephenson and Dunn, *George Washington,* II, 410-411. Washington did not reject a third term as a matter of principle; see Charles W. Stein, *The Third Term Tradition* (New York, 1943), pp. 17-30.

CHAPTER THREE

ANGLO-AMERICAN WAR CLOUDS

Although no longer a dependency of the British Empire, the thirteen Provinces of the American Commonwealth are not regarded by Britons as a land of strangers. The mutual animosities of the war of the American revolution are already extinguished. Britons and Americans now think of each other only as brethren; a kindred descent, a common language, congenial character, a strong alliance of institutions, arts, and manners render them to one another reciprocally interesting, perhaps much more than, in similar circumstances, any third nation would be to either.—H. Neuman, "The Translator's Preface," La Rochefoucauld-Liancourt, *Travels Through the United States.*

A wise govt. will never, in a free country go to War against *the feelings of the People—but it will often refuse to go to war to indulge the heat of the public mind—Its chief value in this respect is to check impolitic wars.*—William Vans Murray, Commonplace Book, August 11, 1795.

* * * * *

As DURING the years of the Confederation, American foreign policy under the new Constitution was concerned most with England and France. "Great Britain and France," pointed out a British diplomatist, "have the most essential influence on the interests of this country [the United States], as well commercial as political."[1] From the beginning of the new government foreign policy problems became issues in emerging national politics; the government's foreign policy inspired support or opposition for partisan political reasons.[2]

---

[1] Hammond to Grenville, Philadelphia, March 7, 1793, Henry Adams Transcripts.
[2] Relations with Spain were important and are not ignored. But they are

The immediate foreign-policy problems of the Washington government were not new; they were carry-overs from the Confederation period. So it was with Anglo-American relations, the most pressing of immediate foreign-policy issues. Old grievances, particularly English violations of the treaty of 1783, discriminatory policies directed against American shipping, and the failure of the British government to establish normal diplomatic relations angered Americans. The British, moreover, gave encouragement to secessionist sentiment in Vermont.[3]

In May, 1785, the Congress of the Confederation initiated diplomatic overtures toward Great Britain by appointing John Adams minister to the London government. England did not reciprocate. When Adams terminated his mission in February, 1788, the United States did not send a successor to London: formal diplomatic relations with Great Britain, consequently, were nonexistent.[4] When, in 1789, the new federal government was launched, one of President Washington's first tasks in foreign affairs was to open normal diplomatic intercourse with Great Britain. Without such intercourse the outstanding difficulties between the two countries appeared to stand little chance of being reconciled amicably.

Acting upon the advice of Alexander Hamilton and John Jay, even before a Secretary of State had been appointed, Washington worked unofficially to approach the British through a special execu-

---

touched upon only as they relate to the diplomacy and politics of the French alliance, or as they influenced domestic politics which in turn affected the French alliance. For Spanish-American relations in this period see Arthur P. Whitaker, *The Spanish-American Frontier: 1783-1795* (Boston, 1927) and his *The Mississippi Question 1795-1803* (New York, 1934); Samuel F. Bemis, *Pinckney's Treaty: A Study of America's Advantage from Europe's Distress, 1783-1800* (Baltimore, 1926); and Isaac J. Cox, *The West Florida Controversy 1793-1813* (Baltimore, 1918).

[3] For accounts of the grievances, British as well as American, see Bemis, *Jay's Treaty . . .* , pp. 1-36; Bemis, "Relations Between the Vermont Separatists and Great Britain, 1789-1791," *American Historical Review*, XXI (April, 1916), 547-560; Burt, *The United States, Great Britain, and British North America . . .* , pp. 53-105; Darling, *Our Rising Empire . . .* , pp. 110-115; Harlow, *The Founding of the Second British Empire*, pp. 448-491.

[4] Adams complained that while in England he was treated with "dry decency and cold civility which appears to have been the premeditated plan from the beginning." Adams to John Jay, London, Feb. 14, 1788, in Adams, *Works*, VIII, 476.

tive agent, Gouverneur Morris.[5] Morris, who had been in France
on private business, reached London in March, 1790. His assign-
ment was to open formal diplomatic relations, to obtain a commercial treaty, and to begin settlement of outstanding disputes between the two countries; he attained none of his objectives.[6] In
the case of the commercial treaty, for example, rumors were current at the time that the English government wished such a treaty
with the United States. Morris found that the British wished to
evade a commercial treaty while not peremptorily rejecting one.
Construing this as a rejection, he left without a treaty. Not until
a crisis between Great Britain and Spain seemed likely to burst into another world-encompassing war did the British government
manifest any favorable reaction to the purposes of Morris's mission.[7]

The crisis, usually referred to as the Nootka Sound controversy,
involved a clash on the outposts of the British and Spanish empires
on the northwest coast of North America.[8] In 1789 the British
attempted to establish a base on Nootka Sound on Vancouver
Island's west coast. This, however, was territory claimed by Spain
and closed to all foreigners. Enforcing their claim, the Spaniards
drove out the English and captured their ships. Both countries
alerted allies and prepared for war. Reports reached the American
government that "the rage for war & desire to seize on Spanish treas-
ures, & punish, as they express themselves, an insult to the British
flag, pervades all ranks of people in London." Newspaper stories
and other reports stressed that war was inevitable.[9]

[5] Freeman, *Washington*, VI, 239; Henry M. Wriston, *Executive Agents
in American Foreign Relations* (Baltimore, 1929), pp. 369-371.

[6] For Morris's instructions, see *American State Papers, Foreign Relations*,
I, 122. Hereinafter cited as *ASP FR*.

[7] The rumors were reported by William Short to Secretary of State, Paris,
March 3, 1790, National Archives, State Dept. Diplomatic Despatches, France;
Morris to Washington, London, May 1, 1790, *ibid*.

[8] The standard work on the Nootka Sound subject is William K. Manning,
"The Nootka Sound Controversy" in *Annual Report of the American Historical Association for the Year 1904* (Washington, 1905), pp. 279-478; see
also Frederick Jackson Turner, "English Policy toward America in 1790-
1791," *AHR*, VII (July, 1902), 706-735 and VIII (Oct., 1902), 78-86.
These contain reproductions of documents from the English Public Record
Office.

[9] The quotation is from William Short to Secretary of State, Paris, May
11, 1790, National Archives, State Dept. Diplomatic Despatches, France; the

Spain's major ally, France, was in revolution; Spain could not count on her for essential aid. Realizing that she alone could not cope with English might, Spain bowed before a British ultimatum. In the Nootka Sound Convention of 1790 she agreed to restore British property and acknowledged the right of Englishmen to trade and to settle in territory formerly claimed as exclusively Spanish.[10]

Although essentially a problem in European diplomacy and a conflict between rival empires, the Nootka Sound controversy brought to a head critical questions in American diplomacy and politics. When Washington learned of the impending Anglo-Spanish conflict, he feared that America might become a battle-ground, that England would attempt to strike at Spanish terri-tory to the south—Louisiana, Florida, and New Orleans. To do this by land Britain might demand permission to move troops across American soil. In the face of such a demand, what should the government do? In August, 1790, Washington turned to his ad-visers for their views.[11] Refusal might mean war with Great Britain; acquiescence in the demand, on the other hand, might lead to hostilities with Spain. The implications of the French alliance had also to be considered. What if France entered the probable war on the side of Spain? Would the United States be compelled to fight England if the Franco-American alliance were subsequently invoked?

Conflicting views in Washington's official family resulted in confusing advice. At this early date, in their written opinions, Hamil-ton and Jefferson revealed fundamental differences. Their differing

---

Maryland Gazette (Annapolis), July 8, 1790, printed a letter from London of June 21, 1790, which emphasized the inevitability of war. "I wish," declared the correspondent, "America may profit by the follies of others." The issue of Oct. 28, 1790, still stressed the inevitability of war, as did Sir John Temple to Duke of Leeds, New York, Jan. 5, 1791, Henry Adams Transcripts.

[10] The text of the convention is in Manning, "Nootka Sound Controversy," pp. 454-456.

[11] Washington: Queries to the Heads of the Departments, United States, Aug. 27, 1790, in Fitzpatrick, *Washington's Writings,* XXXI, 102-103. If circumstances had permitted, Washington would have preferred a strict neutrality in the crisis—to profit from it by selling to the belligerents "good things of subsistence." Washington to Marquis de Lafayette, New York, Aug. 11, 1790, p. 87. Washington's fears were groundless; Professor Bemis's re-searches in British archives revealed that British plans for attack on Spanish territory were based on naval operations. *Jay's Treaty* . . . , p. 71.

philosophies disclosed that they clashed over the basic framework of the Washington government—the Hamiltonian system.

What Jefferson dreaded most as the result of a war was a British victory. Instead of "two neighbors balancing each other," he feared, there would be after the conflict only one, whose possessions would encircle the United States. That encircling power would be America's former enemy—Great Britain. To avoid this, he would, if necessary, have had the United States go to war. For the moment he suggested delay, neutrality, and use of the American position as a lever to force to an issue frontier grievances with both England and Spain.[12] He had turned, for instance, to France for assistance in forcing Spain to give to the United States New Orleans and even Florida, arguing that Spain's possessions west of the Mississippi would then benefit from an American guarantee offered in exchange.[13]

The Secretary of State advised a policy of opportunism and watchful waiting; he wished to use the newly acquired bargaining position of the United States to fullest advantage. Hamilton did not. Basic in his thinking was the idea that at almost any cost the United States must keep peace with Great Britain. Without that peace his system was doomed. Spanish resentment or retaliation was of far less consequence. A refusal, he reasoned tortuously, may give "the complexion of partiality to Spain, and of indisposition towards Britain, which may be represented as a deviation from the spirit of exact neutrality." As to any special considerations which Spain might claim because of her alliance with France, Hamilton was emphatic. "The Ally of our ally has no claim, as such," he said, "to our friendship."[14]

[12] Jefferson, "Opinion on Course of United States towards Great Britain and Spain," [Aug. 28, 1790], in Ford, *Writings of Jefferson*, V, 238-239.

[13] See Frederick Jackson Turner, "The Policy of France toward the Mississippi Valley in the Period of Washington and Adams," *AHR*, X, 258; Jefferson to William Short, New York, Aug. 10, 1790, and following "Heads of Consideration on the Navigation of the Mississippi, for Mr. Carmichael," [Aug. 22, 1790], in Ford, *Writings of Jefferson*, V, 218-220, 229.

[14] Hamilton to Washington, New York, Sept. 15, 1790, in Lodge, *The Works of Alexander Hamilton*, IV, 20-49. Vice-President John Adams wanted no war but advised that the answer "should be a refusal in terms clear and decided, but guarded and dignified." Adams to Washington, New York, Aug. 29, 1790, in Adams, *Works*, 497-500.

Although unaware of these official American concerns and of the split among Washington's advisers, the British government did know that Hamilton and his followers were convinced that the commercial tie with England was indispensable, that there existed in the United States a party in the "British interest." Through Major George Beckwith, a special paid agent, with no official diplomatic status, of the Governor-General of Canada, it had maintained for a number of years intimate contact with Americans who nursed British proclivities. Beckwith had rushed back from Canada when the Nootka Sound affair threatened. Immediately after his return to New York in July, 1790, he had resumed an earlier friendship with Hamilton.[15]

Beckwith carried on an informal diplomacy, some of which was known to General Washington, with Hamilton, with friendly Senators, and with lesser pro-British government officials. He had hinted to Hamilton that Great Britain might be willing to settle her differences with the United States. She might, he added, even be willing to enter an alliance. On this point Hamilton was quick to inform the President and the Secretary of State. Although eagerly sought, a British *rapprochement* on such terms would injure the French alliance. It was with this situation in mind that Washington had sought the advice of his department heads.[16]

Even though Great Britain had no official diplomatic relations with the United States, her interests within the Washington government were well-guarded through Beckwith and Hamilton. Always present at social and even official functions, Beckwith aroused uneasiness and some suspicion. "The stationing of this Person about

[15] See Dorchester to Beckwith, Quebec, June 27, 1790, Nos. 20, 21, Douglas Brymner, *Report on Canadian Archives* (Ottawa, 1891-1892), pp. 143-144; Bemis, *Jay's Treaty. . . ,* p. 68. The British Consul-General at New York, Sir John Temple, reported to the Duke of Leeds, for example, that in case of war between England and Spain the United States would observe an exact neutrality. New York, Aug. 5, 1790, Henry Adams Transcripts.

[16] For Hamilton's memorandum of his conversation with Beckwith, see Hamilton to Washington, July 8, 1790, in Lodge, *The Works of Alexander Hamilton,* IV, 5-7; in a subsequent interview with Beckwith, Hamilton asked for particulars on the proposed alliance. Hamilton to Washington, July 22, 1790, *ibid.,* pp. 7-10; for Washington's reaction, see John C. Fitzpatrick, ed., *The Diaries of George Washington, 1748-1799* (4 vols., Boston, 1925), IV, 137-140, diary entry of July 8, 1790; Freeman, *Washington,* VI, 269-271.

Congress," observed a British consular official, "hath indeed disgusted not a few, who heretofore leaned towards Great Britain. 'An Envoy, say they, from a Colony Governor, to a Sovereign Power, is a business, heretofore unheard of! he can be considered in no other light than as a petty Spy.' "

With Hamiltonians, nonetheless, Beckwith earned respect and confidence. Hamilton, in fact, told him that Jefferson, the Secretary of State, because of his French "predilections," could be by-passed; that Washington could be reached, when necessary, through himself.[17] In 1790-91 Anglo-American diplomacy was thus channeled not through the Secretary of State but informally through the Secretary of the Treasury, who considered foreign policy a vital implementing force in his over-all governmental program. In this he was not alone; he had the support of well-organized and powerful elements in and out of government.

Just as the Nootka Sound affair created anxiety in the American government over British policy, it caused concern in the British government over American policy. In London there were those who feared that Americans would grasp the opportunity offered by Anglo-Spanish hostilities to bring to an issue grievances with Great Britain. They might, among other things, use force to take the Northwest posts. For the first time the British government was ready to make concessions in its American policy.

Toward Morris the British attitude changed; toward relations with the United States in general cordiality became a keynote. Orders went out to British commanders along the frontier to avoid friction with Americans.[18] In view of British reaction to possible

[17] The quotation is from Sir John Temple to Duke of Leeds, New York, May 23, 1791, Henry Adams Transcripts. Temple knew nothing of the purpose of Beckwith's mission. John Hamilton to Duke of Leeds, Norfolk, April 10, 1791, *ibid.*, also reported that Beckwith aroused uneasiness. Beckwith's report of Hamilton's sentiments is reproduced in Darling, *Our Rising Empire. . . ,* p. 142; see also Samuel F. Bemis, "Jefferson," *The American Secretaries of State and Their Diplomacy,* ed. by Samuel F. Bemis (10 vols., New York, 1927-29), II, 29; Hamilton's *de facto* dominance in Anglo-American relations is discussed in Bemis, *Jay's Treaty. . . ,* pp. 44-45, 75-76; Malone, *Jefferson and the Rights of Man,* p. 419.

[18] The British attitude toward the United States in the Nootka Sound crisis is discussed in detail in Burt, *The United States, Great Britain, and British North America. . . ,* pp. 106-113; Bemis, *Jay's Treaty . . . ,* pp. 52-58, 67-68.

American moves in North America Jefferson's suggested policy of opportunism appeared to have had a sound basis. With the passing of the Nootka Sound crisis, however, the divergent British policies of Jefferson and Hamilton were not put to the test. The impending foreign-policy crisis, nevertheless, had demonstrated the basic differences between the two men before those differences came to a head in domestic matters.

* * * * *

After he had been in office but six months Jefferson found his foreign policy challenged, sabotaged, or otherwise vitiated by another presidential adviser. The Secretary of the Treasury was attempting to establish a foreign policy differing fundamentally from that which he, the Secretary of State, desired to implement. This clash in the views of the two men showed clearly in the issue of American commercial foreign policy.

American foreign policy immediately following independence tried to surmount mercantilism and to make treaties with European nations based upon commercial reciprocity. To carry out such a policy, James Madison, in the first Congress of the new federal government in April, 1789, proposed a tariff system favoring those countries having commercial treaties with the United States and discriminating against those which did not. Although the House of Representatives adopted Madison's legislation, the conservative, British-oriented Senate killed it. In its stead Congress adopted the revenue-producing but basically protective tariff structure of 1789.[19]

Directed against Great Britain, Madison's proposal continued essentially the commercial policy favored by the Confederation government—preferential treatment for friends and retaliation against enemies.[20] Under the new national government such a

[19] Madison's proposals are discussed in Brant, *James Madison, Father of the Constitution. . . ,* pp. 246-254; in Schachner, *The Founding Fathers,* pp. 36-46. Hamilton's influence in defeating the Madison measures was decisive. Bemis, "Jefferson," in *The American Secretaries of State. . . ,* II, 26; for a British reaction to the tariff and tonnage duties see Society of Ship-Owners of Great Britain, *Collection of Interesting and Important Reports and Papers on the Navigation and Trade of Great Britain, Ireland and the British Colonies in the West Indies and America, with Tables of Tonnage and of Exports and Imports* (London, 1807), pp. 47 ff.; it contains, also, a detailed treatment of Anglo-American commerce.

[20] For British discriminations against American shipping, see Emory R.

policy was now possible. France had a commercial treaty with the United States; Great Britain did not. By a retaliatory policy, therefore, France would be favored at the expense of England; the French alliance would be buttressed.

Such a policy, of course, ran counter to the Hamiltonian thesis of no conflict with Great Britain.[21] Commercial war with England would have struck down the Hamiltonian system before it had had a chance to function properly; revenues from British imports were indispensible to its survival. As finally passed, the tariff and tonnage laws of 1789 and 1790 gave certain advantages to American ships over foreign competitors, but they made no distinction between foreign countries. In practical application on foreign commerce, however, they were not impartial; they favored Great Britain[22] because most American trade still flowed to England, and with no change in government policy the flow would continue in established channels. What, however, favored England injured France. In view of the special trading privileges and the 1778 commercial treaty France had granted to the United States, American policy appeared particularly galling to her. Good treatment, concluded the French, was repaid with indiscriminate blows. Americans made no distinction between friend and foe.

Johnson and others, *History of Domestic and Foreign Commerce of the United States,* II, 11-12. At this time the country was recovering from a business depression that had begun in 1785; its economy was relatively sound, and hence it could have embarked, despite inherent risks, upon a policy of commercial retaliation with some chance of success. *Ibid.,* p. 3.

[21] For a summary of Hamilton's views on commerce, see Vernon G. Setser, *The Commercial Reciprocity Policy of the United States 1774-1829,* pp. 102-103.

[22] Tench Coxe, political economist and Assistant Secretary of the Treasury under Hamilton, analyzed American and British trade restrictions, condensed them into a table of two parallel columns, and concluded that American commercial regulations were much more favorable to Britain than were British regulations to the United States; see his *A View of the United States of America* . . . (Philadelphia, 1794), pp. 242-245. For background of Britain's trade policy toward the United States, see Gerald S. Graham, *Sea Power and British North America 1783-1820: A Study in British Colonial Policy* (Cambridge, Mass., 1941), pp. 19-35. The tariff and tonnage laws created a keen interest in the British government; Lord Grenville (William Wyndham), Secretary of State for Home Affairs, referred them to the Committee of the Privy Council on Trade and Plantations for study and report. Bemis, *Jay's Treaty.* . . , p. 41.

Whatever the French attitude might be, it had no effect on Hamilton. Before either Hamilton or Jefferson had come into the government, the foreign-policy question of commercial discrimination had become a political issue which divided Congress. As a political issue it loomed large in the Jefferson-Hamilton feud and in the formation of political parties.[23]

* * * * *

After he had had an opportunity to study Anglo-American relations, Jefferson saw in the policy of commercial retaliation a key to his foreign policy. In comparison to the major powers of Europe the United States was insignificant; it had no army, no navy, nor any important weapons of coercion in international relations except one—the threat of trade reprisals. His view was logical. Nations react to pressure. Punish enemies and reward friends.[24]

The Secretary of State believed that the threat of trade retaliation might force England to change her ways; she might accede to American demands for a commercial treaty, for evacuation of the Northwest posts, for compensation for abducted Negroes, for an exchange of ministers, and for a general settlement of Anglo-American problems. As in the Nootka Sound crisis the differences between Hamilton and Jefferson were clearly established before they came out into the open over the issue of the bank in 1791.[25]

On several occasions as the year 1791 opened Jefferson pressed for a policy of commercial reciprocity or discrimination against England. The first opportunity arose as a result of French protests

[23] For political views of Congress on the matter of British policy, see Bemis, *Jay's Treaty.* . . , pp. 64-66.

[24] Anglo-American trade was indispensable to the prosperity of England; no English government could survive an inexcusable loss of the American market. *Ibid.,* p. 35. John Adams, for example, while he was minister to Great Britain urged a policy of trade discrimination and retaliation against England to bring her to heel. Setser, *The Commercial Reciprocity Policy.* . . , p. 98. Adams emphasized as a diplomatic axiom "that he always negotiates ill who is not in a condition to make himself feared." He concluded also "that we have no means to make an impression on them [the British] but by commercial regulations." Adams to John Jay, Auteuil, May 5, 1785, in Adams, *Works,* VIII, 242.

[25] Malone, *Jefferson and the Rights of Man,* pp. 327-328; Jefferson's policy of retaliation had a good chance of success; this is indicated in the fears of British commercial and manufacturing interests. Setser, *The Commercial Reciprocity Policy.* . . , pp. 126-127.

against the tonnage laws of 1789-90 which Washington submitted to the Senate on January 19, 1791. Contending that the laws violated the 1778 treaty of amity and commerce because they made no exception in favor of French shipping, the French asked that the laws be modified in favor of their vessels. The protests carried the implied threat that the favorable status France granted American commerce might be scuttled. Although Jefferson, who had drawn up the President's report, would not grant that the treaty had been violated, he favored relaxing the tonnage laws on a reciprocal basis—*quid pro quo*.[26] This action would strengthen the 1778 alliance by placating the French and so advance his diplomacy. But relaxation of the laws needed congressional sanction, and Congress was dominated by Hamilton.

Jefferson's hopes for a strong commercial tie with France were also in danger of being dashed by the French themselves. American trade had thus far brought no profit, and the French appeared no longer concerned with it. Attachment of Americans to British commerce seemed too firm to be broken. While still friendly, the French, in view of the realities of trade and of established American commercial policy, felt ill-used.[27]

Doubting the seriousness of the French threat but fearing even more British resentment, Hamilton stood against Jefferson's plan. "My commercial system," he said, "turns very much on giving a free course to trade, and cultivating good humor with all the world." Free trade was essential as long as 90 per cent of it was with Great Britain. Controlled by Hamilton supporters and giving evidence of strong anti-French sentiment, the Senate advised Jefferson to deny the French demand for exemption from the tonnage laws. Commerce and the tie to England, observed a Jeffersonian Senator, "I fear has already revived our ancient prejudices against France. Should we differ with France, we are thrown inevitably into the hands of Britain; and, should France give any occasion, we have thousands and tens of thousands of anti-Revolutionists ready to blow the coals of contention."[28]

[26] For the French documents and the text of Jefferson's reply, see *ASP FR*, I, 109-116.
[27] See William Short to Jefferson, Paris, Oct. 21, 1790, *ibid.*, pp. 120-121; Malone, *Jefferson and the Rights of Man*, p. 330.
[28] For the quotation from Hamilton, see Hamilton to Jefferson, Jan. 13,

Again, in his report to Congress of February 1, 1791, on the state of the cod and whale fisheries, the Secretary of State struck at the British by urging bounties for American fishermen and reprisals against British commerce. Englishmen, he said, were "mounting their navigation on the ruin of ours." Only by countermeasures, he added, could that policy be foiled. Clinging to his conviction that with England the United States had a natural commercial rivalry and with France a natural friendship, Jefferson with this report once more clarified his own foreign policy and his politics. They were the antipodes of the Hamiltonian system.

The pro-French implications of the report were immediately apparent to the British. The report, designed to arouse "coldness and dislike" toward Great Britain, reflected Jefferson's anti-British bias and his pro-French policy, said one British consul, a policy which appeared to the British to be gaining ground. Soon it would gain sufficient following to force anti-British measures through Congress. On February 14, Washington presented Congress with the last of the Jefferson-inspired anti-British reports—the report of the failure of the Morris mission to England.[29]

When Jefferson had taken office in March, 1790, the President had turned the Morris negotiation over to him. By December Jefferson had concluded that the mission was a lost cause and that Morris should be recalled. So concerned was Morris over the failure of his mission that he had urged closer ties with France and a policy of retaliation against Britain. He wanted to strike at the merchants who dominated English trade policy toward the United States. Jefferson believed that England would make no commercial

---

1791, in Lodge, *The Works of Alexander Hamilton,* IV, 54; Schachner, *Alexander Hamilton,* p. 296; Malone, *Jefferson and the Rights of Man,* pp. 329-330; for the Senate's action, see *Journal of the Executive Proceedings of the Senate of the United States of America,* I, 77, dated Feb. 26, 1791; the anti-French, pro-British sentiment of the Senate is reflected in *Journal of William Maclay* . . . , pp. 390-395, entry of Feb. 26, 1790.
[29] Sir John Temple to Duke of Leeds, New York, March 19 and May 23, 1791, Henry Adams Transcripts. The reaction of Phineas Bond, British consul in Philadelphia, to the Duke of Leeds (March 14, 1791) is in Schachner, *The Founding Fathers,* p. 167. The report on cod and whale fisheries, Feb. 1, 1791, is in Lipscomb, *Jefferson's Works,* III, 120-144; it was submitted to Congress on Feb. 4, 1791; see Malone, *Jefferson and the Rights of Man,* pp. 332-333; the report on the Morris mission, with pertinent documents, is in *ASP FR,* I, 121-127.

treaty without a treaty of alliance designed "to undermine our obligations with France."[30] This fitted the objective of weaning the
United States from the French alliance.

While Washington accepted Jefferson's advice and terminated
the Morris mission, he waited two months before presenting the data
to Congress. Hamilton and Jefferson differed completely on the
basic foreign policy and political considerations involved and so on
the kind of message the President should send to Congress dealing
with the failure of the mission.[31]

In the House of Representatives the cumulative impact of the
Jefferson reports revived proposals for retaliatory legislation against
British commerce. In 1789 and 1790 there had been unsuccessful
efforts in both houses to secure the enactment of discriminatory
trade laws. The mood of Congress in February, 1791, was different.
Out of committee in the House of Representatives came a navigation bill—similar to British navigation laws—which discriminated
against British shipping. The bill threatened to destroy at one
blow Britain's most valuable commerce and Hamilton's elaborate
system. Jefferson's anti-British policy seemed about to triumph.[32]

But all was not lost. Through Hamilton's influence and timely
action the bill "vanished" before it could be brought to a final vote;
sidetracked, reported the British consul at Philadelphia, "to prevent
any hasty measures which might interrupt the [commercial] Intercourse with Great Britain."[33] Jefferson had expected his policy to
carry in the next session of Congress. When the discriminatory
measures collapsed, he suffered a personal political defeat.

[30] See Morris to Washington, London, Sept. 18, Nov. 22, 1790; to Robert
Morris [Sept., 1790], in Beatrix Cary Davenport, ed., *A Diary of the French
Revolution by Gouverneur Morris, 1752-1816, Minister to France during the
Terror* (2 vols., Boston, 1939), I, 604, 613, 616; Bemis, *Jay's Treaty. . . ,* p.
49; Jefferson: Report on British Negotiations [Dec. 15, 1790], in Ford, *Writings
of Jefferson,* V, 262.
[31] Woolery, *The Relation of Jefferson to American Foreign Policy. . . ,*
p. 90; Malone, *Jefferson and the Rights of Man,* pp. 331-332.
[32] Setser, *The Commercial Reciprocity Policy. . . ,* p. 110; *The Annals
of the Congress. . . ,* 1st Cong., 3rd sess., Feb. 22, 23, 1791, pp. 2020-2022.
[33] Phineas Bond to Duke of Leeds, Philadelphia, March 14, 1791, Henry
Adams Transcripts. Bond also reported that increasing anti-British sentiment
was a cause for alarm. See also Malone, *Jefferson and the Rights of Man,*
p. 335; Setser, *The Commercial Reciprocity Policy. . . ,* p. 111; Bemis, *Jay's
Treaty. . . ,* p. 87.

The British, in the meantime, had decided to send an accredited minister to the United States. Even though the American navigation law was proposed after the British decision, it undoubtedly served to accelerate opening of full diplomatic relations. In England government officials and traders reacted with alarm to the growth and evident strength of the anti-British Jeffersonian coalition in the American government. Anti-British and pro-French activities, they believed, were being pushed by a vigorous "French party in America." This party had disseminated the pernicious impression that England would enter no commercial negotiation *"and that she* treated America with ineffable contempt."[34] Basically, the threat of commercial discrimination, not the discriminatory legislation itself, had been instrumental in forcing Great Britain to send a minister to the United States.[35]

The first British minister to the United States, twenty-seven-year-old George Hammond, arrived in October, 1791, bringing with him instructions to combat anti-British legislation, and to keep a sharp eye "for renewing former Alliances or forming new Connexions" between the United States and France, but otherwise limited severely in his powers. This, seven years after independence, was a step motivated by British self-interest. President Washington reciprocated by sending to London as American minister Thomas Pinckney of South Carolina, a man satisfying to the British government, and one described by Hammond as belonging to the party of the British interest.[36]

* * * * *

[34] B. P. Colquhoun to Lord Grenville, Aug., 1791, London, Great Britain, Historical Manuscripts Commission Reports, *The Manuscripts of J. B. Fortescue, Esq., Preserved at Dropmore* (No. 30, 10 vols., London, 1892—), II, 157. Hereinafter cited as *Dropmore Papers*.

[35] See Grenville to George Hammond, Whitehall, Sept. 1, 1791, in Bernard Mayo, ed., *Instructions to the British Minister to the United States 1791-1812* in *AHA Ann. Rep.* (1936) (3 vols., Washington, 1941), III, 17. Hammond was instructed that the projected retaliatory commercial legislation was to be a principle object of his attention immediately on arriving in America. Hammond's initial instructions are in pp. 2-13.

[36] George Hammond to Lord Grenville, Philadelphia, Jan. 9, 1792, in *Dropmore Papers*, II, 250; Samuel F. Bemis, "The London Mission of Thomas Pinckney, 1792-1796," *AHR*, XXVIII (Jan., 1923), 228-247. It had been understood that if Great Britain would send a minister the United States would appoint one to London.

Chronologically, Hamilton and Jefferson clashed first over foreign policy; actually, the differences between the two men, over both foreign and domestic affairs, crystallized almost simultaneously; and, politically, the lines of battle were drawn on most fronts at approximately the same time. Foreign policy and domestic politics were of the same fabric; what affected one affected the other. Jefferson and his supporters opposed not only the financial aspects of the Hamiltonian system, but its political, diplomatic, and constitutional aspects as well.[37]

Before the outbreak of war between France and England and before the fight over the bank, Hamilton and Jefferson were steering collision courses. The political philosophies of both men antedated establishment of the national government, as did their attitudes toward England and France and their views of the French alliance. American policy toward England and France had its roots in the Confederation period, changing little in the transition to a new centralized government. This was so because of the Hamilton system and the resulting resistance of Hamiltonians to any policy change which would discriminate against England to bring her to terms.

Hamilton met the threat of tariff discrimination against Great Britain with the argument that it would choke off needed revenues from British imports, that it would lead to commercial warfare in which the young nation was not strong enough to engage, that it would destroy his "system." He met the threat against the bank with the cogent argument of loose construction. To conduct his campaign he had to be a versatile general. The foreign policy he espoused was not subservient to a domestic financial policy; both were part of the same thing—his total program.

At this time (1791) Hamiltonians diverted the threat of retaliation; Britain retained her advantages in America. Fearful of future trade reprisals she acceded somewhat to American desires by opening full diplomatic relations. France, with cause, felt discriminated against. Hamilton and those of the "British interest" carried the day on all fronts. The pro-British foreign policy, upon which

[37] See Malone, *Jefferson and the Rights of Man,* p. 304; Schachner, *Alexander Hamilton,* pp. 293-294; White, *The Federalists. . . ,* pp. 212-214, 222-232.

the entire Hamiltonian structure rested, had been saved. But its greatest crisis had yet to be met.

* * * * *

Officially, Great Britain's first minister to the United States conducted his relations with the American government through Thomas Jefferson, the Secretary of State. His relations with Jefferson, were, in fact, nominal, mere formalities. As he reported, he considered the Secretary of State "as the devoted instrument of a French faction." The substance of his relations with the United States were through Alexander Hamilton, the Secretary of the Treasury. Where Beckwith had left off George Hammond continued, cultivating not only the valuable Hamilton, but also others in government in the "British interest."[38]

For over a year Hammond went through shadow-motions of diplomacy with Jefferson. In conversations which were from the outset practically meaningless the two men negotiated over outstanding differences between their two countries. So restricted were Hammond's powers that he could do little more than talk. He had no authority to make a treaty or any other kind of agreement. His mission was to delay positive action.

Even in these foredoomed negotiations with Hammond, Hamilton wrecked Jefferson's case. The Secretary of the Treasury told the British minister that Jefferson's views could be ignored with impunity; they were not a true reflection of government policy.[39] In his own field of operations the Secretary of State had been checkmated by an intra-administration feud, by domestic political con-

[38] Hammond wrote to his superiors that he preferred working with Hamilton privately and that he would have relations with Jefferson only when absolutely necessary. Hammond to Grenville, Philadelphia, April 2, Nov. 7, 1793, Henry Adams Transcripts. The relationship between Hammond, Jefferson, and Hamilton is discussed in Bemis, *Jay's Treaty. . .* , pp. 89-108; and the Hammond-Jefferson negotiations are summarized also in Malone, *Jefferson and the Rights of Man,* pp. 396-399.

[39] For Hamilton's thwarting of Jefferson's diplomacy, see Hammond to Grenville, Philadelphia, June 8, 1792, Henry Adams Transcripts; Bemis, *Jay's Treaty. . .* , pp. 106-107; Schachner, *The Founding Fathers,* pp. 207-211. Jefferson was aware of "the intimacy of their [Hamilton and Hammond] communications"; he believed that Hamilton "communicated to Hammond all our views & knew from him in return the views of the British court." The Anas, March 11, 1792, in Ford, *Writings of Jefferson,* I, 186.

siderations, and by foreign-policy objectives pursued by Hamilton. Jefferson was a Secretary of State committed to a foreign policy of his political enemy, to a foreign policy he wished to overthrow.

Despite the dominance of Hamilton's views and the dark outlook for Jefferson's policy all hope was not lost. British delaying actions for a while inspired hopes in Jefferson that the French alliance might be reinforced and that his foreign policy views might eventually prevail with the President. Aroused by the British tactics of delay Washington almost returned to the embrace of France. He instructed Jefferson "to endeavor to effect a stricter connection with France." In view of "the circumstances of dissatisfaction between Spain Gr. Brit & us," he said, "there was no nation on whom we could rely at all times but France, and if we did not prepare in time some support in the event of rupture with Spain & England we might be charged with a criminal negligence." This pleased Jefferson. "The very doctrine," he said, "which had been my polar star."[40]

Even though aware of mounting anti-British sentiment, the British had reason to be content with the status of American diplomacy; it was tailored to objectives of their commercial policy. American discriminatory legislation against their shipping had been quashed; their traders had not been compelled to grant concessions to Americans; their commerce continued to dominate the American market; and within the country the dominant political alliance was British-oriented. With the covert aid of Hamilton, who readily admitted to the British minister the importance of British commerce to his system, and with the help of those of the "British interest," Hammond's diplomacy of delay at the end of its first year succeeded.[41]

* * * * *

On the Northwest frontier, while Jefferson and Hammond conferred, Anglo-American relations smoldered. Continued occupation by the British of the Northwest posts in violation of the peace treaty of 1783 caused the greatest resentment. The British, regretting the generosity of that peace settlement, wanted to revise the boundary.

[40] The Anas, Dec. 27, 1792, *ibid.,* p. 212.
[41] Hammond to Grenville, Philadelphia, Jan. 9, 1792, Henry Adams Transcripts; Bemis, "Jefferson," in *American Secretaries of State. . . ,* II, 36.

With the American violations of the treaty as an excuse, British officials in Canada continued to hold the posts.

A parallel objective in England's policy on the Northwest frontier was creation of an Indian buffer state in American territory in the region of the occupied posts. Nominally independent, the Indian state was conceived as a dike holding back the expanding American frontiersmen, a protective cordon of wilderness for British Canada. Although ostensibly neutral, the Indian state, controlled by the British, would have hemmed in the American nation, confining it to the Atlantic seaboard. British motives for championing the Indian state were complex, but profit from the valuable fur trade in the region and protection of British North America against a growing United States were important.[42]

As the American frontier advanced across the Ohio, challenging the British frontier policy, Indians in the virgin lands resisted the alien encroachment. British officials in Canada supplied the Indians with the weapons they used to attack American settlers. In many instances British agents intrigued with Indians and encouraged them in their attacks.

Added to this were British fears that punitive expeditions sent out by the American government against Indians were in reality aimed at the British-occupied posts. American frontiersmen, on their part, demanded government protection against Indians. When aroused to suspicion, in some cases supported by evidence of British-Indian intrigue, they became bitterly anti-British. The butchering of their friends and relatives by savages of the forest wielding British weapons, no matter how justified by their own actions, had an intense emotional impact on frontiersmen.[43]

[42] For details on British-American relations on the Northwest frontier, see Burt, *The United States, Great Britain, and British North America. . . ,* pp. 82-140; Bemis, *Jay's Treaty. . . ,* pp. 109-133, 161-183. On the Spanish-American frontier to the south Spain also wished to erect an Indian barrier between its lands and the aggressive Americans. Whitaker, *The Spanish-American Frontier. . . ,* p. 43.
[43] See Beverly W. Bond, Jr., *The Civilization of the Old Northwest,* p. 253; James H. Perkins, *Annals of the West* (2nd ed., rev. and enlarged by J. M. Peck; St. Louis, 1851), pp. 361-365; narrative of Thomas Rhea, June 30, 1791, contains evidence of British connivance with Indians, in *American State Papers, Indian Affairs,* I, 196-197. Even President Washington took note of the "notoriety" of British assistance to the Indians, Washington to Secretary of State, Mount Vernon, April 4, 1791, in Fitzpatrick, *Washington's*

Frontier grievances had a continuing impact on American politics and foreign policy.[44] Men of the Northwest frontier, already Jeffersonian in outlook, pressed their grievances with the national government. They demanded protection against Indian depredations—protection which would carry with it possibility of Anglo-American conflict. At the same time, the frontiersmen became stronger supporters of the Jeffersonian party. Thus Anglo-American relations, Indian policy, the advancing frontier, and rising political parties came to a focus at approximately the same time. Collectively they built a fire under the Washington administration.[45]

Washington moved to pacify the Indians with federal arms. The first expeditions against the Indians failed. General Josiah Harmar was routed in the spring of 1790 and an expedition under General Arthur St. Clair in the winter of 1791 was "cut to pieces, hacked, butchered, and tomahawked." News of the disaster unleashed Washington's rage—he angrily labeled St. Clair "worse than a murderer."[46] Anti-administration forces capitalized on the defeat. Politicians demanded the general's scalp; both sides in Congress called for and obtained an investigation of the entire affair.[47]

Although the Harmar and St. Clair expeditions proved fruitless, their execution had posed a threat to British control over Indians south of the 1783 treaty line; the armies had come too close to the occupied posts; they had endangered British frontier objectives.[48]

Writings, XXXI, 267-268; Washington to David Humphreys, Philadelphia, July 20, 1791, _ibid.,_ p. 320.

[44] The relationship between the local frontier problem of defense against Indian attack and the national problem of foreign affairs is noted also in Russell J. Ferguson, _Early Western Pennsylvania Politics,_ p. 136.

[45] See the remarks of William Branch Giles, congressman from Virginia, in _Annals of the Congress,_ 3rd Cong., 1st sess., Jan. 25, 1794, pp. 315-322. Giles listed the Algerine war as another ground of complaint against Great Britain, asserting that it had been brought on by her "artifices."

[46] Washington is quoted in Stephenson and Dunn, _George Washington,_ II, 305-307; for details on the Indian expeditions, see William Henry Smith, _The St. Clair Papers_ . . . (2 vols., Cincinnati, 1882), I, 167-185; Bond, _The Civilization of the Old Northwest,_ pp. 250-252.

[47] Results of the investigations of the Harmar and St. Clair expeditions and pertinent documents are in _American State Papers, Military Affairs,_ I, 20-39.

[48] Henry Hamilton, for example, reported to the Duke of Leeds, April 10, 1791, that St. Clair's "real intentions are to attack Detroit & the other

Hammond was given orders to press for British mediation and to attempt to secure the Indian barrier state which his government desired. In his dealings with both Jefferson and Hamilton the British minister urged these projects upon them. Not even Hamilton could embrace the proposals; they were politically dangerous and a desertion of American rights. No external intervention could be allowed, he told Hammond. Indian relations within the acknowledged borders of the United States were internal matters to be handled exclusively by Americans.[49]

Indian atrocities on the frontier continued; British agents intrigued with the Indians and anti-British sentiment continued to spread. With congressional backing Washington once more tried to crush Indian resistance. He placed General "Mad" Anthony Wayne in command of the frontier forces on the Ohio. From summer 1792 to winter 1793 Wayne prepared his forces for the northern expedition.[50]

During this period Anglo-American frontier relations rose to a crisis. British frontier officials saw in Wayne's army a threat to Canada; they believed that his real objectives were the occupied posts. As 1793 closed, the threat of war between Great Britain and the United States hovered over the Northwest frontier. On this front the foreign policy of the Hamiltonians appeared headed for disaster. In Europe in the meantime, events posed the same threat —Anglo-American hostilities.

* * * * *

Except for existing differences, the opening events of the French Revolution did no immediate violence to Franco-American relations. As the Revolution picked up momentum, its course avidly studied by Americans, it divided emerging political party groupings

---

forts in the possession of Great Britain." Norfolk, Va., Henry Adams Transcripts.

[49] Grenville to Hammond, Whitehall, March 17, 1792, in Mayo, *Instructions to the British Ministers. . . , AHA Ann. Rep.* (1936), III, 25-27; Lord Dorchester to Dundas, London, March 23, 1792; Hammond to Grenville, Philadelphia, June 8, 1792, Henry Adams Transcripts. For details, see Burt, *The United States, Great Britain, and British North America. . . ,* pp. 119-126; Bemis, *Jays' Treaty. . . ,* pp. 117-123.

[50] Bond, *The Civilization of the Old Northwest,* pp. 254-255; Stephenson and Dunn, *George Washington,* II, 307.

in the United States and gave them emotion-arousing national issues. Foreign affairs, the position of the United States *vis à vis* France or England, became internal issues; domestic politics and foreign policy became one. The French Revolution "drew a redhot plough-share through the history of America as well as that of France."[51]

At first Americans greeted the French Revolution with favor; when France went to war against monarchical enemies in April, 1792, they sympathized with her; she was fighting against "Tyrants leagued for the subversion" of liberty.[52]   Aside from its effect on American attitudes the first international conflict of the French Revolution did not threaten vital American interests.   Neither American commerce nor American neutrality was endangered by France's fight against the alliance of Austria and Prussia in 1792; there was no question of being dragged into the European war by the 1778 Franco-American alliance.   Uninhibited by threat of in-volvement and seeing in the French cause a fight for commonly espoused democratic principles, Americans, regardless of political faith, cheered French military successes and establishment of the First Republic.

With news of the execution of Louis XVI, of the French invasion of the Austrian Netherlands, and of the subsequent French war declaration of February 1, 1793, against Great Britain, Holland, and Spain, American attitudes and American policy changed.   Federalists reversed their previously expressed sympathies for the French Revo-lution.[53]   As they had done in the past, they rallied to the defense of England.   Republicans more than ever became pro-French, pro-Revolution, and anti-English.   As a contemporary Federalist poli-tician analyzed the situation, the events and theories of the con-tinuing French Revolution—"this temper so congenial to a fac-tious & disorganized mind"—were seized by Republicans for political

---

[51] Quoted in Charles D. Hazen, *Contemporary American Opinion of the French Revolution,* "Johns Hopkins University Studies in Historical and Political Science," XVI (Baltimore, 1897), pp. ix-x.

[52] John Stewart to Genet, Richmond, Va., May 10, 1793, Edmond C. Genet Papers, Library of Congress.   Stewart wished to expatriate himself, become a French citizen, and join the struggle for liberty.

[53] For an example of a reversal of opinion by a prominent Federalist to-ward the French Revolution, a not uncommon experience, see Noah Webster, "To the Public," New York, March 4, 1797, in Harry R. Warfel, ed., *Letters of Noah Webster* (New York, 1953), pp. 145-147.

reasons. Through propagation of the "disorganizing principles" of the French they gained reputation. The reason for this, he concluded, was that the affected adoption of French theory was connected with the great cause of "French Freedom, so dear to all americans [*sic*]."[54]

War between England and France did not bring anything new into the already established foreign-policy orientation of political parties. What it did was to cast into sharp focus already existing differences; it made the foreign-policy objective of the Hamiltonian system the disputed issue in national politics; it plunged the French alliance into American politics. "The war between France and England," Jefferson said, "has brought forward the Republicans & Monocrats in every state so openly, that their relative numbers are perfectly visible."[55] Grasping the new issue of the expanded French Revolution as a matter of expediency rather than as the result of predetermined policy, Republicans in Virginia, for example, concentrated on it to consolidate party lines.[56]

In addition to providing a national issue for emerging political parties the Anglo-French war also created foreign-policy dilemmas over problems of neutrality, particularly the rights of neutrals at sea, trade, and treaty obligations. These in turn, because of the intimate interrelationship between politics and foreign policy, accentuated party bitterness. New plus old grievances, combined with political pressures, led to a foreign-policy crisis that almost thrust the nation into war with Great Britain and that did give the *coup de grâce* to the aimless Hammond-Jefferson conversations.

* * * * *

Simultaneously the new diplomatic problems destroyed whatever unity still fronted the Washington administration. Federalists believed that war with Great Britain was national suicide. The British knew this. Hamilton's system, Hammond reported, constitutes "the most material props of the government, and were they

[54] William Vans Murray Papers, Commonplace Book, July 28, 1795 (Princeton).

[55] Jefferson to Madison, June 29, 1793, in Ford, *Writings of Jefferson*, VI, 326.

[56] Cunningham, "The Jeffersonian Party to 1801. . . ," p. 85; Ammon, "The Formation of the Republican Party in Virginia," *Journal of Southern History*, XIX, 310.

to be too hastily removed, it is not impossible that the whole fabric which they tend to support, might crumble into ruin."[57]   But crumble into ruin Hamilton's program might.   Bound to the French alliance "forever," the United States in time of war was obligated to defend the French West Indies against the enemies of its ally. France's enemy was Great Britain, the anchor in the Hamiltonian system.

Startled, though not surprised, by news of the Anglo-French war and confronted with a major foreign-policy decision, Washington as usual turned to his department heads for advice.[58]   Again Hamilton and Jefferson differed.   Hamilton saw this as an opportunity to jettison the French alliance and to steer the United States closer to England.   Jefferson contended that the treaties were not between governments but between nations and so could not be abrogated unilaterally; the French alliance was still in effect.[59]

While not challenging the validity of the French treaties, Washington essentially accepted Hamilton's advice.   On April 22, 1793, he promulgated a proclamation of neutrality.   On the surface it appeared as a compromise, yet its purpose was obvious.   It declared the United States at peace with both England and France and warned American citizens to refrain from hostile action against the belligerent powers.[60]

[57] Hammond to Grenville, Philadelphia, March 7, 1793, No. 5.   In No. 8 of the same date Hamilton is cited as deeply concerned over the failure of Great Britain and the United States to settle their differences.   Henry Adams Transcripts.   At the same time the French feared that their allies might be "reduced by our enemies."   Otto to Genet, Paris, March 8, 1793, Genet Papers, Library of Congress.

[58] War was not unexpected, but the French declaration of it was.   Charles M. Thomas, *American Neutrality in 1793: A Study in Cabinet Government* (New York, 1931), p. 24; Questions Submitted to the Cabinet by the President, Philadelphia, April 18, 1793, in Fitzpatrick, *Washington's Writings,* XXXII, 419-420.

[59] Young John Quincy Adams in "Marcellus" III contended that America's obligation under the French alliance was "dissolved or at least suspended"; the law of nature, he contended, "which supersedes all others," commanded Americans to remain at peace, neutral.   Reprinted from the *Columbian Centinel* (Boston), May 11, 1793, in Worthington C. Ford, ed., *Writings of John Quincy Adams* (7 vols., New York, 1913-1917), I, 142-146.

[60] Washington expressed his desire for neutrality in the European war to David Humphreys and to Gouverneur Morris, Philadelphia, March 23, 25, 1793.   Fitzpatrick, *Washington's Writings,* XXXII, 399, 402; the proclamation is in *ASP FR,* I, 140.

Politically, the proclamation pleased neither Federalists nor Republicans. But as Washington was a Federalist and, because the proclamation favored Great Britain, Republicans denounced the President, the proclamation, Great Britain, and Federalists in general. Critics of the administration attacked the proclamation because they believed it abrogated the French alliance "from which we have long enjoyed important advantages" and because it disregarded the nation's plighted faith. It was not a true neutrality proclamation in that it would provoke France to hostilities against the United States, "a consequence naturally to be expected from the violation of solemn treaties."[61] Deploring Anglophilism in the Cabinet, Jefferson advised that only the "ardent spirit" of Republicans could prevent American neutrality from becoming a "mere English neutrality."[62]

More than in almost anything in the past Republicans attempted to make political capital out of this unpopular foreign-policy decision. Desperate, Federalists were driven to defend the obviously pro-English neutrality policy. Defense was almost political suicide; with Hamilton's system at stake, however, they had no choice.

Washington was alarmed by the violent anti-administration reaction to the proclamation of neutrality, coupled with enthusiastic pro-French outbursts on behalf of Citizen Edmond C. Genet, the French Republic's new minister to the United States, on his trip through the South. Rumors reached him as to the agitated state of public opinion and of plans of anti-administration forces in Virginia to attack him and his policies. To test the rumors and to sample public opinion, Washington, in July, 1793, sent Attorney General Edmond Randolph to Virginia. On his return Randoph reported that basically Virginia liked the President's policies, that public opinion supported the administration's foreign policy. The opposition, he explained, was limited to a personal antagonism toward Hamilton.[63]

[61] "Veritas" in the *National Gazette* (Philadelphia), June 8, 1793, quoted in Woodbury, *Public Opinion in Philadelphia. . . ,* pp. 64-65. Republicans, basically, wanted to aid France and still remain neutral; this was a difficult position to maintain as they thus appeared to be in favor of war against England. Brown, *First Republicans. . . ,* p. 98.

[62] Jefferson to Madison, May 13, [1793], Henry A. Washington, ed., *The Writings of Thomas Jefferson,* III, 557.

[63] Ammon, "Republican Party in Virginia. . . ," *JSH,* XIX, 301-302; see

Republicans, who controlled the House of Representatives, saw in the proclamation of neutrality evidence of mercantile influence and of the pro-British faction at work. They insisted that Congress had to decide questions of war and peace. Washington's action, they contended, was a high-handed, unconstitutional usurpation by the executive of legislative power. Republicans thus cast themselves in the role of defenders of the Constitution, defenders of popular government against dictatorship. But fundamentally they opposed the proclamation for political reasons. It was not a pro-French neutrality in support of the 1778 alliance, and that was a major flaw. "It wounds the national honor," Madison said, "by seeming to disregard the stipulated duties to France."[64]

Regardless of the bitter partisanship the proclamation had inspired, Washington's deed, in its wider implications and in at least two important particulars, was of precedent-making significance. First, in foreign affairs it was a bold step in the direction of establishing the claim of the Executive Branch to exclusive right to determine policy. Such a right is not explicit in the Constitution or elsewhere. Yet Hamilton maintained that the President had the right unilaterally to proclaim neutrality; he insisted that such a proclamation was merely an executive act and that the executive power rested solely with the President.[65] There was ample reason to conclude with equal justification that the Senate should be consulted in policy-making, that the making of foreign policy was something of a partnership between the Executive and the Senate. Indisputably the power to declare war rested with Congress. This was a power in foreign relations of the most critical kind. Conversely, the power to determine foreign policy, as pointed out by Jeffersonians, was

---

also Jefferson to James Madison, July 21, 1793, in Ford, *Writings of Jefferson*, VI, 355.

[64] See James Monroe to Jefferson, Albemarle, June 23, 1793, in Stanislaus M. Hamilton, ed., *The Writings of James Monroe* (7 vols., New York, 1898-1903), I, 261-267; James Madison, Letters of Helvidius, August-September, 1793, No. V, in Gaillard Hunt, ed., *The Writings of James Madison*, VI, 182-183. Madison's quotation (Madison to Jefferson, June 10, 1793) is on p. 127 n. The issue of the Proclamation of Neutrality is summarized in Thomas, *American Neutrality. . . ,* pp. 13-52.

[65] Hamilton, Pacificus No. 1, June 29, 1793, in Lodge, *The Works of Alexander Hamilton*, IV, 135-147.

the power to make war or peace. Thus the proclamation represented another Hamiltonian victory.

Secondly, and again in line with Hamilton's views, the President's proclamation decision contributed to the strengthening of the central government at the expense of its components. When the Executive Branch acted, it acted for the nation as a whole; its policy was a national policy. In this instance a vital national policy was determined, as was to be the case again and again, solely by the Executive without consultation with the legislative branch where the sectional units of the government were represented.[66] In a sense then, even though Washington sought to placate the sensibilities of pro-French Republicans by omitting the word "neutrality" from the proclamation, it was a political document.

With the issue ready-made, Republicans intensified their attack on the administration. Their tactics succeeded; popular support rallied to their side. They pushed the country toward war with England. But their tactics alone did not bring the country virtually to war; they had assistance from the British government.

* * * * *

Washington was in a difficult diplomatic position. By the French treaty of amity and commerce of 1778 the United States was committed to the practice and enforcement of maritime principles which Great Britain had never recognized and which she constantly violated in time of war. Prominent among those principles were: that free ships make free goods, the acceptance of a broad definition of contraband of war, and the freedom of neutrals to trade in non-contraband goods with belligerents or between belligerent ports.[67]

To attempt to enforce these "small navy" principles against British maritime power might mean war with England. Not to enforce them, in the view of many, violated the French alliance and might mean war with France. President Washington seemingly was in trouble whichever course he chose. Furthermore, any foreign-policy decision involved dangerous political decisions. On

[66] See White, *The Federalists. . . ,* pp. 62-63.

[67] Great Britain made clear that she did not and would not recognize such principles as free ships, free goods. See, for example, Grenville to Hammond, Whitehall, March 12, 1793, in Mayo, *Instructions to the British Ministers. . . , AHA Ann. Rep.* (1936), III, 38.

this foreign-policy question Republicans and Federalists held ir-reconcilable positions.

With the opening of war against England, France, aware of her inferior sea-power status, threw open her previously jealously guarded West Indian trade to the United States (it had been partial-ly open before). By the hundreds American ships flocked into the French Caribbean ports; profits soared; Franco-American com-merce flourished.[68] For a while the strengthened commercial tie with France which Jefferson desired appeared a reality. But the flow of commerce into French channels did not last long.

Beginning in June, 1793, Great Britain throttled this lucrative trade. By three orders-in-council, that is executive orders, of June, 1793, November, 1793, and January, 1794, the British govern-ment enforced the dictum that commerce prohibited in time of peace would not be allowed in time of war. Known as the Rule of 1756 from its first application by England in the Seven Years' War, this rule decimated American commerce with the French.[69]

In enforcing the orders-in-council British naval officers without warning swooped down upon American vessels trading with the French in the Caribbean. They stripped Americans of property and dignity; confiscated their vessels and their cargoes; impressed American seamen, tossed them into dungeons, beat them, or other-wise humiliated them. The British thus partially paralyzed Ameri-can Caribbean commerce and endangered American lives.[70]

---

[68] Unrestricted Caribbean trade was what American merchants had antici-pated; many had wanted war between England and France so that they as neutrals could take over the British and French carrying trade. Their profits, despite seizures and losses, were enormous. Freedom of the seas was a practi-cal dollars-and-cents policy. See Robert G. Albion and Jennie B. Pope, *Sea Lanes in Wartime: The American Experience 1775-1942* (New York, 1942), pp. 65-69.

[69] For details, see Anna C. Clauder, *American Commerce as Affected by the Wars of the French Revolution and Napoleon, 1793-1812*, pp. 27-36; for a useful chronological table of British and French restrictions on American trade, see pp. 9-12. A clear account of the British Orders in Council may also be found in W. Allison Phillips and Arthur H. Reede, *Neutrality: Its His-tory, Economics and Law*, Vol. II, *The Napoleonic Period* (New York, 1936), pp. 37-49. Hammond transmitted the order of June 8, 1793, to Jefferson on Sept. 12, 1793, *ASP FR*, I, 240; for the Orders in Council of Nov. 6, 1793, and Jan. 8, 1794, see pp. 430-431.

[70] See the reports of Fulwar Skipwith from St. Eustatia of March 1 and

In American newspapers reports of Caribbean confiscations and indignities received wide circulation. American tempers boiled, anti-British sentiment mushroomed, and Federalists despaired. The British had given Republicans a ready-made issue—one on which political crusades are built and elections won. Adherents of the French alliance and Republicans in general tried to increase the violence of popular feeling against England.

Their tactics were effective; they placed the government's pro-English foreign policy on the defensive. George Hammond realized that the government had "to temporize, to practice half-measures, and to wait until it shall be able to repress or direct the popular will." This policy actuated the Federalist administration, he said, "and prevents it from pursuing with steadiness and decision that course of uniform neutrality which it perceives to be essential to the security as well of its constitution, as of its commercial importance."[71]

The opposition press attacked Hamilton's system, Great Britain, and British tyranny as synonymous evils. "Certain fashionable and courtly maxims of the day," wrote "Americanus," attempted to inculcate "that peace, and a good understanding with Great-Britain, must be preserved at any price; that by pursuing this policy alone can the infant system of our government take root and stability; and that America ought, imperceptibly, to grow to greatness, like the trees of her wilderness, in the midst of silence and retreat." These maxims are repugnant to the essential interests of the nation, he said, and "in the opinion of the great body of the yeomanry of America, flow from the influence of that partial system of things, wherein the advantage of the many is made subservient to the emolument and aggrandizement of the few; a system already too

7, 1794, to the Secretary of State, *ASP FR,* I, 428-429; Albion and Pope, *Sea Lanes in Wartime. . . ,* pp. 73-76.

[71] Hammond wrote to Grenville, Philadelphia, July 7, 1793, that "the public prints teemed with the grossest abuse of Great Britain," and that pro-French, anti-British demonstrations were connived at by state governors for political reasons. The quotation in the text is from Hammond to Grenville, Philadelphia, June 10, 1793, Henry Adams Transcripts. In North Carolina, where public sentiment was pro-French, the federal government even approached popularity as prospect of war with England loomed. Delbert H. Gilpatrick, *Jeffersonian Democracy in North Carolina* (New York, 1931), p. 62.

well understood. . . ."[72]   While Anglophobia increased, the Anglo-American frontier situation reached its most dangerous crisis.

Lord Dorchester (Sir Guy Carleton), Governor-General of Canada, in February, 1794, told a delegation of Indians from the American Northwest that American settlements in that region were unauthorized.   Soon, he indicated, they would be able to recover the settled lands because within the year Great Britain and the United States would be at war.   These hostile Indians were among those General Wayne was preparing to punish.   Undoubtedly Dorchester's intemperate utterances stiffened Indian resistance toward the United States.   At approximately the same time Dorchester had ordered occupation by British troops of Fort Miami, sixty miles southwest of Detroit and in territory clearly American.[73]   The subsequent occupation violated American sovereignty.

News of the Governor-General's speech to the Indians and that of the Caribbean outrages reached the American people at the same time.   Public rage against Great Britain mounted, war talk became common, and Republican political advantage increased.   So persistent was the talk of war that rumors reached England of an American declaration of war against her.   Insurance rates on American bottoms went up.[74]   Anglo-American relations dropped to their lowest point since the American Revolution.   The Caribbean spoliations, the frontier crisis, the festering grievances arising out of the 1783 treaty, and the failure to obtain a commercial treaty, combined with bitterly anti-British Republican political propaganda, produced early in 1794 an Anglo-American war crisis.[75]

In Congress in bitter partisan debates retaliatory measures against

[72] *National Gazette* (Philadelphia), Dec. 8, 1793.

[73] Dorchester's words and actions, however, had not been authorized by his government; see Grenville to Hammond, Downing Street, Aug. 8, 1794, in Mayo, *Instructions to the British Ministers. . . , AHA Ann. Rep.* (1936), III, 62; for details, see Burt, *United States, Great Britain, and British North America. . .* , pp. 133-138; Bemis, *Jay's Treaty. . .* , pp. 174-176.

[74] *Virginia Herald and Fredericksburg Advertiser* (Fredericksburg), Nov. 14, 1793.

[75] William Vans Murray Papers, Commonplace Book, July 28, 1795 (Princeton).   Some Englishmen, fearing that such action would bring on war with the United States, cautioned restraint in seizures of American vessels.   "Iris," in *Sheffield Register* (Sheffield, England), Jan. 3 and Feb. 7, 1794.   Cited in Alice B. Keith, "Relaxations in the British Restrictions on the American Trade with the British West Indies, 1783-1802," *Journal of*

Britain were proposed.[76] Seizing this as the right time to strike, Jefferson, in one of his last acts as Secretary of State, sent to the House of Representatives on December 16, 1793, a long-postponed report on the state of American commerce.[77] With this report he refurbished his long-cherished weapon of trade reprisals against Great Britain. He pointed out that whereas France and others treated American commerce relatively well, Britain crushed it with restrictions. To meet this evil he urged adoption of a policy based on reciprocal favors and retaliation and recommended what he had always espoused—closer commercial ties with France.[78] Infuriating to Federalists and obvious in its implications, Jefferson's report was another well-timed anti-British political measure.

In the House of Representatives James Madison, who after Jefferson's resignation had taken over leadership of Republicans in government, pushed Jefferson's recommendations as well as similar proposals of his own. He offered seven resolutions calling for discriminatory duties and for legislation against British shipping.[79] After a week's delay, Madison's resolutions touched off full-scale debate on commercial and foreign policy. As Federalism's mouthpiece, William Loughton Smith of South Carolina took the lead. Expressing Hamilton's ideas, he charged that Jefferson slanted his

---

Modern History, XX, 10. For a brief summary of the crisis, see Raymond C. Werner, "War Scare and Politics, 1794," *Quarterly Journal of the New York State Historical Association,* XI (Oct., 1930), 324-344.

[76] Hammond reported as time went on that Congress received "with avidity every tale of falsehood and calumny that might be propagated with respect to Great Britain. . . ." Hammond to Grenville, Philadelphia, April 17, 1794, Henry Adams Transcripts.

[77] The report is in *ASP FR,* I, 300-304, and Lipscomb, *Jefferson's Works,* III, 261-283. In the report Jefferson countered Hamilton's ideas as expressed in the report on manufactures. Caldwell, *Hamilton and Jefferson,* p. 224.

[78] "France," declared Jefferson, "has, of her own accord, proposed negotiations for improving, by a new treaty, on fair and equal principles, the commercial relations of the two countries." *ASP FR,* I, 304. The British saw clearly the anti-British impact of the report. Hammond reported that "the avowed undisguised tendency of the whole report is to recommend a closer connexion with France, and to inculcate the expediency of a direct system of commercial hostility with Great Britain." Hammond to Grenville, Philadelphia, Feb. 22, 1794, Henry Adams Transcripts. See also the précis on American affairs, 1794 [Sept.-Oct.], in the *Dropmore Papers,* III, 526.

[79] The resolutions are in *Annals of the Congress,* 3rd Cong., 1st sess., Jan. 3, 1794, pp. 155-156.

report to favor France by exaggerating British commercial hostility. Sarcastically, he said that Americans were accustomed to "a constant panegyric on the generous policy of France towards this country in commercial relations" and to "a constant . . . philippic on the unfriendly, illiberal, and persecuting policy of Great Britain towards us in the same relations."[80] This was not a true picture, he said; France was selfishly motivated and hostile and little could be expected of her. Commercial discrimination against Great Britain, he feared, would lead to war and to America's ruin.[81]

Madison and other Republicans who joined in the debate, which lasted over a month, would not accept this reasoning. In his final rebuttal Madison attacked Smith's argument and defended his own resolutions. Among other things, he stressed that his proposals would draw France and the United States closer together, which was precisely what Federalists did not want.[82] In their opposition to the Madison resolutions in the light of increasing public resentment against England, Federalists were characterized as "slaves of British gold," who raised incessantly the cry of war during the entire congressional session. "The hireling printers and funding dependents caught the sound," later explained a Republican writer, "and war, war was echoed through the land. And what was the mighty cause? Why some propositions were made, upon what terms we could regulate our intercourse with nations, to whom we were under no obligations. What would a stranger, who knew nothing of the relation subsisting between us and Great Britain, have thought & most undoubtedly, that we were dependent, and that basely so."[83]

[80] For Smith's speech, see *ibid.*, Jan. 13, 1794, pp. 174-209; Brant, *James Madison: Father of the Constitution . . .*, p. 191, elaborates on Hamilton's authorship of Smith's speech; Hamilton's outline of Smith's speech is in Lodge, *The Works of Alexander Hamilton*, III, 423-441; Jefferson recognized Hamilton as the author of the speech; see Jefferson to Madison, Monticello, April 3, 1794, in Ford, *Writings of Jefferson*, VI, 501-502. In his home town, Charleston, Smith was burned in effigy for defending Great Britain. Bemis, *Jay's Treaty . . .*, p. 190.
[81] For another Federalist attack on Madison's resolutions, see the speech of Fisher Ames, Jan. 27, 1794, in *Works of Fisher Ames*, Compiled by a number of his friends (Boston, 1809), pp. 26-57.
[82] See *Annals of the Congress . . .*, 3rd Cong., 1st sess., Jan. 29-30, 1794, pp. 366-395; Brant, *James Madison: Father of the Constitution . . .*, pp. 392-393.
[83] "Junius Americanus" in the *New York Journal*, reprinted in the *Virginia Herald and Fredericksburg Advertiser*, June 26, 1795.

Madison's first resolution carried, but before Congress acted on the others, war hysteria hardened its grip upon the nation. Action was postponed, and the resolutions were lost in a flood of legislation aimed at war. They were debated by Republicans, Hammond complained, "on their political expediency alone. Here an ample range was afforded for the former topics of abuse of Great Britain."[84] "Mr. Madison's plan," pointed out a Jefferson supporter, "does not go far enough: Let us at one stroke stop all trade with the English, till justice is done, and our merchants indemnified. Great Britain could not resist the stroke. She must acquiesce in the measures, and her necessities would at once compel her to act right." Another writer reviewed the grievances against Great Britain and then concluded that "we had better be at open war with a perfidious nation; than be thus murdered by inches."[85]

Spurred by an enraged public opinion, Congress pressed anti-British legislation which in its war-provoking potential surpassed the Madison resolutions. On March 26, 1794, Congress laid a temporary one-month embargo against foreign shipping (directed primarily against Great Britain), and later extended it for another month; it discussed and passed various defense measures, among which was a bill to fortify harbors, and another calling out eighty thousand militia, as well as one for additional military stores. In the Senate a nonintercourse bill was defeated only by the vote of Vice-President John Adams.[86]

Bills for sequestration of British debts to offset seizure of Ameri-

[84] Hammond to Grenville, Philadelphia, Feb. 22, 1794, Henry Adams Transcripts. Hammond maintained that Madison's proposals "excited the most universal attention." The political effect of the resolutions was clearly recognized by Americans of both parties. The existence of two parties in Congress was now clear. "Whether the subject be foreign or domestic—relative to war or peace—navigation or commerce—the magnetism of opposite views draws them wide as the poles asunder." John Taylor, *A Definition of Parties, or the Political Effect of the Paper System Considered* (Philadelphia, 1794), p. 2 (the date of writing was given as April 5, 1794).

[85] "Plain Truth" and "A Native of Columbia," in the *Independent Chronicle and the Universal Advertiser* (Boston), Jan. 30 and Feb. 24, 1794.

[86] For the legislation and proposed legislation, see *Annals of the Congress . . .* , 3rd Cong., 1st sess., March 26, 1794, p. 531; April 17, 1794, pp. 597-598; Bemis, *Jay's Treaty . . .* , pp. 194-198; Dauer, *The Adams Federalists,* pp. 86-87. Adams's vote on several occasions was decisive in foreign policy matters; he usually voted anti-French.

can ships appeared, and resolutions were passed to increase the federal army. The resolutions and legislation, much more than trade retaliation, carried seeds of war; hostility to Great Britain, "which pervades the whole Continent," increased rapidly.[87] Americans caught the war spirit; they volunteered for defense preparations and began drilling in volunteer companies. British sailors and officers suffered at the hands of aroused anti-British mobs; some mobs, in places such as Norfolk and Baltimore, tarred and feathered pro-British Americans.

Alarmed and overwhelmed Federalists were almost swept into an English war. To defend British actions had become almost impossible. Many Federalists, even Hamilton and Washington, felt that Great Britain had gone too far. William Loughton Smith, for example, changed his tune and urged preparations for war.[88] "Even the Monocrat papers," reported Jefferson, "are obliged to publish the most furious Philippics against England." Yet the war in the making was a Republican war. Federalists wanted none of it; to them it was national suicide. "You cannot imagine," said John Adams, "what horror some persons are in, lest peace should continue. The prospect of peace throws them into distress."[89]

Certain New England Federalists, morever, took a sectional view of difficulties with Great Britain. They maintained that the South, because of its debts to England, acted to generate irritation with England and thereby plunge the nation into war. The South's opposition to the government, its anti-British attitude, in the opinion of Yankee Federalist Oliver Ellsworth, gave "a baleful ascendancy to French influence."[90] Fisher Ames deprecated Southern violence

[87] For the debate on the sequestration of British debts, see *Annals of the Congress* . . . , 3rd Cong., 1st sess., March 27, 1794, pp. 535 ff. John Quincy Adams wrote to his father that "the sequestration of British debts must be considered as a direct act of hostility. . . ." Boston, April 22, 1794, in Ford, ed., *The Writings of John Quincy Adams*, I, 187; Hammond to Grenville, Philadelphia, May 8, 1794, deprecated hostility to Great Britain, Henry Adams Transcripts.

[88] *Annals of the Congress*, 3rd Cong., 1st sess., March 14, 1794, pp. 506-507.

[89] Jefferson to James Monroe, Philadelphia, May 5, 1793, in Ford, *Writings of Jefferson*, VI, 238; Adams to Wife, Philadelphia, April 19, 1794, in Charles F. Adams, ed., *Letters of John Adams Addressed to His Wife* (2 vols., Boston, 1841), II, 156.

[90] Oliver Ellsworth to Oliver Wolcott, Sr., Philadelphia, April 5, 1794, Gibbs, ed., *Wolcott Papers*, I, 134.

against the British in Norfolk and Baltimore. "Compared with New-England," he sputtered contemptuously, "the multitude in those towns are but half civilized." Then he queried, "Will our Yankees like a war the better for being mobbed into it, and because the South will not pay the British debts?"[91] That the pro-French anti-British influence upon the government was at least in part sectional—Southern—was an idea which persisted in New England Federalist circles. In those circles, in fact, "dissolution of the Union" seemed the only cure for the political, foreign-policy, sectional split.[92]

Believing that sequestration and trade reprisals were certain steps to disaster and that the war-party was sectional and politically motivated, Federalists groped for a way out of their dilemma. To be shoved into a war they did not want ran counter to their political philosophy; they would not act merely to gratify public passion.[93] To save the nation, to save their kind of government, they adopted the strategy of delay, of urging preparation for war while seeking a formula for peace.[94]

Fortunately all hope for peace and for Federalism was not lost. Angered by America's failure to enforce treaty obligations, France for a while retaliated by seizing, wherever possible, American ships carrying goods to England. In the French view the Franco-American alliance obligated Americans to resist British seizures of goods on American ships destined for French ports—the vexing question of free ships, free goods.[95]

[91] Fisher Ames to ———, Philadelphia, May 6, 1794, in Ames, *Works of Fisher Ames*, p. 478.

[92] When Oliver Ellsworth and Rufus King suggested dissolution of the Union to John Taylor of Caroline as the cure for the split between Republicans and Federalists, Taylor saw it as a plot of a "British interest." John Taylor of Caroline to [Madison], May 11, 1794, in John Taylor, *Disunion Sentiment in Congress in 1794. . .* , ed. Gaillard Hunt (Washington, 1905), pp. 22-23.

[93] So certain did war seem that Thomas Pinckney, American minister in London, queried the Secretary of State about moving his family to France when hostilities should break out. Pinckney to Jefferson, Nov. 27, 1793, cited in Bemis, "The London Mission of Thomas Pinckney. . . ," *AHR*, XXVIII, 243.

[94] Bemis, *Jay's Treaty . . .* , p. 194.

[95] For the French decrees of May 9 and 23, 1793, and the correspondence relating to them, see *ASP FR*, I, 243-246. French seizures of American vessels were difficult to stop, related French Minister of Foreign Affairs to Genet, because of the great resemblance between American and English vessels. Paris, March 31, 1793, Genet Papers, VIII, 2690.

After the initial surprise seizures, moreover, England relaxed her orders-in-council and allowed a temporary resumption of American Caribbean trade.[96] England paid for many of the confiscated cargoes, whereas the French did not. In addition, the English wartrade was more lucrative than that of France; even at its height the French war-trade with America was a poor second to that of England. These were factors which mitigated the drive to war. Even more important as a war deterrent was the fact that Federalists controlled the Senate and the Executive Branch of the government.[97] In England, too, there were those who worked to avert war. Realizing that the Washington administration was friendly and pro-British, "His Majesty's Ministers" wanted no war with the United States. At the height of the war hysteria Hammond received instructions to encourage the Federalist government in its "maintenance of a fair Neutrality" and in its policy of friendship toward Great Britain.[98]

Federalists therefore were not committed to a lost cause. After partisan struggles, Federalists in Congress blocked the worst of the anti-British legislation. Next, they tried to avoid an English war in a more decisive manner; as a last minute gamble they decided to send a special mission to London.[99]

[96] See Thomas Pinckney to Jefferson, London, Jan. 9, 1794, and Instructions to Commanders of British Ships, Jan. 8, 1794, *ASP FR*, I, 430-431. Washington, for example, realized that the British Order in Council of Jan. 8 "allayed the violence of the heat." To Tobias Lear, Philadelphia, May 16, 1794, in Fitzpatrick, *Washington's Writings*, XXXIII, 355.

[97] Federalist control of the Senate was close; it depended, oftentimes, on the casting vote of the Vice-President. Gibbs, *Wolcott Papers*, I, 116.

[98] Grenville to Hammond, Whitehall, Jan. —, 1794, in Mayo, *Instructions to the British Ministers. . . , AHA Ann. Rep.* (1936), III, 44. Whether or not England wanted to go to war with the United States was, of course, a vital question to Federalists; see the *Independent Chronicle and the Universal Advertiser* (Boston), May 5, 1794.

[99] Speaking for Federalists, George Cabot remarked: "We all perceive that, bad as our condition is, war would make it much worse, and therefore must be avoided." To Samuel Phillips, Philadelphia, March 8, 1794, in Henry Cabot Lodge, *Life and Letters of George Cabot* (Boston, 1877), pp. 75-77; see also Fisher Ames to Christopher Gore, Philadelphia, March 26, 1794, in Seth Ames, ed., *Works of Fisher Ames* (2 vols., Boston, 1854), I, 139-140.

CHAPTER FOUR

THE JAY TREATY

PRELUDE TO PEACE OR WAR?

*You can have no idea, how deeply the public confidence is withdrawing itself from the President, and with what avidity strictures on his conduct are received; sensible of this, his friends are redoubling their efforts to exalt his name and exaggerate his past services—But all in vain, the vital blow aimed at the Independence & best Interests of his country, by the impending treaty, mark him in indelible character as the head of a British faction, and no longer blinds the public mind.—*John Beckely to James Madison, September 10, 1795.

*The Present crisis appears to me to be most delicate and important since the organization of the Government. The Anti-Federalists, and the personal enemies of the Administration, have rallied with astonishing activity. The circumstances of the Treaty has ranged a variety of parties on their side, and given an imposing appearance to their numbers; and I believe they will now make their last effort to shake the Government.—*William Richardson Davie to James Iredell, Halifax, North Carolina, September 4, 1795.

* * * * *

F ROM its inception the plan of a special mission to England was a political move; politics and personal partisanship dominated almost every step of its development. It was conceived by Federalists to be executed by Federalists for the benefit of Federalists.[1] At

[1] Zephaniah Swift, Federalist congressman from Connecticut, had suggested Oliver Ellsworth from his own state for the mission, but Southern Republicans objected; they had no confidence in him. "Mr. Hamilton was mentioned, but the Southern Democrats made such rout that it was thought best by Hamilton himself to appoint Mr. Jay against whom one would suppose there could be no objection, and yet the Southern Democrats object."

first Hamilton was to be saviour of party and country; but his unpopularity, the strong Republican opposition to him, and Federalist
need for his political talents at home, particularly in his relations
with President Washington, made another choice imperative.[2]

At Hamilton's suggestion, Washington nominated John Jay, the
Chief Justice of the United States, for the mission. Although not
yet involved in the more violent political battles, he was almost
wholly a political choice.[3] On the basis of his record and past diplomatic experience Jay was admirably qualified for the task. But
politically and temperamentally his qualifications were dubious,
particularly to Republicans. A staunch and haughty Federalist, an
Anglophile, and, though of French ancestry, inveterately anti-
French, already unpopular for an ostensible surrender of American
navigation rights on the Mississippi in an unexecuted treaty with
Spain (Jay-Gardoqui Treaty, 1786), Jay lacked the very things
needed most—public confidence and an uncommitted position.

To George Hammond, for instance, he revealed that he desired

Swift to David Daggett, Philadelphia, April 17, 1794, in Franklin B. Dexter,
ed., "Selections from Letters Received by David Daggett, 1786-1802," *Proceedings of the American Antiquarian Society*, n.s., IV, 372. George Cabot
and Caleb Strong, Senators from Massachusetts, Oliver Ellsworth, Senator
from Connecticut, and Rufus King, Senator from New York, headed the
movement for a special mission to England; they acted together and constituted a clique which shaped Federalist policy in the Senate. See the contemporary notes of Rufus King in Charles C. King, ed., *The Life and
Correspondence of Rufus King* . . . (6 vols., New York, 1874-1900), 517-
527, hereinafter cited as King, *Rufus King Correspondence*. See also, Taylor,
Disunion Sentiment in Congress, 1794, p. 8; William G. Brown, *The Life of
Oliver Ellsworth* (New York, 1905), pp. 211, 214-217; Oliver Ellsworth to
Oliver Wolcott, Sr., Philadelphia, April 5, 1794, in Gibbs, *Wolcott Papers*, I,
134-135; Lodge, *Life and Letters of George Cabot*, p. 95; Dice R. Anderson,
"Edmund Randolph," in Bemis, ed., *American Secretaries of State*. . . , II,
112-114; and Joseph Charles, "The Jay Treaty: The Origins of the American
Party System," *The William and Mary Quarterly*, 3rd Series, XII (Oct., 1955),
592-593.

    [2] Secretary of State Randolph opposed Hamilton's appointment; see Mon-
cure D. Conway, *Omitted Chapters of History Disclosed in the Life and
Papers of Edmund Randolph* (New York, 1888), p. 215. Hereinafter cited
as Conway, *Randolph*. See also King, *Rufus King Correspondence*, April 13,
1794, I, 519-520; Washington to Monroe, Philadelphia, April 9, 1794, in
Fitzpatrick, *Washington's Writings*, XXX, 320-321.

    [3] See Hamilton to Washington, Philadelphia, April 14, 1794, in Hamilton,
ed., *Hamilton's Works*, IV, 519-532; Monaghan, *John Jay*, pp. 365-366.

to remove every obstacle to Anglo-American friendship. In accepting the nomination, which he did not welcome and which he foresaw would make him unpopular, he made clear where he stood. He demanded wide discretion in negotiation and that the anti-British measures in the House of Representatives be blocked, or at least that the President not sanction them.[4]

No one but a Jeffersonian would actually have pleased Republicans, but Jay and his notorious record seemed almost as bad as Hamilton. His nomination struck them as a deliberate political challenge.[5] It immediately touched off a furious political wrangle. After three days of Senate debate Federalists on April 19, 1794, by a margin of 18 to 8 finally rammed the nomination through.[6] Even in a Federalist-controlled Senate, it was now obvious that so controversial a matter as Jay's mission would face further buffetings. In Federalist reasoning a matter as vital to party and nation as the Jay mission should not again be set free in the Congress.

Previously Washington had relied upon the Senate for collaboration in the formulation of foreign policy. In addition to obtaining Senate confirmation of envoys the President had followed the practice of seeking its approval of diplomatic instructions. Up to the time of the Jay mission this practice had not caused difficulty, as the Senate was Federalist and dominated by Hamilton; it responded like an amiable partner. At this juncture Federalists saw that the ostensible partnership could no longer function with the harmony Washington cherished; political differences were too deep, even in the still-Federalist Senate. The political challenge of the Republicans had made control of foreign policy by an elite group almost impossible.

[4] Hammond to Grenville, Philadelphia, April 28, 1794, Henry Adams Transcripts; Jay to Mrs. Jay, Philadelphia, April 15, 19, 1794, in Johnston, ed., *Correspondence of John Jay*, IV, 3-6; King, *Rufus King Correspondence*, April 14, 15, 1795, I, 520.

[5] One administration critic later went so far as to demand Washington's impeachment for appointing Jay. This was "Franklin," a pseudonymous writer who wrote fourteen anti-Jay letters in the *Independent Gazetteer* (Philadelphia) between March 11 and June 10, 1795. William Cobbett responded in kind and in defense of the administration in a pamphlet entitled *A Little Plain English*. For a summary of the arguments, see Woodbury, *Public Opinion in Philadelphia . . .* , pp. 82-87.

[6] U. S. Congress. Senate, *Journal of the Executive Proceedings of the Senate of the United States* (Washington, 1828), April 17, 18, 19, 1794, I,

In line with Hamiltonian doctrine of loose constitutional interpretation, the Federalist Senate coterie which had won approval of
Jay's nomination suggested that the practice of executive collaboration with the Senate be abandoned. "From the Difficulty of passing
particular instructions in the Senate," wrote Rufus King, "it seems
to me to be most suitable that the Pr. shd. instruct, and that the
Treaty shd. be concluded subject to the approbation of the Senate."[7]

Senate partnership in formulation of foreign policy was thus
smothered in infancy; the Senate was to be presented with accomplished fact, to be accepted, rejected, or perhaps modified. In this
way Federalists shielded the Jay mission from further attacks; in
this way political expediency impelled the Executive to assume sole
control in execution of foreign policy; in this way Washington
established foreign policy precedent which has endured to this day.[8]

Federalist strategy infuriated Republicans. Before Jay's confirmation they demanded that the President be forced "to inform
the Senate of the whole business." But Federalist votes killed their
demands.

After winning the battle for confirmation, Alexander Hamilton
drew up Jay's instructions. While other Federalist opinion had
been sought, Hamilton's ideas predominated; those of Edmund
Randolph, the new Secretary of State, were ignored.[9] During the
entire negotiation, in fact, Randolph was either ignored or by-
passed. As in the past, when Jefferson held the post, the Secretary

151-152. Rufus King notes April 20 as the date of Jay's approval. King,
Rufus King Correspondence, I, 522.

[7] King, *Rufus King Correspondence,* April 16, 1794, I, 521; for a discussion of the episode, see White, *The Federalists . . . ,* pp. 61-62.

[8] See Ralston Hayden, *The Senate and Treaties: 1789-1817* (New York,
1920), pp. 70-71, 94, 103-105. In a body as numerous and as divided as the
Senate the necessary secrecy in treaty negotiation would have been impossible.
Give and take necessary in diplomatic negotiation, too, would have been im-
possible. Jefferson recognized this and on more than one occasion viewed
conduct of foreign affairs as belonging to the President exclusively. See
"Opinion on the Powers of the Senate," April 24, 1790, in Ford, *Writings of
Jefferson,* V, 161; White, *The Federalists . . . ,* p. 62.

[9] For drafts of Jay's instructions, see Hamilton to Washington, April 22,
1794, Hamilton to Randolph, April 27, 1794, "Part of Instructions to John
Jay," 1794, in Lodge, ed., *The Works of Alexander Hamilton,* IV, 300-308;
Schachner, *Alexander Hamilton,* p. 331; Bemis, *Jay's Treaty . . . ,* p. 210;
Anderson, "Edmund Randolph," in Bemis, ed., *The American Secretaries of
State,* II, 116.

of State went through empty formalities in writing instructions to Jay. Not being a confirmed Federalist, he never knew Jay's real instructions.

* * * * *

In England Jay was as popular a choice as he was an unpopular one in the United States.[10] Received with warmth, he was wined, dined, and flattered. Assessing Jay as "long-winded and self- opinionated," the British reasoned that he "may be attached by good treatment, but will be unforgiving if he thinks himself neglected"; they were aware that "Mr. Jay's weak side is *Mr. Jay*."[11] Conciliation was the British theme. Even though as an opponent the United States might seem inconsequential, England wanted no war if it could be avoided without sacrifice. Her primary foe was France; any new conflict would detract from the main war. In Parliament, moreover, English merchants made their weight felt. Dreading the loss in trade from their largest and most profitable customer, they opposed an American war.[12]

Jay's conduct and Britain's conciliatory attitude did not stem Anglophobia in the United States. On the streets aroused Americans still attacked British sailors and officers. In complaining of "the *uniformly* unfriendly treatment that British officers have experienced in American ports," Hammond said the American government must adopt "some effectual mode of protecting from popular

[10] Thomas Pinckney, the regular American minister to London, was recognized by the British as being less disposed than Jay to make concessions. See Count Woronzow to Lord Grenville, Harley Street, June 21, 1795, and J. B. Burgess to Lord Grenville, Downing Street, June 28, 1795, *Dropmore Papers*, III, 78, 87; Bemis, "The London Mission of Thomas Pinckney . . . ," *American Historical Review*, XXVIII, 243; Bemis, *Jay's Treaty . . .* , p. 208.

[11] Lord Auckland to Grenville, Beckenham, June 22, 1794, *Dropmore Papers*, II, 578.

[12] Most informed Britons, apparently, recognized the seriousness of difficulties with the United States and also the importance of keeping the former colonies from being driven once again into the arms of France. Even Lord Hawkesbury, president of England's Board of Trade, who had long opposed relaxation of the British commercial system in favor of Americans recognized this. See Hawkesbury's memorandum to Lord Grenville, n. d., in Bradford Perkins, ed., "Lord Hawkesbury and the Jay-Grenville Negotiations," *Mississippi Valley Historical Review*, XL (Sept., 1953), 293-304. Other evidence of attempted British conciliation is revealed in Josiah T. Newcomb, "New Light on Jay's Treaty," *American Journal of International Law*, XXVIII (1934), 685-93.

insult and aggression the British officers in its ports; or it will be otherwise impossible for them to quit their ships in security."[13] Although Jay's negotiations fanned anti-British sentiment, it was his treaty that enraged Anglophobes and Republicans.

Jay's instructions were not on the surface an abandonment of American rights; they contained much that even Republicans could approve. In their very nature, therefore, they stressed provisions which Great Britain under no circumstances would accept.[14] In the four-month negotiation the British held the trump cards. William Wyndham Grenville (Lord Grenville), the British foreign minister, had a copy of the State Department's secret cypher, but, more important, he had in Alexander Hamilton an invaluable ally. Even if he had set his heart on it, Jay was committed to a game he could not win.

In Jay's instructions Randolph had incorporated the suggestion that Jay consult with Russian, Swedish, and Danish representatives on the possibility of common action in forming an armed neutrality to resist high-handed British maritime practices. "The principles of the armed neutrality," Randolph pointed out, "would abundantly cover our neutral rights." Jay was to "sound those ministers upon the probability of an alliance with their nation to support those principles." In March, 1794, Sweden and Denmark formed an armed neutrality, and shortly after Jay's departure for England had invited the United States to join. American adherence was precisely what Great Britain did not want; to block it she was apparently willing to make concessions. This proved unnecessary. President Washington and his Federalist Cabinet rejected the invitation on the basis of a desire to avoid entangling alliances.[15]

Although the British knew of the invitation, they did not know, at first, of the American rejection. In the Jay-Grenville negotiations the threat of joining the armed neutrality was almost the only

[13] Hammond to Grenville, New York, Aug. 3, 1794, Henry Adams Transcripts.

[14] The instructions, dated Philadelphia, May 6, 1794, are in *ASP FR*, I, 472-474.

[15] The quotations are from *ibid.*, p. 473; for more information on the armed neutrality, see Samuel F. Bemis, "The United States and the Abortive Armed Neutrality of 1794," *AHR*, XXIV (Oct., 1908), 26-46; Phillips and Reede, *Neutrality* . . . , II, 91-94.

coercive weapon the United States possessed. If the British government learned of the Washington administration's decision on the armed neutrality the United States would be in the position of a petitioner hopeful of small favors in the negotiation. That happened.

Fearful of the slightest threat to his pro-English foreign policy, Hamilton assured Hammond beforehand that the American government would not join the armed neutrality. The settled policy of the American government, he told the British minister, was "to avoid entangling itself with European connexions, which could only tend to involve this Country in disputes, wherein it might have no possible interest, and commit it in a common cause with allies, from whom in the moment of danger, it could derive no succour." Later Hamilton told Hammond that the Cabinet had discussed the armed neutrality and that—as he had predicted—it had decided against joining.[16] Apparently not even Jay could be trusted completely to implement the Hamiltonian program as Hamilton wished it.

Except in two controversial points, Jay's Federalist-inspired, Federalist-controlled instructions were but recommendations. Few American diplomats have been allowed the discretion that was Jay's.[17] Two only were the rules from which he was not to deviate. First, he could do nothing contrary to American engagements to France; secondly, he could sign no commercial treaty that did not recognize those obligations to France. Basically the instructions directed him to obtain an agreement in trade reciprocity, "particularly to the West Indies." Among other things, he was to adjust grievances arising from the 1783 treaty, gain British recognition of America's neutral rights, obtain compensation for British seizures of American ships and property, and, if possible, negotiate a commercial treaty.

Fundamental in the instructions was the simple objective—peace. Regardless of other desirable recommendations Jay was to make great concessions for peace—a peace upon which was grounded the entire Federalist structure of government. Yet, Hamilton had in-

---

[16] Hammond to Grenville, New York, Aug. 3, and Philadelphia, Jan. 5, 1795, Henry Adams Transcripts.
[17] See Monaghan, *John Jay,* p. 368; Bemis, *Jay's Treaty . . . ,* p. 212.

structed Jay that he was not to do anything which might be interpreted as an abdication of American rights. Obviously the instructions were contradictory. Some of the very concessions Jay was allowed to make were considered American "rights." Consequently
the treaty that Jay signed on November 19, 1794, failed to comport
with his instructions, even with the two imperatives upon which he
was not to retreat. By ignoring most of his confusing instructions Jay
achieved his fundamental objective, peace with England.[18]

In comparison Great Britain's concessions appeared minor. Her
most important concession was the signing of the treaty, a treaty of
commerce that did not include admission of American vessels, on
a reciprocal basis, into the British West Indies. A second British
concession consisted of a promise—a valuable promise Britain had
given in the peace treaty of 1783 but had not carried out—to evacuate the frontier posts. A third concession was another promise, a
promise to pay for spoliations under the orders-in-council. The
spoliations themselves, however, were not repudiated and were to
continue. Aside from these and a few other limited privileges, Jay
obtained no commercial concessions the United States had not
enjoyed before the treaty. The one explicit privilege of trade with
the British West Indies embodied in article twelve was so restrictive
that not even a Federalist Senate could accept it.[19]

The treaty's most ominous feature was its blighting effect on the
French alliance. In this it fitted British foreign policy and Federalist
objectives; in this it reflected its political as well as its diplomatic
character. Considering the treaty's major provisions, its objectives,
and the motives of people responsible for it, the stipulation that
nothing in it should violate any treaty the United States had with
another nation appeared meaningless.[20] While the Jay treaty gained

[18] Monaghan, *John Jay*, p. 369; Carlton Savage, *Policy of the United States
towards Maritime Commerce in War* (2 vols., Washington, 1934), I, 15; for
the text of the treaty with notes, see Miller, *Treaties and Other International
Acts of the United States of America*, II, 245-274.

[19] Bemis, *Jay's Treaty . . .* , p. 258; Robert R. Rankin, *The Treaty of
Amity, Commerce, and Navigation between Great Britain and the United
States* (Berkeley, Calif., 1907), p. 30.

[20] For a critical appraisal of the Jay treaty, see George A. King, *The French
Spoliation Claims,* Senate Document No. 451, 64th Cong., 1st sess. (Washington, 1916), p. 7. King maintained that article XXV of the Jay treaty
directly contravened obligations to France. With the Jay treaty, he de-

the laudable objective of peace with England when war might have
been disastrous, it laid the basis for another war which might have
been equally disastrous—a war with France.[21]

The treaty ignored maritime principles Americans had bound
themselves to uphold: free ships make free goods, freedom of neutrals to trade with belligerents in noncontraband goods, and a restricted contraband list. By including naval stores as contraband and
by acquiescing in the British Rule of 1756 and in other big-navy
British maritime practices the United States deserted principles it had
obliged itself to observe by previous treaties, particularly by the
French treaties of 1778.[22] Legalistically and realistically—in view of
feeble American sea power—the United States could not have been
called upon to force British compliance with these principles. Yet
the American government's abandonment of its maritime principles
was, in the view of many, incompatible with treaty obligations to
France. Indeed, American acquiescence in the British practices
seemed, especially to the French, unconscionably eager.

Technically the Jay treaty could have been interpreted, and was
by Hamiltonians, as being harmless to France.[23] But such an interpretation seemingly evaded the treaty's real intent. The treaty violated the spirit if not the letter of the 1778 treaties. Under it
Great Britain's position in relations with America was more favorable than that of America's French ally. Frenchmen viewed it as
a negation of the alliance.[24] Many Americans did also. Was the

---

clared, the United States "committed a flagrant breach of our plighted
faith for which she [France] might well call upon us to make reparation."
Ibid., p. 8.

[21] One Federalist praised the treaty because it brought a peace which would
give the country in the "vigour of youth room to expand into that gigantic
size which will in 20 years outgrow the Insolence of Britain & render the
U. S. too Formidable to be trifled with." William Vans Murray Papers,
Commonplace Book, July 28, 1795 (Princeton).

[22] Before the treaty had been negotiated Hamilton had revealed to Hammond that the United States was ready to abandon its established maritime
principles. Bemis, *Jay's Treaty* . . . , pp. 199-201.

[23] Professor Bemis believed that the Jay treaty did not violate the French
treaties. See his "Washington's Farewell Address: A Foreign Policy of Independence," *AHR,* XXXIX (Jan., 1934), 251 and his *John Quincy Adams
and the Foundations of American Foreign Policy* (New York, 1949), p. 46.

[24] La Rochefoucauld-Liancourt, *Travels* . . . , II, 518; C. S. Hyneman,
"Neutrality during the European Wars of 1792-1815," *AJIL,* XXIV (1930),
292. Frenchmen had feared an Anglo-American *rapprochement.* Genet, for

treaty a breach of neutrality? Some Americans thought so. Could a state at peace, according to international practice, alter its relations with belligerents without compromising its neutrality?[25]

Jay's treaty has often been called Hamilton's treaty because Hamilton sabotaged negotiations on the issue of the armed neutrality. Regardless of the real significance of that episode (probably it did little to alter the basic structure of the treaty or even the tenor of the negotiations), Jay's treaty was Hamilton's treaty more than that of any other man. As had been planned, it saved his system.[26] Not only had he had a hand in its inception and dominated its negotiation; he was to be its leading defender, working it through the Senate and being responsible for its execution. This treaty, because of the violent reaction it inspired in France, for a short time made Federalists popular.

*   *   *   *   *

The Jay treaty said little about the frontier-Indian question. While Jay had been negotiating, "Mad" Anthony Wayne had been fighting. At one stroke, in the Battle of Fallen Timbers (August 20, 1794), he settled the immediate Indian problem on the Northwest frontier. Immediately following the American victory it appeared that Anglo-American tension in the region would lead to a collision. With arrival of news of the Jay agreement, suspense ended. By the treaty of Greenville of the following year (August 3, 1795), facilitated by the stipulation in Jay's treaty that the posts were to be surrendered, the United States made a lasting peace with the Indians. With the Jay treaty and the treaty of Greenville there was peace with both British and Indians on the Northwest frontier.[27]

---

example, had been instructed to thwart any Anglo-American negotiations for a commercial treaty. LeBrun to Genet, Paris, May 9, 1793, Genet Papers, IX, 2765.

[25] James Madison, James Alexander Dallas, and others believed the Jay treaty a breach of neutrality; see C. S. Hyneman, *The First American Neutrality: A Study of the American Understanding of Neutral Obligations during the Years 1792 to 1815* (Urbana, Ill., 1934), pp. 42-45; Anderson, "Edmund Randolph," in Bemis, ed., *American Secretaries of State*, II, 142.

[26] Bemis, *Jay's Treaty . . .* , p. 271; Setser, *Commercial Reciprocity Policy . . .* , p. 130.

[27] For details, see Schachner, *The Founding Fathers*, pp. 334-335; Bond, *The Civilization of the Old Northwest*, pp. 254-255; Darling, *Our Rising Empire . . .* , pp. 207-213.

In the meantime national politics, with foreign affairs predominant, continued in ferment. In every step of the way to a treaty Jay had been vilified. The real abuse was not loosed fully until the contents of the treaty were publicly known. Then popular scorn fell upon Jay and the Federalist treaty. Any treaty with England would have suffered at the hands of Republicans and Anglophobes; and so great an abdication of alleged national principle did the Jay treaty seem that even Federalists hung their heads. Some confessed that the treaty "in the opinion of the most candid [is] *quite* as favourable to the B[ritish] as to ourselves."[28]

With the treaty the Washington administration had met a severe crisis in foreign affairs. But this did not settle the problem of foreign policy towards England and France; the explosive political implications of the treaty had to be dealt with. The treaty was now before the Senate, partially exposed to public opinion, and President Washington confronted the beginning of his greatest political crisis.[29]

Washington, displaying little liking for the treaty, had feared the public reaction that would follow its promulgation. The treaty had reached the United States in March, 1795; he then smothered it in secrecy until a special session of Congress could assemble in June. During the four months the President attempted to shield it from attack; but rumors and garbled interpretations reached the public.

How would Washington handle this political treaty now that politics had been woven into American national life and consequently into the treaty-making machinery? There was no precedent to follow; what he did might establish precedent. For the

[28] Timothy Williams to Timothy Pickering, Boston, July 17, 1795, Timothy Pickering Papers, Massachusetts Historical Society, Boston (microfilm copy). Governor Sam Johnston of North Carolina confessed, for example, that various objectionable articles *"have greatly lessened my opinione of Mr. Jay's abilities as a negotiator. . . ."* Johnston to Iredell, Williamston, N. C., Aug. 1, 1795, in J. Griffith McRee, *Life and Correspondence of James Iredell* (2 vols., New York, 1858), II, 450. Fifteen days later Johnston wrote: "The whole continent appears to be highly enraged against Mr. Jay and his Treaty." *Ibid.*, II, 453.

[29] "There is nothing brilliant in it," remarked William Vans Murray of the treaty, but it avoided war. This seemed to be an estimate shared by other Federalists. William Vans Murray Papers, Commonplace Book, Aug. 3, 1795 (Princeton). In Pennsylvania the Jay treaty was an effective agent in crystallizing party demarcation. Tinkcom, *The Republicans and Federalists in Pennsylvania, 1790-1801,* p. 99; see also Henry Adams, *The Life of Albert Gallatin,* p. 159.

first time constitutional procedure for making and approving treaties was to undergo a full test.

Critics maintained that the Senate did not know that Jay was to negotiate a treaty. How then, they asked, "could it be demonstrated a treaty negociated with the advice and consent of the Senate?" If the President could thus dispense with the advice of Senators he could just as well dispense with their consent "and render their participation with him in matters of treaty altogether nugatory."[30]

So fearful were Federalists of the adverse impact that the document would have on the public that they pledged each Senator not to divulge the treaty's contents.[31] For eight days the Senate debated the treaty. Republicans charged to the attack, particularly against article twelve; Federalists defended Jay's work. Words seemed not strong enough to describe Jay's "betrayal" of his country with this "dishonorable" treaty; so, at least, it appeared to Republicans. Although they wanted the treaty approved just as Jay had negotiated it, Federalists realized that Senate consent was impossible in that form, and that retreat was essential. They struck out the most offensive part of the treaty, article twelve, which article imposed a limit of seventy tons upon American ships trading with the British West Indies. As expressed by James Madison, this would have been trade "in canoes." With not a single vote to spare and according to party alignment the Senate on June 24, 1795, consented to the treaty by a vote of 20 to 10.[32]

Still bound by the pledge of secrecy, the Senate resolved that the treaty, even though its contents were in the main already known, should not be divulged to the public until the President should so decide. Up to this point not even George Hammond, the British minister, had seen the official treaty.[33] In view of the political heat centering on the treaty, the attempt at secrecy was foolish. The effort failed; in a few days the terms leaked out.

[30] "Atticus" in the *Aurora* (Philadelphia), July 23, 1795.

[31] See *Annals of the Congress . . .* , 3rd Congress, 2nd sess., June 8, 1795, p. 855.

[32] See *ibid.*, June 24, 1795, p. 862. From the Senate, only news of the treaty's approval reached the public, none of the treaty itself. *Maryland Gazette* (Annapolis), July 2, 1795; see also Rankin, *The Treaty of Amity, Commerce, and Navigation . . .* , pp. 30, 37-40.

[33] Hammond to Grenville, Philadelphia, June 25, 1795, Henry Adams Transcripts.

An anti-Federalist Virginian, Senator Stevens Thomson Mason, did not regard himself as bound by the pledge. He made the treaty articles available to Benjamin Franklin Bache, one of the more scurrilous Republican editors. In his *Aurora,* Bache flooded Philadelphia with a summary, and then with the full contents of the treaty.[34] Mason, critics maintained, released the treaty to embarrass the government. "This artifice," George Hammond said, "has been too successful in its operation."[35] Immediately the treaty was reprinted in pamphlet form and in other newspapers and widely distributed.

Public reaction was overwhelmingly hostile; Americans denounced the Jay treaty in prose and rhyme. Odes such as this expressed anti-British sentiment:

> Is it again the patriot's fate,
> To mourn his country's fallen state,
> To weep her honour lost;
> To see her bend at Britain's throne,
> No wrongs redress'd, her freedom gone,
> Her independence grown an empty boast?
>
> . . . .

[34] There is evidence that Senator Mason sold a copy of the treaty to Pierre Auguste Adet, the French minister in Philadelphia, who gave it to Bache for publication. See Bernard Faÿ, *The Two Franklins: Fathers of American Democracy* (Boston, 1933), pp. 239-241; Howard C. Rice, "James Swan: Agent of the French Republic, 1794-1796," *New England Quarterly,* X (Sept., 1937), 480-481. The *Virginia Herald and Fredericksburg Advertiser,* July 7, 1795, for example, carried the text of the treaty preceded by a letter from Mason in which he stated that he sent a "genuine" copy of the treaty to the press for the information of Americans. For further details, see Timothy Pickering to John Quincy Adams, Sept. 10, 1795, in Octavius Pickering and C. W. Upham, *The Life of Timothy Pickering* (4 vols., Boston, 1867-73), III, 200-203. Federalists also revealed official information about the treaty to foreign diplomats. Oliver Wolcott, for instance, passed on the substance of Senate proceedings leading to approval to Hammond. Anderson, "Randolph," in Bemis, ed., *The American Secretaries of State . . . ,* II, 140. Adet reported that he had purchased a copy of the treaty from a Senator, probably Mason, and, without its being suspected that he, Adet, had a hand in it, had it published in Bache's *Aurora.* Adet to Committee of Public Safety, Philadelphia, July 3, 1795, in Frederick J. Turner, ed., "Correspondence of the French Ministers to the United States, 1791-1797," *Annual Report of the American Historical Association for the Year 1903,* II (Washington, 1904), 741-743. Hereinafter cited as Turner, *CFM.*

[35] Hammond to Grenville, Philadelphia, July 18, 1795. Earlier, June 28, Hammond had told Grenville that after the Senate's approval of the treaty there was a state of general tranquillity in the United States such as he had not witnessed since his arrival. Henry Adams Transcripts.

Ay yes! unless her suns arise
To rend the curst infamous ties
and break the magic spell,
No more by Britain's art beguil'd
O let us spurn the base born child
The Imp of slavery begot in hell.[36]

In pleading for organized opposition to the treaty a Virginia Republican declared that the nation had been "dragooned into a treaty with barbarians," a treaty that was "obtained by British influence."[37] "Sir John Jay" became the most hated man in America. Seldom in time of peace had a treaty aroused such violent public reaction. While much of the reaction against the treaty arose spontaneously, Republicans organized some of it for political purposes; they had a popular national issue around which to rally the party; they would not let that opportunity slip by.[38] That the treaty violated the "rights of friendship, gratitude and alliance which the republic of France may justly claim from the United States" was a foremost criticism of Jay's work, a criticism with great popular appeal.[39]

Politically, the treaty doomed Jay. Even though recently he had been elected governor of New York, after publication of the treaty

[36] From the *Aurora*, reprinted in the *Virginia Herald and Fredericksburg Advertiser*, July 3, 1795.

[37] W. Wilson to Joseph Jones, Sept. 14, 1795, Joseph Jones Papers, Duke University Library.

[38] Alexander J. Dallas, prominent Pennsylvania Republican, for example, wrote numerous articles attacking the treaty. His most pretentious work, a twenty-two-thousand-word essay entitled "Features of Mr. Jay's Treaty," was published in five parts in the *American Daily Advertiser* between July 18 and August 17, 1795. Dallas warned that his work should not "be regarded as an instrument of faction, nor made the foundation of slander and abuse," for the issue at stake was "too momentous to be treated as the football of contending factions." Walters, *Alexander James Dallas,* pp. 66-68. The essay is reprinted in George M. Dallas, *The Life and Writings of Alexander J. Dallas* (Philadelphia, 1871), pp. 160-207.

[39] The quotation is from a memorial emanating from a mass meeting of citizens in Philadelphia, July 25, 1795, cited in Woodbury, *Public Opinion in Philadelphia . . . ,* p. 88. "Junius Americanus," in an essay in the *New York Herald* (reprinted in the *Virginia Herald and Fredericksburg Advertiser,* June 26, 1795), attacked the administration for neglecting France and surrendering to Great Britain's tyranny. For a French commentary on American public opinion in regard to the Jay treaty, see La Rochefoucauld-Liancourt, *Travels . . . ,* I, 381-382.

he lost political appeal. "YES, Sir, you have bitched it; you have indeed put your foot in it Mr. Jay—for shame, Sir,—" expressed certain public reaction to Jay's diplomacy.[40] At one time prior to the treaty negotiation Jay had been considered a leading candidate to succeed Washington when the great man chose to step down. Gouverneur Morris went so far as to declare that much of the outcry against the Jay treaty stemmed from a plot to eliminate Jay as a successor to Washington. Regardless of motivation the result was the same—damnation of Jay.

Jay, England, and the treaty were damned. The Jay treaty, said the Republican press, was "degrading to the national honor, dangerous to the political existence and destructive to the agricultural, commercial, and shipping interests of the people of the United States."[41] France, the ten senators who had "refused to sign the death warrant of American liberty," and, particularly, the pledge-wrecking Mason, were praised. Handbills proclaimed that "France is our avowed Friend. . . . Great Britain is the universal Foe of Liberty." To be a supporter of the treaty was to be a friend of England and an enemy of France, which was anathema to Republican patriots.[42]

Caught unprepared by the popular outburst, the Federalists at first were numbed. Timothy Pickering, for example, viewed popular opposition to the treaty "in a very serious light" and was "alarmed at the effect it may have on the French Government, and the advantage they may be disposed to make of the spirit which is at work to cherish a belief in them that the treaty is calculated to favor Britain at their expense."[43]

Soon, however, Federalists recovered; they returned Republican barbs in kind. To them Republican opposition represented "all

[40] "Atticus" in the *Alexandria Gazette,* reprinted in the *Virginia Herald and Fredericksburg Advertiser,* Aug. 11, 1795.

[41] *Charleston City Gazette,* July 14, 1795, quoted in Ulrich B. Phillips, "The South Carolina Federalists," *AHR,* XIV (July, 1909), 735. In South Carolina as elsewhere the Jay treaty was the source of intemperate party strife.

[42] Monaghan, *John Jay,* p. 391. In New Jersey the Jay treaty caused more public meetings, petitions of protest, and more political feeling than anything since the government was established. Walter R. Fee, *The Transition from Aristocracy to Democracy in New Jersey, 1789-1829,* p. 69.

[43] Pickering to Edmund Randolph, July 29, 1795, in Pickering, *The Life of Timothy Pickering,* III, 185.

the detestable arts, all the machinations of disappointed demagogues, and all the malice of even Hell itself, employed to deceive the people and destroy our government. . . ." Opposition to the treaty was the work of a "violent Jacobin Party" which was determined "either to throw this country into war and anarchy, or reduce us to a *Province of France.*"[44] Regardless of popular outcry, Federalists took the stand that the treaty was good; come what may the United States now had the faith of the British nation "plighted for Amity."

Previously, because of America's attachment to France, there existed a strong spirit of resentment toward the United States in the British cabinet. That resentment, reasoned Federalists, was blunted by the Jay treaty. The treaty saved the nation not only from war, they pointed out, but also from civil strife.[45]

The popular furor over the treaty did not move the Federalists to change their views. According to their political philosophy, "treaties or any other difficult subject when honestly acted upon by the proper constitutional authority" were to be "acquiesced in though not understood by the people. If the government do a legitimate act; it has done its duty—it is no less binding because ignorance do not see its policy—Citizens ought either to qualify themselves to Judge understandingly or to submit without refractoriness to things or obligations Constitution[al] formed by *their own govt.*—This if true at all, is doubly urgent as a duty in a Free Representative Republic like ours—Where the appointment of the legislature is actually in the peoples' hands—"[46]

To stem the antitreaty tide unloosed by men with "hell in their hearts and faction on their tongue," Hamilton brought his pen into service. At the call of President Washington, Hamilton came out of private life to save the Jay treaty. From his pen poured most of the words in thirty-eight letters defending the Jay treaty which appeared and reappeared in the nation's press under the signature of "Camillus." Rufus King and John Jay collaborated with Hamilton in thus producing a Federalist manifesto on foreign policy.[47] Ignor-

[44] Monaghan, *John Jay,* p. 395; Timothy Williams to Timothy Pickering, Boston, July 17, 1795, in Pickering, *The Life of Timothy Pickering,* III, 177.
[45] William Vans Murray, Commonplace Book, July 19, 28, 1795, Murray Papers (Princeton).
[46] *Ibid.,* July 23, 1795.
[47] The "Camillus" series began in the New York *Argus* on July 22, 1795,

ing the treaty's weaknesses, praising its stronger points, labeling opponents as "rabble," evil Francophiles, and Jacobins trying to plunge the country into war with England, Hamilton made a brilliant defense of a weak case. He even stumped for the treaty. In New York when he attempted to speak in its defense angry antitreaty partisans stoned him. With blood on his brow he remarked, "If you can use such knockdown arguments I must retire."[48]

Hamilton did not retire. In Jefferson's words he was "a collossus to the anti-republican party," a "host within himself."[49] Hamilton understood the issue as few men did. War at this time, he pointed out, would destroy the nation's prosperity and stunt its growth. Peace, above all, should be the goal of American foreign policy. Yet "a numerous party among us," he said, "though disavowing the design, because the avowal would defeat it, have been steadily endeavoring to make the United States a party in the present European war, by advocating all those measures which would widen the breach between us and Great Britain, and by resisting all those which would tend to close it." With tongue in cheek, undoubtedly, he insisted that in the treaty the British gave more than did Americans, that there were no improper concessions, that the treaty did not violate the French alliance or other international obligations, and that it was in the interest of the United States.[50]

---

and ran for twenty-five numbers; the remainder appeared first in the New York *Minerva;* all thirty-eight letters are in Lodge, *The Works of Alexander Hamilton,* IV, 371-524, V, 3-332. See also King, *Rufus King Correspondence,* II, 9-13; Monaghan, *John Jay,* 395; Schachner, *The Founding Fathers,* pp. 367-368. Under the pseudonym of "Curtius" Noah Webster, with the aid of James Kent, also enlisted his pen in defense of the Jay treaty. Along with Hamilton, his efforts were important in reversing antitreaty sentiment. Warfel, *Webster,* pp. 233-234.

[48] Quoted in Schachner, *Alexander Hamilton,* p. 350.

[49] Jefferson to James Madison, Monticello, Sept. 21, 1795, in Ford, *Writings of Jefferson,* VII, 32.

[50] The quotation is from Camillus No. I. Lodge, *The Works of Alexander Hamilton,* IV, 374-375; see also Monaghan, *John Jay,* pp. 397-398; Schachner, *Alexander Hamilton,* pp. 350-351. Many Federalists shared Hamilton's views. It was Federalist dogma that war with Great Britain was suicide. William Vans Murray, echoing views of Federalist leaders, saw no virtue in any kind of war with Great Britain, even if American arms were victorious. Canada, he pointed out, would be the only conquest and it was not worth the candle. He confessed to Oliver Wolcott, Jr., that avoidance of war was about the only argument he had with which to counter attacks against the treaty. William

Distorted though Hamilton's views might be, Washington concurred in them. Despite the popular outcry and abuse "by progeny
of dirt," to which Washington as well as Jay had been exposed, the
President on August 14, 1795, ratified the treaty. On that day
George Washington, in the eyes of Republicans, fell as had Lucifer.
On that day an ardent Republican confided to his diary sentiments
which many undoubtedly shared. "Washington now defies the
whole Sovereign [people] that made him what he is—and can un-
make him again," he said. "Better his hand had been cut off when
his glory was at its height, before he blasted all his Laurels."[51]

From this time on Washington became increasingly a target for
political abuse, a fate which has often befallen American presidents.
With his acceptance of the Jay treaty he lost his seeming immunity
from political attack. Some critics said Washington ratified the Jay
treaty because of a "clear manifestation of an unjust and ungrateful
Partiality towards Great Britain."[52] "Had the meridian blaze of the
President's popularity continued much longer," said one attacker,
"the lamp of American liberty would have been extinguished forever. Happily for humanity a change has taken place before it
was too late, and the consecrated ermine of Presidential chastity,
seems too foul for time itself to bleach." No longer, the writer continued, would the name of Washington be fatal to any man against
whom it was directed. "The real character of the man is known";

Vans Murray Papers, Commonplace Book, Aug. 4, 1795, and Aug. 7, 1795
(Princeton).

[51] Diary of Dr. Nathaniel Ames, Aug. 14, 1795, in Charles Warren, *Jacobin
and Junto* (Cambridge, Mass., 1931), pp. 12 and 63. Ratifications were exchanged Oct. 28, 1795. Washington's ratification led to a concerted effort
among Republican newspaper editors to make public life so unpalatable that
he would virtually be driven from office. Donald M. Stewart, "The Press and
Political Corruption During the Federalist Administrations," *Political Science
Quarterly*, LXVII (Sept., 1952), 436. Certain Federalists had recognized
Washington's dilemma. Wrote William Vans Murray: "From . . . my heart
I feel for the President in his dilemma. He must take a more high & decisive
Responsibility than he ever has since his election. He must risk the most
alarming discontent if he ratifies & war if he does not." Yet, Murray hoped
that Washington would not ratify the treaty; he wanted negotiations con-
tinued. William Vans Murray Papers, Commonplace Book, Aug. 15, 1795
(Princeton).

[52] Phineas Bond to Grenville, Philadelphia, Jan. 22, 1796, Henry Adams
Transcripts.

in "abandoning and deceiving a tried friend and ally [France], he has forfeited the confidence and the affections of the real patriots of America."[53]

Critics even deprecated Washington's revolutionary exploits. "With what justice," asked "Portius" in an open letter to Washington, "do you monopolize the glories of the American revolution?" Among other important factors, the critic pointed out, "the success of our revolution must be attributed to the French alliance. . . ," which, according to Republicans, was being destroyed by the Jay treaty and by Washington.[54] The President had his defenders. In a "Cursory Review of the Past Year [1795]," one of them highlighted Washington's fall from grace in Republican eyes. "It has been reserved for the deep reproach of America in the past year to troduce [sic] a name more glorious than that of the proudest conqueror, or most patriotic king . . . the envenomed shafts of malice have fallen on the champion of freedom, and Washington has been classed with tyrants, and calumniated as the enemy of his country. Gratitude, whither art thou flown! . . . Weep for the national character of America, for, in ingratitude to her Washington, it is sullied and debased throughout the globe!"[55]

* * * * *

Washington's ratification of Jay's treaty had been hastened in part by the alleged improper conduct of Secretary of State Edmund Randolph, but more by the astute political maneuverings of the British minister, George Hammond, and by certain Federalist leaders. As the only remaining member of the Cabinet who was not a thorough-going Federalist and the only Cabinet member who had opposed ratification of the Jay treaty, Randolph had incurred the enmity of Federalists and of the British. Considering him pro-French, Hammond, for example, disliked Randolph; he complained that "acrimony and intemperance" pervaded Randolph's letters to him, and that the new Secretary of State would not reject but rather would "improve upon the prevarication and subterfuges practiced

---

[53] "Pittachus" in the *Aurora* (Philadelphia), Oct. 26, 1795.
[54] *Aurora,* reprinted in the *Virginia Herald and Fredericksburg Advertiser,* Oct. 6, 1795.
[55] *Western Centinel,* reprinted in the *Federal Gazette and Baltimore Daily Advertiser,* Jan. 21, 1796.

by his predecessor." In his despatches Hammond deprecated Randolph.[56] Hammond, it appeared, would have distrusted anyone who was not as cordial as Hamilton. Indeed, both Federalists and Republicans distrusted Randolph because he tried to be politically neutral.[57]

Randolph had urged Washington not to sign the treaty. He told the President that "it is not the interest of the U. S. to be on ill terms with France, lest we thereby throw ourselves too much on G. britain [*sic*] so vice versa, the U. S. ought to be on good terms with both. It is at least doubtful, whether it be the interest of the U. S. that there should be only *one* dominant power or game-cock in Europe." Randolph recommended that if "new negotiations could not be opened up" which might remove some of the obnoxious features of the treaty it "ought to be absolutely broken up."[58] Even though the Secretary of State was alone in his stand, Washington, for the time being at least, had agreed with his conclusions. Randolph, after all, was Secretary of State. A few days later (July 15) the President left Philadelphia for Mount Vernon without signing the treaty. This alarmed inveterate Federalists in the Cabinet and the British minister.[59]

[56] Hammond to Grenville, Philadelphia, Feb. 22 and April 28, 1795, Henry Adams Transcripts; John Adams noticed animosity between Hammond and Randolph. See Adams to Wife, Philadelphia, May 26, 1794, in C. F. Adams, ed., *Letters of John Adams Addressed to His Wife,* II, 162.

[57] Randolph admitted that he was "a man of no party," distrusted by both Republicans and Federalists. Edmund Randolph, *A Vindication of Mr. Randolph's Resignation* (Philadelphia, 1795), p. 97.

[58] Randolph to Washington, Philadelphia, July 12, 1795, in Worthington C. Ford, ed., "Edmund Randolph on the British Treaty, 1795," AHR, XII (April, 1907), 596-597. For Washington's unfavorable view of the treaty, see his letter to Randolph, Mount Vernon, July 22, 1795, in Fitzpatrick, *Washington's Writings,* XXXIV, 244. See also Randolph to Thomas Pinckney, Philadelphia, July 25, 1795, Rufus King Papers, Huntington Library; this reflects Randolph's opposition to the treaty; John Marshall, *The Life of George Washington* (2 vols., Philadelphia, 1846), II, 362.

[59] Hammond apparently felt deceived by Randolph. Earlier he had reported that Randolph had indicated that the President would sign the treaty if stipulations were met—"that the President's determination was formed antecedently to the Manifestation of the popular dislike of the Treaty. . . ." Hammond to Grenville, Philadelphia, July 18, 1795, Henry Adams Transcripts. Generally accepted opinion, however, seemed to be that Washington would not ratify the Jay treaty. When he did, it surprised many. Robert Atkinson to Joseph Jones, Sept. 7, 1795, Joseph Jones Papers, Duke University. Vice-President John Adams thought that Washington should not have hesitated

Already distasteful to his Federalist colleagues, Randolph now, to their utter disgust, had set himself up as the sole barrier to consummation of a treaty upon which existence of the party, and, insofar as they were concerned, existence of the nation hinged. So, like his predecessor, the second Secretary of State was out of harmony with the dominant political party in its government—the only source of discord in an otherwise thoroughly Federalist administration. Unlike Jefferson, however, he was not a powerful political figure in his own right; he had no dedicated partisans to do battle for him.[60] His predicament illustrated what later came to be a truism in American political life: in addition to being a statesman, a Secretary of State, to be successful and to escape partisan attacks motivated by those seeking political advantage, must usually be a political figure of consequence.

When Randolph complained of British violations of American neutrality Hammond responded by outlining French violations of the same neutrality and noted England's sufferings thereby. Attacking the Franco-American alliance, he told the Secretary of State, ". . . I can scarcely imagine that it is your intention to maintain, that the treaty concluded by France and the United States, is obligatory on the commanders of his Majesty's ships of war, as to render it requisite for those officers to be conversant with the precise tenor and import of any stipulations which may be comprehended in that instrument."[61]

Randolph's opposition to pro-British Federalist dominance of the government was the real source of enmity. Federalists and the British had determined that he must go, even if in ruin. Nothing

---

a moment in signing the treaty. Adams to Abigail Adams, Philadelphia, Jan. 7, 1796, in C. F. Adams, ed., *Letters of John Adams Addressed to His Wife,* II, 188.

[60] Hamilton had no confidence in Randolph; he regarded the new Secretary of State as a nonentity. Hamilton to Washington, New York, Oct. 16, 1795, in Hamilton, ed., *Hamilton's Works,* VI, 48. Jefferson treated Randolph with contempt, as a chameleon. Philip M. Marsh, "Randolph and Hamilton," *Pennsylvania Magazine of History and Biography,* LXXII (July, 1948), 252; Jefferson to Monroe, Philadelphia, May 5, 1793, in Ford, *Writings of Jefferson,* VI, 239; Gibbs, ed., *Wolcott Papers,* I, 176, 205-206.

[61] Hammond to Randolph, Philadelphia, April 10, 1795, Rufus King Papers, Huntington Library; Randolph's response is dated April 13, 1795, *ibid.* See also Bassett, *The Federalist System . . . ,* 131; Anderson, "Randolph," in Bemis, ed., *The American Secretaries of State. . . ,* II, 151.

must stand in the way of the Jay treaty, of British ascendancy in American politics, and of salvation of the Hamiltonian system.

When informed of President Washington's hesitation in signing the Jay treaty and of Randolph's opposition of ratification, George Hammond took the step that brought Washington to sign immediately and led to Randolph's ruin.[62] The events leading to Hammond's action started on the high seas. In March, 1795, a British warship captured a French corvette carrying despatches from the French minister in the United States, Joseph Fauchet, to his government. In a salvaged package of papers the British discovered a despatch "No. 10" written by Fauchet in the autumn of 1794. To investigators looking for sinister connections contents of the despatch indicated intrigue between the French minister and the American Secretary of State, and possible corruption on the part of the latter.

In the despatch Fauchet referred to certain revelations Randolph had made to him concerning the Whiskey Rebellion.[63] Apparently Randolph looked upon the Whiskey Rebellion—as did many Americans and most Republicans—as an unnecessary exhibition of force by Hamilton and perhaps as a first step to absolute power. Fauchet indicated that Randolph had spoken of many things—of feuds between Jeffersonians and Hamiltonians, of Washington's attitude toward France and England. Among other things, Randolph explained to Fauchet that British agents were attempting to convert the Whiskey Rebellion into a civil insurrection. He implied that Fauchet might foil British intrigue if he were to work through three or four key men, Americans. But those "key" men were in debt to the British and hence under British influence. Randolph stressed that the fate of the republic might hang on the expenditure of "some thousands of dollars." He suggested that Fauchet lend the "key" men sufficient funds to wean them from British influence. In his captured despatch Fauchet had remarked that "thus the consciences of pretended patriots in America have already a price."[64]

Lord Grenville, after receiving the captured despatches, sent

[62] Irving Brant, "Edmund Randolph, Not Guilty!" *WMQ*, 3rd Series, VII (April, 1950), 182; Conway, *Randolph*, pp. 265-269.

[63] The despatch, Fauchet to Commissioner of Foreign Relations, Philadelphia, Oct. 31, 1794, is in Turner, *CFM*, pp. 444-445; Conway, *Randolph*, pp. 272-281; see also Baldwin, *Whiskey Rebels*, pp. 265-269.

[64] See *ibid.;* also Brant, "Edmund Randolph, Not Guilty!" *WMQ*, 3rd Series, VII, 183.

Fauchet's "No. 10" to Hammond in Philadelphia. The Fauchet despatch reached Hammond in July, 1795, not long after the Senate had approved the Jay treaty. Believing that "if properly treated" the despatch would "tend to effect an essential change in the public sentiment of this country with regard to the character and principles of certain individuals, and to the real motives of their conduct," Hammond wanted to make use of the document so that it would "be productive of the most beneficial effects to the general interests of His Majesty's service."[65]

Hammond set in motion the train of events which were to destroy Randolph and banish French influence from Washington's Cabinet. The day before writing to Grenville, July 26, 1795, he had given Fauchet's despatch to Oliver Wolcott, Jr., Hamilton's successor as Secretary of the Treasury. Wolcott showed the document to Secretary of War, Timothy Pickering, who with the aid of a French dictionary and grammar laboriously translated it into English.[66] They called on Attorney General William Bradford for consultation. The three men agreed; a crisis was at hand; Washington should be called back to Philadelphia.[67]

On August 11, 1795, Washington read Pickering's translation of the Fauchet letter. That Randolph was fishing for French gold seemed clear—gold capable of transforming the Whiskey Rebellion into a civil war. Next day Washington called a Cabinet meeting and his advisors debated the Jay treaty. In opposition to ratification Randolph again stood alone; the others urged ratification as the alternative to national disaster. Again, personal partisanship, domes-

[65] Grenville to Hammond, Downing Street, May 9, 1795, in Mayo, *Instructions to the British Ministers, AHA Ann. Rep.* (1936), III, 83; Hammond to Grenville, Philadelphia, July 27, 1795, Henry Adams Transcripts; Anderson, "Randolph," in Bemis, ed., *The American Secretaries of State . . . ,* II, 151-152.

[66] For Wolcott's account see Gibbs, ed., *Wolcott Papers,* I, 232-233. At this time Pickering feared that Washington might not sign the Jay treaty. Pickering to Timothy Williams, no place, no date, Pickering, *The Life of Timothy Pickering,* III, 181-182.

[67] Except for the Fauchet letter, Federalist opinion held that Washington would not have ratified the Jay treaty without further British concessions. William Vans Murray Papers, Commonplace Book, Dec. 10, 1795 (Princeton). For Pickering's account of the Randolph affair, see Pickering, *The Life of Timothy Pickering,* III, 216-219; also G. Cabot to Christopher Gore, Philadelphia, Jan. 5, 1796, in Lodge, *Life and Letters of George Cabot,* pp. 91-94.

tic political considerations, and foreign meddling hastened or perhaps even produced a decision in foreign policy fraught with serious
national and international implications. Washington forced Randolph on August 18, 1795, to deliver the ratified treaty to Hammond.[68] Hammond had indeed played his cards with skill.

Randolph's fate was decided on dubious evidence. The day after
handing Hammond the ratified treaty, Washington confronted Randolph with the Fauchet despatch in the presence of his hostile colleagues.[69] Openly humiliated, Randolph was driven to resign. Undoubtedly the Secretary of State had been indiscreet in dealing with
Fauchet. His most serious crime appears to have been that he favored the French side of national politics and diplomacy, that he was
more Republican than Federalist. Except for the unproved charge
of corruption, Randolph had been no more flagrant than had been
Hamilton and other Federalists in their disclosures of national secrets
to agents of a foreign government.[70]

Even though Fauchet exonerated Randolph of treasonable corruption and even though Randolph later wrote and published *A
Vindication* of his conduct, blaming the "British faction" for his
fate, he was in Federalist eyes condemned.[71] To Federalists Fau-

[68] Pickering to Washington, July 31, 1795, in Pickering, *The Life of
Timothy Pickering*, III, 188-189; Wolcott, Jr., to John Marshall, June 9, 1806, in
Gibbs, ed., *Wolcott Papers*, I, 241-246; John Beckley to De Witt Clinton,
Philadelphia, July 24, 1795, De Witt Clinton Papers, cited in Charles, "Jay
Treaty. . . ," *WMQ*, 3rd Series, XII, 599; Brant, "Edmund Randolph, Not
Guilty!" *WMQ*, 3rd Series, VII, 184-186.

[69] Pickering told William Vans Murray that the President wished to dismiss
Randolph immediately upon discovery of Fauchet's letter but that important
business held him back for about a week. William Vans Murray Papers,
Commonplace Book, Dec. 14, 1795 (Princeton).

[70] See Brant, "Edmund Randolph, Not Guilty!" *WMQ*, 3rd Series, VII, 190;
an interesting but unreliable account of the Randolph episode is in Faÿ, *The
Two Franklins*, pp. 250-263. The French recognized Randolph as being the
member of the Washington government most attached to the French cause;
they believed that the disgrace of Randolph had been designed to harm France
and that it led Washington to sign the Jay treaty. Reinhard to Committee
of Public Safety, Nov. 9, 1795, AAE CP EU, Vol. XLIV, f. 377.

[71] Edmund Randolph, *A Vindication of Mr. Randolph's Resignation*, p. 98.
Randolph maintained that he sought always to have the "United States shake
off all dependence of French and English interference in our affairs," but
that he was opposed to ingratitude toward France in favor of England.
According to an anti-Randolph contemporary, the book, which came out on
Friday, Dec. 18, 1795, sold a thousand copies in two hours and the publisher
derived a $3000 profit from it. William Vans Murray Papers, Commonplace

chet's exonerating statement, in fact, seemed to offer proof that there existed an alliance between Republicans and the French government designed to overturn the Washington government.

Before the *Vindication* appeared certain Federalists prejudged it, condemning it unseen as an attack on the administration and "a slurring of the president."[72] To his misfortune Randolph had been trapped in the crossfire of a fierce political war, had been condemned on meager evidence, and had had against him men who viewed opposition to their principles as treason. Republicans did nothing for him. "Every man of that party," said Phineas Bond, "seems willing to let this ruined Bark [Randolph] sink of itself and to shun the vortex, which hurries it to the bottom."[73]

From the Federalist viewpoint, Randolph's disgrace is understandable; it was essential in saving the Hamiltonian system and perhaps in countering French influence in the United States. Ever since the signing of the Treaty of Paris of 1783, as one high Federalist spokesman maintained, the French government had shown "a steady determination to distract divide & injure this country." The French, he continued, wished to force us into that distracted state that would put us in their power and oblige us to look to them only for aid. Since the French Revolution they had pursued the same end, varying only their means. Fauchet's letter was a demonstration of this. If published, he went on, the letter would do much "towards demolition of that Jacobin faction wh. now distracts the govt." The clamor against the Jay treaty had been based on the presumed indifference to the interests of France. Fauchet's letter proved too clearly France's views; of course, he concluded, it would do away with those feelings in her favor which she did not deserve.[74]

Book, Dec. 20, 1795 (Princeton). This is some indication of the intense interest in the Randolph affair, in politics, and in foreign affairs at this time. Murray maintained, also in line with Federalist doctrine, that the *Vindication* proved that Randolph was guilty of the crime of favoring the Republican party. For an example of the violent Federalist attack against Randolph and his *Vindication,* see William Cobbett, *A New Year's Gift to the Democrats* (Philadelphia, 1796).

[72] William Vans Murray to James McHenry, no place, no date, in Steiner, *The Life and Correspondence of James McHenry,* pp. 159-160.

[73] Phineas Bond to Grenville, Philadelphia, Dec. 20, 1795, Henry Adams Transcripts.

[74] Oliver Ellsworth as cited in William Vans Murray Papers, Commonplace Book, Dec. 8, 1795 (Princeton).

The Randolph affair wrecked any remaining illusions that Washington and his administration were above party. With gusto the Republican press now pilloried him as few presidents have ever been. Washington reacted with pain and surprise.[75] In vain he sought a replacement for Randolph. Turning to such men as William Patterson of New Jersey, Thomas Johnson of Maryland, Rufus King of New York, Charles Cotesworth Pinckney of South Carolina, and Patrick Henry of Virginia, Washington met one refusal after another. With the affairs of the nation in "violent paroxysm" and threatening "to embroil us in the disputes of Europe," the highest appointive office in the land went begging.[76] Not only was the job unpopular, but also, because of the intimate interrelationship between foreign affairs and domestic politics, acceptance of the office seemed equivalent to committing political suicide. As a last resort, Washington placed Timothy Pickering in the State Department post. At first the appointment, which Pickering did not want, was conditional. Pickering agreed to serve for three months while the President sought a permanent appointee. Then, in December, 1795, he became permanent Secretary of State.[77]

Although Hammond earlier in the year had mistakenly characterized Pickering as being blindly hateful of Great Britain, the British themselves could not have contrived a better appointment.[78] An admirer and devoted follower of Alexander Hamilton, Pickering was an uncompromising New England Federalist. He had served with distinction under Washington during the American Revolu-

[75] Federalists now complained that the press had become the vehicle for unfounded personal abuse. *Ibid.*, Oct. 12, 1795. The press attacks against Washington at this time are discussed in Philip M. Marsh, "John Beckley: Mystery Man of the Early Jeffersonians," *PMHB*, LXXII (Jan., 1948), 59-62. For the first time Washington faced intense personal opposition. Warren, *Jacobin and Junto*, pp. 63-64; Marshall Smelser, "George Washington and the Alien and Sedition Acts," *AHR*, LIX (Jan., 1954), 327.

[76] Henry J. Ford, "Timothy Pickering," in Bemis, ed., *The American Secretaries of State . . .*, II, 164; Sears, *George Washington*, p. 460.

[77] Pickering accepted the post only at the importunities of Oliver Wolcott, Jr., and the President. Pickering to Hamilton, Philadelphia, Nov. 17, 1795; Pickering to Stephen Higginson, Dec. 12, 1795, Pickering Papers; Pickering, *The Life of Timothy Pickering*, III, 249-250. From Aug. 19 to Dec. 10, 1795, Pickering held the office *ad interim*, during which time he was also Secretary of War; on Dec. 10, 1795, he received his permanent appointment.

[78] Hammond to Grenville, Philadelphia, Jan. 5, 1795, Henry Adams Transcripts.

tion, and, early in Washington's first administration, had become Postmaster General, then a non-Cabinet post, and had achieved Cabinet rank on January 2, 1795, when he succeeded General Henry Knox as Secretary of War.

Pickering, detesting the French alliance and loathing the French Revolution, harbored an anti-French obsession which became the basis of the foreign policy he would have the nation follow. He believed that France sought to destroy American independence by overthrowing the Washington regime and instituting mob rule; he was convinced that the major bulwark in American foreign policy was the British fleet. To thwart nefarious French designs, he held that American foreign policy must align itself with that of Great Britain. From the French viewpoint Washington could not have made a less satisfactory appointment.[79]

In the meantime as the pro-British orientation of Washington's government became more pronounced, England had accepted the modified Jay treaty. Ratifications were exchanged in London on October 28, 1795. On February 29, 1796, Washington proclaimed the treaty as law of the land.[80]

*   *   *   *   *

Randolph's career was not the only one blasted by the violent partisanship engendered by the Jay treaty. John Rutledge, prominent South Carolina statesman, hero of the American Revolution, jurist, and a founding father of the Constitutional Convention, suffered a similar fate.[81]

Immediately after Jay had resigned as Chief Justice (June 29, 1795) to become governor of New York, President Washington (July 1, 1795) offered the barely vacant post to John Rutledge.[82] At that time the *Aurora* published the Jay treaty. The treaty provisions

[79] For a short, competent sketch of Pickering, see William A. Robinson in *Dictionary of American Biography;* for Pickering as Secretary of State, see Ford, "Pickering," in Bemis, ed., *The American Secretaries of State . . . ,* II, 161-244.

[80] Miller, *Treaties. . . ,* II, 245.

[81] Accounts of Rutledge's life may be found in Ralph Barry, *Mr. Rutledge of South Carolina* (New York, 1942); Henry Flanders, *The Lives and Times of the Chief Justices of the Supreme Court of the United States* (2 vols., New York, 1855-58), I, 431-645.

[82] Washington to Rutledge, Philadelphia, July 1, 1795, in Fitzpatrick, *Washington's Writings,* XXXIV, 225-226.

and news of his appointment reached Rutledge together. While
usually Federalist in politics, Rutledge disliked the treaty; it was "a
damned thing made to plague the French."[83]   Such sentiments were
not unique in Charleston, where Americans dragged the British flag
through the streets and burned it before the doors of the British
consul; in few cities was antitreaty sentiment more violent.[84]

At St. Michael's Church on July 16, 1795, Charlestonians gathered to vent antitreaty sentiments.   There they heard prominent
leaders denounce the treaty; conspicuous among the denouncers
was the newly appointed Chief Justice *ad interim,* John Rutledge.
In a spellbinding, hour-long speech, which one listener reported
as "sufficient to raise the tombstones in the nearby graveyard," he
attacked the Jay treaty.   Stressing the improprieties of negotiations
of any kind with Great Britain, he denounced the treaty as an
acknowledgment of American dependence upon the mother country, as a prostitution of American freedom.   At the same time he lav-
ished praise on France.   Shortly thereafter he left for Philadelphia
to take up the duties of his new post in the August term of the
Supreme Court.[85]

In the meantime, towards the end of July, the Charleston papers
carrying reports of Rutledge's July-sixteenth speech arrived in the
North.   Accounts of the speech whipped Federalists to fury, and
false and garbled reports circulated in Northern Federalist papers
kept their wrath boiling.   One version, widely copied from a leading Federalist journal of Boston, the *Columbian Centinel,* described

[83] For political affiliation, see George Van Santvoord, *Sketches from The
Lives and Judicial Services of the Chief Justices of the Supreme Court of the
United States* (New York, 1954), p. 178; Barry, *Mr. Rutledge . . . ,* p. 400,
maintained that Rutledge was "neither Jeffersonian nor Hamiltonian."   The
quotation in the text is from Flanders, *The Lives and Times of the Chief
Justices . . . ,* I, 633.

[84] For an account, based on memory, of the antitreaty, anti-British sentiment in Charleston, see Charles Fraser, *Reminiscences of Charleston* (Charleston, 1854), pp. 45-46; for examples of Charleston feeling, see the "Address
of the Citizens of Charleston (South Carolina) to the President. . . ." (July
19, 1795) in Mathew Carey, ed., *The American Remembrancer* (3 vols., Philadelphia, 1795-96), II, 51-52; "Speech of Charles Pinckney" (Charleston, July
22, 1795), I, 5-20; Pinckney concluded that the Jay treaty was "ungrateful to
our allies."

[85] Rutledge's speech, published in the *Charleston City Gazette,* is ab-
stracted in Flanders, *The Lives and Times of the Chief Justices . . . ,* I, 633-
636; the quotation is from Barry, *Mr. Rutledge . . . ,* p. 356.

the jurist as "mounted upon the head of a hogshead, haranguing a mob assembled to reprobate the treaty and insult the Executive of the Union . . . insinuating that Mr. Jay and the Senate were fools or knaves, duped by British sophistry or bribed by British gold . . . prostituting the dearest rights of freemen and laying them at the feet of royalty." Another reported that he had declared "he had rather the President should die (dearly as he loved him) than he should sign that treaty."[86]

Rutledge's friends denied the accuracy of such accounts, but with true Federalists such denials made little difference.[87] In their view no man who opposed the Jay treaty should be confirmed to high government office. According to Edmund Randolph, Wolcott, Jr., and Pickering saw Rutledge's conduct as offering substantiation of anonymous reports that he was insane. After all, how could a sane man oppose the treaty? Attorney General William Bradford, Jr. wrote to Hamilton that "the crazy speech of Mr. Rutledge, joined to certain information that he is daily sinking into debility of mind and body, will probably prevent him receiving the appointment. . . ." Pickering informed Washington that "private information, as well as publication of his recent conduct, have fixed my opinion that the commission intended for him ought to be withheld." In Hamilton, Rutledge's conduct produced "pain, surprise and mortification."[88]

If it were to be judged by the national sensation it created, Rutledge's opinion of the Jay treaty was important. The Federalist press circulated reports concerning it and subjected Rutledge to merciless attack. The *Columbian Centinel* of Boston announced that he could not pay his debts, assailed his private character as well at his political views, and said that "the President's motives, however,

[86] Letter of "A Real Republican" in the *Columbian Centinel,* Aug. 26, 1795, and the *Farmer's Weekly Museum,* Aug. 11, 1795, quoted in Charles Warren, *The Supreme Court in United States History* (rev. ed., 2 vols., Boston, 1935), I, 130.

[87] "A South Carolinean" maintained, for example, that "the Speech of the Chief Justice, relative to the treaty, was never fairly represented in the newspapers." From the *Columbian Centinel,* reprinted in the *Connecticut Courant and Weekly Intelligencer* (Hartford), Sept. 14, 1795.

[88] The quotations, with citations, are in Warren, *The Supreme Court in United States History,* I, 130-131; see also Hamilton, "Camillus," No. V, in Lodge, *The Works of Alexander Hamilton,* IV, 417 n.; Chauncey Goodrich to Oliver Wolcott, Jr., Hartford, July 30, 1795, in Gibbs, ed., *Wolcott Papers,* I, 220.

cannot be questioned; everyone knows and confesses his integrity and zeal to do right, but he cannot know every man in the United States and the information he got from others cannot always be relied upon." Rutledge was not without defenders. The *Salem Gazette* spoke for him warmly and termed the attack against him "more licentious than anything which the pen of faction has yet produced."[89]

While the furor raged, Rutledge arrived in Philadelphia, took the oath of office, and as the new term began, assumed his seat upon the Supreme Court bench. During this term he presided over two sessions, wrote one opinion, and delivered another orally. With the close of the term he left Philadelphia for Circuit Court duty. He was not to return to the Court. Although Rutledge's Federalist friends from the South tried to obtain his confirmation, their efforts did little good. Their pleas could not move Northern Federalists. "The virtuous motives which have induced the treating with regard, men who avow and act upon principles inconsistent with the preservation of order, to influence them to a more just conduct, have been and will be ineffectual," said Oliver Wolcott, Sr.; "I hope, therefore, however disagreeable it may be to imply an error of judgment in the President in appointing Mr. Rutledge, that he will not be confirmed in his office."[90]

Before the Senate convened and could act on Rutledge's appointment, Federalists gathered evidence of his unfitness for office. They pounced on the reports that the judge suffered from intermittent attacks of insanity. If such were true it would interfere with the proper performance of his judicial duties. Hamilton counseled Rufus King, Senator from New York, that Rutledge's qualifications should be scrutinized carefully. "If there was nothing in the case but his imprudent sally upon a certain occasion, I should think the reasons for letting him pass would outweigh those for opposing his

[89] See Flanders, *The Lives and Times of the Chief Justices. . . ,* I, 637; the quotations are in Warren, *The Supreme Court in United States History,* I, 133, dated Sept. 1, 1795, and Sept. 12, 1795. Many Southerners, Federalist and Republican, shared Rutledge's views on the Jay treaty. Mrs. St. Julien Ravenel, *Life and Times of William Lowndes of South Carolina, 1782-1822* (Boston, 1901), pp. 33-34.

[90] To Oliver Wolcott, Jr., Litchfield, Nov. 23, 1795, in Gibbs, ed., *Wolcott Papers,* I, 268.

passage. But if it be really true that he is sottish, or that his mind is otherwise deranged, or that he has exposed himself by improper conduct in pecuniary transactions, the bias of my judgement would be to negative." It is "of infinite consequence," he said, "that our judiciary should be well composed."

Whether or not the charges were true made little difference (Rutledge's biographer maintained they were unfounded); Rutledge's fate in the Federalist Senate was certain.[91] On December 15, 1795, by a partisan vote of 14 against 10, he failed of confirmation.[92] Ostensibly the Senate rejected Rutledge because of his alleged insanity, but, as Rutledge himself was not interrogated and no medical report was called in evidence, the conscientiousness of the investigation is questionable.

"This is as it should be," a Federalist organ said, "and what he ought to have expected, after the imprudent and virulent attack he made on their characters. . . . he has been judged (all politicks apart) to be a very unfit person for a Chief Justice of the United States." Approving of the rejection along the same lines, one Federalist looked to the future. "The conduct of the Senate will, I hope," he remarked, "teach demagogues that the road to preferment in this enlightened country is not to revile and calumniate government and excite mobs in opposition to their measures."[93]

Republicans took a different view. Jefferson, seeing the political implications of the action, warned that "the rejection of Mr. Rutledge by the Senate is a bold thing, because they cannot pretend any objection to him but his disapprobation of the treaty. It is of course a declaration that they will receive none but tories hereafter into any department of the government."[94] Another Republican commented from Philadelphia that "such is the violence of party spirit, the force of stockjobbing influence and the prejudice of our

[91] Hamilton to King, Dec. 14, 1795, in Hamilton, ed., *Hamilton's Works*, VI, 76-77; for a discussion of Rutledge's sanity, see Barry, *Mr. Rutledge . . .* , pp. 357-58, 399.

[92] The vote is in U. S. Congress. Senate, *Journal of the Executive Proceedings of the Senate . . .* , I, 195-196.

[93] *Columbian Centinel*, Dec. 26, 1795; William Plumer to Jeremiah Smith, Jan. 1, 1796; cited in Warren, *The Supreme Court in United States History*, I, 137.

[94] Jefferson to William Branch Giles, Monticello, Dec. 31, 1795, in Ford, *Writings of Jefferson*, VII, 44.

Anglomen here that it is regarded as wise in the Senate to keep out of office everyone who has spoken disrespectfully of the treaty lately made or Mr. Jay. . . . Mr. Hamilton who manages the Senate, has become a perfect terrorist, and his satellites and votaries disseminate with uncommon industry the following principle: that it is ruinous to admit into administration any man who may refuse to go all lengths with it; that our citizens who expressed their disapprobation of the commercial treaty are enemies to the general government; that most of them are in the pay of France, and the object of their service is the overthrow of the Constitution."[95]

Rutledge's criticism of the Jay treaty had a profound influence on the course of American constitutional development. Except for his Charleston speech it seems certain the Senate would have confirmed him, and if it had, it seems unlikely that President Adams would have appointed John Marshall to the Supreme Court. "Thus upon the event of one chance speech regarding a British treaty hinged the future course of American constitutional law."[96]

* * * * *

By no means did the Randolph and Rutledge affairs or the exchange of ratifications end the political struggle over the Jay treaty. It continued stronger than ever. To Federalists the crisis appeared "to be the most delicate and important since the organization of the Government." They were aware that Republicans would marshal forces for a decisive assault on the treaty and hence on the government.[97] Such was the case. With Washington's proclamation of the treaty public frenzy again burst forth and, in the words of John Marshall, "seemed to rush through the Union with a rapidity and violence which set human reason and common sense at defiance."[98] Again men burned the treaty in public gatherings; again they hanged effigies of "damn Sir John Jay"; and again, more vehe-

[95] Quoted in Warren, *The Supreme Court in United States History*, I, 138.

[96] *Ibid.*, p. 139.

[97] William R. Davie to James Iredell, Halifax, Sept. 4, 1795, in McRee, *The Life and Correspondence of James Iredell*, II, 454.

[98] John Stokes Adams, ed., *An Autobiographical Sketch by John Marshall* (Ann Arbor, 1937), p. 16. Marshall, in the House of Representatives, played a key role in getting the treaty implemented. For his summary of the treaty agitation, see pp. 16-19.

mently than before, they vilified President Washington, the man who critics said "had completed the destruction of American freedom." In Virginia men drank to the toast, "A speedy Death to General Washington," and elsewhere an anti-Federalist wrote a series of articles attempting to prove that the President was a thief. In Charleston irate citizens constructed a gallows and from it suspended effigies of the pro-treaty Federalist hierarchy—John Jay, John Adams, Timothy Pickering, and others.[99]

Republicans did not limit their strategy to epithets and public demonstrations. They circulated all sorts of rumors. One reached Federalist ears to the effect that under the aegis of Jefferson the anti-treaty men of Virginia had met to plan strategy for opposing the treaty in the next session of Congress. Such procedure, of course, was "subversive of the Constitution & . . . poisonous to our national faith."[100] From the Federalist viewpoint, it was to be feared because it might succeed. To execute the treaty the Washington government would need financial legislation originating in the House of Representatives. The House, however, was the Republican stronghold; there as nowhere else Republicans might be able to destroy the Jay treaty.

Washington sent the Pinckney treaty with Spain to the Senate shortly before he placed the ratified Jay treaty before it and the House. His timing was good. The Pinckney treaty, which opened the Mississippi to Americans and settled boundary difficulties with Spain to American advantage, was as widely acclaimed as the Jay treaty was hated. In the West, for example, it mollified antiadministration frontiersmen; they were more agreeable to the Jay treaty because they now obtained free navigation of the Mississippi.[101]

[99] "A Calm Observer," in the *Aurora* (Philadelphia), Oct. 23, 27, 29 and Nov. 5, 1795. John James Beckley, first clerk of the House of Representatives, first librarian of Congress, and ardent Republican, appears to have been the author of the articles. See Marsh, "John Beckley . . . ," *PMHB*, LXXII, 59-60; Monaghan, *John Jay*, p. 400; Fraser, *Reminiscences of Charleston*, p. 45.

[100] William Vans Murray Papers, Commonplace Book, Nov. 2, 1795 (Princeton).

[101] One Senator remarked that "the Spanish Treaty was so favorable, that if the Spanish Government had asked the American Minister to dictate his own terms, he could scarcely have asked for better." James Iredell to Mrs. Iredell, Philadelphia, March 3, 1796, in McRee, *Life and Correspondence of James Iredell*, II, 462-463. For details on the influence of the Jay treaty on Pinckney's treaty, see Bemis, *Pinckney's Treaty*, pp. 249-279. Considering the

Edward Livingston, Republican from New York, touched off
the battle in the House of Representatives by moving that the President be asked to lay before the House the papers of the Jay negotiation.[102] After long debate, by a vote of 62-37 the House adopted
Livingston's resolutions. The House asked Washington for the Jay
papers. Upon the advice of Hamilton, of his Cabinet, and of Chief
Justice Oliver Ellsworth, Washington refused the request.[103] Again
political considerations brought to an issue a basic foreign policy
and constitutional question: to what extent did the constitutional
right of control over money appropriations give the House power
to participate in the treaty-making or treaty-approving functions of
the government? Again Americans answered a fundamental question and established a fundamental precedent largely on the basis of
political partisanship.

Federalists contended that the Constitution restricted the treaty-
power to the President and to the Senate, and excluded the House.
They controlled the Executive Branch and the Senate. According to
Federalist interpretation the President negotiated treaties and the
Senate approved or disapproved them; the House merely lent its
aid in fulfilling treaties when made constitutionally.[104] Representa-

---

Jay treaty a virtual alliance with England, Spain, in short, consented to the
Pinckney treaty. For pertinent documents, see *ASP FR,* I, 533-549; for Western
reaction, see Ferguson, *Early Western Pennsylvania Politics,* p. 138. Washington sent the Pinckney treaty to the Senate on Feb. 26, 1796, and the Jay treaty
to House and Senate on March 1, 1796. Fitzpatrick, *Washington's Writings,*
XXXIV, 477, 481.

[102] See *Annals of the Congress . . . ,* 4th Cong., 1st sess., March 2, 1796, pp.
400-401. Federalists were aware that Livingston's resolution was a well-
calculated attack on the Jay treaty, difficult to combat. See "A Yankee" in
the *Columbian Centinel* (Boston), April 13, 1796.

[103] Washington to the Secretaries of State, Treasury, War, and the Attorney General, Philadelphia, March 25, 1796, in Fitzpatrick, *Washington's
Writings,* XXXIV, 505; Hamilton to Washington, New York, March 7,
1796, Hamilton, ed., *Hamilton's Works,* VI, 90-91. Judge Iredell saw the
conflict over the Jay papers "as a real difference of opinion, and not as an
affected one on either side." To Mrs. Iredell, Philadelphia, March 31, 1796,
in McRee, *The Life and Correspondence of James Iredell,* II, 465.

[104] For summaries, see Brant, *James Madison: Father of the Constitution . . . ,* pp. 434-439; Channing, *A History of the United States,* IV, 143-147;
Rankin, *Treaty of Amity, Commerce, and Navigation. . . ,* pp. 41-44; William
Vans Murray Papers, Commonplace Book, Sept. 18, 1795 (Princeton), contains a contemporary analysis of the constitutional issues.

tives could not, in the view of Hamilton, control or hamper the President in foreign affairs by presuming to have a veto power over the means for execution of treaties. In his concept of the conduct of foreign affairs, the House could not deliberate whether it would appropriate or pay the necessary money, "the *mode* of raising and appropriating the money, only remains a matter of deliberation."[105]

Republicans, on the other hand, maintained that if the House voted funds to implement a treaty without considering the appropriation, and consequently the treaty, on its merit, it would be in fact not an independent legislative organ but one subject to control of another branch of government.[106] According to Republican Constitutional interpretation the treaty powers rested with the Executive and the Senate, but in all cases touching upon legislative powers given explicitly to either branch of Congress the assent of the whole Congress was necessary. If this were not so, continued Republicans, the Senate and the Executive could, in essence, vitiate the exclusive power of the House to initiate money appropriations; under the guise of a treaty they could actually and in fact initiate various kinds of money appropriations. It was the "right" and the "duty" of the House to consider whether or not a treaty should be put into effect, to judge whether it be "to the public good." If this right were not upheld, would not "the immediate representatives of the People" be reduced "to mere Cyphers in the government?"[107]

In support of this view the House, under the leadership of Madison, reprimanded the President and upheld its asserted right to reject the treaty by a vote of 57 to 35. Next, Republicans presented the House with a motion to put the treaty into execution—a motion designed to make possible rejection of the treaty.

All through April, 1796, the House debated the issue. Echoes of

[105] Hamilton to William [Loughton?] Smith, March 10, 1796, in Hamilton, ed., *Hamilton's Works,* VI, 92-93.

[106] John Adams, for example, voiced Federalist sentiment in his belief that if the House withheld the appropriation the Executive and the Senate would be reduced to virtual nullity. To Abigail Adams, Philadelphia, March 13, 1796, in C. F. Adams, ed., *Letters of John Adams Addressed to His Wife,* II, 210.

[107] John Clopton to James Apperson, Philadelphia, April 4, 1796, John Clopton Papers, Duke University. For an analysis of the constitutional aspects of the Jay treaty debate, see Wilfred E. Binkley, *President and Congress,* pp. 43-44; see also Adams, *The Life of Albert Gallatin,* pp. 160-166; White, the *Federalists . . . ,* pp. 63-64.

the debate penetrated everywhere. "Nothing," reported an English diplomatist, "has occurred which has so much agitated the public mind as the Discussion of this question" [appropriation of funds for the execution of the Jay treaty]. "Every man of Reflection seemed to think the Fate of the country rested upon the Event."[108] Federalists fought hard. "When a measure passes by the proper authorities," they asked, "shall it be stopped by force?"[109] Vice-President Adams saw "a prospect of foreign war and civil war in conjunction" with the battles over the treaty and related constitutional issues. "We are a poor, divided nation," he said, "in the midst of all our prosperity."[110]

Events in the House of Representatives created a sensation in England, according to the Vice-President's son, John Quincy Adams, who had been in London when the news of the treaty debate arrived. Englishmen felt that the House was going to repudiate the Jay treaty. Young Adams saw behind the antitreaty agitation in the House "all the weight of French influence." Consummation of the Jay treaty, he told his father, would have been a "death blow" to all French hopes "of engaging the United States in the war, and they well knew it was inevitable, if the treaty did not first meet with non-compliance on our part." Then he repeated twice, "as a certain fact," that "the French policy of the present day is determined upon involving us yet in the war." A war with Great Britain, he thought, would bring dissolution of the union. The French, it was obvious, had no "dispositions at all favorable to the American union."[111]

Certain Republican leaders, on the other hand, saw the Jay treaty as a threat to the French alliance. John Nicholas of Virginia, for example, saw it as such and declared that the American people "were not ready to transfer their alliance from France to Great Britain."[112]

[108] Phineas Bond to Grenville, Philadelphia, May 4, 1796, Henry Adams Transcripts.

[109] Fisher Ames to ———, Philadelphia, March 9, 1796, in Ames, *Works of Fisher Ames*, p. 482; William Vans Murray Papers, Commonplace Book, April 9, 1796 (Princeton).

[110] John Adams to Abigail Adams, April 19, 1796, in C. F. Adams, ed., *Letters of John Adams Addressed to His Wife*, II, 222-223.

[111] John Quincy Adams to John Adams and to Charles Adams, The Hague, June 6, 9, 1796, in Ford, *Writings of John Quincy Adams*, I, 490-494.

[112] *Annals of the Congress. . .* , 4th Cong., 1st sess., April 16, 1796, p. 1014.

As the showdown approached, Republicans, their confidence in their strength based upon past votes in the House, practically touched victory. On April 18, 1796, Madison estimated that Republicans had a safe majority of 21; defeat of the treaty seemed certain. But Madisonians had not anticipated the exertions of desperate Federalists nor had they realized the power of the moneyed elements behind the treaty. As they had in the previous summer, bankers and merchants rescued Jay's treaty. With the aid of the clergy, they headed a campaign which reversed the tide of sentiment against it.[113]

A large part of the change in sentiment was not so much pro-treaty as it was pro-Washington. Capitalizing on the President's popularity, Federalists attempted to reduce the struggle to one of loyalty to the man. " 'Washington & Peace' was the exclamation in every Circle & in every Street of the Town," reported a Federalist lawyer of Baltimore.[114] "Political preaching" in favor of the treaty, particularly in New England, became common, and was apparently a persuasive factor in formulating public opinion. "The Clergy," said one antitreaty man of the cloth in disgust, "are now the Tools of the Federalists." Petitions in favor of the treaty flooded Congress; pressures, varied and constant, caused wavering congressmen to change their stand.[115]

[113] See Brant, *James Madison, Father of the Constitution* . . . , pp. 438-439. Stephen Higginson, Boston merchant, believed, for example, "that the good Citizens must come forward in support of Government to counteract the intervention of the bad," particularly in the case of the Jay treaty. Another Bostonian also equated the principal merchants with the best people and with those favorable to the treaty. Higginson to Timothy Pickering, Timothy Williams to Pickering, Boston, Aug. 13 and July 17, 1795, Pickering Papers, Massachusetts Historical Society (microfilm copy). For further evidence of merchant protreaty activity, see Theodore Lyman to Pickering, Boston, July 23, 1795, in Pickering, *The Life of Timothy Pickering*, III, 178-179; J. D. Forbes, *Israel Thorndike: Federalist Financier* (New York, 1953), p. 43. In Philadelphia over 400 merchants and traders signed a protreaty petition. *Gazette of the United States*, reprinted in the *Maryland Gazette*, Aug. 27, 1795. On April 10, 1796, New York merchants met and established a committee to correspond with "other trading towns in the United States to gain support for the treaty in the House of Representatives. *Columbian Centinel* (Boston), April 30, 1796.

[114] James Winchester to James McHenry, Baltimore, April 22, 1796, in Bernard C. Steiner, ed., "Maryland Politics in 1796—McHenry Letters," *Publications of the Southern History Association*, IX (Nov., 1905), 375; Adams, *The Life of Albert Gallatin*, p. 164.

[115] The quotation is from William Bentley, *The Diary of William Bentley,*

The decisive propaganda device which treaty supporters constantly called forth was the apparition of civil and foreign war. Fear proved to be the treaty's most potent ally. That refusal to carry the treaty into effect meant war was an almost unanswerable argument.[116]

Yet, was war the inevitable alternative to voting funds to implement the treaty? If the House had directed the President to seek modifications of the treaty before implementing it with necessary funds, would Great Britain have answered with the sword? Great Britain and the United States were at peace, and even before the ratification of the Jay treaty the most serious frictions between the two countries had been removed.[117]

As long as Federalists continued in power it appeared unlikely that the American government would take aggressive action against Great Britain. England, of her own accord, would hardly have made a fighting enemy of the United States—her best customer, a source of important supplies, with a government controlled by a pro-English party. The Republican contention that implementation of the Jay treaty meant war with France—which in time it did—appeared just as logical. France would not stand by and watch her treaty of alliance with the United States vitiated; see the United States become, in effect, an ally or semi-ally of her enemy.

Fisher Ames, New England Federalist, "Colossus of Monocrats," semi-invalid, and superb orator, is usually credited with breaking the opposition to the Jay treaty in one magnificent speech. His "superlative demagogy" just before the vote was taken on the Republican motion to reject the treaty swayed the House with moving pleas on the Federalist theme that the treaty, more than anything else, was the only means of avoiding war. Opposition to the treaty was political, he explained, designed to arouse public passion against

---

D.D. (4 vols., Salem, 1905-1914), II, 129, entry of Feb. 25, 1795. Republicans, of course, resented the attacks from the pulpit; the outcry against political preaching increased in volume from 1795; see Vernon Stauffer, *New England and the Bavarian Illuminati* (New York, 1918), pp. 119-120.

[116] The war-scare theme can be traced in the House debates; see, for example, *Annals of the Congress . . . ,* 4th Cong., 1st sess., April 26, p. 1174, 1198.

[117] This view is expanded in Adams, *The Life of Albert Gallatin,* p. 165; see also Charles, "Jay Treaty. . . ," *WMQ,* 3rd Series, XII, 609-610.

the government. Any treaty with Britain, he said, would suffer similar treatment.[118]

John Adams and Judge James Iredell sat in the gallery over-whelmed. "My God! how great he is," gasped Iredell. "Noble," responded Adams. "I never heard anything so great since I was born," sobbed Iredell. "Not a dry eye in the House," explained Adams, "except some of the Jackasses who had occasioned the necessity of the oratory."[119]

Overawing though Ames was, his speech probably did not save the treaty. Astute Federalist politicians undoubtedly did not run the risk of trusting the fate of their vital treaty to the unpredictable effect of a last-minute speech. The oration probably did not change one vote; grass-roots politics and fear had probably already decided the issue.

The following day, April 29, 1796, in committee of the whole, the House of Representatives voted 50 to 49 to accept the motion and to make appropriations for implementing the treaty. The Federalist Speaker of the House had cast the decisive vote.[120] After defeating a Republican amendment labeling the treaty "objectionable" and "injurious," the House sitting as a legislative body on April 30 accepted the motion to implement the treaty by the vote of 51 to 48.[121]

Once again Federalists had snatched victory from defeat.[122] While the narrow Federalist victory in the Republican House of Representatives was in effect a political triumph, it did not remove

[118] The speech, delivered April 28, 1796, is in Ames, *Works of Fisher Ames,* pp. 58-93; see also Brant, *James Madison, Father of the Constitution . . . ,* p. 438; Bassett, *The Federalist System. . . ,* p. 135; Channing, *A History of the United States,* IV, 146.

[119] John Adams to Abigail Adams, Philadelphia, April 30, 1796, C. F. Adams, ed., *Letters of John Adams Addressed to His Wife,* II, 226-227; McRee, *Life and Correspondence of James Iredell,* II, 475 n.; for another contemporary impression of Ames's eloquence, see Theophilus Parsons, *Memoir of Theophilus Parsons* (Boston, 1859), p. 115; even Albert Gallatin called Ames's speech "brilliant and eloquent." Adams, *The Life of Albert Gallatin,* p. 155.

[120] *Annals of the Congress. . . ,* 4th Cong., 1st sess., p. 1280.

[121] *Ibid.,* pp. 1282-1292. Fear of war with England, apparently, was too great to be overcome; it swung the House majority behind the treaty. La Rochefoucauld-Liancourt, *Travels . . . ,* II, 517.

[122] By destroying all opportunities for extensive experimentation in the regulation of foreign trade at this time, Jay's treaty was also a marked triumph for the economic aspects of Hamilton's program. Setser, *The Commercial Reciprocity Policy,* p. 130.

Jay's treaty from the brawling of domestic politics.[123] The struggle
was a prelude to the presidential election of 1796—an election dominated by foreign-policy issues, of which the Jay treaty and the
French alliance were foremost.[124]

While the Jay treaty intensified the interaction of domestic politics and foreign affairs and while it may not have saved the country
from war with England, it did at least remove the threat of such
a war, and by so doing it became the first major step since the
American Revolution toward an Anglo-American *rapprochement*.[125]

The battles over its acceptance were an early example of how a
political party out of power would use a critical and controversial
foreign-policy issue as a partisan weapon to gain political preferment.
As it turned out, the campaign boomeranged. Instead of riding to
victory on the crest of an unpopular foreign-policy issue, Republicans lost strength, and fell temporarily in popular estimation. Yet,
in their basic contentions, they were correct. The Jay treaty brought
with it another threat—war with France. Never since independence
had the French alliance and Franco-American relations in general
dropped so low.

[123] The Virginia legislature, for example, passed a resolution calling for
an amendment to the Constitution which would make the House of Representatives a part of the treaty-making power; see Albert J. Beveridge, *The
Life of John Marshall* (4 vols., Boston, 1916-1919), II, 117. A Virginia congressman was convinced and pleased that his constituents were still vehemently opposed to the treaty. John Clopton to ———, Philadelphia, May 1, 1796,
John Clopton Papers, Duke University.
[124] The House vote of April 30, 1796, to implement the Jay treaty caused
Jefferson to decide to run for President in 1796. William E. Dodd, *Thomas
Jeffersons rückkehr zur politik 1796* (Leipzig, 1899), pp. 84 ff.; Charles,
"Adams and Jefferson," *WMQ*, 3rd Series, XII, 445.
[125] This was recognized by contemporaries in England as well as in America; see a letter from London of Aug. 22, 1794, in the *Maryland Gazette* (Annapolis), Oct. 30, 1794. This is emphasized in Bradford Perkins, *The First
Rapprochement: England and the United States, 1795-1805* (Philadelphia,
1955), pp. 1-2.

CHAPTER FIVE

FRANCO-AMERICAN COMMERCE

AN UNREALIZED HOPE

*America is singularly situated. . . . Her maxims of commercial policy
will differ from every other nations* [sic]. *Her policy will be mixed—:
it will be partly possessed of the liberality of commercial enlargement; &
partly of the restrictions that must govern a national habit of agricultural
economy. She must manufacture, a little—her agriculture will elicit the
great natural resources wh. which she is endow'd by nature—the manufactures will grow, where impelled by necessity and encouraged by the
discovery of the natural advantages—and in a short time she may establish
those acts of navigation & monopoly that produce navies & marine
respectability.*—William Vans Murray, Commonplace Book, April, 1787.

*The influence which our commercial connections with England have
upon our politics, is the chief cause of the alienation of our administration from France and predilection for Britain. And this cause will operate until the French can rival the British with their manufactures in our
market; or until the agricultural part of our nation determine no longer
to draw their politics with their merchandize from our commercial cities.*
—Benjamin Franklin Bache, 1797.

* * * * *

W HILE American friendship with France had receded from the
highwater mark of the Revolutionary years, it remained a vital
bond. Even though some influential Americans had begun to express a distrust of France and to reveal a partiality for England,
most Americans in assessing Franco-American relations in the year
1789 could find considerable reason for assuming that the war-begot
amity between the two nations would continue to grow.

Between France and America there were no exacerbating grievances. Both distrusted England, and each needed the other as a
balance against British power. In contrast to England's policy of
commercial discrimination, France had given the United States
special trading privileges within her mercantilist empire.[1] While
England refused to enter into formal diplomatic relations, France
for a decade had not only recognized the American nation as independent but also had established proper diplomatic relations. With
France there were no outstanding treaty grievances and there was
no common frontier as a breeding ground for conflict.

It seemed, too, that France and the United States were striving
for common ideals. Within France a revolution had begun that
was liberalizing French life and society—a revolution based in part
upon American precedent. To many Americans France appeared
more a kindred spirit than ever before. They admired France as
a nation, not just as an ally. She became, in the minds of many,
identified with democracy.[2] Frenchmen, too, believed that common
bonds of democracy were drawing the two countries close. Those
familiar with America thought that the French Revolution would
strengthen the Franco-American alliance.[3]

Americans of all classes approved of the new federal government's seeming friendliness toward France. In the beginning of the
Washington administration Americans had abundant cause for resentment against England and little evident reason for antagonism
toward France. As Washington himself phrased it, "the welfare of
the french [*sic*] Nation cannot but be dear to this country; and that
its happiness may in the end be established on the most permanent

[1] A large part of the shipping to French islands in the Caribbean was
American. France did not discriminate against American shipping in Europe
or in her colonies. Bemis, *Jay's Treaty. . .* , p. 21 n. The privileges granted
to the United States constituted a "revolution" in French economic practice.
See Edmund Buron, "Statistics on Franco-American Trade, 1778-1806," *Journal
of Economic and Business History*, IV (May, 1932), 573-574.

[2] Washington, for example, wrote to Gouverneur Morris at this stage that
"the revolution which has been effected in France is of so wonderful a nature
that the mind can hardly realize the fact." New York, Oct. 13, 1789, in
Fitzpatrick, *Washington's Writings*, XXX, 443; see also Faÿ, *The Revolutionary Spirit in France and America*, p. 271; Adams, ed., *An Autobiographical
Sketch by John Marshall*, pp. 13-14.

[3] Louis-Guillaume Otto to [Minister of Foreign Affairs], New York, Jan.
19, 1790, Genet Papers, VII, 2180, Manuscripts Division, Library of Congress.

and liberal foundation is the ardent wish of every true American. . . ."[4]

* * * * *

Of the Franco-American diplomatic questions Washington inherited from the Confederation period, that of commerce and trade was, at first, most important. Later, primary concern centered on the problems of American neutrality, French prizes and privateers, the future relations of France to the Mississippi Valley, and the position of England in the context of Franco-American relations. These latter problems emerged from the wars of the French Revolution—and particularly the struggle between England and France— and involved the nature of the relationship between France and the United States under the 1778 alliance. In the beginning, however, the political relationship seemed to depend for its strength upon the economic bond between the two countries.

In the Confederation period, as has been seen, France had nourished the objective of strengthening commercial ties with the United States, of replacing England in an almost monopolistic domination of American trade and finance. Even in that period, despite French concessions and English discriminations, American commerce continued to flow, as it had in colonial days, to England.[5] To those hoping for viable, growing commercial ties with France, the fact that in these early years American mercantile interests had begun to reveal a hostility toward France and an almost unswerving attachment to Great Britain was disconcerting.[6] This attachment to England came to dominate the foreign policy of Washington's administrations. In the face of rising popular resentment against Britain merchants, bankers, and men of substance stood fast in their preference for the mother country. Those, on the other hand, who had from the first feared and distrusted England promoted the idea

[4] Washington to Comte D'Estaing, Philadelphia, Sept. 7, 1791, in Fitzpatrick, *Washington's Writings,* XXXI, 360.

[5] Trade relations with France during the Confederation period, despite the Franco-American alliance and commercial treaty, were slight. Buron, "Statistics on Franco-American Trade," *JEBH,* IV, 572.

[6] See, for example, J. Franklin Jameson, ed., "Letters of Stephen Higginson, 1783-1804," *Annual Report of the American Historical Association for the Year 1896* (Washington, 1897), I, to ————, April, 1784, p. 715; to John Adams, Boston, Aug. 8, 1785, pp. 719-725; to John Adams, Boston, July—, 1786, pp. 738-39; to John Adams, Boston, Dec. 21, 1789, p. 772.

of supplanting England with France as America's most-favored commercial nation by adopting commercial policies toward France more advantageous than those then existing, which favored Great Britain.[7]

Despite meager results, the French government strove to build a commercial bond with the United States. Through most of 1789 it continued to consider means of interesting recalcitrant French merchants in the American market. In America French officials wrote home about advantages which would accrue to France from increased trade with the United States, urging at the same time special privileges for American traders in France.[8] For months the last minister of the *ancien régime,* Count de Moustier, studied American economic conditions with the objective of placing France in a strategic position in America's foreign commerce. To counteract England's favored commercial position, he had, among other things, recommended from the beginning a new commercial treaty with the United States.[9]

With the establishment of the new Constitution and a stronger national government, French officials saw greater hope than ever before for French economic opportunity and commercial security. As one official saw it, the new federal government provided the means for securing national trade legislation unfavorable to Great Britain and advantageous to France. In accord with this reasoning Moustier urged the French government to lend its support to renewed efforts by French merchants to win American trade. Such ideas were well received in high places; the Count de Montmorin, French foreign minister, favored them.[10] Prospects for a flowering

---

[7] William Short in Paris wrote in glowing terms on the possibilities of increasing Franco-American trade. To Secretary of State, March 3, 1790, no. 20, National Archives, State Dept., Diplomatic Despatches, France; cited also in Setser, *The Commercial Reciprocity Policy. . . ,* p. 119 n.

[8] *Ibid.,* p. 91; Nussbaum, *Commercial Policy in the French Revolution,* pp. 30-31.

[9] Le Comte de Moustier to le Comte de Montmorin, New York, Feb. 14, 1788, AAE CP EU, Vol. XXXIII, ff. 37-42; Moustier, "Les Etats-Unis au lendemain de la guerre de l'indépendance. . . ," *Revue d'histoire diplomatique,* VI, 521. Later Moustier also recommended special concessions to Americans in French West Indian possessions (July 2, 1789); see Rayford W. Logan, *The Diplomatic Relations of the United States with Haiti, 1776-1891* (Chapel Hill, N. C., 1941), pp. 29-30.

[10] Moustier to Montmorin, June 1, July 2, 1789, AAE CP EU, Vol. XXXIV, ff. 139-146, 217-220, cited (with wrong vol. no.) in Setser, *The Com-*

of the Franco-American trade were good. President-to-be Washington wrote favorably of France's overcoming English commercial pre-eminence in the United States. For a while after becoming President he continued to hold such views.[11]

* * * * *

The pro-French orientation of the United States was logical. England, diplomatically and commercially, was still an enemy; France was a friend and ally which many Americans believed the foreign policy of the new government would favor. They believed that the commercial power given to Congress had been placed in the Constitution to strengthen American commercial foreign policy, and was to be used as a weapon of retaliation, to aid friends and to punish enemies. They sympathized with French commercial objectives and expected the economic tie with France to be strengthened.[12]

As the first reports of the French Revolution reached the United States, many came to feel that the liberalizing changes in France would contribute to a rejuvenated Franco-American commerce. Some thought that events in France would redound in other ways to the material benefit of Americans. "It seems," Oliver Wolcott said, "as though all the events in Europe were concurring for the benefit of America."[13] While the outbreak of the French Revolution had

---

mercial Reciprocity Policy. . . , p. 92; Montmorin to Moustier, Versailles, June 23, 1788, in Henry E. Bourne, ed., "Correspondence of the Comte de Moustier with the Comte de Montmorin, 1787-1789," *AHR,* VIII (July, 1903), 729. An interesting example of efforts to increase Franco-American commerce at this time were the activities of James Swan, Boston merchant and financier. In 1789-90 the French consul at Boston, Létombe, had translated into French and published in Paris a refurbished memorial on Franco-American commerce which Swan had prepared, apparently in 1784, at the suggestion of Lafayette. The English title was *Causes Which Have Hindered the Growth of Trade between France and the United States, with the Means of Stimulating It.* See Howard C. Rice, "James Swan: Agent of the French Republic, 1794-1796," *New England Quarterly,* X (Sept., 1937), 466-468. See also Nussbaum, *Commercial Policy in the French Revolution,* p. 31.

[11] Washington to Moustier, Mount Vernon, Aug. 17 and Dec. 15, 1788, in Fitzpatrick, *Washington's Writings,* XXX, 43-47, 160-163; George F. Zook, "Proposals for New Commercial Treaty between France and the United States, 1778-1793," *South Atlantic Quarterly,* VIII (July, 1909), 275.

[12] See Setser, *The Commercial Reciprocity Policy. . . ,* p. 119; in France similar views were held, Nussbaum, *Commercial Policy in the French Revolution,* pp. 36-41.

[13] The quotation is from Oliver Wolcott, Jr. to Oliver Wolcott, Sr., New

disrupted plans for a new Franco-American commercial treaty, the outlook for Franco-American trade continued to appear hopeful. William Short, American *chargé d'affaires* in Paris, for example, wrote that "the shackles of commerce" which hitherto have prevented the extending of our commercial connections with France are about to be destroyed. In the future, he went on, both countries will find those connections mutually advantageous. "The manufactures of France," he concluded, "are undergoing a sensible change which will adapt them to our choice."[14]

Not only did the French National Assembly look favorably toward the United States, but also the French committees on commerce agreed that French policy should give American trade a more favorable status than it then had. Lafayette and Ducher, among others, urged upon the Committee of Agriculture and Commerce a policy of trade as free as was possible to achieve. A treaty-based program of full reciprocity appeared the best way to implement such a policy. The French legislature acknowledged this, but did not act. With some justification the French believed that the commercial concessions they had already given to the United States had not been reciprocated.[15] How could they be certain that additional concessions would elicit desired American reciprocity?

French fears were not groundless. The first step in the Hamiltonian "system," the tariff and tonnage laws of 1789 and 1790, struck directly at any Franco-American commercial partnership, contemplated or otherwise. Those laws ran counter to the popular understanding that the government would use its power of commercial retaliation as an economic and diplomatic weapon which would discriminate between friend and foe. James Madison had proposed the laws in an effort to favor France against Great Britain; his

York, May 8, 1790, in Gibbs, *Wolcott Papers,* I, 46; Wolcott, Jr., to Wolcott, Sr., New York, Dec. 2, 1789; Wolcott, Sr., to Wolcott, Jr., Litchfield, Dec. 23, 1789, pp. 24, 33; Short to Secretary of State, Paris, Aug. 27, 1790, No. 40, National Archives, State Dept., Diplomatic Despatches, France; Hazen, *Contemporary American Opinion of the French Revolution,* p. 144.

[14] Short to Secretary of State, Paris, March 3, 1790, No. 20, National Archives, State Dept., Diplomatic Despatches, France.

[15] Short to Secretary of State, Paris, Oct. 25, 1790, *ibid.;* Short to Jefferson, Paris, Oct. 21, 1790, *ASP FR,* I, 120-121; Nussbaum, *Commercial Policy in the French Revolution,* pp. 45-46; Zook, "Proposals for a New Commercial Treaty. . . ," *SAQ,* VIII, 277.

efforts were thwarted by Hamiltonians, who viewed the proposed discrimination as an attempt "to wage commercial war with England." Fisher Ames, for example, was puzzled by Madison's "passionate attachment to discrimination. It is a favorite point with the Frenchmen in town." Did Madison, he asked, who was "very much devoted to the French," urge discrimination to affront England, and "to create a closer connection with her enemy?"[16] Hamiltonians would not allow Great Britain to be affronted. By placing France on the same footing with Great Britain, the laws as passed in effect discriminated against America's friend and ally, since they made no distinction between a country granting commercial favors and one enforcing trade penalties. The tariff and tonnage laws began the break with France that was to grow until the alliance was destroyed.[17]

In judging these first foreign commerce laws of the new federal government, the French saw them not only as a gauge of American sincerity in the purported desire for increased French trade, but also as a test of American political loyalty to the alliance of 1778. Protesting vigorously against the American laws, commercial interests within France used them as an argument against further relaxation of the French mercantile system in favor of American traders.[18]

[16] Fisher Ames to George Richards Minot, New York, May 29, July 2, 1789, in Seth Ames, ed., *Works of Fisher Ames,* I, 48, 58. Ames maintained that actually discrimination would not benefit France; see also Hamilton, *History of the Republic. . . ,* IV, 4-7; James P. Baxter, III, "Our First National Shipping Policy," *United States Naval Institute Proceedings,* XLVI (Aug., 1920), 1262-1263.

[17] Acidulous William Maclay saw this. See his *Journal* entry of May 26, 1789, p. 50, and his "unequivocal opinion" of June 17, 1789, p. 76, that lack of discrimination in favor of France was contrary to the spirit of the 1778 commercial treaty and that probably the tonnage laws would arouse French resentment. For a British reaction to the tariff and tonnage laws, see Society of Ship-Owners of Great Britain, *Collection of . . . Reports,* (pp. 47 ff.; it contains also a detailed account of Anglo-American commerce between 1783 and 1791.

[18] For the documents exchanged on the tonnage laws, see *ASP FR,* I, 109-116. When the merchants of Havre complained of the heavy tonnage duties to which they were subjected in the United States, Short warned his superiors that this example would be taken up by other Frenchmen "as soon as they can find time to attend to their commercial regulations" unless there were some change in the laws. To Secretary of State, Paris, Aug. 4, 1790, No. 38, National Archives, State Dept., Diplomatic Despatches, France. See also Malone, *Jefferson and the Rights of Man,* p. 328 n.

In contending that the tonnage duties discriminated against France, the French maintained that the duties violated the fifth article of the treaty of amity and commerce of 1778 and that in general they were also inconsistent with the spirit of the alliance.

The French argument appeared sound. Article 5 excused American vessels in French ports from payment of duties similar to those now imposed by the United States. The French said they had included that article in the treaty in recognition of the situation existing at the time in the United States; Americans did not at the time collect alien tonnage duties in their ports. Regardless of French argument, French friendship, and the French alliance, Senate opposition to the French protests was vigorous and deep-rooted. "God forgive me if I wrong some people," an anti-Hamilton senator said, "but there certainly have been more censorious conclusions than to charge some people with a design of breaking our connection with France!"[19] That accusation was not far from the mark; the French alliance was under attack.

To Secretary of State Jefferson the French protest seemed invalid. He responded that nothing in article 5 or in any part of the 1778 treaty prevented the United States from levying tonnage and tariff duties as long as it did not disturb France in her most-favored-nation status. Under the tonnage laws her duties were the same as those of the most-favored nation. Not satisfied with this interpretation of her rights under the treaty, France persisted in asserting that they had been violated. Franco-American relations had been injured and subsequent developments aggravated the injury.[20]

While Jefferson did not accept the French view of the 1778 treaty in its technical application, he did feel that France had legitimate cause for complaint. Having been minister to France during the Confederation years, Jefferson knew that the French government had, in spite of protests by merchants, granted generous favors to American commerce. He knew that the French believed the American interpretation of the commercial treaty to be a violation of

[19] Maclay, *Journal,* entry of Jan. 31, 1791, p. 371.
[20] Jefferson to Washington, report of Jan. 18, 1791, *ASP FR,* I, 109-110. William Maclay was puzzled by Jefferson's apparent anti-French stand. "There is certainly a design of quarreling with France," he realized, "and that Jefferson should seem to countenance this! What can this mean? I am really astonished at all this." *Journal,* entry of Feb. 7, 1791, p. 375.

faith; he knew that the French government was sensitive to internal political pressures and that French merchants still opposed the governmental policy of special favors for American commerce. Finally, he realized that France might retaliate against the tonnage duties by revoking privileges previously granted to American traders in French ports. He urged Congress to relax the tonnage laws in favor of France if it could be done without allowing other nations with a most-favored-nation status in their treaty relations with the United States to obtain the same concession without equivalent compensation.[21]

The Secretary of State suggested, therefore, that Congress specify a tonnage concession as *quid pro quo* for France's earlier nontreaty favors to American shipping. In this way no other nation could demand, without an equal concession, the same privilege. Since the suggested commercial concessions to France were to be made by legislation rather than by treaty, the entire scheme hinged on Congress, and in Congress the dominant factor was the political power of the Hamiltonians.

To implement his plan, as has been indicated earlier, Jefferson had also to overcome Hamilton's opposition within executive councils; this proved impossible. When consulted on the Jefferson proposal, Hamilton threw his weight against it. In so doing and by winning Washington to his view, Hamilton aroused Jefferson to do battle against him. This, as Jefferson later complained, was evidence of Hamilton's interference in the realm of foreign affairs to force a policy on the government the reverse of that which Jefferson, as Secretary of State, sought to implement.[22]

Hamilton concurred in Jefferson's rejection of the French interpretation of the 1778 treaty but protested the proposed easing of the tonnage laws in favor of France. Paradoxically, Hamilton based his objection on the argument that there was no binding reciprocity on the part of France in Jefferson's proposed arrangement, even though there was a "collateral consideration." French vessels in

[21] Jefferson to Washington, report of Jan. 18, 1791, *ASP FR,* I, 110-111; Malone, *Jefferson and the Rights of Man,* p. 328.

[22] See Jefferson to the President of the United States, Monticello, Sept. 9, 1792, in Ford, *Writings of Jefferson,* VI, 102-105. Jefferson maintained that he had been "duped" by Hamilton and was at first used as "a tool forwarding his schemes." See also Caldwell, *Hamilton and Jefferson,* pp. 222-223.

American ports, under the Jefferson proposals, would be placed on a footing of equality with American ships, but France would not be bound to grant the same treatment to American ships in French ports. Such a practice, he said, might set an evil precedent. Even though not of immediate and major consequence, French shipping, the Secretary of the Treasury feared, might grow so as to threaten American commerce. Also, the tonnage duties provided important revenues for his "system." If they were lowered or abolished, another revenue-producing source would have to be devised.

Hamilton suggested incorporating concessions to France into a new commercial treaty that would protect reciprocal advantages permanently. The new treaty would, perhaps, be less offensive to Great Britain than the proposed legislation. In essence, Hamilton revealed that he favored reciprocity when it was to Britain's advantage, but was opposed to it when it was not.[23]

In the Senate Jefferson's recommendations favoring special commercial consideration for French shipping were referred to a committee of dedicated Hamiltonians, two members of which, Oliver Ellsworth and Rufus King, voiced strong anti-French sentiments. After long and deliberate delay the Hamilton-dominated Senate killed the proposal. In its resolution the Senate advised rebuffing the French gently, that the government inform them of the American position "in the most friendly manner."[24]

To certain anti-Hamiltonians the shape of the opposition to the French alliance had already begun to take form. One outspoken anti-administration Senator said "that the vote against discrimination which had involved us in difficulties with France was the work of the President, avowedly procured by his influence; and that he

---

[23] See Hamilton to Jefferson, Philadelphia, Jan. 11 and 13, 1791, in Lodge, *The Works of Alexander Hamilton,* IV, 52-55. Hamilton feared, apparently, that trade concessions would create an adverse reaction in England. Nonetheless, he rationalized his position and stressed the importance of foreign policy to his system in these words: "My commercial system turns very much on giving a free course to trade, and cultivating good humor with all the world."

[24] U. S. Congress. Senate, *Journal of the Executive Proceedings of the Senate of the United States* (Washington, 1828), I, 77 (Feb. 26, 1791). Jefferson had feared that Senate opposition to his proposal would "prove too strong." To George Mason, Philadelphia, February 4, 1791, in Ford, *Writings of Jefferson,* V, 276; for other accounts, see Setser, *The Commercial Reciprocity Policy. . . ,* p. 120; Malone, *Jefferson and the Rights of Man,* p. 330.

did it to facilitate a connection with Great Britain, thus offering direct offence to France and incurring the contempt of Great Britain, for she has spurned every overture made to her." The spurned overtures were those of Gouverneur Morris. Not only had Hamiltonians succeeded in launching their campaign of undermining the French alliance, but they had succeeded also in getting the powerful backing of the President. Yet, at this time in his peace-treaty difficulties with Great Britain, Washington had sought a way out by trying to heal the breach with France. According to Senator William Maclay, "the measure is right, but his motives wrong." The President's crooked policy, said Maclay, has involved us in difficulty. Unless the tonnage laws were repealed, he concluded, "we lose forever the friendship of France."[25]

A few days later Maclay noted in his journal "that there has been a design to sacrifice French interest as a peace-offering to the British court I can not doubt; but that this should be persisted in after the disappointment attending Gouverneur Morris' management is strange indeed." Already, he feared, "our ancient prejudices against France" have been revived.[26]

* * * * *

The Jeffersonian commercial policy was founded on the 1778 alliance and extended commerce and friendship with France. In striving to attain the trade objective, Jefferson needed not only political support at home but also co-operation from the French government and merchants—co-operation he could use politically to aid him in putting across his policy.

Hamilton, of course, was in the same position with respect to England, yet, despite grievances and popular hostility against Great Britain, his position was the stronger of the two. Not only were the dominant figures in American government almost wholly pro-British in outlook, sympathy, philosophy, and financial and personal connections, but also the important merchants and bankers who would be the key men in any rejuvenated French trade were almost all of the Hamiltonian "British interest." They comprised, in large

[25] Maclay, *Journal,* entries of Feb. 14, 15, 1791, pp. 381-383. Maclay confessed that he could never contemplate the insult offered to France "without feeling resentment."

[26] *Ibid.,* entry of Feb. 26, 1791, pp. 90, 95.

part, the very group that Hamilton had made the heart of his system
—the most favored people in the Hamilton scheme.[27]

Jefferson and the French, furthermore, had to overcome the
handicaps of lack of common language, heritage, and culture, and
the earlier, not-wholly-eradicated anti-French inheritance of Americans. They faced the disadvantages of a fully established and widely accepted preference for English goods, the superiority of the
British industrial and commercial system, and English domination
of the seas. The Secretary of State consequently exerted continual
pressure on the French government to support him and his policy
with action and legislation.

But convincing evidence that French commercial policy was of
greater advantage to the United States than that of England was
practically impossible to obtain.[28] In a sense it did not exist.[29]
Since enacting the legislation of 1787-88, lowering some of the barriers of her mercantilist empire to American shipping, France had
made no special overtures to American traders. In comparison to
England's discriminatory practices, of course, the French concessions were milestones in America's struggle for commercial recognition. Yet, if the Jeffersonian policy were to prevail in spite of the
obstacles before it, it was imperative for France to initiate even more
trade concessions. On the other hand, it was not essential that
England concede anything to support Hamilton. English merchants already controlled the bulk of American trade; they were

[27] So close was the merchant-banker connection with England that even
New England merchants at one time deplored their too-intimate dependence
on English credit. See Morison, *The Maritime History of Massachusetts,
1783-1860*, p. 169. Perkins, *The First Rapprochement*, pp. 7, 10, 14, stresses
Anglo-American commercial ties.

[28] See, for example, Gouverneur Morris to Washington, Paris, Jan. 22, 1790,
ASP FR, I, 381. In seeking more trade advantages Morris informed Montmorin, the French foreign minister, that if such advantages were not obtained
the United States might be driven into British arms. Instead of using threats,
Jefferson, on the other hand, stressed anti-British reciprocity as the means of
winning French trade concessions. Jefferson to Short, Philadelphia, March 15,
1791, in Lipscomb, *Jefferson's Works*, VIII, 146-149.

[29] One reason for this was the rapacity and monopolistic practices of French
merchants. By 1785, for example, French merchants had sacrificed an opportunity to win at least a portion of the American trade to the greed of the
Farmers-General, a financial ring monopolizing the tobacco trade. See Frederick L. Nussbaum, "American Tobacco and French Politics," *Political Science
Quarterly*, XL (Dec., 1925), 497-516.

satisfied with the situation as it was. They were aware that profit-minded, British-connected American businessmen would not turn from an established and basically satisfying commercial policy to one based on sentiment and on possible future benefits, particularly when those merchants were also committed politically to other parts of the British-oriented Hamilton program.

As in the United States and England, middle-class mercantile interests were now powerful in the French government. Unlike British merchants, however, French traders did not profit from American trade. They believed that France had extended most of the favors and had received few of the benefits. Looking upon American commerce as a losing proposition, French merchants wished to rescind the trading privileges already granted to Americans rather than to extend them. With the intention of making American trade profitable, they sought enactment of discriminatory mercantile legislation similar to that of England, which seemed, indeed, to be no handicap to profits.[30]

Convinced that relaxations of the mercantilist system by the old regime had injured them, French merchants and bankers found in the National Assembly an outlet for their resentments. As a result of banker-merchant political power revolutionary France denounced the Eden treaty of 1786, which had taken her a considerable distance toward free trade with Great Britain.[31] As the French Revolution progressed and as nationalism increased, high tariffs and a navigation system similar to that of Great Britain became a part of French policy.[32] Such a policy, it was obvious, ran counter to Jeffersonian policy. So, while the political and ideological complexion

[30] Short to Jefferson, Paris, Oct. 21, 1790, *ASP FR*, I, 120-121; Woolery, *The Relation of Thomas Jefferson to American Foreign Policy. . .*, p. 100.

[31] For the Eden treaty, see Sir Adolphus W. Ward and G. P. Gooch, eds., *The Cambridge History of British Foreign Policy, 1783-1919* (3 vols., Cambridge, 1922), I, 164-170; Eli F. Heckscher, *The Continental System: An Economic Interpretation* (London, 1922), pp. 18-25. The National Assembly, apparently, was so governed by questions of local interest and internal politics, as was the Minister of Foreign Affairs, that it did not see the danger of killing existing and hoped-for commerce with the United States. Faÿ, *Revolutionary Spirit*, p. 303.

[32] Setser, *The Commercial Reciprocity Policy. . .*, p. 121. The French trade laws of the revolutionary years were intended to injure Great Britain by excluding her goods and also to serve as protectionist measures designed to benefit French industries. Heckscher, *The Continental System*, p. 28.

of the French Revolution drew Americans to France, its nationalism and the attitudes of its middle-class merchants tended economically to alienate the United States.

According to William Short, Jefferson's former secretary and successor in Paris as American *chargé d'affaires,* some members of the French National Assembly considered the United States "so much attached to England & to English manufactures, that every sacrifice which France could make to encourage commercial connexions with us, would be lost—they say that the experience of seven years has sufficed to shew this.—others suppose that the commerce with the United States is a losing commerce,—they are supported in this opinion by many of their merchants who tell them there is no instance of a French house having undertaken the commerce without having lost by it."[33]

Understandably that state of affairs disturbed Short, for to him fell the difficult, if not hopeless, task of trying not only to wring new and more favorable commercial treatment from France but also to retain the concessions already acquired, concessions that Jefferson considered "the sheet anchor of our connection with France."[34]   Throughout 1790 and into 1791 Short fought for better treatment of American commerce. He regularly attended sessions of the National Assembly's committee of commerce, pressing for a program of reciprocal concessions. The power of French merchants in the committee, however, proved too great to counteract. One by one the French stripped previously granted privileges from the American trade.[35]

In his lobbying activities Short tried, for example, to obtain special treatment for American tobacco and to fight legislation for a pending French tobacco monopoly. "I have brought over a few members [of the French legislature]," he reported, "to the opinion in favor of rendering this article free in commerce—one obstacle which I found with all of them, was my being an American—ignorant themselves they were afraid to listen to a person whom they considered as interested. I attempted to persuade them that the

[33] Short to Secretary of State, Paris, Oct. 21, 1790, National Archives, State Dept., Diplomatic Despatches, France.

[34] Jefferson to Short, Philadelphia, March 15, 1791, in Lipscomb, *Jefferson's Works,* VIII, 147.

[35] Setser, *The Commercial Reciprocity Policy. . . ,* p. 122.

interests of France & America were the same in this matter." Sometimes Short lost his temper over the ignorance of the French legislators. Earlier, when the committee of the Assembly met and proposed in effect to shut out American commerce in tobacco, he said that "it is useless to add all the stupid reasoning I have heard on the subject."[36]

Short's work was to no avail. After considerable debate, in March, 1791, the National Assembly passed two decrees against this major American commodity, one reinstituting a tobacco monopoly and the other levying a discriminatory and almost prohibitive duty on the importation of tobacco in American ships.[37] The United States protested vigorously. Jefferson, who had not expected such an act of hostility against American navigation from a friend and ally, exclaimed, "A moment's consideration must convince anybody that no nation on earth ever submitted to so enormous an assault on the transportation of their own produce. Retaliation, to be equal, will have the air of extreme severity and hostility." He warned that it would undoubtedly crush American desires for a new and more liberal commercial treaty "as wished for by the real friends of both [nations]." A repeal of the decree against American shipping by the Assembly, he said, was imperative.[38]

Neither Jefferson's threats of discriminatory legislation by Congress nor his entreaties brought results. American traders, however, were not stymied. Using deception and other means, they eluded the trammels of the French decree and carried tobacco to French ports. In two years, nevertheless, rather than improving Franco-American trade, the French Revolution had practically smothered it

[36] Short to Secretary of State, Paris, Oct. 30 and Aug. 22, 1790, National Archives, State Dept., Diplomatic Despatches, France.

[37] For the laws and debates, see *Archives parlementaires de 1787 à 1860...*, ed. by Jérôme Mavidal, Émile Laurent, and others (Ser. 1, 82 vols., Paris, 1862-1913), XIII, 153, 162-168, 173, Sessions of Feb. 12-14, 1791; XIII, 669, session of March 5, 1791; XIV, 221-223, session of March 20, 1791. Short reported that in enacting the discriminatory legislation French legislators were unaware of its rigor—a rigor which would of course invite retaliatory laws. To Secretary of State, Amsterdam, March 4, 1791, National Archives, State Dept., Diplomatic Despatches, France.

[38] Jefferson to Short, Philadelphia, July 28, 1791, Aug. 29, 1791; Lipscomb, *Jefferson's Works,* VIII, 217, 237-238, 239; Jefferson to Joseph Fenwick, Philadelphia, Aug. 30, 1791, National Archives, State Dept., Diplomatic and Consular Instructions.

in infancy. By the close of 1791 France and the United States were virtually committed to a trade war.[39]

Yet French government officials were anxious, and had been all along, to improve Franco-American trade. Montmorin, the minister of Foreign Affairs, wanted American commerce on a reciprocal basis with that of France, and Ternant, the new French minister to the United States, exerted himself in urging various French commercial committees to treat American shipping more favorably.

So strongly did those officials press the trade-reciprocity idea based on a new commercial treaty that Short advised caution against entering such a treaty in view of the instability of the French government. Then he counseled that "time cannot but strengthen the demands of the U. S.—Their increasing numbers & commerce & general prosperity will render their connexions more valuable" and in particular such growth will make American friendship essential to nations with Caribbean possessions. Although without possessions there, he said, the United States will have the power to keep the colonies in the hands of nations to whom the colonies belong and will itself be attached to those countries who offer the greatest commercial advantages in their West Indies. "France of course will be enlisting us by our interest in the guarantee of her possessions in the Islands," he concluded, "instead of having it on paper only."[40]

Despite the growing commercial barrier between the two countries, the ties of French-American friendship were still strong. News of Benjamin Franklin's death (April 17, 1790) served to spark French enthusiasm for the United States and for things American once again. So great was the popular tribute to Franklin in France that the accompanying feeling of warmth toward the United States spilled over into renewed attempts "to cement the friendship and interests of the two nations."[41] French overtures, however, were

[39] Louis-Guillaume Otto to [Minister of Foreign Affairs], Philadelphia, June 17, 1791, complained of American evasions of the tobacco decree. Genet Papers, Library of Congress; Setser, *The Commercial Reciprocity Policy. . . ,* pp. 122-123.

[40] Short to Secretary of State, Paris, May 3, 1791, No. 65, National Archives, State Dept., Diplomatic Despatches, France.

[41] The National Assembly voted to wear mourning for three days in tribute to Franklin. Rosenthal, *America and France,* pp. 243-245. See Jefferson to the President of the National Assembly of France, Philadelphia, March 8, 1791, in Lipscomb, *Jefferson's Works,* VIII, 137-138; Faÿ, *Revolutionary*

received in the Senate "with coldness that was truly amazing," according to William Maclay, who concluded that that body cared not a fig for the French, Franklin, or freedom.[42]

Despite the obstacles in the French legislature, efforts to improve American relations continued. On June 2, 1791, the efforts bore fruit in a decree adopted unanimously by the Assembly calling for negotiation of a new American commercial treaty.[43] Insofar as French desires were concerned this was nothing new; it merely formalized an earlier and frequently expressed desire "that the two countries should form a treaty on the footing of the most perfect reciprocity" such as might increase commerce and other bonds.[44] But, even though the decree became law the day after it was adopted, the French executive took no steps to implement it.

The new French minister to the United States, Colonel Jean Baptiste de Ternant, left France about three weeks after the June 2 decree was adopted and arrived in the United States in August, but he had not been instructed to negotiate a new commercial treaty with the United States. He was directed to propose to President Washington that the American minister in Paris be authorized to negotiate such a treaty. Jefferson did not like this; he wanted the negotiations to take place in the United States.[45] For almost six months Jefferson waited for another French overture in the light of the June decree. Finally he took the initiative by directing Short to inform the French that the United States was "perfectly disposed

---

Spirit. . . , pp. 286-294; Zook, "Proposals for New Commercial Treaty. . . ," *SAQ,* VIII, 278; Hazen, *Contemporary Opinion of the French Revolution,* pp. 148-149.

[42] Maclay, *Journal,* entry of Jan. 26, 1791, pp. 368-369.

[43] *Archives parlementaires. . . ,* XXVI, 710; Short to Secretary of State, Paris, June 6, 1791, National Archives, State Dept., Diplomatic Despatches, France.

[44] Short to Secretary of State, Paris, Aug. 4, 1790, *ibid.*

[45] Jefferson to Short, Philadelphia, Nov. 24, 1791, in Lipscomb, *Jefferson's Works,* VIII, 258; Short to Secretary of State, Paris, Jan. 25, 1792, National Archives, State Dept., Diplomatic Despatches, France. In an earlier despatch (May 3, 1791), *ibid.,* Short had reported mistakenly that Ternant, who favored a new commercial treaty, was authorized to negotiate one. Lord Gower, the British ambassador in Paris, also reported that Ternant had received instructions to obtain a new commercial treaty. Despatch of June 3, 1791, Paris, in Oscar Browning, ed., *The Despatches of Earl Gower* (Cambridge, 1885), p. 93.

to meet such overtures, and to concur in giving them effect on the most liberal principles."[46]

In the United States, meanwhile, Ternant took a keen interest in the possibility of arranging a new commercial treaty. Washington, too, showed interest. In his very first conversation with the French minister the President brought up the subject of the treaty by referring to the French decree of June 2.[47] Although the treaty issue was clouded by domestic political concerns, Washington's government did not minimize the importance of French commerce.

In his instructions to Gouverneur Morris as he was to take over the American legislation in Paris, Jefferson, as was to be expected, also again stressed the value of French trade. He pointed out that "the most important of your charges" is "the patronage of our commerce and the extension of its privilege, both in France and her colonies; but most especially the latter." Again in later instructions he adverted to this subject and to the commercial treaty; he urged Morris to exert himself to re-establish American "commerce with *France* on the footing on which it was at the beginning of their revolution."[48]

The first direct proposal for negotiation of a new treaty came from the Secretary of the Treasury of the United States, not from the Secretary of State, who most cherished the object. In October, 1791, while Jefferson and Washington were out of town, Hamilton had a four-hour discussion with Ternant. The Secretary of the Treasury indicated that oustanding difficulties between France and the United States could be settled if they made a new commercial treaty, and indicated that he favored such a treaty. He also hinted that the tonnage duties would be adjusted to meet French desires.[49]

Ternant, for his part, informed Hamilton that France already

[46] Jefferson to Short, Philadelphia, Jan. 5, 1792, National Archives, State Dept., Diplomatic and Consular Instructions; also in Lipscomb, *Jefferson's Works*, VIII, 258.

[47] Ternant to Montmorin, Philadelphia, Aug. 13, 1791, in Turner, *CFM*, p. 44.

[48] Jefferson to Morris, Philadelphia, Jan. 23 and June 16, 1792, National Archives, State Dept., Diplomatic and Consular Instructions; also in Lipscomb, *Jefferson's Works*, VIII, 291, 379.

[49] Ternant to Montmorin, Philadelphia, Oct. 9, 1791, in Turner, *CFM*, pp. 57-60; Malone, *Jefferson and the Rights of Man*, p. 395; Setser, *The Commercial Reciprocity Policy. . .* , p. 123; Zook, "Proposals for New Commercial Treaty. . . ," *SAQ*, VIII, 279.

had granted enough gratuitous privileges to the United States, and that unless Americans reciprocated properly, she would do nothing further without appropriate compensation. In referring to the French position on the tonnage law, Ternant remarked that he believed the American government should execute the old treaty before worrying about a new one.

Hamilton's expressions of attachment to France at this time are difficult to reconcile with his other words, deeds, and sympathies. Nevertheless, he did take the initiative in bringing the question to Jefferson and Washington, proposing that the Secretary of State engage Ternant in conversations to draw up a plan for the proposed commercial treaty. The completed plan would be sent to the French government for consideration. From the beginning Jefferson objected to the Hamilton proposal. He pointed out that an unsolicited treaty draft would be binding on the United States but not on France. The main result of such a procedure would be to disclose gratuitously how far the United States was preparing to go for the desired treaty.

Washington, believing that the plan should be tried, brushed aside these objections and backed Hamilton. Jefferson then asked Ternant what the basis for a new commercial treaty should be. Ternant responded that such a treaty should hinge on a single article establishing mutual naturalization privileges. Jefferson devised a brief draft for the proposed commercial treaty which, in essence, called for each nation to receive and treat the citizens, products, and ships of the other nation in its ports on the same basis as its own nationals and shipping.[50] It excepted tariff duties from national treatment; they were to remain as they stood unless they exceeded a certain percentage.

Hamilton, objecting to the low schedule of duties set forth, drew up a much higher one, increasing tariffs on certain French imports as much as 25 to 50 per cent according to Jefferson, who summarized Hamilton's reciprocity in these words: "So they were to give us the privileges of native subjects, and we, as a compensation, were to make them pay higher duties."[51]

[50] Ternant to Montmorin, Philadelphia, Oct. 24, 1791, in Turner, *CFM,* pp. 61-62.

[51] Jefferson's Anas, dated 1791 but written March 11, 1792, in Ford, *Writings of Jefferson,* I, 185-186; for the treaty project and duty schedule, see

Hamilton's sudden interest in the French treaty showed the marks of another astute political maneuver. In his next move the Secretary of the Treasury suggested a similar treaty parley with the newly arrived British Minister, George Hammond. Again Washington supported Hamilton. Concluding that Hamilton had proposed the negotiation of a French treaty—a treaty which undoubtedly he would have defeated if it had been consummated—as a necessary preliminary for overtures to Hammond, Jefferson at this time blocked action on a commercial treaty with either France or England.

Although forced by political considerations to give up temporarily further action on a new French commercial agreement, Jefferson did not abandon hope ultimately of obtaining it. It was while pressing for repeal of the discriminatory French commercial legislation of 1791 that he also impatiently prodded the French government for proposals implementing the National Assembly's decree of June 2, 1791.[52]

Finally, in April, 1792, Jefferson informed Ternant "openly and frankly" that the American government desired negotiation of a new commercial treaty. Stressing his attachment to the 1778 alliance, he explained how important it was for the Franco-American alliance that he be able to present France's position to Congress in a favorable light. Continued discriminatory legislation, he warned, would be to the advantage of England.[53]

Before closing the long interview with the French minister, Jefferson presented his earlier-conceived plan for the proposed commercial treaty. Embodying the idea that citizens of each country should be entitled to the same privileges as natives in ports of the other, such a treaty would have opened wide France's West Indian trade to Americans, and it would have given French traders a favored status in American ports. It might, in addition, have provided a solid economic base for Jefferson's objective of strengthening the

"Clauses for Treaty of Commerce with France" and "Questions to be Considered Of," [Nov. 26, 1791], *ibid.*, V, 397-400; see also Malone, *Jefferson and the Rights of Man*, p. 397.

[52] Jefferson to Short, Philadelphia, Jan. 5, 1792; to Gouverneur Morris, Philadelphia, March 10, 1792, in Lipscomb, *Jefferson's Works*, VIII, 283, 311.

[53] Ternant to Lessart, Philadelphia, April 8, 1792, in Turner, *CFM*, pp. 108-114.

French alliance. Such an economic connection accorded, moreover, with the thinking of French ministers then in power. So strong, in fact, was their faith in the power of economic ties that they looked askance at alliances without economic bonds.

While it responded favorably to the plan, the French ministry could do little; it was in too precarious a position to formulate long-range foreign policy.[54] Soon it toppled from power. Hopes for immediate action on a new commercial treaty were blocked following the establishment of the Republic in France in September, 1792. In spite of long effort, the treaty was not made; Franco-American commercial relations did not improve; and the 1778 alliance was not supported by the solid economic foundation it needed.

Still Jefferson persisted in his efforts to get discriminatory French trade legislation repealed. Within France, too, hope for a strong economic connection survived troubled times. Certain officials believed that through the unifying bonds of common republican principles the French and American peoples could now be drawn into a firmer alliance in defense of republican government. One of the advantages of such an ideological alliance would be better and more advantageous trade relations, the most solid basis for a common connection.[55] In proposing a renewed commercial alliance, French republican officials pointed out that the United States produced what France consumed and was capable of consuming what France produced. Why not, suggested one agent, send a commissioner to the United States empowered to propose and to negotiate a treaty embodying political as well as economic and commercial questions?[56]

War pushed aside theories and ideas. The clash with Great Britain in February, 1793, gave the French government new interest in Jefferson's proposed mutual naturalization agreement. Such a treaty would have permitted virtually untrammeled trade between

[54] See Morris to Jefferson, Paris, July 10, 1792, *ASP FR*, I, 332. In view of the uncertainty of the French government Morris advised not to press for a decision at this "unpropitious moment." See also Gilbert, " 'New Diplomacy' of the Eighteenth Century," *World Politics*, IV, 33-34.

[55] "Alliance entre les républiques française et américaine," par M. Ducher [probably Sept. 20, 1792], AAE CP EU, Vol. XXXVI, ff. 154-155.

[56] "Projet d'un pacte commercial et economique avec les Etats-unis de l'Amérique," signed d'Hauterive, Oct. 29, 1792, Genet Papers, Library of Congress, VIII, 2470-2471.

France, the French possessions, and the United States; its wartime value would have been incalculable.

Faced with the dominating might of British sea power and consequently forced to turn to American shipping for certain essential supplies, the French government saw more clearly than before the advantages in Jefferson's plan. Internal developments, too, underscored the need for the treaty. In France's southern provinces in the winter of 1792 there was a shortage of wheat and flour; more than ever the French needed American provisions in American ships. One of the first acts of the French government following the outbreak of war, therefore, was to place American ships and products on the same status as those of French citizens in French ports.[57] Concurrently it sought to open negotiations with the United States to gain reciprocal advantages for French commerce in American ports. War, in effect, had driven the French to embrace Jefferson's proposals without obtaining equivalent concessions; war had thrust them into the role of suppliant.

Shortly before the war ministers of the Republic had written their ideas on a commercial treaty into the instructions of Edmond Charles Genet, Republican France's first minister to the United States. One of his major objectives was to gain liberal mutual naturalization concessions embodied in a commercial treaty. Reflecting the thinking of republican officials in France, Genet proposed "a true family compact" embodying political as well as commercial objectives.

Alarmed, the Washington administration interpreted Genet's overtures, correctly, as an effort to revise the treaty of alliance as well as the commercial treaty of 1778.[58] With France at war with England such a compact would alienate Great Britain to the extent

[57] The food shortage is discussed in Étienne Cathalan, American Consul at Marseilles, to Gouverneur Morris, Sept. 10, 1792, National Archives, State Dept., Diplomatic Despatches, France. The decree of the National Convention of Feb. 19, 1793, is in *ASP FR*, I, 147.

[58] See "Instructions to Genet," Dec., 1792, in Turner, CFM, p. 202; Genet to Jefferson, Philadelphia, May 23, 1793, *ASP FR*, I, 147; Randolph to Monroe, Philadelphia, June 1, 1795, *ibid.*, pp. 707-708. Here Randolph reviews in part the history of the attempt to negotiate a new commercial treaty; France's concessions and increased desires for a closer commercial connection, he pointed out, were the result of the war. See also Nussbaum, *Commercial Policy in the French Revolution*, p. 203.

that it bound the United States more closely to France. To Hamilton and his Federalist followers such a revitalized alliance was out of the question. The question of closer commercial connections with France now took on deeper political coloring. Friendship for France, proponents of a tighter trade connection asserted, was sufficient for a new treaty favorable to French commerce. Opponents, on the other hand, declared that in view of the "unnatural convulsed state" in France, this was no time to form a "closer alliance than already existed with a people who had so far transgressed the bounds of humanity," nor was it a time "to alter either our commercial or political connexion with France. . . ."[59]

Franco-American relations became so entangled in the complexities of war, neutrality, and American politics that the proposed commercial treaty never received full consideration. Never enthusiastic about the alliance and closer commercial relations with France, Washington's administration—aside from Jefferson—became more than ever opposed to closer ties with France. Yet it did not discard the ultimate objective of improving Franco-American trade. At Jefferson's suggestion, Washington approved a proposal urging the French government to include in the instructions of Genet's successor powers to negotiate on a possible new commercial treaty.[60]

Both of Genet's immediate successors (Fauchet and Adet) were, in fact, instructed to negotiate a new commercial treaty, but without results. Even though Republicans and others continued to complain of America's economic vassalage to England and continued to urge as a counterbalance a reorientation of American commerce in favor of France, England continued her near-monopoly of American commerce.[61] With American acceptance of the Jay treaty the chances for making a new French commercial treaty were lost in increasing Franco-American hostility. With them was lost, but not forgotten, the Jeffersonian hope of intimate economic ties with France as a means of fortifying the alliance of 1778.

[59] *Annals of the Congress.* . . , 3rd Cong., 1st sess., Moore of Virginia, Jan. 25, 1794, pp. 321-322.

[60] See Jefferson's Anas, Aug. 23, 1793, in Ford, *Writings of Jefferson*, I, 261-262; Jefferson to Washington, Aug. 22, 1793, Jefferson to Morris, Philadelphia, Aug. 23, 1793, *ibid.*, VI, 395-396.

[61] For an attack on the Anglo-American commercial connection as unfavorable to the United States and as being supported by American aristocrats, see the *Independent Chronicle and Universal Advertiser* (Boston), Jan. 13, 1794.

CHAPTER SIX

THE FRENCH FRENZY

The success of the French arms has been celebrated throughout the country with every demonstration of festivity; and every exertion has been employed to combine the cause of France with the preservation of American liberty. By such artifices as these the public mind is worked upon, and unless speedily checked, may be gradually led on from the dislike of partial grievances to a decided and open opposition to the government.—George Hammond to Lord Grenville, Philadelphia, March 7, 1793.

The arrival and conduct of Mr. Genet excited great sensation throughout the southern states. We were all strongly attached to France—scarcely any man more strongly than myself. I sincerely believed human liberty to depend in a great measure on the success of the French revolution. My partiality to France however did not so pervert by understanding as to render me insensible to the danger of permitting a foreign minister to mingle himself in the management of our affairs, and to intrude himself between our government and people.—John Marshall, *Autobiography.*

* * * * *

Fᴙᴇɴᴄʜ diplomatic representatives to the United States, because of the French alliance and the critical importance of French relations, occupied influential posts.[1] Their conduct and their opin-

[1] For a contemporary appraisal of French ministers in the United States during the Washington administrations, see Moreau de Saint Méry, *Voyage aux États-Unis de l'Amérique, 1793-1798*, pp. 295-296; for an English translation see Kenneth and Anna M. Roberts, eds. and trans., *Moreau de St. Méry's American Journey, 1793-1798*, pp. 275-276; see also Turner, *CFM*, p. 12. Moreau believed that France's choice of ministers, on the whole, was unfortunate, and manifested little effort to win American friendship. His view, it should be noted, was a biased one. Turner, too, was not impressed by the French ministers.

ions had a marked impact not only on Franco-American diplomacy but also on domestic politics. Even before Washington became President, this was evident—strikingly so in the case of Éléonor François Élie Moustier, first the Count and later the Marquis de Moustier.[2]

Appointed minister to the United States in 1787, the Count de Moustier, accompanied by his sister-in-law, Mme de Bréhan, arrived in October to take over his new post. At first he seemed pleased with the friendliness of influential Americans toward France and made shrewd observations as to the course of Franco-American relations under the new Constitution. George Washington, he reported, maintained that most Americans "still felt a vivid and sincere gratitude for the King and French nation; but that self-interest alone could regulate relations between nations; that it was very easy to grant that it entirely belonged to His Majesty to see to it that the interests of the United States be closely connected with His own." This conclusion, pointed out Moustier, was worthy of note "as General Washington will become President of the United States if he so wishes, and . . . his power and influence in that capacity will be of utmost importance under the terms of the new Constitution." He praised the Constitution, indicating that the French government considered it desirable and viewed it as a means of strengthening the 1778 alliance. "This way of speaking," he wrote home, "seems to me useful and even necessary, if we consider that the thing is in a way accomplished and that the only course left is to make the most of it."[3]

Following Washington's inauguration, Moustier gave a magnificent ball in his honor. On this well-chosen occasion (May 14, 1789) he sought to impress Washington and his government with the central position of the French alliance in American foreign policy. He did this by presenting two sets of cotillion dancers in complete

[2] Biographical sketches of Moustier are in *Nouvelle biographie générale* (46 vols., Paris, 1853-66), XXXVI, 803; *Biographie universelle, ancienne et moderne* (52 vols., Paris, 1811-62), XXX, 343-346. Scattered details may be found also in Frédéric Masson, *Le Departement des affaires étrangères pendant la révolution, 1787-1804* (Paris, 1877).

[3] Moustier to Montmorin, New York, Nov. 18, 1788, in Gilbert Chinard, ed., *George Washington as the French Knew Him: A Collection of Texts* (Princeton, 1940), pp. 89-90.

military costume, one group wearing French colors and the other the buff and blue of the American Revolution. While the dancers celebrated the French alliance they reminded onlookers of war-bred French friendship.[4]

Such auspicious aspects of Moustier's mission appeared to justify the warm recommendations Jefferson, Lafayette, and other notables had given him. He "would give the most perfect satisfaction in America," predicted Jefferson. To Madison he spoke of Moustier in glowing terms. "He is a great enemy to formality, etiquette, ostentation and luxury. He goes with the best dispositions to cultivate society, without poisoning it by ill example. He is sensible, disposed to view things favorably, and being well acquainted with the constitution of England, her manners and language, is better prepared for his station with us. But I should have performed only the lesser, and least pleasing half of my task, were I not to add my recommendations of Madame de Bréhan." Then Jefferson pulled all the stops. "She is goodness itself. You must be well acquainted with her. You will find her well disposed to meet your acquaintance, and well worthy of it. The way to please her, is to receive her as an acquaintance of a thousand years." Getting back to Moustier, Jefferson described him as "remarkably communicative. With adroitness he may be pumped of anything. His openness is from character, not from affection. An intimacy with him, may on this account, be politically valuable."[5] To Moustier Jefferson offered advice on American conditions, saying that he would "find the affections of the Americans by circumstances, embracing what they loathe, they realize the fable of the living and dead bound together."[6]

So different were later appraisals of Moustier by other Americans that it does not appear possible that they described the same man. Although recognized as a man of energy, talent, and intelligence, he struck bourgeois Americans as an obnoxious, haughty, and vain French aristocrat, alienating government officials by his persistent advocacy of French recovery of Louisiana. In addition, he alienated

---

[4] See Rufus W. Griswold, *The Republican Court, or American Society in the Days of Washington* (New York, 1867), pp. 157-158.

[5] Jefferson to Madison, Paris, Jan. 30, 1787; to Jay, Paris, Feb. 1, 1787; to Madison, Paris, Oct. 8, 1787, in Lipscomb, *Jefferson's Works*, VI, 67, 85, 335-336.

[6] Jefferson to Le Comte de Moustier, Paris, Oct. 9, 1787, *ibid.*, p. 339.

highly placed Americans by his personal conduct and alleged eccentricities.

He heartily disliked American cooking, and at times apparently took his own food with him when invited out to dine. On another occasion he is reputed to have told Cyrus Griffin, last president of the Continental Congress, that he "was but a tavern-keeper."[7] These foibles did not endear him to American officials; one critic remarked pointedly that "if France had wished to destroy the little remembrance that is left of her and her exertions in our behalf, she would have sent just such a minister."[8]

Most damaging to American sensibilities, however, was the appearance of "an improper Connection" between the Count and Mme de Bréhan. As Jay wrote to Jefferson, "You can easily conceive the Influence of such an opinion on the minds and feeling of such a people as ours."[9] In all, Moustier's conduct in the United States was felt by Americans to be "politically and morally offensive." American officialdom, at best lukewarm toward the French alliance, concurred and requested his recall. It was the first such request by the American government touching a foreign minister.

Jay, then American Secretary for Foreign Affairs, handled the matter through Jefferson in France. Jefferson considered the question to be a delicate one, for in the event either of failure or of mismanagement friendship with France would be jeopardized. With the help of the Marquis de Lafayette, Jefferson brought the problem before the French Minister of Foreign Affairs, the Count de Montmorin, who desired close relations with the United States.[10]

[7] Griswold, *The Republican Court*, p. 83 n.; Moreau de Saint Méry, *Voyage.* . . , ed. Mims, p. 295; Faÿ, *Revolutionary Spirit*. . . , pp. 274-75; Malone, *Jefferson and the Rights of Man*, p. 197. An unbiased appraisal of Moustier is difficult to obtain. Renaud de Moustier, for example, in "Les Etats-Unis," *Revue d'histoire diplomatique*, VI, 520, called him "an impartial, experienced diplomat."

[8] John Armstrong to General Gates (n.p., n.d.), quoted in Monaghan, *John Jay*, p. 266.

[9] Jay to Jefferson, Nov. 25, 1788, quoted in *ibid*. Such insinuations must have hurt Jefferson, who was on intimate terms with Mme de Bréhan, considering her "goodness itself." For the correspondence between Mme de Bréhan and Jefferson, see Gilbert Chinard, ed., *Trois Amitiés Françaises de Jefferson*, pp. 13-61.

[10] Jefferson to Jay, Paris, Feb. 4, 1789, in Lipscomb, *Jefferson's Works*, VII, 279-282.

Although Montmorin was willing to call Moustier back to France, he contended that there was no grievance of sufficient gravity against him to justify a recall. He had, moreover, no vacant post to which he could send Moustier if he were recalled. Finally, Montmorin hit upon the device of calling Moustier back to France on leave of absence, ostensibly in response to Moustier's own earlier-expressed desires. Without the difficulties of an actual recall, the Count de Moustier left the United States in October, 1789, never to return. [11]

After Moustier's departure the French government left the American ministry vacant for over a year. During that time American affairs were in the capable hands of *chargé d'affaires,* Louis-Guillaume Otto, later the Count de Mosloy. Otto worked at keeping Franco-American friendship active. On the alliance's twelfth anniversary, February 6, 1790, he celebrated the occasion with a large entertainment attended by Vice-President John Adams, the heads of departments, the Senate, the Speaker of the House of Representatives, Chief Justice John Jay, Governor George Clinton, and Chancellor Robert R. Livingston of New York, and the diplomatic body and other foreigners of distinction.[12]

So, shortly after the Washington government began not only were full diplomatic relations with Great Britain not established, but also the post of French minister to the United States was vacant. The two most important powers in America's foreign relations were not represented formally or adequately in the United States. Furthermore, as it named no immediate successor to Jefferson in France, the Washington administration did not have adequate representation in the British and French capitals.

Before Jefferson left France governmental authorities consulted him about the next ministerial appointment to the United States. Although there were some doubts as to the congeniality and per-

---

[11] *Ibid.;* Monaghan, *John Jay,* p. 267. By his contemporaries Moustier was considered a capable statesman and diplomat: he was twice offered the post of Minister of Foreign Affairs, and later distinguished himself in a number of important diplomatic posts. See the biographical sketches in *Nouvelle biographie générale,* XXXVI, 803, and *Biographie universelle. . . ,* XXX, 343-346.

[12] Griswold, *The Republican Court,* p. 217; for brief sketches of Otto see *Biographie universelle. . . ,* XXXII, 246; Masson, *Le Departement des affaires étrangères. . . ,* pp. 242-243.

sonal qualities of Colonel Jean Baptiste de Ternant, Jefferson approved of his appointment to the post. To make sure of American acceptance, Montmorin through Lafayette later approached Gouverneur Morris on sending Ternant to the United States. Morris took this as evidence of Montmorin's sincere desire "of cultivating a good understanding with the United States." Important factors in the selection of Ternant seem to have been his knowledge of the United States and his being on the whole a person agreeable to the American government, having served with valor as an officer in the American Revolution. In addition, he spoke English as if it were his own tongue.[13]

* * * * *

In striking contrast to his predecessor, Ternant proved popular with Americans.[14] But following Moustier's departure France paid little attention to her diplomatic representatives in the United States. Neither Otto, who was responsible for American affairs until August, 1791, nor Ternant, who was France's minister from August, 1791, to May, 1793, was in close touch with the home government. Ternant felt keenly his neglected status, and in his correspondence complained frequently of his being abandoned.[15] With the demise of the constitutional monarchy in September, 1792, the new French government ended Ternant's uncertainty by deciding to replace him. It apparently distrusted his attitude and loyalty toward the Republic.

France's neglect of American diplomacy at this juncture reflected her immediate domestic and European concerns. Involved first in domestic revolution and then in foreign wars, the French naturally

[13] Jefferson to John Jay, Paris, Feb. 4, 1789, in Lipscomb, *Jefferson's Works*, VII, 281; Morris to Washington, Paris, Jan. 22, 1790, *ASP FR*, I, 381-382; A. Bertrand, "Les Etats-Unis et la révolution Française," *Revue des deux mondes*, XXXIII (May 15, 1906), 398; Monaghan, *John Jay*, p. 267.

[14] George Hammond ascribed Ternant's popularity to his service in the American Revolution and to his friendship with Lafayette. To Grenville, Philadelphia, Oct. 3, 1792, Henry Adams Transcripts.

[15] Ternant's neglect is reflected in AAE CP EU, vols. XXXVI and XXXVII and in his correspondence in Turner, *CFM*, pp. 43-200, particularly pp. 145, 161, 166 (at one time he received only one letter in reply to sixty he had sent to the home government). For an evaluation of Ternant's mission in the United States, see Bertrand, "Les Etats-Unis. . . ," *RDM*, XXXIII, 400-403; see also Faÿ, *Revolutionary Spirit. . . ,* p. 304.

devoted their energies to the most pressing affairs and allowed secondary matters, such as relations with the United States, more or less to drift by themselves.[16] This neglect did not mean that French officialdom considered the 1778 alliance valueless; rather, in the turmoil of revolution and continental wars the American alliance, it was felt, could do nothing to affect the outcome. To the United States, however, French relations, quiescent or otherwise, were of primary concern.

The French preoccupation with domestic and European affairs was reflected in the diplomatic problems growing out of the August, 1791, Negro-slave insurrection on the French Caribbean island of Saint Domingue.[17] Unable to secure aid from France, the colonial assembly on the island appealed directly to the United States for assistance. It sent agents to Philadelphia to obtain arms and supplies necessary to suppress the uprising. At first Ternant disregarded normal diplomatic protocol by appealing directly to President Washington for money and munitions to put down the insurrection and to save the most important possession of America's ally.[18] Soon, however, he became alarmed. The appeal of French colonists directly to the American government he regarded as a disturbing manifestation of independence, a manifestation that was by no means new. Fearing American designs on the island, Ternant saw the situation as a threat to French dominion in the Caribbean.

The French planters of Saint Domingue seemed more determined to defend their own interests than to save the colony for France. Some had even appealed to the British in Jamaica for aid.[19] The islanders' direct diplomacy and the consequent threat to French-American friendship also disturbed Jefferson. An independent

[16] Turner, *CFM,* p. 12.

[17] Sylvanus Bourne, American consul at Cap Français, predicted the horrors of civil war. Charles C. Tansill, *The United States and Santo Domingo, 1798-1873* (Baltimore, 1938), p. 7.

[18] Ternant to Jefferson, March 3, 1792, AAE CP EU, Vol. XXXVI, f. 48; to Hamilton, March 7, 1792, f. 49; Ternant to Washington, Philadelphia, Sept. 22, 1791, National Archives, State Dept., Notes from the French Legation; Mary W. Treudley, "The United States and Santo Domingo, 1789-1866," *Journal of Race Development,* VII (July, 1916), 103-104.

[19] See Ternant to Montmorin, Philadelphia, Sept. 28, Nov. 24, and Dec. 10, 1791, in Turner, *CFM,* pp. 45-51, 76-84; Logan, *The Diplomatic Relations of the United States with Haiti, 1776-1891,* p. 33.

Saint Domingue would be easy prey for the British, and in British hands Saint Domingue's valuable commerce with the United States would be destroyed.

After assuring both the French government and Ternant that the United States had no desire to conquer Saint Domingue, Jefferson informed the island's agents that they would have to work through the French Minister to obtain American aid.[20] They did. Out of the revolutionary debt due France, then seven years in arrears, the American government supplied French colonial authorities with funds to purchase arms, foodstuffs, and other supplies necessary to combat the uprising. Without American assistance in the early days of the insurrection the French planters on the island would have been in almost impossible straits.[21]

As slave rebellion and the fervor of the French Revolution swept over Saint Domingue many of the refugee French planters fled to the safety of the United States; other planter-aristocrats sought sanctuary under the British flag, principally in Jamaica. Americans opened hearts and purses to the French refugees, especially after the great and pitiful influx of the summer of 1793. Towns and villages raised subscriptions for refugee-relief; various state governments appropriated funds, as did Congress. Not only did the influx tax American resources but also the presence in the United States

[20] Ternant to Montmorin, Philadelphia, Nov. 17, 1791, in Turner, *CFM,* pp. 72-75; Jefferson to Short, Philadelphia, Nov. 24, 1791, in Lipscomb, *Jefferson's Works,* VIII, 259-263. The role of Saint Domingue's commerce in Franco-American relations is discussed in Logan, *The Diplomatic Relations. . . ,* pp. 26-31; see also Ludwell L. Montague, *Haiti and the United States, 1714-1938* (Durham, N. C., 1940), p. 33.

[21] Hamilton, however, raised objection to the legitimacy of the existing French government, questioning its authority to give sufficient receipt. Essentially, his objection was political rather than financial. Jefferson countered his arguments successfully in this instance. See Hamilton to Washington, Treasury Dept., Nov. 19, 1792, in Hamilton, ed., *Hamilton's Works,* IV, 328-331; Woolery, *The Relations of Jefferson to American Foreign Policy,* p. 104; Jefferson to Ternant, Philadelphia, Nov. 20, 1792, in Lipscomb, *Jefferson's Works,* VIII, 440-442. Ternant was given advance payments on the French debt. Too, the American government did not attempt to liquidate the debt in depreciated French currency, but paid an equitable compensation. See Alphonse Aulard, "La Dette Américaine envers la France sous Louis XVI et sous la révolution," *La Revue de Paris,* XXXII (May-June, 1925), 531; Logan, *The Diplomatic Relations. . . ,* p. 36; Treudley, "The United States and Santo Domingo. . . ," *JRD,* VII, 110; Montague, *Haiti and the United States. . . ,* p. 33; Tansill, *United States and Santo Domingo. . . ,* p. 8.

of thousands of French aristocrats, loyal to the Old Regime, created a political-diplomatic problem.[22]

At first most of the important figures in the American government, including Washington and Hamilton, favored helping their French ally restore its authority over Saint Domingue.[23] As the influence of the French Revolution made headway on the island, however, Federalist opinion turned against the restoration of French rule, which now meant "Jacobin" instead of aristocrat-planter rule. Federalists and refugee-aristocrats agreed that the old order could be maintained only by British intervention. Jefferson, however, opposed this; and despite his sympathy for the French *emigrés* and his distaste for Negro uprisings, he wished the island insurrectionists well in their fight for liberty.[24]

The situation on Saint Domingue, complicated by the interweaving of French revolutionary doctrines, the horrors of a slave uprising, and political-diplomatic considerations, met with mixed reactions in the United States. Sometimes sympathy for displaced and suffering humanity overcame political considerations, and sometimes politics came first. Despite its racial aspects and its emotional overtones, the Saint Domingue situation struck Americans as another point of difference between Hamiltonians and Jeffersonians, another irritant among other disturbing factors in Franco-American rela-

---

[22] Treudley, "The United States and Santo Domingo. . . , *JRD*, VII, 111-115; Logan, *The Diplomatic Relations. . . ,* p. 40. Refugee planters in the United States tended to split into two groups, pro-French Revolution and anti-French Revolution; see Frances S. Childs, *French Refugee Life in the United States, 1790-1800: An American Chapter of the French Revolution* (Baltimore, 1940), p. 155. American generosity toward the refugees was also mixed with harsh treatment; see Moreau de Saint Méry, *Voyage. . . ,* ed. Mims, pp. 294-295. Refugees from France, too, flocked to the United States—"many People of fortune and fashion and some of Title." "Occurrences from 6 Aug. to 1 Sept., 1790," signed P. Allaire, Henry Adams Transcripts.

[23] See, for example, Washington to Ternant, Mount Vernon, Sept. 24, 1791, in Fitzpatrick, *Washington's Writings,* XXXI, 375-376 and note; Malone, *Jefferson and the Rights of Man,* p. 394.

[24] Jefferson later wished that the French "aristocrats & monocrats" could be distributed "among the Indians, who would teach them lessons of liberty & equality." To Martha Jefferson Randolph, Philadelphia, May 26, 1793, in Ford, *Writings of Jefferson,* VI, 268. Jefferson, and Hamilton too, however, wanted to exact whatever advantages (within the limits of their political views) were possible from France's difficulties. Logan, *The Diplomatic Relations. . . ,* p. 39.

tions. In the critical war year of 1793 it was to be another complicating element in the politics and diplomacy of the French alliance.

* * * * *

Basic differences had disturbed French-American relations from the beginning of American independence. The effect of those differences, however, had been to slow the development of closer ties between the two countries rather than to threaten seriously those existing at the beginning of that period. With the arrival of Edmond Charles Genet, Ternant's successor, in April, 1793, following destruction of the French monarchy and establishment of the First Republic, Franco-American relations entered a new and dangerous phase. This turn of events, although rooted in other causes as well, can be traced to the unfolding French Revolution, the reactions it aroused in the United States, and the American interests it either threatened or appeared to threaten.

From its beginning Americans had, with few exceptions, hailed the French Revolution with sympathy and enthusiasm; they had looked upon it as adding new strength to already existing French ties. As the Revolution progressed, American interest in it seemed to grow; Americans took pride in what seemed to them an implementing of American ideals adopted by the French, ideals which had become common in both countries.[25] In the first three years of the French Revolution, while there were no frenzied public demonstrations in its behalf, as there were to be later, it did win the overwhelming favor of the American people.

Despite the temper of the American populace there were exceptions to the general feeling. Influential conservatives, such as Wash-

[25] William Vans Murray Papers, Commonplace Book, July 28, 1795 (Princeton); Aratus No. II in the *National Gazette* (Philadelphia), Nov. 24, 1791; Madison to Edmund Randolph, New York, Oct. 17, 1788, in Gaillard Hunt, ed., *The Writings of James Madison*, V, 276; Jefferson to Dr. Price, Paris, Jan. 8, 1789, in Lipscomb, *Jefferson's Works*, VII, 253. For an example of extravagant Franco-American sentiments given expression as a consequence of the French Revolution, see the address of twelve Americans, including Joel Barlow and John Paul Jones, to the National Assembly, July 10, 1790, in Robert F. Durden, "Joel Barlow in the French Revolution," *William and Mary Quarterly*, 3rd Series, VIII (Jan., 1951), 332-333 (note also the French response); Hazen, *Contemporary American Opinion of the French Revolution*, pp. 140-143; Rosenthal, *America and France*, pp. 155-156, 296-298, 252.

ington, Hamilton, John Adams, and Gouverneur Morris, were skeptical of the events in France from the first. Later they were horrified.[26] Vice-President John Adams, for example, was so disturbed by the political and social principles of the French Revolution, particularly when the single assembly became the heart of the new French government, that he felt compelled to express his views in print. This step led to a series of incidents which ruptured the long-standing friendship between John Adams and Jefferson.[27]

Proud of their Revolutionary accomplishments, the French praised and defended their new governmental system, as well as their new political doctrines, in books and pamphlets. Even before the Revolution French thinkers gave their political theories wide circulation. One writer, the Marquis de Condorcet, an honorary citizen of New Haven, Connecticut, had in 1788 published a small treatise in which he criticized views expounded by John Adams and in which he also advised Americans to change their constitution in accord with French ideas by concentrating power in a single legislative body.[28] Condorcet's ideas, given additional importance by his prominent role in the French Revolution, presented a challenge which Adams could not resist.

Adams wrote a series of thirty-two essays which were published in John Fenno's *Gazette of the United States* beginning in April, 1790, and running for a year. These papers, the *Discourses on*

[26] For the conservative reaction, see Albert J. Beveridge, *The Life of John Marshall*, II, 21-24; Adams, *Works*, I, 452-453; for a shrewd contemporary assessment of the effect of the French Revolution on the United States by a French royalist in the United States, see "An Unknown Correspondent to William Windham," June 1, 1793, in William Windham, *The Windham Papers* (2 vols., Boston, 1913), I, 121-124. In later years John Adams estimated that the American reaction to the French Revolution was one third opposed, one third in favor, and one third neutral. Adams to James Lloyd, Quincy, Jan., 1815, Adams, *Works*, X, 110-111.

[27] For details, see Gilbert Chinard, *Honest John Adams*, p. 231; Samuel F. Bemis, *John Quincy Adams and the Foundations of American Foreign Policy*, 26-29; Zoltán Haraszti, *John Adams and the Prophets of Progress* (Cambridge, Mass., 1952), 38-40, 165-166, 236; Alfred Iacuzzi, *John Adams, Scholar* (New York, 1952), pp. 141-156.

[28] Condorcet wrote his *Lettres d'un bourgeois de New-Heaven* [sic] to refute the first volume of Adams's *A Defence of the Constitutions of Government of the United States of America* (London, 1787). Condorcet's refutation appeared in 1788 in the first volume of Philip Mazzei's *Recherches historiques et politiques sur les États-Unis* . . . (4 vols., Paris, 1788).

Davila, attacked French Revolutionary doctrines and expressed Adam's own governmental theories, which to opponents appeared antidemocratic and smacked of monarchy. To Adams democracy was unworkable, the first step toward anarchy. He warned the French to abandon their illusory idea that men were by nature good.[29] Convinced that the best government was one of checks and balances, on the English or American model, he lashed out at the idea of government by a single legislative assembly, to him the framework of despotism.

To Jeffersonians, Adam's articles were like a red rag waved before an enraged bull. Many felt that Adams should not go unanswered. Although he had no desire to lock horns with the Vice-President, Jefferson shared these sentiments, and, quite unexpectedly, was thrust into the role of challenger.

Tom Paine's *The Rights of Man* had been published in England early in 1791. Written as a direct reply to Edmund Burke's *Reflections on the French Revolution,* Paine's pamphlet was a defense of the French Revolution (a second part, appearing a year later, attacked the English government). In defending the French Revolution, Paine coupled it with the American Revolution, a connection which seemed logical to Jeffersonians, but which seemed sacrilegious to Hamiltonians, who were wedded to Burke's thesis. William Vans Murray, for example, was to label Paine's reply "a work designed to loosen every sort of Government. . . ."[30]

The first part of the work was scheduled for almost immediate republication in the United States, John Beckley, clerk of the House of Representatives, having made arrangements for the reprinting of a copy of the English edition which he owned. Before sending it to the printer he loaned it to James Madison, who passed it on to Jefferson. To avoid further delay, Beckley asked Jefferson to send it directly to the printer. With the pamphlet Jefferson sent the printer an explanatory note in which he stated that he was pleased to see that at last something would "be publickly said against the political

[29] According to Adams, just as "cold will still freeze, and fire will never cease to burn," man will be corrupted by disease and vice. Hazen, *Contemporary American Opinion of the French Revolution,* p. 156. All the Davila articles are reprinted in Adams, *Works,* VI, 223-403.

[30] William Vans Murray Papers, Commonplace Book, Aug. 9, 1795 (Princeton).

heresies which have sprung up among us. . . ."[31] Believing that
the note would help sell the Paine volume, the printer on his own
initiative included it in the preface to the American edition.

When the book was published in May, 1791, Jefferson was "sincerely mortified." While he approved of Paine's work and had
never made a secret of being "anti-monarchical and anti-aristocrati-
cal," Jefferson had no desire to take issue publicly with his old
friend.[32] Regardless, the lines were drawn. Jefferson had publicly
approved of Paine's work, Adams despised it; Jefferson had appeared
as the foremost American defender of the French Revolution, John
Adams as its leading American antagonist.

At this time John Quincy Adams, a young lawyer of twenty-four
waiting for clients and eager to make his mark in the world, wrote
a number of articles under the pseudonym of "Publicola," attacking
Paine's arguments.[33] For ambitious young men of the period, the
writing of anonymous political tracts for the press on current controversial subjects was a not unusual way to attract public attention.
But young Adams had still another purpose: to defend his father
against Jefferson's public charge of political heresy. So well-done
were the *Letters of Publicola* that at first almost everyone, including
Jefferson, attributed them to the Vice-President. Regardless of origin, the assaults against Paine invited vehement counterattacks all
over the country.

Clearly, the French Revolution and the "storm over the rights of
man" had laid bare the deep ideological split between the Vice-
President and the Secretary of State. As a result of the controversy
over Paine's work, the public began to divide on the questions of
the French Revolution and the doctrines it embodied. No longer

[31] With Jefferson the central figure, the entire episode is treated in Malone,
Jefferson and the Rights of Man, 354-359; see also Adams, *Works,* I, 454-455;
Moncure D. Conway, *The Life of Thomas Paine* (3rd ed., 2 vols.; New York,
1908), I, 291-292.

[32] The quotations are from Jefferson to Washington, Philadelphia, May 8,
1791, in Ford, *Writings of Jefferson,* V, 329; the phrase "storm over the
rights of man" is taken from the title of chap. xxi, Malone, *Jefferson and the
Rights of Man.*

[33] *The Letters of Publicola* were printed in the *Columbian Centinel* of
Boston in the summer of 1791 and then reprinted throughout the land. Bemis,
John Quincy Adams and the Foundations of American Foreign Policy, pp.
26-28. The *Letters* are reprinted in Ford, ed., *The Writings of John Quincy
Adams,* I, 65-110.

was American foreign policy concerned almost exclusively with the politics and diplomacy of Anglo-French rivalry, or with the economics of the French alliance. With the burgeoning of the French Revolution, it, and American domestic politics as well, became enmeshed in the "battle of sentiments and ideas" of the expanding ideological struggle between England and Revolutionary France.[34] To the public Jefferson became the leader of a crusade of democracy against monarchism and, as a result of this, the leading opponent of the Hamiltonian system. In view of the acclaim given Paine's pamphlet few doubted that Jefferson had quite consciously placed himself at the head of this popular cause, even though he had been thrust there by the force of circumstances.

France's adoption of her first written constitution, the Constitution of 1791, provided another source of dissension. This liberal constitution, resembling in many respects that of the United States, was greeted by most Americans who were at all concerned with it with admiration and approval. While not yet a republic, France appeared to approach the American political ideal in progressing from an absolute monarchy to a liberal constitutional monarchy. To democrats this was cause for rejoicing. To conservatives— including most Hamiltonians—the new constitution, with its seemingly undue extension of popular rights and popular election, was detestable.[35]

With American publication of the main framework of the French Constitution of 1791, which the French had put into effect piecemeal since the summer of 1789 as each section was ready, there appeared one of the first noticeable divisions in the general unanimity Americans had shown in hailing the Revolution in France. Although not

[34] Malone, *Jefferson and the Rights of Man*, 356; Brant, *James Madison: Father of the Constitution. . . ,* 340-341; Bowers, *Jefferson and Hamilton: The Struggle for Democracy in America,* pp. 208-211.

[35] Gouverneur Morris, for example, denounced the new French constitution as "good for nothing." Morris to Washington, Paris, Dec. 27, 1791, in Beatrix Cary Davenport, ed., *A Diary of the French Revolution by Gouverneur Morris, 1752-1816, Minister to France during the Terror,* II, 332-333. John Adams did not know "what to make of a republic of thirty million atheists. The Constitution is but an experiment, and must and will be altered. I know it to be impossible that France should be long governed by it." To Richard Price, New York, April 19, 1790, Adams, *Works,* IX, 564. Washington, too, was losing confidence in the French Revolution. Malone, *Jefferson and the Rights of Man,* p. 403.

major, this division in American sentiment, seen with that exposed by the Jefferson-Adams episode, foreshadowed a major split in American politics. The French Revolution by the close of 1792 had become an undeniable factor in American politics. In 1793 it became a dominant factor in American foreign policy as well. "The sensations it [the French Revolution] has produced here, and the indications of them in the public papers," Jefferson said, "have shown that the form our own government was to take depended much more on the events of France than anybody had before imagined."[36]

*   *   *   *   *

Before the year 1792 ended and as the French Revolution became more violent, American interest in it, while no longer approaching almost unanimous approval, increased enthusiastically.[37] In December, 1792, slow sailing vessels from Europe brought electrifying news from France—the Tuileries had been stormed, the Prussians had been stopped at Valmy, the monarchy was no more, a republic had been declared. These events, reported in varying detail, were reprinted in American newspapers and the news spread through the countryside. A French frenzy rolled over the land. America became hysterical.

Thrilled by the achievements of their fellow-republicans in France, Americans followed the progress of French armies against the massed bayonets of monarchism. With news of the propaganda Decree of November 19, 1792, which appeared to transform the

[36] To Thomas Mann Randolph, Philadelphia, Jan. 7, 1793, in Ford, *Writings of Jefferson*, VI, 157; a contemporary Federalist account of that party's change of view toward the French Revolution is in William Vans Murray Papers, Commonplace Book, Aug. 9, 1795, Sept. 21, 1795 (Princeton). In South Carolina, as in other states, domestic politics reflected the influence of events in France and Europe. On January 9, 1793, high state officials attended a "feast" in celebration of France becoming a republic. *City Gazette* (Charleston), cited in John H. Wolfe, *Jeffersonian Democracy in South Carolina* (Chapel Hill, N. C., 1940), p. 72. Similar sympathy for France was expressed in Rhode Island and Virginia; see Mary Ellen Loughrey, *France and Rhode Island, 1686-1800* (New York, 1944), p. 43; David K. McCarrell, "The Formation of the Jeffersonian Party in Virginia," (unpublished Ph.D. dissertation, Dept. of History, Duke University, 1937), p. 101.

[37] According to George Hammond, at this period the French Revolution did not "appear to have excited so much admiration and applause as might have been expected" in the United States. To Lord Grenville, Philadelphia, Nov. 1, 1791, *Dropmore Papers*, II, 223.

French Revolution into an armed crusade on behalf of "liberty" and against "oppression," American joy became epidemic.[38] Public demonstrations and celebrations hailed news of each success of French arms. Feasts, civic and private, honoring the rights of man, liberty, equality, or variants thereof, became commonplace. Republicanism became increasingly popular; the cause of France, in the minds of many, became coupled with the preservation of American liberty. Americans decried titles and all that smacked of monarchy. Men and women addressed each other as "Citizen" and by such contrived female variants as "Citess." They raised liberty poles and wore the tricolored cockade everywhere; they sang French songs; and they drank toasts to French principles.[39] These things happened everywhere but in Federalist households. Disapprove though they might, Federalists were helpless to stem the tide of republican zeal, "the spirit of Licentiousness utterly averse from regular government."[40]

Clergymen too, at this time, joined in to give ecclesiastical blessings to pro-French Revolution, prorepublican festivities.[41] At one

[38] For the decree, see John H. Stewart, ed., *A Documentary Survey of the French Revolution* (New York, 1951), p. 381.

[39] This verse sung at a Boston "festival" honoring the French achievements seemed to express popular feeling:
> "See the bright flame arise,
> In yonder Eastern skies
> Spreading in veins;
> 't is pure Democracy
> Setting all Nations free
> Melting their chains."

From the *Columbian Centinel* (Boston), Jan. 26, 1793, reproduced in Beveridge, *The Life of John Marshall,* II, 19; in McMaster, *A History of the People of the United States. . . ,* II, p. 90 n., are printed the words of the French Republican song, *Ça ira;* George Hammond changed his tune—the French frenzy alarmed him. To Grenville, Philadelphia, March 7, 1793, Henry Adams Transcripts (see quotation at the head of this chapter).

[40] William Vans Murray Papers, Commonplace Book, July 28, 1795. John Adams lamented that "Dragon's teeth have been sown in France and come up monsters." To wife, Philadelphia, Jan. 14, 1793, in C. F. Adams, ed., *Letters of John Adams Addressed to His Wife,* II, 120.

[41] In the main, however, the clergy tended to be anti-French Revolution and to support Federalists, particularly in New England. An important factor in the political attitude of the clergy was the sympathy of Republicans for the French Revolution. See William A. Robinson, *Jeffersonian Democracy in New England,* p. 129; Anson E. Morse, *The Federalist Party in Massa-*

day-long public demonstration of January 24, 1793, in Plymouth, Massachusetts, the religious sanction was as obvious as the way to parish church.   After beginning the day's festivities with the discharge of fifteen cannon, the town folk gathered in the Meeting House, where their leaders addressed them on the principles and foremost events of the Revolution in France.   Then followed the word of the minister, who spoke to them in the language, appropriate to the occasion, of the Prophet Daniel. "Blessed be the name of God forever and ever: for wisdom and might are his and he changeth the times and seasons. *He removeth Kings."*

Choir selections were in keeping with the ministerial theme. "'Down with these earthly Kings,' thundered the majestic bass. 'No King but God,' was the sublime response."   A parade through town followed the church service, during which a song written by a local citizen, an Ode to Liberty, which was "composed in a moment of happy inspiration, was repeatedly sung. . . ."   Fittingly, "a cheerful ball closed the enjoyment of this agreeable day."[42]

*   *   *   *   *

In April, 1793, having been detained for about three months by wind and storm, news-bearing ships from Europe finally brought reliable word of the execution of King Louis XVI, of France's February declaration of war against Great Britain, Holland, and Spain, and of the coming of the French Republic's first minister to the United States, Citizen Edmond Charles Genet.   In the wake of this news the popular clamor for France, for republicanism, and for liberty became louder.   America's ally was now pitted against America's old enemy, England.   To many, particularly to Republicans, this indeed offered cause for renewed rejoicing.[43]

chusetts to the Year 1800 (Princeton, 1909), pp. 88-115; for the political influence of the clergy, see pp. 116-139.

[42] *Columbian Centinel* (Boston), Jan. 30, 1793, quoted in Hazen, *Contemporary American Opinion of the French Revolution,* p. 170.

[43] Jefferson's concept of the ideological interdependence between France and the United States, for example, was strengthened by the establishment of the French republic.   See Jefferson to Brissot de Warville, Philadelphia, May 8, 1793, in *Writings of Jefferson,* VI, 249; to Madison, Philadelphia, May 19, 1793, p. 261, he identified American interests with those of France and scored France's enemies as "the confederacy of princes against human liberty"; to Harry Innes, Philadelphia, May 23, 1793, he expressed his fear for America's future if France were defeated; "This summer," he summed up, "is of im-

Federalists now shed their cloak of public helplessness and came out openly in defense of England and in opposition to the Revolution and France. Having at first embraced the French Revolution as had Jeffersonians, Federalists, in unconcealed horror, now recoiled from it.[44] Accounts of violence and bloodshed, of the apparent decline from constitutional monarchy to control by the mob under the Girondins, terrified American conservatives. The trial and beheading of Louis XVI, acclaimed friend of the United States, upset Republicans as well as Federalists. "Ninety-nine of our citizens out of a hundred," remarked a prominent doctor, "have dropped a tear to his memory."[45] Louis's execution caused more than tears in the Federalist camp; it and the declaration of war against England removed any doubts remaining in Federalist minds that the French Revolution was an evil thing. With Federalists it now became party dogma that the effect of the French Revolution upon the minds of the American people must be counteracted.[46]

* * * * *

mense importance to the future condition of mankind all over the earth, and not a little so to ours," p. 266; see also Bemis, "Jefferson," in Bemis, ed., *The American Secretaries of State. . .*, II, 61.

[44] Robert Goodloe Harper is a good example of a pro-French Revolution politician whose views changed with the progress of the Revolution so that he became a vigorous anti-French Revolution Federalist. See his *Select Works of Robert Goodloe Harper* (Baltimore, 1814), "Observations on the Dispute between the United States and France" (Philadelphia, May 25, 1797), pp. 50-51. John Jay, too, at first had welcomed the Revolution and then turned against it. "This revolution had, in my eye, more the appearance of a woe than a blessing. It has caused torrents of blood and tears, and been marked in its progress by atrocities very injurious to the cause of liberty and offensive to morality and humanity." To Robert Goodloe Harper, New York, Jan. 19, 1796, in Johnston, *Jay Correspondence,* IV, 201-202; another example of change from pro-Revolution sentiment is Noah Webster; see Harry R. Warfel, *Noah Webster: Schoolmaster to America* (New York, 1936), p. 226.

[45] Benjamin Rush to John C. Letsam, Philadelphia, April 26, 1793, in Lyman Butterfield, ed., *Letters of Benjamin Rush,* II, 635. Remarked William Bentley, Unitarian clergyman, liberal in politics and theology, Jeffersonian Republican, and personal friend of Jefferson: "The melancholy news of the beheading of the Roi de France is confirmed in the public opinion, & the event is regretted most sincerely by all thinking people. The french loose [*sic*] much of their influence upon the hearts of the Americans by this event." March 25, 1793, in Bentley, *Diary of William Bentley, D. D.,* II, 13.

[46] Federalist philosophy in this regard is expounded in William Vans Murray Papers, Commonplace Book, July 28, 1785. Murray, though a minor

Into the midst of this pro-French hysteria and into a hail of Federalist scorn stepped "Citizen" Genet, French republicanism's emissary to the United States. In the new order of things, the French Republic had sent Genet to Philadelphia to strengthen the alliance which had been "too much neglected by the ancient diplomacy of the royal government." He was to attach Americans to French republican principles, to convince them that they were the new France's natural allies, and thus to fortify them in support of the 1778 alliance. Ironically, a prime reason for selecting Genet for such a mission was to forestall the very reaction and alienation that followed news of the execution of the King.[47]

Realizing that Louis's death might be ill-received in the United States, where Americans respected him as the benefactor of their independence, certain Girondin leaders, among them Thomas Paine, Jacques Pierre Brissot de Warville, and Genet, conceived the idea of rescuing Louis's neck and at the same time buttressing American friendship by exiling the deposed monarch to the United States. Far-fetched though it might seem, such a plan accorded with the Girondin policy of attempting to build a fraternal union between the world's two great republics, a union whose foundation would be the moral force of a common democracy and the practical force of an increased mutual trade.[48]

figure, was a representative Federalist thinker. An example of efforts "to represent the Republic of France as unfriendly to the United States" so as to influence American public opinion is recorded by Harry Toulmin, a young English liberal, in his journal, Norfolk, July 23, 1793; see Marion Tinling and Godfrey Davies, ed., *The Western Country in 1793: Reports on Kentucky and Virginia by Harry Toulmin* (San Marino, Calif., 1948), pp. 4, 21.

[47] Minister of Foreign Affairs (Le Brun) to the President of the National Convention, Paris, Oct. 20, 1792, Genet Papers, Library of Congress, VIII, 2498; Provisory Executive Council of the French Republic to President Washington, Jan. [?], 1783, National Archives, State Dept., Notes From the French Legation. These objectives should not obscure the main goal of Genet's mission: to obtain all possible support from the United States in the imminent war with England and Spain. Maude H. Woodfin, "Citizen Genet and His Mission" (unpublished Ph.D. dissertation, Dept. of History, University of Chicago, 1928), p. 77. For a brief analysis of Girondist foreign policy and the Genet mission, see Richard K. Murdoch, "The Genesis of the Genet Schemes," *French American Review*, II (April-June, 1949), 81-87; see also Frederick A. Schminke, *Genet: The Origins of His Mission to America* (Toulouse, 1939).

[48] Davenport, ed., *A Diary of the French Revolution. . . ,* II, 595-596; Faÿ, *Revolutionary Spirit. . . ,* pp. 320-321; Meade Minnigerode, *Jefferson, Friend*

To carry out this plan, the individual who had been slated to be the new minister to the United States was, in November, 1792, replaced by Genet, who had been privy to the plot from its inception and whose Girondin connections were unimpeachable. Officially, Genet was to be minister plenipotentiary to the United States, but privately he was to convey the King and royal family to the United States, where the deposed Bourbon was to become "an American planter."[49]

The plan for Louis's American banishment was never carried into effect. Lack of political sagacity and courage by Girondins and the clamor for the monarch's death by radical Jacobins of the Mountain sealed his doom. While Genet waited to take the King with him to America, he watched his former sovereign's trial; "the most mournful spectacle I ever witnessed," he confessed. Only Thomas Paine had the courage to plead openly for Louis's life. "France has today but one friend," he said, "the American Republic. Do not give the United States the sorrow, and the King of England the joy, of witnessing the death upon the scaffold of a man who has aided my American brethren in breaking the fetters of English despotism."[50] Without King or royal family, Genet boarded the frigate *L'Embuscade,* and in mid-February, 1793, sailed for the American shore he was destined never to leave.

When Genet sailed from France he left behind him a notable family, which had been high in governmental and court circles of the Old Regime, influential and high-placed friends, and for a young man of thirty, an amazing career.[51] The eldest of his four sisters

---

of France, 1793: The Career of Edmund Charles Genet, Minister Plenipotentiary from the French Republic to the United States as Revealed by His Private Papers, 1763-1834 (New York, 1928), pp. 125-129. Hereinafter cited as Minnigerode, *Genet.*

[49] Woodfin, "Citizen Genet and His Mission," p. 69; Eloise Ellery, *Brissot de Warville* (New York, 1915), p. 315; memorandum by Genet (n.p., n.d.) in Moncure D. Conway, ed., *The Writings of Thomas Paine* (4 vols., New York, 1894-1896), IV, xii.

[50] Quoted in Minnigerode, *Genet,* p. 133. Later Paine's efforts on behalf of Louis XVI almost sent him to the guillotine. *Maryland Gazette* (Annapolis), Feb. 6, 1794.

[51] Biographical data on Genet drawn from Minnigerode, *Genet;* J. J. Jusserand, "La Jeunesse du citoyen Genet d'après des documents inédits," *RHD,* XLIV (1930), 237-268; George Clinton Genet, *Washington, Jefferson and "Citizen" Genet, 1793* (New York, 1899); Greville Bathe, *Citizen Genet,*

was the celebrated Mme Campan, first lady in waiting to Queen Marie Antoinette, and another was beautiful Mme Angine, mother-in-law of Marshal Michel Ney.

From his father, Edmé Jacques Genet, who had been head of the Bureau of Interpreters in the Ministry of Foreign Affairs at Versailles, Edmond, a precocious child, had received the best in education and had inherited an unusual linguistic proficiency. At six Edmond could read French and English and could recite Greek; at fourteen or younger he translated, with some assistance, the *History of Eric XIV* from Swedish into French, with his own footnotes. Published copies of his work were presented to the King and Queen, and the King of Sweden sent him a gold medal for the translation. By the time he was fifteen, Genet spoke six languages in addition to his native French—Latin, Greek, Italian, Swedish, German, and English.

Before he had reached his fifteenth birthday he began to learn the vocabulary and the mechanics of diplomacy. He became a secretary in his father's bureau where he translated documents dealing with the American Revolution.[52]   In 1781, following the death of his father, eighteen-year-old Edmond Charles took over as Clerk-in-Chief of the Bureau of Interpreters. Since his first appointment, he had, of course, traveled and had held other diplomatic posts of trust in government, having been secretary to the French Embassies in Berlin and Vienna, 1780 and 1781. His new position, however, placed him in the center of European diplomacy, and once more put him in touch with American affairs.

After the death of Vergennes in 1787, the government, for reasons of economy, abolished Genet's bureau. Friends at Court then obtained a diplomatic appointment for him at the Court of Catherine II in St. Petersburg. Leaving for Russia in the autumn of 1787, he saw for the last time the France of the Old Regime.

At St. Petersburg, handsome young Genet, in the brilliant uniform of the First Regiment of Dragoons, made an immediate and

---

Diplomat & Inventor (Philadelphia, 1946); Woodfin, "Citizen Genet and His Mission"; Woodfin's sketch in the *Dictionary of American Biography;* and Genet's Memoirs in the Genet Papers, Library of Congress.

[52] In these early years he met many Americans; John Adams, among others, dined with the Genets. Woodfin, "Citizen Genet and His Mission," p. 7; Genet, *Washington, Jefferson and "Citizen" Genet. . . ,* p. 2.

striking impression on Queen Catherine; she even presented him with diamond knee buckles. But the Queen's favor did not last. When *chargé d'affaires* Genet began expressing revolutionary sentiments and revealed his loyalty to the French Constitution of 1791, he became obnoxious to the Queen. Forbidden to appear at Court and placed under surveillance, Genet was expelled from Russia in mid-1792. Later, he maintained that he had no personal enemies in Russia; his functions were the source of difficulty, "after having enjoyed a consideration which has often excited the jealousy of my Colleagues."[53]

On Genet's return to Paris the then dominant Girondins welcomed him warmly into the highest circles of their party. His obvious talents and his display of revolutionary zeal had not gone unnoticed, and they were not to go unrewarded. In the circle of Mme Roland he mixed with ease; his charm and talents had found a congenial setting. At Mme Roland's, moreover, after a brief special diplomatic mission in Geneva, his mission to the United States was born and Louis's banishment was first suggested. "No, no," protested Mme Roland, "it is not royal heads that we must strike, but royalty."[54]

This is the background of the brilliant young French republican, often described as "ardent," "eloquent," "impulsive," "rash," who on April 8, 1793, was acclaimed by the populace of Charleston, South Carolina.[55]

* * * * *

As Genet basked in the ovation given him in Charleston, Washington's government moved to resolve the critical foreign-policy question thrust upon it by the Anglo-French war and made press-

[53] Memoirs, n.p., n.d., Genet Papers, Library of Congress, Box 38; Woodfin, "Citizen Genet and His Mission," p. 44, states that Genet was not satisfied in Russia and sought to get out. See also Genet, *Washington, Jefferson and "Citizen" Genet. . . ,* pp. 10-13.

[54] The quotation is from Genet's Memoirs, Genet Papers, Library of Congress, Box 38. Brissot, apparently, proposed Genet as minister to the United States. Ellery, *Brissot de Warville,* p. 315; see also Cl. Perroud, ed., *Mémoires de Madame Roland* (2 vols., Paris, 1905), II, 266-267.

[55] Woodfin, "Citizen Genet and His Mission," p. 456, lists contemporary epithets directed against Genet. George Cabot called him "that feather-headed Frenchman," and to youthful John Quincy Adams he was "a beardless foreigner, a petulant stripling."

ing by the Genet mission—the question of neutrality. When in April, 1792, the first war of the French Revolution began, the war of the first coalition, France was pitted only against Austria and Prussia; the conflict was restricted to land campaigns on the European continent. This, as has already been indicated, had little effect on American diplomacy, commerce, or neutrality. Despite American sympathy for the French cause, American interests were not involved. Americans were by force of circumstances and geography compelled to remain neutral save in thought.

As it became obvious that the scope of the European conflict would widen to include England and so involve the interests of the United States, American statesmen turned their thoughts to the new nation's position in such a conflict. At the end of February, 1793, Hamilton and Jefferson prepared a number of questions on the French treaties. All of them, in one way or another, touched upon problems of neutrality and alliance later faced by the government.[56]

In April, 1793, with news of the war's expansion to include England, Holland, and Spain, action succeeded speculation. On April 13, 1793, the President rushed from Mount Vernon, where he was first apprised of events, to Philadelphia that he might deal personally with the foreign policy crisis. On April 18, the day following his arrival in the national capital, he sent to his Cabinet a circular and thirteen questions dealing with the country's "delicate situation" relative to the French-British war and the French alliance.[57]

In summary, Washington asked advice on these questions: Shall we issue a proclamation of neutrality? Shall we receive a minister from the French Republic? If we receive one, should it be with or without qualification? Under present circumstances are we com-

[56] Woolery, *The Relation of Thomas Jefferson to American Foreign Policy. . . ,* pp. 105-106; England expected war with France and moved to counteract action between the French and American allies. Grenville instructed Hammond, Whitehall, Jan. 4, 1793, ". . . you will be particularly attentive to discover what Negotiations may be on Foot for cultivating a more intimate Correspondence between the French Government and the United States," and urged the utmost vigilance on this point. Mayo, *Instructions to British Ministers, American Historical Association Annual Report for the Year 1936,* III, 33.

[57] The circular and questions are printed in Fitzpatrick, *Washington's Writings,* XXXII, 419-421; the French knew of the circular and questions; there is a copy in AAE CP EU, Vol. XXXVII, ff. 221-222.

pelled by good faith to adhere to the French treaties of 1778? If we
are obliged to adhere, is it expedient to do so? If we have the right
to renounce the treaties, would it be a breach of neutrality to consider them still in operation? If the treaties are still binding, does
our pledged guarantee of French possessions in America in the
treaty of alliance apply to a defensive war only? Is France presently
engaged in a defensive war? If the war is not defensive, does the
guarantee, under any event, still apply? What is the effect of the
guarantee? Do the treaties grant special privileges to French warships in American ports? If the future regent of France were to
send a minister, should he be received? In view of the European
crisis, should I call Congress into session?[58]

The next day, April 19, when Washington met his official family,
all weighed and debated each question. First and most pressing
was the problem of the neutrality proclamation. The President's
sentiments were clear. He believed it necessary for the United
States "to maintain a strict neutrality" to prevent Americans "from
embroiling us" with France or Great Britain.[59] In deciding for
this policy of neutrality he had the support of all his advisers; in
implementing it he brought on Cabinet dissension.

While agreeing that the United States must remain neutral,
Jefferson and Hamilton attacked the question of the proclamation
of neutrality from differing premises. To Jefferson the European
war provided an opportunity for Americans to gain important advantages and to increase trade at European expense. He realized
that neutrals would reap the profits of war; the United States was
then caught in a financial panic and needed an economic transfu-
sion.

The Secretary of State opposed an immediate proclamation of
neutrality as being against the best interests of the United States. He
favored holding it back, making the belligerents "bid for it," the

[58] The authorship of the questions has long been debated. Madison and
Jefferson considered Hamilton to be the author, and undoubtedly he was.
For a discussion as to the authorship, indicating Hamilton as the author,
see Thomas, *American Neutrality in 1793: A Study in Cabinet Government*, pp. 27-33; Schachner, *Thomas Jefferson, a Biography*, I, 481.
[59] See Washington's letters to Jefferson and Hamilton, Mount Vernon,
April 12, 1792, in Fitzpatrick, *Washington's Writings*, XXXII, 415-416.

price to be "the *broadest privileges* of neutral nations."[60]   Here was the opportune time to force commercial concessions and concrete definitions of neutral rights from the warring powers.   This approach favored France at the expense of England, which did not lessen its attraction for Jefferson.   In reporting Jefferson's views to his government, George Hammond wrote that "Mr. Jefferson is so blinded by his attachment to France, and his hatred of Great Britain, as to leave no doubt upon my mind, that he would without hesitation commit the immediate interests of his country in any measure which might equally gratify his predilections and his resentments."[61]

Jefferson's second objection had its basis in strict constitutional construction.   The Constitution gave the power to declare war to Congress.   Technically, a neutrality declaration was an announcement that the United States would not go to war.   This, he maintained, was merely the negative side of the war-power entrusted solely to Congress; the Executive Branch had no right to encroach on that power.[62]

From opposite premises Hamilton argued for an immediate proclamation of neutrality.   In his view the President had ample authority to proclaim neutrality, at least until Congress again convened.   Declaring neutrality, he retorted to Jefferson, was merely an executive act, and in its entirety the executive power lay with the President.   Constitutionally, then, the President had the requisite power to issue a proclamation of neutrality.   Countering Jefferson's contention that at that time it would be unwise to issue the proclamation, Hamilton insisted that unless immediate action were taken any potential profits would be outweighed by the dangers of involvement in war.   In view of America's present weakness and meager resources, such a policy would be suicidal.[63]

[60] Jefferson to Madison, n.p., June 23, 1793, in Ford, *Writings of Jefferson,* VI, 315-316; Thomas, *American Neutrality. . . ,* pp. 35-37; Schachner, *Thomas Jefferson. . . ,* I, 479-482.

[61] Hammond to Grenville, Philadelphia, March 7, 1793, No. 6, Henry Adams Transcripts.

[62] Opponents of the administration, long after the proclamation had gone into effect, continued to attack it as unconstitutional. See the resolution of the Democratic Society of Pennsylvania of April 10, 1794, in Woodbury, *Public Opinion in Philadelphia, 1789-1801,* p. 70.

[63] Thomas, *American Neutrality. . . ,* pp. 38-39; Hamilton's reasoning is in "Pacificus" No. 1, June 29, 1793, Hamilton, ed., *Hamilton's Works,* IV, 135-145.

When Britain went to war with France, Hammond received instructions to "make every practicable exertion to counteract" any effort to implement the Franco-American alliance.[64]   In following these instructions, he turned to Hamilton for inside information on the American government's stand on the alliance and neutrality. At first he feared *"secret* engagements" beyond those in the original alliance. His mind was set at ease by "Mr. Hamilton and others of consequence in this Government" that there were none. Hamilton further assured Hammond that the United States, in spite of the French alliance, would maintain a strict neutrality and would not honor French treaty obligations if in conflict with such neutrality. Hammond learned, moreover, "that the President concurs in sentiment with Mr. Hamilton."[65]   Strict neutrality, as envisaged by Hamiltonians, was precisely what Great Britain wanted. Such neutrality, in view of American treaty obligations to France, was of great advantage to England and distinctly disadvantageous to France. In effect, it nullified advantages of the 1778 alliance.

Yielding before the strength of the opposition, although not convinced by its argument, Jefferson consented to the issuing of the proclamation of neutrality. "If we preserve even a sneaking neutrality," he confessed to Monroe, "we shall be indebted for it to the President, & not to his counsellors."[66]   Hamilton's victory on this issue, as has been seen earlier, was of precedent-making significance. Control of the Executive over the determination and implementation of foreign policy was strengthened by broad constitutional interpretation. Washington's administration had struck a blow against the French alliance, pleased Great Britain so as to pave the way for the Jay treaty, and possibly fended off war in support of the French alliance.[67]

[64] Grenville to Hammond, Whitehall, Feb. 8, 1793, No. 3, in Mayo, *Instructions to British Ministers. . . , AHA Ann. Rep.* (1936), III, 35.

[65] Hammond to Grenville, Philadelphia, March 7, 1793, No. 6, April 2, 1793, No. 11, Henry Adams Transcripts.

[66] Jefferson to James Monroe, Philadelphia, May 5, 1793, Ford, *Writings of Jefferson,* VI, 239; for an analysis of Jefferson's ideas on neutrality and other aspects of foreign policy, see Wiltse, *The Jeffersonian Tradition, in American Democracy,* pp. 191-200.

[67] White, *The Federalist: A Study in Administrative History,* pp. 62-63; the proclamation convinced the British government of American desires to shun a pro-French neutrality and hence was a factor leading to the Jay treaty, Thomas, *American Neutrality. . . ,* pp. 49-50. When Thomas Pinckney, for

On April 22, 1793, Washington issued the proclamation of neutrality with the ostensible backing of all his Cabinet. To sweeten
Jefferson's defeat the word "neutrality" did not appear in the text,
but that the declaration was a proclamation of neutrality was recognized by Federalist and Republican alike.[68] To Republicans it was
a desertion of the French alliance. "The cause of France is the
cause of man," a Western critic said, "and neutrality is desertion."
America, bound by alliance to France, should assist her and if necessary go to war with England. Not only by treaty of alliance, he
added, are we bound to France, but also "by a higher principle,
if our assistance could avail; the great law of humanity . . . the heart
of America feels the cause of France."[69]

With the question of neutrality seemingly settled, the Cabinet
on April 19 next debated the second question, the problem of receiving an envoy from the French Republic. Involved in this also were
precedent-making foreign-policy principles; the acceptance of a
French Minister meant recognition of the legality of the French
Republic. This time Jefferson set the precedent, one which has
been followed by successive governments to the days of Woodrow
Wilson, and taken up again by the Herbert Hoover administration
to become once more the established recognition policy of the
United States. Actually, the question of recognition had been settled before the meeting of the Cabinet.[70]

---

example, informed the English government of America's decision to observe
a strict neutrality, there was great satisfaction in England. *Maryland Gazette*
(Annapolis), May 9, 1793.

[68] The proclamation is in *ASP FR,* I, 140. It was drafted by Edmund
Randolph, although often its authorship has been attributed to Jay. Thomas,
American Neutrality. . . , pp. 43-45. Rufus King expressed his pleasure over
the neutrality proclamation but deplored even the small sop allowed Jefferson.
He lamented: ". . . I would have wished to have seen in some part of it the
word "Neutrality" which every one would have understood and felt the force
of." King to Hamilton, April 24, 1793, in King, *Rufus King Correspondence,*
I, 439. Vice-President Adams also supported the proclamation. Dauer, *The
Adams Federalists,* p. 86. See also C. S. Hyneman, *The First American Neutrality: A Study of the American Understanding of Neutral Obligations during
the Years 1792 to 1815,* p. 13.

[69] Hugh H. Brackenridge in the *National Gazette,* April 20, 1793, and
July 27, 1793, quoted in Claude M. Newlin, *The Life and Writings of Hugh
Henry Brackenridge* (Princeton, 1932), pp. 132-133.

[70] Thomas, *American Neutrality. . . ,* p. 70; Schachner, *Thomas Jefferson. . . ,* I, 483.

With the President's support, the Secretary of State had, on March 12, 1793, instructed Gouverneur Morris, the American minister in Paris, to recognize the National Assembly as France's legal government. "We surely cannot deny to any nation," he explained at the time, "that right whereon our own government is founded, that every one may govern itself according to whatever form it pleases, and change these forms at it's [sic] own will; & that it may transact its business with foreign nations through whatever organ it thinks proper, whether king, convention, assembly, committee, president or anything else it may chuse. The will of the nation is the only thing essential to be regarded."[71]

Hamilton seems to have been the only Cabinet member who favored reversing the decision by not receiving Genet. In view of his isolated position, Hamilton surrendered on this point, and the Cabinet agreed unanimously that the President should receive the French minister. So divided were the President's advisors, however, that on the remaining questions Washington allowed them to prepare written opinions.[72]

Of these questions, those dealing with the status and applicability of the French treaties were the most important. By the treaty of alliance of 1778 the United States guaranteed "forever" against all other powers the possessions of the "Crown of France" in America.[73] Under the commercial treaty the United States and France agreed that if either were at war, the warships and privateers of the belligerent power should have the right to bring captured prizes into the other's ports. Those prizes were to be immune from arrest, seizure, search, duties, and examination concerning their lawfulness. The warships were to have the right at all times to depart with their prizes. Similar privileges were not to be extended to the enemy of either signatory.[74]

[71] Ford, *Writings of Jefferson*, VI, 199.

[72] Anas, April 18, 1793, *ibid.*, I, 226-227; Hamilton to Jay, April 19, 1793, Lodge, *The Works of Alexander Hamilton*, VIII, 297-298; Woolery, *The Relations of Thomas Jefferson to American Foreign Policy*, p. 107.

[73] Article 11, Miller, *Treaties and Other International Acts of the United States of America*, II, 39; Hammond, under this article, believed that any attack on the French West Indies "might justly be considered as *causus foederis.*" To Grenville, Philadelphia, March 7, 1793, No. 6, Henry Adams Transcripts.

[74] Article 17, Miller, *Treaties. . . ,* II, 16-17.

Other significant articles forbade citizens of either nation, under the penalty of being punished as pirates, to apply for or to accept any commission or letters of marque to privateer against the shipping and subjects of the other country.[75] Each country was prohibited from fitting out privateers of the other's enemies, as well as forbidden to sell such privateers supplies in its ports or to permit sale of their prizes.[76]

Those provisions obviously were incompatible with the strict neutrality Washington's government sought. If the treaties were still binding, which legally they were, it would take some involved diplomatic maneuvering to keep the United States at peace. England could well look upon fulfilment of the treaty obligations by the United States as cause of war. Hamilton and his cohorts saw no dilemma. As quickly as possible, they believed, the United States should deny any objectionable obligations and scuttle the alliance. Jefferson and his partisans also wanted to avoid war-breeding commitments; in doing so, however, they did not want to antagonize France.[77]

In their written opinions on yet-unanswered questions Hamilton and Jefferson marshaled evidence to support their differing views. Hamilton expounded the thesis that the French treaties were not applicable to the present circumstances, hence not binding upon the United States. When the legitimate government of France was re-established, they might then be continued. If, however, such continuance ran counter to the interests of the United States, they might then be renounced. This policy of suspension during the European conflict, he believed, would free the United States from interpreting and applying the onerous treaty articles, preserve American neutrality, and avoid conflict with Great Britain.

Involved though Hamilton's argument was, several points stand out. First, he maintained that the treaties had been made with Louis XVI. Since Louis had been driven from the throne, he

[75] Article 21, *ibid.,* p. 19.
[76] Article 22, *ibid.,* pp. 20-21. Only articles 17 and 22, maintained Hammond, conferred considerable advantage on the French. These articles plus the guarantee in the alliance "are the only stipulations which include anything like common principles of offense or defence against any other power. . . ." Hammond to Grenville, Philadelphia, March 7, 1793, No. 6.
[77] See Thomas, *American Neutrality. . . ,* p. 55.

said, it would be unfair of the United States to turn the agreements (eventually) against his heirs. It would be moral and just to suspend the treaties until the outcome of the war determined the permanent government of France.

Hamilton's argument further noted, correctly, that the alliance was defensive. Since France was engaged in an offensive war, the treaties were not applicable.[78] How he would determine what a defensive war was, he did not make clear. His most effective point was that the United States would be in a grave position if it aided the Revolutionary government of France and the royalists should emerge victorious. Undoubtedly the best solution was to suspend the treaties until the situation in France were clarified.[79]

In an extension of his argument on the nonapplicability of the French treaties, the Secretary of the Treasury urged that, although it had been decided to receive a French republican minister, Genet be accorded a qualified reception. The United States, he said, should reserve "to future consideration and discussion the question—whether the operation of the treaties. . . ought not to be deemed temporarily and provisionally suspended."[80] If the United States failed to add such a condition to Genet's reception, the applicability of the treaties would, he believed, be conceded. France's enemies would consider the United States France's committed ally and therefore an enemy, and the United States would be plunged into war.[81]

Jefferson could not accept that reasoning. Denying that the French treaties were inapplicable, in whole or in part, he countered Hamilton's argument almost point by point in his written answers to Washington's questions.[82]

[78] Genet, however, was instructed to place the blame for war on England; he was to convince Americans that France resorted to force only after using all means of conciliation within her power. Minister of Foreign Affairs (Le Brun) to Genet, Paris, Feb. 3, 1793, Genet Papers, Library of Congress, VIII, 2632-2633.

[79] Hamilton to Washington, April and May 2, 1793, in Lodge, *The Works of Alexander Hamilton,* IV, 74-112; the questions are discussed in Thomas, *American Neutrality. . . ,* pp. 53-90.

[80] Lodge, *The Works of Alexander Hamilton,* IV, 75.

[81] *Ibid.,* pp. 95-99. Such reasoning was in line with assurances Hamilton had given Hammond that although the 1778 alliance "could not be considered as null," it would not be enforced to such an extent as to "involve the United States in any difficulties or disputes with other powers." Hammond to Grenville, Philadelphia, April 2, 1793, No. 11, Henry Adams Transcripts.

[82] Jefferson: "Opinion on French Treaties," April 28, 1793, in Ford, *Writ-*

Regardless of change in the government in either France or the United States, the Secretary of State said, the treaties were binding. King or no king, treaties bound nations, not governments. If the treaties were binding they could not be suspended. Violation of treaty obligations could be justified only if the performing state were incapable of carrying out its commitment or were in imminent danger of self-destruction. This, he argued, was not the case with the United States at that time. Treaty obligations could not be suspended, as Hamilton would have it, because they were distasteful or dangerous—all political treaties were dangerous. Danger does not vitiate the commitment.

The clearest danger obviously was possible war with England over the "guarantee" of the French West Indies. Jefferson recognized this, but insisted that it was not an imminent danger, and so could not justify suspension of the treaties. The United States, moreover, might never be called upon to implement the guarantee; Jefferson doubted that France would invoke it at all.[83] If France did invoke the alliance, the question of applicability could be met at that time, but not before. To decide whether the Anglo-French war was offensive or defensive, or to decide which side began it, was also a premature and unnecessary action on the part of the United States, and a gratuitous insult to France.

Instead of avoiding war and preserving neutrality as Hamilton contended, Jefferson maintained that his colleague's policy would do just the opposite. "An injured friend is the bitterest of foes," he warned, "& France had not discovered either timidity, or over-much forbearance on the late occasions."

In conclusion Jefferson said that "not renouncing the treaties now is so far from being a breach of neutrality, that the doing it would be the breach, by giving just cause of war to France." He denied, too, that there was any connection between the applicability of

_____

ings of Jefferson, VI, 219-231; Thomas, American Neutrality. . . , pp. 60-65; Woolery, The Relation of Thomas Jefferson to American Foreign Policy, pp. 109-110.

[88] He recognized that "we shall be more useful [to France] as neutrals than as parties by the protection which our flag will give to supplies of provision." Jefferson to Morris, Philadelphia, April 20, 1793, in Ford, Writings of Jefferson, VI, 217; see also Darling, Our Rising Empire. . . , pp. 150-151.

the alliance and the reception, qualified or otherwise, of the French minister.[84]

In developing their opposing views on the question of the conditions of Genet's reception, Hamilton and Jefferson had again divided upon the theoretical and practical aspects of governmental recognition. The mere act of recognition, according to Jefferson, implied nothing more than acknowledgment of a *de facto* situation, that a government was in actual control and functioning over a given territory, and that there was no implied commitment or obligation, as Hamilton believed, in such recognition. Reservations to Genet's reception were not necessary to safeguard American neutrality; there was no need to correct any implied approval of the French government through the mere act of recognition. The French alliance had never been renounced; recognition of the new French government, even before receiving its envoy, had continued it in effect. There was nothing in the 1778 treaties on the reception of diplomatic envoys; governments sent diplomats and received them under the common usage of nations.

Jefferson's program of benevolent neutrality toward France to the detriment of England was, in the light of his foreign-policy ideas, logical and by no means unusual. In past conflicts third states had seldom been strictly impartial in their neutrality; usually they had been benevolently neutral in favor of one or the other belligerent.[85]

With the Cabinet split on the issues raised by his questions and with his two leading foreign-policy advisers far from neutral on the problem of neutrality, Washington made the final decision. In this instance he sided with Jefferson. Privately, the President had never doubted that the alliance was binding. At least he so told Jefferson.[86] With the positive decision on Genet's unqualified recep-

[84] The quotations are from "Opinion on French Treaties," April 28, 1793, in Ford, *Writings of Jefferson*, VI, 225, 231.

[85] For a discussion of neutrality obligations in the light of existing international law, see C. S. Hyneman, *The First American Neutrality*, pp. 15-16, 153-154; and his "Neutrality during the European Wars of 1792-1815," *American Journal of International Law*, XXIV (1930), 281-309.

[86] Jefferson was not alone in his stand; Randolph agreed with him on most points. Anas, April 18, 1793, in Ford, *Writings of Jefferson*, I, 227; Schachner, *Thomas Jefferson*. . . , I, 485; Thomas, *American Neutrality*. . . , p. 76; even stanch Federalist Rufus King maintained that Hamilton was on weak ground in declaring the French treaties suspended. To Hamilton, April 24, 1793, in King, *Rufus King Correspondence*, I, 439.

tion coupled with acceptance of the French treaties as binding, Washington set another foreign-policy precedent—American adherence to and respect for the sanctity of treaties.

The question of the issuing of a neutrality proclamation, as has been noted, brought into question the scope of the President's control over foreign affairs under the Constitution. Other questions were to raise similar problems. The Constitution was vague on specific responsibilities for the conduct of foreign affairs, and at this time there were no established precedents to serve as guides in the making of foreign policy. Decisions taken then were to become the precedents of later years. In this state of uncertainty under an untried four-year-old Constitution it was to be expected that Jefferson, Hamilton, and others, in view of their differing political ideas, would disagree as to the constitutional basis of foreign-policy decisions. The problem of responsibility for control of foreign affairs was implicit in the thirteenth and last of the President's questions. Should he call Congress into special session because of the European crisis?

Jefferson, holding the view that the Constitution granted Congress a considerable role in the conduct of foreign affairs (which by precedent has since accrued to the Executive), proposed that Congress be convened. His colleagues in the Cabinet took the opposite view. While Jefferson's stand was an outgrowth of his interpretation of the Constitution, doubtless it was dictated also by partisan political considerations. By this time he realized that the administration was Federalist-dominated and could not be changed from within. By this time he had set his course in politics, and it was a collision course with that of the administration.

If the administration was not favorably disposed toward republican France, popular sentiment was. This sentiment would, perhaps, spread to Congress and help to mold foreign policy.[87] In the newly elected Congress, Republicans would, for the first time, have a dominant voice; they would control the House, and the Senate would be divided about evenly with Federalists. By supporting a call for a

[87] Fear of popular support for France was an important factor, in fact, which motivated other members of the Cabinet in opposing Jefferson's proposal. "Knox," for example, "sd we shd have had fine work if Congress had been sitting these last two months. The fool [Knox] thus let out the secret." Anas, Aug. 3, 1793, in Ford, *Writings of Jefferson,* I, 255.

special session and emphasizing the role of Congress in the formulating of foreign policy, Jefferson would hasten the day when his party would have an important voice in the conduct of foreign policy and could perhaps counterbalance Federalist predominance in the Executive Branch.

After seeing that Hamilton's views on the other questions dealing with the alliance and recognition of the French Republic did not prevail whereas his own did, the Secretary of State realized that at this time the aid of Congress was not essential to prevent implementation of extreme Federalist policies toward France. He therefore joined with the other Cabinet members in advising against calling Congress into immediate session.[88] Again Washington's government set a precedent for retaining foreign-policy initiative almost solely in the Executive.

* * * * *

While Washington and his advisors debated problems of neutrality and alliance, Genet in Charleston had begun his questionable activities which were to test American neutrality and the French alliance. Even though, as Jefferson had anticipated, Genet's instructions did not call for invoking the 1778 alliance to bring America into the war, they did imply that being an ally of France and remaining impartially neutral in the ally's fight were incompatible. While France preferred American neutrality to belligerency, the neutrality she desired was one weighted in her favor to a degree which involved serious risks for the United States.[89]

[88] For details, see Thomas, *American Neutrality. . .* , pp. 66-68.

[89] The alliance and guarantee of the French West Indies were in the French view of little value at this time. Their value lay in the future. The United States was a country whose resources were increasing incalculably and hence its value as an ally increased in proportion. Supplement to Genet's instructions, n.p., n. d., in Turner, *CFM*, p. 210. Too, the French hoped that the lure of unrestricted commerce with their West Indies would be sufficiently strong so that Americans would not allow them to fall into British hands. Woodfin, "Citizen Genet and His Mission," p. 78. Later, too, the French continued to maintain that American neutrality was of greater advantage than participation in the war. Statement of François Joseph Noël in Charles F. Adams, ed., *Memoirs of John Quincy Adams, Comprising Portions of His Diary from 1795 to 1848* (12 vols., Philadelphia, 1874-77), I, 125 (diary entry of Oct. 20, 1795, The Hague). In view of international practice, France's view on American neutrality was logical; see Hyneman, *First American Neutrality*, pp. 15-16.

George Hammond saw the situation of the French Republic clearly. "Exposed to formidable enemies in Europe, and unsupported by a single alliance upon that continent," he wrote of France, "it is by no means a matter of surprize, that its present rulers should direct their views to the United States and should entertain the hope that a supposed similarity of sentiment, heightened by the offer of commercial advantages, may induce this country to extend still farther its connexions with France."[90] For England the status of the 1778 alliance was critically important. Even though England's ministers believed that France would not invoke the alliance, they sought in every way to counteract any attempt to implement it. With the spread of the European war, therefore, the French alliance became an important international pledge.[91]

Genet's instructions had directed him to fortify Americans in the principles which led them to unite with France against England in 1778 and to convince them that France was their natural ally.[92] He was to work for compliance with the treaties of 1778, and to obtain from the American government as favorable a construction of them as possible. Accordingly, he was to see to it that articles which favored French shipping and commerce were executed fully; in American ports French maritime activities were to have the advantage over those of the enemy.

Particularly noteworthy were instructions to begin negotiation for a new and stronger treaty to supersede that of 1778, an alliance that would bind closer the world's leading republics.[93] France now was ready to bring into the open negotiations for the new commercial treaty Jefferson and "Citizen" Ternant had discussed. Genet was to negotiate a treaty combining commercial with political in-

[90] Hammond to Grenville, Philadelphia, March 7, 1793, No. 6, Henry Adams Transcripts.

[91] Grenville to Hammond, Whitehall, Jan. 4 and Feb. 8, 1793, Mayo, *Instructions to British Ministers, AHA Ann. Rep.* (1936), III, 33, 34-35. The British view on the alliance was that France was conducting an offensive war and hence would not venture to invoke the 1778 alliance.

[92] Instructions to Genet, Dec., 1792, in Turner, *CFM*, p. 202; additional instructions, dated Jan. 4, 1793, are in AAE CP EU, Vol. XXXVII, ff. 13-14.

[93] Hammond, of course, was directed to thwart any such treaty. Grenville to Hammond, Whitehall, Jan. 4, 1793, in Mayo, *Instructions to British Ministers, AHA Ann. Rep.* (1936), III, 33.

terests, an alliance that would establish an intimate co-operation that would serve to expand the "Empire of Liberty."

Other important aspects of Genet's instructions included plans for the conquest, with American assistance, of Spanish America and of Canada, the latter to go to the United States. Embodying the grandiose revolutionary schemes of the Venezuelan adventurer, Francisco de Miranda, France's plans for overthrowing Spain in South America actually antedated the Genet mission. To draw the United States into an anti-Spanish partnership of revolution and conquest France offered American statesmen the Floridas. Jefferson, apparently, snapped at the bait.[94]

While awaiting American aid Genet was to sow French revolutionary principles in Louisiana, Kentucky, and other provinces bordering the United States, and to work to open the Mississippi to navigation from Kentucky. To carry out this part of the mission he had a supply of blank naval and military commissions to be issued to Americans, Frenchmen, and Indian chiefs who would fight France's enemies, and was to support in other ways agents who might aid him in achieving those objectives. He was to use his diplomacy to secure payment of the debt the United States still owed to France, and with the payments furnish his government with sorely needed provisions and foodstuffs. Secret instructions directed him to propagandize Americans, to influence them so they would favor France in her struggle. Assured of the favorable disposition of Jefferson and Madison, he had orders to tamper with American domestic politics for whatever advantage might accrue to France.[95]

[94] The Anas, Feb. 20, 1793, Ford, *Writings of Jefferson,* I, 217-218; William S. Robertson, *The Life of Miranda* (2 vols., Chapel Hill, N. C., 1929), I, 122-130; Frederick J. Turner, "The Policy of France toward the Mississippi Valley in the Period of Washington and Adams," *American Historical Review,* X (Jan., 1905), 259-260; Albert Sorel, *L'Europe et la révolution française* (8 vols., Paris, 1885-1904), III, 157-175.

[95] Instructions to Genet, Dec., 1792, in Turner, *CFM,* pp. 204-206; the need for provisions in France was stressed by the Minister of the Interior, who asked the Minister of Foreign Affairs to instruct Genet to obtain them. Paris, Jan. 13, 1793, AAE CP EU, Vol. XXXVII, ff. 53-54. The British knew or guessed the main points in Genet's instructions; Hammond was directed to be vigilant in detecting provision shipments to France; he was to inform British commanders in American waters of such shipments. Grenville to Hammond, Whitehall, March 12, 1793, Mayo, *Instructions to British Ministers, AHA Ann. Rep.* (1936), III, 37-40. Tampering with politics and politicians,

The objectives of Genet's mission were logical ones for a country fighting a desperate war. That he might do everything possible to cripple Spain and England and to aid France required that he strive for American assistance in realizing his objectives.[96] Without it his mission was destined to fail. The possibility of such assistance, limited though it might be, caused alarm in Great Britain and led to preparations for appropriate countermeasures. If all this was not sufficient to plunge the United States into war, it certainly contravened the Washington administration's deliberate policy of impartial neutrality.[97]

Genet's first appearance in America—the landing at Charleston—portended trouble. Why had he landed at a place so remote from the seat of government? Philadelphia was no farther from France than Charleston. According to Genet, contrary winds rather than his own wishes had dictated the choice of landing site; others have discerned more sinister reasons for the choice. In any case, his conduct at Charleston was enough to arouse suspicion, even where none had existed previously. Remaining in Charleston eleven days instead of pushing on immediately to Philadelphia to present his credentials, he started promptly to implement his instructions.[98]

of course, was inconsistent with the specific and clear instructions that Genet was not to interfere in internal American affairs. Taking advantage of known party divisions and seeking out favorable political leaders to advance French principles certainly was interfering in internal affairs. See Lebrun to Genet, Feb. 24, 1793, in Turner, *CFM*, p. 215 n.; Woodfin, "Genet and His Mission," p. 78; Richard K. Murdoch, "The Genesis of the Genet Schemes," *FAR*, II (April-June, 1949), 81-82. To tamper with American politics was the intention of the Girondist government. Jefferson was told that Genet would strengthen too-long neglected Franco-American relations. [Minister of Foreign Affairs] to Jefferson, Paris, Jan. 13, 1793, Genet Papers, VIII, 2588.

[96] Subsequent instructions usually emphasized this. [Minister of Foreign Affairs] to Genet, May [?], 1793, "Observations sur les reproches faits au Citoyen Genet," May, 1793, AAE CP EU, Vol. XXXVII, ff. 384-385, 388-399.

[97] Grenville to Hammond, Whitehall, March 12, 1793, Mayo, *Instructions to British Ministers, AHA Ann. Rep.* (1936), III, 37-40. Great Britain expected the United States to uphold neutrality.

[98] The question of Genet's Charleston landing is discussed in Thomas, *American Neutrality. . . ,* pp. 79-80. For Charleston's reaction to Genet's activities, see Ulrich B. Phillips, "The South Carolina Federalists," *AHR*, XIV (April-July, 1909), 733. Charles Biddle in *Autobiography of Charles Biddle, 1745-1821* (Philadelphia, 1883), p. 251, asserts that Genet landed at Charleston in an effort to gage American public opinion—if the United States would join

Aided by Governor William Moultrie of South Carolina and by the enthusiastic citizenry of Charleston, Genet quickly established prize courts to dispose of prizes brought in by *L'Embuscade,* and at the same time outfitted privateers to cruise against British shipping. With Michel Ange Mangourit, French Consul in Charleston, he laid the groundwork of plans to raise two American armies, composed of frontiersmen, which were to invade neighboring Spanish provinces. Here his blank commissions came into use. George Rogers Clark of Kentucky, for example, was commissioned major-general to head an American frontier army aimed at conquest of New Orleans. After launching these projects, Genet headed for Philadelphia.[99]

Instead of taking the easier and faster trip by sea, Genet sent *L'Embuscade* to Philadelphia while he proceeded overland. His journey northward was a triumphant procession; Republicans, Francophiles, Anglophobes, and ordinary Americans by the score turned out to welcome him and to wave him on. It took him twenty-eight days rather than the expected two weeks to reach Philadelphia. Few, if any, cities outdid the national capital in acclaiming the French republican emissary; to him the acclaim was "a triumph for Liberty."[100] The succession of joyful public demon-

France in the war. A French royalist maintained that Genet landed at Charleston because the French government wished "to raise the spirit of the people of the Western States in favour of the pretensions of the french republic." An unknown correspondent to William Windham, Philadelphia, June 1, 1793, in Windham, *Windham Papers,* I, 128.

[99] Genet to Minister of Foreign Affairs, Charleston, April 16, 1793, in Turner, *CFM,* pp. 211-213; for details on Clarke, see James A. James, *The Life of George Rogers Clark* (Chicago, 1928), pp. 411, 419-420; Richard K. Murdoch, *The Georgia-Florida Frontier 1793-1796: Spanish Reaction to French Intrigue and American Designs* (Berkeley, Calif., 1951), pp. 9-14; Richard Lowitt, "Activities of Citizen Genet in Kentucky, 1793-1794," *Filson Club History Quarterly,* XXII (Oct., 1948), 252-254; Bemis, "Jefferson," in Bemis, *American Secretaries of State. . . ,* II, 78.

[100] The quotation is from Genet to Minister of Foreign Relations, Philadelphia, May 18, 1793, in Turner, *CFM,* pp. 214-215. Prominent Pennsylvania Republicans had decided that Genet's Philadelphia reception should surpass all others. Such a welcome would emphasize America's regard for her sister republic, and, more important, it would aid Republicans in organizing for the autumnal gubernatorial election. From the beginning, consequently, it came to be that Genet's mission was thrust into the hustings of embryonic party politics in the United States; see Raymond Walters, Jr., *Alexander James*

strations and the warm response of Americans he had met personally up to this time were undoubtedly sufficient to convince him that
the United States would go to almost any extreme to support France.
He was destined, nonetheless, for a rude fall from exhilarating
heights.

Genet's first jolt in the United States came with news of the
proclamation of neutrality, news he heard in Richmond, Virginia;
the President delivered the second personally. The cool official
reception Washington gave him was far different from the warmth
of the people's embrace. Even before the French envoy reached the
United States the President had decided, as Hamilton had advised,
to receive him without "too much warmth or cordiality." As a
description of the actual audience, this was an understatement.[101]

In presenting his letters of credence Genet did not ingratiate himself with the Federalist administration. At the time, he made clear
that his government considered the 1778 alliance in force and applicable under present circumstances and that it had the right to demand guarantee of its West Indies possessions. He declared, however, that France did not wish to invoke the alliance.[102]

There was little doubt, particularly in the minds of Federalists,
that Genet and his activities would be fatal to American neutrality;
many thought that he had secret instructions to involve the country
in the war against Great Britain.[103] In the popular enthusiasm he

---

Dallas: Lawyer-Politician-Financier, pp. 43-44. Later Philadelphia Republican leaders gave evidence of their hostility to Washington's policies. At a
dinner in Philadelphia in June, 1793, for example, they used Genet and the
occasion as a means of protest against administration policies. Woodfin,
"Citizen Genet and His Mission," pp. 234-238.

[101] The quotation is from The Anas, March 30, 1793, in Ford, *Writings of
Jefferson,* I, 224. Later, Genet remarked about Washington's coldness; he
believed that royalist refugees had influenced Washington and had turned the
President against the French Revolution. He felt also that through Hamilton
and Gouverneur Morris, they had turned Washington against the alliance.
Genet to Minister of Foreign Affairs, New York, Oct. 7, 1793, *CFM,* pp. 244-
246.

[102] Remarked Jefferson: "It is impossible for anything to be more affectionate, more magnanimous than the purport of his mission. . . . In short he
offers everything & asks nothing." To Madison, Philadelphia, May 19, 1793,
in Ford, *Writings of Jefferson,* VI, 260-261.

[103] William Vans Murray Papers, Commonplace Book, July 28, 1795. The
British minister was aware that despite the general appearance of good will
toward Genet "his general conduct has been very far from making a favorable

aroused, furthermore, he posed a threat to Federalist political ascendancy. Fearful of the publicly demonstrated attachment of Americans to Revolutionary France, Federalists were struck numb by
the "terrorism excited by Genet."[104]   Although Jefferson thought
otherwise, the proclamation of neutrality and Genet, as France's
minister, could not for long coexist. One or the other had to go.
The Girondist emissary's ensuing activities underscored this.

---

impression on the President and the other members of his Government."
Nonetheless Hammond was convinced that Genet sought to form a party to
overawe, if not subvert, Washington's government. Hammond to Grenville,
June 10, 1793, No. 13, July 7, 1793, Henry Adams Transcripts.

[104] So recounted John Adams twenty years later to Jefferson, Quincy, June
30, 1813, in Adams, *Works,* X, 47.

CHAPTER SEVEN

GENET AND NEUTRALITY

INCOMPATIBLES

France, then, being on the offensive in the present war, and our alliance with her being defensive only, it follows that the casus foederis, *or condition of our guaranty, cannot take place; and that the United States are free to refuse a performance of that guarantee if demanded.*—Alexander Hamilton in *"Pacificus"* No. II, July 3, 1793.

It is certainly intolerable arrogance in the President and other officers in the federal government to differ from M. Genet, in his construction of the French treaty. Had not this gentleman a right to determine what its meaning was and act accordingly without consulting America?—"Ca Ira" in *Columbian Centinel* (Boston), September 11, 1793.

* * * * *

THE FRENCH REPUBLIC, fighting for her national existence, devoted her main energies to European affairs and to the war. In comparison, relations with the United States mattered little. She did not need her American ally's active participation in the war; direct American aid probably would have had little effect on the war's outcome. Yet, by treaty the United States was France's ally "for ever." In the then state of French affairs the strategic role of the United States, while not decisive, was not inconsequential.

The United States was more valuable to France as a neutral ally than as a feeble cobelligerent; it was valuable as a source of supplies and as a neutral carrier of French goods.[1] France needed money,

---

[1] France, as the inferior naval power, needed all the neutral help she could get. Heckscher, *The Continental System*, p. 47; Aulard, "La Dette Américaine. . . ," *La Revue de Paris*, XXXII, 540. To take advantage of the neutral American flag, French traders would change their vessels from French to American registry by mock sales or other means, or they would load French

provisions, and foodstuffs badly, and these might be had from a friendly United States. Cut off from her colonies by the British fleet, her vessels swept from the seas, France also looked to the United States to supply her West Indies possessions with necessary provisions.[2]

As a cobelligerent the United States would be cut off from France and her possessions by the British fleet. In the over-all strategy of the war, a belligerent United States would be useful to France only as a force diverting some English energies away from the main struggle.[3]

As the naval inferior in the war, France, dependent on the United States for bases and shipping, at first sought to find in America seamen she could use on her privateers sailing against the British.[4] To carry out this program, to make in effect the neutral United States a base and protected sanctuary for operations of French privateers, called for a broad interpretation of French privileges under the 1778 treaties.[5] If, however, these privileges were exploited fully, as Genet's instructions proposed, the United States might well have

---

goods on American ships as American property; see, for example, John Bach McMaster, *The Life and Times of Stephen Girard: Mariner and Merchant* (2 vols., New York, 1918), I, 176, 180. Gouverneur Morris was aware that France "may, as a nation, derive greater advantage from our neutrality than from our alliance," and so informed Washington. To Washington, Paris, March 2, 1793, *ASP FR*, I, 396.

[2] Albion and Pope, *Sea Lanes in Wartime, The American Experience, 1775-1942*, p. 71. Cut off from Baltic sources by the war, France also sought to obtain naval stores and timbers from neutral United States. Robert G. Albion, *Forests and Sea Power: The Timber Problem of the Royal Navy, 1652-1862* (Cambridge, Mass., 1926), pp. 347-348.

[3] Bemis, "Washington's Farewell Address: A Foreign Policy of Independence," *American Historical Review*, XXXIX, 250-251.

[4] So complete was British naval ascendancy at this time that French and British operations in North American waters were little more than "sideshows." Gerald S. Graham, *Empire of the North Atlantic: The Maritime Struggle for North America* (Toronto, 1950), pp. 217-218.

[5] This is reflected in an unsigned essay dated merely 1793 and entitled: "Reflexions sur les traites d'alliance & d'amitié entre la France et l'Amérique par un ami des deux Républiques" in AAE CP EU, Vol. XXXVII, ff. 147-153. According to the author, f. 151, even though under the terms of the alliance she could invoke American aid in the war, always-generous France wanted nothing but impartial neutrality from the United States under the terms and privileges of the 1778 treaties. Such privileges precluded an impartial neutrality.

plummeted into war with England. This, as has been indicated, was the critical factor in Hamilton's domestic and foreign policy, in important aspects of developing national politics, and in the formulating of American foreign policy, particularly in the agreed-upon neutrality.

While both the United States and France had an obvious stake in American neutrality in 1793, America's concept of neutrality and of her treaty obligations differed from the French view. Without French help the United States probably could not have emerged a nation in 1783. For this aid Americans were in 1793 still grateful. Yet the sense of obligation, strong though it was, could not in the long run be expected to override considerations of self-interest and national existence.[6] America's struggle for national survival still continued; was still precarious.

To survive as a small nation, without being either a French or English pawn, the United States had to steer its course between French and British foreign policies. This meant a policy of cautious neutrality, not of partisan neutrality as France would have it. In French eyes, of course, because of British naval supremacy, strict neutrality was a partial neutrality favorable to England. In 1793, as it has been since, it was impossible to be impartially neutral. If the United States had acceded to French desires as set forth in Genet's instructions, England might have plunged the United States into the war, and the American experiment in democracy might have been destroyed before it had been able to sink roots. Any policy of neutrality or of assistance to France, any implementation or interpretation of the French treaties, had to be undertaken with an eye to England's probable reaction.

*   *   *   *   *

News of Genet's Charleston reception reached Philadelphia as Attorney General Edmund Randolph was drafting the proclamation of neutrality. On its heels, a week later, came information which challenged the newly devised proclamation and which raised the

[6] At one time Americans expressed extravagant sentiments such as this: "That America ought to join France against England in two future wars; one to pay the debt of gratitude already contracted, and the other to show ourselves as generous as France had been." John Adams and others did not take such sentimental ideas seriously. Quoted from John Adams to John Jay, Auteuil, April 13, 1785, in Adams, *Works,* VIII, 235-236.

problem of executing it notwithstanding treaty obligations to France. On the voyage to Philadelphia the heavily armed *L'Embuscade* took several English prizes; it captured one of them, the merchant vessel *Grange,* inside Delaware Bay. Other French vessels—privateers fitted out in the United States and manned by Frenchmen and Americans—soon were sailing into American harbors with English prizes in tow, some of them captured in American territorial waters. It was not long before American ports were swarming with French privateers.[7]

Those activities elicited immediate protests from George Hammond; he demanded in particular restoration of the *Grange,* pointing out that the French had captured it within United States territorial waters.[8] On May 3, 1793, Jefferson notified Ternant, who still headed the French legation pending Genet's arrival, of the British protest. He informed the French Minister "that the U. S. being at peace with all parties cannot see with indifference it's [*sic*] territory or jurisdiction violated by either," and asked that the *Grange,* its crew, and cargo be detained until the American government could decide upon a plan of action.[9] Ternant took no action; the matter awaited Genet's arrival.

Meanwhile Washington's Cabinet investigated the case and deliberated America's neutral obligations. Basic in its considerations were two questions, the maritime extent of American territory and the prevention of belligerent hostilities within American territory. In the opinion of Attorney General Edmund Randolph, Delaware Bay was American national territory. The French had seized the *Grange,* therefore, on neutral ground, an illegal act; it should be restored to the British. The Cabinet accepted Randolph's opinion; so Jefferson on May 15, 1793, informed Ternant of the decision. As

[7] For details see Thomas, *American Neutrality.* . . , pp. 91 ff.; Gardner W. Allen, *Our Naval War with France* (Boston, 1909), pp. 5-6; Bemis, "Jefferson," in Bemis, *The American Secretaries of State.* . . , II, 79; Schachner, *The Founding Fathers,* pp. 245-248.

[8] Hammond was not displeased. To Lord Grenville he remarked: "It has been an extremely fortunate circumstance that almost immediately after the appearance of this declaration of neutrality, events should have arisen which have brought the sincerity of it to a practical test." British State Papers, May 17, 1793, No. 14, quoted in Thomas, *American Neutrality.* . . , p. 91.

[9] Jefferson to Ternant, Philadelphia, May 3, 1793, in Ford, *Writings of Jefferson,* VI, 236-237.

if sacrificing a right, Genet, who arrived two days later, acquiesced, and restored the vessel to the British.[10] Almost immediately, reported Hammond, the *Grange* case brought the sincerity of the neutrality proclamation "to a practical test."[11]

While the government disposed of the *Grange* case without much trouble, other problems raised by Genet's activities were more complicated. In addition to equipping privateers in American ports and recruiting American seamen on American soil, Genet challenged American sovereignty by granting French consuls in the United States authority to act as admiralty prize courts for the condemnation and sale of enemy prizes brought into port by French privateers. These activities alarmed Federalists. "These infractions of our neutrality, will, I presume," Oliver Wolcott, Jr., said, "be censored by the government; they must be restrained in the future or this country will inevitably be dragged into the war to the utter ruin of our affairs."[12] Although in agreement on a general policy of neutrality, Washington's official family divided on some specific problems of the implementation of neutrality and the interpretation of the French treaties.

On the issues of privateering commissions conferred by Genet and condemnation of prizes in American ports by French consular courts, the Cabinet did not disagree. Such practices were illegal and had to stop; they were not allowed by treaty practices and violated American sovereignty. The Cabinet decided, in addition, that outfitting privateers in American ports violated neutrality, and should stop. American citizens enlisting in the United States to serve a foreign power would be prosecuted.[13] This, in substance, was

[10] Jefferson to Ternant, Philadelphia, May 15, 1793, *ibid.*, pp. 254-257. The American position provided a famous precedent in international law; see Hyneman, *The First American Neutrality. . .* , pp. 99-100; Woolery, *The Relation of Thomas Jefferson to American Foreign Policy*, p. 113; Bemis, "Jefferson," in Bemis, *The American Secretaries of State. . .* , II, 80; Thomas, *American Neutrality*, pp. 96-97.

[11] Hammond to Grenville, Philadelphia, April 2, 1793, Henry Adams Transcripts. The British government was pleased with Hammond's efforts to make the United States toe the line of strict neutrality. Grenville to Hammond, Whitehall, July 5, 1793, No. 8, in Mayo, *Instructions to British Ministers. . .* , *American Historical Association Annual Report for the Year 1936*, III, 42.

[12] Oliver Wolcott, Jr., to Frederick Wolcott, Philadelphia, May 20, 1793, in Gibbs, ed., *Wolcott Papers*, I, 100.

[13] The President and his Cabinet acted as they did because they believed that

[12] Oliver Wolcott, Jr. to Frederick Wolcott, Philadelphia, May 20, 1793, in

the code of neutrality hammered out in Cabinet meetings by the Washington administration.

In the course of debate over these questions, Jefferson, at times supported by Randolph, favored an interpretation of neutral obligations advantageous to France, while Hamilton, backed by Knox, took an opposite stand. In most instances, Washington decided the issue. Jefferson complained that his colleagues were playing England's game and would thus "force France to attack us."[14] Neither he nor Hamilton, apparently, could divorce neutrality issues from political considerations and from their feelings toward the belligerent powers.

The Secretary of the Treasury had warned the British minister against the Secretary of State, pointing out that *"he* [Hamilton] shall exert his influence to defeat the success of any proposition on the part of France, which tempting as it might appear, might ultimately render it necessary for this government to depart from the observance of as strict a neutrality as is compatible with its present engagements, and which is so essential to its real interests."[15]

While Hamilton carried on his revealing intercourse with Hammond, Jefferson turned to Genet. At first, Jefferson was pleased with Genet, with the great public ovations he received, and with the apparent strength of Republican and pro-French sentiment in the country. He greeted the new French minister cordially, took him into his confidence, explained the political situation, and warned him against Hamilton and the Anglophiles, especially against their influence over the President. Jefferson realized that in government councils the cards were stacked against him, and against Genet, although the Frenchman contributed immeasurably to his own downfall.[16]

American independence depended on a strong assertion of sovereignty; their stand was not predicated on any obligation under international law. See Hyneman, "Neutrality during the European Wars of 1792-1815," *American Journal of International Law,* XXIV, 284, and his *The First American Neutrality,* pp. 118-144; Hamilton, "No Jacobin," No. V, Aug. 16, 1793, in Hamilton, ed., *Hamilton's Works,* VII, 138-139. These problems on Genet and neutrality are treated in detail in Thomas, *American Neutrality,* chaps. iv and v.

[14] The Anas, May 20, 1793, in Ford, *Writings of Jefferson,* I, 230.

[15] Hammond to Grenville, Philadelphia, March 7, 1793, No. 6, Henry Adams Transcripts.

[16] See Schachner, *Thomas Jefferson. . . ,* I, 489-490; Woolery, *The Relation*

Jefferson confided to James Monroe the difficulty of upholding the French side in government councils. He explained that "every inch of ground must be fought in our councils to desperation in order to hold up the face of even a sneaking neutrality, for our votes are generally 2½ against 1½."[17] The split vote was Randolph. Yet Jefferson exerted whatever political influence he could muster to prevent American neutrality from injuring France.[18] Through supplementary personal representations Jefferson tried to soften the shock of official complaints against Genet. Although officially he presented the government's views and adhered to the adopted neutrality decisions, Jefferson disavowed any personal support for the actions taken; he informed Genet that he was to be considered "as the passive spokesman of the President."[19]

In defense of his conduct, Genet contended that the 1778 commercial treaty "expressly" authorized France to arm and to equip privateers in American ports, allowed French privateers to bring their prizes into the ports, and granted French consular prize courts the right to condemn and sell prizes. The treaty did not confer such positive privileges. Article 22 obligated the United States to close its ports to the outfitting of British privateers, and to their prizes, while allowing French privateers and their prizes the use of American ports. This did not, as Genet argued, therefore grant to France what was denied to Great Britain.[20]

Yet Jefferson, along with other Americans, believed that the granting to France of the rights denied to Britain was understood by the United States as well as France. Hamilton saw no such implication.[21] On the basis of convenience and friendship, the United

of Thomas Jefferson to American Foreign Policy, p. 113; Genet to Minister of Foreign Affairs, New York, Oct. 7, 1793, No. 13A, in Turner, *CFM*, p. 245.

[17] Jefferson to Monroe, Philadelphia, May 5, 1793, in Ford, *Writings of Jefferson*, VI, 239.

[18] Jefferson to Madison, May 12, 1793, *ibid.*, pp. 250-251.

[19] Genet to Minister of Foreign Affairs, New York, Oct. 7, 1793, No. 14, in Turner, *CFM*, p. 254.

[20] See Jefferson to Genet, Philadelphia, June 17, 1793, and Genet to Jefferson, Philadelphia, June 22, 1793, *ASP FR*, I, 154-156; Hyneman, *The First American Neutrality*, pp. 74-77; Bemis, "Jefferson," in Bemis, *The American Secretaries of State. . .* , II, 79-80.

[21] *The Anas*, May 20, 1793, in Ford, *Writings of Jefferson*, I, 229; Hamilton, "No Jacobin," No. I, Aug., 1793, Hamilton, ed., *Hamilton's Works*, VII, 118-123.

States could have granted France the right to arm privateers in its ports and to set up prize courts. Such action, however, would have contravened America's avowed impartial neutrality and have served as the invitation for Britain to drag the country into an unwanted war. Despite his French sympathies Jefferson apparently saw the dangers, agreeing that to remain neutral the United States had to prevent France from using American ports as bases for hostile actions.[22]

Rules for neutral conduct could be debated and formulated, but their enforcement was another matter. Despite Jefferson's care in approaching the French minister on neutrality violations and his studied efforts to placate the zealous Frenchman, Genet refused to order offending French privateers from American ports. He had expected something more than merely expressed friendship from the United States; he wanted the tangible support of an ally.[23] The result, by the end of June, 1793, was an open struggle between Genet, backed by Francophile elements, and the Executive authority of the American government.

* * * * *

Factors other than neutrality violations and Genet's intransigence contributed to growing Franco-American frictions and to Franco-Federalist bitterness. In keeping with his instructions, Genet initiated his official correspondence with Secretary of State Jefferson by requesting advance payment of the outstanding American debt to France. Since advance payments had already been made to Ternant, and the original contracts allowed advance payments, this was not an unreasonable request, nor could it be construed as a violation of neutrality. Yet the British, basing their view on an earlier refusal by the United States to make advance payments to France, regarded it "as characteristic of this [Washington's] Government to entangle itself in no new or close connexion with France, and consequently

[22] Bemis, "Jefferson," in Bemis, *The American Secretaries of State. . . ,* II, 80; see Jefferson to Genet and to Hammond, Philadelphia, June 5, 1793, in Ford, *Writings of Jefferson,* VI, 282-283, 285-287.

[23] Genet to Jefferson, Philadelphia, June 8, 1793, *ASP FR,* I, 151; Thomas, *American Neutrality. . . ,* p. 134.

to observe as strict a neutrality as might be consistent with its existing engagements."[24]

As an inducement to advance payment at this time, Genet indicated that the money would be spent in the United States to purchase foodstuffs, provisions, and various supplies for Saint Domingue
and France. Actually, he intended to divert some of the funds to
finance privateers and to raise hostile expeditions against English
and Spanish possessions in the Western Hemisphere.[25]

If the Treasury could stand the drain, Jefferson favored making
advance payments on the debt installments as requested, as he had
with Ternant. Hamilton did not. He wanted a curt refusal without explanation. Finally the Cabinet accepted Hamilton's view,
somewhat modified, and Jefferson came to see that it was to the
government's advantage to refuse advance payment. Washington's
government, therefore, turned down Genet's first request, and also
subsequent demands, for debt payment in advance.[26]

Immediately following his request for advance debt payment,
Genet brought to the attention of the American government another
item prominent in his instructions, the matter of commercial relations. First he announced grandiloquently that the National Convention had by recent decree opened all French home and colonial
ports to Americans on the same footing as if they were Frenchmen.
This concession to free trade between the two countries, an almost
complete breakdown of previous French commercial restrictions,
Genet implied was a special privilege, a token of good will France
granted uniquely to the United States. Actually, as has been seen,
it was a war measure the French promulgated immediately after
the outbreak of hostilities with the objective of luring needed supplies in neutral bottoms into their ports. In principle, nonetheless,

[24] Hammond to Grenville, Philadelphia, April 2, 1793, No. 11, Henry
Adams Transcripts.

[25] Genet to Jefferson, Philadelphia, May 22, 1793, *ASP FR*, I, 142-143;
Frederick J. Turner, "The Origins of Genet's Projected Attack on Louisiana
and the Floridas," *AHR*, III (July, 1898), 665.

[26] See Hamilton to Washington, June 5, 1793, and Jefferson to Washington,
June 6, 1793, in Hamilton, ed., *Hamilton's Works*, IV, 414-417; Darling,
Our Rising Empire. . . , p. 159; Channing, *A History of the United States,*
IV, 131.

it accorded with Jefferson's earlier plan for a Franco-American commercial treaty.[27]

The same decree which opened French ports also directed the French executive to negotiate with the United States for reciprocal concessions; Genet was so instructed. Accordingly, the French minister, immediately after arriving in Philadelphia, opened negotiations for a new treaty, to be actually a political as well as a commercial treaty, "a true family compact" on a liberal and fraternal basis. Earlier there had been considerable sentiment in the American government for such a treaty, without the new political bonds. Now, in the midst of war, such a proposal, even to Jefferson, was like a siren screaming danger. The intimate alliance France proposed would undoubtedly have engulfed the United States in hostilities.[28]

Acting for the administration, Jefferson evaded the issue by delay. He informed Genet that nothing could be done without the advice and consent of the Senate, which would not again convene until autumn. The proposal got no further. Soon caught in the controversy over neutrality and politics, Genet did not again pursue the matter.[29]

* * * * *

By midsummer, 1793, Genet was openly at war with the Washington administration. In effect, he challenged the administration to enforce its own orders. Lacking the necessary means itself, the national government called upon state governors to enforce neutrality regulations. If necessary, the governors were to call out militia to stop and to apprehend the "attackers" of neutrality.[30] Despite this decisive step, it was not easy to meet the French minister's challenge. It proved almost impossible to exclude armed vessels from American ports. Ultimately, despite objections by the Secretary of State, re-

---

[27] Genet to Jefferson, Philadelphia, May 23, 1793, and the Decree of the National Convention of Feb. 19, 1793, in *ASP FR,* I, 147.

[28] See Hamilton, "Camillus" No. XXIV, 1795, in Hamilton, ed., *Hamilton's Works,* VII, 394-395; Schachner, *Thomas Jefferson. . . ,* II, 493.

[29] To Gouverneur Morris for relay to the French government Jefferson explained the reasons for the delay in "making formal accession to their proposition to treat," Philadelphia, Aug. 23, 1793, in Ford, *Writings of Jefferson,* VI, 396. See also Genet to Jefferson, New York, Sept. 30 and Nov. 14, 1793, and Jefferson to Genet, Germantown, Nov. 5, 1793, *ASP FR,* I, 244-246.

[30] For details see Thomas, *American Neutrality. . . ,* pp. 134-135; Woolery, *The Relation of Thomas Jefferson to American Foreign Policy,* p. 113.

sponsibility for enforcement of neutrality regulations fell into Hamilton's hands. Hamilton instructed customs officials precisely in what they were to do to apprehend neutrality violators.[31]

Meanwhile, one of the first attempts to enforce the neutrality orders against American citizens enlisting on French privateers on American soil brought a partial victory to Genet. Two Americans, Gideon Henfield and John Singletary, had enlisted for service aboard a French privateer in Charleston. When this privateer, dubbed the *Citizen Genet,* came into Philadelphia in the latter part of May, 1793, the local authorities arrested the two men for violating the neutrality proclamation and jailed them. Genet immediately protested. He could not understand why bestowing commissions and enlisting men in the service of the French Republic was offensive to the American government. There was ample precedent to justify his action, he contended. He was "ignorant of any positive law, or treaty" prohibiting Americans from serving on French armed vessels.[32]

Genet was right; the federal government in its first four years had passed no law forbidding foreign recruiting on its shores. According to the official opinion of the Attorney General, however, no specific statute was necessary. Referring to Henfield's case, Randolph declared that Henfield was punishable, "because treaties are the supreme law of the land" and his action violated treaties the United States had "with three of the Powers at war with France." Since he had disturbed the peace of the United States, Henfield "was indictable at the common law."[33] When told by Jefferson that Henfield was in civil custody, and so beyond the President's control, Genet proceeded to make a test case of Henfield's trial; he decided to finance the litigation in the first prosecution of an American citizen for aiding the French.

With Hamilton supplying aid and support for the prosecution, with Randolph arguing the case, and with Genet backing the de-

[31] Washington to The Heads of Departments and the Attorney General, Philadelphia, July 29, 1793, Fitzpatrick, *Washington's Writings,* XXXIII, 34; Hamilton, "Instructions to the Collectors of the Customs," Philadelphia, Aug. 4, 1793, in Lodge, *The Works of Alexander Hamilton,* IV, 236-241.

[32] Genet to Jefferson, Philadelphia, June 1, 1793, *ASP FR,* I, 151.

[33] Opinion of the Attorney General, Edmund Randolph, May 30, 1793, *ibid.,* p. 152.

fense, the trial in the Federal Circuit Court in Philadelphia, in July, 1793, became a legal battle between the Executive Branch of the government and the French minister. The prosecution's case convinced the judges, but not the people, and the jury was made up of the people. In their charge to the jury the federal judges declared that Henfield's offense was a crime punishable by existing laws, that it was the jury's task to judge the facts; the judges determined the law. In view of the charge, the jury's role seemed clear; it was to declare Henfield guilty.

But popular sentiment was on the defendant's side. Motivated, apparently, by a widespread sentiment that the administration was attempting to give a mere proclamation the force of law, the public reacted against conviction. This sentiment was reinforced by Republican propaganda. The jury, sharing the popular sentiment for Henfield or perhaps merely reflecting it, declared him not guilty after a two-day deliberation.[34] "A Farmer of the back Settlements" said, "The decision of the jury at Philadelphia cannot be sufficiently extolled, since it avenged the Majesty of the Free American people; which the Executive power, the Attorney General and the Judges, attempted to violate."[35]

Genet gloried in the outcome; he had defeated the administration in an acknowledged test case in its own courts; he had humiliated the great Washington. As one Federalist later expressed it, "He show'd the facility of converting an *American citizen* into a *Frenchman* and soldier in the bosom of the country."[36] Popular rejoicing over the jury's verdict pained Federalists. Popular reaction made the government's task of enforcing neutrality more difficult. The men of the jury, "worthy *sans cullottes*," were paraded triumphantly through the streets. Immediately following the trial Genet cele-

[34] For details on the case, see *The Virginia Herald and Fredericksburg Advertiser*, Aug. 8, 1793; Thomas, *American Neutrality. . . ,* pp. 171-173; Hyneman, *The First American Neutrality,* pp. 130-131, and Charles P. Smith, *James Wilson: Founding Father, 1742-1798* (Chapel Hill, 1956), pp. 362-364; more detailed is the account in Frances Wharton, comp., *State Trials of the United States during the Administrations of Washington and Adams* (Philadelphia, 1849), pp. 49-89; and in Warren, *The Supreme Court in United States History,* I, 112-115.

[35] *The Independent Chronicle and the Universal Advertiser* (Boston), Jan. 20, 1794.

[36] William Vans Murray Papers, Commonplace Book, Aug. 9, 1795 (Princeton).

brated the "victory" with a dinner party for the popular hero, "Citizen" Henfield, who flauntingly re-enlisted on a French privateer. Then, believing his right to enlist Americans had been vindicated legally, the French minister continued openly to flout the neutrality orders; in newspaper advertisements he invited all "Friends of Liberty" to fight in the service of France.[37]

Although Washington and his advisers saw the effect and recognized the implications of the verdict, all was not lost. Since the court had declared that the act was punishable by law, Randolph pointed out publicly "that this verdict does not by any means amount to a decision that it is not unlawful to enlist on board French privateers."[38] This was clear warning against further enlistments in French service; the government gave orders to proper officials to continue to enforce the ban.[39] George Hammond did not stew over the decision; Henfield had been acquitted "through the means of a packed jury" he wrote to his superiors.[40] In all, Henfield's acquittal was not the great triumph Genet imagined it to be. Yet it brought on a crisis sufficiently upsetting to cause the administration to consider seriously the calling of a special session of Congress.[41]

Basically, the government's opposition to Genet's activities was predicated on the principle, as expressed by Jefferson, that "it is the *right* of every nation to prohibit acts of sovereignty from being exercised by any other within its limits, and the *duty* of a neutral nation

[37] Minnigerode, *Genet*, p. 224; Thomas, *American Neutrality. . . ,* pp. 173-176; one French recruiting pamphlet directed able-bodied seamen, particularly natives of Ireland, to apply to the French consul. In serving France, it pointed out, Americans would be imitating French heroes of the American Revolution. Dated Philadelphia, Aug., 1793, Genet Papers, Library of Congress.

[38] Edmund Randolph in the *Federal Gazette* (n.p., n.d.), quoted in Conway, *Randolph*, p. 183.

[39] French consuls, for example, were notified that their exequaturs would be revoked and that they would be liable to prosecution if they violated American neutrality. Jefferson, "Circular to the French Consuls," Philadelphia, Sept. 7, 1793, in Ford, *Writings of Jefferson*, VI, 417.

[40] Hammond to Grenville, Philadelphia, July 7, 1793, No. 16, Henry Adams Transcripts.

[41] Washington to The Heads of Departments and the Attorney General, Philadelphia, Aug. 3, 1793, in Fitzpatrick, *Washington's Writings*, XXXIII, 35-36. Jefferson was the only Cabinet member who favored calling Congress into special session. For the separate opinions of Knox, Jefferson, Randolph, and Hamilton, see Hamilton, ed., *Hamilton's Works*, IV, 455-462.

to prohibit such as would injure one of the warring Powers."[42] Hammond early had made clear that Genet's recruiting of men and his equipping of privateers in the United States injured Great Britain; that these were acts of sovereignty usurped by the French minister which the United States as a neutral country was obligated to stop.[43]

The administration itself did not doubt that the French minister's conduct violated American sovereignty. According to Genet's concepts of neutrality and his interpretations of the 1778 treaties, the prohibitions imposed by the administration were not valid.[44] Backed by American partisans of France and by evidence of extensive popular support, Genet acted according to his concepts, considering the neutrality orders as the workings of the pro-English Federalists in temporary control of the government, and not as representative of national sentiment. Nowhere was his contempt for the authority of the Federal government better illustrated than in the case of the *Little Sarah*.

* * * * *

The *Little Sarah* was a small English merchant vessel that had been caught in Philadelphia by the war in Europe. Arming her with four cannon for protection and loading her with cargo, her owners early in May, 1793, sent the vessel to sea. Not far from the American shore Genet's frigate *L'Embuscade* captured her and brought her back to Philadelphia as a prize. From this point on her story becomes involved in complex questions of law and neutrality.[45] More important for this study, she soon became the center of a crisis in Franco-American relations, a crisis which brought on the downfall of Genet.

[42] Jefferson to Genet, Philadelphia, June 5, 1793, *ASP FR,* I, 150.

[43] Hammond to Jefferson, May 8, 1793, summarized in Thomas, *American Neutrality. . . ,* pp. 120-121; see also pp. 165-166.

[44] See, for example, Genet's views in his note to Jefferson, Philadelphia, June 8, 1793, *ASP FR,* I, 151. A French view of American neutrality was that it cost the French heavily and made dupes of them. T. G. Legury to Genet, Boston, Oct. 30, 1793, Genet Papers, Library of Congress, XII, 3730.

[45] For accounts of the *Little Sarah* affair, see, Thomas, *American Neutrality. . . ,* pp. 137-144; White, *The Federalists. . . ,* pp. 216-217; Henry S. Randall, *The Life of Thomas Jefferson* (3 vols., New York, 1858), II, 157-171; Hamilton, *History of the Republic. . . ,* V, 294-306; McMaster, *History of the People of the United States. . . ,* II, 112-114.

For over a month the *Little Sarah* lay in Philadelphia's port while questions of her restitution and cargo were being argued. Then in the beginning of July the Cabinet learned through Hamilton that Genet was outfitting the vessel, now renamed the *Petite Démocrate,* as a privateer. Hamilton suggested that Governor Thomas Mifflin of Pennsylvania examine the ship. At the request of the Secretary of State the governor verified the report. He found that the *Petite Démocrate* now had fourteen cannon instead of four and that according to schedule she would sail the next day, July 7, 1793.[46]

To avoid using force in detaining the vessel, Mifflin sent his Secretary of State, Alexander J. Dallas, on a midnight mission to Genet to ask him to hold the ship in port. Working himself into a "great passion," Genet denounced Washington as a man misled by evil anti-French advisers. He allegedly indicated that he would appeal over the head of the President to the real sovereigns—the people. In the end he refused to agree to hold the vessel.

On the morning of July 7, 1793, Governor Mifflin informed Jefferson of the turn of events and of his having ordered a detachment of militia to seize the ship. With both Washington and Randolph out of town Jefferson was in a dilemma. If the ship sailed, American neutrality and the authority of the American government would appear meaningless, and England would be offered an excuse to wreak reprisals on the United States. On the other hand, if the government used force against the *Petite Démocrate* Franco-American amity and the French alliance would suffer. This Jefferson would avoid if it were at all possible. On his own initiative he sought personally to resolve the crisis.[47]

Before the militia marched into action Jefferson went to Genet, asking him to keep the vessel in port until Washington returned from Mount Vernon, a matter of a few days. Once more Genet raged. Repeating former complaints, he said the crew would resist the use of force. At the same time he indicated that the ship would not be ready for sea for "some time," but that it would drop down the Delaware River a way; not, however, with the intention

[46] The Anas, July 5 and July 10, 1793, in Ford, *Writings of Jefferson,* I, 235-243.

[47] See *ibid.,* p. 237; Kenneth R. Rossman, *Thomas Mifflin and the Politics of the American Revolution,* pp. 218-219.

of sailing immediately. Jefferson took this plus some gestures as a promise that the vessel would stay. Then he conferred with Mifflin, explaining that the ship would not sail. The governor thereupon dismissed the militia. That left the *Petite Démocrate* unguarded and averted an immediate armed clash.

The crisis, however, was not resolved. Clearly Genet had armed the *Petite Démocrate* in defiance of the President's orders, and clearly he was bent on sending her to sea to attack English shipping. He had admitted as much to Jefferson while denying the President's authority to stop her. "When treaties speak," wrote Genet, "the agents of nations have but to obey."[48]

In view of the neutrality violation and of the French minister's obvious defiance, Hamilton, Knox, and Jefferson met on Monday, July 8, 1793, to map a course of action. Having little faith in Genet or his alleged promise, Hamilton and Knox pressed to prevent the sailing by force if necessary. Located in the Delaware River so as to command the passage to sea was an island called Mud Island. Hamilton and Knox wanted to fortify the island with artillery and to issue orders to fire on the *Petite Démocrate* if she attempted to head for sea.

Not to stop the sailing, argued Hamilton and Knox, would be a flagrant violation of neutrality, sufficient to justify Britain's warring on the United States. Genet's open defiance of the federal government—"a gross outrage upon, and undisguised contempt of the government"—had to be checked or it would precipitate domestic as well as external crises. His conduct, they said, fitted "a regular plan to force the United States into the war." The integrity of the national government was at stake. In consideration of previous assurances of neutrality to England and as a precedent for similar cases confronting state officials, they argued, the government had no honorable alternative but to stop the equipping of the ship and to prevent its sailing.[49]

Critics of the administration, on the other hand, saw the crisis over the *Little Sarah* as evidence of English machinations. "The government," declared one of them under the pen name of "Juba,"

[48] Genet to Jefferson, Philadelphia, July 9, 1793, *ASP FR,* I, 163.
[49] "Reasons for the opinion of the Secretary of the Treasury, and the Secretary at War respecting the Brigantine Sarah," July 8, 1793, in Hamilton, ed., *Hamilton's Works,* IV, 443-448.

"is in an uproar because the French have fitted out a brig in Philadelphia, but appears to slumber over the British armaments that have been made here and the multiplied injuries and insults that our flag has sustained from the pirates under English colours."[50] Others, using pseudonyms such as "Alcanor," "Metellus," "Agricola," and "Dorax," also attacked the government's position. Pro-administration groups and individuals, however, were active, vociferous, and powerful in their proneutrality activities. Merchants and traders in various cities threw their support behind the government. In Philadelphia a merchant group met in July, 1793, to consider action to be adopted in the case of the *Little Sarah.* They demanded of the government strict adherence to the proclamation of neutrality. The proadministration Philadelphia press stressed that the United States would have plunged into war "had not the Proclamation of Neutrality been issued at the crisis at which it was promulgated."[51]

In Boston, too, "merchants and tradesmen" met in support of the government's stand on the *Little Sarah* incident; they sent the President a resolution supporting his neutrality policy. "A Thousand Bostonians," declared an antiadministration journal, assailed the meeting. Those who voted the resolves, it maintained, were old tories, speculators, funding-system men, custom house officers, English merchants, and merchants under English influence. If an English privateer, asked the journal, had been fitting out, would these persons have raised such a protest, "would they not *rather have assisted it?*"[52]

At the Monday Cabinet meeting, meanwhile, Jefferson dissented from his colleagues' argument, declaring that he was satisfied that the *Petite Démocrate* would not sail before Washington's arrival. Placing artillery on Mud Island might prompt a departure not now intended. Then, if the ship attempted the passage and were fired upon, she would return the fire; blood would flow. Moreover, a powerful French fleet, expected momentarily, might arrive and join the fray. Under the circumstances forcible detention might

[50] *National Gazette* (Philadelphia), July 27, 1793, quoted in Woodbury, *Public Opinion in Philadelphia. . . ,* p. 67.

[51] *The American Daily Advertiser* (Philadelphia), Jan. 6, 1794, cited in *ibid.,* p. 80.

[52] *The Mercury* (Boston), July 26, 1793.

lead to war. Such serious responsibility was not to be shouldered by nonelected subordinate officials, particularly when Washington was expected in two days. If the ship did make the open sea British protests could be met with these explanations.

For ten years, Jefferson said, the United States had borne "the grossest insults & injuries" from Great Britain. To rise at a feather against the French, "friends & benefactors," would be grossly inconsistent. Continuing, he maintained that he would not "gratify the combination of kings with the spectacle of the two only republics on earth destroying each other for two cannon; nor would I, for infinitely greater cause, add this country to that combination, turn the scale of contest, & let it be at our hands that the hopes of man received their last stab."[53] In this, as in other issues touching France and Britain, Hamilton and Jefferson differed. Such was the state of public sentiment and such were the divided counsels that greeted Washington when he reached Philadelphia. Lying on his desk, the papers dealing with the affair of the *Petite Démocrate,* were marked ominously "instant attention."

On the basis of his advisers' opinions it appeared that in the foreign-policy crisis confronting him, Washington had the choice of war with France or war with England. Fortunately, the issue did not preclude other alternatives. After reading the material on Genet and the *Petite Démocrate,* but before seeing Jefferson's explanation, he wrote the Secrtary of State, who had gone to his home outside Philadelphia because of illness, a curt letter. "What is to be done in the case of the Little Sarah, now at Chester?" he demanded. "Is the Minister of the French Republic to set the Acts of this Government at defiance, *with impunity?* and then threaten the Executive with an appeal to the People? What must the World think of such conduct and of the Governmt. of the U. States in submitting to it?"[54]

Jefferson replied immediately to his chief's demands, forwarding the formal report on the *Little Sarah* affair that he had drafted a few days before. After weighing the matter and taking into account the difficulties of stopping the *Petite Démocrate* at this late date, Wash-

[53] "Reasons for His Dissent," [July 9, 1793], in Ford, *Writings of Jefferson,* VI, 340-344.
[54] Washington to The Secretary of State, Philadelphia, July 11, 1793, in Fitzpatrick, *Washington's Writings,* XXXIII, 4.

ington—apparently reluctantly—decided against use of force; instead he once more resorted to words.[55] On July 12 Jefferson sent Genet another note informing him that he was not to permit the *Petite Démocrate,* and other vessels in similar status, to depart.[56] A few days later, unhindered, the ship headed for sea, becoming ultimately one of Genet's best privateers and setting a dangerous example for other French privateers in American ports. American neutrality thus appeared a sham, Jefferson's argument was shattered, Washington's authority had been flouted.[57]

As Hamilton had argued, the unhampered sailing of the privateer created an Anglo-American crisis. From repeated assurances by the American government the British had drawn justifiable conclusions that the United States was doing all within its means to prevent breaches of its neutrality. The escape of the *Petite Démocrate,* however, did not conform with the assurances. Obviously it had escaped because the federal government, although sufficiently forewarned, had not taken necessary measures to enforce its neutrality. Such apparent abdication of neutral obligations could be construed by Great Britain as an unneutral act of omission and a cause of war. Surprisingly, Hammond did not seize the opportunity to strike at the United States, as Jefferson had feared. To his government he reported that the privateer had escaped, "and the government [of the United States], from the want of having any cannon or military in readiness, was compelled to submit to the indignity."[58]

Genet's conduct in the *Little Sarah* affair was a first-rate diplomatic blunder. It demolished hope, however, slight, for an American policy of benevolent neutrality toward France as envisaged by Genet and the Girondin regime. Instead, it led the Washington

[55] See "Cabinet Opinion on Privateers and Prizes," July 12, 1793, in Ford, *Writings of Jefferson,* VI, 344-345; the Anas, July 10, 1793 (committed to writing July 13), *ibid.,* I, 242-243; Stephenson and Dunn, *George Washington,* II, 361-362.

[56] Jefferson to Genet, Philadelphia, July 12, 1793, *ASP FR,* I, 163.

[57] Later Genet informed Jefferson that he had sent the vessel to sea to obtain intelligence on coastal waters for the French fleet which was to sail from Norfolk to New York. The Anas, July 26, 1793, in Ford, *Writings of Jefferson,* I, 250.

[58] Hammond to Grenville, Aug. 18, 1793, No. 17, British State Papers, quoted in Thomas, *American Neutrality. . . ,* p. 143.

administration to define its neutral obligations more strictly. The Cabinet grappled with the whole problem of neutrality and Genet; and finally, at the behest of Jefferson, agreed on July 12, 1793, to submit the complex questions of neutral obligations to the Supreme Court.[59]

A careful compilation of American neutrality problems then confronting the government was presented to the Court on July 18, 1793. The judges, for constitutional reasons, refused to consider them.[60] The Cabinet was forced to answer its own questions, a procedure which resulted on August 4, 1793, in the promulgation of "Rules Governing Belligerents."[61]

These rules—eight in number—agreed upon by the Cabinet and accepted by the President, forbade equipping of privateers in American ports and clearly established the American interpretation of Article 22 of the commercial treaty with France. By the first provision not just England, as had been maintained by Genet, but France as well was barred from outfitting ships in American ports. Other provisions clarified specific neutrality obligations which the United States assumed and would enforce. Except for special privileges granted France by treaty, the rules applied in the same degree to both France and England. The eighth rule prohibited foreign

[59] *Ibid.*, pp. 146-147. This action inspired public attacks on Washington. Why, asked "Juba" in the *National Gazette* (Philadelphia, July 27, 1793), if he had any doubts on the subject did the President not consult the representatives of the people in Congress? Then "Juba" answered his own question by indicating that Hamilton's fear of Congress and the people was the reason. Cited in Woodbury, *Public Opinion in Philadelphia. . . ,* pp. 66-67.

[60] See Jefferson to The Chief Justice and Judges of the Supreme Court of the United States, Philadelphia, July 18, 1793, in Ford, *Writings of Jefferson,* VI, 351-352—the questions are on pp. 352-354; Chief Justice Jay and Associate Justices to President Washington, Philadelphia, Aug. 8, 1793, in Johnston, *Jay Correspondence,* III, 488-489. The Court's refusal constituted an important step in establishing the purely judiciary function of the Supreme Court; see Warren, *The Supreme Court in United States History,* I, 111.

[61] The administration knew before the formal reply was received that the Justices would refuse to give an opinion; see Jefferson to Madison, Aug. 3, 1793, in Ford, *Writings of Jefferson,* VI, 362; the rules, dated Aug. 3, 1793, are in *ibid.*, pp. 258-259. The rules were published by means of Hamilton's "Instructions to the Collectors of the Customs," Philadelphia, Aug. 4, 1793, in Lodge, *The Works of Alexander Hamilton,* IV, 236-241; see also Washington to The Secretary of State, Philadelphia, Aug. 4, 1793, in Fitzpatrick, *Washington's Writings,* XXXIII, 37-38.

recruiting on American soil. Backed staunchly by Federalist opinion, the rules provided for effective implementation of the neutrality proclamation and gave assurance to Great Britain that the United States would enforce its neutrality.[62]

Once more Jefferson and Hamilton clashed; this time over responsibility for supervising the neutrality regulations. Responsibility for administering the neutrality provisions, instead of being Jefferson's as Secretary of State, was delegated to customs officials under Hamilton's control in his capacity of Secretary of the Treasury.

In the first week of May, 1793, following adoption of the proclamation, Hamilton had prepared instructions for collectors of customs directing them to supervise adherence to the just-published neutrality regulations and to inform him of infractions. Jefferson had objected to Hamilton's attempted usurping of State Department functions. The collectors of customs, who were predominantly Federalist, Jefferson complained, "are to be made an established corps of spies or informers against their fellow citizens, whose actions they are to watch in secret, inform against in secret to the Secretary of the Treasury." This procedure, he said, "will at least furnish the collector with a convenient weapon to keep down a rival, draw a cloud over an inconvenient censor, or satisfy mere malice & private enmity." Coming to the heart of the matter, he added that he could not "possibly conceive how the superintendence of the laws of neutrality, or the preservation of our peace with foreign nations can be ascribed to the department of the treasury, which I suppose to comprehend merely matters of revenue. It would be to add a new & large field to a department already amply provided with business, patronage, & influence."[63]

Jefferson had proposed that grand juries rather than customs officials be charged with responsibility for investigating neutrality violations. Washington, however, had followed Randolph's suggestion of directing customs collectors to report neutrality infrac-

[62] A sample of Federalist backing was the resolution of September 5, 1793, by a group of Annapolis citizens in support of Washington's neutrality policy and critical of Genet's influence in American affairs. *Maryland Gazette* (Annapolis), Sept. 26, 1793.

[63] Jefferson to Edmund Randolph, May 8, 1793, in Ford, *Writings of Jefferson*, VI, 244-245; White, *The Federalists. . .*, pp. 214-216.

tions to the district attorney in each port. The district attorneys, in turn, were to report to the Attorney General. The Secretary of War, in addition, had instructed state governors to help in enforcing the neutrality regulations by guarding against violations.[64] Neither Jefferson nor Hamilton, therefore, had direct responsibility for enforcing neutrality in the ports at the beginning of the Anglo-French conflict.

The *Little Sarah* crisis, however, led Washington to abandon reliance on state governors for enforcing neutrality and to turn once more to Hamilton's May proposal. At the Cabinet meeting of July 29, 1793, the President had requested his advisors to consider charging customs officials with responsibility of preventing neutrality violations. Emphasizing the need for more stringent regulation, he said "unless this, or some other *effectual* mode is adopted to check this evil in the first stage of its growth, the Executive of the U. States will be incessantly harassed with complaints on this head, and probably when it may be difficult to afford a remedy."[65]

Earlier, Washington had taken for granted that the governors would discover neutrality infractions "in embryo & stop them when no force was requisite or a very small party of militia wd. suffice."[66] He had not anticipated, as in the case of the *Little Sarah,* enforcement in an advanced stage of violation where large force was necessary and where a clash might lead to war. With adoption of the "Rules Governing Belligerents," the government put Hamilton's suggestion into effect; it instructed collectors of customs to enforce the rules. Once more Hamilton's influence with the President proved stronger than that of Jefferson. The Secretary of State, convinced that supervision of neutrality was the responsibility of the State Department and believing that to remove it from his

[64] See Washington to The Secretary of the Treasury, Philadelphia, May 7, 1793, in Fitzpatrick, *Washington's Writings,* XXXII, 451; the circular of governor Henry Lee of Virginia, Richmond, June 8, 1793, in *ASP FR,* I, 606; Conway, *Randolph,* pp. 204-205; Woolery, *The Relation of Thomas Jefferson to American Foreign Policy,* p. 113.

[65] Washington to The Heads of Departments and the Attorney General, Philadelphia, July 29, 1793, in Fitzpatrick, *Washington's Writings,* XXXIII, 34.

[66] Quoted from The Anas, July 15, 1793, in Ford, *Writings of Jefferson.* I, 243.

department demonstrated a lack of confidence in him, offered once again to resign.[67]

This episode exposed one more of the perplexing difficulties that confronted Jefferson in assuming responsibility for foreign relations in a Federalist regime while personally advocating Republican policies. He was not responsible for formulating foreign policy to the degree that other department heads were responsible for the major functions of their departments. As has been illustrated by previous incidents, and particularly by the case of the *Little Sarah,* the President, who constitutionally was in control of foreign policy formulation, insisted upon holding Cabinet deliberations on important foreign policy questions; he preferred collective opinions to the individual counsel of the Secretary of State. On financial questions, on the other hand, while more technical but no more complex and no less vital, he accepted the individual judgment of the Secretary of the Treasury. Executive practice, therefore, made it relatively easy for Hamilton to wield an important influence in formulating foreign policy and in thwarting Jefferson's foreign policy objectives.[68]

While it was true that Hamilton's "system" was anchored on a policy of peace with England, which might have justified tampering with Jefferson's department, it is also true that it was Washington's practice of collective Cabinet decisions on foreign policy issues which gave Hamilton important advantages in implementing his program in areas beyond the scope of normal Treasury Department concerns. Jefferson was never able to put into effect his foreign policy views on major questions without Hamilton's knowledge, interference, or obstructions.

* * * * *

Jefferson, as has been seen, while favoring neutrality, had opposed the neutrality proclamation; when it had been adopted he had sup-

---

[67] See Jefferson to Washington, Philadelphia, July 31, 1793, in Ford, *Writings of Jefferson,* VI, 360-361. There were, of course, other reasons for the resignation offer; see Schachner, *Thomas Jefferson,* I, 500; Randall, *The Life of Thomas Jefferson,* II, 61. Nonetheless, Hamilton's interference in foreign policy was a prominent reason for the resignation; see White, *The Federalists. . . ,* pp. 216-217; Woolery, *The Relation of Thomas Jefferson to American Foreign Policy,* p. 119.

[68] For variations of this theme, see Caldwell, *Hamilton and Jefferson,* p. 228; White, *The Federalists. . . ,* p. 217.

ported it, but he did not do so wholeheartedly.[69] He considered
the "guarantee" provision of the French alliance legally and morally
binding, and looked upon the proclamation of neutrality as merely
a temporary executive expedient; when Congress convened, it would
decide on the proper neutrality legislation. Hamilton, on the other
hand, saw no need for congressional action. Washington's proclamation, he believed, had established rightfully a rigid neutrality
that suspended the "guarantee" to France. If it were not suspended,
he believed, the United States would not then be a true neutral, and
war with England might follow.

With the *Little Sarah* affair the questions of the proclamation of
neutrality and of the nature of the French alliance became a center
of political dispute. But even before the *Little Sarah* affair the proclamation had precipitated a public political battle. By June, 1793,
Hamilton was smoldering under Republican attacks on the proclamation and was upset by the obvious public support Genet and
Republicans were receiving. In defense of the proclamation and
his party's position, he published, under the pseudonym of "Pacificus," seven articles in John Fenno's *Gazette of the United States*
from June 29 to July 27, 1793. The articles outlined Federalist policy
on neutrality, argued in support of its position toward the belligerent powers, and attacked the French alliance.[70]

The most persistent of the Republican thrusts were taunts that
Federalist policy violated the French alliance, that France by treaty
was still an ally whom the United States was obligated to aid if
called upon to do so. Hamilton countered that the alliance was
defensive and that France was the aggressor; she had been first to
declare war. "Self-preservation is the first duty of a nation," he
said. "Good faith does not require that the United States should
put in jeopardy their essential interests, perhaps their very existence,
in one of the most unequal contests in which a nation could be
engaged, to secure to France—what? Her West India islands and

[69] Woolery, *The Relation of Thomas Jefferson to American Foreign Policy*,
p. 115. Privately, Jefferson deprecated the proclamation, labeling it a "milk
and water" pronouncement. Jefferson to Madison, June 29, 1793, postscript
of June 30, in Ford, *Writings of Jefferson*, VI, 328.

[70] The "Pacificus" articles are reprinted in Lodge, *The Works of Alexander
Hamilton*, IV, 135-191; see also Schachner, *Hamilton*, p. 322; Hamilton, *History of the Republic. . . ,* V, 309-311.

other less important possessions in America."[71]   Gratitude for French aid during the American Revolution he cast aside, pointing out that not altruism, not love for Americans had motivated France, but revenge—revenge against England for past humiliations.

In defense of Executive control of foreign policy, Hamilton argued that the President's constitutional powers were broad, not narrow as Jefferson had maintained.   In carrying out his functions the President "must necessarily possess a right of judging what is the nature of the obligations which the treaties of the country impose on the government."[72]

After several of Hamilton's trenchant articles had appeared, Jefferson became alarmed over the possible extent of their influence upon the public if left unanswered.   Urgently, he turned to Madison. "For God's sake, my dear Sir," he wrote, "take up your pen, select the most striking heresies and cut him to pieces in the face of the public.   There is nobody who can & will enter the lists with him."[73] Although disturbed by "Pacificus" and by the proclamation of neutrality which earlier he had labeled "a most unfortunate error" and as violating "the forms and spirit of the Constitution," Madison was reluctant to tangle once more with Hamilton.[74]   Under the signature of "Helvidius," nevertheless, he did challenge "Pacificus," a "most grating" task, he confessed.   To Hamilton's seven articles Madison responded with five letters published in the same paper, beginning August 24, 1793, and ending September 18, 1793.[75]

All five articles attacked Hamilton's first letter.   Labeling Hamilton's argument an appeal to those "who hate our republican government and the French revolution," Madison denied that the proclamation of neutrality meant suspension of the French alliance.   On the basic issue of control over foreign policy he took the narrow constitutional view that only Congress had the power to decide what

[71] The quotations are from "Pacificus" No. II, July 3, 1793, in Lodge, *The Works of Alexander Hamilton,* IV, 159.

[72] "Pacificus" No. I, June 29, 1793, *ibid.,* pp. 142-143.

[73] Jefferson to Madison, July 7, 1793, in Ford, *Writings of Jefferson,* VI, 338; Schachner, *Alexander Hamilton,* p. 323; Brant, *James Madison: Father of the Constitution. . . ,* pp. 377-378.

[74] "I am in hopes of finding that some one else has undertaken it."   Madison to Jefferson, July 18 and July 30, 1793, in Hunt, *The Writings of James Madison,* VI, 135, 138-139.

[75] The "Letters of Helvidius" are in *ibid.,* pp. 138-188.

treaty obligations were binding on the nation. He refuted "the extraordinary doctrine, that the powers of making war, and treaties, are in their nature executive." This vicious doctrine, he pointed out, emanated from British sources; for in Great Britain treaty and war powers "are *royal prerogatives,*" hence executive functions. It would never do for a democracy; it smacked of monarchy—worse still, of British monarchy.[76]

Classical pseudonyms fooled no one; the public recognized in "Pacificus" and "Helvidius" the Secretary of the Treasury and the leading member of the House of Representatives. But Hamilton and Madison did not have the field alone; others plunged in, sporting such cognomens as "Veritas," "Cato," and "Ironicus."[77] Among these, "A Firm Republican" expressed well the Republican position. Referring to the proclamation of neutrality, he wrote that he "always considered it as a thing which had very little good or harm in it; but assumes the one character or the other, as it is differently received." Taken merely as a declaration of America's stand toward the belligerent powers, "it was no more than a promulgation of the law of the land, which every citizen ought to know, conform his actions to; and in that light was a fresh proof of that watchful regard so frequently manifested by him [Washington] towards the people of America." If, on the other hand, it were taken as enjoining neutrality on American citizens "so far as to dispense with the obligations by which we are bound, in our treaties with France, it must be received as a daring affirmation of power, which no man acquainted with his dispositions, can seriously believe he [Washington] ever contemplated."[78]

"Cato" defended the French alliance, urging closer ties with France, and declared that if Great Britain defeated France the United States would be the next victim. Following this reasoning, "A Farmer of the Back Settlement" declared that the United States should have aided France against England even if it meant privations and hardship for Americans.[79] Agitated by the controversy,

[76] The quotations are from "Helvidius" No. I, August-September [1793], *ibid.,* pp. 139, 143, 150; see also Brant, *James Madison: Father of the Constitution. . . ,* pp. 378-379.

[77] Stephenson and Dunn, *George Washington,* II, 355.

[78] *Virginia Herald and Fredericksburg Advertiser,* Dec. 5, 1793.

[79] "Cato" wrote for the *New York Diary;* reprinted in the *Independent*

citizen groups in various towns met and passed resolutions for and against the government's foreign policy and forwarded their re-solves to the President. In Virginia, Federalists such as John Marshall joined the battle.[80] Though various proadministration resolutions they appealed to Virginians to support Washington's neutrality policy. Citizens of Annapolis, Maryland, also expressed satisfaction with government policy and condemned Genet's activities, as did "Columbus," who maintained that Genet, if not stopped, "would have exposed us inevitably to the hostilities of all the great maritime powers of the earth."[81]

Antiadministration resolutions adopted by planters, farmers, and other yeomanry in Caroline County, Virginia, for instance, demanded that the French alliance be safeguarded. They expressed fear that the administration was bent on dissolving the alliance and replacing it with "a more intimate connexion" with Great Britain. Other Virginia counties also passed antiadministration resolutions, patterned after those of Caroline County. Support of the French alliance became a rallying point for organized protest against Washington's foreign policies. From these organized attacks against Washington's French policy Virginia Republicans, for example, gained the confidence that led them to scrutinize critically and then to attack Hamilton's fiscal program. Foreign policy and politics, in effect, fused on the issue of the French alliance.[82]

If not dignified and not in the tradition of European governments, brawling over foreign policy at least was something new and

Chronicle and the Universal Advertiser (Boston), Jan. 6, 1794; "A Farmer" appeared in the Jan. 27, 1794, issue of the latter.

[80] *Virginia Gazette and General Advertiser* (Richmond), Aug. 21, 1793, cited in Ammon, "The Formation of the Republican Party in Virginia," *Journal of Southern History*, XIX, 303.

[81] *Maryland Gazette* (Annapolis), Sept. 26, 1793; "Columbus" appeared in the *Columbian Centinel* (Boston), Nov. 30, 1793.

[82] Citizens of Caroline County did, however, profess esteem for Washington and condemn Genet's activities. *Maryland Gazette* (Annapolis), Oct. 10, 1793; Ammon, "The Formation of the Republican Party in Virginia," *JSH*, XIX, 300, 304-305. Republicans were opposed to administration foreign policy not because it was neutral but because Washington's Federalist-oriented government did not give even moral support to the French alliance. In the neutrality proclamation they saw victory for the pro-British commercial classes. This issue of neutrality and the French alliance divided clearly the two national parties, particularly in pivotal Virginia.

democratic. Here was evidence of widening popular participation in important governmental issues, of policy-makers reaching down to the people. For good or evil, foreign policy issues had been forced to the level of domestic politics and were debated publicly in bids for popular support. Republican attacks had compelled Hamilton, contemptuous of public opinion, to bring his case to the very public he detested. At the beginning of America's national history, as a consequence, the heat of politics gave birth to a democratic approach to foreign policy.

* * * * *

Not only did Republicans and Federalists battle over foreign policy, but they also vied with each other in aiding Great Britain and France, and hence in subverting American neutrality. While French neutrality violations, highlighted particularly by Genet's rash conduct, were at this time numerous and conspicuous, the British and their American partisans also flouted American laws. Many vessels, both British and French, were armed and equipped for offensive action in American ports and escaped detection by American officials, or else sympathetic officials connived at their breaking American neutrality regulations.

As in the case of French violations, a number of attempts to arm and equip British ships in American ports were brought to the attention of the Washington administration. In detecting these British efforts Genet appeared as vigilant and as concerned as did Hammond over the arming of French privateers. The legal grounds for his protest against British violations of neutrality were stronger than those of Hammond. As has been noted, Washington's advisers differed markedly in their interpretations of American treaty obligations to France. With Great Britain there was no problem; the American government was bound to forbid the use of its ports to the British for hostile acts against France. Not only was such conduct unneutral, but it was also prohibited by Article 22 of the commercial treaty of 1778. When they were caught illegally using American port facilities, neither the British nor their Federalist sympathizers could justify their acts by an overfavorable interpretation of a treaty right as did Genet. Great Britain had no treaty with the United States.[83]

[83] For details on this problem, see Thomas, *American Neutrality. . . ,* pp. 159-162; Hyneman, *The First American Neutrality,* p. 81.

Whenever Genet received reports, particularly from French consuls in American ports, that English privateers had been armed in places such as Charleston, Baltimore, and Philadelphia, he protested to the Department of State. A typical example of a British ship adding to her armament in an American port was that of the armed privateer *Jane*. Carrying two unmounted cannon in addition to fourteen cannon already mounted, the *Jane* sailed into Philadelphia's port, pierced two new portholes, and mounted the extra guns on carriages obtained in the United States. On July 9, 1793 (only four days after the alleged violation), Genet protested to Jefferson that the British were adding armament to the vessel in violation of America's treaty obligation to France.[84]

Following usual procedure in such cases, Jefferson brought the matter to Hammond's attention. Contending that Genet's accusations were unfounded and that the *Jane* was not violating American neutrality, the British minister exchanged considerable correspondence with the State Department over the case. To throw Genet's exacerbating conduct into sharp contrast with his own, Hammond tried to be particularly accommodating in the exchanges. These unprovocative intentions were difficult to carry into effect before the concentrated offensive hurled against the *Jane*—the only armed British vessel in the port—by Republicans and other French partisans.

In view of the agitation Hammond finally "judged it most expedient to consent to the alterations suggested" by Jefferson.[85] The British reduced the *Jane's* armament to what it had been when she entered port. Even though he retreated judiciously before Genet's protests and heated popular agitation, Hammond did attain one valuable objective. By his conduct in the *Jane* case, which appeared almost exemplary in comparison to Genet's in similar situations, he placed the French minister in a relatively unfavorably position.[86] He did not openly defy the American government or meet its pro-

[84] Genet to Jefferson, Philadelphia, July 9, 1793, *ASP FR,* I, 163; the Anas, July 29, 1793, in Ford, *Writings of Jefferson,* I, 250.

[85] Hammond to Grenville, Aug., 1793, No. 17, British State Papers, cited in Thomas, *American Neutrality. . . ,* p. 161.

[86] See *ibid.,* pp. 161-162; for details on the action of the American government, see the Anas, July 29, 1793, in Ford, *Writings of Jefferson,* I, 250-251; Cabinet Opinion, Aug. 3, 1793, in Hamilton, ed., *Hamilton's Works,* IV, 457-458.

tests with bitter arguments and impassioned pleas for popular support. Hammond's procedure illustrated well British practice, which was to take whatever advantages were possible by secretly arming vessels in American ports, but when caught, to yield gracefully.

At this time Hammond's task in defending British violations of American sovereignty in the ports was less complicated than that of Genet. As article 17 of the French commercial treaty prohibited British privateers from bringing prizes of war into American ports, the privateers never returned once they left port, nor did exigencies of war compel them to use American ports. The British had other bases in the Western Hemisphere easily available from which privateers could operate.

But the same treaty article gave French privateers the specific right to return to American ports with their prizes. Their bases of operation were limited; they were, to a degree, forced to rely upon American facilities in carrying out their depredations. When the French privateers returned to American ports they often brought trouble with them. Genet, differing treaty interpretations, and the complexion of American politics all aggravated this trouble.

In all, in this period of American neutrality, despite Genet's continuing protests against the equipping of British vessels, British violations of American neutrality in the ports were apparently less than those of the French. Except for special treaty privileges granted the French, American neutrality regulations were applicable in equal degree to both Great Britain and France. By one standard of international conduct the United States was obligated to prevent the use of its ports for the armament of vessels belonging to either belligerent. This allegedly impartial neutrality favored Great Britain and violated the spirit if not the letter of the French alliance, particularly as Republicans and Genet interpreted it. Under the terms of the alliance and in accord with past international practice, Genet and France had expected a benevolent American neutrality, under which French actions, while exacerbating, would not have been construed as violations of American neutrality. This kind of neutrality Genet did not get.[87]

[87] According to past international practice, the neutrality of third states had not been impartial; it had been benevolent usually toward one belligerent. In this period of transition in practice and standards Genet had expected a benevolent neutrality; see Hyneman, *The First American Neutrality*, pp. 153-

154. In this period of transition "there were still fundamental differences of opinion as to the rights of belligerents and neutrals, respectively, under the law of nations." Phillips and Reede, *Neutrality. . .* , II, 16. Grotius, for example, spoke of neutrals as "those who in time of war are in a position between the contending parties," and expected the neutrals to look into the merits of the controversy and to take sides accordingly. He did not stress impartiality. Cited in Charles G. Fenwick, *American Neutrality: Trial and Failure* (New York, 1940), p. 9.

CHAPTER EIGHT

WESTERN INTRIGUE, SELF-CREATED
SOCIETIES, AND A MUTINOUS FLEET

Our self-created societies and clubs, as it appears to me, have a tendency, directly or indirectly, to introduce into the measures of government all the precipitation, all the heat and ungovernable passions of a simple democracy.—Nathaniel Chipman to Alexander Hamilton, Rutland, Vermont, January 9, 1794.

Resolved that we ought to resist to the utmost of our power all attempts to alienate our affections from France, and detach us from her alliance and to connect us more intimately with Great Britain, that all persons who, directly or indirectly, promote this unnatural succession ought to be considered by every free American as enemies to republicanism and their country.—The Democratic Society of Pennsylvania, Resolution of January 9, 1794.

* * * *

GENET did not confine his problem-spawning activities to the seaports; he also caused trouble on the land frontiers. Hatching or abetting various plots, he had planned to launch hostile military expeditions from American soil with American troops against Spanish and English possessions in North America.[1] France's plans to

[1] Some students of this period believe that the real purpose of Genet's mission was to wrest Louisiana from Spain. See, for example, Woodfin, "Citizen Genet and His Mission," Ph.D. Dissertation, University of Chicago, p. 446. Genet's plans for attacks on Florida and Louisiana were at this time war measures directed against Spain, not a part of French policy to establish a new colonial empire in North America. Mildred S. Fletcher, "Louisiana as a Factor in French Diplomacy from 1763 to 1800," *Mississippi Valley Historical Review*, XVII (Dec., 1930), 369-370. For Genet's plans to attack Canada, see Benjamin Sulté, "Les Projets de 1793 à 1810," *Proceedings and Transactions of the Royal Society of Canada*, V (1911), 27-31; Eugene P.

use disgruntled American frontiersmen in the Southwest in the conquest of Louisiana and Florida actually antedated Genet's mission,
as did her designs on Canada.[2]   Genet was to be the instrument
charged by the Girondins with converting plans into action; they
would have given any French minister to the United States the
same responsibilities.   The results of the Genet mission, nonetheless,
were stamped unmistakably with his personal imprint.[3]

Genet's instructions, as has been noted, directed him "to take
every measure" which might "germinate the principles of liberty
and independence in Louisiana and in the other American provinces
bordering on the United States."[4]   He was to do this, if possible,
with aid from the American government, relying upon the alliance
and pro-French sentiment to induce the government to give the
needed assistance.   If he could get no aid, apparently, he was
to proceed alone.   In particular, the instructions emphasized that
he could probably rely on the active support of Kentucky frontiersmen who "burned" to enjoy free navigation of the Mississippi, a
privilege denied them by Spain.   In carrying out his frontier projects Genet was authorized, at his discretion, to spend as much as he
thought necessary.[5]

Genet plotted a three-pronged attack against Louisiana and

Link, *Democratic-Republican Societies, 1790-1800* (New York, 1942), pp.
141-144; "Compte que rend de Mission de Citoyen [Henri] Meriere au Citoyen
Genet, Ministre Plentipotentiare de la République Française près les États-
Unis," New York, Sept. 20, 1793, AAE CP EU, Vol. XXXVIII, ff. 233-238.
Meriere was a secretary of Genet.

   [2] See Frederick J. Turner, "The Origins of Genet's Projected Attack on
Louisiana and the Floridas," *American Historical Review,* III (July, 1898),
651; Richard K. Murdoch, "The Genesis of the Genet Schemes," *French
American Review,* II (April-June, 1949), 81-82; see also Brissot to Servan,
Minister of War, Paris, Nov. 26, 1792, in Cl. Perroud, ed., *J. P. Brissot: Correspondance et papiers* (Paris, [1911]), p. 312; to the Comité de défense
général, Jan. 25, 1793, Brissot reported on the possibility of an attack against
Spanish possessions. F. V. A. Aulard, ed., *Recueil des actes du Comité de
salut public* . . . (26 vols., Paris, 1889-1923), II, 10.

   [3] Turner, "Origins of Genet's Projected Attack. . . ," *AHR,* III, 660; Murdoch, "The Genesis of the Genet Schemes," *FAR,* II, 94; Thomas, *American
Neutrality.* . . , p. 177.

   [4] Instructions of Dec., 1792, in Turner, *CFM,* p. 205.

   [5] Even though Genet's initial instructions had been drafted before France
went to war with Spain and England, subsequent instructions directed him
to proceed with the liberation of Spanish lands. Le Brun to Genet, Paris,
[date illegible], 1793, Genet Papers, Library of Congress, VIII, 2665.

Florida: one expedition was to descend upon East Florida from the Georgia border, another was to be recruited in South Carolina and then hurled against Louisiana, and the third force was to come out of Kentucky via the Mississippi River to conquer New Orleans. He placed the New Orleans expedition under the command of General George Rogers Clark, hero of the Northwest during the American Revolution, who long had dreamed of wrenching the lower banks and mouth of the Mississippi from Spanish control. Clark had, in fact, suggested an attack against New Orleans to the French government as early as the latter months of 1792.[6]

This was encouraging to Genet, particularly when Clark, in February, 1793, had pointed out that he could take the Spanish possessions with ease, that the magic of his name would cause frontiersmen to flock to his cause.[7] All he needed was support from the French government in the form of commissions for himself and his cohorts, and of course, money to buy boats, guns, ammunition, supplies. Not much else was necessary. The fighting men, Clark indicated, could be paid in land captured from the Spaniard. Once initial expenditures were met, the expedition would be self-financing. This, indeed, gratified Genet. He sent to Kentucky a French botanist, André Michaux, with enough funds to start the project and instructions to co-ordinate plans and to arrange details for the expedition.[8]

[6] See Thomas Paine to Dr. James O'Fallon, Passy near Paris, Feb. 17, 1793. This letter reveals also that Jefferson had been sounded concerning Clark's suitability for the task. Louise Phelps Kellogg, "Letter of Thomas Paine, 1793," *AHR*, XXIX (April, 1924), 504-505; John C. Parish, "The Intrigues of Doctor James O'Fallon," *MVHR*, XVII (Sept., 1930), 259-260; Clark to [French minister], Louisville, Feb. 5, 1793, in Frederick J. Turner, ed., "Selections from the Draper Collection in the Possession of the State Historical Society of Wisconsin, to Elucidate the Proposed French Expedition under George Rogers Clark against Louisiana, in the Years 1793-1794," *Annual Report of the American Historical Association for the Year 1896* (2 vols., Washington, 1897), I, 967-971; Turner, "Origins of Genet's Projected Attack. . . ," *AHR*, III, 653; James A. James, *The Life of George Rogers Clark* (Chicago, 1928), p. 411.

[7] Clark to [French minister], Louisville, Feb. 5, 1793, Turner, "Draper Collection," *AHA Ann. Rep.* (1896), pp. 967-971. In AAE CP EU, Vol. XXXIX, f. 90, dated Oct. 7, 1793, is an authorization given by Genet to Clark to take command of the Legion of Revolution and Independence of the Mississippi.

[8] Genet to Michaux, Philadelphia, July 12, 1793, Genet Papers, Library of Congress, X, 3087. Genet authorized Michaux to treat with the French

For various reasons Clark, who had become a major general in the French army in command of French revolutionary legions which he was to recruit in Kentucky, was unable to unleash his planned attack in 1793. In autumn and winter of that year he prepared, instead, for an offensive in the spring. Establishing a base on the Mississippi, he gathered men, boats, and supplies.[9] In the meantime Genet put plans for the other expeditions into motion. One of the expeditions, destined for New Orleans, was to join Clark's forces after descending the Tennessee River; the combined expedition was then to sweep down the Mississippi. While this force attacked from the North, a French naval force was to close the river below New Orleans.[10]

As Clark made preparations in Kentucky, the recruiting of men and general preparations for the invasion of the Floridas progressed under the direction of Michel Ange Bernard de Mangourit, French consul at Charleston. During his short sojourn in Charleston Genet had informed Governor William Moultrie of his plans, set them in motion, and turned over responsibility for them to Mangourit.[11] The French consul succeeded in carrying out his responsibilities;

---

and Indians west of the Mississippi to bring French liberty to Louisiana and to concert with Clark and General Benjamin Logan to raise a corps titled the Legion of Revolution and Independence of the Mississippi; also Instructions to Michaux, Oct. 7, 1793, AAE CP EU, Vol. XXXIX, ff. 82-83; C. S. Sargent, "Journal de André Michaux," *Proceedings of the American Philosophical Society,* XXVI (1889), 91; Genet to Minister of Foreign Affairs, Philadelphia, July 25, 1793, Turner, *CFM,* pp. 221-223.

[9] For a recruiting notice of "George R. Clark Esq. Major General in the armies of FRANCE, and Commander in Chief of the FRENCH REVOLUTIONARY LEGIONS on the Mississippi River," see the *Kentucky Gazette* (Lexington), Feb. 8, 1794.

[10] Instructions for Contre Amiral Sercey, Commandant of the French Republic's Naval Forces in America, Oct. 4, 1793, AAE CP EU, Vol. XXXIX, ff. 99-103. The *Petite Démocrate* was to be a part of this naval force. Turner, "The Origins of Genet's Projected Attack. . . ," *AHR,* III, 668; Thomas, *American Neutrality. . . ,* p. 180. For summaries of Genet-Clark intrigues, see F. R. Hall, "Genet's Western Intrigue, 1793-1794," *Illinois State Historical Society Journal,* XXI (1928), 359-381; Regina K. Crandall, "Genet's Projected Attack on Louisiana and the Floridas, 1793-1794," *Abstracts of Theses, Humanistic Series* (University of Chicago, 1928), V, 263-270.

[11] Genet informed his superiors that Mangourit was "an excellent patriot." To Minister of Foreign Affairs, Charleston, April 16, 1793, in Turner, *CFM,* p. 213. For a sketch of Mangourit as a "dealer in international revolution," see R. R. Palmer, "A Revolutionary Republican: M. A. B. Mangourit," *William and Mary Quarterly,* 3rd Series, IX (Oct., 1952), 483-496.

Charlestonians, it seemed, had gone "recruiting-mad for the French service."[12] More men were enlisted, armed, and ready to join the New Orleans assault from South Carolina than were ready for action in Kentucky.[13]

Success in attaching American frontiersmen to the French cause was not at this time difficult to achieve. Sympathy for France was strong in most Western areas. In many regions of Tennessee and Kentucky, for example, French sympathizers organized democratic societies and sowed French ideas on receptive soil, there to be culti-vated by Genet's agents.[14] Men of the West had grievances against Spain, because, among other reasons, she denied them free use of the Mississippi River as an outlet for their produce. This antago-nism was, in part, also directed against the Federalist regime in Philadelphia because frontiersmen believed that the administration had not exerted itself to gain coveted rights to the mouth of the river.[15]

[12] Quoted from the *Kentucky Gazette* (Lexington), April 5, 1794, citing a letter from Charleston under date of Jan. 3.

[13] Mangourit's preparations are summarized in Richard K. Murdoch, "Citizen Mangourit and the Projected Attack on East Florida in 1794," *Jour-nal of Southern History*, XIV (Nov., 1948), 522-540 and in Murdoch, *The Georgia-Florida Frontier, 1793-1796*, pp. 11-24; for an account of preparations in Georgia, see E. Merton Coulter, "Elijah Clarke's Foreign Intrigues and the 'Trans-Oconee Republic,'" *Proceedings of the Mississippi Valley Historical Association for 1918-1919*, X, Part I (Cedar Rapids, Iowa, 1920), 260-267; for correspondence on Mangourit's preparations, see Frederick Jackson Turner, ed., "Mangourit Correspondence in Respect to Genet's Projected Attack upon the Floridas, 1793-1794," *AHA Ann. Rep.* (1897) (Washington, 1898), 569-679.

[14] Agents reported to Spanish officials, for example, that in Kentucky the democratic societies had hatched a plot "to associate the whole western coun-try" in a separatist movement. James White to Gayoso de Lemos, Mero Dis-trict, Feb. 1, 1794, in Lawrence Kinnaird, ed., "Spain in the Mississippi Valley, 1765-1794," *AHA Ann. Rep.* (1945) (4 vols., Washington, 1946), IV, 252-253.

[15] Westerners welcomed French aid to check English and Spanish intrigues and to reduce the threat of Indian attacks. See E. Merton Coulter, "The Efforts of the Democratic Societies of the West to Open the Navigation of the Mississippi," *MVHR*, XI (Dec., 1924), 378-379; Charles H. Ambler, *Sectionalism in Virginia from 1776 to 1861* (Chicago, 1910), p. 63; Archibald Henderson, "Isaac Shelby and the Genet Mission," *MVHR*, VI (March, 1920), 451. Spanish officials were aware of the pro-French leanings of Westerners. See Gayoso de Lemos, Governor of Natchez, to Baron Carondelet, Governor of Louisiana, Dec. 23, 1793, in Turner, "Draper Collection," *AHA Ann. Rep.* (1896), p. 1028.

To these hardened frontiersmen the federal government had little apparent value. It did not protect them from recurring Indian attacks on their homes and farms nor did it aid them to break Spain's grip on their economic welfare through her control of the Mississippi. Westerners believed, as their political leaders emphasized, that they had "an indisputable right to the undisturbed enjoyment of the Mississippi." Their leaders, for example, stressed that "too long, my fellow citizens have you placed an implicit dependence on the impartiality and virtue of the General Government. . . . Awake from your lethargic indifference. Think & act for yourselves. Let the example of France and her glorious successes animate you in the pursuit of those advantages which nature has bestowed upon your country." Then followed the clinching rhetorical question: "What, my countrymen, has been done for you by the General Government?"[16]

"Nature," declared John Breckinridge, a belligerent Westerner who later, under Jefferson, became Attorney General of the United States, "has done everything for us; Government everything against us." He and his fellow Westerners considered themselves "deluded by Govt., and sacrificed to the narrow local policy of the Eastern States."[17] For them, these pressing grievances transcended vague national loyalties. Any reasonable solution to their dilemma had great appeal and undoubtedly would win their support.[18]

* * * * *

In the summer of 1793, as the federal government attempted to negotiate a settlement with Spain which would resolve the dilemma of Southwest frontiersmen and as Genet's grandiose schemes

[16] "A Centinel" in the *Kentucky Gazette* (Lexington), Feb. 15, 1794. As far back as the Nootka Sound crisis the English had recognized that Westerners, "men hardy, inured to fatigue and danger, expert Marksmen, who live by hunting," are not loyal to the United States; they owe their allegiance to none. P. Allaire, report on occurrences from Aug. 6 to Sept. 1, 1790, Henry Adams Transcripts.

[17] Breckinridge to Samuel Hopkins, Mecklinburg County, Va., Sept. 14, 1794, quoted in Coulter, "The Efforts of the Democratic Societies of the West to open the Navigation of the Mississippi," *MVHR*, XI, 387.

[18] For failure of the government to protect settlers on the frontier see Turner, "The Origin of Genet's Projected Attack. . . ," *AHR*, III, 653; Link, *Democratic-Republican Societies*, p. 68. Some Westerners favored separation from the United States and an accommodation with Spain. Kinnaird, "Spain in the Mississippi Valley," *AHA Ann. Rep.* (1945), IV, p. xxxvi.

began to germinate along the frontier, the United States and Spain headed toward war.[19] Spanish-inspired Indian attacks along the frontier and Spain's uncompromising control of the Mississippi had led to serious protests from the United States in the fall of 1792. Basically American grievances with Spain, like those with England, stemmed from the American Revolution and the peace of 1783.

Spain had obtained Louisiana from France at the close of the Seven Years' War in 1763 to compensate her for the loss of Florida to England. By right of conquest, she had regained Florida from England at the end of the wars of the American Revolution. In once more controlling the Floridas, Spain faced a new neighbor and a perplexing boundary difficulty. In a secret article in the preliminary peace treaty with the United States in 1782 Great Britain had agreed that if Spain took the Floridas the boundary should be the thirty-first degree of north latitude; if not, it would be further north, at the mouth of the Yazoo River, 32°28' north latitude, which had been the boundary of British West Florida since 1764. Great Britain and the United States did not incorporate this secret article into the final peace between them in 1783.[20]

Spain contended, rightly, that as a third power she could not be bound by stipulations of the Anglo-American treaty and especially not by a secret article not incorporated into the final treaty. She had received the Floridas from England without defined boundaries,

[19] Jefferson reported to Monroe, ". . .Spain is so evidently *picking a quarrel* with us, that we see a war absolutely inevitable with her." Philadelphia, June 28, 1793, in Ford, *Writings of Jefferson*, VI, 322. Washington urged precautionary measures against Spain in fear of war. To The Secretary of War, Philadelphia, June 14, 1793, in Fitzpatrick, *Washington's Writings*, XXXII, 502-503; see also Turner, "The Origins of Genet's Projected Attack. . . ," *AHR*, III, 665; Thomas, *American Neutrality. . .*, pp. 181-182; Bemis, "Jefferson," in Bemis, *The American Secretaries of State. . .*, II, 55.

[20] Primary emphasis in this study is on Franco-American politics and diplomacy. The Spanish background is merely summarized and highlighted, primarily from secondary sources, to give adequate background to the main threads of the narrative and analysis. Reliable accounts of Spanish-American diplomacy in this period based on the sources are Arthur P. Whitaker, *The Spanish-American Frontier: 1783-1795* and *The Mississippi Question, 1795-1803*; Samuel F. Bemis, *Pinckney's Treaty*; and Isaac J. Cox, *The West Florida Controversy, 1793-1813*. Arthur B. Darling, *Our Rising Empire. . .*, covers Spanish-American diplomacy in relation to France and England. Pertinent diplomatic documents may be found in *ASP FR*, Vol. I.

and held to her claim for a northern boundary beyond the 31° line, enforcing it by occupation.

In any case, Spain did control two banks of the Mississippi River. For purposes of navigation, the extent of control was not the vital factor. What was crucial to American frontiersmen was that for several hundred miles along the lower shores the Mississippi River was in alien hands. The trans-Allegheny settlements of Kentucky and Tennessee, which in post-Revolutionary years were being populated rapidly, depended for their economic well-being upon unrestricted use of the Mississippi River to the Gulf. As the mountains were almost insuperable barriers to trade with the Atlantic seaboard, the Mississippi River was the logical and only usable large water artery for intercourse with the outside world. Americans saw the danger of relying upon Spain for free use of the river when in 1784 she closed it to American shipping.

Involved with these boundary and navigation difficulties was control of Indian tribes along the frontier and in the disputed lands. Both Spain and the United States claimed sovereignty over these tribes—Creek, Choctaw, Chickasaw, Cherokee—and attempted with treaties and presents to win them over. While making agreements with both sides, the Indians virtually allied themselves with Spain, under whose aegis they carried on border warfare against encroaching American settlers (as did Indians of the Northwest under British tutelage).

These were not the only Spanish problems which faced the government of the Confederation. As with England and France, the United States wanted and needed to work out a program of commercial intercourse with Spain and her colonies, particularly some agreement allowing unstifled trade with Spain's New World possessions. Spain had conceded such privileges willingly to no power. Basic in Spanish policy was a mercantilism which shut off Spanish America from legal trade with all of the world but Spain. As a new and not yet fully united nation, the United States was in no position to bargain with Spain for commercial concessions, let alone for settlement of the other questions; it had no valuable equivalent to offer.

Almost the only diplomatic weapon held by the United States was a threat, a threat that grew with the passing years. American frontiersmen were aggressive and impatient, and their women fecund. Each year they added to their strength; each year the population of the transmontane West increased; each year, as Spanish power declined, American power grew. In time it seemed probable that the Spanish-hating and Indian-fighting Westerner might settle by force what the American government could not solve by diplomacy. There was always the danger that American frontiersmen might sweep aside Spain's lamentable frontier defenses, occupy and hold the disputed border lands, force open the Mississippi, gain control of New Orleans, and impose an illicit commerce on Spain's wealthier domains to the south.

To forestall this, Spain fostered a separatist movement in the Southwest, particularly in the Kentucky area. She hoped to wean the settlers from their American ties and win them to Spanish allegiance through gold and intrigue and through tempting them with special trade privileges on the Mississippi and at New Orleans. Unlike England she was willing to negotiate with the new republic over its outstanding grievances, to make limited concessions to the American viewpoint, but not without some equivalent. In return for American recognition of her exclusive right to control the lower reaches of the Mississippi, Spain was willing to modify her most extensive boundary claims and to agree to a commercial treaty granting trade privileges in certain Spanish European ports to Americans. In order to obtain these limited concessions, the United States would have been compelled to surrender its demand for free navigation of the Mississippi. In its essentials, this was the position taken by Don Diego de Gardoqui, the envoy Spain sent to the United States in 1785 to negotiate over issues then unsettled.

After extended discussions with Gardoqui, the American Secretary of Foreign Affairs, John Jay, in 1786 agreed to a treaty with Spain in which the United States, in return for the Spanish trade concessions, was to "forbear" use of the Spanish portion of the Mississippi for a period of thirty years, but not to yield the "right" of navigation. This proposal split the Congress of the Confederation along sectional lines. To the Southerner it looked as if Jay had sacrificed the Southwest, which was dependent on free navigation of the Mississippi, to the interests of the Northeast, which desired the trading privileges thus secured. As a result of sectional opposition in the Continental Congress, where it was impossible to get the necessary two-thirds vote for approval, Jay never completed the treaty. Spain did not, however, retreat. She continued to control the Mississippi and to keep it closed to Americans.

The pioneer settler's fear that in a government controlled largely by Eastern merchants their welfare would be sacrificed to mercantile interests and the consequent sectional distrust fed Spanish intrigue. Gardoqui, having failed to obtain a treaty, turned his attention to fostering a separatist movement in the Southwest with the goal of creating an independent state amenable to Spanish policy.

A leading figure and convenient instrument for Spanish plans was an American veteran of the Revolution, General James Wilkinson. While holding a commission from the American government, Wilkinson swore a secret oath of allegiance to the Spanish crown. His task, for which he received Spanish gold, was to detach the Southwest from the government of the Confederation. To facilitate their plans of winning over American frontiersmen, Spaniards, under a special licensing system, opened the Mississippi River to American use and even allowed Westerners to land their cargoes at New Orleans. Unwisely, they also opened the region north of the Floridas to American immigration.[21]

Despite Spanish conspiracies and concessions and despite the efforts of Wilkinson and others like him to separate the Southwest from the seaboard communities, the region clung to the new federal government of 1789. In 1790, after North Carolina had relinquished her control of the area to the federal government, the United States established a territorial government in Tennessee, and in 1792, after being released from Virginia, Kentucky became a state. These developments did not dissipate discontent in the Southwest; hatred of Spain and distrust of the central government still prevailed. Indian attacks, abetted by Spain, continued to harry frontier settle-

[21] Much has been written on the dubious and controversial career of Wilkinson. Accounts of his dealings, with varying emphases, may be found in Thomas R. May and M. R. Werner, *The Admirable Trumpeter: A Biography of General James Wilkinson* (New York, 1941), pp. 79-109; James R. Jacobs, *Tarnished Warrior: Major-General James Wilkinson* (New York, 1938), pp. 70-109; Manuel Serrano y Sanz, *El brigadier Jaime Wilkinson y sus tratos con España para la independencia del Kentucky (años 1787 a 1797)* (Madrid, 1915).

ments and the Philadelphia government did not provide protection. Even though under the Spanish licensing system they had been granted generous use of the Mississippi, Westerners wanted no trammels, however slight, placed on their use of the river. Their chafing under Spain's continued grip on the river was unabated, and their resentment against the federal government for not obtaining the desired freedom still smoldered.

Unable to obtain desired federal assistance, the frontiersmen were eager to descend upon Spain's Indian allies—and in several instances they did so—and even upon the Spaniards to protect their lands and livelihood. If not restrained, it appeared that they would plunge the country into war with Spain. As early as the summer of 1791, in fact, English newspapers carried stories that war between the United States and Spain was inevitable and that both sides were pushing preparations for it.[22]

The problems of the Southwest and of relations with Spain were far from settlement when Washington became President. Both the President and his Secretary of State were concerned over the dangerous situation and were aware of the difficulties which had destroyed the Jay-Gardoqui treaty. Jefferson tried to avoid similar difficulties; his idea was to wait for an opportune moment when Spain was mired in European troubles and then to force a solution by diplomacy that was favorable to the United States, and particularly to frontiersmen of the Southwest.

In the Nootka Sound controversy—at the beginning at least—Jefferson saw the awaited opportune moment, the chance, in fact, to force to a favorable issue frontier problems with both Spain and England. He initiated steps for a treaty with Spain whereby the United States would have acquired the Floridas and free navigation of the Mississippi. In return, the United States would have guaranteed to Spain the west bank of the river. When Spain backed down before British power, the threat of war disappeared, and so did Jefferson's hopes of forcing the treaty on Spain.

Next Jefferson attempted to enlist French aid in getting Spain

[22] William Short to Jefferson, Paris, July 24, 1791, National Archives, State Dept., Diplomatic Despatches, France. Jefferson denied that the United States was preparing for war and maintained that the London newspapers lied. Jefferson to Short, Philadelphia, Nov. 24, 1791, in Lipscomb, *Jefferson's Works*, VIII, 258.

to meet American demands on the Mississippi and to accede to American boundary claims.[23] With the help of Lafayette's influence at court, he was successful. The Count de Montmorin, then French foreign minister, transmitted a memorandum embodying the American case to the Spanish foreign minister. Prompted—and perhaps startled—by the French intercession, the Spanish government offered to resume negotiations with the United States on the boundary and river questions. Accepting the Spanish offer, President Washington appointed William Carmichael, then *chargé d'affaires* in Madrid, and William Short, recently elevated to American Minister Resident at The Hague, as joint commissioners plenipotentiary to conduct the Spanish negotiations.

Before negotiations in Madrid could begin, the fabric of European politics and diplomacy was rent by revolution in France. In beheading Louis XVI France destroyed her family alliance with the Bourbon monarchy of Spain. On February 1, 1793, the day that Short joined Carmichael in Madrid, France declared war on Spain. Not long after, on May 25, 1793, Spain and Great Britain signed a treaty of alliance; old friends were now enemies and old enemies were dedicated to a common cause.

So upsetting to American diplomacy was this European diplomatic revolution that the American commissioners in Madrid postponed presenting their case. The new conditions called for new instructions. Soon after news of war between France and Spain reached America, Spanish border intrigues increased, and the attitude and conduct of the Spanish *chargés* in Philadelphia toward the American government became intractable. Jefferson believed that the Spanish agents, now that the international situation as reflected in North America was favorable to Spain, were trying to provoke a war. Faced by two hostile and powerful neighbors who were now allies, the United States at this juncture could see no favorable solution to its border problems.[24] This was far different from the state

[23] "The middle ground held by France between us and Spain," Jefferson told Short at Paris, required that we place full confidence in France and particularly in Montmorin. Philadelphia, March 12, 1791, National Archives, State Dept., Diplomatic and Consular Instructions.

[24] According to Short, who had obtained a copy of the document, the new Anglo-Spanish alliance provided that a rupture with either ally would be cause for both states to unite against a third power. War with Spain at

of affairs at the time of the Nootka Sound crisis in 1790. The international situation, Indian raids along the borders, pressures of domestic politics, plus the dangerous burden of Genet placed the Washington government in a serious dilemma in the summer of 1793.

Carmichael and Short attempted to negotiate, but, as they had little or no bargaining power, their efforts proved fruitless. The Spaniards argued, delayed, and evaded. Under the circumstances no reason existed for acceding to American demands; the United States had nothing to offer to Spain and it was yet to be feared. When Carmichael left for the United States in January, 1794, the commission was dissolved; failure of the negotiation became a fact.

* * * * *

If Genet's plans were successful and Southwestern frontiersmen attacked Spanish Louisiana and Florida, there would be war with Spain. As an ally, an already hostile England was committed to join Spain and under the circumstances the United States might be crushed by two powerful neighbors.[25] Genet, moreover, had designs on Canada, dependent of course upon American support and co-operation, which, if carried out, would surely have arrayed England in open warfare against the United States. In propaganda directed to Canadians, Genet stressed that if delivered from English domination they would enjoy freedom, independence, and could join France and the United States in alliance.[26]

Although war with Spain seemed probable in any case—Jefferson even considering it "absolutely inevitable"—when Washington's Cabinet first heard of Genet's disaster-breeding schemes in the summer of 1793, it took prompt measures to forestall him.[27] As early

---

this time would have meant also war with England. See Bemis, "Jefferson," in Bemis, *The American Secretaries of State. . .*, II, 56.

[25] Spain's governor of Louisiana, Baron de Carondelet, for example, appealed to John G. Simcoe, Britain's lieutenant-governor in Canada, for assistance against Americans in the West. He told his superiors that Spanish and British policies in the West were similar and that the two nations would benefit mutually by aiding each other. Abraham P. Nasatir, "The Anglo-Spanish Frontier on the Upper Mississippi 1786-1796," *Iowa Journal of History and Politics* (April, 1931), XXIX, 181-182.

[26] "Les Français Libres a leurs frères les Canadiens," pamphlet, n.p., n.d., Genet Papers, Library of Congress.

[27] Jefferson to the Governor of Kentucky, Philadelphia, Aug. 29, 1793, *ASP FR*, I, 455; Thomas, *American Neutrality. . .*, pp. 182-185.

as February, 1793, there had been rumors and forewarnings of French designs on Spanish America. In hopes of enlisting Jefferson's support, Genet sounded him out, "not as Secy. of State, but as Mr. Jeff.," on his attitude toward French frontier schemes, particularly as set forth in Genet's instructions to Michaux and his manifesto to Canadians which urged them to shake off England's yoke and to rely on American friendship.[28]

Under the impression that the Kentucky expeditions were to assemble outside the United States, Jefferson cautioned that Americans enlisting in the Louisiana project would "be hung, if they commd. hostilities agt. a nation at peace with the U. S.," then added significantly that he "did not care what insurrections should be excited in Louisiana." According to Genet, he indicated also that "a small spontaneous irruption of Kentuckians into New Orleans would advance" the treaty negotiations then going on in Spain and might help in persuading Spain to concede a treaty along lines suggested by the United States.[29]

At Genet's request, Jefferson now revised a letter of introduction for Michaux to Governor Isaac Shelby of Kentucky. The original letter had recommended Michaux merely as a botanist, the revision implied that he had Jefferson's confidence. The Secretary of State did this even though he knew that Michaux was to carry manifestos calling for rebellion against English rule in Canada and against Spanish rule in Louisiana as well as instructions for organizers of the invasion of Louisiana.[30]

Despite the federal government's promptness in trying to safeguard American neutrality on the frontier, its immediate measures were not effective. Governor Shelby, for example, while at first

[28] Turner, "The Origins of Genet's Projected Attack. . . ," *AHR*, III, 668-669; Jefferson, The Anas, July 5, 1793, in Ford, *Writings of Jefferson*, I, 236.

[29] Genet to Minister of Foreign Affairs, Philadelphia, July 25, 1793, Turner, *CFM*, p. 221.

[30] The Genet Papers, Library of Congress, contain accounts of Michaux's expenditures and Genet's advances to him. Box 46 contains records of secret expenditures. On July 14, 1793, for example, Genet gave Michaux $250.00 and on July 13, $500.00. Sent by Genet to co-operate with Michaux in the expedition aimed at Louisiana was a Louisiana Creole, Auguste Lachaise, who was made a head of brigade. AAE CP EU, [Paris], 1795, ff. 194-195. For details on Jefferson's role, see Bemis, "Jefferson," in Bemis, *The American Secretaries of State. . .* , II, 82.

promising co-operation, refused to prosecute alleged offenders. He pleaded that all citizens had a right to leave the state and that he had no power to prevent them from going and taking arms with them, even if the arms were destined for use against Spain. This had been a good occasion, he said later, to impress upon the national government the need to open the Mississippi.[31] Not understanding the international complications involved, the settlers saw this as an opportunity to take the settlement of the river navigation question into their own hands. Sentiment in Kentucky, commented an astute English observer, indicated "that the project of opening by force the navigation of the Mississippi is not merely a transient sentiment of individuals, but is the fixed universal determination of the great mass of the inhabitants of that part of American territory."[32]

The frontiersmen were in no mood to be stopped by mere admonitions from the government in Philadelphia. Clark and his men were almost ready to crash into Louisiana, and other forces in Georgia and South Carolina were prepared to invade Florida. Fortunately, a combination of circumstances beyond Genet's control blocked the realization of his invasion plans.

Realizing with alarm that the West was in turmoil and perhaps ripe for general insurrection, Washington's government now took decisive steps to meet the peril and to alleviate Western grievances. These were coupled with the measures designed to uphold American neutrality. At this juncture, on December 31, 1793, Jefferson, who had sympathized with Western grievances and who had looked upon Genet's frontier schemes in a more favorable light than had Hamilton and Washington, retired from the State Department. With his resignation Westerners lost their best friend in government.[33] Not long afterward President Washington, on March 24, 1794, issued what was in effect a second proclamation of neutrality. The proclamation's warning was specific. All men taking part in Western expeditions against Spanish lands, it said, would be prosecuted. To give the proclamation teeth, the neutrality act of June 5,

[31] See Shelby's two letters to Jefferson of Oct. 5, 1793, and Jan. 13, 1794, in *ASP FR*, I, 455-456; Henderson, "Isaac Shelby," *MVHR, VI,* 467; Darling, *Our Rising Empire. . . ,* pp. 162-164.

[32] Hammond to Grenville, Philadelphia, June 24, 1794, Henry Adams Transcripts.

[33] Whitaker, *Spanish-American Frontier. . . ,* p. 188.

1794, embodied the proclamation's provisions into statutory law. The new law prohibited foreign enlistments in the United States, a rule which has guided American neutral conduct to the present.[34]

More effective in preserving American neutrality than the government's actions, which came after Genet's enterprises had begun to collapse, were the French minister's desperate need for funds to finance his projects and the sequence of events in Europe. Having been refused advance payment on the American debt to France, Genet had nowhere to turn for the funds essential in equipping the frontier forces. His *coup* against Louisiana, the Spanish governor of the province believed, "failed only because of lack of money."[35] No help could be expected from France, where, by June, 1793, Jacobins had replaced Girondins. So hard pressed in Europe was the Jacobin regime that it could devote little energy, let alone money, to American enterprises. It recalled Genet, disavowed his activities, and abandoned the frontier projects. Then, on March 6, 1794, Joseph Fauchet, the succeeding French minister, issued a proclamation which quashed the projects and Genet's already-completed arrangements.[36]

[34] For the proclamation of March 24, 1794, see Fitzpatrick, *Washington's Writings*, XXXIII, 304-305; for the neutrality act of June 5, 1794, see *The Statutes at Large of the United States of America*, I, 381-384; the legislation is discussed in Hyneman, *The First American Neutrality*, p. 137 and in Thomas, *American Neutrality. . .*, pp. 278-279. While attention has been focused on the more numerous and more significant French neutrality problems, this is not to imply that there were none with the British. The British, for example, hatched plots against French territory. In one case they planned an expedition from American soil against Saint Domingue. *Ibid.*, p. 187 n.

[35] Baron de Carondelet to Juan Delavillebeuvre, New Orleans, April 23, 1794, in Kinnaird, "Spain in the Mississippi Valley," *AHA Ann. Rep.* (1945), IV, 271. The financial deficiency was viewed by contemporary Westerners also as a major handicap; see James White to Gayoso de Lemos, Feb. 1, 1794. White spoke of "large promises" by the French unaccompanied by even a "denier of money." *Ibid.*, p. 252. Judge Henry Innes of Kentucky, Feb. 14, 1794, also wrote to the Spanish governor Gayoso de Lemos in the same vein. He prophesied that the Clark-Genet expedition would "unquestionably fail as it has not the essential ingredients of money and Influence." *Ibid.*, p. 257. Not being paid, Clark's men, for example, took to plunder. *Columbia Gazette* (Columbia, S. C.), June 27, 1794.

[36] *Virginia Herald and Fredericksburg Advertiser*, March 27, 1794, and Turner, "Mangourit Correspondence. . . ," *AHA Ann. Rep.* (1897), p. 629, contain Fauchet's proclamation; see also E. Wilson Lyon, *Louisiana in French Diplomacy, 1759-1804*, p. 72.

If Fauchet had not stopped the projected invasions when he did, the leaders of the projects, despite all handicaps, would at least have attempted them.[37] Apparently the reasoning of French authorities in halting them was that they did not wish to make still another enemy for France, no matter how weak. The Louisiana and Florida projects were violations of American neutrality; to retain the alliance and American friendship France had to abandon them.[38] Events in Europe, furthermore, caused a change in Spanish diplomacy to the advantage of the United States. The Spanish government, increasingly dissatisfied with its English alliance, saw advantages in American friendship. In the summer of 1794, therefore, it made overtures to the United States to renew disrupted negotiations, requesting that Washington send a new plenipotentiary to Madrid. This request gave birth to the Thomas Pinckney mission, which gained what Westerners had been demanding. Europe's troubles had worked to America's advantage, not only to save the United States from an unwanted war but also to settle a festering domestic problem.[39]

* * * * *

[37] Mangourit, for example, tried to convince Fauchet's agent that it was too late to halt the East Florida expedition. Murdoch, "Citizen Mangourit. . . ," *JSH*, XIV, 439; see also Lyon, *Louisiana in French Diplomacy. . .* , p. 77. For Spanish officialdom's reaction to the projected invasions, see "Circular Addressed by the Government to all the Inhabitants of Louisiana, Feb. 4, 1794," by Baron de Carondelet, the governor of Louisiana and West Florida, in Kinnaird, "Spain in the Mississippi Valley," *AHA Ann. Rep.* (1945), IV, 255-257. Despite drawbacks and handicaps faced by the expeditions, chances for success were not illusory because of the pitiable condition of the Spanish defenses. See Baron de Carondelet to Duke de Alcudia, Spanish Secretary of State, New Orleans, Jan. 1, 1794, in Turner, "Draper Collection," *AHA Ann. Rep.* (1896), pp. 1027-1029. Carondelet predicted the loss of Louisiana in case Clark invaded.

[38] Turner, "The Origins of Genet's Projected Attack. . . ," *AHR*, III, 671; Lyon, *Louisiana in French Diplomacy. . .* , pp. 72-73; Fauchet did not completely stop the planned invasions. After Genet's recall a small force landed in Florida and a few French and Americans assembled in Georgia. François Barbé-Marbois, *The History of Louisiana* (Philadelphia, 1830), p. 159.

[39] Whitaker, *Spanish-American Frontier. . .* , pp. 182-183; Bemis, *Pinckney's Treaty*, pp. 239-241; Bemis points out that the decision to send Pinckney to Madrid had been made before the Anglo-American crisis of 1794 which led to the Jay treaty; for the effect of Jay's treaty on the Spanish negotiations, see pp. 249-279; for a "French view of Genet's conduct," [ca. Oct., 1793], see Turner, *CFM*, p. 283-286.

A distinctive feature of Genet's mission and of the American reaction to the French Revolution was the rise of democratic societies. If they did not appear "as if by magic from one end of the continent to the other," as Genet expressed it, these "popular" political organizations did rise swiftly and spread throughout the land in the wake of pro-French Republican sentiment. Philadelphians organized one of the first and most influential of these societies, which were modeled after the Jacobin clubs of France, a few days after Genet's arrival. Its leaders lost no time in approaching the French minister. Asked to pick a name for the newly organized club, which some proposed to call "The Sons of Liberty," Genet suggested the title that was adopted, "Democratic Club."[40] Once organized, the Philadelphia club sent out invitations for the formation of affiliated societies. From all parts of the nation came quick and generally favorable responses.[41] The democratic society of the national capital thus inaugurated something of a national movement.[42]

Complex though the origins of the democratic societies are, this seems clear. They were pro-French alliance, pro-French, and anti-English; they were vociferous in their attachment to the French

[40] Quoted from Minnigerode, *Genet*, pp. 219-220; see also Genet, *Washington, Jefferson and "Citizen" Genet, 1793*, p. 34. Genet, reported Hammond, had been instrumental in re-establishing and supporting a club in Philadelphia affiliated to the Jacobin clubs in France. Philadelphia, July 7, 1793, Henry Adams Transcripts.

[41] The following account of the Democratic Societies, while based also on varied and independent sources, relies heavily on Link, *Democratic-Republican Societies. . . .* Republican leaders in Pennsylvania worked to convert popular interest in the European war into enthusiasm for domestic politics. Alexander J. Dallas, an organizer of the Philadelphia Society, and his cohorts worked to make the society a means of organizing anti-Federalists in the state and nation into a cohesive political group. Walters, *Alexander James Dallas*, pp. 45-46. For a contemporary account of formation of the Philadelphia society by one of its vice presidents, see Charles Biddle, *Autobiography of Charles Biddle, 1745-1821*, pp. 252-253. Biddle's Federalist friends thought he "could be of service by moderating some of the most violent of the party [Republicans] who were inclined to do anything that would involve us in a war with Great Britain." See also Warren, *Jacobin and Junto*, p. 53.

[42] Citizens of Lexington, Kentucky, for example, embraced "the laudable objects of the Philadelphia Society." *Kentucky Gazette* (Lexington), Aug. 24, 1793. Similar society principles were adopted by the Norfolk society. *Virginia Herald and Fredericksburg Advertiser*, June 13, 1793. In Boston, formation of a Democratic Society attracted great attention and excitement. Morse, *The Federalist Party in Massachusetts. . . ,* pp. 74-75.

Revolution; they were antimonarchical, anti-Federalist, and pro-Republican; and they were suspicious of the federal government while sympathetic to Genet.[43] From these societies, which functioned apparently as early political pressure groups, Genet received considerable popular support.

In welcoming Genet, one society deplored that England, "a nation from whom we are descended should be among the first in the conspiracy against liberty."[44] Devotion to France and the French Revolution led a society in Charleston to petition the Jacobin Club in Paris for adoption. "Americans must be alarmed!" declared one of the manifestos; "the interest and preservation of France is that of America." On another occasion it said that "if the present eventful European contest should terminate in the dissolution of the French Republic, we have no doubt but that the craving appetite of despotism will be satisfied with nothing less than American vassalage in some form or other."[45]

In almost all conflicts over neutrality and treaty interpretation between Genet and Washington's government the democratic societies supported the French minister. A foremost tenet in their pro-French crusade was support for the French alliance. Piling resolution on resolution, they demanded that the government honor the alliance. At their festive gatherings they drank to such toasts as "The Alliance between the Sister Republics of the United States and France. May their union be as incorporate as light and heat and their friendship as lasting as time."[46] The club in Portland,

[43] See Link, *Democratic-Republican Societies. . .* , p. 125 ff.; Hazen, *Contemporary American Opinion of the French Revolution,* pp. 194-195; William Miller, "The Democratic Societies and the Whiskey Insurrection," *Pennsylvania Magazine of History and Biography,* LXII (July, 1938), 234; Warren, *Jacobin and Junto,* p. 56.

[44] German Republican Society of Philadelphia to Genet, Philadelphia, May 5, 1793, signed Henry Kammerer, Pres., Genet Papers, Library of Congress, IX, 2785.

[45] The quotations are from a printed pamphlet addressed to the citizens of Charleston, Aug. 20, 1793, in the Genet Papers, Box 49; from *Baltimore Daily Repository,* Sept. 18, 1793, cited in Eugene P. Link, "The Democratic Societies of the Carolinas," *North Carolina Historical Review,* XVIII (July, 1941), 270; see also Hazen, *Contemporary American Opinion of the French Revolution,* pp. 195-196.

[46] This toast was raised in the presence of Genet's successor, Fauchet, in Philadelphia on May 1, 1794. Woodbury, *Public Opinion in Philadelphia. . .* , p. 72.

Maine, declared "that the cause of France is our own, that our Interest, Liberty and public happiness are involved in her fate, that we are bound to support her by every type of principle and gratitude as well as principle of self-preservation."[47]

Another resolution from the Pennsylvania society said that "we ought to resist to the utmost of our power all attempts to alienate our affections from France and detach us from her alliance."[48] Other democratic societies were not so timorous; they called for war by the side of America's transatlantic ally. In cities such as Charleston, Philadelphia, and New York, Americans organized French benevolent and patriotic societies to propagandize for the French Revolution. These French clubs were more akin in their revolutionary zeal and other aspects to the French Jacobin clubs than were the so-called democratic societies, which were more concerned with American political problems.[49]

Little wonder that Genet was swayed. He saw about him evidence indicating that public support for him and the alliance was greater than for the Federalist administration. His efforts to array the United States alongside republican France in her struggle seemed to fit what he construed to be public sentiment. One society even asked its members to arm in defense of the Rights of Man; another, believing war inevitable, called on "all good republican citizens to provide themselves as speedily as possible with such implements of war as may be necessary for their defence."[50]

In keeping with pro-French sentiments, the democratic societies directed some of their wrath against Washington's proclamation of neutrality. In scornful denunciations, they tarred the proclamation as despotic, unconstitutional, and as an attempt to replace republican government with government by proclamation. In the clubs there was talk of need for a change in government to save democracy.

[47] Portland Republican Society Papers, cited in Link, *Democratic-Republican Societies*, p. 128.

[48] The Democratic Society of Pennsylvania, Resolution of Jan. 9, 1794, quoted from Woodbury, *Public Opinion in Philadelphia. . .* , p. 68.

[49] The Newark Democratic Society, for example, concerned itself with the spread of political information and propaganda. See, *Transition from Aristocracy to Democracy in New Jersey. . .* , pp. 40-50.

[50] Link, *Democratic-Republican Societies*, p. 129; Hazen, *Contemporary American Opinion of the French Revolution*, p. 198.

Even Washington himself could not escape attacks by the societies.[51]

With the announcement of the Jay mission to England, the abuse heaped upon the President increased. All the societies apparently passed resolutions condemning Jay's appointment and denouncing the mission. In castigating Jay the New York society declared, a few days after his departure, "We take pleasure in avowing that we are lovers of the French nation; that we esteem their cause as our own." Hence, "he who is an enemy to the French revolution [Jay] . . . ought not to be intrusted with the guidance of any part of the machine of government."

Viewing the war in Europe as "a war of tyrants against liberty," the democratic clubs wanted no dealings with Britain, "the champion of despotism." A society in Virginia pleaded, "Let us unite with France and stand or fall together." Calling for a repudiation of Washington's policies, particularly the Jay appointment, it lamented that Genet had been "abused," France denied her treaty privileges, and Americans wishing to aid France with their arms "prosecuted as traitors." To prevent what it termed despotism and to chastise the executive for what it termed "misconduct," the society urged Americans to "consider well this experiment": to amend the Constitution to limit the President's tenure of office to eight years.[52]

After the contents of the Jay treaty became public, democratic societies organized mass meetings protesting the "British Treaty," published public protests in the newspapers, passed scathing resolutions blasting the Federalist document, and circulated antitreaty petitions. Members of one club, while not willing to indulge in the popular

[51] See, for example, the resolutions of the Democratic Society of Pennsylvania of Jan. 9 and April 10, 1794, Woodbury, *Public Opinion in Philadelphia* . . . , pp. 67-71.

[52] The quotations are from Hazen, *Contemporary American Opinion of the French Revolution*, pp. 200-203, citing the *Independent Chronicle* (Boston), May 19 and Aug. 11, 1794. On the other hand, staunch New England Federalist Harrison Gray Otis wrote to his wife, "Should Great Britain be compelled to yield, it is my opinion that our liberties and independence would fall a sacrifice. She is the only barrier to the dreadful deluge, and when that is broken down, it will be time for us to prepare to be good and dutiful subjects to the French." N.p., n.d., cited in Samuel E. Morison, *The Life and Letters of Harrison Gray Otis*, I, 51.

sport of burning Jay in effigy, left little doubt as to their feelings by indicating, "if the original were here—!"[53]

The opposition of the democratic societies to Washington's foreign policy demonstrates that in their first great crisis in foreign relations, Americans used foreign policy as a political football. Pressure groups everywhere not only opposed the government's foreign policy—in many instances merely for domestic political considerations—but worked also to sabotage it.[54] Their objectives were goals —ideological, political, and economic—which Federalists opposed. They worked against incumbent office-holders, and supported candidates, almost always Republican, who were favorable to their views; they electioneered. In these political activities their more immediate objectives varied according to local conditions, but in opposing the national government, particularly in foreign policy, they shared objectives and features common to all of the clubs. In fighting the Federalists, men of the democratic societies went so far in their opposition to lawful governmental leaders as to look upon a representative of a foreign government as a champion of their principles. They trusted Genet, apparently, more than the Washington administration.[55] In resorting to direct action in the West and in aiding Genet's frontier projects, the democratic societies not only acted against a political opposition they distrusted, but in a sense they also revolted against the federal government.

* * * * *

In attacking the government and in defending France the democratic societies created a widespread clamor, but equally vehement

[53] *South Carolina State Gazette,* Nov. 26, 1795, quoted in Link, *Democratic-Republican Societies. . . ,* p. 133.

[54] When, for instance, the New York Democratic Society was established (Feb., 1794), it was joined by so many members of the Tammany Society that the two organizations became almost identical and hence both took on pro-French political coloring. Edwin P. Kilroe, *Saint Tammany and the Origin of the Society of Tammany* (New York, 1913), p. 92; for evidence of the pro-French attitude of Tammany, see Peter Paulson, "The Tammany Society and the Jeffersonian Movement in New York City, 1795-1800," *New York History,* XXXIV (Jan. 1953), 72-84.

[55] At a dinner party given in Philadelphia by a militia regiment, the guests raised a toast to Genet but refused to do the same for Washington. Link, *Democratic-Republican Societies. . . ,* p. 180; see also Minnigerode, *Genet,* 222.

were the Federalist denunciations of the clubs.[56] How large their national following or how representative of public sentiment the democratic clubs were perhaps will never be known. The mere fact that they aroused frenzied opposition and that their hold upon the public caused alarm would indicate they had a substantial following. Yet Federalists denied that the clamor raised by the societies was, as the Republicans boasted, the voice of the people. They claimed that the societies and the ideas for which they stood represented only a small segment of public opinion, or as one editor said, "Great Cry and Little Wool."[57]

In any case, the "Great Cry" of the democratic clubs frightened anti-Republicans and men of wealth; they were afraid of anything, anybody, any idea which might agitate the populace. To them the societies appeared a threat to order, stability, property, and to the vital financial tie to England; an association of political Jesuits "which must be crushed in its infancy or it would certainly crush the government."[58] Federalists said "the Genet begotten Clubs abuse every man as an enemy to his country who opposes their arrogant assumption of power. These Clubs are become the tyrants of America."[59]

To Hamilton's wealthy followers, of whom a prominent contemporary said "Gain is their God, and present gain is their polar star," the mere mention of the democratic clubs aroused anger. The societies would introduce into government, horrified Federalists warned, "all the heat and ungovernable passions of a simple democracy."[60] One Virginia dame denounced the democratic society in Kentucky as "that horrible sink of treason,—that hateful synagogue

[56] John Quincy Adams, as an illustration, irrespective of political expediency refused to attend "the anarchical dinner" of the Boston society. The clubs, he declared, were "the folly of the day," to John Adams, Boston, Feb. 10, 1793, Ford, *The Writings of John Quincy Adams,* I, 134.

[57] *Independent Chronicle* (Boston), March 2, 1795, quoted in Hazen, *Contemporary American Opinion of the French Revolution,* p. 203.

[58] Noah Webster, "To the Public," New York, March 4, 1797, in Warfel, ed., *Letters of Webster,* p. 146.

[59] *American Minerva,* reprinted in the *Georgia Gazette* (Savannah), June 19, 1794.

[60] The quotations are from Horatio Gates to Madison, n.p., n.d., cited in Link, *Democratic-Republican Societies. . . ,* p. 176; Nathaniel Chipman to Hamilton, Rutland, Vermont, Jan. 9, 1794, in Daniel Chipman, *The Life of Hon. Nathaniel Chipman* (Boston, 1846), pp. 398-399.

of anarchy,—that odious conclave of tumult,—that frightful cathedral of discord,—that poisonous garden of conspiracy,—that hellish school of rebellion and opposition to all regular and well-balanced authority."[61]

Within the Federalist hierarchy the wrathful voices spoke out charging that the clubs sought to overthrow the Constitution and to destroy the federal system. Oliver Wolcott, Jr., warned "that these popular societies speak the sentiments of certain demagogues, and that the clubs consist of hot-headed, ignorant, or wicked men, devoted entirely to the views of France." Fisher Ames denounced the "rabble formed into a club," and ranted that the clubs "were born in sin, the impure offspring of Genet." He said that "they poison every spring; they whisper lies to every gale," but that "such foes are to be feared as well as despised." At election time "they will be as busy as Macbeth's witches."[62]

Behind the societies many saw the specter of Revolutionary France; they were convinced that the clubs stemmed from those of the dreaded Jacobins in Paris.[63] The danger that they might inspire revolutionary changes in the United States as they had in France and that they might force a realignment in wealth and property led Federalists to launch vicious assaults on them. Spurred on by the knowledge that they had much to lose and nothing to gain by social change, political upheaval, and wartime collaboration with France, they threw ethics aside and fought a death struggle.

In Federalist hands a formidable weapon was economic coercion. In Philadelphia in 1793 the large merchants agreed to boycott a marine insurance businessman, Clement Biddle, because of his pro-

---

[61] *Virginia Chronicle*, July 17, 1794, quoted in Link, *Democratic-Republican Societies. . . ,* p. 175. Along the same vein a clergyman described the "Jacobins" of the societies as men with "Hell in their heart, and faction on their tongue." Warren, *Jacobin and Junto*, p. 54.

[62] Oliver Wolcott, Jr., to Oliver Wolcott, Sr., Philadelphia, April 14, 1794, Gibbs, ed., *Wolcott Papers*, I, 134; the Fisher Ames quotations are from Warren, *Jacobin and Junto*, pp. 56-57, and Hazen, *Contemporary American Opinion of the French Revolution*, p. 204.

[63] John Quincy Adams wrote, for public consumption: "And as to the democratic societies, they are so perfectly affiliated to the Parisian Jacobins that their origin from a common parent cannot possibly be mistaken," writing as "Columbus" in the *Columbian Centinel* (Boston), Dec. 4, 1793, reprinted in Ford, *The Writings of John Quincy Adams*, I, 156; see also La Rochefoucauld-Liancourt, *Travels*, II, 516-517.

French activities. The same merchants also coerced their employees. To keep their jobs the employees were compelled to vote Federalist. Even the mails were not safe; members of the societies had to exercise care to keep their mail from being intercepted. At their meetings they had to guard against rowdies who might turn the gatherings into riots and so lend substance to Federalist charges that the societies were riotous. During elections Republicans had to be vigilant against fraud and rigged results. Even physical violence had to be warded off, and often was not.[64]

Among countermeasures designed to destroy the influence of the popular societies Federalists organized antidemocratic societies. While it was true that before the popular clubs had come into existence wealthy conservatives had benefited from organization, and that as Federalists they continued to enjoy powerful support from chambers of commerce and from the Society of Cincinnati, such organizations were not enough. Federalists created the new organizations for the specific purpose of countering the influence of the popular societies, to "check the wild and Jacobinical self-created clubs." In line with these aims they took such patriotic-sounding names as "The Constitutional Association" (Elizabeth-town, New Jersey) and the "Society of Constitutional and Governmental Support" (Norfolk, Virginia). Even George Washington lent his support to these ostensibly patriotic organizations.[65]

More important than the antidemocratic organizations in combatting the popular societies and the Republicans was the Federalist-dominated press. To keep such journals as John Fenno's *Gazette of the United States* (Philadelphia), Noah Webster's *American Minerva* (New York), and Benjamin Russell's *Columbian Centinel* (Boston) financially viable, wealthy Federalists poured money into them. While Republicans may have exaggerated in contending that the country's press was overwhelmingly in Federalist hands, their claims may not have been far from the truth. Even in the 1790's newspapers were substantial businesses requiring capital investment, and as business ventures they were controlled by businessmen. Most of the businessmen were Federalists. Logically, those

[64] Link, *Democratic-Republican Societies. . .* , p. 187.
[65] *Ibid.*, p. 188.

who supported the press controlled it. Most newspapers in the Federalist era were Federalist organs.[66]

Through their subsidized press the Federalists were able to impede or stop the flow of information on activities of the popular societies or of the Republicans. One result of this press dominance was propaganda, widely circulated and widely believed, that the American government was being undermined by "French gold" and that "foreign influence" manipulated the democratic societies. Another piece of effective press strategy directed against the popular clubs was the publication of announcements, without basis in fact, that various clubs had disbanded; this to belittle the societies and to show that they were losing popular support.[67]

In part, the Federalist campaign to discredit the democratic clubs was a scheme to destroy Genet. The Federalists believed that the French republican's popular support came mainly from the democratic societies or was whipped up by their activities; they were convinced that the democratic clubs, "composed of men of superficial minds and low manners" were founded by Genet. To discredit them would be to destroy Genet's influence.[68]

[66] For Federalist backing of Webster's *Minerva*, see Warfel, *Noah Webster*, 223-224. In March, 1794, Webster wrote a pamphlet entitled *Revolution in France, considered in respect to its Progress and Effects*, in which he violently attacked the democratic clubs. Like Washington he detested party spirit which to him was faction—actually opposition—which in turn was death to existing government. *Ibid.*, pp. 228-229. Webster sent a copy of his pamphlet to Washington with an accompanying letter in which he stated that it was "the duty of every good citizen to use his influence in restraining the violence of parties. . . ." Webster to Washington, New York, April 20, 1794, in Warfel, *Letters of Noah Webster*, pp. 117-118. Washington's first administration, according to Washington's latest biographer, enjoyed "the solid endorsement and unqualified esteem of a great majority of the influential newspapers of the land." Freeman, *Washington*, VI, 399.

[67] For details and documentation, see Link, *Democratic-Republican Societies. . .* , pp. 189-190; for political influence of the press see also the comments in Warren, *Jacobin and Junto*, p. 127; the author of a Republican pamphlet in 1800 complained that France in the 1790's received an unfair and even vicious press. Abraham Bishop, *Connecticut Republicanism: An Oration on the Extent and Power of Political Delusion. . .* (Philadelphia, 1800), pp. 48-51.

[68] William Vans Murray Papers, Commonplace Book, Aug. 9, 1795 (Princeton); Link, *Democratic-Republican Societies. . .* , p. 191. The democratic societies were not introduced into the United States by Genet; to him belonged little credit or discredit for them, except in indirect influence. Woodfin, "Citizen Genet and His Mission," p. 486.

Highly placed Federalists, as will be seen, were responsible for spreading the story that Genet not only had defied Washington but also had threatened an "appeal to the people." Such a threat, in the context of the times, carried implications of revolt and mob rule. Whether or not the story was true mattered little; the accusation was sufficient. Repeated often enough, it smothered or made fruitless any denials. In the story's retelling the name Genet seldom was mentioned without a derogatory adjective; overnight the story distorted the popular hero of the societies and Republicans into a villainous monster. In New England, Federalists expanded his villainy to include murder, practically regicide; they jolted people with the fabrication that he had assassinated George Washington.[69]

To malign Genet and to bring about his downfall, Federalists resorted to their greatest public asset, the person and prestige of George Washington. "We go on as usual," wrote John Adams, "Congress resolving one thing and the democratical societies resolving the contrary; the President doing what is right, and the clubs and mobs resolving it to be all wrong."[70] Already a revered figure, Washington was made the object of a Federalist campaign of deification. Federalists apotheosized him in song, story, and poetry. Federalists drank "To Washington—loved as a father, as a god adored." The campaign began not long after he became President. His name, noted William Maclay in December, 1790, was "brought forward as the constant cover to every unconstitutional and irrepublican act."[71] As the government became wholly Federalist, as it lost almost all semblance of being nonpolitical, Federalists increased their efforts to enhance the popular esteem of the President. The war-spawned foreign policy crisis, the democratic societies, and the coming of Genet into the midst of an aroused pro-French public sentiment drove Federalists to exploit Washington and the magic of his name to the utmost.

Even this was not enough. Abandoning, in practice if not in theory, the myth of being above partisan politics, Washington him-

[69] The assassination story is in the *Mirrour* (Concord), Dec. 16, 1793, cited in Link, *Democratic-Republican Societies. . . ,* p. 192.
[70] Adams to wife, Philadelphia, May 10, 1794, C. F. Adams, ed., *Letters of John Adams Addressed to his Wife,* II, 159.
[71] Maclay, *Journal,* Dec. 14, 1790, p. 341; see also Link, *Democratic-Republican Societies. . . ,* pp. 192-193.

self finally battled the democratic societies and Republican opponents of his administration. Angered by their attacks on him and his
government's policies, the President was willing to believe almost
anything about the societies and to impute to them almost any degree
of treachery.[72] When the Whiskey Rebellion broke out, Washington, along with other Federalist leaders, placed the blame on the
democratic clubs. Clearly, he pointed out on August 26, 1794, the
insurrection was "the first *formidable* fruit of the Democratic Societies; brought forth," he forecast ominously, "too prematurely for
their own views, which may contribute to the annihilation of them."
He was convinced that the societies were established "by the *artful*
and *designing* members . . . primarily to sow the seeds of jealousy
and distrust among people, of the government, by destroying all
confidence in the Administration of it. . . ."[73]

In his correspondence and elsewhere, Washington continued to
place the onus for rebellion and general turmoil on the popular
organizations and Genet. "But how can things be otherwise than
they are," he said, "when clubs and Societies have been instituted
for the express purpose though clothed in another garb by their
diabolical leader G[ene]t whose object was to sow sedition, to
poison the minds of the people of this Country, and to make them
discon[tente]d with the Government of it, and who have labored
indefatigably to effect these purposes."[74] Then, in his annual message of November 19, 1794, the President delivered a withering blow,
damning the democratic clubs as "self-created societies" which by
"formal concert" sought to destroy the government.[75]

[72] Sears, *George Washington*, p. 445.
[73] Washington to Henry Lee, Germantown, Aug. 26, 1794, in Fitzpatrick,
Washington's Writings, XXXIII, 475-476. Like other Federalists, Washington
believed that Genet was the "father" of the Democratic Societies.
[74] Washington to Major Gen. Daniel Morgan, Carlisle, Oct. 8, 1794, *ibid.*,
p. 524; see also Washington to Burges Ball, Philadelphia, Sept. 25, 1794, *ibid.*,
pp. 505-507.
[75] The text is in *ibid.*, pp. 28-37. Federalists, of course, echoed Washington's
refrain; see, for example, William Vans Murray to James McHenry, Philadelphia, Dec. 16, 1794, Bernard C. Steiner, *The Life and Correspondence
of James McHenry*, pp. 155-156. Vice-President John Adams, however, while
disapproving of the disorders attributed to the clubs believed that the clubs
had a perfect right to exist, "that political clubs must and ought to be lawful
in every free country." Adams to wife, Philadelphia, Dec. 14, 1794, in C. F.
Adams, ed., *Letters of John Adams Addressed to His Wife*, II, 171.

To James Madison and other Republicans, the "game" was obvious: "to connect the democratic societies with the odium of the insurrection—to connect the Republicans in Cong[res]s with those Societies—to put the P[resident] ostensibly at the head of the other party, in opposition to both. . . ."[76] Even though Republicans saw through and tried to counteract Federalist maneuvers, and even though the democratic societies in general had no connection with the Whiskey Rebellion and were vehement in their denials, Washington's shotgun denunciation was a heavy if not mortal blow.[77] Federalist tactics proved eminently successful. The awesome prestige of General Washington, plus blanket condemnation, plus guilt by association were almost impossible to combat.

One effect of Washington's denunciation, however, was to focus public attention on the societies in many places where in the past they had been practically ignored.[78] Jefferson, for example, defended the popular organizations; Madison termed Washington's denunciation "perhaps the greatest error of his political life."[79] Other Republicans agreed, and even some Federalists believed, that the President was losing his hold on the public imagination. Men began to talk of turning Washington out of office. His support, as mild Federalist Elbridge Gerry later pointed out, came from "the union of the funded, bank, commercial, Cincinnati and anti-revolu-

[76] Madison to James Monroe, Philadelphia, Dec. 4, 1794, in Hunt, *The Writings of James Madison,* VI, 223; Brant, *James Madison: Father of the Constitution. . . ,* p. 417.

[77] Washington's denunciation "was the most powerful cause of the decline and ultimate disappearance of the clubs." Miller, "The Democratic Societies and the Whiskey Insurrection," *PMHB,* LXII, 325, 334. An acute French observer in the United States also concluded that Washington's condemnation completed destruction of the clubs. La Rochefoucauld-Liancourt, *Travels. . . ,* I, 43-44. For a contemporary denial that the societies were instrumental in fomenting the Whiskey Rebellion, supposedly expressing sentiment representing all the societies, see the *Independent Chronicle and the Universal Advertiser* (Boston), Oct. 6, 1794. For an appraisal of Washington's role in the Whiskey Rebellion, see Bennett M. Rich, "Washington and the Whiskey Insurrection," *PMHB,* LXV (July, 1941), 334-352; also in Rich, *The Presidents and Civil Disorder,* pp. 2-20.

[78] Woodbury, *Public Opinion in Philadelphia. . . ,* p. 115.

[79] "The denunciation of the democratic societies is one of the extraordinary acts of boldness of which we have seen so many from the fraction of monocrats." Jefferson to Madison, Monticello, Dec. 28, 1794, Ford, *Writings of Jefferson,* VI, 516; Madison to Monroe, Philadelphia, Dec. 4, 1794, Hunt, *The Writings of James Madison,* VI, 222.

tionary or monarchical interest."[80] The more radical opposition now turned on Washington, denouncing "idolatry for a popular citizen." One Republican club member toasted Washington as "a despot from the South, with Democracy on his lips and tyranny in his heart."[81] More important than name-calling and the personal reaction against Washington were the fundamental issues raised by opponents of the government. With reasoned argument they accused the administration of attempting to muzzle opposition and stifle freedom of expression.[82]

Among Federalists, however, joy reigned; with them Washington's stock soared to new heights. Seizing his formal denunciation, Federalists turned to Congress to place the seal of death on organized "sedition."[83] The Senate, controlled by Hamiltonians, responded promptly to the President; using his own words, it passed a motion of censure on the societies.[84] But in the House of Representatives Federalists could not beat down Republican strength.

For four days the House debated and in the end refused to sanction a blanket condemnation. William Branch Giles, zealous anti-Hamiltonian from Virginia, could not sit silent "when he saw, or thought he saw the House of Representatives about to erect itself into an office of censorship."[85] In attacking the President's phrase "self-created," which the House struck out of the proposed condemnation by a two-vote margin, he raised his voice against guilt

[80] Gerry to John Adams, April 25, 1797, Gerry Papers, quoted in Link, *Democratic-Republican Societies. . . ,* pp. 194-195.

[81] Quoted in *ibid.,* p. 195.

[82] *Baltimore Daily Advertiser,* reprinted in the *Virginia Herald and Fredericksburg Advertiser,* Jan. 15, 1795.

[83] Referring to Washington's denunciation of the societies, Jeremiah Smith, Jeffersonian-hating Federalist congressman from New Hampshire, wrote to Samuel Smith, Nov. 20, 1794, that "we smile and they pout. They feel it. Let their mortification be increased tenfold." John H. Morison, *Life of the Hon. Jeremiah Smith, LL.D.* (Boston, 1845), p. 65. Regardless of the connection between the societies and the whiskey uprising, Federalists were determined to squeeze party advantage from it. See also Link, *Democratic-Republican Societies,* p. 196; Miller, "Democratic Societies and the Whiskey Insurrection," *PMHB,* LXII, 348.

[84] *Annals of the Congress. . . ,* 3rd Cong., Nov. 21, 1794; the vote is recorded on pp. 943-945 (Nov. 27, 1794); Hazen, *Contemporary American Opinion of the French Revolution,* p. 205.

[85] For Giles's comments, see *Annals of the Congress. . . ,* 3rd Cong., Nov. 24, 1794, pp. 899-901.

by association and in support of freedom of thought and lawful organization. In America "there was not an individual who might not come under the charge of being a member of some one or other self-created society," he said, be it religious, political, philosophical, or otherwise. Baptists and Methodists, for example, might be categorized as "self-created." Believing that Congress should avoid legislation designed in any way to circumscribe public opinion, he favored allowing established law to take its course. If the societies were illegal, he said, the law should act; if not, further legislation would be unwise.

Giles was not alone in his stand; others echoed his sentiments. James Madison "conceived it to be a sound principle, that an action innocent in the eyes of the law could not be the object of censure to a Legislative body. . . . Opinions are not the objects of legislation." A proper function of Congress, he believed, was to investigate public servants, but the democratic societies were private, not public agencies. Censure such as that proposed might easily be extended to freedom of speech and the press. The people had to be protected from congressional condemnation when not sanctioned by law. In answering Federalist contentions, he said "it is vain to say that this indiscriminate censure is no punishment." Then he touched a heart-beat of democracy. "If we advert to the nature of Republican Government," he said, "we shall find that the censorial power is in the people over the Government, and not in the Government over the people."[86]

To such declarations Federalists had responded that whenever such action was debated "there were certain gentlemen in that House, who shook their backs, like a sore-backed horse, and cried out The Liberties of the people." Congressional condemnation, they said, would discourage the clubs, "by uniting all men of sense against them." Theodore Sedgwick, consecrated New England Federalist, believed the censure salutary; it "would have a tendency to plunge these societies into contempt, and to sink them still further into abhorrence and detestation." The conduct of the "despised and repenting societies," he said, "differed as far from a fair and honorable investigation as Christ and Belial."[87]

[86] The text in *ibid.,* Nov. 27, 1794, pp. 934-935; quoted also in Brant, *James Madison: Father of the Constitution. . . ,* p. 418.

[87] Uriah Tracy, quoted from *Annals of the Congress. . . ,* 3rd Cong.,

Federalist oratorical salvos were not sufficient to win the battle; the House of Representatives adopted only a mild resolution, omitting a general damnation of the popular clubs. Federalists recognized this as a Republican victory and as a rebuke to Washington. He did not take the rebuke in silence; in a partisan blast at the House's action he called upon the patriotism of the people to check the "artful approaches" to rebellion.[88]

To James Madison and other leading Republicans, it was obvious that Washington was deep in party politics. Here, patently, was a political appeal for legislators of his own party. One reason for their defeat, felt wrathful Federalists, was that there were too many members of the societies in Congress; Jacobinism and Gallomania were too strong. The legislature must be cleansed; "mobocrats" must be weeded out and excluded.[89]

While Washington's descent into party politics did not crush opposition or destroy immediately all popular societies, his denunciations undoubtedly led to their loss of influence and hastened their demise. Although they retreated before the Federalist assault, for awhile they fought back and were influential in electing several Republicans to congressional posts. A few scattered societies were formed after Washington's condemnation. They had been stigmatized, however, and were on the way to obscurity.[90]

Another important factor hastening their end was the attack on the clubs made by leaders of the clergy.[91] In the theological mind the societies were associated with the irreligion and exaggerated outrages of the French Revolution. One fire-spouting preacher

Nov. 24, 1794, p. 903; Sedgewick quoted from *ibid.*, Nov. 25, 1794, p. 911; see also Hazen, *Contemporary American Opinion of the French Revolution*, pp. 206-207.

[88] Washington to the House, Nov. 29, 1794, *Annals of the Congress.* . . , 3rd Cong., p. 950.

[89] See Madison to Monroe, Philadelphia, Dec. 4, 1794, Hunt, *The Writings of James Madison*, VI, 219-227; Brant, *James Madison: Father of the Constitution.* . . , p. 419.

[90] Link, *Democratic-Republican Societies.* . . , pp. 200-203; Hazen, *Contemporary American Opinion of the French Revolution*, pp. 207-208; Federalists, however, were still fearful of the societies; see for example, Jay to Pickering, New York, Aug. 17, 1795, in Pickering, *The Life of Timothy Pickering*, III, 197-198.

[91] Vernon Stauffer, *New England and the Bavarian Illuminati*, pp. 111-112; Link, *Democratic-Republican Societies.* . . , p. 197.

assigned the French to perdition as "execrable monsters" who had desecrated the Sabbath, denied God, immortality, and the resurrection. They had butchered 2,000,000 people, men, women, and children, including 24,000 men of the cloth! As mothers pleaded for their children, their outstretched hands were chopped off. The inhuman perpetrators of these deeds were the wretched sponsors of the popular societies. Obviously then, the societies were sowers of sedition infiltrating the country to divide and weaken it. Seen thus as an aspect of the French Revolution, the societies prompted clergymen to throw their potent influence behind Federalists.[92]

In addition, Pinckney's treaty, by winning navigation of the Mississippi, calmed pro-French Westerners; Jay's treaty, although thunderously damned, placated many frontiersmen because it brought actual evacuation of the British-held Northwest posts; "Mad" Anthony Wayne's victory at Fallen Timbers and the ensuing Treaty of Greenville freed the Northwest from the Indian menace and ushered in a period of comparative peace and security. With these developments the immediate grievances of the Westerner against the government lost some of their urgency, and the societies lost some of their support. Without much external distraction men could now devote themselves to exploiting the trans-Appalachian wilderness.

Events in France, too, contributed to alienating American support for the popular societies and to quenching pro-French ardor in the United States. As the French Revolution became more violent, as Jacobins replaced Girondins, not only did the French-oriented democratic societies fall under a cloud but also some Republicans became alarmed. Newspaper stories and Federalist propaganda, much of it based on facts, most of it exaggerated, branded Jacobin leaders as blood-stained villains whose regime was one of terror, mob violence, and murder. Many Americans, and particularly the Federalists, were convinced that the democratic societies were also committed to alleged Jacobin extremes.

[92] The preacher was David Osgood of Medford, Mass., and is quoted in Link, *Democratic-Republican Societies. . . ,* pp. 197-200; for an example of clerical condemnation hailed by Federalists, see Osgood's *The Wonderful Works of God Are to Be Remembered: A Sermon Delivered on the Day of Annual Thanksgiving, November 24, 1794* (Boston, 1794), 29 pp. This was published at the request of the hearers.

In the course of the violent public reaction against the Jay treaty certain of the Federalist hierarchy expressed fear that the "American Jacobins" would invite the French Republic to "rescue" American freedom and would unite with the French to overthrow Washington's government. This "horrible" deed would be done, one Federalist said, on the pretense that the American government was in the hands of the British. Such pretense fitted one objective of the "Democratic Clubs"—to render the government odious to the people.[93] The Boston Jacobins, warned another Federalist, evinced an unconquerable disposition "either to throw their country into war & anarchy, or reduce us to a *province* of *France*. Notwithstanding the failure and overthrow of their *Brother* Jacobins in france [*sic*] they, like the wounded snake, still retain all their rage and venom, & would fatally wound, if they could, our *tender* but I hope, immortal Constitution." Members of the societies, he continued, "are offended by being called Jacobins; but there cannot be a more appropriate term for them; in all its horror, & as understood in France." They "assume the exclusive title of Patriots" and "believe that patriotism was *born* in the year 1775, that it, & a hatred of the British are synonymous." They had set up French idols and sacrificed to them. "They have *always* wished, & now ardently long to join the F[rench] and put at risque our peace & happiness, & the fairest form of Government the World could ever boast of."[94]

These fears spread, the membership of the clubs was divided and decimated, and some of their most prominent leaders were either alienated from or withdrew from them. Sectional splits, as that over the Whiskey Rebellion, also reduced membership. Federalists exploited the internal dissensions. When the National Convention denounced and proscribed the French Jacobin clubs Federalists were delighted; it "gave a shock to their brethren here & gave a confidence to all good Federalists."[95] While the furor over the Jay treaty aroused the societies to new activity, by 1795-96 most of them had apparently disappeared. Weakened from within and

[93] William Vans Murray Papers, Commonplace Book, Aug. 4, 1795 (Princeton).

[94] Jacob Williams to Timothy Pickering, Boston, July 17, 1795, Pickering Papers, Massachusetts Historical Society, Boston.

[95] William Vans Murray Papers, Commonplace Book, Sept. 21, 1795 (Princeton).

assailed from without, they did not survive Washington's second term.

Associated intimately with the growing Republican party and devoted to the French alliance, the democratic societies were, for a while, important instruments in molding pro-French public sentiment. But like Genet, with whom they were also closely connected, they intensified the hatred and opposition of Federalists and Anglophiles. By sharpening issues and by challenging those in power the societies, nonetheless, made important contributions to then emerging political parties and to the growth of a democratic foreign policy.[96]

* * * * *

Not only were American politics rent by Genet's activities, by the rise of the democratic societies, and by the violent French and English proclivities of the citizenry, but Frenchmen and Englishmen, supported by their American partisans, brawled on American soil and clashed in American waters. Americans as individuals were not neutral; American neutrality was a precarious thing. So intense was party spirit and so excited was the public mind that tavern brawls and street battles between French and English sailors caused little stir in various port cities in midsummer 1793.[97] Toward the close of July, 1793, however, two events did stir Americans and drove them almost to riot. One was a sea duel off Sandy Hook, New York, between the British frigate *Boston* and the French frigate *L'Embuscade*. The other was the arrival of a French fleet giving France a temporary and illusory supremacy in American waters.[98]

Commanded by a Captain Courtney, the *Boston* had been sent

[96] The role of the societies in party politics is not clear. Link, *Democratic-Republican Societies. . . ,* p. 206, maintains that "the democratic societies laid the ground work for the Republican party." Cunningham, "The Jeffersonian Party to 1801," maintains that "there is no substantial evidence that any of the popular societies . . . functioned as an element in a party organization." He makes a good case that the societies did not constitute a party. *Ibid.,* pp. 101-103.

[97] Such riots and brawls involving French sailors seemed to be commonplace in these years; see, for instance, the *Virginia Herald and Fredericksburg Advertiser,* Sept. 5, 1793, and May 29, 1795; the *Maryland Gazette* (Annapolis), Sept. 5, 1793, Jan. 30, 1794, April 10 and May 22, 1794; McMaster, *A History of the People of the United States. . . ,* II, 121.

[98] Genet boasted to Jefferson of the strength of the French naval force. The Anas, July 23, 1793, in Ford, *Writings of Jefferson,* I, 249.

from Halifax to New York with orders to end the pillage of British commerce by French cruisers and privateers "daily chasing vessels bound in and out" of American ports. Through an error in recognition, or perhaps through planned deception, the French took the *Boston* as their frigate *La Concorde*. Captain Bompard of *L'Embuscade* sent out an officer and about a dozen men in a small boat to welcome his ostensible comrade-in-arms. As the small boat drew up to the ship, the French officer became suspicious of her nationality, but his fears were allayed as she hoisted French colors. Climbing aboard he found that he had delivered himself and his men into British hands. Republicans, Francophiles, and Frenchmen fumed over Courtney's ruse; they demanded revenge for his "vile" English trick.

The Englishman did not hesitate. At the Tontine Coffee House on July 29, Courtney posted a challenge to meet "Citizen" Bompard and his now famous *L'Embuscade* off Sandy Hook. The French captain promptly grasped the challenge.[99] The news spread throughout the city; the populace became excited; business practically stood still. Everyone, it appeared, was willing to place money on the outcome of the clash; the stakes in money and prestige were large. As the frigates prepared to do battle on August 1, 1793, off Long Branch on the New Jersey coast, partisan spectators lined the shore and filled the topsides of the vessels which were being used as floating grandstands to give spectators a closer view of the hostilities.

For almost two hours the cannon of the two ships spewed fire, glass, nails, and assorted hardware; both sides suffered severe damage and many casualties. Then, with Captain Courtney slain, the *Boston* fled.[100] While *L'Embuscade* was in hot pursuit, which lasted for five hours, a French fleet of some fifteen ships sailed past Sandy Hook into the bay.[101] The appearance of the French fleet, flags

[99] Courtney's challenge and Bompard's response are in the *Maryland Gazette* (Annapolis), Aug. 8, 1793.

[100] Federalists, particularly Hamilton and Henry Knox, were mortified by the battle; they heaped "unqualified abuse" and "censures" on Courtney. *The Anas*, Aug. 3, 1793, in Ford, *Writings of Jefferson*, I, 255.

[101] For details of the *Boston-L'Embuscade* episode, see McMaster, *A History of the People of the United States. . .* , II, 121-123; Hyneman, *The First American Neutrality*, p. 108; Minnigerode, *Genet*, pp. 236-238; Woodfin, "Citizen Genet and His Mission," pp. 328 ff.; for Genet's report on the

flying and salutes booming, coupled with the Bompard victory, sent the populace, particularly the pro-French elements, into raptures. The French admiral was immediately surrounded by thousands of celebrating Americans. The French fleet had sailed into a ready-made reception; and when *L'Embuscade* returned thousands greeted her, lining the shore in shouting, waving multitudes.[102]

The French warships, however, brought neither strength to the French cause and to the alliance, nor harmony to deteriorating Franco-American relations. They bore, instead, seeds of more trouble. Crowded with royalist refugees and manned by mutinous sailors who had been swept into the sea by armed blacks in Saint Domingue, the warships, in company with a large merchant convoy, had at first limped into American ports for sanctuary, rather than in search of a base for operations against the English. The ships, the sailors, and the refugees were remnants of a white dominance in Saint Domingue which was never to return.

With the development of the Revolution in France the home government's control over its Caribbean possessions had weakened, strikingly so in Saint Domingue where a strong rule had until then kept class and racial discord under control. Following the outbreak of the Revolution, Creoles, or Frenchmen born on the island, elected assemblies in each province and seized control of the island's governmental machinery. Their power, however, was short lived; the island was turbulent. Planters, poor whites, royalists, and democrats all distrusted each other, and each sought dominance. To this was added further complication when mulattoes, with some support from members of the National Assembly in Paris, entered the power struggle by demanding social and political equality. Soon Negro slaves took advantage of the turmoil to demand freedom.

Violence was inevitable. A freedman's revolt flared up in 1790 and was savagely suppressed. In the following year mulattoes joined

---

affair, see Genet to Minister of Foreign Affairs, Philadelphia, Aug. 2 and 5, 1793, in Turner, *CFM,* pp. 236-238; for a critical contemporary analysis of the battle, see Biddle, *The Autobiography of Charles Biddle. . . ,* p. 254; for an "authentic" (French) version of the battle, see the *Maryland Gazette* (Annapolis), Aug. 8, 1793.

[102] *Virginia Herald and Fredericksburg Advertiser,* Aug. 15, 1793; Captain Bompard became a popular hero. To the Tammany society of New York he presented the colors of the victorious vessel; his victory, in addition, won him a promotion. Woodfin, "Citizen Genet and His Mission," pp. 593-596.

a white royalist faction in a revolt against the Creole government. Then, in August, 1791, Negro slaves rose suddenly against their white masters, indiscriminately slaughtering and destroying through most of the plantation areas. This placed self-emancipated Negroes in control of the country's northern rural districts while whites and mulattoes fought for power around Port-au-Prince in the west. Only in the southern districts did French planters retain effective control.

The National Assembly of France, which had added to the turmoil by granting, in May, 1791, a limited franchise to free mulattoes, sent three commissioners to Saint Domingue in 1791 to investigate affairs there and to use special executive powers in an attempt to restore order. They failed. In the meanwhile the Legislative Assembly in France had decreed, in April, 1792, that men of color were entitled the same political rights as white Creoles. To replace the first commission, to enforce the political decree, and to restore peace, the Girondin government sent to Saint Domingue three new commissioners with supreme power. Supported by six thousand troops—four thousand National Guards, and two thousand soldiers of the line—in fifteen ships, the civil commissioners arrived in September, 1792. Of the three commissioners, the most active and most powerful was Léger Félicité Sonthonax, a confirmed Jacobin.

In reorganizing the colony's government so as to concentrate power into the hands of the commission he headed and particularly in consorting with and leaning upon mulattoes for support, Sonthonax alienated the various white groups. Then, by turning to the blacks for support, he lost his mulatto backing. So intense was the resentment of the whites against Sonthonax that when France, in January, 1793, went to war against Great Britain and Spain and Saint Domingue was thus placed in peril of foreign conquest, they would have supported foreign troops against the arch-commissioner's regime.

Into this supercharged situation in May, 1793, sailed the new Governor-General of the colony, General Thomas Francis Galbaud. Although an appointee of the Revolutionary regime in the homeland, Galbaud was a conservative soldier who held property in Saint Domingue, having married a local heiress. Under the circumstances, and having apparently no one else at the time to turn to, the whites placed their faith in him. When he landed at Le Cap Français the anti-Revolutionary whites greeted him with a tumultuous reception. Sonthonax, realizing that once the General was established the commission's power would vanish, moved swiftly to forestall Galbaud's taking control.

Backed by mulatto militia, Sonthonax, in June, 1793, declared Galbaud's credentials invalid and forced the General and his staff aboard a ship to be returned to France. But the Jacobin commissioner's coup miscarried. Infuriated by this high-handed treatment of the Governor-General, the sailors and regular troops stationed on the ships of the fleet in the harbor mutinied. Sweeping their officers along with them, they rallied around Galbaud and offered to fight to re-establish his authority. On June 20, 1793, Galbaud, at the head of several thousand armed and trained fighting men, landed at Le Cap Français. Immediately, the antirevolutionary whites of the city rushed to his standard.

Sonthonax, supported mainly by men of color, was unable to withstand Galbaud's counterstroke; Galbaud's forces drove him back to the edge of the city. Beaten and facing further defeat, he took a momentous step. Summoning prisoners, slaves, and insurgent slaves who surrounded the city, he armed them, promised them pardon and freedom, and gave them freedom to loot and sack the city. Blacks in massive thousands crashed into the city. Galbaud's forces, intoxicated with initial victory, wine, and loot, were smashed or pushed into the sea. With them, back to the ships, fled over ten thousand white refugees; there was no sanctuary on land.[103] Unchained, the black fury killed, plundered, and destroyed indiscriminately. Ultimately the Negroes fired the city, leaving it in ashes. All that remained of white domination on Saint Domingue were the ashes of Le Cap Français.

Leaving behind them the holocaust of Le Cap Français, Galbaud, the mutinous sailors, and the thousands of terror-stricken refugees sailed in a convoy of over a hundred merchant vessels and warships for the United States. This was the first batch of new *emigrés*

---

[103] On his retreat Galbaud freed British prisoners who then fought by the side of French soldiers and sailors—former enemies—against the black fury; Galbaud took these Englishmen with him to America. *Maryland Gazette* (Annapolis), July 18, 1793.

which made its way to Chesapeake Bay. Later others followed, creating relief and political problems in a number of American ports. This was the fleet Americans greeted so joyfully as it sailed into New York Harbor.[104]

[104] For detailed accounts of the events in Saint Domingue, see T. Lothrop Stoddard, *The French Revolution in San Domingo* (Boston, 1914); Bryan Edwards, *An Historical Survey of the Island of Saint Domingo . . . and a History of the War in the West Indies in 1793 and 1794 . . .* (London, 1801); Cyril L. R. James, *The Black Jacobins: Toussaint L'Ouverture and the San Domingo Revolution* (New York, 1938); for a detailed bibliography, see Logan, *Diplomatic Relations of The United States with Haiti,* pp. 459-496; for some eye-witness comments, see also McMaster, *The Life and Times of Stephen Girard,* I, 193-211.

CHAPTER NINE

THE CAUSE OF MANKIND AGAINST TYRANTS

As to the present cause of France, although I think that they have been guilty of many excesses, that they have many men amongst them who are greedy of power for themselves and not of liberty for the nation, and that in their present temper they are not likely to have a very good government within any short time, yet I firmly believe their cause to be that of mankind against tyrants. . . . So far I think we are interested in their success; and as to our political situation, they are certainly the only real allies we have had. . . . although Mr. Genet is a man of abilities and firmness, he is not endowed with that prudence and command of his temper which might have enabled him to change the opinion of our Executive in those points where they might be in the wrong.—Albert Gallatin to Miss Hannah Nicholson, August 25, 1793.

The town is less frenchified than it was. Citizen Genet is out of credit; his rudeness is as indiscreet as it is extraordinary, and everybody is provoked with him. I like the horizon better than I did; there are less clouds.—Fisher Ames to Thomas Dwight, Boston, August, 1793.

* * * * *

W HEN the French warships sailed into New York harbor on the first day of August, 1793, they aroused varied emotions.[1] Genet had

---

[1] The precise number of French ships reaching the United States is difficult to ascertain. According to George Hammond, who made it his business to record movements of French ships, some 15 armed vessels—ships of the line, frigates, and sloops—together with some 120 merchantmen arrived at Norfolk between July 7 and 11. The greater part of the merchant vessels proceeded to Baltimore. One ship went to Europe, some went to Boston, some cruised along the coasts. Some of the merchant vessels, moreover, had the appearance of warships. Hammond to Grenville, Philadelphia, Aug. 10,

high hopes—not to be realized. He had grand plans for the fleet. With the ships his projected invasion of Louisiana and Florida would be easier; he might recapture the islands of St. Pierre and Miquelon, destroy British fisheries in Newfoundland, raid British shipping in North American waters, and support the liberation of Acadia.[2]

The British looked upon the French fleet as a threat to their naval ascendancy in North American waters.[3] Hammond protested the stay of the war vessels in a neutral port. Jefferson replied that the same privileges were available to English ships; this was precisely the admission Hammond sought. The American position did not imply that the administration was undisturbed by the threat to its neutrality policy posed by the presence of the armed vessels. The popular receptions Americans showered on the French ships in the ports were particularly upsetting.[4]

1793. Henry Adams Transcripts. These figures approximate those given by Genet. See Genet to Minister of Foreign Affairs, Philadelphia, July 28, 1793, Turner, *CFM,* p. 225; a list of the ships drawn up by Genet is in AAE CP EU, Vol. XXXVIII, f. 143, dated July 31, 1793.

[2] Genet to Minister of Foreign Affairs, Philadelphia, Aug. 2, 1793, New York, Oct. 7, 1793, in Turner, *CFM,* pp. 234-235, 264-265; Woodfin, "Citizen Genet and His Mission," p. 420. It was dangerous to send the ships back to France because Great Britain controlled the seas; on this basis, in line with what he conceived to be the desires of his superiors, Genet worked out his plans to use the ships. Logan, *The Diplomatic Relations of United States with Haiti. . . ,* p. 45; Woodfin, "Citizen Genet and His Mission," p. 421; instructions for Contre Amiral Sercey, Commandant of the French Republic's Naval Forces in America, AAE CP EU, Oct. 4, 1793, Vol. XXXIX, ff. 99-103. These included plans for attacks on Quebec, New Orleans, etc. In essence, the admiral was instructed to hit the English wherever possible and cause as much damage as possible. Similar instructions, n.p., n.d., are in the Genet Papers, Library of Congress, XI, 3527.

[3] Yet Hammond reported that the ships which arrived in New York were in no condition to fight or to proceed on expeditions; they needed repairs, supplies, and seamen. Some thought that the ships would be used against Halifax, the Bermudas, or the Bahamas; others believed that Genet would use the warships to overawe the Federalist government. Hammond to Grenville, Philadelphia, Aug. 10, 1793, Henry Adams Transcripts. Spaniards told Hammond that they feared that Clark's expedition would be supported by the French fleet in New York. *Ibid.,* March 7, 1794; see also the précis on American affairs, 1794 [Sept.-Oct.], *Dropmore Papers,* III, 524-525.

[4] See Cabinet Decisions, Sept. 7, 1793, in Ford, *Writings of Jefferson,* VI, 411; Jefferson to Hammond, Philadelphia, Sept. 9, 1793, *ibid.,* pp. 422-424; Thomas, *American Neutrality. . . ,* p. 163 n. When news reached Halifax that the French squadron had reached New York and was laying up warm clothing, the British feared an attack there or on Newfoundland. Gerald S.

A complicating factor in the pattern of Franco-American amity was the problem created by the new influx of royalist and Revolution-hating French refugees. Once established in the United States, these refugee-planters, monarchists in sentiment, constituted a grave danger to the French alliance. Many of them were eager to deal with the enemies of the French Republic. Rather than subject themselves to rule by men of color—their former slaves in many instances—rather than accept the Revolutionary doctrine of equality, these colonial *emigrés* plotted to turn over their island to the enemy of France—to England.[5]

If the United States returned the refugee-planters to Saint Domingue they would be a constant threat to French republican hegemony; if they remained in the United States they would constitute a continuing menace to the French alliance. Genet met the problem; he opposed returning them to Saint Domingue and at the same time sought to make them harmless in the United States. Immediately after the arrival of the French squadron in New York, Genet warned Jefferson that refugee-planters were plotting to organize in the United States an expedition designed to overthrow the French authorities in Saint Domingue.[6] As to the mutinous sailors, Genet drew up no stern measures; he believed royalist whites and Galbaud, who took advantage of their strong racial feelings, had duped them into fighting against the authority of delegates of the French Republic. He was particularly bitter against Galbaud for having jeopardized the safety of Saint Domingue.[7]

Graham, *Empire of the North Atlantic: The Maritime Struggle for North America*, p. 220; Woodfin, "Citizen Genet and His Mission," p. 420.

[5] Minnigerode, *Genet*, 297-299; Woodfin, "Citizen Genet and His Mission," p. 416; Carl L. Lokke, "Saint Domingue in Anglo-Spanish Diplomacy in 1795," *Hispanic American Historical Review*, XVI (May, 1936), 251, and Lokke's "London Merchant Interest in the St. Domingue Plantations of the Emigrés, 1793-1798," *American Historical Review*, XLIII (July, 1938), 795; McMaster, *A History of the People of the United States. . .* , II, 124-125. For some of the exchanges between Genet and the refugees see Frances S. Childs, *French Refugee Life in the United States, 1790-1800: An American Chapter of the French Revolution*, pp. 142-144.

[6] Jefferson to Genet, Philadelphia, Aug. 7, 1793, in Ford, *Writings of Jefferson*, VI, 366. Jefferson informed Genet that "effectual measures" would be taken to stop the expedition; see also Minnigerode, *Genet*, pp. 297-298.

[7] Galbaud was brought to the United States a prisoner by the officers of the fleet who blamed him for their defeat and charged him with plotting to

To give his personal attention to the problem of disaffection in the French squadron, Genet in the first week of August rushed north to New York. Night and day he labored, or so he declared, to supply the squadron's needs, to remove the cancer of mutiny, to republicanize the sailors and soldiers, and to counteract the influence among them of "the traitor or imbecile Galbaud," whom he tried to send back to France for trial. Galbaud, with his wife, warned the disaffected men that Genet was plotting their destruction, and that if they allowed the minister to take him ashore his life would be snuffed out.[8]

Genet's efforts failed; the soldiers and sailors obeyed no authority; their officers were powerless to control them. Going ashore as they pleased, the defiant men created bedlam. Their behavior did not endear the French to Americans. Estimates placed the number of Frenchmen in New York in August, 1793, as high as five thousand. Logically, many Americans feared the violence and potential danger from so many armed and apparently uncontrollable foreigners. Some perceived in their presence a sinister design by Genet against the peace of the country. The British added to the turmoil. Hammond and his agents worked to keep alive the disaffection on the French ships. With the aid of French traitors they succeeded. In a letter to the home office Hammond boasted of the obstacle he had planted to prevent Genet from using the fleet against British North American possessions.[9]

turn Saint Domingue over to the British. Woodfin, "Citizen Genet and His Mission," p. 417. Before Galbaud arrived in the United States, Moissonier, French consul at Baltimore, told Genet that Galbaud should be punished. He implied that Galbaud's concern for wealth and property and his consorting with men of property was the cause of trouble in Saint Domingue. Baltimore, July 16, 1793, Genet Papers, Library of Congress, X, 3139; see also Genet to Minister of Foreign Affairs, Philadelphia, July 28, 1793, in Turner, *CFM*, pp. 224-225.

[8] Genet maintained that the squadron had placed itself under his direction of its own accord. Genet to Jefferson, 1797, in Genet, *Washington, Jefferson, and "Citizen" Genet, 1793*, p. 27. For details see Genet to Minister of Foreign Affairs, Philadelphia, July 28, 1793, New York, Aug. 15, 1793, Sept. 19, 1793, and Oct. 5, 7, 1793, in Turner, *CFM*, pp. 223-227, 238-241, 242-243, 244-251, 259-260; Minnigerode, *Genet*, pp. 299-306. Hammond reported that Genet went to New York to prevail on the men and officers of the French ships to proceed on an expedition against British possessions. To Grenville, Philadelphia, Sept. 1793, No. 19, Henry Adams Transcripts.

[9] "I have regularly received the fullest information of all its proceedings,

From ship to ship Genet carried his pleas, urging loyalty and obedience to the officers of the French Republic. With the aid of port authorities, he attempted to police the anchorage, but his labors were in vain. He could not move the defiant crews; they threatened him and his representatives with violence. The mutineers, moreover, would have nothing to do with Genet's plans to create from among them a volunteer corps to take the ships back to Saint Domingue; what they wanted was to return to France.[10]

At the end of August, with the connivance of certain sailors, Galbaud and his wife escaped; by the middle of September they had made their way to Canada. Soon after the general's escape the mutiny in the French squadron in New York ended. Vainly Genet tried to apprehend Galbaud and his party. He obtained warrants for the general's arrest, but pro-English sympathizers, who rallied around the fleeing French royalists, thwarted his plans.[11]

---

from a French Gentleman of distinction," boasted Hammond, "who, at my instigation, exerted his influence, to discover and frustrate any project, in which this fleet might have been employed to promote the views of the ruling party of France. . . ." To Grenville, Sept. 17, Philadelphia, Sept. 17, 1793, No. 19, Henry Adams Transcripts; see also Hammond to Grenville, Lansdowne, Oct. 12, 1793, *Dropmore Papers,* II, 443-444. Gov. Mifflin of Penn., for example, to preserve the peace in Philadelphia, asked Genet to keep mutinous sailors aboard the French ships or to see to it that when they came ashore they behaved with decorum. Philadelphia, Aug. 3, 1793, Genet Papers, Library of Congress, X, 3217. A list of the ships in the New York squadron is in AAE CP EU, Vol. XXXVIII, f. 143, dated July 31, 1793, and signed by Genet. In it Genet listed nine ships of varying armament.

[10] For an exchange between the mutinous crew of the warship *Jupiter* (justifying its conduct) and Genet, see the *Maryland Gazette* (Annapolis), Aug. 29, 1793. Unsuccessfully, Genet tried to send men from another ship aboard the *Jupiter* to disarm the mutineers. Finally, Genet placed Captain Bompard in command of the *Jupiter.* "Council of War gathered to organize the forces of the Republic," New York, Aug. 18, 1793, Genet Papers, Library of Congress. See also Minnigerode, *Genet,* pp. 301-303; Woodfin, "Citizen Genet and His Mission," p. 426. Hammond reported that Genet, eventually, was obliged to flee New York because of attacks by French sailors. They broke into his house, smashed windows, and destroyed furniture. To Grenville, Lansdowne near Philadelphia, Oct. 12, 1793, No. 20, Henry Adams Transcripts.

[11] "Rapport de l'officier de Garde du 29 aout 1793," AAE CP EU, Vol. XXXVIII, ff. 381-383. Earlier the General and Mrs. Galbaud complained of their confinement; two American physicians visited them, reported that both were ill and needed exercise, and requested that they be allowed to come ashore for a change of situation. Michael Bayley and James Tillany to Genet, New York, Aug. 19, 1793, Genet Papers, Library of Congress, X, 3273.

Galbaud did not remain in his Canadian sanctuary long; in December he returned to the United States. From New York he feuded publicly with Genet. He threatened to sue the French minister, denounced him for alleged crimes, and in other ways debased him.[12] Public sentiment was, for other reasons, turning against Genet; Galbaud's attacks poured oil on the fire.

Genet's need for money was now desperate. The frontier expeditions had been mired because of lack of funds, and now his warships were immobilized in American ports, never to be used in his sweeping plans. As George Hammond had forecast, the ships created a dilemma for Genet and the American government.[13]

In desperation Genet turned to Hamilton for advances from the debt owed to France, "particularly to supply the urgent wants of the fleet and Squadron of the Republic which are just arrived from Saint Domingo."[14] He got no satisfaction. Still he persisted in his pleas to an ally. "Two thousand seamen and soldiers," he told Jefferson, "whom I support are on the eve of wanting bread. The repairs of our vessels are at a stand. The indispensable expeditions of subsistence for our colonies and France are suspended." When his pleas reached Hamilton, the Secretary of the Treasury advised against advancing funds, especially "when the means of execution are uncertain."[15]

Shortly after reaching Philadelphia, Genet, perhaps unknowingly, had laid the precedent for uncertain execution. American merchants not long before had supplied the French West Indies, in particular Saint Domingue, with provisions and the authorities there had given them bills drawn on a former French consul-general in the United States and later on Genet. When Genet did not pay the bills—not

[12] For an example of Genet's anti-Galbaud pronouncements, see that of Sept. 16, 1793, directed "to the Crews of the French squadron on the American Station," the *Maryland Gazette* (Annapolis), Sept. 19, 1793; for Galbaud's views, see the public letter he addressed to Genet, New York, Dec. 24, 1793, printed in the *Virginia Herald and Fredericksburg Advertiser*, Jan. 9, 1794.

[13] Hammond to Grenville, Philadelphia, July 7, 1793, No. 16, Henry Adams Transcripts.

[14] Genet to Hamilton, Philadelphia, July 19, 1793, Genet Papers, Library of Congress, X, 3144.

[15] Genet to Jefferson, Philadelphia, Nov. 11, 14, 1793; Jefferson to Genet, Germantown, Nov. 24, 1793; Hamilton to Washington, Treasury Dept., Nov. 23, 1793, in *ASP FR*, I, 185-186.

for lack of desire but for lack of funds—the American government, feeling that it had underwritten the advances of its citizens to the French, paid them, in some instances to save traders from bankruptcy.[16] Knowingly, or otherwise, Genet had made a serious blunder. He had alienated important mercantile interests, the backbone of Washington's Federalist government, interests essential to hoped-for Franco-American trade, interests he needed most to convert to the support of the French alliance. In not paying the Saint Domingue bills Genet created another serious misunderstanding with the Washington administration. "His conduct has been such as to have created a distrust, which never can be surmounted," said George Hammond. Genet's breach of contract, he added, "will throw innumerable impediments in the way of any future money concerns between the Government of France and the government and individual citizens of the United States."[17]

Meanwhile, bitter attacks against Genet by the refugee royalists continued. Defying his authority, they held mass meetings and formed expeditions in American ports to be launched against French republicanism in Saint Domingue, conspiring all the while with the English against the Republic. Little wonder that Genet granted the refugees relief out of his meager funds grudgingly and only in order to divert public criticism. Their activities smacked of treason; he could not help distrusting them, and his distrust was shared by his colleagues in consular posts.[18] Genet demanded that the American government, as a helpful ally, arrest traitorous royalist-refugees. He asked also that the United States prohibit further royalist immigration from Saint Domingue, and even suggested that it allow French frigates to detain American vessels not provided with passports from

[16] Genet to Jefferson, Philadelphia, June 18, 1793; Jefferson to Genet, Philadelphia, June 23, 1793, *ibid.*, pp. 158-159; the Anas, July 5, 1793, in Ford, *Writings of Jefferson*, I, 235.

[17] Hammond to Grenville, Philadelphia, July 7, 1793, No. 16, Henry Adams Transcripts. By this time Hammond was convinced that Genet sought to form a party to overawe if not subvert the American government.

[18] See Childs, *French Refugee Life. . . ,* pp. 164-171; for additional details on proroyalist and prorepublican activity in the United States, see Allen J. Barthold, "French Journalists in the United States, 1780-1800," the *Franco-American Review,* I (Winter, 1937), 222-223. See also Logan, *The Diplomatic Relations. . . ,* p. 45.

him so that he could prevent enemies of French republicanism who had escaped the vigilance of American officials from landing.

Jefferson pointed out, rightly, that many of Genet's requests were out of the question, although some had substance. Genet appealed to him, as a friend of liberty, to curtail the flood of royalist-aristocrats "who inundate your continent." No longer did he appeal merely for the help of an ally; France, he said, entreated the American government not to aid in her destruction, "not to conspire in the loss of a colony which you ought to defend" under the terms of the alliance. In the name of the French people he begged "that you will not suffer poniards, for their assassination, to be forged in your territory."[19]

Not only did the Saint Domingue fleet bring mutiny and royalist refugees to harass Genet, but also some Americans believed it brought yellow fever, a plague which swept through Philadelphia in the summer of 1793. Surely this was punishment visited by the Lord upon heretics who followed Genet's banner.[20]

In addition, the French ships brought trouble with Hamilton's customs officials. When the French merchant ships arrived, even though their cargoes were not destined for the United States, customs officials demanded payment of the usual tonnage dues. The French captains protested that "by the 19th and 26th articles of the treaty of Alliance [commercial treaty] they are not to be subject to any duties in the harbours of the United States." Their vessels, pointed out the captains, sought refuge not by destination, but because of distress; "the rigorous severity in the application of the revenue laws of [the United States]," they said, "forms an unpleasing contrast with the fraternal reception which the French people receive from the inhabitants."[21]

[19] Genet to Jefferson, New York, Sept. 6 and Nov. 29, 1793; Jefferson to Genet, Philadelphia, Sept. 12 and Nov. 30, 1793, *ASP FR*, I, 177, 187-188; Minnigerode, *Genet*, 308-312. When Genet asked for arms to defend the French West Indies against English-royalist attacks, Hamilton apparently maintained that this would mean war with Great Britain and the request was refused. Genet, *Washington, Jefferson, and "Citizen" Genet*, p. 19.

[20] McMaster, *The Life and Times of Stephen Girard*, I, 212; Hazen, *Contemporary American Opinion of the French Revolution*, p. 185; for details on the plague, see J. H. Powell, *Bring Out Your Dead: The Great Plague of Yellow Fever in Philadelphia in 1793* (Philadelphia, 1949).

[21] "Protest of Captains of Commercial Vessels Assembled Under Hauterive, Consul of the French Republic," New York, July [?] 1793, Genet Papers,

Lending his support to the captains, Genet also protested. True, some of the captains had unloaded goods and sold them in American ports, but this was not premeditated; they did it out of desperation to obtain funds for revictualling. Genet also insisted that article 19 of the commercial treaty gave the ships sanctuary without payment of duties.[22] Hamilton was adamant; he refused to make an exception for the French merchantmen, claiming they did not fall within the category of shipping mentioned in the commercial treaty. Although the Frenchmen had to pay the duties, public sentiment was in their favor. After the Attorney General ruled that relief could come only from the legislature, Genet, through private hands, sent a petition to Congress, and it passed an act remitting the duties.[23]

The tonnage-duties episode coupled with further frustration—in particular a seemingly successful English invasion of Saint Domingue connived at by *emigré* planters in London—sent Genet's temperature boiling. His experiences with the 1778 alliance had been so circumscribed by misadventure that he saw in it nothing of advantage to France. Fume as he might about the alliance, about ingratitude and treaty violations, his day as French envoy in the United States was coming to a close.

$$* \quad * \quad * \quad * \quad *$$

Genet's turbulent career in the United States was an important factor in the emergence of national political parties. What he did

Library of Congress, X, 3186. The vessels, in addition to the refugees, were loaded with the annual production of Saint Domingue and had been destined originally for France under escort by the warships.

[22] See Genet to Minister of Foreign Affairs, New York, Oct. 8, 1793, in Turner, *CFM*, p. 263; Jefferson to Washington, Monticello, Oct. 3, 1793, in Ford, *Writings of Jefferson*, VI, 435; Jefferson to Hamilton, Philadelphia, Sept., 12, 1793, *ASP FR*, I, 178.

[23] Randolph to Hamilton, Germantown, Nov. 15, 1793; Hamilton to Jefferson, Treasury Dept., Nov. 30, 1793, in Hamilton, ed., *Hamilton's Works*, IV, 487-488, 490-491. Hamilton maintained that the ships "are liable by law to the payment of the duty of tonnage, from which it is not within the compass of executive discretion to relieve them, whatever circumstances of hardship may exist." Cabinet Decisions, Dec. 7, 1793, in Ford, *Writings of Jefferson*, VI, 462-463; "Report of a Committee of the House of Representatives. . . ," 3rd Cong., 1st Sess., *ASP FR*, I, 314; *Annals of the Congress*. . . , 3rd Cong., pp. 1418-1419, "Act for Remission of Duties," approved March 7, 1794. The tonnage duties situation is discussed also in Minnigerode, *Genet*, pp. 313-314.

and said was partly influenced by the conviction that he had behind him the support of most Americans, whereas the Washington administration did not. In this belief he was encouraged by public manifestations of sympathy on his behalf and in support of the French alliance, particularly by anti-administration politicians seeking political advantage. Failing to get support for the alliance from the government Genet had turned to the people. In so doing he found a party already and conveniently formed, George Hammond said, "and *the individuals,* who composed this faction, were willing to avail themselves of the influence arising from his official character, his nation and his principles, in their efforts to increase the ascendancy of the democracy, both in the federal government, and in the separate states. Thus actuated they readily coalesced. . . ."[24] In this way Genet quickened party growth and demarcation.

Some of Genet's troubles were not of his own making and were beyond his power to control. Much of his conduct, however, was arrogant, tactless, defiant, self-defeating, and, if nothing worse, imprudent. His intemperate deeds, his plots, and his flouting of the authority of his host government in time alienated many who from the first had been pro-French alliance and who had been among his most ardent supporters, and even threw off some of the politicians who had tried to use him for party purposes.[25]

Thomas Jefferson, a few months earlier, had praised the Frenchman as affectionate, magnanimous, as one who "offers everything & asks nothing."[26] But not long after Genet's arrival, Jefferson expressed his disgust with the French envoy's actions. "Never in my opinion," he said to another prominent Anglophobe, "was so calamitous an appointment made, as that of the present Minister of F[rance] here. Hot headed, all imagination, no judgement, pas-

[24] Hammond to Grenville, Philadelphia, July 7, 1793, No. 16, Henry Adams Transcripts.

[25] In some instances the reaction against Genet and republican France was so strong as to carry men from espousal of radical democracy to firm conservatism and into the bosom of the Federalist party. Too, the Saint Domingue slave uprising and the influence of royalist refugees in the South turned many former adherents from the French cause. Liberty and equality for the Negro was a doctrine which had negative appeal in the South. See Ulrich B. Phillips, "The South Carolina Federalists," *AHR,* XIV (April and July, 1909), 733-734.

[26] To Madison, Philadelphia, May 19, 1793, *ibid.,* pp. 260-261.

sionate, disrespectful & even indecent towards the P[resident] in his written as well as verbal communications, talking of appeals from him to Congress, from them to the people, urging the most unreasonable & groundless propositions, & in the most dictatorial style, & c, & c, & c."[27]

In alarm, Madison insisted that Genet "must be brought right if possible. His folly will otherwise do mischief which no wisdom can repair. Is there no one through whom he can be *effectually* counselled?"[28] It was too late. The *Little Sarah* affair was the last straw; it convinced Washington that he should get rid of Genet. Hamiltonians, who welcomed anything that might destroy Genet, now pounced upon the very thing that caused Jefferson concern— Genet's alleged threat to go over Washington's head in a direct appeal to the people. With this, they succeeded in turning popular feeling against Genet and reversing a hitherto hostile public sentiment.[29] At the same time, aroused Federalist leaders launched a powerful campaign against the French alliance, attempting to show that from the beginning France had sought to keep the United States low, imbecile, and dependent, that she was more an enemy than an ally.[30]

As was often the case, Hamilton put into motion events which accelerated the public reaction.[31] With Henry Knox he had heard second hand from Governor Mifflin of Pennsylvania details of the midnight interview between Alexander J. Dallas and Genet over detention of the *Petite Démocrate*. Hamilton then repeated what he had heard to John Jay and Rufus King, stressing Genet's alleged threat to appeal from the President directly to the people. When

[27] Jefferson to Madison, July 7, 1793, in Ford, *Writings of Jefferson*, VI, 338-339.

[28] Madison to Jefferson, July 18, 1793, in Hunt, *The Writings of James Madison*, VI, 135; Woodfin, "Citizen Genet and His Mission," pp. 253, 381.

[29] Confident that he had public sentiment behind him, Genet had planned, as he had done on his Southern trip, "a journey thro the northern states, to feel the pulse of the people." It never came off; the plan was lost in the furor over his alleged threat to appeal to the people. The *Minerva*, reprinted in the *Herald: A Gazette for the Country* (New York), Dec. 17, 1796.

[30] George Cabot to Rufus King, Beverley, Aug. 2, 1793, Henry Cabot Lodge, *The Life and Letters of George Cabot*, pp. 73-75.

[31] See Hamilton to Rufus King, Philadelphia, Aug. 13, 1793, in Hamilton, ed., *Hamilton's Works*, V, 574-576, also undated letter of Aug., 1793, pp. 576-577; Minnigerode, *Genet*, pp. 319-320; Bassett, *The Federalist System. . . ,* p. 96; Woodfin, "Citizen Genet and His Mission," pp. 364, 371.

King and Jay returned to New York from Philadelphia early in August, 1793, they in turn spread among their friends what they learned from Hamilton. Soon rumors flew from tongue to tongue. Such a threat from a foreign diplomat was serious and dangerous; directed, as it was, against venerated Washington it had a sensational effect. Hamilton's strategy was superb. The appeal-threat reduced the issue of the French alliance to an emotion, to patriotism, to a personal duel between Washington and Genet.[32]

Americans privy to the rumors were dumbfounded; some were outraged, others were incredulous, their various reactions colored by their political leanings. Finally, newspapers took notice. Certain pro-French or Republican writers asked Jay and King, as the source of the rumors, either to authenticate them or to deny them. Jay and King certified publicly that what had passed as rumor was fact. Acknowledgment that they had spread the story, written on August 12, 1793, appeared in *The Diary; or Loudon's Register* (New York); the statement noted that "Genet, the French Minister, had said he would appeal to the People from certain decisions of the President."[33]

Everywhere Federalist newspapers reprinted the Jay-King certificate, making the most of an emotion-charged issue. With the issue now a struggle between Genet, an impetuous young foreigner, and Washington, a revered hero and lawful President, patriotism carried the day. The country rallied to Washington's support. Even Genet could see the turn in the current of public opinion. Washington's name and position, the attacks of high government figures, such as Jay and King, had their desired effect. Republican ranks and Genet's pro-French adherents were thinned out as if raked by grapeshot.[34]

[32] Woodfin, "Citizen Genet and His Mission," p. 364.

[33] A fascimile of the Jay-King certificate is in Minnigerode, *Genet*, p. 320; for details and pertinent documents, see King, *Rufus King Correspondence*, I, 455-480; Monaghan, *John Jay*, pp. 355-356; the certificate is also reprinted in Henry B. Dawson, ed., "The Citizen Genet," *Historical Magazine*, X (Nov., 1866), 329; the important newspaper correspondence dealing with the Jay-King accusation is reproduced on pp. 329-346.

[34] Federalists were elated that "Citizen Genet is out of credit" and that "everybody is provoked with him." Fisher Ames to Thomas Dwight, Boston, Aug., 1793, Seth Ames, ed., *Works of Fisher Ames*, I, 129; McMaster, *A History of the People of the United States . . .* , II, 139; Monaghan, *John Jay*, p. 256; Woodfin, "Citizen Genet and His Mission," pp. 364 ff., 381.

Hard-core elements of the Republican press and of the democratic societies still clung to Genet and fought in his defense. They denounced the "certificate men" and cried that all was a Federalist plot to ruin Genet, destroy Franco-American friendship, and undermine the French alliance. Federalist attacks against the French minister, they declared, were nothing new; from the first he had been the object of their scurrility and slander. What was new, they pointed out, were the open efforts of high government officials to ruin and discredit him.[35]

Even Hamilton, who had directed the offensive against the French minister, had entered the fray openly. He who detested appeals to the mob had turned to the people. In a series of four articles appearing in the New York *Daily Advertiser* in August, 1793, under the title "No Jacobin," Hamilton turned his pen against Genet and the French alliance, exposing and dissecting the entire controversy over prizes, neutrality, and Genet's defiant conduct. He denounced "the very disrespectful treatment we have experienced from the agents of France, who have acted towards us from the beginning more like a dependent colony than an independent nation." Hamilton never completed his attack; yellow fever cut it short.[36]

* * * * *

When first confronted with the Jay-King certificate, Genet did not take it seriously. Being false, he maintained, it merited no reply. At the same time he did not conceal from his home government his contempt for the Washington administration; the "weak" American government, he wrote, "deserves such an appeal."[37] But the

[35] Philip Marsh, "James Monroe as 'Agricola' in the Genet Controversy, 1793," the *Virginia Magazine of History and Biography*, LXII (October, 1954), 472-476. Genet believed that the certificate publication was part of the Federalist government's design "to discard our alliance and to cement one with England. . . ." Genet to Jefferson, 1797, in Genet, *Washington, Jefferson, and "Citizen" Genet*, p. 28.

[36] The articles, written ostensibly in reply to criticisms appearing in the press signed "Jacobin," are reproduced in Lodge, *The Works of Alexander Hamilton*, IV, 198-229; the quotation is from "No Jacobin," No. II, p. 216; see also Schachner, *Alexander Hamilton*, pp. 323-324; for Jefferson's comment, see his letter to Madison, Philadelphia, Aug. 11, 1793, in Lipscomb, *Jefferson's Works*, IX, 179-180; Woodfin, "Citizen Genet and His Mission," p. 371.

[37] Genet to Minister of Foreign Affairs, New York, Aug. 15, 1793, in Turner, *CFM*, p. 241.

public furor stirred up by the "certificate" episode could not be dismissed so easily. Even Jay and King had been disturbed deeply by it and had turned to Hamilton for additional support. The Federalist chieftain had obliged on August 13 by outlining the facts of the Dallas-Genet midnight conversation as he knew and interpreted them and by indicating what they might use in their anti-Genet campaign. "The charge," he advised, "ought to be insisted upon."[38]

Genet's friends, too, were concerned; they suggested that he disavow the Federalist accusations. He did not need much urging. Promptly, and perhaps unthinkingly, on August 13 he wrote directly to the President, later publishing the letter. This was rash; it appeared to lend credence to the Federalist charge. For, in effect, the letter and its later publication constituted an appeal to the people. It was indeed an extraordinary document for a diplomat to address to a head of state. In it Genet angrily demanded of Washington that he dissipate the "dark calumnies" directed against him by "an explicit declaration that I have never intimated to you an intention of appealing to the people. . . . A publication of your answer will be the only reply which shall be given to those party men, who never fail to confound the individual with affairs of state."[39]

Three days later, on August 16, Jefferson replied that the President had received the letter. "I am desired to observe to you," he told Genet, "that it is not the established course for the diplomatic characters residing here, to have any direct correspondence with him. The Secretary of State is the organ through which their communications should pass. The President does not conceive it to be within the line of propriety or duty for him to bear evidence against a declaration which, whether made to him or others, is perhaps immaterial: he therefore declines interfering in the case."[40]

Genet considered the reply evasive; but in his own letter to Washington he had evaded the question of whether or not he had made the threat of appeal to Dallas. Jay, King, and other Federalists

[38] Hamilton to King, Philadelphia, Aug. 13, 1793, in Hamilton, ed., *Hamilton's Works*, V, 574-576.

[39] The letter to Washington is reproduced in Dawson, "The Citizen Genet," *HM*, X, 330; see also Minnegerode, *Genet*, pp. 321-323; McMaster, *A History of the People of the United States. . .* , II, 140.

[40] Jefferson's letter is reproduced in Dawson, "The Citizen Genet," *HM*, X, 331; see also Minnigerode, *Genet*, pp. 323-324; McMaster, *A History of the People of the United States. . .* , II, 140.

were quick to catch the omission and to point to the disingenuous-
ness of Genet's statements. Having found its way into print, the
entire affair now became public property. When stripped of propaganda and counterpropaganda—if that were possible—the people
could see for themselves in Genet's letter to Washington what was
and was not evasive.

With publication of his intemperate letter to Washington, Genet's
popular following melted away faster than ever; even some of his
staunchest supporters now deserted him; he became a lost cause.[41]

Jefferson, who earlier had seen the political danger of too close a
tie to Genet, now cut his lines. "Genet has thrown down the gaunt-
let to the President by the publication of his letter and my answer,"
he told Madison, "and is himself forcing that appeal to the people,
and risking that disgust, which I had so much wished should have
been avoided." It would "be true wisdom in the Republican party
to approve unequivocally of a state of neutrality," he was convinced,
and "to abandon G.[enet] entirely with expression of strong friendship & adherence to his nation. . . in this way we shall keep the
people on our side by keeping ourselves in the right—I have been
myself under a cruel dilemma with him. I adhered to him as long
as I could have a hope of getting him right . . . finding at length
that the man was absolutely incorrigible, I saw the necessity of quit-
ting a wreck which could not but sink all who should cling to it."[42]

Sharing Jefferson's concern, Madison recounted his observations.
He revealed that the anti-Genet revulsion ran so strong throughout
Virginia that he found it necessary to attempt to get the people to
discriminate between France and her minister's conduct.[43] Genet's
conduct, he wrote, "as exhibited in the newspapers, is as unaccount-
able as it is distressing. The effect is beginning to be strongly felt
here in the surprise and disgust of those who are attached to the
French cause, and viewed this minister as the instrument for cement-
ing instead of alienating, the two Republics. These sensations are
powerfully reinforced by the general and habitual veneration for the

[41] Woodfin, "Genet and His Mission," p. 253.
[42] Jefferson to Madison, Aug. 11, 1793, quoted from the Madison Papers
in Stephenson and Dunn, *George Washington,* II, 363; Jefferson to Madison,
Philadelphia, Aug. 25, 1793, in Lipscomb, *Jefferson's Works,* IX, 211.
[43] Brant, *James Madison: Father of the Constitution. . . ,* 382-383; McMaster, *A History of the People of the United States. . . ,* II, 140.

President."[44] Even pro-Genet Governor Moultrie of South Carolina warned the French minister that his behavior had offended and alarmed friends of France; he could not insult highly respected President Washington and still remain popular in the United States.[45]

Not all of his followers deserted the French minister; some stayed and continued the fight with him. But the battle was lost. Throughout the country men pledged their support to Washington, through letters, resolutions, pamphlets, and public rallies.[46] Federalist leaders, in addition, pressed home their attack. Jay wrote to Hamilton that he was tired of Genet's evasions. Why not, he asked, sink him in one blast by getting Jefferson to acknowledge publicly that Genet had made a threat of appeal to him?[47] The Chief Justice's politics were naïve; he failed to distinguish between Jefferson the patriot and Jefferson the politician.

Little doubt remained that Republican leaders were worried and that the French alliance was foundering. This danger to the alliance struck James Monroe with special force. He warned Jefferson that "the state into which the conduct of an indiscreet man on the one part and some very wicked men on the other part has thrown us in respect to France fills me with extreme concern." Clearly, he said, the Hamiltonians are trying "to separate us from France & ultimately unite us with England;" obviously "the certificate of Messrs. Jay & King was concerted at Phila[delphia] as the means of bringing the subject before the publick." Nevertheless, Monroe considered "the whole however as a mere trick and which will ultimately recoil on the authors of it."[48]

As if to embarrass his supporters and to lend proof to the Federalist charge of attempting to subvert the government, Genet continued to cross swords with Washington. In October, 1793, Washington revoked the exequatur of Antoine C. Duplaine, French vice-con-

[44] Madison to Jefferson, Sept. 2, 1793, in Hunt, *The Writings of James Madison*, VI, 191; Stephenson and Dunn, *George Washington*, II, 363.

[45] *New York Journal*, Oct. 23, 1793, cited in McMaster, *A History of the People of the United States. . .* , II, 140.

[46] Similar support by last-ditch supporters poured in for Genet. Minnigerode, *Genet*, p. 327.

[47] Monaghan, *John Jay*, p. 357.

[48] Monroe to Jefferson, Staunton, Sept. 3, 1793, in Stanislaus M. Hamilton, ed., *The Writings of James Monroe*, I, 273-274; Minnigerode, *Genet*, p. 329.

sul at Boston, for using armed force from a French warship in the harbor to rescue a French privateer from the custody of an American "officer of justice." Duplaine's action—consistent with Genet's orders to the French ships in New York to use force against American officials in protecting privateers in the port—had outraged the Cabinet. Three times the United States district attorney at Boston brought civil charges against Duplaine, and three times a sympathetic jury, apparently supported by a sympathetic public opinion, failed to sustain the charges. Up to this point the Duplaine case had the appearance of another Henfield case. Finally, however, Washington ordered Duplaine's exequatur revoked. Jefferson followed this up with a "Circular to the French Consuls" which defined the limits of their jurisdiction.[49]

During the furor Genet did not attempt to defend Duplaine's deed; he defied Washington, challenging the President's power to dismiss a French representative. He declared that under the Constitution the President did not have the power to revoke an exequatur. When notified officially of Duplaine's dismissal, he responded with a violent protest which he published in the newspapers before delivering it to the Secretary of State; in it he refused to admit the "validity" of the dismissal, an "arbitrary" presidential act.[50]

Like Genet's other deeds this touched off a newspaper battle. John Quincy Adams, this time writing as "Columbus," defended the Executive's power to revoke an exequatur or to dismiss a foreign minister and attacked Genet's actions as incitement to insurrection. In so doing he delivered a warning against "the interference of foreigners upon any pretense whatever, in the dissensions of fellow-citizens." Such meddling, he said, "must be inevitably fatal to the liberties of the State." Under the name "Americanus," the inevitable opponent rose to Genet's defense. Congress, which has the power to declare war, he said, not the President, had the power to revoke an exequatur.[51]

[49] The "Circular," Philadelphia, Sept. 7, 1793, is in Ford, *Writings of Jefferson*, VI, 417.

[50] The Duplaine affair is recounted in Thomas, *American Neutrality. . . ,* pp. 212-220; Woolery, *The Relation of Thomas Jefferson to American Foreign Policy,* p. 120; Minnigerode, *Genet,* pp. 238-239.

[51] The Duplaine affair is described also in Bemis, *John Quincy Adams and the Foundations of American Foreign Policy,* pp. 37-38; see Jefferson to

In spite of mounting complications, for a while it appeared that Genet's counteroffensive might cause Jay and King's certificate to recoil. On November 14, 1793, Genet wrote to Jefferson and to Attorney General Randolph demanding that the Federal government prosecute Jay and King for libel. Their certificate, he said, was "a public insult to my nation and to myself" which greatly injured "the cause of my country."[52] "The lie having effected its purpose," he said, "I can unfortunately for justice, but too slowly follow it with detection." With its topsy-turvy mixture of foreign policy and domestic politics, the battle to sink Genet had brought forth the demand of a foreign diplomat that his host government prosecute for libel its highest judicial officer.

On November 26, 1793, the press carried another Federalist certificate—this one from Hamilton and Knox. In it they declared that Jay and King had obtained their information on Genet's alleged appeal from them, and that they in turn had gotten it from Governor Thomas Mifflin of Pennsylvania, who had heard it directly from Dallas and Jefferson.[53] In the final analysis, this new "certificate" indicated that in order to clear up the matter, Mifflin, Dallas, and Jefferson—Republicans all—had to affirm the certificates. Both Republicans and Federalists realized this. Monroe wrote to Jefferson that upon his testimony depended the outcome of the affair.[54] To Jay this was painfully apparent. He regretted that Jefferson and Mifflin remained in the background; he wondered when Jefferson was going to come forward to affirm the Hamilton-Knox certificate.

Duplaine, Oct. 3, 1793, *ASP FR,* I, 178; appended documents are on pp. 179-182. Young Adams's "Columbus" letters first appeared in the *Columbian Centinel* (Boston) in Nov., 1793, and are reprinted in Ford, *The Writings of John Quincy Adams* I, 148-178. In later years, John Adams, relying perhaps too much on tricky memory, asserted that his son's writings first turned the tide against Genet and the French frenzy. John Adams to William Cunningham, Oct. 13, 1808, *ibid.,* p. 148 n.

[52] Genet's letter is reproduced in Dawson, "The Citizen Genet," *HM,* X, 331; see also Minnigerode, *Genet,* p. 329; Monaghan, *John Jay,* p. 358. Despite the brave front, Genet by this time had grown weary. He complained of lack of instructions and that day by day his mission had become more difficult. Genet to Minister of Foreign Affairs, Nov., 1793, Genet Papers, XIII, 3910.

[53] The Hamilton-Knox certificate is reproduced in Dawson, "Citizen Genet," *HM,* X, 335.

[54] Monroe to Jefferson, Philadelphia, Dec. 4, 1793, in Hamilton, *The Writings of James Monroe,* I, 279.

While Jefferson and Mifflin remained silent, or until their silence was accounted for, he realized that little could be done. He even urged that Jefferson's original report to the President on the conversation with Genet over the *Petite Démocrate* be published.[55]

Jefferson and Mifflin refused to clarify the situation to the advantage of Federalists. While recognizing Genet as a political liability and eager to be rid of him, they would not contribute knowingly to any further discrediting of him, of their party, and of the French alliance. All this was logical, particularly as Jefferson had acknowledged privately that Dallas told him that Genet had made the threatened appeal.[56]

Alexander J. Dallas, the key figure in the matter of the alleged "appeal," indicated publicly that neither Jefferson nor Mifflin could substantiate the "certificate men." Several days later, December 9, 1793, in the *American Daily Advertiser* of Philadelphia Dallas gave the purported "facts, relative to Mr. Genet's conversation with me." Dallas was, for those who would believe him, quite detailed and specific. "I now most solemnly say," Dallas wrote, "that Mr. Genet never did, in his conversation with me, declare 'that he would appeal from the President to the People,' or that he would make any other appeal which conveyed to my mind the idea of exciting insurrection and tumult." He said that neither Jay, King, Hamilton, nor Knox had consulted him before publishing their certificates.[57]

Truly the situation had become ludicrous. In effect, a foreign diplomat had succeeded in labeling as liars several of the nation's highest officials. Whether or not Genet had threatened an "appeal" in the presence of Dallas mattered little. In Federalist eyes, his actions, his deeds, his entire diplomatic career in the United States constituted an appeal to the people over the head of Washington.

Republicans maintained that he was driven to this because Washington's Federalist-oriented government defied popular will and

[55] Monaghan, *John Jay*, pp. 358-359; Minnigerode, *Genet*, p. 332.

[56] See The Anas, July 10, 1793, in Ford, *Writings of Jefferson*, I, 241; for a sketchy treatment of Mifflin's role, see Kenneth R. Rossman, *Thomas Mifflin and the Politics of the American Revolution*, pp. 220-221.

[57] Dallas's statement is reproduced in Dawson, "The Citizen Genet," *HM*, X, 336-337; also in King, *Rufus King Correspondence*, I, 464-469; for a discussion centering on Dallas's role, see Walters, *Alexander James Dallas*, pp. 48-50. Dallas had submitted a copy of his statement to Jefferson before publication.

sabotaged the French alliance. This was politics, and in political battles truth often is the first casualty. In politics statesmen must be politicians. Name-calling, groundless accusations, guilt by association, lies, deception, and hysteria are thrown into the same cauldron. In 1793 this cauldron was American democracy—just beginning to boil.

Federalists were outraged by what Rufus King called Dallas's "apostacy"; they accused the Pennsylvania Republican of collusion with Genet.[58] Collusion or not, the French minister, thinking he now had the upper hand, once more sprang to the offensive. He directed another letter to Attorney General Randolph on December 16 demanding prosecution of Jay and King for libel. He asked Jefferson, in addition, to "prevail" upon the President to direct Randolph "to commence as speedily as possible, a suit which the honor of France and my own are essentially concerned."[59] Jefferson acted, but not entirely to Genet's satisfaction. First he told Randolph that Washington recommended prompt action in the case, "as it concerns a public character peculiarly entitled to the protection of the laws." At the same time he added the proviso that "our citizens ought not to be vexed with groundless prosecutions." Randolph then told Genet that "this case will not sustain the prosecution which you meditate."[60]

Even though Randolph had turned him down, Genet was not without champions. Several lawyers, among them Edward Livingston, offered to take his case. On December 23, 1793, they told him that in the light of Dallas's statements they believed that Jay and King "committed an offense, not only against the local law of this country, but against the law of nations, for which they may be indicted and punished." They recommended prosecuting Jay and King, probably in the Supreme Court.[61]

Armed with legal support, Genet was determined to go ahead with the lawsuit. He notified Randolph that "since you refuse to

[58] Rufus King in the *American Minerva* (New York), Dec. 11, 1793, reprinted in King, *Rufus King Correspondence*, I, 462-464.

[59] The letters to Randolph and Jefferson are in Dawson, "The Citizen Genet," *HM*, X, 341-342.

[60] Jefferson to Randolph, Philadelphia, Dec. 18, 1793, Randolph to Genet, Philadelphia, Dec. 18, 1793, *ibid.*, pp. 342-343.

[61] Minnigerode, *Genet*, pp. 333-334.

cause to be rendered to my Nation, the ally of yours, the justice claimed by its representative, I will apply immediately to the Judges; and should they refuse to admit my complaint, I will cover myself with the mantle of mourning, and will say America is no longer free."[62] A truly noble threat. There is something of the child in most people, and here spoke the child in Genet.

When the "certificate men" learned that Washington, through Jefferson, had authorized the Attorney-General to act as he saw fit in response to Genet's demands for a libel suit, they were horrified. Jay and King considered Washington's action "as extraordinary as it authorized inferences unfavorable to our characters, and such indeed as both the President and Mr. Jefferson were sensible we did not merit."[63] They rushed an angry letter directly to the President. In it they denounced Randolph and Jefferson and demanded a certi-fied copy of Jefferson's report on the Dallas-Genet interview which they wished to be allowed to publish. Washington was in a dilemna. The politics and "faction" he abhorred were splitting his government and were driving a wedge between him and his staunchest sup-porters.

Randolph urged the President to reply to the critics, justifying his course of action. Hamilton, on the other hand, advised him to release a copy of Jefferson's report to Jay and King. Knox wanted to restore party harmony; he wished to prevent a complete rupture between Jay and King on the one hand and the President on the other. He searched for "some middle course which would satisfy no one, but end in burying the affair in oblivion." To achieve this goal he asked Jay and King to take back their angry letter to Wash-ington; they refused. They wished to settle the matter, but they believed the President should confer with them directly.[64]

Washington subsequently invited Jay to Philadelphia, where the two men thrashed out the entire affair. Complaining of the severity of the Jay-King letter to him and pointing out that neither Jeffer-son nor Randolph had meant anything harmful or unfriendly, Washington had written out a defense of his conduct in the episode.

[62] Genet to Randolph, Philadelphia, Dec., 1793, reprinted in Dawson, "The Citizen Genet," *HM*, X, 344.

[63] Statement of Rufus King, Feb., 1794, in King, *Rufus King Correspond-ence*, I, 476-480.

[64] The entire episode is aired in *ibid*.

The President emphasized the difficulty of his position and the fact that he had to proceed with "caution." His entire Cabinet was involved in this unsavory affair. The Chief Justice was being sued for libel and was accused of propagating slanders against the plenipotentiary of an allied power; and Washington himself was involved, as Jefferson had made the official report to him. Finally, after some animated exchanges, Washington expressed his friendship for both Jay and King and agreed to release Jefferson's report. They had reached an understanding and had avoided a permanent rupture. They agreed that if Genet, the source of all the trouble, were not recalled soon by his government, Washington would dismiss him.

Within a few days King called on the President to make his peace. The two men went through proper rituals. King handed Washington the original of the Jay-King letter. Then Washington took the written defense of his own conduct and set fire to both documents, and thus reduced dissension to ashes. To seal the bargain, Washington gave King the desired extract of Jefferson's report on the Dallas-Genet conversation.

As to Genet's threatened lawsuit against King and Jay, it turned out almost as Knox had desired. Caught in the flow of other events and recalled finally by his own government, Genet dropped the suit. His successor, Fauchet, who arrived in February, 1794, made clear that he would abandon the legal action.[65]

* * * * *

Immediately following the escape of the *Petite Démocrate*, President Washington had decided that the French minister must go and had taken steps to implement his decision. Among the factors which influenced that decision were the activities of George Hammond, who had learned through Hamilton of the sentiment for Genet's recall before the French government had decided upon it and had contributed every assistance to bring it about. He was motivated by the idea that if the United States could be awakened to a sense of wrongs suffered from France, Americans would react so as to de-

[65] Thirty years later Genet still denied having appealed to the people, insisting that a threat to appeal to Congress was not a threat to appeal to the people. Genet to the *Albany Argus*, Sept. 29, 1823, cited in Woodfin, "Citizen Genet and His Mission," p. 474; Minnigerode, *Genet*, p. 363; Turner, *CFM*, p. 279 n.

prive France of her only ally capable of supplying desperately needed provisions. But Hammond's assistance in alienating the two allies was hardly necessary in view of Genet's official conduct, which had harmed the alliance and caused the American government to decide to get rid of him.[66] During the public airing of the affair of the "threatening appeal," Genet's American career as a diplomat was ruined; fight as he might, the fatal decisions had been made.

Jefferson, as has been seen, by early summer 1793 had come to consider Genet a liability to the French alliance and to the budding Republican party. Fearing "that he will enlarge the circle of those disaffected to his country," Jefferson was doing everything in his power "to moderate the impetuosity of his [Genet's] movements." Genet's conduct, he added later, "is indefensible by the most furious Jacobin. I only wish our countrymen may distinguish between him & his nation, & if the case should ever be laid before them, may not suffer their affection to the nation to be diminished." A crisis was imminent; Jefferson, though he felt that there was blame on both sides, admitted that there was more on Genet's side.[67]

As might have been expected, Hamilton took the initiative. In a Cabinet meeting of July 13, 1793, he moved that Washington ask the French government to recall Genet; Knox suggested that in the meantime the President suspend Genet's functions. Jefferson opposed Hamilton's motion and suggested a milder approach. Washington said nothing.[68] This was a delicate matter; if it were not handled properly American neutrality would be imperiled. Hamilton even told the British minister not long after that the American government looked forward to war with France as "neither improbable nor distant."[69]

Ten days later Washington reintroduced the problem of Genet's status to his Cabinet. He believed he should bring Genet's conduct to the attention of the French government through Gouver-

[66] Hammond to Grenville, Philadelphia, Aug. 10, 1793, No. 17, Henry Adams Transcripts.

[67] Jefferson to Monroe, Philadelphia, June 28 and July 14, 1793, in Ford, *Writings of Jefferson,* VI, 323, 348-349; Woolery, *The Relation of Thomas Jefferson to American Foreign Policy,* p. 118.

[68] The Anas, July 10, 1793, committed to writings July 13, in Ford, *Writings of Jefferson,* I, 243.

[69] Hammond to Grenville, Philadelphia, Aug. 10, 1793, No. 17, Henry Adams Transcripts; also cited in Thomas, *American Neutrality. . . ,* p. 227.

neur Morris, the American minister in Paris, and ask for his recall. At the same time he wanted to draw "a clear line between him & his nation, express[in]g our fr[ien]dship to the latter but insist[in]g on the recall of Genet, and in the mean time that we should desire him either to withdraw or cease his functions." Supported by Knox, Hamilton urged the President to take strong action; if not, he warned, the government would lose all public support and might even be overthrown by a faction.[70] The Cabinet took no action at this meeting; not until August 1, 1793, after Jefferson had prepared translations of Genet's correspondence for the Cabinet members to read, did it reach a final decision.[71]

Washington's advisers agreed to send a full statement of Genet's conduct and a copy of his correspondence to the French government and to request his recall. Knox suggested sending off Genet himself, but the others rejected the suggestion. Jefferson confided to Madison that "we have decided unanimously to *require* the *recall of Genet. He will sink the republican* interest if they do not *abandon him. Hamilton presses eagerly an appeal i.e.* to the *people*. It's [*sic*] consequences you will readily seize, but *I hope we shall prevent it* tho the *Pr. is inclined* to it."[72]

As Secretary of State, Jefferson had the task of writing the letter Morris would transmit to the French government. Randolph, as Attorney General, compiled a list of charges noting five specific points of misconduct by Genet. Included were Genet's commissioning of privateers after he had agreed to stop the practice, his use of French consuls as admiralty courts after he promised to stop such usage, the escape of the *Petite Démocrate,* his insulting language toward Washington, and his interference with the American judiciary in its efforts to prosecute Americans who had enlisted on French privateers.[73]

Jefferson and Hamilton clashed once more, this time over phrase-

[70] The Anas, July 23, 1793, in Ford, *Writings of Jefferson*, I, 247; Woolery, *The Relation of Thomas Jefferson to American Foreign Policy*, p. 118.

[71] The Anas, Aug. 1, 1793, in Ford, *Writings of Jefferson*, I, 252-253; Thomas, *American Neutrality. . . ,* p. 228.

[72] Jefferson to Madison, Aug. 3, 1793, in Ford, *Writings of Jefferson*, VI, 361; see also the record of Cabinet meetings, Aug. 23, 1793, in Fitzpatrick, *Washington's Writings*, XXXIII, 58 n.-59 n.

[73] Randolph to Jefferson, Aug. 4, 1793, cited in Woolery, *The Relation of Thomas Jefferson to American Foreign Policy*, pp. 118-119.

ology in the letter requesting Genet's recall. On the wording of that request much depended—war or peace perhaps? George Hammond thought so and noted that "should the national convention determine to support its minister—this order of things must issue in war between France and this country."[74] Jefferson was equal to the occasion and produced a document which is, in the view of some, a diplomatic "masterpiece." With "great delicacy" he reviewed in eight thousand words Genet's career in the United States, making a clear distinction between the man and his government, pointing out that "our first duty, therefore, was to draw a strong line between their intentions, and the proceedings of their minister." Adroitly he emphasized the "constant and unabating" friendship of the United States for France. In other hands, undoubtedly, a harsher document would have resulted. As it was, despite the strained circumstances the administration made an effort to preserve the 1778 alliance from a mortal blow. Jefferson sent this request for Genet's recall to Gouverneur Morris in Paris on August 16, 1793.[75]

Several months would elapse before a reply to the letter could be expected. What to do with Genet in the meantime perplexed Washington's official family. To Federalists he became more and more unbearable and to Republicans he became more and more an embarrassment. Washington was out of patience and ready for peremptory action; he wanted to suspend the Frenchman's functions while waiting for a reply to the request for recall. Jefferson opposed this precipitate action, defending "France the only nation on earth sincerely our friend" and pointing out that it was not fair to force a belligerent to remain several months without a representative in a neutral country.[76] Washington did not suspend Genet's functions immediately; Genet continued to harass the government.

[74] Hammond to Grenville, Philadelphia, Aug. 10, 1793, No. 17, quoted in Thomas, *American Neutrality. . . ,* p. 229; Woodfin, "Citizen Genet and His Mission," p. 393.

[75] The text of the letter is in *ASP FR,* I, 167-172; the quotation is from p. 167.

[76] The Anas, Nov. 8, 1793, in Ford, *Writings of Jefferson,* I, 265-267; in getting rid of Genet some had suggested to Washington that Congress pass a resolution to dismiss him, but this was opposed by Federalists "on the ground that it was throwing the Apple of Discord into Congress, and would inevitably produce a violent struggle and convulsion." Genet was still a power to be feared because of popular sentiment. Quoted from Rufus King's statement of Feb., 1794, in King, *Rufus King Correspondence,* I, 479.

Another question the Cabinet discussed was whether or not the government should inform Genet immediately of the request for his recall. Overruling Jefferson, the presidential advisers decided to inform him. On September 15, after the ship carrying the request for recall was beyond reach of ships which might be sent out by Genet to overtake it, Jefferson gave the French minister a copy of the recall letter. He told Genet that he would be permitted to retain his functions only "so long as they shall be restrained within the limits of the law as heretofore announced to you."[77]

Although staggered by the blow, Genet responded quickly. On September 18 he gave his answer. He said that he had done nothing wrong, that he had merely obeyed superior orders, that he had attended strictly to his duty, and "that the President of the United States took on himself to give to our treaties arbitrary interpretations, absolutely contrary to their true sense."[78] Laboring under the illusion that the executive action could not stick, that the next Congress would repudiate the President and vindicate him, and that his Republican allies would rally to his side, he failed to catch the real import of the administration's action. He wrote home that Washington called him a "Jacobin anarchist" and threatened to have him recalled because he did not yield to the Federalist party. This, he said, did not bother him; he had the trust of the people whose opinions differed greatly from those of the government.[79] Genet was mistaken; his faith in the people and in Congress was misplaced; they would not support him in defiance of President Washington, the man he called "the living idol which the Americans have set up for themselves."[80]

Several of Genet's advisers and American friends dissuaded him from making an appeal to Congress. Such an appeal, they said, would strengthen the now widespread belief that the French minister sought to create faction and confusion and to drive the United

[77] Jefferson to Genet, [Sept. 15, 1793], in Ford, *Writings of Jefferson*, VI, 429-430; Thomas, *American Neutrality. . . ,* pp. 232-233.

[78] Genet to Jefferson, New York, Sept. 18, 1793, *ASP FR*, I, 172-174.

[79] Genet to Minister of Foreign Affairs, New York, Sept. 19, 1793, in Turner, *CFM,* pp. 242-243.

[80] Genet in effect, refused to admit the power of the President to dismiss him. Such might have been expected; Genet had expressed the same view in the controversy centering on Antoine C. Duplaine. See above, pp. 290-291.

States into war. They tried, in addition, to keep him from publishing his instructions, a step he had threatened to take. It would be sheer folly, they warned. Washington was hedged about with such divinity, they said, "that he is and will forever remain, unapproachable to any personal attack." They even believed that the breach between Genet and the President might be closed. A sympathetic triumvirate of John Taylor of Caroline, Edward Livingston, and Albert Gallatin, representing a caucus of Republican congressmen, actually tried to achieve a reconciliation.[81]

Here again, as on previous occasions, Genet appeared to be his own worst enemy. Hamilton and the Federalists wanted publication of the French minister's correspondence. In fact, at the fatal Cabinet meeting of August 1, 1793, Hamilton had moved that this be done, with a statement of the proceedings leading to the request for recall. He wanted this done as an appeal from the administration to the people, as a political stroke designed to paralyze opposition.[82]

Washington at first favored the move as a step to thwart selective publication by Genet and as a step to strengthen public confidence in the administration. Only Jefferson's vigorous opposition stopped publication at this time. Without mincing words, he labeled the plan an attempt to make the President "the head of a party instead of the head of a nation." Publication, he said, would only reveal Cabinet dissensions to the public; it would be undignified; it would thrust the President more than ever into a contest with Genet for public support.[83] Although not convinced by Jefferson's arguments, Washington accepted Randolph's suggestion that he postpone publication and public appeal until it could be ascertained whether such action was necessary to win popular support. When the new Congress met in December, Washington laid the Genet correspondence, together with an explanation for the requested recall, before it.[84]

[81] Minnigerode, *Genet*, p. 342; for Gallatin's views on the Genet-Washington feud, see Gallatin to Hannah Nicholson, Philadelphia, Aug. 25, 1793, in Henry Adams, *The Life of Albert Gallatin*, p. 104. Gallatin considered the President to be in the right.

[82] The Anas, Aug. 1, 1793, in Ford, *Writings of Jefferson*, I, 252-253.

[83] *Ibid.*, Aug. 2, 1793, pp. 253-254.

[84] Thomas, *American Neutrality. . .* , pp. 234-235. John Adams remarked: "How a government can go on publishing all their negotiations with foreign nations I know not. To me it appears as dangerous and pernicious as it is

Political opportunist that he was, Jefferson in drafting Washington's accompanying message of December 5 had succeeded in including several paragraphs on relations with Great Britain. Sections of Hammond's correspondence were published over Hamilton's objections. Britain's conduct up to this point had not been exemplary, and a double publication, Hamilton realized, would offset any adverse reaction against France. Publication of the Genet correspondence only, however, would direct all public resentment against France alone. Jefferson won out; against the advice of Randolph, Hamilton, and Knox, Washington authorized a complete publication.[85] Publication of Genet's correspondence left little doubt in the minds of even pro-French Republicans "that he is a man totally unfit for the place he fills." In his violence and conceit, they believed, "he has hurted the cause of his country here more than all her enemies could have done."[86]

When this new blow fell Genet could be restrained no longer; to counteract the administration's action he was determined to go directly to Congress. He persisted in his mistaken notion that Congress was the final source of authority in the United States. From the beginning of his mission he had looked forward to the convening of Congress, arguing continually that the various decisions he had opposed in the Executive should have been made by the legislature. His reasons were obvious. Popularity and public enthusiasm were his; Congress was the popular branch of government. Logically, he concluded, Congress would support him on most matters where the pro-English Executive would not.[87]

---

novel; but upon this occasion it could not, perhaps, have been avoided." To his wife, Philadelphia, Dec. 19, 1793, C. F. Adams, ed., *Letters of John Adams Addressed to His Wife,* II, 132-133.

[85] Washington's message to Congress of Dec. 5, 1793, is in *ASP FR,* I, 141-142; the Genet and Hammond papers follow to p. 246; see also The Anas, Nov. 28, 1793, in Ford, *Writings of Jefferson,* I, 271, 272. Jefferson remarked that this was the first time he had seen Washington taking the opinion of one of his advisers against that of three others. Hammond, of course, was upset, but he realized that Jefferson's motives were political. For details, see Thomas, *American Neutrality. . . ,* pp. 243-245.

[86] Albert Gallatin to his wife, Philadelphia, Dec. 6, 1793, in Adams, *The Life of Albert Gallatin,* p. 111; to John Adams, Jefferson seemed "as little satisfied with the conduct of the French minister, as any one." To his wife, Philadelphia, Dec. 5, 1793, C. F. Adams, ed., *Letters of John Adams Addressed to His Wife,* II, 130.

[87] When Congress convened and threw its support behind Washington,

In his stress on popular government and legislative predominance, Genet was not alone; many Republicans shared such views, among them Thomas Jefferson. The Virginian had also questioned the competence of the Executive to settle certain neutrality questions and foreign policy issues. Like Genet, he favored an early session for Congress. As Genet became more vehement in his concept of complete legislative dominance, Jefferson attempted to disabuse him, lecturing him privately on the subject several times. To such lengths did Genet carry his concept that Jefferson believed it endangered France's reputation and hence the alliance in the United States. While concerned politically about Genet's irritatingly expressed views and while attempting to moderate them, the Secretary of State did not abandon his own convictions concerning the limits of executive power.[88]

Moderation was not in Genet's make-up. Through Benjamin Bache, after Washington had given the correspondence to Congress, he published an extract of his instructions and then sent a supply of the publications to the President for distribution to Congress. Jefferson bounced the papers right back at Genet. Once again he lectured the minister on Presidential powers and prerogatives. Communications between the executive and legislative branches of the government, he said, were none of the French diplomat's business; the President was the sole judge of what papers should be submitted to Congress.[89]

Beaten, but not yet ready to acknowledge it, Genet could not grasp the fact that Congress had not supported him and that it would not. He continued to believe that public opinion, even at this late hour, would rally to his side to vindicate him and save the 1778 alliance as he interpreted it. Not all his American friends, despite the late hour, abandoned him. Some still argued that Genet

Genet, obviously, was disappointed. He wrote home that "Congress has convened, Washington has been unmasked, America has decayed." Genet to Minister of Foreign Affairs, New York, Dec. 10, 1793, No. 27, in Turner, *CFM*, pp. 277-279; Thomas, *American Neutrality.* . . , pp. 236-237; Minnigerode, *Genet*, 349-350.

[88] See Thomas, *American Neutrality.* . . , pp. 236-237; for Cabinet Opinions (Aug., 1793) on convening Congress early, see Hamilton, ed., *Hamilton's Works*, IV, 455-462.

[89] Jefferson to Genet, Philadelphia, Dec. 31, 1793, in Ford, *Writings of Jefferson*, VI, 495-496.

was being condemned publicly on unsubstantiated charges alone and pleaded "that every friend to the French Republic should wait for *authentic proofs* before they judge his conduct."[90]

Events in France, meanwhile, also had turned against him. The Girondins had fallen from power; Jacobins ruled. Not only were the Jacobins unsympathetic to him and willing to assent to the request of his recall, but also they wanted his neck.[91] On the morning of October 8, 1793, Gouverneur Morris had interviewed the French minister of foreign affairs and had won the promise that Genet would be recalled immediately.[92] The French ministry had not wasted time. In November it had composed Genet's recall and had informed him that he was to be replaced. It ordered Fauchet, his successor, to arrest him and to send him back to France for trial and probable execution. Morris boasted that he "favored, or rather excited the idea," believing that such a procedure would serve as an example to future French diplomats and would "place in a contemptible light the faction connected with M. Genet."[93]

On January 20, 1794, Washington delivered the news to Congress. The new French government "unequivocally disapproved" Genet's conduct and expressed "strongest assurances" that the minister's "recall should be expedited without delay." It was timely assurance; Washington had stood enough; Genet's activities in sponsoring the Western expeditions had placed him on the verge of

[90] "Caution" in the *Independent Chronicle and the Universal Advertiser* (Boston), Jan. 13, 1794.

[91] Not long after the Jacobins had come to power Genet received evidence of their displeasure with his conduct, a scorching reprimand. The new Minister of Foreign Affairs, François-Louis-Michel Deforgues, had upbraided him in strong language: "You are ordered to treat with the *Government* and not a *portion of the people,* to be an instrument of the French Republic before Congress, and not the leader of an American party. . . . Dazzled by a false popularity, you have alienated the one man [Washington] who must be for us the spokesman of the American people. . . . I can in no way endorse the means you have used to reach the patriots and the laudable goal which you have in view." Minister of Foreign Affairs to Genet, Paris, July 30, 1793, No. 12, in Turner *CFM,* pp. 228-231; for the change in the French ministry of foreign affairs, see Masson, *Le Département des affaires étrangères* . . . , pp. 285-305.

[92] Morris to Jefferson, Paris, Oct. 10, 1793, National Archives, State Dept., Diplomatic Despatches, France.

[93] See "Instructions to the Commissioners," Nov. 15, 1793, in Turner, *CFM,* p. 289; Morris to Washington, Paris, Oct. 19, 1793, *ASP FR,* I, 398.

peremptory dismissal before the recall arrived.[94] There was little chance this time for a reprieve. Jefferson, on December 31, had left the government; there was now no one in the Cabinet to restrain Hamilton or to placate Washington.

In February Fauchet and three commissioners arrived in the United States. Immediately Fauchet took steps to undo Genet's work in the West. On March 6, 1794, newspapers carried his proclamation prohibiting all Frenchmen from violating American neutrality and revoking all commissions tending to violate such neutrality. Ironically, Fauchet's proclamation stopped what presidential proclamations had not prevented. Washington's government was satisfied. As we shall see, however, the French government did not abandon the broad view of the 1778 alliance; it insisted instead on its binding force.[95] The menace of Genet was no more; his own government had repudiated him. "Poor Genet, I fear, is undone," John Adams said; "Bad as his conduct has been, I cannot but pity him. What will become of him, I know not."[96]

Washington did not allow Fauchet to carry out the decree of the Committee of Public Safety ordering Genet's arrest. Fauchet had planned to send Genet to France by return trip on the ship in which he himself had arrived. But Genet, knowing of the death of many of his Girondin friends and fearing the implacable Robespierre, decided not to return to France. The President informed Fauchet that he did not desire Genet's punishment; he had wanted Genet's recall, nothing more. Randolph quieted Genet's fears of punishment

[94] Washington to Congress, Jan. 20, 1794, *ASP FR*, I, 314; Stephenson and Dunn, *George Washington*, II, 365; Minnigerode, *Genet*, pp. 353-355.

[95] Minnigerode, *Genet*, pp. 361-362; Genet, *Washington, Jefferson, and "Citizen" Genet*, p. 331; in striking at Genet, Robespierre's Jacobin government did not condemn his methods or repudiate him; it aimed primarily at the Girondists, of whom Genet was an important representative. Daniel Walther, *Gouverneur Morris: Witness of Two Revolutions*, trans. Elinore Denniston (New York, 1934), p. 254. Some thirty years later Jared Sparks interviewed Genet, who remarked that he still remained an "arrant Democrat" even though he had long suffered for his "democratical diplomacy." Interview of Oct. 10, 1826, in Herbert B. Adams, *The Life and Writings of Jared Sparks* (2 vols., Boston, 1893), I, 529. See also Phillips and Reede, *Neutrality. . .*, II, 50.

[96] Adams to his wife, Philadelphia, Feb. 23, 1794, in C. F. Adams, ed. *Letters of John Adams Addressed to His Wife*, II, 143; Minnigerode, *Genet*, pp. 358-359.

by the Jacobins by telling him in confidence that he still had many American friends. For a while, however, Genet lived in fear of being kidnaped and went around with an armed guard. Having married Cornelia Tappen Clinton, daughter of governor George Clinton of New York—a staunch Republican—he remained in the United States for the rest of his days, becoming an American citizen in 1804.

* * * * *

In later years John Adams commented to Thomas Jefferson on Genet and the American enthusiasm for France. "You certainly never felt the terrorism excited by Genet, in 1793," he said, "when ten thousand people in the streets of Philadelphia, day after day threatened to drag Washington out of his house, and effect a revolution in the government, or compel it to declare war in favor of the French Revolution and against England. The coolest and the firmest minds, even among the Quakers in Philadelphia, have given their opinions to me, that nothing but the yellow fever . . . could have saved the United States from a fatal revolution of government."[97] Undoubtedly Genet terrified Federalists; that he brought the United States to the brink of revolution is difficult to substantiate. That he brought enthusiasm to the French cause in the United States, that he tried to align the United States behind Republican France in her struggle against England, that he wanted broad implementation of the 1778 alliance, and that he attempted to use the United States to achieve French objectives there is little doubt. Yet Genet was not the fool he often has been depicted; in French eyes he appeared a man of talent and good intentions.[98]

Almost any minister from France would have run into difficulty in 1793 if he had come with Genet's instructions. Granted, Genet was headstrong, impatient, and intemperate in his actions, and often he created his own difficulties. Yet, usually, he attempted merely to carry out instructions of his lawful superiors. Even Ham-

[97] Adams to Jefferson, Quincy, June 30, 1813, in Adams, *Works*, X, 47.
[98] Jusserand, "La Jeunesse du citoyen Genet. . . ," *Revue d'histoire diplomatique*, XLIV, 237; Adams, *Memoirs of John Quincy Adams*, diary entry of March 18, 1795, The Hague, I, 97; "View of Genet's Conduct," [Oct., 1793], AAE CP EU, Vol. XXXIX, f. 144, printed in Frederick J. Turner, ed., "Documents on the Relations of France to Louisiana, 1792-95," *AHR*, III (April, 1898), 505-507.

mond observed that "however intemperate, reprehensible, and un-warrantable his conduct may have been he has not essentially ex-ceeded the spirit of his instructions."[99]   Unfortunately for Genet, those instructions ran counter to the plans and desires of the domi-nant party in the American government, a party-in-the-making which in principle was predicated on Anglo-American friendship. "Citizen" Genet was not a wild-eyed revolutionary; he was a cul-tured, educated, and intelligent young man possessing many of the traits long admired by Americans—honesty, straightforwardness, devotion to duty, and patriotism.[100]

One of Genet's basic difficulties—and one which was to bedevil his immediate successors—was that he overestimated the strength of the pro-French element in the United States and underestimated the influence of the pro-English element. The pro-French element apparently had the largest following among the people and was the most vocal, but the pro-English Hamiltonians dominated the govern-ment and were the most influential members of society. Many of them did not hesitate to intrigue with English agents to combat French influence. More important undoubtedly, as was recognized by Republicans in some instances, was the fact that the tie of blood and commerce to the mother country had been little weakened by the American Revolution even among those who were most hostile to the Federalist government. This tie to England, reinforced by manners, customs, and an admiration of England as a powerful, enlightened nation with a "government the most perfect that existed in our time," was something that was beyond the power of Genet or any other French minister to overcome. Americans directed their enmity against the British government, not against the English people, and in the struggle against France the English people as well as the government were involved.[101]

[99] Hammond to Grenville, Philadelphia, Feb. 22, 1794, No. 2, Henry Adams Transcripts; Woodfin, "Citizen Genet and His Mission," p. 429; Minnigerode, *Genet,* pp. 367-368; Murdoch, "Genesis of the Genet Schemes," *FAR,* II, 94.

[100] After the Jacobin reaction, French officials spoke highly of Genet. One of his successors maintained that he was worth more than the entire commission that had succeeded him. Adams, diary entry of July 17, 1795, The Hague, *Memoirs of John Quincy Adams,* I, 118-119.

[101] See, for instance, the views of "A Farmer of the back Settlements" as he explained the American predilection for England in the *Independent Chronicle and the Universal Advertiser* (Boston), Jan. 20, 1794.

Much of Genet's difficulty came from bad advice; he listened too readily to American sycophants who were eager to use him to advance their own political interests; he was too easily overcome by flattery and outward evidence; he did not penetrate beneath the glittering surface of Franco-American friendship, nor see beyond the written bond of the French alliance.[102]   At the age of thirty, imbued with fresh hopes and sparkling ideals which were for the benefit of "mankind against tyrants," who might not have been turned by the public demonstrations, the mass adulations, and the evidence on every hand that he was the lion of the hour and that public favor was his for the asking?

Ironically, by the time his mission had reached its dénouement, Genet had contributed immeasurably to the injury of the French alliance, the cause he had come to America to aid.   At the same time he had damaged the status of the budding Republican party, upon which the cause of France largely depended.   By meddling in American politics and attempting to gain control over American foreign policy, Genet set a precedent which led finally to the undoing of the alliance his actions were designed to strengthen.   Each of his successors from the French Republic ultimately followed his precedent and each damaged the alliance further.

A main bulwark of the 1778 alliance was Thomas Jefferson.   The French knew that Jefferson was eager to resign as Secretary of State. Early in his mission, therefore, Genet received instructions to influence the selection of Jefferson's successor, to see to it that the new Secretary of State was pro-French alliance.   Although cautioned to act prudently, Genet's task was to block any pro-English appointment.   "In this regard," his instructions said, "you are to use great circumspection so as not to compromise the source of your popularity and the confidence you have inspired."[103]

As Genet's mission closed, confidence would be the last thing

[102] As one French apologist put it, Genet's intentions were not bad, "but he fell into bad hands upon his arrival in America, and was impelled to his offensive conduct by people of the country, who wanted to produce a discord between your Government and our Minister to serve their personal views." Adams, diary entry of March 18, 1795, The Hague, *Memoirs of John Quincy Adams,* I, 97.

[103] Minister of Foreign Affairs (Lebrun) to Genet, Paris, April 10, 1793, AAE CP EU, Vol. XXXVII, f. 208; also in the Genet Papers, Library of Congress, VIII, 2698.

one could say he had inspired. To the contrary, as one critic put it, he had irritated and disgusted a whole nation of "well wishers to the establishment of liberty, order and good Government in France. . . ."[104] Along with his emotion-arousing neutrality-defying activities, Genet had also given impetus to beginning political align-ments in the United States. Jefferson's departure from the govern-ment, as has been seen, coincided with the end of Genet's mission, and the end of the mission marked the establishment of a definite one-party government; Washington had cast aside his efforts at non-partisanship. With Genet a contributing cause, American national politics continued at increased tempo to interact with foreign policy.

In this interaction Genet's mission, like foreign policy itself, became a tool of feuding political parties. In attacking administra-tion foreign policy, Republicans, for example, coupled Genet's mis-sion with the Jay treaty. One critic declared that the administration "to keep the minds of the populace quiet with their sufferings from England, and the ungrateful return of our government to France," began the quarrel with Genet and that "every wretched scribbler on the continent set to try his talents at abuse; as Indians tye their unfortunate prisoners to trees, and then set their popooses [*sic*] to shoot at them." He did not imply that Genet was blameless. Ad-mitting that the Frenchman was guilty of several faults, he said nonetheless that "those were such as a patriot would be liable to fall into, and were greatly exaggerated by calumny." In conclusion, he prophesied "that future disinterested times will think the quarrel unnecessarily begun and shamefully managed."[105]

Although it cannot be divorced from basic foreign policy issues of the time, Genet's quarrel with the Washington administration, in its political aspects, had little to do with principles of neutrality or with principles of an emerging foreign policy being forged by neutral uncommitted statesmen. If this had been the case the differ-ences between Genet and Washington might have been reconciled. As it was neither Genet nor Washington's Federalists wanted an impartial neutrality. Instead of using American politics to advance his cause, as he believed he was doing, Genet was used by Amer-

[104] "Henry" in the *Connecticut Courant* (Hartford), Nov. 11, 1793.

[105] "Junius Americanus" in the *New York Journal,* attacking administration foreign policy toward France and Great Britain. Reprinted in the *Virginia Herald and Fredericksburg Advertiser,* Jan. 26, 1795.

ican politicians—Federalist and Republican—to advance their own interests and to gain political advantage.[106] It is not surprising therefore that in 1793 the French alliance suffered mortal wounds.

[106] Similar ideas with varying emphasis are expressed in Hammond to Grenville, Philadelphia, July, 1793, No. 16, Henry Adams Transcripts; Woodfin, "Citizen Genet and His Mission," pp. 400-401.

CHAPTER TEN

GOUVERNEUR MORRIS

ANACHRONISM IN PARIS

The fact is, that Gouverneur Morris, a high flying monarchy-man, shutting his eyes & his faith to every fact against his wishes, & believing everything he desires to be true, has kept the President's mind constantly poisoned with his forebodings.—Thomas Jefferson, The Anas, March 12, 1792.

There is here an American who takes infinite pains. His name is Morris, and there are positive proofs, that he is acknowledged by the government. He has neutral passports of the United States of America.

He lives in great style, is very magnificient, and besides being rich himself, he has quantities of guineas at his disposal, and he understands scattering them, as well as florins and louis, wherever occasion requires.

He hath the art of winning the good graces of the ladies; he is a very devil in political gallantry, notwithstanding his wooden leg.—Letter from Berlin, August, 1796, the *Kentucky Gazette* (Lexington), January 25, 1797.

* * * * *

Genet in 1793 was not unaided in destroying the French alliance. In Paris Gouverneur Morris, a man whose actions and attitudes the French resented as bitterly as Americans resented those of Genet in Philadelphia, represented the United States. A confirmed aristocrat, a counterrevolutionary, and a dabbler in royalist intrigue, Morris had irritated French governments since the Revolution.[1] When

[1] For details, see Walther, *Gouverneur Morris*, p. 254; A. Esmein, *Gouverneur Morris: Un témoin Américain de la Révolution Française* (Paris, 1906), pp. 34-35; Washington to the Senate, May 27, 1794, *ASP FR*, I, 463. Fauchet reported that he had asked for Morris's recall (informally) and that the

Washington requested Genet's recall, the Jacobin government saw the awaited apportunity to get rid of Morris, so as *quid pro quo* it asked Morris's recall.

A descendant of an officer in Cromwell's armies who had left Restoration England for America, Morris by birth and upbringing belonged to New York's landed aristocracy. In his youth he had acquired conservative ideas which, although modified by time, were to remain with him for the rest of his life. He had apparently always been opposed to revolution and to "the worst of all possible dominions," that of the "riotous mob." Until he was forced to a decision by the bloodshed at Lexington, he had opposed revolt against England. He had trembled at the consequences of a "democratic" revolution, from fear of the social upheaval which generally accompanied such activity; he dreaded the possibility of violence to established interests, to men of property and status.[2]

Nonetheless, he played an active and significant role in the struggle against England. While still in his middle twenties he sat in the Continental Congress. He contributed to vital tasks and decisions, and he gained valuable political and diplomatic experience, all the while clinging to his conservative ideas. After being defeated in his quest for continued political preferment in New York in 1779, he moved to more congenial surroundings in Philadelphia. There he soon plunged again into political activities. From 1781 to 1785 he was concerned with the economics of the embryonic republic as assistant to Robert Morris (not a relation), the Superintendent of Finance.

A believer in a strong executive and a centralized government, Morris was eager to see the government of the Confederation either strengthened or replaced. His chance to do something about it came when he was elected to represent Pennsylvania at the Constitutional Convention. There he achieved lasting renown as the stylist of the

President had agreed. Fauchet to Minister of Foreign Affairs, Philadelphia, April 21, 1794, AAE CP EU, Vol. XLI, f. 183. For evidence of French dissatisfaction with Morris before Genet's mission, see Ternant to Minister of Foreign Affairs, Philadelphia, Feb. 13 and March 7, 1793, in Turner, *CFM*, pp. 170, 187; The Anas, Feb. 20, 1793, in Ford, *Writings of Jefferson*, I, 216-217.

[2] See, for example, Morris to Penn, New York, May 20, 1774, in Jared Sparks, *The Life of Gouverneur Morris* (3 vols., Boston, 1823), I, 25.

Constitution and became a leading political figure. There he found men of his own persuasion, men like Hamilton, who wanted a strong centralized government controlled by the rich and the well-born and with an executive whose tenure of office should be for life. Nursing contempt for "democracy," he believed that elective offices should be kept out of the hands of the "mob."[3] On foreign policy, too, Morris had set ideas, some of them critical of the Constitution he had helped to establish.

During the American Revolution, he later maintained, he had opposed what appeared to him "a rage for treaties." In his view the Constitution, insofar as treaty-making was concerned, favored foreign nations because it made treaties the supreme law of the land. Foreign powers, he said, hence "can violate their contracts with us, but we cannot violate our contracts with them; neither have we, perhaps, any constitutional means of annulling our obligations, when they shall have broken their engagements." He advised "that we should be cautious *what treaties we form, and with whom. What treaties,* because, if contingent engagements become onerous to us, we *must* comply with them; whereas, should they become onerous to those with whom contracted, they *may* release themselves."

As general guides to foreign policy Morris believed that the United States should avoid as much as possible being "drawn into the vortex of European politics." Secondly, he advised that "the less we are fettered by diplomatic engagements, the better shall we be able to preserve a firm and equal conduct in difficult cases." Thirdly, he suggested that "in most controversies between European Powers, we should preserve an exact neutrality." He was convinced "that a neutrality may be most easily preserved, when no belligerent Power can rightfully claim any privilege; because, by conferring such privilege at our pleasure, we can sufficiently punish either of the parties for the injuries and indignities we may have cause to complain of." Lastly, in reference to treaties and negotiations, he concluded "that our present, compared with our future situation, is such that, in treating now, we must make bad bargains, even were

[3] In recalling Morris's activities in the Constitutional Convention, Madison in later years remarked that Morris was "an able, an eloquent, and an active member" and that certainly he did not "incline to the democratic side." Madison to Sparks, Montpelier, April 8, 1831, *ibid.,* p. 284.

there any tribunal to enforce the performance in a peaceable way."[4]

In these and similar ideas Morris was in tune with his Federalist colleagues. He regarded the French alliance as an onerous obligation which should be jettisoned. For a brief time it appeared that the French government held similar views. Charles-François Dumouriez, French Minister of Foreign Affairs for a few months in 1792, informed Morris that "his System of Politics was extremely simple. That a Power so great as France stood in no Need of Alliances and therefore he was against all Treaties other than those of Commerce."[5]

Despite his antialliance convictions, Morris, after the death of Louis XVI, told another French minister of foreign affairs that he truly wished the alliance to be "strictly preserved." In this he attempted to quash French rumors that the United States was headed for an alliance with Great Britain. England, he said, was hostile to the United States "and an attempt at alliance with her idle." Of course, he pointed out, the British minister in the United States "would exert himself to inculcate the opinion that our treaty having been made with the King was void by the Revolution." "Absurd," responded the French Minister. Morris agreed, and then took care to emphasize that the "whole conversation was unofficial and unauthorized" on his part.[6] Later, however, Morris's antipathy to the French Revolution led him to consider the salvation and prosperity of England essential to the welfare of America.[7]

Morris's ideas on foreign policy were important not only because of his political influence in the United States but also because they influenced his conduct as a diplomatic representative of Washington's government in Europe, particularly in France. His career

[4] These ideas are summarized in Morris to Randolph, Sainport, May 31, 1794, *ASP FR,* I, 408-409. For Morris's other views on treaties in regard to the Constitution, see Max Farrand, ed., *The Records of the Federal Convention of 1787* (rev. ed.; 4 vols., New Haven, 1937), II, 197, 417, Aug. 7 and 25, 1787.

[5] Morris to Jefferson, Paris, June 10, 1792, in Davenport, ed., *A Diary of the French Revolution. . . ,* II, 439.

[6] Morris to Jefferson, Paris, Feb. 13, 1793, No. 19, National Archives, State Dept., Diplomatic Despatches, France; also printed in *ASP FR,* I, 349-351.

[7] J. B. Burges to Lord Grenville, [London], June 28, 1795, *Dropmore Papers,* III, 87-89.

abroad began not long after he had completed his work at the Philadelphia convention; he was sent to France by Robert Morris, arriving there in February, 1789. In Paris his principal duty was to press American claims against the Farmers-General, claims which had arisen out of difficulties connected with certain tobacco contracts.[8] While engaged in his official tasks, he did not neglect his own fortunes and found occasion to dabble in numerous profitable speculations.[9]

At first Morris delighted in the Parisian world and formed an affection for the France of the monarchy. His wealth, culture, family background, aristocratic orientation, affability, and knowledge of French opened for him the doors of the French nobility, and even those of the court circle. After Jefferson's departure Morris, for a time, became the most influential American in Paris. With the ladies, too, he was a success. Through his mistress, the Countess de Flahaut, he came to know Charles Maurice de Talleyrand-Périgord, soon to become one of France's outstanding statesmen.

In March, 1790, Morris interrupted his duties and his pursuit of pleasure in Paris to go to London for President Washington on a special mission as America's first executive agent to attempt a *rapprochement* with Great Britain.[10] The mission failed, in part because of Morris's shortcomings and in part because the time was not ripe for success. The English knew he had dabbled in French politics and they believed at this time that he was inclined to be anti-English and pro-French.[11] Abandoning hope of success in his

[8] There is reason to believe that Morris at this time acted aslo as a special agent in France for John Jay, Secretary of Foreign Affairs; see Henry M. Wriston, *Executive Agents in American Foreign Relations,* p. 24.

[9] Walther, *Gouverneur Morris,* p. 93; Howard Swiggett, *The Extraordinary Mr. Morris* (New York, 1952), p. 139. Morris apparently had contracted with the French government for the supply of a considerable quantity of flour. Short to Secretary of State, Paris, Nov. 7, 1789, No. 7, National Archives, State Dept., Diplomatic Despatches, France.

[10] See Davenport, ed., *A Diary of the French Revolution. . . ,* I, 458 ff. For Washington's instructions, New York, Oct. 13, 1789, see pp. 462-464.

[11] Sir John Temple to the Duke of Leeds, New York, March 19, 1791, Henry Adams Transcripts. Temple believed that Morris was pro-French and that he was in the pay of the French government. For Morris's views on the failure of his mission, see his letters to Washington, London, April 10, 1792; to Robert Morris, no date, in Davenport, ed., *A Diary of the French Revolution. . . ,* I, 614-617. Jefferson blamed the British for the failure of

London diplomacy, Morris returned to France. The French Revolution germinated as he observed, recorded, advised, judged, and criticized. It was under these circumstances that Morris wrote his remarkable eyewitness commentaries on the French Revolution.[12]

Ironically, this man who loved pleasure and hated turmoil lived to witness at first hand two of the world's great revolutions. Favoring a constitutional monarchy for France, Morris did his best to save Louis XVI, going so far as to draft a plan for rescuing Louis from his virtual imprisonment in the Tuileries. He schemed and contrived to carry out the plan.

Despite these compromising activities, Morris was fortunate politically. In George Washington he had a reliable friend, one who still nourished the illusory ideal of a nonpolitical government—although to most posts he appointed Hamiltonians. Morris, whose friendship went back to the dire days of Valley Forge, fitted this pattern. He was a conservative with ability—a man the President could trust.[13]

When Jefferson relinquished his Paris post, Washington did not immediately appoint another minister in his place. Instead William Short, as *chargé d'affaires,* represented the United States in the French capital. With the post open, pressures to make an appointment beset Washington. "Mr. [Robert] Morris wishes his namesake, Gouverneur (now in Europe selling lands for him)," said Senator Maclay, "placed in some conspicuous station abroad." Then he belittled Gouverneur Morris's diplomatic activities, stating that "he has acted in a strange kind of capacity, half pimp, half envoy, or perhaps more properly a kind of political eavesdropper about the British court, for some time past."[14]

Despite Morris's inauspicious diplomatic record, when Washington chose to fill the French post, he appointed him.[15] Jeffersonians

---

the mission and Hamilton blamed Morris. Malone, *Jefferson and the Rights of Man,* pp. 331-332.

[12] The latest and unexpurgated edition of these commentaries is Davenport, ed., *A Diary of the French Revolution. . . .*

[13] See Stephenson and Dunn, *George Washington,* II, 345-346.

[14] Maclay, *Journal,* entry of Feb. 25, 1791, p. 389.

[15] About Morris's appointment the Secretary of State asserted with positiveness that "No man upon earth knew he was to be appointed 24 hours before he was appointed but the President himself. . . ." Jefferson to Short, Oct. 16, 1792, in Ford, *Writings of Jefferson,* VI, 122.

in the Senate and elsewhere bitterly opposed the appointment. "He is a monarchy man," said James Monroe, "& not suitable to be employed in this country, nor in France."[16] "Our new Government," said another Jeffersonian, "is a Government of Stock jobbing and favouritism."[17] Morris's nomination, and those of two other candidates to fill posts at The Hague and Madrid, were submitted to the Senate in December, 1791. For a while it looked as if the Senate would approve the other appointments but reject that of Morris. Senate hostility to Morris appeared so strong that it overcame the deference usually accorded Washington. Active and intense support from Rufus King and Hamilton, added to the prestige and backing of Washington, finally got the nomination through by the narrow vote of 16 to 11.[18] Certain Republicans surmised that the appointment was the consequence of "an anti republican influence in the President and Senate."[19]

Opposition to Morris appeared soundly based. In his mission to London he had shown ineptitude as a diplomat, in his plottings with royalists he had compromised himself with ruling elements in the French government, and his outspoken aristocratic views were well-known and resented by the French. Morris's most important qualifications were his political affiliations and views, views that the Hamiltonians shared. In a political government a diplomat should represent the government's viewpoint, even though such a viewpoint may be the source of trouble with the government to which he is accredited.

Washington wrote candidly to Morris about the difficulties encountered in getting the nomination approved, informing him that the congressmen had accused him of "levity and imprudence of conversation and conduct." Some emphasized, Washington said, "that your habits of expression indicated a *hauteur* disgusting to those, who happen to differ from you in sentiment . . . that in France

[16] The quotation from Monroe is cited from King, *Rufus King Correspondence*, I, 421; see also Walther, *Gouverneur Morris*, p. 171.

[17] G. Mason to James Monroe, Gunston Hall, Feb. 9, 1792, James Monroe Papers, Library of Congress.

[18] *Journal of the Executive Proceedings of the Senate*, I, 92-97; the vote, dated Jan. 12, 1792, is on p. 97; see also King, *Rufus King Correspondence*, I, 421; Swiggett, *The Extraordinary Mr. Morris*, pp. 224-226.

[19] "A Firm Republican" in the *Virginia Herald and Fredericksburg Advertiser*, Nov. 28, 1793.

you were considered as a favorer of Aristocracy, and unfriendly to
its Revolution. . . . That under this impression, you could not be
an acceptable public character, of consequence you would not be
able, however willing, to promote the interest of this Country in an
essential degree."[20]   The President pointed out, too, the criticism
based on the failure of the London mission.

When news of Morris's appointment reached Paris, the French
protested. Some were disappointed in the appointment because
they felt it was inappropriate and because they regretted the departure of William Short, who in their view had acquitted himself well
as *chargé d'affaires*. Short had hoped for and expected the ministerial appointment himself. Washington sent him, instead, to The
Hague.[21] The Duchesse d'Enville, writing to Jefferson to express
her disappointment over Short's departure and her alarm over
Morris, said that "his [Morris's] opinions are so different from those
which prevail today that people suppose Congress is little informed
of what is going on among us. The national assembly has expressed
itself so strongly as holding opinions entirely opposed to those which
your successor professes, that I would almost dare to say that if those
who appointed him had been well informed they would have sent
him to Holland and would have left in France a young man who
has all the maturity one could wish, and reason joined to the most
conciliating spirit."[22]

In view of Morris's personal unpopularity with the men in control
of the French government he could do nothing favorable for the
French alliance. Critics denounced him for having filled Paris for
two years "with invectives against every principle of liberty," as
"being personally detested by all leaders of the Revolution," and as
being "the banker, protector and correspondent of the most obnoxious emigrants." Thomas Paine and other Americans living in
Paris considered his appointment a horrible mistake.[23]

[20] Washington to Morris, Philadelphia, Jan. 28, 1792, in Fitzpatrick, *Washington's Writings*, XXXI, 468-470; Stephenson and Dunn, *George Washington*,
II, 346.

[21] Myrna Boyce, "The Diplomatic Career of William Short," *Journal of
Modern History*, XV (June, 1943), 108-110; later there was dissatisfaction with
Short too; see Ternant to Minister of Foreign Affairs, Philadelphia, March 7,
1793, in Turner, *CFM*, p. 187.

[22] Quoted in Walther, *Gouverneur Morris*, pp. 175-176.

[23] *Ibid.*, pp. 176-177; see also Thomas Paine to Jefferson, London, Feb.

Even Lafayette, a personal friend of Morris, deplored the appointment. He maintained that "as a private man" he had been satisfied with Morris. But Lafayette told Washington, "the aristocratic, and indeed counter revolutionary principles he has professed unfitted him to be the representative of the only nation whose politics have a likeness with ours, since they are founded on the plan of a representative democracy." Declaring that he hated whatever resembled despotism and aristocracy, Lafayette continued, "I can not help wishing the American and French principles were in the heart and on the lips of the American ambassador to France."[24]

Morris was conscious of his difficult situation and of the low esteem in which he was held both at home and in France. Since many Frenchmen tended to place a certain responsibility for France's difficulties on the United States, almost any American minister would have run into trouble in France at this time. Writing to his mentor Robert Morris, the new minister confessed that his mission "must be a stormy one" and that France "is split up into Parties whose Inveteracy of Hatred is hardly conceivable and the Royalists and Aristocrats consider America and the Americans as having occasioned their Misfortunes. . . . the Republicans consider every Thing short of downright Democracy as an Abandonment of political Principle in an American."[25]

Some Frenchmen placed the onus for the Morris appointment on the French foreign minister, Montmorin. Many French leaders looked upon the appointment as evidence that the United States had abandoned the principles of liberty and had turned against France and the 1778 alliance. They were convinced that Morris preferred despotism to liberty.

13, 1792, in Philip S. Foner, ed., *The Complete Works of Thomas Paine* (2 vols., New York, 1945), II, 1322-1323. Paine mentioned that French newspapers gave evidence of French distaste for the appointment. Several French officials attempted to block Morris's appointment; when this proved too late they sought from the beginning to have him recalled. Short to Jefferson, May 17, 1792, Short Papers, Library of Congress, cited in Boyce, "The Diplomatic Career of William Short," *JMH*, XV, 111-112.

[24] Lafayette to Washington, Paris, March 15, 1792, in Louis Gottschalk, ed., *The Letters of Lafayette to Washington 1777-1799* (New York, 1944), p. 361.

[25] G. Morris to R. Morris, London, Feb. 15, 1792, in Davenport, ed., *A Diary of the French Revolution. . .* , II, 366-367.

Having been appointed while on a visit to London and being uncertain of his reception in France, Morris did not allow his new
duties to hasten his return. When he arrived in Paris early in May,
1792, he heard rumors that the government would not receive him
but did not attach much importance to them.[26] Morris presented
his credentials to Charles-François Dumouriez, who in March had
become Minister of Foreign Affairs. Dumouriez regretted Short's
departure and disliked the Morris appointment, but he accepted the
choice of the American government. Nonetheless, he let Morris
cool his heels; not until June 3, 1792, did he present Morris to the
King.[27]

Almost as soon as Morris officially took over his post, he gave
evidence of a persecution complex; he seemed beset by petty annoy-
ances. First he was annoyed at being compelled to pay customs
duty on his luggage at Calais; next he complained of being the
object of "patriotic curiosity"; he complained that the French censored his mail; he expressed anger at being stopped in the streets for
identification. These were minor irritants; greater difficulties soon
obscured them.

A major dilemma which soon confronted Morris was that of making arrangements to pay the debt the United States owed to France,
a debt stemming from French loans made during the American
Revolution. Already, under Hamilton's astute guidance, the United
States had paid the interest and part of the principal. Before Morris
became minister Washington had authorized Short to negotiate
loans with Holland to facilitate liquidation of the debt. When
Morris began his official duties, therefore, there was in the hands of
Dutch bankers at Amsterdam a large sum of money destined for
payment of America's public debt. As a consequence he early
pressed the ministers of foreign affairs for a settlement and was confident he would get one.[28] Morris and Short made plans with the

[26] Morris recorded, for example, in his diary on May 12, 1792, rumors
that the French foreign minister did not wish to receive him and "that the
Idea of not receiving me was started by Short, but I do not believe it." *Ibid.*,
II, 427. Mme de Flahaut told Morris on his return from England that Du-
mouriez would not receive him as America's minister. Esmein, *Gouverneur
Morris,* p. 30.

[27] Walther, *Gouverneur Morris,* p. 180; Davenport, ed., *A Diary of the
French Revolution. . . ,* II, 436 (entry of June 3, 1792).

[28] Morris to Jefferson, Paris, July 10, 1792, *ASP FR,* I, 331.

French government for payment. They made those plans and agreed to them before August 10, 1792.[29]

On August 10 the French overthrew the monarchy. That confronted Morris with the question of whether or not he was bound to the same obligations toward the new government as toward the monarchy. This was the same problem which the government back home had to resolve and which split Jefferson and Hamilton. Morris's dilemma became complicated at the end of August because of the demands of Pierre-Hélène-Marie Le Brun, the new French Minister of Foreign Affairs.

Aware that American service of the French debt provided for payments to the French minister in the United States so that he could purchase supplies for Saint Domingue, and that a payment of four hundred thousand dollars was due in the United States on December 1, 1792, Le Brun on August 29 had invited Morris to the office of foreign affairs. There, having in mind large American credits in Amsterdam, Le Brun asked the American minister to anticipate the December 1 payment by sixty days, to make it in Paris, and to double it.[30]

Morris said he had no authority to make such a transaction and that he "had no Powers to treat with the present Government."[31] He did indicate that he would write to his superiors and recommend payment. To French officials this was evasion; speed was essential; correspondence across the Atlantic took months. They were also upset by Morris's "pretended insufficiency" of powers. Le Brun wrote cuttingly to the American minister that "according to the principle that you are not authorized by your instructions to treat with the new French Government your functions would be nil. . . . The King being suspended from his functions must change nothing, Sir, in the dispositions of a nation with which we have

[29] For details see Hamilton to Short, to Washington, to Jefferson, Philadelphia, April 13, 14, 15, 1791, in Hamilton, ed., *Hamilton's Works*, IV, 152-156; Davenport, ed., *A Diary of the French Revolution. . .* , II, 501-504; Walther, *Gouverneur Morris,* pp. 181-182; Sparks, *The Life of Gouverneur Morris,* I, 387-389; Swiggett, *The Extraordinary Mr. Morris,* pp. 246-249; Theodore Roosevelt, *Gouverneur Morris* (Boston, 1888), pp. 280-281.

[30] Morris's diary entry of Aug. 29, 1792, in Davenport, ed., *A Diary of the French Revolution. . .* , II, 518.

[31] Morris to Jefferson, Paris, Aug. 30, 1792, No. 9, *ibid.* 519-523; also in *ASP FR,* I, 336-337.

links of friendship and of interest and whose independence is our work." He concluded that "the Government being immutable and always existent no representative may, without an express order from his Court or his constituents, refuse to treat directly with it."[32]

These bold words did not settle the problem as to Morris's powers to deal with the new Revolutionary French government. But Thomas Jefferson's instructions did. When Jefferson learned of the situation he directed Morris to carry on with the new French government and at the same time he announced in clear-cut terms, as has been indicated earlier, what came to be the basic recognition policy of the United States.[33]

In the meantime Morris had replied immediately to Le Brun's remarks, stating once more his own position. Unfortunately, in so doing he referred more than once to the American government as "my Court." Insignificant in itself, the phrase, coming from the representative of a sister republic, shocked the French and reverberated across the Atlantic. Morris, it appeared, deliberately flaunted his aristocratic predilections and royalist sympathies. Regardless of the motives behind the use of the expression, it was a thoughtless gesture, doing harm to intangibles in Franco-American amity. Morris, in effect, had driven another nail into his diplomatic coffin.[34]

Previously Morris had said he was determined to remain in Paris and had been the only foreign diplomatic representative to remain there during the Reign of Terror.[35] At this point, however, he became indignant over the August 30 letter and demanded his passport; he would leave Paris. Le Brun hastened to mollify him, declaring that he had misunderstood the letter. "Besides," explained the French minister, "you Sir who were born in the midst of a free people, should regard the present affairs of France from a different point of view to all the foreign ministers resident in Paris. We uphold the same cause as that of your country, therefore our principles

---

[32] Le Brun to Morris, Paris, Aug. 30, 1792, in Davenport, ed., *A Diary of the French Revolution. . .* , II, 527.

[33] Jefferson to Morris, Philadelphia, March 12, 1793, in Lipscomb, *Jefferson's Works,* IX, 36-37.

[34] Morris to Le Brun, Paris, Sept. 1, 1792, *ibid.,* II, 528-531; also the note on the use of the word "court."

[35] Morris to Jefferson, Paris, Aug. 22, 1792, National Archives, State Dept., Diplomatic Despatches, France. At this time Morris described the fleeing diplomats and announced his intention to stay.

and yours should be the same and by a chain of natural consequences no reason can oppose your residence in Paris."[36]

Although ruffled, Morris reconsidered immediately and told Le Brun, "I resume my intention of staying on and awaiting the orders of my Court. As to my personal opinions, Sir, they are of no importance in so grave a matter, but you may rest assured that I have never questioned the right of every People to be governed as they please. For many years I have sincerely wished that France should enjoy all possible liberty and happiness, and I am certain of carrying out the intentions of the United States in assuring you that these wishes are shared by all my compatriots."[37]

Regardless of the fine words, little had been changed; to Frenchmen Morris was a menace to amicable relations between their country and the United States. They suspected him of purposely creating difficulties between the two allies. "His ill will is proved," one official said; he betrays Americans "as well as us."[38]

Upset because Morris's conduct caused concern in the government and believing that a close accord between France and the United States should continue, Le Brun asked Ternant, then French minister to the United States, to convey to Jefferson the French version of what had transpired and to inform the American Secretary of State of Morris's hostile attitude.[39]

The distrust was mutual; Morris harbored suspicions concerning the French ministers. He told Jefferson that he "had good reasons to believe that a private Speculation was at the Bottom of the Proposals made to me."[40] Soon the Secretary of State heard from other sources that "the French Ministers are entirely broken with Gouvr. Morris, shut their doors to him & will never receive another communication from him." This same witness reported that he had

[36] Le Brun to Morris, Paris, Sept. 16, 1792, in Davenport, ed., *A Diary of the French Revolution. . . ,* II, 544-546.

[37] Morris to Le Brun, Paris, Sept. 17, 1792, *ibid.,* p. 547.

[38] Clavière, Minister of Public Contributions, to Le Brun, Sept. 10, 1792, quoted in Walther, *Gouverneur Morris,* p. 187.

[39] Le Brun's remarks (n.p., n.d.) to Ternant are quoted in *ibid.,* p. 188; for Ternant's reaction see his despatches to the Minister of Foreign Affairs, Philadelphia, Feb. 13 and March 7, 1793, in Turner, *CFM,* pp. 170, 187; The Anas, Feb. 20, 1793, in Ford, *Writings of Jefferson,* I, 217.

[40] Morris to Jefferson, Paris, Sept. 27, 1792, in Davenport, ed., *A Diary of the French Revolution. . . ,* II, 549.

heard Morris curse "the French ministers as a set of damned rascals" and that "the king wd. still be replaced on his throne."[41]

Weighing his every motion, the French read hostility into most of Morris's actions. When in his letter of September 1, in which he threatened to leave Paris, he had requested a passport to England, French officials suspected that he planned to go to London to plot against their government. Classing Morris an enemy of the French Republic, they accused him of fomenting trouble with the American government and of seeking to transform the French alliance into an Anglo-American alliance. His recall was already in the making. His presence in Paris, declared General Dumouriez, posed "an enigma for the two republics"; France should no longer deal with "this insolent and vile man." When confronted by the French complaints, even Washington realized that Morris must go, that he "cd. be no longer contind. there [Paris] consistent with the public good."[42]

Ironically, the world's two major republics, both created by revolution and allies by treaty, sent to each other's capital not emissaries of good will but propagators of distrust. Both men, Genet and Morris, were intelligent, cultured, and patriotic, but both were antipathetic to the host government. Even though each did his duty as he saw it and each in his own way carried out instructions of the home government, both committed the cardinal sin of diplomacy. They did not act diplomatically.

* * * * *

Morris's doubts concerning the legal status of the new French government, particularly in the problems of recognition and accreditation and payment of debts to the new government, were shared by others. His predecessor, Short, had also believed that the debt payments to France should be suspended and that payments should be made only to the King or to officials of the government to which Morris originally had been accredited. The Dutch bankers, too, had opposed payment; they raised the problem of what receipt France would give, questioning the legality of any receipts unless

[41] Report of Col. W. S. Smith to Jefferson summarized in The Anas, Feb. 20, 1793, in Ford, *Writings of Jefferson*, I, 216-218.

[42] Washington's reaction is paraphrased in *ibid.*, p. 217; Dumouriez to Le Brun (n.p., n.d.) is quoted in Walther, *Gouverneur Morris*, p. 189.

signed by the King.[43] Even Jefferson concurred and urged caution and suspension of payment until the political situation in France clarified.[44] As soon as Hamilton heard of the King's suspension, he directed Short to stop all payments until he received new instructions.[45]

Although he had serious doubts as to the legitimacy of the new government and as to his powers to deal with it, particularly on the debt question, Morris nevertheless had insisted on paying the money to France as planned. In his view "the Debt from the United States was to the *Nation* and not to the *King* of the French, much less to *his most Christian Majesty.*" He wished "to adhere to the original Nature and Form of the present Payment" because the arrangement was financially advantageous to the United States; not to adhere to the payments, moreover, would have been politically unwise. As to the form of receipt, he believed the objections of the Dutch bankers could be met or overcome if the United States would accept *"a Bill on the Commissaries"* of the French treasury. There was little danger, Morris felt, of not being credited with the payment. This comprised but one small installment; the debt remained large and other payments were still pending. In the final adjustment with any other French government, he said, the United States could insist that the payment in question be credited in full.[46]

Payment was made, in the end, not as French officials had wanted nor as Short had stipulated, but in the form and with the receipt upon which Morris had insisted.[47] Morris had viewed the situation

[43] Boyce, "The Diplomatic Career of William Short," *JMH,* XV, 112; Walther, *Gouverneur Morris,* p. 182; Short to Morris, The Hague, Aug. 28 and Sept. 4, [1792], in Davenport, ed., *A Diary of the French Revolution. . . ,* II, 508-510.

[44] Jefferson to Morris, Philadelphia, Oct. 15, 1792, in Ford, *Writings of Jefferson,* VI, 120-121.

[45] See Hamilton to Short, Newark, Oct. 1 and Philadelphia, Oct. 16, 1792, and Philadelphia, Nov. 5, 1792, in Hamilton, ed., *Hamilton's Works,* IV, 318-322.

[46] Morris to Short, Paris, Sept. 20, 1792, in Davenport, ed., *A Diary of the French Revolution. . . ,* II, 512-513. Morris and Short engaged in a quarrelsome correspondence over the debt payments; see pp. 504-515; Boyce, "The Diplomatic Career of William Short," *JMH,* XV, 112-113; Swiggett, *The Extraordinary Mr. Morris,* pp. 250-251.

[47] Morris to Jefferson, Paris, Dec. 21, 1792, National Archives, State Dept., Diplomatic Despatches, France. Here Morris summarized his views on the debts question.

correctly; successive French governments did not question the validity of the payment. An important factor which facilitated unquestioned settlement of the debt-payment issue was the attitude of Robespierre when his government assumed power. Eager to recover lost initiative in the French alliance for his government, he placed no real obstacle in the path of settlement.[48]

* * * * *

While problems of debt payment and recognition had embittered French officials toward Morris and had been important influences in strengthening the convictions that Morris must go, these were by no means the only factors which had made him *persona non grata* to the French Republic. French republican distrust was also grounded on other evidence. Despite Washington's and Jefferson's admonitions against meddling in French domestic politics and despite a promise to Dumouriez that he would not do so, Morris not only entangled himself in French revolutionary politics, but he also took a hand in royalist intrigue. Before he became America's official emissary, Morris had compromised himself by engaging in royalist plots and counterrevolutionary activity. Whatever the moral rightness or wrongness of such activity or the human values involved, the diplomat implicated always runs serious risk. If the side he supports wins in the struggle for power, he may be acclaimed as a hero; if the side he backs loses, however, not only does he embitter relations between his government and the new government which comes to power in the country to which he is accredited, but also he is a failure as a diplomat and must suffer the consequences.

Morris, who had been accepted by and had enjoyed the lavish hospitality of French nobility during his years in France and who had strong aristocratic views anyway, was concerned over the fate of various French aristocrats, particularly those who were his friends, at the hands of vengeful republicans. His home and the American legation became an asylum for French nobles fleeing the guillotine. Among the French aristocrats to whom Morris gave the protection of his home was Count Charles Hector d'Estaing, well-known naval commander in the wars of the American Revolution.[49] Aware that,

[48] See Masson, *Le Département des affaires étrangères. . .* , p. 295.

[49] See Morris's diary entries of Aug. 10-16, in Davenport, ed., *A Diary of the French Revolution. . .* , II, 489-491; for Estaing, see p. 519 n.

in his position as American minister, the new French authorities would find fault with his receiving and protecting royalists, he would not turn them out; "it would be inhuman to force them into the hands of these assassins."[50]

This activity, while humanitarian and laudable, violated French laws, and when engaged in by a foreign diplomat provided justifiable cause for serious action by the host government. Actually, Morris had begun aiding and offering sanctuary to royalists while still a private citizen, but he did not cease this counterrevolutionary and antigovernmental activity when he became the American minister.[51]

Noteworthy among Morris's counterrevolutionary activities was his role in a plot to snatch Louis XVI and his Queen from the claws of the republicans and to spirit them out of Paris to sanctuary. The plan was conceived at one of the dinner parties Morris gave for Parisian luminaries in the middle of July, 1792. In a garden conversation with one of the royalist ministers, he discussed the King's fate; it was by then clear that execution awaited the French monarch. When, in the course of the conversation, the Frenchman asked what should be done in the present situation, Morris urged that the King get out of Paris. From this evolved the plot to save the King. They exchanged ideas, and those involved later met at Morris's house. Of the various plans concocted, Louis preferred Morris's detailed scheme which promised a possibility of success.[52]

Even at this crucial time the monarch vacillated; nothing was done. Finally, on July 24, 1792, Louis gave tangible evidence of his trust in Morris by asking the American minister to take custody

[50] Quoted in Henry Cabot Lodge, *Historical and Political Essays* (Boston, 1892), p. 102; Roosevelt, *Gouverneur Morris*, p. 264.

[51] The most reliable printed source on Morris's proroyalist activities is Davenport, ed., *A Diary of the French Revolution. . .* , II, 245-246, *et passim.* For other accounts, see Anne Cary Morris, ed., *The Diary and Letters of Gouverneur Morris* (2 vols., New York, 1888), I, 555 ff.; Walther, *Gouverneur Morris*, pp. 190-191; Sparks, *The Life of Gouverneur Morris*, I, 380-385. Esmein, *Gouverneur Morris*, pp. 25-26, maintains that Morris's attachment to the Bourbon dynasty lasted as long as he lived.

[52] Morris's diary entry of July 17, 1792, in Davenport, ed., *A Diary of the French Revolution. . .* , II, 467; subsequent diary entries should be read in conjunction with an unsigned, undated document addressed "Son Altesse Royale," written probably by Morris in 1796 to explain the events of the summer of 1792, *ibid.,* pp. 473-479.

of his papers and money; Morris would not accept the papers, but did take the money, which, unlike the papers, "bore no mark of ownership." He was to use the money on bribes and the hiring of soldiers to cover the King's escape.[53]

After the slaughter of the Swiss guards on August 10, escape seemed impossible. Revolutionary authorities got wind of the plot and seized and condemned one of the men privy to it. Fortunately, he died without betraying his conspirators. Others who were under suspicion were saved by judicious bribery, by using the King's money in Morris's possession. With the failure of the plot, rumors reached America that Morris had lost his life as a consequence of his involvement. Though the rumors were false, it appeared obvious that "Mr. Morris is not, at this time, a very popular character at Paris."[54] Morris had run a great risk. He had compromised his diplomatic status and had endangered American relations with the French government. Those in power knew of his intimate relations with the royalists. Until it could get rid of Morris, the French government determined to ignore him or bypass him as a channel to the American government and people.

* * * * *

Another problem which confronted Morris concerned the Marquis de Lafayette, America's adopted son. From the beginning, Lafayette had been a staunch but moderate supporter of the French Revolution, gaining prominence as a defender of the constitutional monarchy and of the King. After the overthrow of the constitutional monarchy on August 10, 1792, and the taking of the Tuileries, Lafayette was placed in an untenable position. First he attempted to save the monarchy by a march on Paris but failed to arouse a sufficient following. Soon the National Assembly ordered his arrest. His army melted away, leaving him to take care to preserve his own life. On August 19, 1792, he escaped from France across the Belgian border into Luxembourg. There he fell into the hands of the Austrians, who threw him into prison.

Lafayette immediately wrote to William Short at The Hague that he was no longer in the French service, that he was now "an American citizen, an American officer," and that he desired the

[53] *Ibid.*, p. 477.
[54] *Maryland Gazette* (Annapolis), May 9, 1793.

assistance of American diplomacy to effect his release.[55] "You must," he wrote to Short on August 30, "immediately, in the name of the United States, and in common with the other American ministers, intervene in our affair and free us."[56] In anxiety Short turned to Morris and to Thomas Pinckney in London for guidance.[57] Pinckney and Morris calmed the alarmed Short; Morris advised that "Monsieur de La Fayette is a Frenchman, and it is as a Frenchman that he is taken and is to be treated." Although sympathetic and desirous of alleviating Lafayette's distress, Morris could not see the validity of the Marquis's claim to American citizenship. Logically, he believed that the United States could not intervene in the affair without becoming a party to the quarrel. He suggested recourse "to Prayer and Solicitation."[58]

Morris was not alone in his view that the American diplomats should not meddle in the Lafayette affair; Pinckney and Jefferson agreed with him.[59] While frowning on any overt efforts, Jefferson, nevertheless, did direct Morris to do his utmost to secure Lafayette's release.[60] As soon as Morris heard that the Marquis was in dire want, having lost his fortune, he sent the prisoner ten thousand florins. Madame Lafayette and her children also benefited from Morris's and the American government's generosity. Morris loaned her money to pay off debts, and, when she was imprisoned, he saved her from death.[61] These were laudable activities, but they did not

[55] Lafayette to Short, Nivelle, Aug. 26, 1792, in Sparks, *The Life of Gouverneur Morris*, I, 398-399.

[56] Quoted in Walther, *Gouverneur Morris*, p. 194.

[57] See Short to Morris, The Hague, Sept. 7, 1792, *ASP FR*, I, 341; Boyce, "The Diplomatic Career of William Short," *JMH*, XV, 113.

[58] Morris to Short, Paris, Sept. 12, 1792, in Davenport, *ed., A Diary of the French Revolution. . .*, II, 556-557.

[59] See Pinckney to Morris, London, Sept. 14, 1792, *ibid.*, pp. 558-559. Washington followed the advice of his diplomatic representatives in not making Lafayette's plight a subject of formal diplomatic intervention. Bemis, "The London Mission of Thomas Pinckney. . .," *American Historical Review*, XVIII, 245; see also Washington to Jefferson, Philadelphia, March 13, 1793, in Fitzpatrick, *Washington's Writings*, XXXII, 385-386.

[60] Jefferson to Morris, Philadelphia, March 15, 1793, in Ford, *Writings of Jefferson*, VI, 202-203.

[61] Morris to W. & J. Willink (Dutch bankers), Paris, Jan. 27, 1793, in Davenport, ed., *A Diary of the French Revolution. . .*, II, 561; see also Sparks, *The Life of Gouverneur Morris*, I, 404-412.

make Morris any more palatable to the Revolutionary government to whom Lafayette was an enemy of the state.

* * * * *

Thomas Paine was also trapped by the French Revolution. Imprisoned by the French, he too appealed to Morris for help as an American citizen. Morris and Paine disliked each other intensely. Since the days of the American Revolution Morris had nursed a contempt for Paine, a contempt which Morris's biographers have shared; Theodore Roosevelt, for example, labeled him "the filthy little atheist."[62] The paths of the two men crossed several times in London and Paris after American independence. In the first years of the French Revolution Paine had achieved high status within the Girondin hierarchy, playing a not inconsiderable role in the revolutionary drama. Morris believed that during these years, and particularly after he became the American minister, Paine plotted against him.[63]

Morris complained, not without justification, that Paine had arrogated rights to himself which were not his to assume, particulary in meddling in affairs of a diplomatic nature which were within the province of the American minister. Paine, moreover, had plunged dangerously into French politics and had acted to undermine Morris's already precarious status with French authorities by stressing that the American minister was hostile to the French Revolution, which, of course, was true. Morris, he pointed out, was unpopular in the United States, as he was with Americans resident in France whom he had antagonized. Following the fall of the Girondins Paine became harmless to Morris. On December 23, 1793, on the orders of Robespierre, the French clapped Paine into prison; he appeared destined for the guillotine. He immediately claimed rights as an American citizen. Morris ignored his pleas; he told Robespierre that he did not acknowledge Paine's right to pass as an American citizen.[64]

[62] Roosevelt, *Gouverneur Morris,* p. 289, and the latest biographer, Swiggett, *The Extraordinary Mr. Morris,* pp. 7-8, 63-64; Walther, *Gouverneur Morris,* p. 247; Sparks, *The Life of Gouverneur Morris,* I, 416.

[63] Morris in the summer of 1793 (June 25, 1793) wrote to Robert Morris that he suspected that Paine had intrigued against him and was "confirmed in the idea." Morris, ed., *The Diary and Letters of Gouverneur Morris,* II, 48. For a discussion of the Morris-Paine antagonism by a partisan of Paine, see Moncure D. Conway, *The Life of Thomas Paine,* II, 77-127.

[64] A biographer and partisan of Paine has claimed that Morris, by hinting

Now desperate, Paine turned again to Morris for help in obtaining freedom. "Though you and I are not on terms of the best harmony," he pleaded, "I apply to you as the Minister of America" for aid, and "I expect you to make Congress acquainted with my situation."[65] Morris had written unenthusiastically to the French Minister of Foreign Affairs, Deforgues, pointing out that Paine, born an Englishman, had become an American citizen and then a French citizen. He concluded that Paine was out of his jurisdiction.[66] To Jefferson, Morris had commented officially that against his better judgment he had claimed Paine as an American.[67] Later he remarked parenthetically that "lest I should forget it, I must mention, that Thomas Paine is in prison, where he amuses himself with publishing a pamphlet against Jesus Christ. . . . I incline to think that, if he is quiet in prison, he may have the good luck to be forgotten," while if he attracts attention to himself, "the long suspended axe might fall on him." Morris then expressed doubt as to the validity of Paine's claim to American citizenship. Even if he were to recognize such a claim, he now indicated, it would at this time do little good.[68] Paine remained in prison until Morris's successor gained his freedom for him.[69]

* * * * *

As the French Revolution unfolded, Morris became increasingly hostile to it. This hostility, coupled with his aristocratic sympathies, colored his views toward the French government, and those biased

---

that Paine had fomented the trouble between Genet and Washington, had set in motion the procedure which led to Paine's imprisonment. Moncure D. Conway, ed., *The Writings of Thomas Paine,* III, 158; see also Walther, *Gouverneur Morris,* p. 248; Sparks, *The Life of Gouverneur Morris,* I, 416-418.

[65] Paine to Morris, Luxembourg, Feb. 24, 1794, in Philip S. Foner, ed., *The Complete Works of Thomas Paine,* II, 1338-1339.

[66] Morris to Deforgues, Paris, Feb. 14, 1794, in Conway, *The Life of Thomas Paine,* II, 120.

[67] Morris to Jefferson, Sainport, March 6, 1794, National Archives, State Dept., Diplomatic Despatches, France.

[68] Morris to Jefferson, Paris, June 21, 1794, *ASP FR,* I, 402.

[69] Partisans of Paine, as most of his biographers have been, have maintained that Morris conspired to keep Paine in prison and that if he had not Paine would have been released quickly. See Foner, *The Complete Works of Thomas Paine,* II, Introduction, xxxv; Conway, *The Life of Thomas Paine,* II, 113-115; William M. Van der Weyde, *The Life and Times of Thomas Paine* (10 vols., New York, 1925), I, 245.

views found expression in the reports he sent home.[70] Not only did he correspond officially with Jefferson, but also, because of his personal friendship with Washington, he went over the head of the Secretary of State and corresponded directly with the President.

Given Washington's conservative outlook and the Hamiltonian make-up of his government, it followed logically that Morris's biased reports on the French Revolution increased the President's apprehensions over French occurrences and created new fears. During the summer of 1792 Morris had reported on French events to Jefferson, concluding that "the best picture I can give of the French nation is that of cattle driven before a thunder storm."[71] As Jacobin activity increased, so did his alarm. "We stand on a vast volcano," he said; "we feel it tremble, and we hear it roar; but how, and when, and where, it will burst, and who may be destroyed by its eruptions, it is beyond the ken of mortal foresight to discover."[72]

With the monarchy overthrown and with Paris in turmoil Morris surveyed his situation and turned to the Secretary of State for guidance. Even though his credentials were to the deposed monarchy "and not to the Republic of France," and even though other foreign diplomats were fleeing, he indicated he would remain.[73] While it took courage to remain in Paris, Morris's action in staying was not the heroic deed that it has been often portrayed. He was not ordered to leave; the other ministers, in most instances, were. Most of the other diplomats represented monarchs and governments committed to antirevolutionary principles; Morris represented an ally and a sister republic; the French expected him to stay. As he admitted, to flee would have given the appearance "of taking part against the late Revolution." Morris's sojourn in Paris during the terror, nonetheless, was not without personal danger.[74]

[70] For an example of Morris's correspondence reflecting his views toward the French and the 1778 alliance, see his long letter to Washington, London, Feb. 4, 1792, in Davenport, ed., *A Diary of the French Revolution. . .* , II, 349-358. In the letter Morris summed up the Paris situation and reported a secret royalist message to the effect that despite overtures to England the Bourbons were still loyal to the American alliance.

[71] Morris to Jefferson, Paris, June 10, 1792, *ASP FR*, I, 330.

[72] Morris to Jefferson, Paris, June 17, 1792, *ibid.*, p. 331.

[73] Morris to Jefferson, Paris, Aug. 22, 1793, in Davenport, ed., *A Diary of the French Revolution. . .* , II, 531-533.

[74] Even Talleyrand had urged Morris to flee; see Morris's diary entries of

As the Revolution swirled about him, Morris wrote home more and more of debaucheries he witnessed, dwelling on all that was evil in the Revolution. In September he reported that "we have had one Week of uncheck'd Murders in which some thousands have perished in this City." To Washington in the following month he alluded to the "sanguinary Events which have taken place" and promised to entertain the President "with the Recital of many Things which it would be improper to commit to Paper, at least for the present."

Washington in his responses reflected Morris's pessimistic view of French events, noting that "gloomy indeed appears the situation of France at this juncture."[75] When Morris expressed horror at events in Paris, deprecated venality and corruptness in the government, and made clear his sympathy for deposed royalists, Washington replied that events in France had more than made good Morris's gloomiest predictions.[76] In Jefferson's words, Morris had "kept the President's mind constantly poisoned with his forebodings."[77]

In Jefferson, Morris could not arouse a spark of sympathy. The Secretary of State knew that Morris was bypassing him and that Morris's influence with the President counteracted his own. Morris, on his part, knew Jefferson's views toward France. On one occasion he told Jefferson that it gave him "Pain to write and will I am sure give you pain to read the distressful State of a Country for which we have both a sincere Regard."[78] Jefferson was disturbed by Morris's one-sided reports, by the somber colors he used in painting the revolutionaries' side of the French picture. In indirect but meaningful ways Jefferson expressed his displeasure with Morris. For long

---

Aug. 31, Sept. 5, 7, 1792, *ibid.,* II, 536-538; Roosevelt, *Gouverneur Morris,* p. 277.

[75] The quotations are from Morris to Jefferson, Paris, Sept. 10, 1792, Morris to Washington, Paris, Oct. 23, 1792, Washington to Morris, Philadelphia, Oct. 20, 1792, in Davenport, ed., *A Diary of the French Revolution. . . ,* II, 540, 565, 584.

[76] Washington to Morris, Philadelphia, Oct. 20, 1792, in Fitzpatrick, *Washington's Writings,* XXXII, 188-190. Even before Morris had become minister to France Washington had written to him privately that his reports "will be treasured up, to be acted upon as circumstances will warrant, and as occasions may present." Philadelphia, June 20, 1792, p. 61.

[77] The Anas, March 12, 1792, in Ford, *Writings of Jefferson,* I, 188.

[78] Morris to Jefferson, Paris, Sept. 19, 1792, National Archives, State Dept., Diplomatic Despatches, France.

periods he would not answer Morris's letters, leaving him in the dark as to instructions and events at home.[79] Between the two men understanding and sympathy appeared lost.

* * * * *

By the beginning of 1793 it had become impossible for Morris to stay much longer in Paris; his situation was intolerable. He confessed to Jefferson that leaders in the government's Diplomatic Committee "hate me cordially, tho'," he remarked naïvely, "it would puzzle them to say why...."[80] One reason was that French republican officials viewed with mounting ill humor the asylum he offered under the cloak of his diplomatic status. They were convinced that he remained in Paris as a spy for England and Austria, particularly after France had gone to war with England in February, 1793. Morris's house had been visited by armed men, he was prevented from traveling in France, and newspapers discussed his execution. "I am told," he wrote to Robert Morris, "that the London gazetteers have killed me, besides burning my house, and other little pleasantries of the kind."[81] His mail was opened and pried into and he was molested in other ways. In the United States it was rumored that so odious had Morris become to the French that to protect him from public vengeance, "excited by his monarchical and aristocratic manoeuvres," he was provided with a guard.[82] Finally Morris could stand no more; he complained to Le Brun.[83]

Morris's frequent meetings with the British ambassador to France, Earl Gower, and his wife, provided another reason for French dis-

[79] Morris complained often of his neglect by Jefferson, stating at one time that "amid the political storms which vex this hemisphere, the opinion of the United States is the polar star which should guide my course, but which is totally concealed from my view." Morris to Jefferson, Sainport, March 6, 1794, ASP FR, I, 404; see also Morris to Randolph, Sainport, April 15, 1794, ibid., p. 406, in which Morris expresses distrust of Jefferson; see his earlier complaint of neglect to Robert Morris, March 10, 1793, in Morris, The Diary and Letters of Gouverneur Morris, II, 56-58.

[80] Morris to Jefferson, Paris, Feb. 13, 1793, No. 19, National Archives, State Dept., Diplomatic Despatches, France; also in ASP FR, I, 350.

[81] Morris to Robert Morris, March 15, 1793, in Morris, The Diary and Letters of Gouverneur Morris, II, 38; Walther, Gouverneur Morris, p. 238.

[82] "A Farmer of the back Settlements" in the Independent Chronicle and the Universal Advertiser (Boston), Jan. 20, 1794.

[83] Morris to Le Brun, March 29, 1793, in Morris, The Diary and Letters of Gouverneur Morris, II, 41.

trust. But this liaison ended in August, 1792, when Gower was recalled. Now almost alone in Paris and at odds with the authorities, Morris realized that his diary, reflecting as it did his dubious activities, was a compromising document. On January 15, 1793, he closed it. To continue his entries, he realized, "would compromise many people."[84] At the same time he became more circumspect in his letter-writing, particularly to those at home, referring to the tampering with his mail as "patriotic curiosity."

Finally, in April, 1793, Morris left Paris, moving to Sainport, some twenty miles away, where he had purchased a house on the banks of the Seine. In the comparative calm of Sainport he spent whatever time he could reading and writing. Business, politics, and diplomacy, however, made inroads. He had to look, for example, into the affairs of American sailors seized by the French. All the time he was at Sainport, in fact, he sent a stream of letters to the French Minister of Foreign Affairs protesting the seizure of American ships in an attempt to secure agreements to prevent further seizures.[85]

Le Brun, the French Minister of Foreign Affairs, assured Morris that the attacks against American shipping were unintentional. France wished to do nothing to injure friendship with America. It was difficult, he explained, in carrying on the sea war against British shipping "to contain, within just limits, the indignation of our marines and in general of all French patriots against a people who speak the same language, and having the same habits, as the free Americans. The difficulty of distinguishing our allies from our enemies has often been the cause of offenses committed on board your vessels."[86]

Other complications arose from the demands of American adventurers in France employed or financed by the French to outfit ships under the American flag for the French service, or from Americans who, with an eye to the huge profits to be made, had outfitted privateers on their own. These men sought American passports from Morris. He refused them, maintaining that "real American vessels have their registry and other papers in proper order, consequently,

---

[84] Diary entry of Jan. 15, 1793, *ibid.*, p. 24.

[85] For the correspondence on the seizures, see *ASP FR,* I, 359 ff.

[86] Le Brun to Morris, April 14, 1793, quoted in James W. Gerard, "French Spoliations Before 1801," *Magazine of American History,* XII (July, 1884), 35.

[they] do not need any documents which we can give, and which, in fact, we are not authorized to give."[87]   Angry American ship captains interned at Bordeaux also made life difficult for Morris. Complaining that he did nothing on their behalf, they turned to Thomas Paine for help.[88]

In fleeing to Sainport, Morris did not escape trouble. His country seat, like his Paris house, became an asylum for royalist friends. Particularly vexing to French republicans was the haven he gave to Countess de Damas, against whom the Paris Committee of General Safety had issued a warrant of arrest. Climaxing Morris's other activities, this affair became the alleged immediate cause of his recall. Morris, convinced that his diplomatic status permitted him to shelter his friends, refused to give up the Countess. Despite protests of French authorities, who pointed out that a French citizen could not invoke the American's diplomatic immunity and thus defy the laws of France, he persisted in protecting the wanted royalist.[89]   In the meantime Genet's activities had their effect on Morris's diplomatic status.

When Morris had learned that Genet was appointed minister to the United States he had gathered what information he could about him and informed Washington that Genet "is a Man of good Parts and very good Education, Brother of the Queen's first Woman."[90] After being introduced to the new minister by Thomas Paine, Morris had dined with him on December 28, 1792. He subsequently reported to Washington that Genet "has I think more of Genius than of Ability and you will see in him at first Blush the Manner and Look of an Upstart." Morris ventured further. "I think that in the Business he is charg'd with," he said, "he will talk so much as

[87] Morris to Pinckney, Paris, Feb. 18, 1793, *ASP FR*, I, 355; Swiggett, *The Extraordinary Mr. Morris,* pp. 262-263.

[88] For Morris's protest to the French government in behalf of the captains, see Morris to Deforgues, Sainport, Aug. 20, 1793, *ASP FR*, I, 373-374; the appeal of the captains to the National Convention of France, Aug. 22, 1793, is on p. 374. The episode is treated in detail in Conway, *The Life of Thomas Paine,* II, 83-85.

[89] Granting sanctuary to Countess de Damas, Morris was warned, did harm to continuing Franco-American accord. Committee of Public Safety to Morris, Paris, Nov. 18, 1793, AAE CP EU, Vol. XXXIX, f. 298; for details, see Walther, *Gouverneur Morris,* pp. 240-243.

[90] Morris to Washington, Paris, Dec. 28, 1792, in Davenport, ed., *A Diary of the French Revolution. . .* , II, 594.

to furnish sufficient Matter for putting him on one Side of his Object should that be convenient."[91]

Morris complained that Le Brun had slighted him "by sending out Mr. Genet without mentioning to me a Syllable either of his Mission or his errand, both of which nevertheless I was early and sufficiently informed of." He then revealed he had discovered that Genet had "three hundred blank Commissions for Privateers" to be used secretly in America. By these measures, he surmised, the French hoped to involve the United States in war with Great Britain. Such a policy he considered unsound "since they may as a Nation derive greater Advantage from our Neutrality than from our Alliance."[92]

As Girondin control over France weakened, Morris in his reports on French developments concluded accurately that if events continued in the same vein Genet undoubtedly would be replaced.[93] In the meantime Genet had laid the groundwork for Morris's recall. Not long after his arrival in the United States he had approached Jefferson informally on securing Morris's recall, indicating that "we all depend on you to send us a good minister there [Paris], with whom we may do business confidentially, in place of mr. [sic] Morris."[94] This was the view of the French foreign office, which believed that Morris's reports were gradually destroying the American friendship basic to the 1778 alliance. An important objective of Genet's mission, in fact, was to offset Morris's malevolent influence on Franco-American relations. French officials wanted an American envoy who sympathized with their revolutionary principles, and Morris did not.[95]

Involved as he was in more pressing activities, Genet did not go beyond his "confidential observations" on Morris until he knew that his own recall was imminent. In retaliation he then detailed reasons for French dissatisfaction with Morris. Summarizing his government's major complaints and adding a few new ones, he

[91] Morris to Washington, Paris, Jan. 6, 1793, ibid., p. 595.
[92] The quotations are from Morris to Jefferson, Feb. 13 and March 26, 1793, and Morris to Pinckney, March 2, 1793, ibid., pp. 596-597.
[93] Morris to Washington, Sainport, Jan. 25, 1793, ASP FR, I, 397.
[94] Jefferson to Washington, Dec. 11, 1793 (quoting Genet), in Ford, Writings of Jefferson, VI, 465.
[95] Le Brun to Genet, Paris, March 31, 1793, and later in 1793 (no day and month), Genet Papers, Library of Congress, VIII, 2693; IX, 2765-66.

accused Morris of being a "counter-revolutionary" and of "having
been the channel of the counsels which conducted Lafayette into the
prisons of Prussia." Denying Genet's charges, Morris labeled them
folly and falsehoods.[96] Morris had the satisfaction of seeing the
French minister replaced; indeed, it was he who handled the negotiations for Genet's recall.[97] The triumph soon tarnished; Morris's
recall followed shortly.

In the meantime, Morris maneuvered to influence the character
of the mission of Genet's successor and so influence Franco-American
diplomacy on the other side of the Atlantic. Morris informed Washington that, "knowing the public and *private* views of the *parties,*"
he had suggested to Deforgues, the new French Minister of Foreign
Affairs, that it might be well if the new French minister to the
United States were to declare early that France was determined
"not to meddle with the interior affairs of other nations. . . ."[98] He
also forwarded details on the diplomatic commission the French had
decided to send to America to replace Genet. Fauchet, the new
minister, he had heard, was a young man of "genius and information." This time Morris believed French assurances of friendship
for the United States, "because America is the only source from
whence supplies of provisions can be drawn to feed this city [Paris],
on which so much depends."[99]

Morris's outlook appeared sound; the French were concerned
over the status of the American alliance. The National Convention dominated by Robespierre had decreed that in her foreign relations France would be terrible to her enemies and generous to her
allies and that she would adhere faithfully to the American alliance.
In particular, the decree stressed "drawing still closer the bonds of
alliance and friendship" which united France and America.[100]

[96] Genet to Jefferson, New York, Sept. 18, 1793, *ASP FR,* I, 173; Morris
to Randolph, Sainport, July 23, 1794, p. 411.
[97] See Morris to Jefferson, Paris, Oct. 10, 1793; to Deforgues, Paris, Oct.
8, 1793, and Deforgues to Morris, Paris, Oct. 10, 1793, *ibid.,* pp. 372-373, 375.
[98] Morris to Washington, Paris, Oct. 19, 1793, *ibid.,* p. 398.
[99] Morris to Washington, Paris, Nov. 12, 1793, *ibid.,* p. 398.
[100] Robespierre was responsible for this statement; for an English translation of the decree of Nov. 17, 1793, which stated succinctly the Jacobin foreign
policy, see Stewart, *A Documentary Survey of the French Revolution,* pp.
475-476; see also Jean Kaulek, ed., *Papiers de Barthelemy: ambassadeur de
France en Suisse, 1792-1797* (6 vols., Paris, 1886-1910), III, 246-247.

French concern for American friendship did not, however, include continuance of Morris as minister in Paris. Armed with a demand for Morris's recall, Fauchet after reaching America lost no time in presenting it to Washington. In view of the circumstances of Genet's recall Washington could neither refuse nor evade the request.[101] While maintaining, perhaps wishfully, that Morris "had too slight an influence here [Paris] to be dangerous," the French were convinced that if American friendship and the alliance were to survive, he must go.[102]

Morris's mission had embittered Franco-American relations, and as it came to a close it touched off a conflict between the Executive and Congress over the control of foreign relations. When the Senate learned of French dissatisfaction with Morris, it voted by a majority of one to call for his correspondence so that it could examine his conduct. Certain Republicans took the view that Morris was the key figure in Federalist diplomacy abroad. One critic assumed that the consuls and the American ministers in London and at the Hague all modeled their conduct after his.[103] Washington refused to comply with Senate demands. Under the injunction of secrecy, Secretary of State Randolph did supply the Senate with selections from the correspondence. This, although a major concession, did not please the senators; the Executive had again asserted and maintained control over foreign policy.[104]

Morris's mission ended as it had begun, with partisan conflict in

[101] Fauchet communicated the request for Morris's recall on April 9, 1794. Randolph to Morris, Philadelphia, April 29, 1794, National Archives, State Dept., Diplomatic and Consular Instructions; Fauchet to [Minister of Foreign Affairs], Philadelphia, April 21, 1794, AAE CP EU, Vol. XL, f. 183; Fauchet to Randolph, April 9, 1794, AAE CP EU, Vol. XL, f. 378. Morris was aware that Fauchet had been instructed to ask for his recall; he told the French foreign minister that "if this Government wished for any person in my place, the best way would be to tell me so, and I would apply for my own recall." Morris to Randolph, Sainport, July 23, 1794, ASP FR, I, 411.

[102] The Committee of Public Safety, quoted from Walther, Gouverneur Morris, p. 257; Masson, Le Département des affaires étrangères. . . , p. 345.

[103] "A Farmer of the back settlements," commenting on Franco-American relations since the French Revolution, in the General Advertiser reprinted in the Independent Chronicle and the Universal Advertiser (Boston), Jan. 20, 1794.

[104] Monroe to Jefferson, Philadelphia, March 3, 1794, March 16, 1794, in Hamilton, The Writings of James Monroe, pp. 283-284, 288-289; Swiggett, The Extraordinary Mr. Morris, p. 280; Conway, Randolph, pp. 213-214.

the Senate. Morris pondered his recall; in his opinion it was unwise. "If the government here were fixed on any permanent basis," he said, "it would be proper for America to have here a man agreeable to the rulers of the country, provided always that he did not, to render himself agreeable, sacrifice the interests intrusted to his care. But during the changes which hourly (as it were) take place, it is impossible for any man to do the business he is called on to perform unless he have the consciousness of support from home, and unless those who are here be well convinced that he cannot be removed at the will and pleasure of any faction or party in the country where he resides."[105] Several months later he told Randolph that "whenever a stable Government shall be established in France it will certainly be right to have here a man agreeable to that government, and I think a coincidence of mutual interests will render the place of such a man easy and pleasant. Until that period . . . I think a firm and decisive tone and conduct will best preserve the peace as well as the dignity of our Country."[106]

Through all of this Washington had approved of Morris's conduct; when he recalled his friend he made it clear that he did so only because the French demanded it. He informed Morris privately that their friendship was still solid and "that notwithstanding your recall, you held the same place in my estimation that you did before it happened." Then he added "that not until some considerable time after Mr. Fauchet had arrived in this country" did he realize that France was dissatisfied with Morris and wanted him replaced; "for until then," he said, "I had supposed you stood well with the powers that were." The aging President's memory had slipped. On February 20, 1793, Washington, realizing French hostility to Morris, had suggested that Jefferson, who possessed the confidence of both sides, replace Morris at Paris. On December 11, 1793, Jefferson had again informed him of French "dissatisfaction" with Morris, alluding to the previous expressions of French distaste for Morris.[107]

[105] Morris to Robert Morris, Sainport, March 10, 1794, Morris, *The Diary and Letters of Gouverneur Morris,* II, 56-57.
[106] Morris to Randolph, Paris, Aug. 31, 1794, National Archives, State Dept., Diplomatic Despatches, France.
[107] Washington to Morris, Mount Vernon, June 25, 1794, Fitzpatrick, *Washington's Writings,* XXXIII, 413-414. Compare The Anas, Feb. 20, 1793

Morris's lack of sympathy for the France of the Revolution had closed to him, from the beginning of his mission, many of the avenues of diplomacy which should have been his in an allied country. Distrust of and lack of confidence in Morris had influenced French behavior toward the United States. The French government by-passed him in matters wherein he should have been consulted and tended to rely too much on the biased reports of its own ministers for knowledge of America—men who were too much swayed by Jeffersonians in their appraisal of American affairs.

Morris, who represented and reflected the Federalist viewpoint of Washington's administration, might have served as a counterforce to the often biased, unsound, pro-French, pro-Republican reports which reached French authorities from their own agents. But Morris's viewpoint appeared to the French so extreme that he could gain no acceptance for his views or those of his government. Under the circumstances perhaps no man except an extreme partisan of the French Revolution would have been acceptable in Paris. If such were the case, Morris, within the context of his own limitations and those imposed by events, might be considered to have performed his diplomatic functions capably. Yet he acted undiplomatically, appearing at times to go out of his way to antagonize his host government. Franco-American friendship and the 1778 alliance could not long survive two such missions as those of "Citizen" Genet and "monarchy man" Morris.

<hr />

(paraphrasing Washington), and Jefferson to Washington, Dec. 11, 1793, in Ford, *Writings of Jefferson,* I, 217, and VI, 465-466; see also Stephenson and Dunn, *George Washington,* II, 380.

CHAPTER ELEVEN

SCHOOL FOR SCANDAL
JAMES MONROE IN PARIS

Monroe's house has been a school for scandal against his country, its government and governors, Mr. Jay and his treaty, &c.—John Adams to his wife, Philadelphia, January 14, 1797.

I cannot believe that an American minister would ever forget the connections between the United States and France, which every day's experience demonstrates to be in the interest of both Republics still further to cement.—James Monroe to the Committee of Public Safety, Paris, December 27, 1794.

* * * *

FOLLOWING Morris's recall, the Federalists appeared to face a dangerous foreign policy dilemma. On the one hand the United States staggered toward war with Great Britain, and, on the other, its relations with France floundered in suspicion and misunderstanding, following the ill-starred Genet and Morris missions. In an attempt to avoid war and to salvage what he could from a perilous situation, Washington had sent Jay to London. This, however, aggravated the French problem; to Frenchmen and to American Francophiles, Jay's mission constituted a betrayal of the French alliance, an alliance they considered the foundation stone of American foreign policy.

To repair the damage wrought by the Morris mission among the French and to counter the revulsion occasioned by the Jay appointment among Jeffersonians, Washington appeared eager to choose a minister for the Paris post whom both the Republicans and the French would accept, one who would allay French suspicions of Jay. Randolph assured Fauchet that "we have been anxiously seeking a successor [to Morris] who may be as acceptable to the French republic as the successor of Mr. Genet is to our own."[1]

In his initial effort at filling the vacancy Washington did consider a Hamiltonian; writing confidentially, in April, 1794, he asked Jay if he would accept the permanent post of minister to Great Britain. If he would, Thomas Pinckney, who was then regular minister in London, would be shifted to Paris before Jay arrived in London. Washington's intention may have been to assuage Pinckney's feelings, which had been ruffled by Jay's special mission. Jay refused the permanent appointment, however, and Pinckney did not go to Paris.[2]

The President then turned to the ranks of anti-Federalists to find a man for the Paris legation. According to James Monroe, Washington's administration "was reduc'd to the dilemna [sic] of selecting from among its enemies or rather those of opposite principles, a person who wo.ᵈ be acceptable to that nation [France]."[3] James Madison and Robert R. Livingston were considered and both turned down proffered appointments. Aaron Burr, then in the Senate, was also suggested.[4]

Finally Washington turned to James Monroe, Senator from Virginia and an outspoken critic of his administration. After deliberating and consulting with Madison and other friends, Monroe accepted the appointment "upon the necessity of cultivating France."[5] Re-

[1] Randolph to Fauchet, April 21, 1794, quoted in Conway, *Randolph*, p. 240; Bemis, "Washington's Farewell Address. . . ," *American Historical Review*, XXXIX, 254; Schachner, *The Founding Fathers*, p. 321.

[2] Washington to Jay, Philadelphia, April 29, 1794, Fitzpatrick, *Washington's Writings*, XXXIII, 345-346.

[3] Monroe to Jefferson, Philadelphia, May 4, 1794, Hamilton, *The Writings of James Monroe*, I, 295.

[4] *Ibid.*, p. 296; Monroe to Jefferson, May 26, 1794, p. 298. Washington offered the Paris post to Jay and Livingston on the same day; see Washington to Livingston, Philadelphia, April 29, 1794, Fitzpatrick, *Washington's Writings*, XXXIII, 345; see also Brant, *James Madison: Father of the Constitution . . .*, p. 400; William P. Cresson, *James Monroe* (Chapel Hill, N. C., 1946), pp. 127-128; Arthur Styron, *The Last of the Cocked Hats: James Monroe and the Virginia Dynasty* (Norman, Okla., 1945), 170; Matthew L. Davis, *Memoirs of Aaron Burr with Miscellaneous Selections from his Correspondence* (2 vols., New York, 1855), I, 408-409; Nathan Schachner, *Aaron Burr: A Biography* (New York, 1937), pp. 136-137.

[5] Believing himself "among the last men to whom it wod. be made," Monroe was surprised by Washington's offer. Monroe to Jefferson, Phila-

publicans, "real friends of their country," rejoiced "that the important trust of drawing closer the ties which unite the sister republics should be placed in hands so worthy of the confidence of republicans."[6] The French were delighted with Monroe's appointment. Fauchet described him as "a true friend of liberty" who wished to strengthen the bonds uniting France and the United States.[7] To the British, on the other hand, the appointment spelled danger. Hammond, who described Monroe as "a man of moderate abilities and of embarrassed circumstances," noted that he was distinguished by his hostility to Great Britain and his admiration for the principles of the French Revolution.[8]

The Washington administration knew what manner of man it had chosen for the Paris legation. It would have preferred to retain Morris, but the administration did not have an alternative to a Republican nomination if it were to placate the French and Republicans; it is unlikely that they would have accepted another Morris. In sending Monroe to Paris while Jay negotiated in London, however, the real purpose of the Jay mission could be camouflaged. By placating the French and offsetting Republican alarm, Monroe was to serve as a cat's paw for Federalist foreign policy.[9]

* * * * *

Monroe, like Washington, Jefferson, and Madison, was a Virginian. Born in Westmoreland County and educated at the College of William and Mary, he left his studies to enlist as a lieutenant in

---

delphia, May 27, 1794, in Hamilton, *The Writings of James Monroe*, I, 299-300.

[6] *Maryland Gazette* (Annapolis), June 5, 1794.

[7] Fauchet and Le Blanc to the Minister of Foreign Affairs, Philadelphia, May 5, 1794, June 4 and 9, 1794, in Turner, *CFM*, pp. 333, 377, 392.

[8] Hammond to Grenville, Philadelphia, May 27, 1794, No. 22, Henry Adams Transcripts.

[9] George Hammond and Phineas Bond believed that Washington's motive in appointing Monroe was to avoid war. Hammond to Grenville, May 27, 1794, and Bond to Grenville, Jan. 22, 1796, cited in Beverly W. Bond, *The Monroe Mission to France, 1794-1796* (Baltimore, 1907), pp. 99-100; Bemis, "Washington's Farewell Address. . . ," *AHR*, XXXIX, 254; Gibbs, ed., *Wolcott Papers*, I, 139; James T. Austin, *The Life of Elbridge Gerry* (2 vols., Boston, 1828-1829), II, 175; Sears, *George Washington*, pp. 439-440. Jefferson later maintained bitterly that Monroe was appointed "merely to get him out of the Senate." Jefferson to Dr. John Edwards, Monticello, Jan. 22, 1797, in Ford, *Writings of Jefferson*, VII, 112.

a Virginia regiment and took an active part in the American Revolution until wounded at the battle of Trenton. He then resumed his work as a law student. During this period he formed an important connection with Thomas Jefferson, then war-governor of Virginia, a friendship that lasted until Jefferson's death in 1826.

In 1782 Monroe was elected to the Virginia legislature. In the following year he won a seat in the Congress of the Confederation. Passed over as a delegate to the Philadelphia convention in 1787, he did not become a founding father. When the Constitution emerged, he opposed it, a logical stand for a confirmed sectionalist representing constituents with strong sectional views. Primarily, he maintained, he was against the Constitution's centralizing features, "the absence of a Bill of Rights, or any express provision limiting the general powers of the government."[10] When the federal government was established, nonetheless, he sought a post in it. In 1788 he ran against Madison for election to the First Congress, suffering a bad defeat. Two years later he was appointed to a vacancy in the Senate, where he remained until he accepted the Paris appointment.

During this time he drew closer to Jefferson, moving near Jefferson's beloved Monticello. While he was a Senator Monroe's political ideas crystallized. From the beginning he criticized the Washington administration. He opposed almost all of the Hamiltonian program—the establishment of the Bank, the selection of Morris as minister to France, the Jay mission. In 1792 he served on the Senate committee which investigated charges that Alexander Hamilton had mishandled public funds. In the course of the investigation Hamilton revealed his sordid affair with Mrs. Maria Reynolds. From this episode Monroe emerged somewhat tarnished although not guilty of dishonorable conduct toward Hamilton.[11]

Despite the unfavorable impression the execution of Louis XVI had made on the American people, Monroe was convinced that they were in favor of the French Revolution.[12] When the Anglo-

[10] "Monroe in the Virginia Convention of 1788," Hamilton, *The Writings of James Monroe*, I, 189.

[11] For details, see Cresson, *James Monroe*, pp. 155-169; Schachner, *Alexander Hamilton*, pp. 365-372.

[12] In Virginia Monroe found scarcely "a man unfriendly to the French revolution as now modified." Monroe to Jefferson, Fredericksburg, March 27, 1793, Albemarle, May 28, 1793, in Hamilton, *The Writings of James Monroe*, I, 252, 257; Cresson, *James Monroe*, p. 119.

French war broke out in 1793 he distinguished himself as a French partisan and supporter of the French alliance. Great Britain, not France, he was convinced, had most to gain by forcing a rupture with the United States. He favored a policy of neutrality because it conferred greater advantage on France than would American belligerency. To join France, he maintained, would do her, as well as the United States, more harm than good and would "but benefit the party we meant to injure," meaning Great Britain. Under a policy of benevolent neutrality "the ports and the bottoms of America will be free to France; in addition to which every act of gratuity & favor which a generous and grateful people can bestow, without infringement on the other side, will be shewn. France may greatly profit from this situation, for under a wise management immense resources may be gathered hence to aid her operations & support her cause."[13] At first, therefore, Monroe had considered the proclamation of neutrality unnecessary but harmless; later, as Washington enforced it against France, he came to look on it as "both unconstitutional & impolitick."[14]

Like most Republican leaders, Monroe had supported Genet. Unlike many of them he continued to plead Genet's cause even after men like Jefferson had lost patience with the French minister. Soon he too trimmed his sails; after appraising Jefferson's views and testing the prevailing winds of the "publick mind," he abandoned "Citizen" Genet. In so doing he expressed "extreme concern" with the effect of Federalist politics and Genet's conduct on the French alliance. To counter these effects he prepared a "pointed" attack on Gouverneur Morris and his conduct in France, which apparently he never published.[15]

[13] Monroe to Jefferson, Albemarle, May 28, 1793, in Hamilton, *The Writings of James Monroe*, I, 256-260.

[14] Monroe to Jefferson, Albemarle, June 27, 1793, *ibid.*, pp. 261-267.

[15] Monroe to John Brackenridge, Albemarle, Aug. 23, 1793; to Jefferson, Staunton, Sept. 3, 1793; to Madison, Albemarle, Sept. 25, 1793, *ibid.*, I, 272-278; Cresson, *James Monroe*, pp. 122-123; Styron, *The Last of the Cocked Hats...*, p. 158. Until August, 1793, Monroe was convinced that the administration had seized on the Genet incident merely to stir up public opinion against France, "thinking to separate us from France & pave the way for an unnatural connection with Great Britain" and at the same time advance the fortunes of the "monarchy party." He was satisfied, however, that public sentiment was still overwhelmingly pro-French. See also Philip Marsh,

Shifting politics brought to Philadelphia in December, 1793, a Congress in which Republicans controlled the House of Representatives. In the Senate, which was divided equally, Monroe and other Republicans fought for control. In the struggle Monroe rose to importance. On the issue of the Jay mission, for example, he jumped into the front ranks of the antiadministration forces. When he learned that the administration was considering Hamilton for the London journey, he appealed personally to President Washington to block the appointment.[16] If there must be an emissary, he believed that Hamilton must not be the one chosen. In objecting to Hamilton's appointment, Monroe scored his pro-British affiliations, contending that Hamilton would use the mission for political intrigue against "republicanism" in the United States and "against our connections with France." The French reaction in particular caused him concern; it would be so unfavorable, he claimed, as to create a situation "as mortifying as it would be alarming" to the cause of American friendship with France.[17]

While Jay, who "had well nigh bartered away the Mississippi," was more palatable than Hamilton, appointment of the Chief Justice did not allay Monroe's fears. He wanted no special mission to England, and especially not a Federalist inspired and controlled mission. He saw the Jay mission as an executive plot to break the French alliance and tie the United States to England.[18]

* * * * *

Monroe, his appointment confirmed, sailed for France in June, 1794. At sea for over a month on a storm-free passage, he had time to digest his instructions. In summary, they were to assure France of the President's friendship and that he did not recognize the right

"James Monroe as 'Agricola' in the Genet Controversy, 1793," *The Virginia Magazine of History and Biography*, LXII (Oct., 1954), 472-476.

[16] Monroe to Washington, Philadelphia, April 8, 1794, in Hamilton, *The Writings of James Monroe*, I, 291-292; for details on this episode see the notes on pp. 291-293. This raised, apparently for the first time, the issue of the right of a senator to criticize a nomination before it was made; see also Washington to Monroe, Philadelphia, April 9, 1794, in Fitzpatrick, *Washington's Writings*, XXXIII, 320-321. Washington stressed that he *alone* was responsible for the nomination.

[17] Quoted in Cresson, *James Monroe*, p. 125.

[18] Monroe to Jefferson, Philadelphia, May 4, 1794, Hamilton, *The Writings of James Monroe*, I, 292-296.

of foreign intervention in the affairs of the French Republic and to make clear that our policy of neutrality, from which France "did not desire us to depart," was to continue. With respect to Jay's mission, he was to allay French suspicions by saying Jay's instructions limited his negotiations to discussions of English spoliations on American shipping and to the question of the Northwest posts. He was to say also that Jay's instructions forbade him to weaken America's treaties with France. While "we are unable to give her aids of men or money," Monroe was to stress that the United States had no "distant intention to sacrifice our connection with France to any connection with England."

The instructions enjoined Monroe specifically to "obviate" the impression, conveyed in the reports to France of Genet and Fauchet, that there were two "irreconcilable" parties in the United States, "one republican, and friendly to the French revolution; the other monarchical, aristocratic, Britannic, and anti-Gallican." This caveat revealed the Washington government's anxiety to remove suspicion of a pro-British policy.

Among other things, Monroe was explicitly prohibited from entering into negotiations on a treaty of commerce. As to an alliance, and particularly as to the guarantee clause in the existing alliance, Monroe was to do nothing but give "testimony" of American attachment to the French cause. All questions touching on these matters, except those on which he had specific instructions, were to be referred to Philadelphia. He was to insist on compensation for spoliations, press claims for repayment of funds expended on French refugees from Saint Domingue, and seek French aid in securing a treaty with the Dey of Algiers and in securing *"free navigation of the Mississippi"* from Spain. In effect, he was directed to obtain favors without being empowered to insure reciprocal advantages. Monroe, nonetheless, was to *"let it be seen, that in case of war, with any nation on earth, we shall consider France as our first and natural ally."*[19]

Although one-sided and lacking in positive commitments, the instructions indicated clearly that the administration wished to maintain close ties with France and they implied that the restricted nature

[19] Dated Philadelphia, June 10, 1794, the instructions are in *ibid.*, II, 1-9; the quotations are taken from this text; the italics are Monroe's.

of Jay's objectives were such as to make French fears groundless. In comparing Jay's instructions with Monroe's, it can be seen that Jay had far greater leeway and that in several particulars Monroe's instructions were deceptive. Monroe's own fears concerning the London mission were calmed, though they did not disappear; before he left the United States Jefferson and Robert R. Livingston had impressed their suspicions of the London mission on him.[20]

When in the beginning of August, 1794, Monroe established himself in Paris, all appeared turmoil; no other nation had a recognized diplomatic representative there; hardly a week before, Robespierre had been put to death. Frigidity, if not hostility, stemming from resentment toward Morris, suspicions of the Jay mission, and lack of confidence in American friendship by some government officials, marked the greeting given to Monroe in the Committee of Public Safety, which was then the executive organ.[21]

Uncertain as to when he might be received, Monroe, after cooling his heels for some ten days, resolved on direct action. To "attract public attention" to his situation, he bypassed the executive body by appealing directly to the president of the National Convention, the head of the legislative body wherein lay "the sovereign authority of the nation," for a time as to when he might be received. His direct diplomacy worked. Almost immediately the National Convention agreed to receive him.[22]

On August 14, in a ceremony lasting an hour and a half, the assembled delegates received Monroe "into the bosom of the Convention." Greetings and expressions of fraternity between the French and American peoples were exchanged. Monroe presented two resolutions from the American Congress. Reflecting the political situation in the United States, the letter from the Senate expressed little more than general good will toward the French nation. The message from the House of Representatives was warmer; in florid

[20] Bond, *The Monroe Mission,* pp. 13-15; Cresson, *James Monroe,* p. 129; Sears, *George Washington,* pp. 439-440; for Jay's instructions (Philadelphia, May 6, 1794) see *ASP FR,* I, 472-474.

[21] Monroe to Madison, Paris, Sept. 2, [1794], Hamilton, *The Writings of James Monroe,* II, 37-41; Bond, *The Monroe Mission. . . ,* p. 15; Cresson, *James Monroe,* pp. 129-130.

[22] Monroe to the President of the National Convention, Paris, Aug. 13, 1794, in Hamilton, *The Writings of James Monroe,* II, 11-12; to Randolph, Aug. 25, 1794, to Madison, Sept. 2, pp. 31-41.

language it stressed the common bond between the two countries, voicing full sympathy for America's ally in her struggle for liberty. Its anti-British overtones pleased the French.

In making the presentation Monroe delivered an ardent speech, emphasizing the close union between the two nations and his own desire to promote harmony between them. His words were greeted with applause; "the effect," he reported, "surpassed my expectation." Speaking for France, the president of the Convention responded that "it is not merely a diplomatic alliance" which unites our peoples, "it is the sweetest fraternity." Then, "in the midst of universal acclamations of joy, delight, and admiration," the president conferred the kiss and fraternal embrace upon Monroe, who received the accolade in the name of the American people. As a climax the Convention decreed that "the flags of the United States of America shall be joined to those of France, and displayed in the hall of the sittings of the Convention in sign of the Union and eternal fraternity of the two people[s]."[23]

As his instructions had specified, Monroe had not committed the United States "by any specific declarations" to anything he was prohibited from doing. His worst sin, "in giving testimony of our attachment" to the cause of America's ally, was indiscretion. Although he did not violate the letter of his instructions in expressing sentiments which he had always held and which were well known to the administration, Monroe's actions caused a sensation in Federalist and pro-British circles, setting off a chain reaction of displeasure; party presses rang with partisan thunder. Republicans, of course, applauded.[24]

Across the channel John Jay fumed. Delicate negotiations involv-

[23] As proof of friendship for its ally the Convention offered to provide Monroe with a house at the expense of the state. Monroe declined because of constitutional prohibition. The congressional resolutions, Monroe's speech, the speech of the president of the Convention, the house offer and response are in *ASP FR*, I, 672-675. The Convention's decree is in Hamilton, *The Writings of James Monroe*, II, 34 n. For details on the flag episode, see McMaster, *A History of the People of the United States. . . ,* II, 257.

[24] Bond, *The Monroe Mission. . . ,* p. 17, maintained that by his public reception Monroe "exceeded his instructions." For the American reaction see Fauchet, La Forest, and Petry to Commissioner of Foreign Relations, Philadelphia, Oct. 22, 1794, Fauchet to the Commissioner, Philadelphia, Nov. 15, 1794, in Turner, *CFM*, pp. 442-443, 474-476.

ing the welfare of the nation lay at stake, he warned. An exhibition such as Monroe's could upset everything. It had caused a "disagreeable sensation" in England. In Jay's unneutral view Monroe's partisan language had compromised American neutrality.[25]

The President, disapproving of Monroe's conduct, agreed with Jay that the American minister in Paris had "stepped over the true line" of neutrality. Yet Washington felt that his language "was susceptible of two views." The Secretary of State, however, delivered to Monroe notice of official displeasure. He stressed in admonishment that the administration had expected a private reception; it had hoped Monroe's words would be "so framed as to leave heartburning no where," and therefore disapproved of the "warm glow" of parts of his speech. In his future conduct, Randolph recommended "caution."[26] Although he feared that Monroe may have exceeded his instructions, Randolph personally did not share his own officially expressed admonition. He was "delighted" with the conduct of his friend Monroe and so told Fauchet, the French Minister in Philadelphia, confidentially.[27]

While Monroe had anticipated that his words would be "scanned with unfriendly eyes in America"—by the Federalists—he responded to Randolph's official censure with "surprize and concern." Asserting that he did not merit reproof, he denied that he had exceeded his instructions. His language, after all, was no stronger than that in the congressional resolutions. In justifying his conduct, Monroe pointed out that when he reached Paris the French were hostile to the United States; Franco-American relations were "in the worst possible situation"; they hung "upon a thread" which "would have been broken" if France were not conciliated and America's preference for her reiterated. Under the circumstances he thought that by his conduct "every thing was to be gained and nothing to be

[25] Lord Grenville made Monroe's "unneutral" effusions the subject of private protest to Jay, Sept. 7, 1794, cited in Bemis, *Jay's Treaty...*, pp. 242 n.- 243 n. See also Jay to Washington, London, Sept. 13, 1794, March 6, 1795, in Johnston, *Jay Correspondence*, IV, 58-60, 163; Jay to Hamilton, London, Sept. 11, 1794, in Hamilton, ed., *Hamilton's Works*, V, 27-28; Washington to Jay, Philadelphia, Dec. 18, 1794, in Fitzpatrick, *Washington's Writings*, XXXIV, 61.
[26] Randolph to Monroe, Philadelphia, Dec. 2, 1794, *ASP FR*, I, 689-690.
[27] Fauchet (paraphrasing Randolph) to Minister of Foreign Relations, Philadelphia, Dec. 1, 1794, in Turner, *CFM*, p. 490.

lost"; that if he had not acted as he had, the United States might have been dragged into war.[28]

Given the pro-French and anti-British state of public sentiment in the United States at the time, Federalist politicians and administration officials confined most of their displeasure to private expression; they dared not at this point risk making a political issue of Monroe. With the Jay mission a desperate one-party gamble to head off war with Great Britain, they dared not arouse public debate which would endanger the negotiation. Such debate might expose the Jay negotiation as inimical to the still popular French alliance. If the London negotiation failed and if at the same time France were alienated, then the United States instead of one would have two powerful enemies ready to crush it.[29]

Secretary Randolph, governed by these considerations and by his personal views, followed his reprimand to Monroe with a peace offering almost immediately. As if in repudiation of his official censure, which he attempted to soften, Randolph instructed Monroe to cultivate French friendship "with zeal," and "to remove every suspicion of our preferring a connexion with Great Britain, or any manner weakening our old attachment to France."[30] Randolph wrote this before he had received Monroe's response to the reprimand.

* * * * *

Soon after his reception Monroe had turned his attention to outstanding American grievances against France. As he had indicated in his reports, Franco-American relations were in a parlous state; American grievances were many. In accord with his instructions he insisted upon compensation for damages to American commerce. He pointed out, in summarizing the American case, that French seizures of British goods on American ships violated the principle of free ships, free goods as given in the Franco-American commercial treaty of 1778. While Great Britain might commit the same deeds, he said, the case was different; she was not an ally and was not bound

[28] See Monroe to Madison, Paris, Sept. 12, [1794], to Randolph, Feb. 12, 1795, in Hamilton, *The Writings of James Monroe*, II, 40, 193-206.
[29] Believing that the Jay negotiation might fail, Randolph wished to court France. See Randolph to Monroe, Philadelphia, Sept. 25, 1794, *ASP FR*, I, 678; Bond, *The Monroe Mission. . .*, pp. 18-19.
[30] Randolph to Monroe, Philadelphia, Dec. 5, 1794, *ASP FR*, I, 690-691.

by treaty to abstain from such actions. France, however, was committed by treaty not to act in such manner against her ally.

Complaining of onerous commercial restrictions on American shipping in French ports, Monroe asked, too, that they be lifted and that French ports be opened to American vessels. Such a policy, he claimed, would be to France's advantage. Then, though still pressing the American claims, he softened his case by stating that his instructions did not ask him to complain of France's departure from certain other specified articles of the 1778 commercial treaty. On the contrary, if such departure produced "solid benefit" to France (which he asserted it did not), he said, "the American government, and my countrymen in general, will not only bear the departure with patience, but with pleasure."[31]

In view of his indiscreet disclosures, it is not surprising that the French at first ignored Monroe's complaints. Seizing upon his voluntary concessions, members of the Committee of Public Safety told him later that it would be detrimental to French interests to comply fully with other provisions in the commercial treaty. They had therefore decided that France's immediate interest would not permit them to admit free enemy goods in American ships even though that principle was embodied in the commercial treaty. This would not be the first time, they said, that the needs of one party and the conciliatory spirit of the other had made possible a deviation from a treaty. Several times in a special interview they asked if he would insist upon execution of the treaty. Parrying the queries, Monroe said, "I had nothing new to add to what I had already said on that head."[32] In Philadelphia Monroe's inept diplomacy—it appeared so to Federalists—aroused consternation. Washington was incensed; in his view (expressed in later years) Monroe had weakened "the pivot" on which American claims rested. Again Randolph informed Monroe of administration displeasure.[33]

[31] Monroe to the Committee of Public Safety, Paris, Sept. 3, 1794, *ibid.*, pp. 676-678.
[32] The French felt also that they did not profit from the 1778 treaties. Most-favored-nation treatment appeared meaningless and the tonnage laws made no distinction in favor of France. Opinion on Monroe's note of Sept. 3, 1794, AAE CP EU, n.p., n.d. [1794], Vol. XLII, ff. 26-27; Monroe to Secretary of State, Paris, Nov. 7, 1794, *ASP FR,* I, 681-683; Darling, *Our Rising Empire. . .* , p. 234; Bond, *The Monroe Mission. . .* , p. 21.
[33] Washington's Remarks on Monroe's "View of the Conduct of the Execu-

Regardless of its ineptitude in Federalist eyes, Monroe's diplomacy had a salutary effect on French relations. Within a few months his complaints brought results; not only did the French listen to them, they also acted. Monroe's arguments alone did not induce a change in the French; ironically, English action reinforced his case. To ease the way for the Jay negotiation, England set aside her provision order of June, 1793.[34] In response to this action and to Monroe's arguments, French authorities issued two decrees, one in November, 1794, the other in January, 1795, which re-established American privileges under the treaty of 1778 and revoked the obnoxious decree of May, 1793, which had allowed seizure in French ports of neutral ships carrying goods to enemy countries. Then she also promised fair treatment for American seamen, again recognized the principle of free ships, free goods, allowed American shipping free use of French ports, and promised to settle claims for past spoliations. While France paid no immediate compensation, and even though some of the re-established privileges were conditioned upon English actions, in the light of the previous low state of Franco-American relations Monroe's contribution proved substantial.[35]

* * * * *

"We are particularly concerned to understand the true state of the different sects of politics" in France, read Monroe's instructions. Accordingly he sent home long reports on conditions there and on European affairs in general. In one of his reports in October, 1794, he outlined briefly the history of the Jacobins in the French Revolution, depicting early Jacobins as "enemies of the ancient despotism"

tive of the United States," [March, 1798], in Fitzpatrick, *Washington's Writings,* XXXVI, 198; Randolph to Monroe, Philadelphia, Dec. 2, 1794, *ASP FR,* I, 690; Cresson, *James Monroe,* 135.

[34] Monroe to Secretary of State, Paris, Dec. 2, 1794, and Jan. 13, 1795, Grenville to Jay, Downing Street, Aug. 1, 1794, *ASP FR,* I, 687, 691, 481-482; Bemis, "Washington's Farewell Address. . . ," *AHR,* XXXIX, 254; the British Order-in-Council of Aug. 6, 1794, British Record Office, Foreign Office, 5:13, which in part revoked the June 8, 1793 Order-in-Council is printed in Newcomb, "New Light on Jay's Treaty," *American Journal of International Law,* XXVIII, 686 n.

[35] For the French decrees of Nov. 15, 1794, and Jan. 4, 1795, see *ASP FR,* I, 752-753, 642-643; for discussions of the decrees and Monroe's diplomacy, see Darling, *Our Rising Empire. . . ,* pp. 234-235; Bond, *The Monroe Mission. . . ,* pp. 22-23.

who, as they gained power, established a tyranny of their own. Monroe had written the sketch not to denounce the Jacobins but to show how their virtues had been perverted, how they had "well nigh ruined the Republic itself."[36]

Unknown to Monroe, the sketch became political fodder for Federalists. Reaching the United States at a time when the Federalists were attacking the democratic societies for their nefarious "Jacobin" connections, the report appeared to them like manna from the devil. The administration pounced eagerly on the providentially timed evidence from the pro-French American minister in Paris. "Your history of the Jacobin societies," Randolph said, "was so appropriate to the present times in our own country, that it was conceived proper to furnish the public with those useful lessons; and extracts were published, as from a letter *of a gentleman in Paris to his friend in this city.*"[37]

Although the sketch at first appeared without signature, Monroe's identity as the writer was easily discernible. Madison explained why the administration used the comments on the Jacobin Societies and pointed out they had been extracted from his despatches and printed out of context. "In New York," he wrote, "they have been republished with your name prefixed." Not liking what had happened, Monroe denounced the "wicked forces" which had taken advantage of him. Madison, in informing him of what had happened, had in effect reprimanded him and cautioned the use of more "reserve" in his communications. Fortunately, the publication of his remarks did not do him as much harm in France, as might have been expected. With the Jacobins out and in ill repute, the new French authorities welcomed criticism of them.[38]

* * * * *

Monroe was also instructed to watch for "an opening for *France to become instrumental in securing to us the free navigation of the Mississippi.*" He awaited his opportunity, and when it arose, under odd circumstances, he grasped it. Twice, in October and in Novem-

[36] For the sketch, see Monroe to Randolph, Paris, Oct. 16, 1794, in Hamilton, *The Writings of James Monroe*, II, 80-85; for a discussion, see Styron, *The Last of the Cocked Hats*, pp. 175-176.

[37] Randolph to Monroe, Philadelphia, March 8, 1795, *ASP FR*, I, 699.

[38] Madison to Monroe, March 11, 1795, in Hamilton, *The Writings of James Monroe*, II, 81 n; Styron, *The Last of the Cocked Hats*, pp. 176-177.

ber, 1794, Don Diego de Gardoqui, Spain's minister of finance, asked him to intercede with the French government so that it would allow him to visit certain baths in France. Monroe concluded quickly that this merely disguised an effort to open peace negotiations, France and Spain still being at war.[39] Unless the issue of Mississippi navigation and allied Spanish-American boundary questions were settled at the same time, he perceived also that such a peace was not to America's advantage.

Ignoring the French channel suggested by Gardoqui, Monroe revealed the correspondence to the French government. With this approach he sought to forewarn the Committee of Public Safety of Spanish peace moves, give convincing proof of American friend-ship, and gain an opportunity to enlist French diplomacy in Amer-ica's behalf in the Mississippi question. To strengthen his position he pointed out that "it was the wish of the Spanish Court to com-mence a negotiation, and that it had addressed itself through me, to inspire a distrust in me by creating a belief that the United States were more friendly to Spain and Britain than to France."[40]

The Committee of Public Safety advised Monroe to suggest to Gardoqui that he approach the Committee directly. The French then made a request of their own. Would the United States, they asked, grant financial aid in the coming campaign against England? Although he had "no power on the subject" and so indicated, Mon-roe saw this as the opportunity for enlisting French diplomacy against Spain on the Mississippi question which he sought; he now had a bargaining point with which to secure concessions. He inti-mated to the members of the Committee that perhaps "considerable" funds might be forthcoming if they gave satisfactory assurances that they would consider America's points at issue with England and Spain in any ensuing peace negotiations with Spain or England.[41] America's cause, responded the Committee, would be treated as its own. Monroe thus enlisted the French in an effort to force conces-sions from Spain. At the same time he had been instrumental in

[39] Monroe to the Committee of Public Safety, Paris, Nov. 13, 1794, in Hamilton, *The Writings of James Monroe*, II, 109-112.

[40] Monroe to the Secretary of State, Paris, Nov. 20, 1794, *ibid.*, p. 120.

[41] See Monroe's "Observations Submitted to the Consideration of the Diplo-matic Members of the Committee of Public Safety," [Nov. 20, 1794], *ibid.*, pp. 124-127.

convincing France that Spain desired peace.[42] In the meantime
other developments beclouded Monroe's controversial diplomacy.

* * * * *

Monroe's handling of Thomas Paine, from the administration
and Federalist viewpoint, was another blunder. Paine still lan-
guished in prison when Monroe took over the American legation.
There the revolutionary author nursed his grievances against Morris
and Washington, and soon after Monroe's arrival he sent him desperate appeals for aid.[43] Monroe immediately began informal negotiations and finally, through an official request, secured Paine's
freedom.[44] Ill and aged beyond his sixty years, Paine, after granting
a promise that he would not write on political issues while a guest
in his home, accepted Monroe's hospitality. The aged writer stayed
for ten months.

As soon as Paine had recovered his health he ignored his promise
and began to write upon politics and American affairs. Working
as a propagandist for the French government, he wrote anti-English
articles for circulation in England and in the United States. This
embarrassed Monroe.[45] The worst came after Paine left. Believing,
wrongly, that Washington had connived at his imprisonment, Paine
published a scorching attack on the President, labeling Washington

[42] Le comité de salut public à Barthélemy, Paris, May 22, 1795, in Kaulek,
Papiers de Barthélemy, VI, 38.

[43] See Paine to Monroe, Luxembourg, Aug. 17, 18, 25, Oct. 4, 13, 20,
Nov., 1794, in Foner, *The Complete Works of Thomas Paine,* II, 1341-1375.

[44] Monroe to the Committee of General Surety, Paris, Nov. 1, 1794; to
Randolph, Paris, Nov. 7, 1794, in Hamilton, *The Writings of James Monroe,*
II, 96-98, 107-108. Monroe also was instrumental in securing the release from
imprisonment of Mme Lafayette; see Monroe to Randolph, Paris, Feb. 12,
1795, *ibid.,* pp. 204-205; Styron, *The Last of the Cocked Hats,* p. 180.

[45] Cresson, *James Monroe,* p. 149; Conway, *The Life of Thomas Paine,*
II, 152-180; Faÿ, *The Revolutionary Spirit in France and America,* p. 380.
An example of Paine's writing at this time is his pamphlet "The Decline and
Fall of the English System of Finance," written in Paris and completed on
April 8, 1796. It was published simultaneously in France, England, and the
United States; it is printed in Foner, *The Complete Works of Thomas Paine,*
II, 651-674. Commented the Federalist *New Hampshire and Vermont Jour-
nal: Or, The Farmer's Weekly Museum* (Walpole, N. H.), Sept. 6, 1796,
Paine has published a six-penny pamphlet to prove that Britain was on the
verge of bankruptcy. His "talent for writing for illiterate minds has never
been exceeded," it said; he "is a man of little reading and erudition; but he
makes that little go farther than any man living."

a "hypocrite" who was "treacherous in private friendship."[46] Federalists were appalled. "Tom, you are surely mad," said one critic.
"Thou hast escaped the *guillotine,* but thy terrors have prepared thee
for a *strait-jacket!*"[47]

Monroe's efforts to stop Paine failed. He feared that he would
be considered to have instigated Paine's attack and that Paine would
compromise him by publishing things he had picked up in his
house.[48] His fears were realized. His hospitality to Paine did not
enhance his already forlorn status with the Washington administration; Federalists charged, with some justification, that he had been
influenced by Paine's anti-administration views.

Although aware that the administration back home would view
dimly almost anything he did, Monroe even in little things seemed
to act so as to irritate his official superiors and political opponents.
For example, Gouverneur Morris had thought that from the beginning Monroe had taken the "wrong tone" at Paris.[49] Despite his
recall Morris retained considerable political influence. In dealing
with him, therefore, Monroe should have been tactful, yet he tried
rather to act in a manner that would not offend French authorities,
who detested and distrusted the former American minister. In so
doing, however, Monroe aroused Morris's ire in an incident involving a passport for Morris, who had chosen to remain in Europe.[50]

Another minor incident in which Monroe, in acting with the
intention of improving French good will, ended by irritating the
Federalists, was that of the exchange of French and American flags.
As we have seen, the National Convention had decreed that the
American flag should hang with that of France in the hall where
its members assembled. Accompanied by "glowing" words Monroe
sent an American flag, which the French received in a public ceremony wherein the bearer delivered a speech and received the kiss

---

[46] Paine's "Letter to George Washington," Paris, July 30, 1796, is in Foner,
The Complete Works of Thomas Paine, II, 691-723.

[47] "No-Painite" in the *Minerva* reprinted in the *Herald: A Gazette for the
Country* (New York), Aug. 17, 1796.

[48] Monroe to Madison, Paris, July 5, 1796, Hamilton, *The Writings of
James Monroe,* III, 19-27.

[49] Diary entry of Oct. 12, 1794, in Morris, ed., *The Diary and Letters of
Gouverneur Morris,* II, 70.

[50] Monroe to Washington, Paris, Nov. 19, 1794, in Hamilton, *The Writings
of James Monroe,* II, 112-114; Bond, *The Monroe Mission. . . ,* p. 28.

and fraternal embrace. With similar ceremonies the French later presented their tricolor to the United States. While nothing of consequence came from the incident, Monroe did not report it to Philadelphia for six months. To an administration keenly sensitive to "public ceremonies" in republican France this episode proved another irritant among many.[51]

* * * * *

Meanwhile developments across the channel created a major crisis in Franco-American relations and led to Monroe's undoing as minister to France. Successful though he was in winning French good will, Monroe was never able to overcome French fears concerning the Jay mission. During the Jay-Grenville negotiations French distrust deepened as rumors emanated from London, despite his efforts to counteract their effect.[52]

To divert French "suspicions" Monroe's instructions had told him to say that Jay "is positively forbidden to weaken the engagements between this country and France" and to declare *the motives of that mission to be, obtain immediate compensation for our plundered property, and restitution of the posts."* Accordingly Monroe had met French uneasiness with assurances that Jay's mission was confined to questions of compensation for depredations on American commerce and the surrender of the Western posts.[53] The Secretary of State had stressed that it was indispensable that Monroe "should keep the French Republic in good humour with us."[54] As rumors of a treaty became too convincing even for Monroe, he wrote home that he could no longer believe that Washington had chosen him "to be the organ of an honest and not a double and perfidious

[51] Monroe to the President of the National Convention, Paris, Sept. 9, 1794; Monroe to Randolph, Paris, March 6, 1795, postscript of March 9, Hamilton, *The Writings of James Monroe*, II, 54-55, 229; Styron, *The Last of the Cocked Hats*, p. 174; McMaster, *A History of the People of the United States. . .* , II, 257; Bond, *The Monroe Mission. . .* , pp. 28-29; Beckles Willson, *America's Ambassadors to France (1777-1927)* (New York, 1928), p. 69.

[52] Monroe to Madison, Paris, Nov. 30, 1794, in Hamilton, *The Writings of James Monroe*, II, 136-137. The Jay negotiations and French distrust, Monroe declared, have "produc'd repellant disposition towards me not from any real distrust in me, but from a distrust of the Ex: adm'n."

[53] Instructions, June 30, 1794, *ibid.*, II, 3; Memorandum of a conversation in Nov., 1794, between Monroe and two members of the Committee of Public Safety, *ibid.*, III, 395 n.-396 n.

[54] Randolph to Monroe, Philadelphia, Sept. 25, 1794, *ASP FR*, I, 678.

policy."[55]   At the same time he continued to receive instructions to cultivate French friendship with zeal and "to remove every suspicion of our preferring a connexion with Great Britain, or in any manner weakening our old attachment to France."[56]

French suspicions were soon confirmed; "like a stroke of thunder," Monroe said, the reports on the Jay treaty "produced upon all France amazement." Jay signed his treaty on November 19, 1794, and on January 5, 1795, the French government announced officially its knowledge of the treaty. In the interval a great deal had happened. Within a week after the treaty had been signed Jay notified Monroe, informing him "that nothing contained in it shall be construed to operate contrary to existing treaties between the United States and other powers"; there was no cause for French anxiety. Then he said, "as the treaty is not ratified, it would be improper to publish it." He did promise, however, to reveal the treaty provisions to Monroe, *confidentially*.[57]

A month later the Committee of Public Safety, in view of the "vague report" concerning "a treaty of alliance and commerce" signed by Jay, invited Monroe to explain as soon as possible what he knew about the treaty. "It is the only means," the Committee said, "whereby you can enable the French Nation justly to appreciate those reports so injurious to the American government and to which that treaty gave birth."[58]   When Monroe accepted the invitation and appeared before the Committee he had not received the letter in which Jay had indicated that he would reveal the contents of the treaty *confidentially*, but had received earlier letters from Jay in

[55] Monroe to Randolph, Paris, Dec. 18, 1794, in Hamilton, *The Writings of James Monroe*, II, 154-163.

[56] Randolph to Monroe, Philadelphia, Dec. 5, 1794, *ASP FR*, I, 690.

[57] Monroe to Jefferson, Paris, June 23, 1795, in Hamilton, *The Writings of James Monroe*, II, 303; in this letter Monroe sketched the state of Franco-American relations, pp. 292-304. Jay to Monroe, London, Nov. 24, 25, 28, 1794, *ibid.*, 169 n., 170 n., 180 n.

[58] Committee of Public Safety to Monroe, Dec. 27, 1794, *ibid.*, II, 169 n. Official French reaction to the signing of the Jay treaty, publicly at least, was at first reserved; see Frances S. Childs, "French Opinion of Anglo-American Relations, 1795-1805," *French-American Review*, I (Jan.-March, 1948), 22. Although it placed the news at the top of the first column on the front page, the official organ of the French government, the *Gazette Nationale ou Moniteur Universel*, Dec. 27, 1794, reported tersely with no comment that Jay and Grenville had signed a treaty of commerce and navigation.

which the latter indicated that the English treaty did not violate treaty obligations to France. Monroe so informed the Committee members. Then, apparently unwittingly, he committed the mistake that was to plague him. "I am altogether ignorant of the particular stipulations of the treaty," he said, "but I beg leave to assure you that as soon as I shall be informed thereof, I will communicate the same to you." Touching on the obligation of the French alliance, he then added, "I take it, however, for granted, that the report is without foundation; for I cannot believe that an American minister would ever forget the connections between the United States and France, which every day's experience demonstrates to be the interest of both Republics still further to cement."[59]

On January 16 Monroe received Jay's letter offering to reveal the treaty contents confidentially. This placed him in an impossible position; he had already rashly pledged to communicate its terms to the French. In his dilemma he sent a personal messenger to Jay for the treaty. In explaining his situation he pointed out "that as nothing will satisfy this government but a copy of the instrument itself, and which, as our ally, it thinks itself entitled to so it will be useless for me to make to it any new communication short of that."[60]

Jay, who had little confidence in Monroe anyway, rejected the request. "It does not belong to ministers who negotiate treaties," he said, "to publish them even when perfected, much less treaties not yet completed, and remaining open to alteration, or rejection."[61] He then sent copies of Monroe's letter and his reply to the Secretary of State.

Resentful of Jay's sarcasm, which he knew was intended more for eyes in Philadelphia than for his own, Monroe too voiced his indig-

[59] Monroe to the Committee of Public Safety, Paris, Dec. 27, 1794, in Hamilton, *The Works of James Monroe*, II, 162-163. Jay, Monroe said, has not "informed me of a single article the treaty contains, nor even the title of it—perhaps because that Gentleman and myself are not in habits of intimacy nor always united in our politics." Dec. 27, 1794, *ibid.*, 163 n. At first the French were satisfied with Monroe's assurances that the Jay treaty was not inconsistent with the 1778 alliance; see, for example, J. Q. Adams to Randolph, The Hague, May 19, 1795, in Ford, *The Writings of John Quincy Adams*, I, 352.
[60] Monroe to Jay, Paris, Jan. 17, 1795, in Hamilton, *The Writings of James Monroe*, II, 180-181; Monroe to Secretary of State, Feb. 1, 1795, National Archives, Dept. of State, Diplomatic Despatches, France.
[61] Jay to Monroe, London, Feb. 5, 1795, *ASP FR*, I, 517.

nation to the Secretary of State. In outlining his difficulties with Jay he emphasized his own embarrassing position and the threat to his reputation and that of the United States in France. While he did not wish to grant the French a right of inspection, he did wish to satisfy them that the treaty did not violate the 1778 alliance. He concluded the defense of his course by saying that "between nations allied as we are, and especially, when past and recent circumstances are considered, I deem it the most magnanimous as well as the soundest policy."[62]

Soon after refusing Monroe's request Jay had his secretary, the artist Colonel John Trumbull, "commit the treaty, verbatim, to memory," and sent him to Paris. There Trumbull informed Monroe that he was authorized to repeat the treaty provided the minister promised "that he would not make any communication of the same to any person whatsoever, especially not to the French government." Jay justified forwarding the information "in *perfect confidence*" on grounds that Monroe was an American minister to whom it might prove useful. Monroe refused to receive the information "upon the terms on which it was offered," and Trumbull withheld his communication. To Monroe the dilemma was painful. "If I accepted and withheld the communication from the committee," he said, "I should violate my engagement with that body; and if I gave it, I subjected myself not only to the probable imputation of indiscretion, but likewise certainly to that of breach of promise."[63]

Trumbull was known to be Jay's secretary, and by his presence in Paris aroused the suspicion of the French government that Monroe knew the contents of the Jay treaty and was engaged in a plot to withhold the information. To counter these misgivings the American minister felt obligated to reveal his correspondence with Jay and so show why the treaty terms had been kept secret. The French replied that the treaty and the secrecy surrounding it, "could not otherwise than excite uneasiness in the councils of this government, when it was observed that in the height of their war with the

---

[62] Monroe to Randolph, Paris, March 17, 1795, in Hamilton, *The Writings of James Monroe,* II, 229-236.

[63] Theodore Sizer, ed., *The Autobiography of Colonel John Trumbull* (New Haven, 1953), p. 185; Jay to Monroe, London, Feb. 19, 1795, *ASP FR,* I, 518; Monroe to Randolph, Paris, April 14, 1795, Hamilton, *The Writings of James Monroe,* II, 238-245.

coalesced powers, and with England in particular, America had stept forward and made a treaty with that power, the contents of which were so carefully and strictly withheld from this government: for if the treaty was not injurious to France, why was it withheld from her? Was it prudent for one ally to act in such manner in regard to another, and especially under the present circumstances, and at the present time, as to excite suspicions of the kind in question?"

Again Monroe assured the French officials that "the treaty contained in it nothing which could give them uneasiness; but if it did, and especially if it weakened our connection with France, it would certainly be disapproved in America." Then, within a few days, he received his first inkling of the treaty terms—a garbled summary from Benjamin Hichborn, a Massachusetts lawyer then in Paris. Monroe suspected Jay's hand behind this as Hichborn said he obtained his information "in some free conversation with Colonel Trumbull." Why, surmised Monroe, should so trustworthy a man as Trumbull disclose the contents to a private individual when he had been instructed to impart them to the American minister who was to be sworn to reveal them to no one else? Hichborn had concluded, moreover, with the obvious hint that "if this information can be of any service to you in your public capacity, you may make use of it in any manner you may think fit."[64]

In spite of the dubious source of this "most informal of all informal communications," Monroe sent Hichborn's letter to the French with the surety "that they might confide in the credibility of the parties." Stressing the innocuous quality of the treaty, Hichborn, in his deceptive summary, said it declared simply "that the parties shall remain at peace." This accorded with the assurances Monroe had been making to the French government, and, apparently, with the impression Trumbull had wished, or had been instructed, to convey.

In the meantime Trumbull remained in Paris, and grasped every opportunity to spread the story that the Jay "treaty contained

---

[64] *Ibid.*, pp. 240-244; Hichborn to Monroe, Paris, March 31, 1795, *ibid.*, 243 n.; Bond, *The Monroe Mission. . .* , pp. 33-35, summarizes the Monroe-Trumbull-Hichborn episode. Fauchet's suspicions also were aroused by the secrecy surrounding the Jay negotiations; see Fauchet to Commissioner of Foreign Relations, Philadelphia, Feb. 4, 1795, in Turner, *CFM*, p. 562.

nothing contrary to the engagement of existing treaties." His continued presence proved galling to French authorities, who so informed the American minister. Monroe, through Hichborn, then advised Trumbull to leave France without delay. Trumbull demurred but finally took up a long-delayed errand to Germany.[65]

Pacified temporarily by Monroe's and Jay's assurances as to the innocuousness of the Jay treaty, but still distrustful of Jay's diplomacy, the French waited to gather more details and remained relatively quiet through the spring of 1795. In Philadelphia developments took on an ominous hue. The administration upheld Jay in his policy of secrecy.[66] Although skeptical that the treaty would be approved as it stood, Randolph informed Monroe that the treaty provided no "reasonable ground for dissatisfaction in the French republic." It would be held secret, he confided, until June 8, 1795, when the Senate would meet to consider it.

On another occasion the Secretary of State had said that "there is no ground for charging that treaty as being offensive or defensive; that the obligation of all prior treaties is *expressly* saved . . . and that the confining of its contents to the President and Secretary of State, is not from any thing sinister towards France, but from the usages in such cases. . . ."[67] Clearly, administration policy was to keep Monroe in the dark until the Jay treaty was ratified and to leave France with the impression that the treaty did nothing to impair the French alliance.

When, despite the administration's policy of secrecy, the treaty contents leaked, Madison passed on information still "a profound secret," to Monroe. "It is possible," he warned, "that articles may be included that will be ominous to the confidence and cordiality of France towards the U. S. . . ."[68] Not until several months had passed did Monroe receive official notice that a copy of the treaty was being sent to him.

[65] Col. John Trumbull to John Jay, London, July 23, 1795, in Johnston, *Jay Correspondence,* IV, 180; Sizer, *The Autobiography of Colonel John Trumbull,* p. 185; Cresson, *James Monroe,* p. 141.

[66] Randolph to John Jay, March 8, 1795, cited in Bond, *The Monroe Mission. . . ,* p. 35.

[67] See Randolph to Monroe, Feb. 15, March 8, April 7, 1795, *ASP FR,* I, 695-696, 699-700, 701.

[68] Madison to Monroe, March 26, 1795, Hamilton, *The Writings of James Monroe,* II, 154 n.-156 n.

Taking cognizance of French uneasiness and of Monroe's fears, Randolph at the same time sent a long review of Franco-American relations from the beginning of the European war, outlining the President's policy and refuting "the imputation of an alienation from France." Among other things, he upheld the policy of secrecy on the Jay treaty, denied any "deception on the French republic," and said that Monroe's instructions, although they did not reveal Jay's full powers, "were commensurate with fact and propriety" and "were *literally* true" because the motives behind the Jay mission "*were* the vexations of our commerce and the posts." Anticipating trouble, he concluded with the plea that "if injuries are complained of, let us reason together like cordial allies; and compensate where either may have been in fault. But let it be the last blot in the annals of the world, that the United States and France cease to be, what they ought to be, friends, who will endure no separation."[69]

When finally the Secretary of State did forward the treaty with a note of his exchanges with Pierre Auguste Adet, the new French minister in the United States, concerning it, he followed up with comments on the unpopularity of the treaty in the United States. Expressing doubt that the President would ratify the treaty, he concluded that "the present may be well considered as a crisis, taken either upon the supposition of a ratification or rejection."[70] The tenor of these last letters, obviously, was far different from the correspondence in the period of secrecy. They reflected administration knowledge that Monroe was in a difficult position in France and needed ammunition for defense of a treaty the administration had told him repeatedly did no violence to the French alliance.

In those summer months Monroe's position deteriorated. "My situation," he said, "since the report of Mr. Jay's treaty has been painful beyond any thing ever experienc'd before. . . . I have, however, done everything in my power to keep things where they shod. be, but how long this will be practicable under existing circumstances I know not."[71] Meanwhile French distrust mounted. Monroe's

[69] Randolph to Monroe, June 1, 1795, *ASP FR,* I, 705-712; the italics are Randolph's. Bond, *The Monroe Mission. . . ,* p. 50, maintains that the Secretary of State's words proved intentional deception by the administration toward Monroe and the French.

[70] See Randolph to Monroe, Philadelphia, July 14, 21, 1795, *ASP FR,* I, 719.

[71] Monroe to Jefferson, Paris, June 27, 1795, in Hamilton, *The Writings of James Monroe,* II, 311.

friendship for France had been insincere, some Frenchmen thought. His assurances of American friendship, in the face of administration policy, smacked of nothing more than a diplomatic ruse to cover an Anglo-American *rapprochement*.[72] During this period of increasing tension Monroe, in spite of the obstacles in his way, attempted to carry out other parts of his instructions.

* * * * *

Of prime importance among these was that concerning navigation of the Mississippi. Despite the difficulties over the Jay negotiations Monroe for a while succeeded in securing French support for the American case. French assistance in gaining freedom of the Mississippi, he said, would go far in proving that French friendship for the United States exceeded that of England, and would strengthen the 1778 alliance.[73] As a result of Monroe's behavior in the earlier Gardoqui episode the French government used him in opening peace negotiations with Spain and promised in the peace negotiations at Basel to press the American side in the Mississippi controversy.[74]

When Thomas Pinckney, the newly appointed American minister to Spain, arrived in Paris on his way to Madrid, Monroe briefed him on the state of the Mississippi question and suggested that he go to the French and request their assistance in his coming negotiations with Spain. Knowing the terms of the Jay treaty, Pinckney shied from this. Monroe had advised that he assure the French the Jay treaty contained nothing injurious to France; Pinckney responded he could not do that without exposing the contents of the still-secret treaty. If he did reveal the treaty provisions, French

[72] See Fauchet to Committee of Public Safety, Philadelphia, April 3, 1795, Turner, *CFM,* p. 619.

[73] See Monroe to the Committee of Public Safety, Paris, Jan. 25, 1795; also "Notes Respecting the River Mississippi," Paris, Jan. 25, 1795, in Hamilton, *The Writings of James Monroe,* II, 182-186.

[74] Monroe to Randolph, Paris, March 6, 1795, postscript of March 9 and the note, J. C. Mountflorence to Monroe, n.p., n.d., *ibid.,* pp. 228-229 and 228 n.-229 n.; Monroe to William Short, Paris, May 30, 1795, *ibid.,* pp. 289-290. For more details on the Mississippi question, see Beverly W. Bond, Jr., "Monroe's Efforts to Secure Free Navigation of the Mississippi River during His Mission to France, 1795-1796," *Publications of the Mississippi Historical Society,* IX (1906), 255-262; Bond, *The Monroe Mission. . . ,* pp. 36-41.

assistance in his negotiations, it appeared, would vanish.[75] When the French did learn what the Jay treaty provided, they suspected the worst of Spanish-American negotiations in Madrid, linking them to the devious diplomacy of the Jay treaty.

Even though the French had promised Monroe they would try to win navigation of the Mississippi for the United States from Spain "in reliance that our treaty with England contained nothing injurious to France," they had from the first feared that Pinckney sought an alliance from Spain whereby the United States would obtain Louisiana and the Floridas. Such acquisitions ran counter to French policy; such an aggrandizement would place Anglo-Americans in control of Mississippi commerce upon which French colonies relied.[76]

In their negotiations at Basel, therefore, the French made a determined effort to recover Louisiana from Spain, bearing hard on Spain's fears of American aggression. If Spain returned Louisiana to France, the negotiators pointed out, France would close the Mississippi to check American expansion westward.[77] Monroe, in placing too much faith in the bond of the French alliance, was, it appeared, naïve in believing that France would assist the United States to gain free use of the Mississippi.

In their appraisal of French motives, the British were closer to the mark. As Phineas Bond pointed out, the French would not assist Americans in obtaining free usage of the Mississippi when that usage under the Jay treaty would also accrue to the British.[78] Yet the British also feared that Pinckney would make an alliance with Spain for navigation of the Mississippi. Secretary of State Timothy Pickering put them at ease by saying "that as it has been the Policy of this Government to avoid every sort of compact and Connexion which might implicate it in Disputes with the European

[75] Monroe to Randolph, Paris, June 14, 1795, to Madison, Paris, Sept. 8, 1795, in Hamilton, *The Writings of James Monroe*, II, 283-284, 355.
[76] See Monroe's "A View of the Conduct of the Executive," *ibid.*, III, 412-414; "Extrait de deux memoires de le passage qui traitent de St. Domingue et de La Louisiane," AAE CP EU, n.p., n.d., Vol. XLVII, ff. 179-180.
[77] See Le Comité de Salut Public a Barthélemy, Paris, Sept. 16, 19, 1795, in Kaulek, *Papiers de Berthélemy*, VI, 150-151, 155; see also instructions, May 12, 14, 1795, *ibid.*, pp. 25, 27.
[78] Bond to Grenville, Philadelphia, Dec. 20, 1795, No. 20, Henry Adams Transcripts.

Nations, the necessity of pursuing this system of Conduct was more
and more felt, and would be persisted in to the total Rejection of
all defensive Alliances." Then Pickering criticized the French alliance, adverting "to the great inconvenience which it had occassioned
in this Country," ascribing the alliance "to the particular Exigencies
at the Moment it was made, and to the impossibility of foreseeing
the Embarrassments which it had produced."[79]

Even though Monroe believed otherwise, neither his diplomacy
nor French aid contributed to the success of Pinckney's treaty. As
a contemporary Federalist viewed the situation, an exhausted Spain
had made peace with France, violating her alliance with Great Britain. Fearing British vengeance, she wished to stand well with the
United States. Events beyond the control of American diplomacy
made possible the favorable Pinckney treaty.[80]

* * * * *

As Franco-American relations deteriorated and as Monroe became convinced of his untenable position under the Federalist administration, he turned more and more to his Republican friends.[81]
Monroe was buttressed in his anti-British, antiadministration, and
pro-French views by letters from his Republican friends, recounting
in one way or another the violent opposition to the Jay treaty in the
United States.[82] In his own letters to them he justified his conduct

[79] Bond to Grenville, Philadelphia, Jan. 2, 1796, No. 1, *ibid*.

[80] William Vans Murray Papers, Commonplace Book, March 10, 1796
(Princeton). Pinckney maintained that whatever French aid had been prom-
ised at Madrid was revoked when France learned of the Jay treaty contents
and that he did not seek French aid because of the Jay treaty dissatisfaction.
Rufus King's note of Aug. 30, 1796, in King, *Rufus King Correspondence*,
II, 82. See also Frederick J. Turner, "The Policy of France toward the Missis-
sippi Valley in the Period of Washington and Adams," *AHR*, X, 67; Arthur
P. Whitaker, "The Retrocession of Louisiana in Spanish Policy," *AHR*,
XXXIX (April, 1934), p. 459; and Whitaker's *The Spanish-American Fron-
tier*, pp. 203-207; Bemis, *Pinckney's Treaty*, pp. 278-279.

[81] See Monroe to Jefferson, Paris, June 23, 30, 1795, in Hamilton, *The Writings of James Monroe*, II, 292-304, 310-312; Bond, *The Monroe Mission. . . ,*
pp. 46-48.

[82] Despite his untenable position Monroe maintained that he did not resign
because by so doing, "I should not only have admitted the misconduct of the
administration . . . but likewise my own, since it would have exposed me to
the suspicion of having accepted the trust to serve a particular purpose, and
withdrawing after that was accomplished." By remaining he thought he

and attacked administration policy. His criticisms, which made excellent political propaganda, received wide circulation in the United States. Basically, he expressed distrust of England and the conviction that the sheet anchor of American foreign policy was the French alliance. These letters, counteracting news from France written from the British viewpoint, were even printed in the press.[83] No administration could long tolerate such activities on the part of one of its diplomats.

Despite Monroe's efforts, as summer faded so did the French alliance. In August American newspapers arrived with the text of the Jay treaty and with accounts of the Senate's approval. After reading the press versions Monroe feared the treaty would sweep away the foundations of Franco-American amity. Yet he did not lose all hope, believing still "that if timely and suitable attempt be made to engage the aid of this government [France] in support of our claims upon England it may be accomplished upon fair and houourable terms."[84]

Privately, he blasted the treaty in detail, saying that "no body will I presume attempt to vindicate the head which dictated it." Labeling it "one of the most extraordinary transactions of modern times," he said it formed "an important epoch in the history of our country." The belief that President Washington would not ratify the document remained his main consolation. In place of the treaty, which contained not "one single stipulation in our favor," he suggested seizure of British possessions in America—the Northwest posts, Bermuda, Canada—to gain respect in France and in Great Britain. In Monroe's words such action would be "a decisive and powerful diversion in favour of France," a tangible support to the French alliance.[85]

might stave off French reprisals. Monroe's "A View of the Conduct of the Executive," in Hamilton, *The Writings of James Monroe*, III, 416.

[83] Monroe offered to supply the Republican press with regular despatches of developments in France. Monroe to George Logan, Paris, June 24, 1795 [dated incorrectly 1796], in Hamilton, *The Writings of James Monroe*, III, 6-7; Marsh, "John Beckley. . . ," *The Pennsylvania Magazine of History and Biography*, LXXII, 58-59.

[84] Monroe to Secretary of State, Paris, Aug. 17, 1795, No. 20, National Archives, Dept. of State, Diplomatic Despatches, France.

[85] Monroe to Secretary of State, Paris, Sept. 8, 1795, No. 24, *ibid.;* Monroe to Madison, Paris, Sept. 8, 1795, in Hamilton, *The Writings of James Monroe*, II, 347-359.

Not far from Paris another American diplomat, John Quincy Adams, also received letters "and papers with accounts of popular movements in opposition to the [Jay] treaty." Although the popular reaction was not unexpected, he responded far differently from Monroe. Indeed, the news gave him "great anxiety" and "solicitude," since he believed the violent opposition to the treaty renewed the danger of war which he had hoped had blown over. "It is a danger," he told his father, "so much the more formidable, because I believe the intention is to draw the United States into it [the European war], merely to make tools of them, in order to procure advantageous terms for others, who would leave us in the well, after using our weight to get themselves out of it. It would be a war in which we should have everything to lose and nothing to gain; a war commenced against the will of almost the whole people, and which therefore under such a government as ours could not be carried on with success."

Distrustful of the French and certain that they wished to draw the United States into the war for their own selfish reasons, Adams also believed that " the conduct of the British government is so well adapted to increasing our danger of war, that I cannot but suppose they are secretly inclined to produce it." Yet he doubted that in case of conflict with Great Britain the French alliance would be of much value, that "the French government would be disposed to contract any engagements which would bind them to a common cause with us. They would give us as many fair words as we could wish, but would stipulate nothing without a consideration more than adequate to it. But if they should even tempt us by the most unlimited obligations of inseparable participation, the present state of their affairs is such as can inspire but little confidence in the permanency of their cooperation." Then he said "the only safe connection that can exist with them is that which would not be liable to follow the fate of their internal revolutions."[86]

In Paris Monroe, although he received no immediate official pro-

[86] John Q. Adams to John Adams, The Hague, Sept. 12, 1795, in Ford, *The Writings of John Quincy Adams*, I, 408-417. Earlier young Adams had sounded similar warnings that France sought to make use of the United States as she did the conquered Dutch provinces, "that is, as an instrument for the benefit of France, as a passive weapon in her hands against her most formidable enemy." To John Adams, The Hague, May 22, 1795, *ibid.*, p. 356.

test from the French government, did not remain long in ignorance of the French reaction to the Jay treaty. "Believe me," he said, "that since the reports of that treaty transpired I have rested on a bed of thorns." Later he wrote that "the appearance of the treaty excited the general disgust of France against the American government," a disgust which "diminished" as knowledge of the violent American reaction against the treaty became known in France. Early in October he learned directly that the French foreign office considered the Jay treaty "as injurious to France." By promising to deliver a copy of the expected Adet-Randolph correspondence dealing with the treaty, Monroe on this occasion headed off a formal protest by the French.[87]

Within a few weeks Fauchet arrived in Paris, "extremely dissatisfied" with the Jay treaty; he confirmed the incredible news that Washington had ratified it.[88] At the same time the French government changed; the Directory succeeded the National Convention. Not until the beginning of December did Monroe receive official confirmation of Fauchet's news. At that time Timothy Pickering, who had succeeded the now disgraced Randolph as acting Secretary of State, so informed him. In his first communication, because unfavorable French reaction "may be apprehended," Pickering outlined his reasons why France had no valid grievances. "In our new engagements we violate no prior obligation," he said, and stressed *"that the negociation has not proceeded from any predilection in our Government towards Great Britain."* In defense of his conduct, Monroe responded bitterly, pointing out that "the course of events" had placed him "in a very delicate and embarrassing dilemma."[89]

As the year 1796 opened Franco-American relations were on the

[87] Monroe's "A View of the Conduct of the Executive," in Hamilton, *The Writings of James Monroe,* III, 422, 425-426; see also the note of J. H. Purviance, Paris, Aug., 1796, pp. 426 n.-427 n.

[88] *Moniteur* (Paris), Nov. 16, 1795, carried the news of ratification with no comment. The next day and thereafter it carried reports of American criticism and expressed doubt that the treaty would be implemented. *Moniteur,* March 29, 1796. According to the official French view the American people did not want the treaty; obviously, therefore, it was the result of British intrigue and collusion with the Washington administration. Cited in Childs, "French Opinion of Anglo-American Relations. . . ," *FAR,* I, 23.

[89] Pickering to Monroe, Dept. of State, Sept. 12, 1795, *ASP FR,* I, 596-598; Monroe to Pickering, Paris, Nov. 5, Dec. 6, 1795, in Hamilton, *The Writings of James Monroe,* II, 410, 422-427.

verge of collapse.   In January Randolph's *Vindication* reached
France; its uncomplimentary references to the French Revolution
added to French dissatisfaction.   Then the text of Washington's
December address to the opening session of Congress arrived.   In
it the President discussed foreign affairs, touched upon the Jay treaty,
but omitted any favorable or even specific reference to France.   This
oversight or slight, according to Monroe, disturbed the French government.[90]

With no evidence of attempted conciliation of the affronted
French by the Washington government, the expected reprisal was
not long in coming.   In the middle of February the Minister of
Foreign Affairs informed Monroe that the Directory considered
the Franco-American alliance as "ceasing to exist" from the moment
the Jay treaty was ratified, that it would recall the French minister
to the United States and would send a special envoy to Philadelphia
to present the abrogation of the alliance.   In the French view the
Jay treaty aligned the United States with the anti-French "coalesced
powers."[91]   France appeared determined to break off diplomatic
relations.

France's warlike threat was soon picked up by others, exaggerated, and relayed to Philadelphia. Gouverneur Morris wrote privately to Washington that "a fleet is to conduct to you the new
french Minister, who will be directed to exact in the Space of fifteen
Days a categorical Answer to certain Questions.   What these are I
can only conjecture but suppose that you will, in effect, be called
on to take Part decidedly with France.   Mr. Munroe [*sic*] will no
Doubt endeavor to convince the Rulers of that Country that such
Conduct will force us into the War against them, but it is far from
impossible that the usual Violence of their Councils will prevail."[92]

Alarmed, Washington turned to Hamilton, now a private citizen,
for counsel.   Among other things, he feared the rumored ultimatum
might demand the "dissolution of the Alliance," or the repudiation
of the Jay treaty, with war as the alternative.   "Were it not for the

[90] Monroe's "A View of the Conduct of the Executive," *ibid.*, III, 436; for
Washington's address, Dec. 8, 1795, see *ASP FR*, I, 27-29.
[91] Monroe to Pickering, Paris, Feb. 16, 1796, in Hamilton, *The Writings
of James Monroe*, II, 454-456.
[92] Morris to Washington, March 4, 1796, in Fitzpatrick, *Washington's
Writings*, XXXV, 38 n.

unhappy differences among ourselves," he said, *"my* answer wd. be short and decisive, to this effect. We are an Independent Nation, and act for ourselves." Then he added, "we will not be dictated to by the Politics of any Nation under Heaven, farther than Treaties require of us." This situation has "been brought on us by the misconduct of some of our own intemperate people; who seemed to have preferred throwing themselves into the Arms of France . . . to that manly, and Neutral conduct which is so essential, and would so well become us, as an Independent Nation." Washington's view that disloyal Americans had brought on the difficulties with France was not unique; other Federalists shared it and echoed it in the press.[93]

Hamilton, stating in his reply to the President that there was "nothing in it [the Jay treaty] to change the nature of our relations with France," advised that, if France insisted on repudiation of the Jay treaty, the answer should be that such repudiation would be "too humiliating and injurious to allow us to believe that the expectation can be persisted in by France, since it is to require a thing impossible, and to establish, as a price of the continuance of friendship with us, the sacrifice of our honor by an act of perfidy, which would destroy the value of our friendship to any nation." If France should claim that the treaty violated the principle of free ships, free goods, "the answer," Hamilton suggested, could be that the Executive is disposed to enter a new negotiation for a new treaty to modify the 1778 treaties, "so as may consist with a due regard to mutual interest and the circumstances of parties." Referring specifically to the alliance, he added that "if the guarantee of the West Indies should be claimed, the answer may be 'that the decision of this question belongs to Congress, who, if it be desired, will be convened to deliberate upon it.' I presume and hope they will have adjourned—for to gain time is every thing."[94] Fortunately, Washington was never forced to follow Hamilton's advice; the French ultimatum was never delivered; the alliance was never put to that critical test.

[93] Washington to Hamilton, Philadelphia, May 8, 1796, *ibid.,* pp. 38-41; extract from a letter of an American citizen dated Paris, Feb. 14, 1796, in the *New Hampshire and Vermont Journal: Or, The Farmer's Weekly Museum* (Walpole, N. H.), May 31, 1796.

[94] Hamilton to Washington, New York, May 20, 1796, in Hamilton, ed., *Hamilton's Works,* VI, 122-125.

Meanwhile, astounded by the French blow, Monroe had acted to divert it. Arguing that the French action would smack of war, that it would convey to the world that "the issue of war and peace was suspended on the issue of the mission," he pointed out that it would give comfort to the enemies of both countries who alone would profit by destruction of the Franco-American alliance. The French minister countered that "independently of any treaty with England," which treaty "annihilated" the 1778 treaties, "France had much cause of complaint against" the United States; that under the circumstances his government's action was "mild" and that France "had rather have a [*sic*] open enemy than a perfidious friend."[95]

Monroe made clear that France would have just such an open enemy if she persisted in this harsh policy. Realizing that sentiment for strong measures had taken firm hold in French councils, he had explained confidentially that such drastic measures were not necessary to make the United States change its French policy. "You well know," he told Charles Delacroix, the French foreign minister, "the number of your friends in America is considerable, and that this number is daily increasing. . . . At the present moment they are acting with great energy in America in your favor. . . . They wish to serve you but having no fleet they see not the means. But the moment you take a step of that eclat against them denouncing as it were the whole nation to the world, for you cannot distinguish between the government and the People, and pressing a crisis in their affairs, it merits consideration whether it would not rather dampen their spirits and diminish their zeal in your favor rather than increase it."

Such action, Monroe said, "would do harm both to you and to us, and certainly no good. Left to ourselves everything will I think be satisfactorily arranged and perhaps in the course of the present year: and it is always more grateful to make such arrangements ourselves than to be pressed to it." In other words Monroe implied that the coming elections (1796) in the United States would bring a pro-French Republican administration to power. "If you will cast

[95] Monroe to Pickering, Paris, Feb. 20, 1796, in Hamilton, *The Writings of James Monroe*, II, 457-460; to Madison, Paris, Feb. 27, 1796, *ibid.*, pp. 460-463.

your eyes upon the United States at the present moment," he said, "you will see them actually in the convulsions of a great crisis, and which is occasioned by this treaty with England and you may be sensible that the injuries we have received from England in the seizure of our vessels, and other outrages whilst you have shewn a different conduct, towards us, tend greatly to increase our attachment to you, whilst it excites our indignation against her."[96]

This argument, although unofficial and unknown to Monroe's superiors, impressed Delacroix. Particularly effective was the point that 1796 was a crisis election year in the United States. After the election, reasoned the French, we can always return to our stern policy if the results are not to our liking. The French government agreed to send its representations to the United States "through the ordinary channel," and, as Monroe had requested officially, to present him with its specific complaints.[97]

Monroe headed off the sending of a special envoy, not by defending, but by undermining administration foreign policy. Unorthodox and unauthorized though it was, Monroe's diplomacy did avert a crisis the government was unprepared to meet. The French minister in the United States reported that the decision not to send a special envoy calmed the fears of the Washington administration and that Secretary of State Pickering behaved like a schoolboy putting on a courageous front in asserting France would not dare take vigorous action against the United States because she needed American friendship.[98]

Pickering's attitude had not been all bravado. Lord Grenville, Great Britain's Secretary for Foreign Affairs, had heard the same rumor that Gouverneur Morris had forwarded to President Washington. Acting promptly, he had instructed Robert Liston, the new British minister in Philadelphia, "to assure the American Govern-

[96] Monroe to Minister of Foreign Affairs, Paris, Feb. 17, 1796, AAE CP EU, Vol. XLV, ff. 146-147; a portion of this document is quoted in Bemis, "Washington's Farewell Address. . . , AHR, XXXIX, 258.

[97] "Observations sur la lettre de M. Monroe, au Ministre de Relations Extérieure," n.p., n.d., AAE CP EU, Vol. XLV, ff. 148-149. To Pickering Monroe reported that his efforts to prevent the French special mission were successful without explaining why. Paris, March 10, 1796, in Hamilton, *The Writings of James Monroe*, II, 463-464.

[98] Adet to Minister of Foreign Relations, Philadelphia, June 16, 1796, in Turner, *CFM*, pp. 922-923.

ment that, if France should commence Hostilities against it" as a result of the Jay treaty, Great Britain "will be ready to enter into such engagements with the United States as may appear best calculated to repel an aggression of this nature and to make common Cause against an Attack which can be dictated by no other motive than by a desire, to prevent the Establishment of a good understanding between Great Britain and the United States and grounded on no other hope than that of exciting internal discontents" in America.

Grenville instructed Liston to encourage the Washington government and the "well disposed party" (Federalists) to resist French pressures. This was precisely what Federalists wanted. In Hamilton's phrase, "a frigate or two to serve as convoys would not be amiss. If the English had been wise, they would neither have harrassed our trade themselves, nor suffered their trade with us to be harrassed. They would see this a happy moment for conciliating us by a clever little squadron in our ports and on our coast." Then he added, "a *hint* might not perhaps do harm."[99]

In Paris, on March 11, 1796, the Minister of Foreign Affairs presented Monroe with a summary of French grievances. Under three main headings he listed specific complaints against the United States, beginning with "the inexecution of treaties." The second heading dealt with "the impunity of the outrage made to the [French] republic" by the arrest of Fauchet in American waters by the British, and the third covered the Jay treaty in which the United States "have sacrificed, *knowingly* and *evidently,* their connexion with the republic; and the rights, the most essential and least contested, of neutrality."

Under the first head the French charged that the United States had by various interpretations of its neutrality policy deprived them of treaty-conferred maritime advantages in American ports. Specifically, they stressed alleged violations of certain articles of the commercial treaty and of the consular convention of 1788. They complained that while they should have benefited as a matter of treaty right from an American policy of benevolent neutrality, they did

[99] Grenville to Liston, Downing Street, March 18, 1796, No. 2, Secret, in Mayo, *Instructions to the British Ministers to the United States, AHA Ann. Rep.* (1936), III, 113-114; Hamilton to Oliver Wolcott, Jr., June 15, 1796, in Lodge, *The Works of Alexander Hamilton*, VIII, 404.

not; whereas Great Britain, their enemy who had no such treaty rights, did benefit.

The second heading was self-explanatory. In the third the French minister struck at American policy with vigor and logic. He contended that, by acquiescing in and accepting in treaty form Great Britain's large-navy maritime principles, the United States had abandoned its principles of small-navy neutrality and had injured France, its ally. Specifically, by agreeing in the Jay treaty to extend the contraband list to include provisions, the United States acknowledged England's paper blockade of French colonies and of France herself. Jay's treaty, he concluded, thus violated neutrality as accepted by the smaller maritime powers and vitiated the treaty of alliance because the United States had contracted to defend French Caribbean possessions, not to acquiesce in their blockade.[100]

Monroe's response in defense of American conduct was long and specific. Although he did not deny the basic charges, he did stress extenuating circumstances. Referring to the Jay treaty and the status of American neutrality, he pointed out that while small-navy principles of neutrality were still "extremely dear" to the United States, England had never "acceded to them." How, he asked, could the United States, alone and without a fleet, compel powerful England to recognize those principles? And if it was impossible for the United States to force Britain to respect those principles, then the American government was not at fault. Despite his argument Monroe could not have believed that the United States was free from fault, as the French complaints were, in substance, similar to those he himself had made against the Jay treaty.[101] He had, moreover, admitted to the French his own view that administration policy was wrong and should be changed.

When the French charges and Monroe's reply reached Philadelphia, Pickering declared officially that the American minister's statement was "sufficient to obviate" the charges although "a more forci-

---

[100] Minister of Foreign Affairs to Monroe, Paris, March 11, 1796, *ASP FR*, I, 732-733; "Exposé sommaire des griefs de la république française contre le Gouvernment des états unis de l'amérique," by the Minister of Foreign Affairs, dated Paris, March 9, 1796, AAE CP EU, Vol. XLV, ff. 232-325; see also Bemis, *Jay's Treaty. . .*, p. 267.

[101] Monroe to Minister of Foreign Affairs, Paris, March 15 and 20, 1796, in Hamilton, *The Writings of James Monroe*, II, 467-482; Monroe to Pickering, Paris, May 2, 1796, *ibid.*, pp. 489-492.

ble explanation" might have been expected. Privately, however, the acting Secretary of State told President Washington that the "statement is as feeble as could have been desired," and that it confirmed the suspicions of several months that Monroe's "ominous letters" were part of a plot to advance "party purposes" in the United States. Implicit in the "solemn farce," he said, were defeat of the Jay treaty, a change in administration, and possibly war with England. Pickering, in effect, accused Monroe of working against his own government and discredited his diplomacy.[102]

* * * * *

In Paris, too, Monroe's diplomacy became more and more discredited. For a while he heard nothing from the Directory; internal affairs and the war in Europe commanded its full attention. Then in June the French learned that the House of Representatives had supported Washington's administration and had voted to implement the Jay treaty. All hope that the Americans would not put the treaty into force was now gone; the treaty was an accomplished fact.[103] In keeping with French objections, the Minister of Foreign Affairs then informed Monroe officially that the Jay treaty, "concluded in the midst of hostilities," had broken the 1778 alliance, had ended Franco-American friendship and American neutrality, and had terminated the commercial treaty. The Directory therefore considered the treaty stipulations concerning neutrality "as altered and suspended." Although Monroe challenged the Directory's action he did not deny that the Jay treaty was advantageous to France's enemy and injurious to France.[104]

Still clinging to the conviction that it was to the advantage of the United States not to break with France, Monroe, working in the dark, uncertain as to how long he could bear what he termed his mortifying situation, strove to prevent a complete rupture. He warned Pickering that French discontent had rooted deeply and

[102] Pickering to Washington, July 21, 1796, *ibid.*, p. 482 n.

[103] See Monroe to Pickering, Paris, May 25, 1796, June 12, 28, 1796, and Monroe to Delacroix, [June 26, 28, 1796], *ibid.*, III, 1-6, 9 n.-10 n.

[104] Delacroix to Monroe, Paris, July 7, 1796, Monroe to the Minister of Foreign Affairs, Paris, July 14, 1796, *ASP FR*, I, 739-740; Bond, *The Monroe Mission. . .* , p. 70.

that French officials wanted to give the United States some signal proof of it.[105] He also managed to block the appointment of Mangourit as *chargé d'affaires* in the United States to replace Adet. To send Mangourit to Philadelphia would have insulted the Washington government.[106]

Monroe's success was transitory. He heard rumors that new French reprisals were in the making, among them "seizures of neutral vessels destined for England." Then followed the blow he had labored most to avoid. The Directory recalled Adet without appointing a successor and declared "that the customary relations between the two nations shall cease." The reason advanced for this was the Jay treaty—the honor of France, it was claimed, would be tarnished if she acted otherwise. Monroe, although professing not to see the full consequences of the French action, did see that "if the same councils prevail in America the alliance is at an end." There was little doubt as to Monroe's personal feelings. "I have detained them seven months," he said, "from doing what they ought to have done at once."[107]

Not until October did the French notify Monroe officially of the reprisals; the delay, he concluded, was intentional. With the official communication the French gave him a copy of the July decree authorizing their warships to deal with American vessels "as these suffer the English to treat them." This, in effect, repudiated the commercial treaty of 1778 in which France had agreed to observe "freedom of the seas" toward neutral United States. The note, in addition, revealed that he had taken too pessimistic a view of the French actions. "Ordinary relations," the French told him, were not to be suspended; they were to be conducted by the consuls. The French did not want a complete rupture; what they wanted was to break the United States' recent accord with Great Britain and to drive it

---

[105] Monroe to Pickering, Paris, July 24, 1796 [dated incorrectly, 1797], No. 36, National Archives, Dept. of State, Diplomatic Despatches, France.

[106] Monroe to Madison, Paris, July 5, 1796, Monroe to Pickering, Paris, Aug. 4, 15, 1796, in Hamilton, *The Writings of James Monroe*, III, 23-25, 48-51, 51 n. Oliver Wolcott, Jr., of Mangourit: "The violence of this man's character, if he has been in fact appointed, is no good omen." To Oliver Wolcott, Sr., Philadelphia, Oct. 17, 1796, in Gibbs, ed., *Wolcott Papers*, I, 387.

[107] Monroe to Pickering, Aug. 27, 1796; to Madison, Paris, Sept. 1, 1796, in Hamilton, *The Writings of James Monroe*, III, 51 n.-52 n., 52-54.

back into the French camp.[108] The French timed their retaliation, moreover, so as to influence the presidential campaign then being waged, a campaign, as Monroe had pointed out, critical to the survival of the alliance.

* * * * *

In Philadelphia administration dissatisfaction with Monroe and his diplomacy culminated in a successful movement to recall him. Such dissatisfaction had early been apparent to Monroe; but he stayed on, he claimed, to prevent the rupture between France and the United States which he dreaded.[109] That such a rupture would have meant war had it not been for Monroe's dubious but effective diplomacy seems clear. While the Directory was split over the severity of its policy toward the United States, at least one Director, Lazare Nicholas Marguerite Carnot, pushed vigorously for war. Having won access to the Directors, Monroe parried the war sentiment with convincing arguments, particularly with the argument that war between France and the United States would drive America into England's waiting arms. The French alliance would then be supplanted by an English alliance.[110] Playing for time, he hoped that in the 1796 election Jefferson would win the Presidency and preserve peace with France.

Monroe's play for time had not taken into account the sharp pen of Timothy Pickering. Even though Monroe realized that his own politics were in opposition to those of the administration and that his diplomacy was not above criticism, he was stunned by Pickering's biting censure of June, 1796, which he described as being addressed "as from an overseer on the farm to one of his gang."[111] Pickering charged Monroe with responsibility for the dangerous state of French relations. The American minister, he said, had failed to explain the views of the administration on the Jay treaty, which

[108] Delacroix to Monroe, Paris, Oct. 7, 1796, Monroe to Pickering, Paris, Oct. 6, 21, 1796, *ASP FR*, I, 745; Bond, *The Monroe Mission. . .* , p. 72.

[109] Monroe to Madison, Paris, July 5, 1796, in Hamilton, *The Writings of James Monroe*, III, 22-23. Monroe thought that Pickering sought a rupture with France.

[110] Louis Marie Larevellière-Lépeaux, *Mémoires de Larevellière-Lépeaux* (3 vols., Paris, 1895), II, 257-260.

[111] Monroe to Madison, Paris, Sept. 1, 1796, in Hamilton, *The Writings of James Monroe*, III, 53.

if effectively presented must have served the purpose "of removing objections and dispelling jealousies" in the French government. Pickering further pointed out that the President "expressly" preferred written communications between Monroe and the French government to personal interviews; he wanted Monroe to transmit complete copies of all communications to Philadelphia.[112]

Federalist plans to replace Monroe had long been brewing.[113] Opponents had attacked his diplomacy and had subjected his personal conduct to innuendo. Rumors, in Alexander Hamilton's phrase, were "industriously circulated" that the American minister in Paris had engaged in French speculations, "largely in French confiscated estates," and that he had mismanaged government funds.[114] Washington, too, was aroused by personal grievance against Monroe. He suspected the American minister of being involved somehow in the situation whereby a personal letter from the President to Gouverneur Morris fell into the hands of the Directory. Using the letter to discomfit the President, the Directory hinted that it contained evidence of American surrender to English hegemony.[115] Another source of irritation seemingly fostered by Monroe stemmed from the 1796 Fourth of July celebration in Paris in which he participated. The Americans present quarreled over a

[112] Pickering to Monroe, Dept. of State, June 13, 1796, *ASP FR*, I, 737-738. For Monroe's reply, see his letter to Pickering of Sept. 10, 1796, in Hamilton, *The Writings of James Monroe*, III, 54-62. Monroe answered that the charge was "unjust and unexpected" and that the supporting evidence was "inapplicable and inconclusive."

[113] The English, too, had wanted Monroe removed. After he had completed negotiations for the treaty with England, Jay had suggested the recall of George Hammond from Philadelphia. Lord Grenville agreed but coupled compliance with the suggestion that Monroe be recalled from Paris. Bemis, *John Quincy Adams and the Foundations of American Foreign Policy*, p. 70.

[114] Hamilton to Wolcott, Jr., New York, June 9, 1796, in Lodge, *The Works of Alexander Hamilton*, VIII, 403; William Vans Murray Papers, Commonplace Book, Dec. 10, 1795 (Princeton). Monroe was hit hard by the rumors. See Monroe to George Clinton, Paris, July 25, 1796, in Hamilton, *The Writings of James Monroe*, III, 36-39. Yet he had been warned by friends that his enemies would use the charge of speculation in working for his recall. Bond, *The Monroe Mission. . .* , pp. 77-78.

[115] Monroe to Washington, March 24, 1796, in Hamilton, *The Writings of James Monroe*, II, 483; Washington to Monroe, Philadelphia, Aug. 25, 1796, to Pickering, Philadelphia, Sept. 12, 1796, in Fitzpatrick, *Washington's Writings*, XXXV, 187-190, 208-210.

toast to President Washington; the outcome was uncomplimentary to the President and unsavory for the American minister.[116]

Dissatisfaction with his personal and political conduct led Cabinet members and highly placed Federalists through spring and summer of 1796 to advocate Monroe's recall. French relations, Hamilton said, were "extremely serious. The government must play a skilful card, or all is lost"; it must immediately set out "in earnest about averting the storm." To do that it must recall Monroe; "we must stop the channels by which foreign poison is introduced into the country," warned Oliver Wolcott, Jr., "or suffer the government to be overturned."[117] "A new minister," reasoned Federalists, "will be able to conciliate this late event [the Jay treaty], with explanation, with the duties the U. S. owe as an ally to France."[118]

Hamilton had in mind several replacements for Monroe, all Federalists. Some Federalists thought "the measure has been too long delayed because they fully believe that the french [*sic*] Executive has been *invited to bully* us for daring to be so independent as to be just to ourselves." Unfortunately "for our own country," such Federalists lamented, "a fact of this kind however true is not very susceptible of proof." Yet, they pointed out, "it has been frequently said by Americans coming from France that the execrations of our government were confined chiefly to that circle of society of which Mr. M[onroe] was the center—whatever may be the final destiny of our national system it cannot be doubted that those who are entrusted with the administration will have the concurrence of every honest citizen in displacing fruitless officers & disgracing treacherous ones."[119]

Pickering let no opportunity evade him whereby he could impress upon Washington the advisability of replacing Monroe. His tactics in the John Churchman episode, for example, followed a

[116] Monroe to Madison, Paris, July 5, 1796, in Hamilton, *The Writings of James Monroe*, III, 19-20; this episode long plagued Monroe; see Monroe to Enoch Edwards, Albemarle, Feb. 12, 1798, *ibid.*, pp. 98-100.

[117] Oliver Wolcott, Jr., to Alexander Hamilton, Philadelphia, June 14, 17, 1796, in Gibbs, ed., *Wolcott Papers*, I, 359, 361; Hamilton to Wolcott, Jr., New York, June 15, 1796, in Lodge, *The Works of Alexander Hamilton*, VIII, 403-404.

[118] William Vans Murray to McHenry, Aug. 29, 1796, in Steiner, *The Life and Correspondence of James McHenry*, p. 189.

[119] George Cabot to Pickering, Brookline, Mass., Aug. 31, 1796, Timothy Pickering Papers, XX, 344 (Mass. Hist. Soc.).

standard Federalist tactic in discrediting Monroe. After residing in Paris for two or three years, Churchman, a Maryland scientist, had returned to the United States in July, 1796, bearing a letter from Monroe to Pickering. In the course of discussion involving the letter's broken seal Pickering asked about "the sentiments of the French people towards America & particularly the *government*," and "whether he had observed any material change of sentiment, especially on account of the Treaty with Great Britain." Churchman "answered that he had observed no material change; that very little was said by *Frenchmen* about the treaty—tho' much was said against it by the *American Citizens* in Paris."[120] Pickering relayed this to Washington, on whom the inference was not lost: Monroe could not be trusted; he and other antiadministration Americans in Paris were causing trouble with France for party purposes.

The Federalist plans to get rid of Monroe were known to the French. From Philadelphia the French minister reported that finally the enemies of France felt sufficiently strong to brave public opinion and force Monroe's recall, and to replace him with "a spy of the English court." Happily, but mistakenly, he did not think the President would dare recall Monroe.[121]

* * * * *

Washington's reaction to Monroe's conduct was far different from what the French minister would have had it. When first impressed with the seriousness of the French reaction to the Jay treaty, concerned about the political situation at home, he reacted as he had in the English and Spanish diplomatic crises; he considered sending a special envoy to France to deal with the new crisis. But could he send such an envoy, he asked of Hamilton and his Cabinet, without Senate approval and while the Senate was in recess? Other questions also bothered him. Believing Federalist dogma that the difficulties with France "have been brought on us by the misconduct of some of our own intemperate people" who threw

[120] Pickering to Washington, July 29, 1796, in Hamilton, *The Writings of James Monroe*, II, 494 n. Several years earlier Churchman, in his scientific pursuits, had sought congressional support for a proposed voyage to find the magnetic pole. *Annals of the Congress. . . ,* 2nd Cong., 1st sess., Jan. 6, 1792, pp. 312-315.

[121] Adet to Minister of Foreign Relations, Philadelphia, June 19, 1796, in Turner, *CFM*, pp. 925-926.

"themselves into the Arms of France," he wondered about the inter-connection between the Directory's reception of such a move and the Republican reaction in the United States. Where could he find the man who had the proper qualifications "for such a Mission; and would not be obnoxious to one party or the other"; and what, he asked, should be done with Monroe in such a case?[122]

Pouncing upon the opening for a fatal thrust against Monroe, the Cabinet agreed that the President had not the power to send a special envoy "in the recess of the Senate." Washington's advisers believed he could meet the crisis only by recalling Monroe and creating a vacancy. They urged the recall so the United States could have in Paris "some faithful organ to explain their real views" and to ascertain the real views of the French. Monroe's conduct, they pointed out, "exposed the United States to all the mischiefs which could flow from jealousies and erroneous conceptions of their views and conduct." His attachment to the cause of France, they said, "rendered him too little mindful of the interests of his own country."[123]

One factor among many available to them which Federalists chose to support their argument on this occasion was a letter writ-ten by Monroe to George Logan, Philadelphia Quaker and Republi-can, which they contended accorded with other evidence of Mon-roe's "political opinions and conduct." The letter, copies of which Monroe sent to four other prominent Jeffersonians, criticized the Jay negotiation and deplored the weakening of the French alliance. Worse still, in the covering letter Monroe had sent to Logan, he explained to the Quaker that he had "no objection" to having his letter published in Bache's *Aurora*. It could be done anonymously— "from a gentleman in Paris to his friend in Philadelphia"—and per-haps Monroe might send similar letters regularly if Logan approved.

[122] Washington to Pickering and to Hamilton, Mount Vernon, June 24, 26, 1796, in Fitzpatrick, *Washington's Writings*, XXXV, 96-97, 101-102; the quotation is from Washington to Hamilton, Philadelphia, May 8, 1796, *ibid.*, p. 41. Capture of the American vessel *Mount Vernon* by the French privateer *Flying Fish* served to convince Washington more than ever that relations with France had become critical; for the episode, see Bassett, *The Federalist Sys-tem. . .*, p. 222.

[123] Pickering, Wolcott, Jr., and McHenry to Washington, Philadelphia, July 2, 1796, in Worthington C. Ford, ed., *The Writings of George Washington* (14 vols., New York, 1889-[93]), XIII, 216 n.

In this way Americans could be "more correctly informed" of the progress of the French Revolution than in the past, when most of their information derived from the English press.[124]

How they got the private letter the department heads did not disclose. They used it to stress Monroe's political treason rather than any harm he may have done to American foreign policy. A minister who made "confidential correspondents" of the "notorious enemies of the whole system of the government," they pointed out, could not be trusted to do his duty to his government. They attempted, also, to connect Monroe to other anonymous letters from France. "These anonymous communications from officers of the United States in a foreign country, on matters of public nature, and which deeply concern the interests of the United States, in relation to that foreign country, are proofs of sinister design," they said, "and shew that the public interests are no longer safe in the hands of such men."[125]

As usual, Hamilton proffered the counsel that Washington followed. Although the Federalist chieftain's advice, prepared after consultation with Jay, agreed in its main points with that of the Cabinet, it was more perceptive. Hamilton felt that the French crisis was not sufficiently dangerous at the time to warrant a special envoy. He and Jay believed that Monroe's successor "ought to be at the same time a friend to the government and understood to be not unfriendly to the French Revolution." General Charles Cotesworth Pinckney was "the only man" they could think of who filled the requirement. They doubted, however, that he would accept the post, as in the past he had turned down other high offices offered him by Washington. If Pinckney declined, they advised, someone else must be sent. Hamilton feared that in view of French discontent "serious

[124] Monroe to Jefferson, Paris, June 23, 1795, in Hamilton, *The Writings of James Monroe*, II, 292-304; he sent copies to Logan, Aaron Burr, John Beckley, and Robert R. Livingston. The covering letter, Monroe to Logan, Paris, June 24, 1795 (dated erroneously 1796) is in *ibid.*, III, 6-7; see also Frederick B. Tolles, *George Logan of Philadelphia* (New York, 1953), pp. 143-144; Cresson, *James Monroe,* pp. 151-152.
[125] Pickering, Wolcott, McHenry to Washington, Philadelphia, July 2, 1796, in Ford, *The Writings of George Washington,* XIII, 216 n.-217 n. Attorney General Charles Lee concurred in the Cabinet opinion, maintaining that it was "not only expedient but absolutely necessary" that Monroe be recalled. Lee to Washington, Alexandria, July 7, 1796, in Fitzpatrick, *Washington's Writings,* XXXV, 126 n.

censure" would fall upon the Executive if he did not attempt another explanation of the American position. "It will be said," he warned, "that it did not display as much zeal to avoid misunderstanding with France as with Great Britain; that discontents were left to rankle; that if the agent of the government in France were negligent or unfaithful, some other mode ought to have been found."[126]

Washington did not hesitate. Within a few days he confidentially set in motion the procedure for Monroe's recall. Simultaneously he sought a replacement "who will promote, not thwart the neutral policy of the Government." Although having "proofs, little short of positive" that John Marshall would not accept the appointment, he offered it first to him. After Marshall's refusal he turned to Charles Cotesworth Pinckney. In almost the same words as Hamilton's he described the desired qualifications to Pinckney. "Where then," he asked, "can a man be found that would answer this description better than yourself?" In urging acceptance Washington again echoed Federalist political dogma. "It is a fact too notorious to be denied," he said, "that the greatest embarrassments under which the Administration of this government labours, proceed from the concentration of people among ourselves; who are more disposed to promote the views of another than to establish a national character of their own; and that unless the virtuous, and independent men of this country will come forward, it is not difficult to predict the consequences. Such is my decided opinion."[127]

Pinckney accepted the appointment.[128] Monroe remained a problem. Apprehensive that when the recall became known it would "set all the envenomed pens to work," the President cautioned his Cabinet officers against unofficial discussion of causes for the recall. He did feel, however, that "it will be candid, proper and necessary to apprize Mr. Monroe" of the motives "which have im-

[126] Hamilton to Washington, July 5, 1796, in Lodge, *The Works of Alexander Hamilton,* VIII, 407-408; Hamilton, of course, influenced the Cabinet's reply. For a discussion of Monroe's recall see Bond, *The Monroe Mission. . . ,* pp. 84-91.
[127] See Washington to Pickering, Marshall, and C. C. Pinckney, all three letters dated Mount Vernon, July 8, 1796, in Fitzpatrick, *Washington's Writings,* XXXV, 126-131.
[128] Pinckney to Washington, Charleston, July 27, Aug. 2, 1796, National Archives, State Dept., Diplomatic Despatches, France.

pelled it."[129] So well guarded was Washington's action that it completely surprised Adet, the French Minister in Philadelphia, who did not learn of the recall until Pinckney was ready to depart.[130]

Secretary Pickering informed Monroe of Pinckney's appointment and of his pending recall. Pinckney would deliver the formal letters of recall, he told Monroe. The reasons for the recall, for the "uneasiness and dissatisfaction of the President," were apparent; he had spelled them out in an earlier letter, Pickering pointed out curtly. There were, he added, "other concurring circumstances" to which he referred without elaboration. To maintain "the obligations of his office," and in particular to maintain "the honor and interests of the United States in relation to foreign nations," the President was obliged to make the replacement.[131]

Early in November Monroe received Pickering's notice, and not long afterward Pinckney arrived in Paris with the letters of recall terminating his mission. Pinckney's arrival heralded not only the end of the Monroe mission, but also the virtual end of the French alliance. The French foreign office viewed Monroe's recall as a deliberate affront, as nothing more than a political move by Washington against Monroe and his party, a move it would not accept. While willing to maintain at least the semblance of diplomatic relations with Monroe, a minister they knew to be sympathetic to the alliance even though his government was not, the French would have nothing to do with a Federalist committed to the policy of the Jay

---

[129] Washington to Pickering, Mount Vernon, Aug. 10, 1796, to Wolcott, Jr., same date, in Fitzpatrick, *Washington's Writings,* XXXV, 174-175, 176-177. Pinckney's acceptance was delayed for about a month because Washington's original letter offering the appointment was lost in the mails. Washington to Marshall, and to Pinckney, Mount Vernon, Aug. 10, 1796, *ibid.,* pp. 175-176. Washington was right; the recall was criticized. After hearing Monroe's side of the recall story Albert Gallatin, for example, was convinced "that the American Administration have acted with a degree of meanness only exceeded by their folly, and that they have degraded the American name throughout Europe." He was convinced, too, that the administration had used Monroe as a scapegoat. Gallatin to his wife, June 28, 1797, in Adams, *The Life of Albert Gallatin,* pp. 186-187.

[130] Adet to Minister of Foreign Relations, Philadelphia, Oct. 3, 1796, in Turner, *CFM,* p. 950. Adet, not far from the mark, interpreted the recall as a result of the "hateful" work of Hamilton and his Federalist cohorts.

[131] Pickering to Monroe, Dept. of State, Aug. 22, 1796, *ASP FR,* I, 741-742; the letter of recall was dated Sept. 9, 1796, and is on p. 742.

treaty. The Directory, therefore, refused to receive Pinckney.[132] In the words of Tom Paine, "the recall of Mr. Monroe cut everything asunder, for though here [France] they were enraged at the American government, they were not enraged at him. They had an esteem for him, and a good opinion of him; they would listen to him, and he could soften them. But to recall him and to send in his place the brother of the man who was concerned in forming Jay's treaty was stupidity and insult to both." Such action tended to confirm French suspicions that "Mr. Monroe was sent for the purpose of amusing them while Jay was to act a contrary part in England."[133]

Although bitter over what it considered deception practiced ungratefully against a generous ally, the French government exonerated Monroe of complicity in it, choosing rather to believe that he had been deceived as much as they. Before he took leave, therefore, the Directory emphasized that its quarrel was with the Federalist administration. It informed Monroe "that it will no longer recognize nor receive a minister plenipotentiary from the United States, until after a reparation of the grievances demanded of the American government." At the same time it hastened to emphasize that its grievances were not with the American people but with the government, that it held the American people in affection "grounded on former good offices and reciprocal interest, an affection which you have taken pleasure in cultivating by all the means in your power."[134]

Monroe's last official act, though brief and unostentatious, touched the same theme as did his first controversial public appearance in Paris. In his farewell appearance before the Directory he said there was no object he had always had "more uniformly and sincerely at

---

[132] Adet warned the Directory against Pinckney, a conservative South Carolina Federalist, cautioning it not to fall into an American trap as American protests of friendship were false. To the Minister of Foreign Relations, Philadelphia, Oct. 3, 1796, in Turner, *CFM*, p. 950. Upon landing in France Pinckney learned first hand that France was disgusted with American conduct, that it viewed the Washington government as antagonistic, and that with the Jay treaty the United States had thrown itself into the arms of France's bitter enemy. In effect, he learned that France considered the 1778 alliance shorn of meaning. Pinckney to Secretary of State, Bordeaux, Nov. 17, 1796, No. 1, National Archives, State Dept., Diplomatic Despatches, France.

[133] Paine to Jefferson, Havre de Grace, France, April 1, 1797, in Foner, *The Complete Works of Thomas Paine*, II, 1387, 1389.

[134] Minister of Foreign Affairs to Monroe, Paris, Dec. 11, 1796, *ASP FR*, I, 746-747; Austin, *The Life of Elbridge Gerry*, II, 179.

heart than the continuance of a close union and perfect harmony between" France and the United States. He had accepted the mission with the view of using his utmost efforts "to increase and promote this object"; he never deviated, he said, from pursuing it. The French reply, while complimentary to Monroe, criticized the American government's action. Indeed, it labeled the recall a "very strange spectacle" for Europe to observe. Again, the French distinguished between the American people, who "will always possess our esteem," and their government. Monroe, they declared, knew "the true interests" of America; he departed to their regret.[135]

Monroe remained in Europe for several months and did not sail for the United States until spring, 1797. Arriving in New York in July, he saw immediately that he and his mission were a focus of political controversy. In attacks in the Federalist press and in Congress, Monroe was even accused of being a traitor who sold his country for French gold. In the words of John Adams, his house in Paris had been "a school for scandal against this country, its government and governors, Mr. Jay and his treaty."[136] Republicans did not agree with this version of Monroe's activities. "The Washington faction," said a Monroe defender, "had affected to spread it abroad that James Monroe was the cause of rupture between the two Republics." Not so, was the reply; it was "the ingratitude and clandestine manoeuvering of the government of Washington, who caused the misunderstanding by signing a treaty injurious to the French Republic."[137]

Nursing a deep resentment against the Federalist government for its treatment of him, Monroe added to the heat of partisan strife over foreign policy, particularly in his feud with Pickering over the reasons for his recall. Finally, like Randolph before him, Monroe presented his case to the people. In December, 1797, he pub-

[135] Monroe to the Directory, [Paris, Dec. 30, 1796] and the President of the Directory to Monroe, *ASP FR*, I, 747. According to a report on public opinion in Paris dated Jan. 2, 1796, the Directory's stand on Monroe's recall was popular. François V. A. Aulard, ed., *Paris pendant la réaction thermidorienne et sous le Directoire* (5 vols., Paris, 1898-1902), III, 672.

[136] Létombe to Delacroix, Philadelphia, July 16, 1797, in Turner, *CFM*, p. 1045; Adams to wife, Philadelphia, Jan. 14, 1797, in C. F. Adams, ed., *Letters of John Adams Addressed to His Wife*, II, 240.

[137] Thomas Paine to the editors of the *Bien informé*, Paris, Sept. 27, 1797, in Conway, *The Writings of Thomas Paine*, III, 368-369.

lished *A View of the Conduct of the Executive, in the Foreign Affairs of the United States, connected with the mission to the French Republic, during the years 1794, 5, & 6,* a pamphlet in which he reviewed his mission, defended his conduct, reiterated his belief that to preserve the French alliance "was the true interest of America," and attacked administration foreign policy.[138]

In Paris, meanwhile, Pinckney had protested to the French government that the sentiments of the American people and those of their government were the same and were misunderstood. With regret he protested that he was "not permitted even to attempt to explain" the position of the Washington administration. The French government refused to listen to his explanation. As he had no official status, Pinckney was informed, he had better leave France; otherwise, he would be subject to arrest under the local police regulation requiring all foreigners to have a passport signed by their ministers in Paris and countersigned by the Minister of Foreign Affairs. Pinckney had no passport, nor could he obtain one. In February, 1797, he retreated to Amsterdam to await instructions from home.[139]

Before leaving Paris Pinckney had observed that within the French government some felt that "America is not of greater consequence . . . nor ought to be treated with greater respect, than Geneva or Genoa." Others, he reported, "who regard us as being of some consequence, seem to have taken up an idea that our Government acts upon principles opposed to the real sentiments of a large majority of our people, and they are willing to temporize until the event of the election of President is known; thinking that, if one public character is chosen, he will be attached to the interest of Great Britain; and that, if another is elected, he will be . . . devoted to

[138] See Monroe to Pickering, Philadelphia, July 6, 1797, in Hamilton, *The Writings of James Monroe*, III, 66-67; the pamphlet is printed on pp. 383-457; see also Daniel C. Gilman, *James Monroe* (Boston, 1898), pp. 67-70.

[139] Pinckney to Pickering, plus enclosures, Paris, Dec. 10, 20, 26, 1796, Amsterdam, Feb. 18, 1797, *ASP FR*, II, 5-10. Fearing that the French refusal to receive Pinckney might mean war, Tom Paine urged the French foreign minister to regard Pinckney—appointed in a recess of the Senate—as in "suspension" until confirmed by the Senate. In this way Pinckney would not be received and an act of outright hostility would not be committed. Paine's counsel was not followed; such a course was not "dignified." See Conway, *The Writings of Thomas Paine*, III, 368 n., citing AAE CP EU, Vol. XLVI, f. 425. See also Faÿ, *Revolutionary Spirit. . .*, p. 381.

the interests of France; entertaining the humiliating idea that we are a people divided by party, the mere creatures of foreign influence, and regardless of our national character, honor, and interest. To eradicate this ill-conceived and unfounded opinion will be the work of time and labor, so greatly have they been prejudiced by misrepresentation."[140] This misrepresentation could be traced, in the Federalist view, to Monroe.

[140] Pinckney to Pickering, enclosed in the letter of Dec. 20, 1796 (Paris), *ASP FR,* II, 8.

CHAPTER TWELVE

A METEOR FOLLOWS A COMET

Fauchet was rec'd. with the most profound attention by the party hereto-fore opposed to his country & his cause. 'Tis probable they might hope the fate of his predecessor wo'd. warn him to shun not only his errors but likewise the friends of France, upon the idea they wo'd. be the friends of Mr. Genet. . . . He must soon find that the republican party here are the only friends of that cause in his own country. . . . —James Monroe to Thomas Jefferson, Philadelphia, March 3, 1794.

Fauchet succeeded Genet. It was a meteor *following a* comet. *No very marked phenomena distinguished his course. But the little twinkling appearances which here and there are discernible, indicate the same general policy in him which governed his predecessor.*—Alexander Hamilton, "France," 1796.

* * * * *

WHILE Monroe labored unsuccessfully to save the French alliance, Genet's successors in Philadelphia meddled in domestic politics to advance French objectives. They too proved unsuccessful; and their activities also contributed to the ultimate destruction of the alliance.[1] Their conduct was not motivated by the desire to alienate the American government; to the contrary, they believed that they were working to strengthen the alliance and to bind the United States more closely to France. Given the state of politics and the pro-

[1] James A. James, "French Diplomacy and American Politics, 1794-1795," *Annual Report of the American Historical Association for the Year 1911* (2 vols., Washington, 1913), I, 163; Fauchet's secretary Le Blanc considered the mission a failure; see the remarks attributed to him in Adams, ed., *Memoirs of John Quincy Adams,* diary entry of July 7, 1795, I, 118-119; Joseph Fauchet, *Mémoire sur les États Unis d'Amérique,* ed., Carl L. Lokke in the *AHA Ann. Rep.* (1936) (3 vols., Washington, 1938), I (introduction), 85. Hereinafter cited as Lokke, *Fauchet Mémoire.*

British orientation of the Federalist government, they saw that they could not reach their objectives through the ordinary channels of diplomacy.

Before resorting to propaganda and threats, Jean Antoine Joseph Fauchet, Genet's immediate successor, tried the diplomacy of concil-iation to achieve French objectives. Although he held the title of minister plenipotentiary, Fauchet did not succeed to all of Genet's powers. Believing that Genet's "imprudent" conduct had illus-trated the danger of conferring powers which critically affected the interests of the French nation on one man (especially one lacking diplomatic experience) when that individual was a great distance away, the Jacobin government sent a commission of four, headed by Fauchet, to replace Genet. Under a division and balance of powers each commissioner had special functions. While Fauchet's main concerns were politics and diplomacy, his colleague La Forest, as Consul-General, was charged with responsibility for matters of com-merce and finance. Le Blanc, the fifty-year old former head of the Paris police department, became Secretary of the Legation and had charge of all French consulates in American ports. Petry took over the consulate at Philadelphia, the national capital.

According to instructions, the commissioners were to act in con-cert, with important decisions requiring majority assent. In purely political matters, Fauchet theoretically had the power to initiate action. In practice, it became almost impossible to extricate the purely political from other actions, particularly when the French governments considered that "the Consuls in the United States are not only commercial agents but also political agents in the states in which they reside."[2]

As is usual in joint diplomatic ventures, the commission almost from the first was torn by dissension. Contemporaries described La Forest and Petry as "two notorious intriguers" and Le Blanc as a man of strong opinions.[3] A prominent French refugee in the United States described Fauchet as "a cowardly slave to the Jacobins"

[2] "Instructions to the Commissioners," Nov. 15, 1793, in Turner, *CFM*, pp. 288-291; Ferdinand M. Bayard, "Sur notre legation près les États-unis de l'Amérique," Paris, Dec. 29, 1795 (contains the quotation), AAE CP EU, Vol. XLIV, ff. 566-567; Gouverneur Morris to Washington, Paris, Nov. 12, 1793, *ASP FR*, I, 398; Conway, *Randolph*, p. 237.

[3] Turner, *CFM*, p. 289 n.

in France.[4] Gouverneur Morris believed that La Forest and Petry would probably sway the conduct of the commission. They expected, he warned, to exert their dominance "by two means; one, their greater knowledge of our country, laws, and inhabitants; the other, a persuasion to be inculcated on the minister and secretary, that they enjoy the confidence of our Government."[5] While the general complexion of the commission at first seemed satisfactory to Federalists, Francophile Republicans had doubts about it. "The political character of these gentlemen," said Madison, "as heretofore understood, give some uneasiness to the Republican party."[6]

As titular head of the mission, Fauchet set the tone in relations with the American government. In those relations and in his personal conduct he was at first as different from Genet as night from day. Unlike Genet, he had had no diplomatic experience, and he spoke no English. A young lawyer of thirty-three, he had been active in the French Revolution and had held a number of governmental posts of varying degrees of responsibility, thereby achieving a minor distinction. He received his American appointment from Robespierre not because of ability or experience, but as a political reward.[7] Estimates as to his abilities vary. In view of some French officials, Fauchet was a man of parts, but "a young man, and not equal to an embassy as important as that of the United States."[8] Gouverneur Morris was told that he possessed "genius and information," whereas George Hammond maintained that "he is inferior to his predecessor not less in abilities than in energy."[9]

Fauchet did not have the immediate popular appeal that Genet had. Four days after his arrival a Philadelphia newspaper remarked

[4] Moreau de St. Méry, *Voyage aux États-Unis de l'Amérique, 1793-1798*, p. 295.

[5] Morris to Washington, Paris, Nov. 12, 1793, *ASP FR*, I, 398.

[6] Madison to Jefferson, Philadelphia, March 2, 1794, in James Madison, *Letters and Other Writings of James Madison*, published by order of Congress (4 vols., New York, 1884), II, 4.

[7] Little is known of Fauchet; brief biographical sketches are in Turner, *CFM*, p. 288 n.; Lokke, *Fauchet Mémoire*, p. 85; James, "French Diplomacy . . .," *AHA Ann. Rep.* (1911), I, 151-163; Conway, *Randolph*, p. 237.

[8] Adams, *Memoirs of John Quincy Adams*, diary entry of March 17, 1795, The Hague, I, 97.

[9] Hammond to Grenville, Philadelphia, Feb. 22 and April 15, 1794, Henry Adams Transcripts.

that he was "not of a very communicative disposition"; John Adams expressed a general estimate in stating that "he is not quite so unreserved as his predecessor" and seemed distressed by popular attention, though "the people have not addressed him or made much noise about him."[10]

Whatever Fauchet's true abilities may have been, he had been entrusted with a difficult task. Robespierre, convinced that Great Britain was working to destroy the 1778 alliance by dividing the United States from France, saw to it that the French commission received special orders to counteract the ill effects of the Genet mission and to re-establish good relations with the United States.[11] Yet he did not relinquish the basic objectives of French foreign policy. English influence in America must be destroyed, his government believed, and France's views must be made known to the American people through the newspapers and with the co-operation of Americans devoted to the cause of liberty. At the same time Fauchet and his colleagues were instructed to win the confidence of President Washington and his Federalist government. What the Jacobins did not realize at this point was that it was impossible to attempt to destroy English influence and seek popular support, and at the same time to win the confidence of Federalists.[12]

Despite these contradictory objectives, the initial instructions reflected a conciliatory and friendly attitude toward the American government. In giving positive assurances of the friendly attachment of France to the United States, the commissioners were to disavow the conduct of Genet and his agents; put a stop to privateering; and recall the letters of marque. On the other hand, they were to see to it that the 1778 treaties were executed according to French interpretation, particularly those articles in the commercial

[10] Adams to wife, March 2, 1794, in Adams, ed., *Letters of John Adams Addressed to His Wife*, II, 145.

[11] "Rapport fait a la Convention Nationale, au nom du comité du salut public, par le citoyen Robespierre, member de ce comité Sur la situation politique de la Republique," Nov. 17, 1793, AAE CP EU, Vol. XXXIX, ff. 279-293. In this report Robespierre denounced Genet and advocated strengthening the Franco-American alliance.

[12] Louis-Guillaume Otto, "Considerations sur la Conduite du governement des Etats unis envers la France, depuis 1789 jusqu'en 1797," June 17, 1797, AAE CP EU, Vol. XLVII, f. 407; "Means to attack and to destroy English influence in America," Nov. 26, 1793, *ibid.*, Vol. XXXIX, ff. 324-325; "Instructions," Nov. 15, 1793, in Turner, *CFM*, pp. 288-294.

treaty allowing French prizes the use of American ports while excluding English prizes. In addition, they were to induce the American government to allow French cruisers and their prizes to take refuge in American ports with the privilege of selling the prizes. In view of the French need for American commerce, the commissioners logically were also to propose a new commercial treaty, more solidly founded than that of 1778.[13]

France's most immediately important goal was the obtaining of food supplies to be sent through the English blockade to relieve shortages she could not alleviate from normal sources then controlled or blocked by France's enemies. The French acknowledged readily their dependence on foreign sources for the needed provisions. American relations were consequently of relatively minor concern to the French war effort in their other aspects.[14] Gouverneur Morris, pointing out that the French desire for cordiality at this time was related closely to the need for provisions of which America was the only source, noted that "everything, then, which opposes this is prejudicial to the most important interests of the [French] republic."[15]

Fauchet and his colleagues arrived in Philadelphia in February, 1794; the anti-British war hysteria was then at its height and the administration despaired over a possible war with England. For the newly arrived commissioners and for the purposes of French diplomacy this was all to the good. In case of war between the United States and England, their later instructions told them, it was essential that France profit from the crisis by proposing a new, closer alliance with the United States, an alliance which would maintain liberty in both countries. At the same time the commissioners were to advise conquest of Canada.[16]

[13] Fauchet's powers in regard to a new commercial treaty bothered Federalists; see Wolcott, Jr., to Hamilton, Philadelphia, Oct. 6, 1795, Pickering to Wolcott, Jr., Oct. 6, 1795, in Gibbs, *Wolcott Papers,* I, 254-255.
[14] In a circular letter, dated Paris, June 6, 1793, to French consulates in the United States, the French Minister of Foreign Affairs, Le Brun, had stressed France's urgent need for provisions from America, a need which continued urgent. Genet Papers, Library of Congress. The continuing need for food is also stressed in Fauchet, La Forest, and Petry to Commissioner of Foreign Relations, Philadelphia, Dec. 30, 1794, in Turner, *CFM,* pp. 525-530.
[15] Morris to Washington, Paris, Nov. 12, 1793, *ASP FR,* I, 398-399; Morris to Deforgues, Minister of Foreign Affairs, Paris, Dec. 9, 1793, *ibid.,* p. 401.
[16] Instructions to French Commissioners in the United States, Paris, Feb.

Despite the ill will stirred up by Genet, from the start all appeared to go well for Fauchet and the objectives of the commission. His first official talks with representatives of the American government pleased him, as did a public expression of fraternity accompanied by the playing of *Ça Ira*. The American government and people, it seemed, favored close ties with the French Republic.[17] Fauchet's conduct, prudent and restrained in contrast to that of his predecessor, made, in turn, a favorable impression on administration leaders. His principal occupation, remarked George Hammond, seemed to be to efface the unfavorable impressions left by Genet and to cultivate the good will of all Americans.[18] According to a Federalist view he was "taught prudence by the follies and ill success of Genet."[19] Even Republicans observed "that Fauchet is going on in the conciliatory plan of reversing the errors of his predecessor."[20] John Quincy Adams found him to be cautious and reserved, but

---

2, 1794, AAE CP EU, Vol. XL, f. 66. Later Fauchet reported that while the people were pro-French and wanted a war against England, the American government was not prepared and wished to remain neutral; nonetheless, the United States sided with France and it was impossible for it to turn against France. [Fauchet], Note, Aug. 9, 1794, AAE CP EU, Vol. XLI, f. 274.

[17] Of all the nations in the world, announced the Committee of Public Safety, free America was the only one which supported the French Revolution. After the Swiss, America is the ally most natural and necessary for France. Politics, commerce, and the identity of civil structure all presage a permanent alliance between the two peoples. N.p., n.d. [probably Jan., 1794], AAE CP EU, Vol. XL, f. 11. Thus it was that French hopes for using the United States and strengthening the alliance were high when Fauchet landed. He landed at Baltimore on Jan. 29, 1794, but because of bad roads he took several weeks to get to the capital. Fauchet's reception, moreover, was not all pleasantness in another respect. Before his arrival Genet had published part of his instructions, causing Fauchet considerable embarrassment; see Commissioners to Minister of Foreign Affairs, Philadelphia, March 21, 1794, in Turner, *CFM*, pp. 306-309, 315; Anderson, "Randolph," in Bemis, *The American Secretaries of State...*, II, 105; Faÿ, *Revolutionary Spirit in France and America...*, pp. 337-338. Later Fauchet insisted that Genet was wrong in publishing his instructions. Joseph Fauchet, *A Sketch of the Present State of Our Political Relations with the United States of North America*, trans. [William J. Duane] (Philadelphia, 1797), p. 22.

[18] Hammond to Grenville, Philadelphia, Feb. 22, 1794, No. 2, Henry Adams Transcripts.

[19] "To the People of the United States," No. II in the *Herald: A Gazette for the Country* (New York), Dec. 21, 1796.

[20] Madison to Jefferson, Philadelphia, March 9, 1794, *Letters and Other Writings of James Madison* (Cong. ed.), II, 6.

committed to a policy of turning the United States against Great Britain: in effect, to a policy of keeping alive the alliance against England.[21]

After the French minister had been in the United States a month and a half, President Washington, too, became impressed by his deportment, remarking that "the manners of Mr. Fauchet, and of Mr. Genet . . . appear to have been cast in very different moulds. The former has been temperate, and placid in all his movements, hitherto; the latter was the reverse of it in all respects. The declarations made by the former, of the friendly dispositions of his Nation towards this Country and of his own inclinations to carry them into effect are strong and apparently sincere."[22] The press also praised Fauchet for just and honorable conduct in controversial matters dealing with problems of neutrality. Later one Federalist journal went so far as to declare that Fauchet was the best of the French ministers sent to the United States by the revolutionary governments.[23]

Republicans, not without "uneasiness" and skepticism, noted the warm reception given Fauchet by Federalists, "the party heretofore opposed to his country & his cause." Probably, observed Monroe, the fate of Genet is taken by Federalists to be sufficient warning to the new French minister to shun not only Genet's errors "but likewise the friends of France, upon the idea they wod. be the friends of Mr. Genet." Fauchet "must soon find," he said, "that the republican party here are the only friends of that cause in his own country, and that it was owing to a zeal for that cause and a belief the man was honest, that his errors were in any degree tolerated by them. As yet the conduct of Fauchet appears to be reserved and prudent, and 'tis to be hoped he will finally take a course correspond'g. with what the interest of his country may require."[24]

[21] Adams, *Memoirs of John Quincy Adams,* I, 36-38, diary entry of July 11, 1794 (Philadelphia).

[22] Washington to Richard Henry Lee, Philadelphia, April 15, 1794, in Fitzpatrick, *Washington's Writings,* XXXIII, 331.

[23] *Columbia Gazette* (Columbia, S. C.), Aug. 1, 1794, quoting a letter of June 3, 1794, from Kingston, Jamaica; *New Hampshire and Vermont Journal: Or, The Farmer's Weekly Museum* (Walpole, N. H.), Nov. 22, 1796.

[24] Monroe to Jefferson, March 3, 1794, in Hamilton, *The Writings of James Monroe,* I, 284-285. Madison remarked that Fauchet's demeanor had the aspect of "moderation." "He takes particular pains to assure all who talk with him of the perseverence of France in her attachment to us, and her

Federalists from the first were pleased with Republican discomfiture over Fauchet's replacement of Genet and their uncertainty as to Fauchet's political orientation in the United States.[25]

Without unnecessary preliminaries, Fauchet plunged into his diplomatic tasks. As has been seen, he dealt quickly with the problem of Genet's disavowal and arrest and stopped the expeditions in preparation against the Spanish lands. At the same time, as Gouverneur Morris had warned, Fauchet attempted to obtain advance payment on the debt owed France by the United States, which it was then meeting by regular installments. Plagued by lack of money and concerned over the plight of the Saint Domingue refugees, Fauchet and the commissioners hoped to relieve their financial embarrassment and to aid the refugees by obtaining from the American government an advance payment of a million dollars in six months' time. Washington, on the advice of the Cabinet, refused to make advance payment; he continued to meet the regular installments. If Fauchet insisted upon the advance payment, Randolph informed him, he could apply to Congress. The French Minister did. The result was a hot debate in the House of Representatives, which voted to make the payment, and a defeat in the Senate. Fauchet did not get the money, and the French mission remained in financial difficulty.[26]

* * * * *

Intimately connected with the debt payments and Fauchet's financial needs was the problem of food supplies for the homeland. English naval power had driven French shipping from the seas. Unable to obtain goods on her own, France counted on neutral bottoms, protected by the small-navy doctrine of free ships make free

---

anxiety that nothing which may have taken place may lessen it on our side," Madison to Jefferson, Philadelphia, March 2, 1794, *Letters and Other Writings of James Madison* (Cong. ed.), II, 3-4.

[25] John Q. Adams to John Adams, Boston, March 2, 1794, in Ford, *The Writings of John Quincy Adams,* I, 180.

[26] Morris to Washington, Paris, Oct. 19, 1793, *ASP FR,* I, 398; for correspondence on the debt question, see pp. 427-428; for the House debate, see *Annals of the Congress. . . ,* 3rd Cong., 1st sess., May 28, 1794, pp. 727-729; May 30, 1794, p. 739. For the Senate's action, June, 1794, see pp. 129-130; see also Anderson, "Randolph," in Bemis, ed., *The American Secretaries of State. . . ,* II, 106; Conway, *Randolph,* p. 241. Fauchet thought at first that he was going to get the million dollars. [Fauchet], Note, Aug. 9, 1794, AAE CP EU, Vol. XLI, f. 274.

goods, to bring them to her ports. In particular, she counted on American shipping; the commercial treaty of 1778 embodied this doctrine. In February, 1793, France had thrown open the ports of her colonies to American shipping. At the same time, to overcome crop shortages, she had made arrangements to purchase grain from the United States, purchases which she hoped to finance with payments on the Revolutionary debt owed to her.[27]

Even though provisions were at times shipped to France as American property, the British blockade was throttling a desperately needed supply for France and a lucrative commerce for the United States. At first the British seized American food ships bound for France on the general principal that the neutral flag did not protect commerce with France. Later, the British made their seizures under a decree of June 8, 1793, which declared corn, flour, or meal contraband of war, and that any vessel loaded wholly or in part with those foodstuffs was subject to seizure. There was, however, the understanding that the British would pay for the seized cargoes.

This was an innovation in international maritime practice, so neutrals protested the British action. But the British persisted in the practice. They argued that France was not waging war according to principles of international law, that France had no recognized government, that the French authorities had taken over the trade in cereals, making that trade an act of the enemy's government, and finally that the plan to starve France into submission was an important means of forcing her to make peace.[28]

France wanted to strike back in kind. American ships carrying British goods, by the 1778 commercial treaty, were protected by the free-ships-free-goods principle. Great Britain was not obligated by treaty to respect the neutral character of American shipping; she had never recognized the free-ships-free-goods principle. By a decree of May 9, 1793, the French authorized their vessels to seize neutral ships carrying goods to England. Since English ships did

[27] The decree of the National Convention of Feb. 19, 1793, is in *ASP FR*, I, 147; see "Cabinet Opinion on French Application," Feb. 25, 1793, wherein the Cabinet advised Washington that funds be advanced to the French for purchase of provisions, in Ford, *Writings of Jefferson*, VI, 190; for French food purchases at this time, see Ternant to Minister of Foreign Affairs, Philadelphia, Feb. 25, 1793, in Turner, *CFM*, pp. 178-179.
[28] Heckscher, *The Continental System*, pp. 43-44.

not respect a neutral flag, decreed the French, neither would theirs. Uncertain, however, about the wisdom of violating the American treaty, the French government responded to strong American protests by exempting (May 23, 1793) American vessels from the decree. Finally (July 27), after experimenting with various decrees, the French did retaliate without exception by declaring that they would seize food-carrying neutral vessels bound for enemy ports.[29] As applied to the United States, this violated the 1778 commercial treaty.

While acknowledging the treaty violation, the French justified it on the principle of retaliation, claiming that in this respect they were not bound by the treaty provisions. If Americans wanted French treaty compliance they would have to force the British to observe small-navy neutrality principles; in effect, they would have to fight for their neutral rights. Against British sea power Americans were helpless and to fight to accommodate France would have been suicidal.[30]

To the French, American protests and insistence upon French respect for American neutral rights as laid down by treaty were puzzling. They could not understand why Americans, as allies, could not see the French position and sympathize with the French dilemma. As allies, reasoned the French, were Americans acting in good faith when they demanded strict fulfilment of treaty obligations which had been contracted to benefit both parties and which no longer did so? Was it right to invoke against an ally a treaty

[29] For details, see Clauder, *American Commerce as Affected by the Wars of the French Revolution.* . . , p. 29; Phillips and Reede, *Neutrality.* . . , II, 27-37; most of the decrees are printed in *ASP FR,* III, 284-285.

[30] Federalist thinking backed up the British view. One Federalist thinker explained that the free-ships-free-goods principle was recognized only by treaty where a nation had relinquished the right of search according to international law. If the nation, such as Great Britain, did not relinquish the right, it could dispute the free-ships-free-goods principle either by reasoning or by force. William Vans Murray Papers, Commonplace Book [c. Aug. 15, 1795] (Princeton). Some French legislators opposed violation of the American commercial treaty, even on grounds of retaliation. Regardless of how much the treaty hurt, France, they maintained, should respect the sanctity of treaties; she should have regard for a faithful ally. The pressures of French vested interests—especially the owners of privateers—appeared, however, to have greater influence than did the sanctity of treaties; see Clauder, *American Commerce as Affected by the Wars of the French Revolution.* . . , p. 29 n.

which had been basic to American independence and which had cost France much in blood and treasure? Was it right to insist upon treaty fulfilment in such a way as to injure France? According to provisions of the 1778 treaty France and the United States promised each other most-favored-nation treatment; yet, reasoned the French, American laws bypassed this principle; they favored no nation. Motivated by political considerations, Congress, it appeared to the French, wished to break the 1778 treaties and to destroy the Franco-American alliance.[31]

Meanwhile the United States protested British seizures. Secretary of State Jefferson in September, 1793, insisted that British capture of food ships was "contrary to the law of nations," that corn, flour, and meal were not contraband, and that Americans had a right to sell them to France. To restrain Americans from sending grain to France while selling it to England smacked of a partiality to Great Britain which may lead to war with France. "This is a dilemma," he said, "which Great Britain has no right to force upon us." Answering Jefferson's protest, Hammond pointed out that writers on international law had stated that provisions were conditional contraband.[32] This conflict over provisions and neutral rights almost led to war with England in the spring of 1794. Finally, in January, 1794, through a mitigating Order-in-Council, the British eased their food seizures.[33]

During this time, even though Americans directed their anger primarily against Great Britain, commercial grievances against France also continued to mount as American merchants suffered at the hands of the French Revolutionary governments. An embargo laid upon foreign vessels in Bordeaux in the summer of 1793 had a crippling effect on Franco-American commerce. In protesting their treatment, American ship captains stranded in Bordeaux pointed out that they had braved great dangers to bring

[31] These views are taken from "Observations sur la neutralité des États-Unis," AAE CP EU (no author or date indicated, but probably spring, 1793), Vol. XXXVII, ff. 270-273.

[32] Jefferson to Pinckney, Philadelphia, Sept. 7, 1793, *ASP FR*, II, 239-240; Hammond to Jefferson, Philadelphia, Sept. 12, 1793, *ibid.*, p. 240.

[33] The order of Jan. 8, 1794, is printed in *ibid.*, III, 264. This order, along with the Jay treaty, contributed to bringing about an Anglo-American *rapprochement*. Letter from London of Aug. 22, 1794, in the *Maryland Gazette*, Oct. 30, 1794.

needed supplies to French ports and in return had received hostile treatment.[34]

When Fauchet arrived in Philadelphia to launch his quest for food supplies, the Bordeaux embargo was still in effect. At that time poor harvests and the British food blockade (supported by allies Russia and Spain, who closed their ports to the French), plus other factors, had produced a severe food shortage in France. Famine threatened Paris. More than ever the French needed American provisions. Fauchet and his colleagues bent every effort to get them. Seeing that the Bordeaux embargo raised a serious obstacle to success—he encountered difficulty getting American ships to carry provisions to France because of it—Fauchet complained to his superiors about it, pleading for the release of detained American vessels.[35] His pleas were heeded.

The French government, in April, 1794, lifted the embargo. In so doing the Committee of Public Safety announced that its action was new proof of French friendship for the United States. The action, for a while at least, removed one American grievance against France.[36] Yet some bitterness lingered. While American captains in Bordeaux obtained partial reimbursement for their losses, they and others too often ran into further complications in obtaining payment for the food cargoes they brought to French ports.[37]

Despite these and other difficulties Fauchet gathered ships and supplies to send to hungry France. So urgent was the French need

[34] Gouverneur Morris had protested the embargo and had been promised daily that it would be removed. He was never able to learn why it had been laid. He suspected that the French were suspicious of the voyages, cargoes, and even of the property of some of the American vessels in Bordeaux. To Jefferson, Paris, Jan. 21, 1794, *ASP FR,* I, 403; for American complaints, see *ibid.,* pp. 373-374; for a discussion of the Bordeaux embargoes (there was a second embargo in 1794), see Clauder, *American Commerce as Affected by the Wars of the French Revolution. . . ,* pp. 38-41.

[35] Commissioners to Minister of Foreign Affairs, Philadelphia, April 4, 1794, May 24, 1794, Turner, *CFM,* pp. 320-321, 348; James, "French Diplomacy. . . ," *AHA Ann. Rep.* (1911), I, 155-156.

[36] "Rapport," AAE CP EU, [n.p., n.d., probably Jan., 1794], Vol. XL, f. 3; Le chargé provisoire du Dept. des affaires etrangeres to Gouverneur Morris, Paris, April 6, 1794, announces the decree of the Committee of Public Safety lifting the embargo.

[37] For continued American grievances and the 1794 embargo, see Monroe to the Secretary of State, Paris, Sept. 15, 1794, *ASP FR,* I, 675; Fulwar Skipwith to Monroe, Paris, Oct., 1794, *ibid.,* 749-752.

that the Paris authorities did not dare risk piecemeal capture of flour-laden vessels from America; instead of trying to run the English blockade with individual vessels they resorted to a convoy system. To guard the convoy, which was to assemble in the United States, the French authorities sent along with Fauchet and the commissioners a small squadron of warships under the command of Rear Admiral Pierre-Jean Vanstabel. In February, 1794, the squadron anchored in Chesapeake Bay, there to await the gathering of the convoy from various ports in the United States and from the French Caribbean islands.[38]

With all means at their disposal Fauchet and the commissioners bought foodstuffs and supplies and stored them in vessels in the various ports, vessels which were to rendezvous with Vanstabel's ships in Hampton Roads to run the English blockade. After unnerving difficulties and delays, the cargo holds were filled and the ships gathered, about 130 strong, to sail under the protecting guns of Vanstabel's meager squadron. Loaded with some 24,000,000 pounds of flour, toward the middle of April they sailed past the Virginia Capes to precipitate the only major naval battle in the first four years of the Anglo-French war.

To get the provisions safely into port, the French risked their battle fleet, sending it to challenge England's control of the sea if the convoy were in danger. In drawing the British channel fleet from the convoy route the French admiral on June 1—the "Glorious First of June," the British called it—suffered a terrible mauling. The sacrifice was not in vain. On June 13 the Franco-American convoy reached Brest without the loss of a single vessel, and American grain helped avert a famine.[39]

---

[38] Vanstabel's squadron, consisting on one 80-gun ship, one of 74 guns, and two 40-gun frigates plus two sloops of war arrived at Norfolk on February 10. Hammond to Grenville, Philadelphia, Feb. 20, 1794, No. 1, Henry Adams Transcripts.

[39] For general accounts of the convoy problem and the ensuing naval battle, see Alfred Thayer Mahan, *The Influence of Sea Power upon the French Revolution and Empire, 1789-1812* (2 vols., Boston, 1892), I, 122-161; Albion and Pope, *Sea Lanes in Wartime. . . ,* pp. 71-73; for Fauchet's activities and complaints in preparing the convoy, see Commissioners to Minister of Foreign Affairs, Philadelphia, March 18, 21, to Minister of Marine, March 21, 1794, in Turner, *CFM,* pp. 305, 307, 319-320. In July reports reached the United States of the merchant fleet's safe arrival. *Maryland Gazette* (Annapolis), July 17, 1794. In autumn, 1794, the French government sent a special pur-

During the time the convoy was forming, anti-British agitation in the Congress came to a head. In the latter part of March Congress debated and finally enacted the thirty-day general embargo mentioned in an earlier chapter, and then extended it for another thirty days, to May 25. While Congress discussed the embargo, which was directed primarily against Great Britain, Fauchet kept in close touch with pro-French congressmen. When passage of the embargo seemed certain "many members of Congress" discussed it with him and asked when the food convoy would be ready to sail, indicating that for France's benefit declaration of the embargo might be postponed until the sailing date.[40] There was, however, no postponement, although the Franco-American convoy did not sail until several weeks after the embargo had been established. This did not escape British notice. Hammond complained that the embargo was discriminatory because it was not enforced against the convoy; he maintained it should have been. Secretary of State Randolph disclaimed partiality in its enforcement.[41]

As the terminal date for the embargo approached, Fauchet, too, turned against it. If continued and enforced, he realized, it might prevent the sending of other vessels to France, vessels for a convoy he had begun to provision in May. He pointed out to friends in Congress that if they extended the embargo again it would harm France, which depended upon American supplies, more than it would England, against whom it was directed originally. Finally, for various reasons, among them a concern over its adverse effect on the Franco-American alliance, the House of Representatives reversed its stand on the embargo. Fauchet claimed that his efforts had influenced the change.[42]

* * * * *

chasing agent, James Swan, to the United States to buy food supplies. For Swan's activities, which were considerable during Fauchet's ministry, see Howard C. Rice, "James Swan: Agent of the French Republic, 1794-1796," *New England Quarterly*, X, 473-480.

[40] Commissioners to Minister of Foreign Affairs, Philadelphia, March 21, 1794, in Turner, *CFM*, p. 317; for a discussion of the embargo and its extension, see *Annals of the Congress. . .* , 3rd Cong., 1st sess., April 17, 1794, pp. 597-598.

[41] Hammond to Randolph, Philadelphia, May 22, 1794, and Randolph to Hammond, Philadelphia, June 2, 1794, *ASP FR*, I, 462, 465.

[42] Commissioners to Minister of Foreign Affairs, Philadelphia, May 29, 1794, in Turner, *CFM*, pp. 357-360; for the congressional debates on the

Fauchet at first tried to avoid politics and attempted to maintain a "just equilibrium" between Federalists and Republicans. Where possible he sought to keep in the good graces of the Washington administration. As he observed political developments more closely—the debates in Congress, the British and French orientation of the political parties—and particularly as he came to realize that the government and Senate were dominated by pro-British Hamiltonians, his attitude changed. In assessing his own position he turned, as Monroe had predicted he would, to the pro-French Jeffersonians for support. Like Genet before him, he began to distinguish between the American people—the majority of whom be believed were pro-French Revolution—and the Federalist government, which he became convinced was pro-English.[43] In this distinction his judgment appeared sound. Most Americans appeared still drawn to the French Revolution and favored close ties with France. In mid-summer 1794 many Americans celebrated the anniversary of the French Revolution. Raising their glasses for the fifteenth time, imbibers at one festive gathering drank to the toast: "Perpetual union between France and America—May the distress of either nation increase the friendship, and call forth the aid of the other."[44]

At this time dissension and intrigue within the commission multiplied Fauchet's problems. He broke with La Forest and Petry, suspecting them of intriguing with Hamilton and Henry Knox. He and Le Blanc, as a consequence, began a separate correspondence with the home government in which they represented the Washington government as sold out to England, Genet as being unjustly persecuted, and their colleagues as being Royalist counterrevolutionaries.[45]

---

embargo's extension see *Annals of the Congress. . . ,* 3rd Cong., 1st sess., May 12, 1794, pp. 675-683; May 29, 1794, pp. 731-734. Congress on June 4, 1794, authorized the President "to lay, regulate, and revoke Embargoes" during the intermission of Congress, *ibid.,* Appendix, p. 1450.

[43] For Fauchet's and the Commissioners' early attitude toward the American government, see their despatch, Philadelphia, March 21, 1794, in Turner, *CFM,* p. 316; for manifestations of change in attitude, see Fauchet to Minister of Foreign Affairs, Philadelphia, May 5, 1794, *ibid.,* pp. 330-334; James, "French Diplomacy. . . ," *AHA Ann. Rep.* (1911), I, 158.

[44] *Columbia Gazette* (Columbia, S. C.), Aug. 1, 1794. The celebration took place in Camden, S. C.

[45] For Fauchet's suspicions of his colleagues, see his despatches to Minister of Foreign Affairs, June 4, 8, 1794, Philadelphia, in Turner, *CFM,* pp. 372-

Although now distrustful of the Washington administration, which he saw correctly as subject to Hamilton's views, and though he now consorted with its political enemies, Fauchet tried to maintain a close touch with it through Edmund Randolph, the only non-Federalist still remaining in Washington's official family. Randolph, declared Fauchet, exhibited the greatest desire to increase Franco-American unity. In "free and friendly conversations" the two men collaborated to maintain this unity. They talked over various measures in advance, agreed upon the steps to be taken, and even sent each other advance copies of letters and communications, "before sending them officially." They consulted with each other and discussed whatever measures they believed might have either a favorable or adverse effect upon relations between their two countries.[46] While it lasted the collaboration had the earmarks of a counterpoise, in part at least, to the Hamilton-Hammond collaboration. Randolph, however, never gained any real influence in the Washington government; so the French pipeline into the Cabinet from the start was of dubious utility.[47]

Among the various factors which complicated Fauchet's mission were the influence and activities of monarchical antirevolutionary French refugees from the colonies and from France, pressures from Republican politicians who would use him for local political advantage, Federalist hatred and distrust, activities and influence of the better-financed British diplomatists, intrigues among the members of his own mission, and finally the neglect he suffered from his home government. In comparison to the effect of the Jay treaty upon Franco-American relations, these were relatively minor irritants.[48] With development of the Jay negotiations whatever rap-

---

373, 389-390, also p. 717 n.; Louis-Guillaume Otto, "Considerations sur le Conduite du government des Etats unis envers la France depuis 1789 jusqu'en 1797," AAE CP EU, [June 17, 1797], Vol. XLVII, f. 407.

[46] Fauchet to Minister of Foreign Affairs, Philadelphia, May 5, 1794, in Turner, *CFM*, p. 333; Anderson, "Randolph," in Bemis, ed., *The American Secretaries of State. . .*, II, 107.

[47] Fauchet characterized Randolph as an "excellent" though "weak character," a partisan of the French Revolution, a man whose secrets were easy to penetrate, and a great aid in helping to foil the machinations of Hamilton. To Minister of Foreign Affairs, Philadelphia, June 4, 1794, in Turner, *CFM*, pp. 276-277.

[48] In his correspondence, Fauchet touched on all these problems, see *ibid.*,

port Fauchet still had in the American government was dissipated. Federalists reversed their attitude toward him; some saw him as the devil incarnate.

Even though Fauchet's suspicions of Federalist designs had been aroused with the first announcement of the Jay mission and though he tried from the beginning to counteract any influence adverse to France which it might generate, he at first labeled the mission "insignificant." America's destiny was, he felt, bound to that of France.[49] His immediate fears had been that an accommodation with England would lead to closer Anglo-American commercial ties and so frustrate French policy. These fears motivated his efforts to influence the appointment of the London envoy; he wanted the post to fall to someone who favored the French alliance. In particular, he did what he could to thwart the selection of so outspoken an Anglophile as Hamilton. Once Jay was appointed, his concerns centered on finding out what his instructions were.[50]

Although Randolph assured him that there was nothing disadvantageous to France in the Jay mission, Fauchet's doubts increased. The mission was no longer "insignificant"; any Anglo-American *rapprochement* posed a threat to the French alliance. He pressed the Secretary of State for specific information. Finally, on the advice of the President, Randolph revealed a part of Jay's instructions to Fauchet—to give "proof" that "Mr. Jay cannot enter into a negotiation contrary to what we owe to France. . . ." He accompanied this with professions of friendship for France, asserting that the two allies should draw closer together and that lovers of liberty supported France while "the partisans of slavery prefer an alliance with England."[51]

---

pp. 287-719; for a discussion of problems and recommendations, see Lokke, *Fauchet Mémoire,* pp. 85-119.

[49] Commissioners to Minister of Foreign Affairs, Philadelphia, May 27, 1794, in Turner, *CFM,* pp. 353-354; James, "French Diplomacy. . . ," *AHA Ann. Rep.* (1911), I, 159.

[50] Fauchet to Minister of Foreign Affairs, Philadelphia, May 17, 1794, in Turner, *CFM,* p. 343; Lokke, *Fauchet Mémoire,* p. 106; for Fauchet's opposition to Hamilton expressed apparently through Randolph, see Rufus King's memorandum of April 13, 1794, in King, *Rufus King Correspondence,* I, 519-520.

[51] Commissioners to Minister of Foreign Affairs, Philadelphia, May 27, 1794, and Fauchet to Minister of Foreign Affairs, Philadelphia, June 4, 1794, in Turner, *CFM,* pp. 354, 374-375; Conway, *Randolph,* p. 245.

As further evidence of American good will Randolph at the same time took up the question of a new commercial treaty which Fauchet had introduced previously. Randolph pointed out that the time was favorable for discussion of the treaty in question. In the next Congress pro-French elements would probably be stronger than the pro-British faction, and in the meantime public opinion could be cultivated by planting articles favorable to a new treaty in the press.[52] The treaty was never to be negotiated.

With Fauchet's apprehensions aroused and mounting, honeyed words and a partial revelation of Jay's instructions were meager palliatives. The French minister, not trusting Petry and La Forest, who he believed were compromising the interests of the French Republic, sent Le Blanc to France to inform government authorities directly that France was being deceived by the American government, and advised them to take "instant measures" to foil the American design.[53]

The air of mystery covering the Jay negotiations and signs of British concessions to the United States tended to confirm Fauchet's grave fears that an Anglo-American commercial system was in the making. That the American government was pro-British became in the words of Edmund Randolph "a copious theme with him."[54]

After Fauchet heard that Jay had signed a treaty and learned something of its general purport, though not its precise content, he came to believe that Jay's instructions had been marked by considerable leeway in negotiation and that the resulting treaty was inimical to French interest. Regardless of this diplomatic setback he still believed that France must attempt to maintain the

---

[52] Fauchet to Minister of Foreign Affairs, June 4, 1794, and to Committee of Public Safety, Philadelphia, April 13, 1795, in Turner, *CFM*, pp. 375-376, 638. When Jay left for London Madison and Monroe urged Fauchet to negotiate a new Franco-American commercial treaty.

[53] See Le Blanc to Commissioner of Foreign Relations, [Sept. 3, 1794], and Fauchet to Commissioner of Foreign Relations, Philadelphia, Sept. 16, 1794, in Turner, *CFM*, pp. 410-411, 421-422; James, "French Diplomacy. . . ," *AHA Ann. Rep.* (1911), I, 160; as a result of Fauchet's complaints the powers of La Forest and Petry ultimately were revoked; they were accused of "aristocracy and misdemeanors"; see Turner, *CFM*, p. 717 n.; James A. James, "French Opinion as a Factor in Preventing War between France and the United States, 1795-1800," *American Historical Review*, XXX (Oct., 1924), 44-45.

[54] Randolph to Monroe, Philadelphia, Sept. 25, 1794, *ASP FR*, I, 678.

alliance and with it her influence over the United States. He therefore suggested that French attacks against American shipping be
stopped and that the French government intercede with Spain that
the Mississippi might be opened to Americans. The latter course,
he believed, might also be a step toward once again securing Louisiana.[55]

Fauchet, in fact, made control of Louisiana a central factor in
"a lasting system to be followed by France towards the United
States." He developed this idea in a plan he sent to his superiors.
In his view, the American alliance, because of the Jay treaty, was
worthless. Even though France might wish to enforce American
compliance with her policy, she had not the means to do so; the
United States was not only free from French control, France was
dependent on the United States. The French Caribbean colonies,
which relied for food upon the United States, were hostages in
American hands. War against the United States would not bring
American policy into line; it would close off trade essential to
France and would sacrifice the hostage colonies.

The best means of keeping America faithful to the alliance, Fauchet suggested, would be to acquire Louisiana. This would furnish
France with raw materials and a market for manufacturers and
would free the West Indies from dependence on the United States.
Through possession of Louisiana France would control the Mississippi and through judicious use of pressure could control the western
growth of the nation. France then could influence American
policy; the alliance could be enforced; no more would it be subject
to the caprices of American politics.[56]

Fauchet's reasoning on Louisiana was more than the musing of

[55] Fauchet to Commissioner of Foreign Relations, Philadelphia, Nov. 19,
1794, and Commissioners to Commissioner of Foreign Relations, Philadelphia,
Feb. 2, 1794, in Turner, *CFM*, pp. 482, 551-553; James, "French Diplomacy. . . , *AHA Ann. Rep.* (1911), I, 160. According to earlier instructions
Fauchet and the Commissioners were to inform the American government
that negotiation with Spain to open the Mississippi was incompatible with
the Franco-American alliance. Turner, "The Policy of France toward the
Mississippi Valley. . . ," *AHR*, X, 264-265.

[56] Fauchet to Commissioner of Foreign Relations, Philadelphia, Feb. 4,
1795, in Turner, *CFM*, pp. 559-571; Turner, "The Policy of France toward
the Mississippi Valley. . . ," *AHR*, X, 265-266; Darling, *Our Rising Empire*. . . , pp. 194-195; see also E. Wilson Lyon, *Louisiana in French Diplomacy, 1759-1804*, pp. 88-89.

a minor diplomatic official; it typified French policy. Although France was still at war with Spain and although it had given up efforts to wrench the territory from Spain by force, the French government had not abandoned its designs on Louisiana. In the ensuing peace negotiations the French argued that a restitution of Louisiana to France would be of great advantage to Spain. It would place a powerful nation between the United States and Spain's American possessions, a barrier which would end the indignities long endured by Spain at the hands of American frontiersmen.[57] But even though it might be controlled by an ally, the United States did not want such a buffer colony on its Western borders. If France persisted in her policy of acquisition of Louisiana, the United States and France could not for long remain allies.

French suspicions of the Jay treaty mounted. Randolph continued to assure Fauchet that there was nothing harmful to France in the Jay agreement; even Madison sought to calm Fauchet's fears on that score. Despite the soft words the Frenchman protested bitterly the secrecy enshrouding the treaty. He was consoled by one development which he felt embarrassed the executive: the treaty would apparently arrive too late to be considered by Congress in its current session. The next Congress, he believed, would have fewer of the British "faction" in it. That, at least, augured well for France.[58]

Up to this time, Fauchet continued to stand well with the American authorities. When they learned that as a result of the fall of Robespierre and the Jacobins he was to be replaced by Pierre Auguste Adet, Randolph expressed regret that the hitherto "acceptable" Fauchet was to be recalled. Although it was unfortunate that a change of party should mean a change of minister, he felt that "the only thing which essentially concerns us, is, that the representative of the French republic in the United States should lay aside all intrigue, and imitate ourselves in a course of plain and fair dealing."[59]

[57] Le comité salut public a Barthélemy, Paris, May 10, 1795; May 12, 1795 (Instructions), in Kaulec, *Papiers de Barthélemy,* VI, 11-12, 14; Lokke, *Fauchet Mémoire,* p. 119 and n.

[58] Fauchet to Commissioners of Foreign Relations, Philadelphia, Feb. 8, 16, 1795, in Turner, *CFM,* pp. 573, 578-581.

[59] Randolph to Monroe, Philadelphia, Feb. 15, 1795, *ASP FR,* I, 696; Ham-

Within a few weeks things changed. On March 8 Jay and his treaty reached Philadelphia.[60] As Fauchet had surmised, they came too late for the current congressional session; Washington, however, called a special session for June 8 to consider the treaty. A few days after the treaty arrived it became, as we have seen, a public issue, touching off a violent newspaper battle as to its terms, still held secret.[61] In Madison's words, "its contents have produced conjectural comments without number." He and other Republican leaders, nevertheless, had a fairly clear idea of what the treaty contained. As did Fauchet, Madison hoped that it would be impossible for any stipulations "inconsistent with the Treaties with France" to be put into effect. He saw, however, a clear possibility "that articles may be included that will be ominous to the confidence and cordiality of France towards the United States. . . ."[62]

The Federalists had no faith in French cordiality. Opposed to the French alliance, they believed it would drag the country into a war from which nothing could be gained and much lost. They were convinced that French interest in the 1778 alliance and in American friendship was predicated on the policy of making the United States a cat's paw in the struggle against Great Britain.

John Quincy Adams, for example, expressed those views to his father, the Vice-President. From his ministerial post at The Hague he warned that it was French policy to make use of the United States as it was making use of the Dutch provinces, "that is, as an instrument for the benefit of France, as a passive weapon in her hands against her most formidable enemy." As to the Jay treaty, he warned, "the whole French influence in America will exert itself

mond maintained that Admiral Vanstabel denounced Fauchet to the National Convention, thus leading to his recall. To Grenville, Philadelphia, Nov. 12, 1794, No. 34, Henry Adams Transcripts. Despite the changes in France many Americans still identified French republicanism with liberty and maintained that America's future happiness depended on the success of the republic. *Philadelphia Gazette and Universal Daily Advertiser*, March 17, 1795.
[60] For Fauchet's views on Jay's return, see Commissioners to Committee of Public Safety, Philadelphia, May 31, 1795, in Turner, *CFM*, pp. 701-703.
[61] See William Cobbett, "Popular Proceedings Relative to the British Treaty," *Porcupine's Works* (12 vols., London, 1801), II, 233-245. Cobbett, violent Federalist editor, believed that Randolph had divulged the treaty terms to Republicans before Jay's arrival, hence his clamor, pp. 238-239.
[62] Madison to Monroe, Philadelphia, March 26, 1795, *Letters and Other Writings of James Madison* (Cong. ed.), II, 40-42.

with more than usual activity to prevent the ratification of the treaty. . . ." He was convinced that France "at all events" wanted war between England and the United States. Why? Because, he continued, the French "are sensible of how much importance our commerce is to Great Britain, and suppose that the loss of it would make that nation outrageous for peace, and compel the Minister to make it upon the terms they are disposed to dictate." French friendship, "tender sympathy," and "amiable fraternity," even if the Jay treaty were not ratified, he concluded, were dangerous; French policy was designed to sacrifice American interests to those of France.[63]

* * * * *

With the Jay treaty a fact, with his pending recall known, and discouraged by lack of instructions, Fauchet felt that he could do little that would be effective to oppose consummation of the treaty.[64] Administration support for it, particularly the prestige of Washington, appeared too powerful to be overcome. In this predicament he looked forward eagerly to Adet's arrival, believing that the new minister with fresh powers could decisively influence the Senate's action. While awaiting Adet he tried as best he could to block the treaty's approval in the Senate. He hoped that in spite of the majority in the Senate which had backed the Jay mission there still might be sufficient votes in that body to stop approval. All that was needed for the Senate to reject the treaty, he reported to his government, was eleven out of the then thirty votes.[65] At this time,

[63] John Q. Adams to John Adams, The Hague, May 22, 1795, in Ford, *The Writings of John Quincy Adams*, I, 353-363. John Adams passed some of his son's letters on to President Washington, who read them. Of the letter quoted the President remarked that it "discloses much important information, and political foresight." Washington to John Adams, Philadelphia, Aug. 30, 1795, in Fitzpatrick, *Washington's Writings*, XXXIV, 279. Another prominent Federalist saw in French designs and tampering with American politics the objective of partitioning the United States. William Vans Murray Papers, Commonplace Book, July 28, 1795 (Princeton).

[64] Fauchet and the Commissioners complained constantly that they were placed in an embarrassing position, maintaining that they received no official despatches, letters, papers, bulletins, or decrees of the Convention. English agents in contrast, they pointed out, were kept informed of developments regularly and they managed to monopolize the American press. Fauchet and Commissioners to the Commission of Foreign Relations, Sept. 1, 1794, AAE CP EU, Vol. XLI, f. 332.

[65] Commissioners to Committee of Public Safety, Philadelphia, June 9, 1795, in Turner, *CFM*, pp. 707-710; Bemis, "Washington's Farewell Address," *AHR*,

too, Fauchet assessed France's position relative to the United States. In his analysis he reported that the political connection as it then existed was practically useless; the American government had shirked its obligations to France. "The treaty of alliance and the reciprocal guarantee which it contained," he said, "was completely nullified."[66]

Meanwhile Fauchet informed the Federalist administration of his dissatisfaction with developments. After trying once more to secure the treaty terms from Randolph and failing, he turned publicly to the Republicans, "the partisans of France," for support. They represented, he was convinced, the great majority of the American people.[67]

Fauchet had protested bitterly to the American government that it had violated the 1778 treaties, rendered the alliance meaningless, and had interpreted the commercial treaty in favor of England. Alluding to the Jay treaty, he reminded the Secretary of State "that France is uneasy." Randolph replied in a stinging letter in which he said "in the name of the President" that "our treaties with France shall be sacred." Fauchet responded that there was "a contradiction between the promises and the performance of them" and "that the United States had not yet established their neutrality upon as respectable a footing as France desired, and had instructed me to demand." The professed friendship of the United States toward France "does not permit them to alter their situation towards our most mortal enemies, to our disadvantage, and amidst hostilities, the origin of which undoubtedly date from the independence of America." He concluded by requesting that the Jay treaty not be ratified until his successor arrived and presented his instructions on the situation.[68]

XXXIX, 256-257; James, "French Diplomacy. . . ," *AHA Ann. Rep.* (1911), I, 161.

[66] Fauchet to Committee of Public Safety, Philadelphia, April 19, 1795, in Turner, CFM, pp. 649-650.

[67] Fauchet to Committee of Public Safety, Philadelphia, April 24, 1795, in *ibid.,* pp. 662-663.

[68] Commissioners to Committee of Public Safety, Philadelphia, March 16, 1795, and Fauchet to Committee of Public Safety, Philadelphia, April 24, 1795, *ibid.,* pp. 605-606, 662-663; Fauchet to Randolph, Philadelphia, May 2, 1795, Randolph to Fauchet, Dept. of State, May 29, 1795, and Fauchet to Randolph, Philadelphia, June 8, 1795, *ASP FR,* I, 608-617; James, "French Diplomacy . . . ," *AHA Ann. Rep.* (1911), I, 161-162; Conway, *Randolph,* p. 248.

In administration eyes Fauchet had thrown off his mask; he was revealed as akin to Genet in his defiant attitude. Like Achilles, he now sulked in his tent, ignoring usual diplomatic amenities and consorting primarily with Republicans. He no longer visited Randolph, whom he now distrusted; and he stayed away from President Washington's receptions. He claimed shattered health as one excuse for his attitude, yet managed to attend Republican celebrations. At a Philadelphia civic festival celebrating a French victory, the "surrender of Holland to liberty," he addressed the crowd, stressing that "alliances between free peoples were like vows taken by men of virtue" and were not suited to evil doers and perverts, that free peoples would not accept as allies despots who war on nations which seek to break their chains.[69]

After such appeals, Fauchet's last letter to Randolph struck Federalists so much as an appeal to the people against the Jay treaty that the administration saw in his protests "an approbation of Mr. Genet's excesses." Randolph therefore made clear the government's position relative to the French minister and to the Jay treaty. While admitting that "a foreign minister has a right to remonstrate *with the Executive* to whom he is accredited, upon any of those measures affecting his country," he cautioned that "it will ever be denied as a right of a foreign minister, that he should endeavor, by an address to the people, oral or written, to forestall a depending measure, or to defeat one which has been decided." Such, he concluded, "is an assertion of the sovereignty of the United States, consistent with what is past, and we trust not likely to be contradicted hereafter." Fauchet did not receive this letter. It was delivered to his successor.[70]

* * * * *

Although his mission was officially closed after Pierre Auguste

[69] Randolph to Monroe, July 29, 1795, quoted in Lokke, *Fauchet Mémoire*, p. 117 n.; see also p. 86; Victor Dupont to Commissioner of Foreign Relations, [March, 1795] and a notice on the Philadelphia Civic Festival, April 6, 1795, AAE CP EU, Vol. XLIII, ff. 93, 431-432. Fauchet's dissatisfaction with the Federalist government was not a sudden reversal; he expressed such sentiments openly and in strong language well before the arrival of the Jay treaty. Hammond to Grenville, Philadelphia, Nov. 12, 1794, No. 34, Henry Adams Transcripts.

[70] Randolph to Fauchet, Dept. of State, June 13, 1795, *ASP FR*, I, 620; Commissioners to Committee of Public Safety, Philadelphia, June 9, 1795, in Turner, *CFM*, p. 708; Conway, *Randolph*, p. 248.

Adet took over in the middle of June, 1795, Fauchet's influence on
Franco-American relations and on American politics, for ill or good,
did not cease. Up to this point, although Fauchet's conduct had
been galling to the administration and to highly placed Federalists,
it had not excited public attention.[71] In comparison to Genet he
had lacked color, fire, qualities which could arouse the public. Before he left for France all this changed. Fauchet became the central figure in the tragic, Federalist-executed disgrace of Randolph.
With dramatic suddenness he was limelighted as a plotting Machia-
vellian manipulating American politics to advance the selfish interests of France. British capture of his despatch No. 10, according to
Federalists, was "a kind of interposition of heaven, by almost a
miracle"; it revealed the treachery of anti-Federalists and stripped
Fauchet of his disguise, revealing that he conspired to overthrow the
Constitution, and to separate "all of the western country from the
Atlantic States."[72] As used astutely by Federalists, the ill-fated despatch damaged the French alliance. It also stained the Republican
party, appearing to compromise some of its main leaders. Pointing out that, if unexplained, the despatch profited the English faction in the United States, Adet urged Fauchet to give Randolph an
explanatory certificate which would meet the criticisms.[73]

Fauchet had broken with Randolph; nonetheless he supplied
the explanation. Randolph, after all, was the only member of the
government who had opposed the Jay treaty and the only one who
in any way inclined toward France instead of England. Fauchet
declared that Randolph had not sold out his country for French
gold.[74] To Federalists, of course, such testimony from a discredited
and distrusted diplomat in defense of a tainted Secretary of State
was not acceptable. "Fauchet's letter," remarked one Federalist,
"read it with disgust—clearly the French Govt. by their ministers
here have had much to do in our parties agt. govt. for three years, or
since Genet's time."[75]

[71] See, for example, W. Bradford to Hamilton, Philadelphia, May 21,
1795, in Hamilton, ed., *Hamilton's Works*, VI, 1.
[72] "To the People of the United States," No. II, *The Herald: A Gazette
for the Country* (New York), Dec. 21, 1796.
[73] Adet to Fauchet, Aug. 20, 1795, AAE CP EU, Vol. XLIV, f. 265.
[74] Fauchet's explanation is in Conway, *Randolph*, pp. 319-321.
[75] William Vans Murray Papers, Commonplace Book, [Dec. 5, 1795]
(Princeton).

Another postmission episode which added to growing Franco-American bitterness was the British attempt to capture Fauchet and his papers as he sailed for France. The French frigate *Medusa*, which was to transport Fauchet, had been bottled up in Newport harbor by a British warship of the line, the *Africa*. Captain Rodham Home of the *Africa*, while patroling outside the harbor, stopped several American ships, plucking seamen from their decks. As he hovered he was irked particularly by the fact that he could not reclaim seamen at liberty on shore while the French captain, as a matter of treaty right, could. Regardless of treaty or American neutrality Home resolved he should receive the same treatment at American hands as did the French. In an ultimatum of July 1, 1795, he so informed the Rhode Island authorities.[76]

The extent of Home's contempt for American neutrality became clear the next day. From New York Fauchet had taken passage on an American coastal sloop, the *Peggy*, bound for Newport. Fortunately for the French diplomat, the *Peggy* was held up by contrary winds. Leaving most of his baggage aboard but taking his most important papers, he left her in a Connecticut port and proceeded north by land. When the *Peggy* neared Newport she was stopped while in American territorial waters by a shot across her bow from the *Africa* and searched by Home's men. Not finding Fauchet, they went through his trunks, scattered his belongings, and left with the few papers they were able to find. Under cover of fog, the *Medusa* with Fauchet aboard slipped out to sea and Fauchet reached France unscathed but burning with resentment against the United States.[77]

The French government in the person of Adet protested that "the neutrality of the United States, and the law of nations, have just been violated in the most serious manner," that the French

[76] Home's ultimatum was in form of a letter to the British vice-consul in Newport to be delivered to the governor of Rhode Island; see Home to J. W. Moore, July 31, 1795, *ASP FR,* I, 667.

[77] For eyewitness accounts of this episode, see the affidavits reproduced in *ibid.,* pp. 662-663; for other accounts see Pickering to Phineas Bond, Sept. 2, 1795, in Pickering, *The Life of Timothy Pickering,* III, 233-237; McMaster, *A History of the People of the United States. . . ,* II, 234-235; Henry J. Ford, "Timothy Pickering," in Bemis, ed., *The American Secretaries of State. . . ,* II, 183-184. The *Medusa* was described as a "remarkable swift sailer." *Maryland Gazette* (Annapolis), Sept. 17, 1795.

Republic had been "outraged," and, in effect, that the American government was derelict in not affording Fauchet the protection to which he was entitled under international law. To compensate for the "insult" he requested a "reparation proportioned to the outrage committed towards the republic of France on the person of my predecessor." Adet pointed out also that the menaces of Captain Home, his use of Newport harbor as a station from which to cruise against French shipping, and his demands for advantages similar to those granted by treaty to the French violated Washington's neutrality proclamation, international law, and the French treaties. The Jay treaty, he had been assured, did not weaken those with France; if the United States did not take steps against the British arrogance and violations, he queried, "of what value are the friendship and treaties which connect" the French and American peoples?[78]

After some delay, during which the *Medusa* made her escape with Fauchet aboard, the Washington administration took action against the aggressive British sea captain, ordering him from American waters. Washington then feared that the French and their "partizans" would maintain "that the order was never intended to be issued until it was known there would be nothing for it to operate upon." Without the requisite force, actually, the American government could have done little. Its demands upon Home and the British government were ineffectual. The most decisive countermeasure taken was to revoke the exequatur of the British vice-consul in Rhode Island who had co-operated with Home in "grossly insulting" the authority of the American government.[79]

Such retaliation was not deemed satisfactory by the French government. As we have seen, when it notified Monroe that the American alliance was no longer in effect, the Directory listed this episode as the second major specific complaint against the conduct of the American government. It charged that the "outrage" against the

---

[78] Adet to Randolph, Philadelphia, Aug. 10, 19, 1795, *ASP FR*, I, 662, 665. Inasmuch as Randolph left office on August 19, Adet's last letter went to Pickering; see also Adet's report to the Committee of Public Safety, Philadelphia, Aug. 25, 1795, in Turner, CFM, pp. 772-773.

[79] Pickering to Adet, Dept. of State, Sept. 5, 1795, and to Gov. Fenner of Rhode Island, same date, *ASP FR*, I, 665-666; other pertinent documents are reproduced on pp. 666-667; Washington to the Acting Secretary of State, Elkton, Sept. 9, 1795, in Fitzpatrick, *Washington's Writings*, XXXIV, 302.

French republic had been committed with "impunity." Monroe at that time answered that the punishment inflicted by the United States was "an adequate one for the offence," pleading that as the United States had no fleet "it was the only one in our power to inflict."[80]

* * * * *

Although it had begun auspiciously and though, in Hamilton's words, "no very marked phenomena distinguished" it, Fauchet's mission ended with Franco-American relations approaching a breaking point. When Fauchet arrived he found the United States on the verge of war with England, French hopes for an American foreign policy and neutrality favorable to French designs seemed within reach, Federalist policy faced destruction, and Republicans and Francophiles were jubilant. When he escaped into the fog of Newport harbor, without, in Washington's idiom, "the most favorable impressions of the views of the government towards his own," a reversal had taken place.[81] The Jay treaty had begun an Anglo-American *rapprochement* which carried the seeds of war with France. Federalist policy had triumphed, Republicans were enraged, French policy toward the United States had failed, and the French alliance appeared shorn of meaning.

The French government recognized the dangerous state of its relations with the United States. The position of France, admitted the Committee of Public Safety, was that of a neglected ally, "one which is betrayed and despoiled with impunity." The United States, the Committee complained, continually evaded its obligations under the alliance. Blame for this state of affairs, obviously, rested with England, and, specifically, with the English party in the United States.[82] Only if Federalist power could be broken might the alliance be salvaged.

This had not been the French view of Federalists at the beginning of the Fauchet mission. At first Fauchet had tried to get

[80] Delacroix to Monroe, Paris, March 11, 1796, *ASP FR,* I, 732; Monroe to Minister of Foreign Affairs, Paris, March 15, 1796, *ibid.,* p. 734.

[81] Washington's quotation is from Washington to Acting Secretary of State, Elkton, Sept. 9, 1795, in Fitzpatrick, *Washington's Writings,* XXXIV, 302.

[82] Le comité de salut public a Barthélemy, Paris, Sept. 16, 1795, in Kaulec, *Papiers de Barthélemy,* VI, 151.

along with the administration and its Federalist supporters, and they in turn greeted him warmly. Now even Randolph, with understandable bitterness, was convinced that "Fauchet has wrapped himself round with intrigue from the first moment of his career in the United States."[83] Party chieftain Hamilton now saw little difference between him and Genet. As if in defiance of Washington, Fauchet had openly patronized the democratic societies. "At the festivals of these clubs he is always a guest," Hamilton pointed out scornfully, "always swallowing toasts full of sedition and hostility to the government." Such conduct "was neither friendly nor decent in a foreign minister"; it was unkind and contemptuous. "But," he went on, "the hostility of the views of this minister is palpable in that intercepted letter of his, which unveils the treachery of Randolph. We there learn, that he pretended to think it was a duty of patriotism to second the Western insurrection; that he knew and approved of a conspiracy which was destined to overthrow the administration of our government, even by the most irregular means."[84]

In embittered sentiments expressed to his own government Fauchet reciprocated Federalist scorn. He believed that he had been deceived and so reported to his superiors.[85] Despite his strong feelings, he blamed French policy as well as Federalist enmity for the deplorable state of Franco-American relations. Negligence and uncertainty, he pointed out, had marked French policy toward the United States since independence. Such policy was indeed in marked contrast to British activity and steadfastness. Putting these ideas and others to paper, Fauchet presented them to the Directory in a seventy-page memoir not long after his return to France.[86] In this memoir he traced past policy, particularly the conduct of his

[83] Randolph to Monroe, Philadelphia, July 29, 1795, National Archives, Dept. of State, Diplomatic and Consular Instructions.

[84] From the essay "France," 1796, in Lodge, *The Works of Alexander Hamilton,* V, 346-347.

[85] See, for example, the comments on Fauchet in William Ellery to Oliver Wolcott, Jr., Newport, Jan. 11, 1796, in Gibbs, *Wolcott Papers,* I, 297.

[86] "Memoire sur les États-Unis d'Amérique," 24 Frimaire, an IV (Dec. 15, 1795) is in AAE CP EU, Vol. XLIV, ff. 457-527, and has been edited and printed. Lokke, *Fauchet Mémoire.* In his note accompanying the memoir Fauchet told the Minister of Foreign Relations that the memoir was the fruit of long meditations and profound researches on the politics and government of the United States. AAE CP EU, Vol. XLIV, f. 450.

predecessors, and plotted what he conceived to be the best path for future French policy towards the United States.

Even though the Jay treaty had already received Senate approval, Fauchet pointed out that if the French government acted promptly the House of Representatives might be influenced to refuse to vote the appropriations necessary to place the treaty in effect. He recommended, therefore, a close accord with the Republican party. French efforts in the forthcoming presidential election should be concentrated on defeating Washington and replacing him with a pro-French executive, preferably Jefferson. If the Jay treaty could not be destroyed and Jefferson did not become President, France, he counseled, should resign herself to the situation. There was little she could do to change matters. Only through acquisition of Louisiana, he advised, could the United States be made to feel the pressure of French influence to the degree necessary to make the government amenable to French policy.

Despite these views, Fauchet valued the 1778 alliance and American friendship. Seeing the United States as a land of vast potential and as a lucrative commercial partner, he stressed its importance to France and recommended a reconciliation. His recommendation that a policy of firmness would be helpful in bringing about a reconciliation influenced the Directory in its American policy.[87] In his analysis Fauchet saw the American political situation clearly. With Federalists in control of the government, French objectives stood no chance of implementation. While his policy of aid to the Republicans meant more and continued trouble with the Federalist-controlled government, in view of anti-French, pro-British Federalist dogma, there seemed to be no logical alternative to it.[88]

As Franco-American relations grew worse, Fauchet expressed his views publicly. In 1797 he published a pamphlet in which he defended French policy towards the United States, expressing ideas similar to those in his memoir. He accused the Federalist government of deserting its ally, an ally which had brought the new nation into being. Yet he pointed out that "the United States, by the

---

[87] E. Wilson Lyon, "The Directory and the United States," *AHR*, XLIII (April, 1938), 514. The Fauchet document provided the basis of the Directory's policy toward the United States in succeeding months.

[88] *Ibid.*, pp. 514-515; Faÿ, *Revolutionary Spirit in France and America. . . ,* pp. 370, 395-396.

extent of their territory, the nature of their population, their character and activity, and by the situation of their coasts, are evidently
called to exercise, in North America, a considerable influence. The
power which shall know how to conciliate them will find in them
an interesting friend, and their neutrality will perhaps be not less
to be courted than their alliance." He advocated in conclusion
a French policy of conciliation. Forget the wrongs of the Federalist
administration, he counseled; "France has a strong interest to preserve a good understanding with America."[89]

Fauchet's venture in American diplomacy had proved a failure.
Like Genet before him, he had injured the French alliance. In his
influential recommendations for future French policy he sowed
seeds for Franco-American conflict and so contributed to the ultimate scuttling of the French alliance.

[89] Fauchet, *Sketch of the Present State of Our Political Relations with the
United States of North America*, pp. 16, 28, 30. Because of the Jay treaty,
Fauchet contended, "it results that England may legally plunder us under
the American flag, and that we are to respect what she places under
that flag." He pictured the Federalist government, moreover, as "the tool
of Great Britain." James A. James, "French Opinion as a Factor in Preventing War between France and the United States, 1795-1800," *AHR*, XXX,
46. After reading Fauchet's pamphlet Albert Gallatin said that "it is candid,
argumentative, well written, and not in the least tainted with the fashionable
French declamation." In addition to refuting Federalist arguments "on
many points, blaming, however, the Directory in many things, he strongly
advises a reconciliation. . . ." To his wife, Philadelphia, Dec. 19, 1797, in
Adams, *The Life of Albert Gallatin*, p. 188.

CHAPTER THIRTEEN

ADET'S WAR WITH WASHINGTON'S GOVERNMENT

There are people in America who to serve certain purposes are forever harping upon the gratitude which they pretend the United States owes to France, and the French themselves are not infrequently disposed to make a merit of what was certainly a very interested policy. The present government are perhaps disposed to cancel our supposed obligations by violating the stipulations of their treaties. It is my opinion that there is a strong debt of reciprocal obligations between the United States and France, or rather, to speak the only honest language upon a political concern, the relations between the two nations were formed upon a very important common interest *which still exists, and must continue long to exist. That common interest prescribes a cordial harmony and a punctual performance of treaties on both sides. The American government is unquestionably and sincerely disposed to cultivate that harmony and faithfully to adhere to its engagements, but it expects a similar return; and I am persuaded that if the French propose to themselves an influence in America by the assumption of a supercilious tone of negotiation, or by disregarding their stipulations, they will fail of success and lose much of the influence which they actually possess.—*John Quincy Adams to Joseph Pitcairn, The Hague, November 13, 1796.

Nothing can be more insolent than Adet's appeal to the people of the United States against their Government, in his note to the Secretary of State; and nothing more extraordinary than the conclusion, where he informs them, though the Directory have determined to act in direct violation of an express article of the [1778] Treaty, that no rupture *is contemplated with the United States. If Congress do not exert themselves with spirit in support of the honor and authority of Government, I shall tremble for the event, and I am not without very painful appre-*

hensions in that respect.—Samuel Johnston to James Iredell, December 25, [1796].

* * * * *

FAUCHET's successor, Pierre Auguste Adet, arrived in the United States at a time when the French alliance faced a dismal future. Not one friend of France remained in the American government. When Randolph was driven from office the last semblance of a nonpartisan government disappeared, the last feeble voice in government councils which spoke for France in opposition to the pro-British stand of the majority was stilled.

Like Genet and Fauchet before him, Adet, in his early thirties when he became France's minister to the United States, was young. Although educated as a chemist, he had had governmental and diplomatic experience. French officials held his diplomatic abilities in high repute, considering him "a very able and very excellent man."[1]

He had been secretary on the first commission the Republic had sent to Saint Domingue. He had then become chief of the administration of the colonies, and subsequently he was appointed a member of the council of marine. At the time of his appointment to the American post he was on a mission in Geneva, a mission he regretted leaving. Arriving in Philadelphia on June 13, 1795, he presented his credentials two days later and then took up his diplomatic activities.[2]

Adet made a good initial impression on Federalist leaders. In Hamilton's judgment he was "more circumspect than either of his predecessors," and to Oliver Wolcott, Jr., he appeared "to be a mild tempered and well educated man and no Jacobin," a minister who "will not be violent or troublesome, though there is reason to think that he will promote what he deems the interest of his country with much sagacity."[3] This impression did not last long. Even

[1] Adams, diary entry of March 18, 1795, The Hague, and of Oct. 20, 1795, *Memoirs of John Quincy Adams*, I, 97, 126.

[2] For biographical details, see Turner, *CFM*, p. 728 n.; *Nouvelle biographie générale*, I, 278; Kaulec, *Papiers de Barthélemy*, VI, 151 n. Adet, actually, was second choice for the American mission. A. Bertrand, "Les États-Unis et la Revolution Française," *Revue des deux mondes*, XXXIII (May 15, 1906), 422.

[3] Hamilton, "France," 1796, in Lodge, *The Works of Alexander Hamilton*, V, 347; Wolcott, Jr., to Mrs. Wolcott, Philadelphia, July 1, 1796, in Gibbs, ed.,

though he was quiet and kept to himself, Adet made it clear that the American mission was personally distasteful, and his antipathy toward America soon became evident.[4] More noteworthy was the fact that his instructions directed him to maintain a close connection with the French party in the United States.

In other respects Adet's instructions were friendly and conciliatory and were not much different in emphasis from those of his predecessor. They covered questions of debt payment, commerce, and navigation, and stressed that he was to see to it that the American government executed the treaties of alliance and commerce and the consular convention. In particular he was to see that articles 17, 21, and 22 of the commercial treaty were enforced. These articles dealt with the admission of French privateers and their prizes into American ports and the exclusion of France's enemies. Among other things, Adet was directed to gain the confidence of Congress and the President, demonstrate that France's cause was America's also, attempt to win exemption from tonnage duties, work for a new commercial treaty and a new consular convention, observe scrupulously the proper form of communication with the President, and obtain a new loan—this last a prime objective of the mission.[5]

Armed with these instructions, Adet reached Philadelphia while the Jay treaty was before the Senate. Not having been forewarned, he was astonished when he learned of the treaty complications. He reported that the treaty filled him with indignation and placed him in an extremely difficult position as to the action he should take toward it. Like his immediate predecessors, he had no actual instructions as to the Jay treaty. He could not wait for instructions;

Wolcott Papers, I, 209. Adet brought with him a handsome wife; "this," remarked Wolcott, Jr., "is a good sign." Like Fauchet, Adet did not speak English. Adet did not mix socially; difficulties in his home life, apparently, led him to keep to himself. See Henrietta Liston to James Jackson, German Town, Oct. 16, 1796, in Bradford Perkins, ed., "A Diplomat's Wife in Philadelphia: Letters of Henrietta Liston, 1796-1800," *William and Mary Quarterly,* 3rd Series, XI (Oct., 1954), 604; Moreau de Saint-Méry, *Voyage. . .* , p. 295.

[4] James, "French Opinion as a Factor in Preventing War Between France and the United States, 1795-1800," *American Historical Review,* XXX, 46.

[5] Originally Adet's instructions were intended for Oudart, the first choice for successor to Fauchet; the instructions, dated Oct. 23, 1794, with additions are in Turner, *CFM,* pp. 721-730.

improvisation and immediate action were imperative.[6] At first he did not publicly show displeasure over the treaty.[7] His indecision did not last long; he soon became convinced that the American government had violated its French treaties and that the alliance was headed for ruin. British gold, promises, and fear, he believed, had dictated the Senate's approval of the treaty.[8]

His views echoed those of his government, which held that with the Jay treaty the United States had plumbed the lowest depth of perfidy in relations with the French Republic, a faithful ally. The treaty was practically a declaration of hostilities between allies; truly England had conquered America, he believed.[9]

When, several months later, Washington signed the Jay treaty, England's conquest appeared complete. Again Adet saw English influence triumph. He turned his rage on Washington. "My conjectures have been verified," he reported; "the President has just signed the dishonor of his old age and the shame of the United States: he has ratified the Treaty of Commerce and Amity with Great Britain, and Hammond, the English Minister, has left New York for Europe . . . with the definite pledge of the blind submission of Washington to the supreme will of [King] George." Adet insisted that "the feelings of subservience" which bound Washington to England "are now displayed in all their strength." The en-

[6] Adet's plight in regard to instructions from home was no different from that of his predecessors. During these years the Revolutionary governments practically ignored their ministers in the United States. This was a source of major complaint in Fauchet's memoir; he complained in his despatches that he had not received instructions for a year. See Fauchet's complaints to Commissioners of Foreign Relations, Philadelphia, Feb. 3, 1795, and to Committee of Public Safety, Philadelphia, April 13, 1795, in Turner, *CFM,* pp. 559, 634-641; Bemis, "Washington's Farewell Address. . . ," *AHR,* XXXIX, 257.

[7] See Wolcott, Jr., to Washington, Philadelphia, July 26, 1795, and to Mrs. Wolcott, same date, in Gibbs, ed., *Wolcott Papers,* I, 217-218. Several times when popular demonstrations against the Jay treaty afforded him an opportunity to vent his feelings, Adet gave the demonstrators no encouragement; Wolcott, Jr., said Adet "conducted himself with strict propriety" and at this early point in the mission described him as "an amiable and honest man."

[8] Adet to Committee of Public Safety, Philadelphia, June 25, 28, 1795, in Turner, *CFM,* pp. 735-738, 739-740; Fauchet, *A Sketch of the Present State of Our Relations with the United States. . . ,* pp. 25-26.

[9] "Comparative Note on the French Treaty with the United States of 1778 and the American Treaty with England in 1795," [Jan.-May, 1795], AAE CP EU, Vol. XLIII, ff. 13-15.

treaties of Randolph and his friends were not sufficient to shake him from his first resolve.[10]

Even though, according to Adet, the Senate and the President had thrown in their lot with Great Britain, one consolation still remained. In the House of Representatives the majority was composed of "patriots" whose views were favorable to France. Their opposition to the treaty could create a split between the President and the legislature and prevent implementation of the treaty.

Before Washington had signed the Jay treaty Adet had taken steps to destroy it. Believing that if the President ratified the treaty all his "efforts to destroy the alliance between the United Sates and England" would be futile, Adet decided to go directly to the American people, to arouse the "patriotic" pro-French majority in America against it. After the Senate approval, he purchased a copy of the still-secret treaty from a Senator, Stevens Thomson Mason of Virginia. Then, in an effort to influence public opinion, he plunged into domestic political controversy by publishing its contents. He believed that publication would arouse sentiment against the treaty and would arouse opposition to the "maneuvers" of the pro-English Washington government.[11] When Bache published the treaty in his *Aurora* it produced the effect desired by Adet; public emotions boiled. "It [the Jay treaty] insidiously aims to dissolve all connections between the United States and France, and to substitute a monarchic, for a republican ally," exclaimed one aroused citizen.[12]

[10] Adet to Committee of Public Safety, Philadelphia, Sept. 2, 1795, in Turner, *CFM*, pp. 776-777; the despatch is printed in translation in Chinard, *George Washington as the French Knew Him*, pp. 106-109. In France, Washington's support of the Jay treaty was considered a tragic mistake and inimical to the 1778 alliance; see George Duruy, ed., *Memoirs of Barras: Member of the Directorate*, trans. Charles E. Roche (4 vols., London, 1895-1896), entry of March 22, 1795, II, 103.

[11] Adet to Committee of Public Safety, Philadelphia, July 3, 1795, in Turner, *CFM*, pp. 741-742; so aroused were Americans by the Jay treaty, as has been seen, that some even passed resolutions urging that Mason be honored for making the treaty public. *Aurora* (Philadelphia), Sept. 14, 1795.

[12] "Americanus" in the *Independent Gazetteer*, reprinted in the *Virginia Herald and Fredericksburg Advertiser*, July 24, 1795. Adet in July sent home copious extracts from newspapers and analyses of public opinion showing that Americans were opposed to the treaty and feared that it would wreck the French alliance. These reports contributed to French belief that the treaty would not be implemented. AAE CP EU, Vol. XLIV, ff. 144-157, 197-200.

Similar sentiments crowded the columns of the Republican gazettes.

Next, Adet went to Randolph and asked in confidence if the published text of the treaty was the same as that ratified by the Senate. Randolph, defending the treaty, insisted that there was nothing in it contrary to French interests. At the same time he pointed out that the Senate did not ratify treaties, it approved them; only the President could ratify treaties and he had yet to ratify the Jay treaty. Then he promised Adet an official copy of the treaty, delivering it the same day. A few days later Adet offered his criticisms. England's favored position under the treaty, he said, precluded negotiation of a new and more favorable Franco-American treaty. The Jay treaty, he concluded, was incompatible with France's special status under the alliance.[13]

In comparison to the reaction within the Directory Adet's protests were mild. Scanning the evidence, French officials were convinced that the Jay treaty violated the 1778 alliance and that the American government had ratified it in defiance of antitreaty public sentiment.[14] What to do under the circumstances was the question. Placing the state of American politics before the Directory, the new Minister of Foreign Affairs, Charles Delacroix, reported that the outrages of the pro-English party in the government had overflowed the cup of forbearance. Yet he believed the people remained constant in their attachment to France. It was up to the Directory to adopt firm measures to recall France's allies to their real interests and to make them denounce England, their natural enemy. To prove the necessity for such measures he outlined the history of recent Franco-American frictions.

"Is it to our interest," the Minister asked, "to declare war against the United States or else is it more in line with our politics to oblige this power to break with England?" Implicitly, he went on,

[13] Adet to Committee of Public Safety, Philadelphia, July 3, 1795, in Turner, *CFM,* pp. 742-743; Adet to Randolph, Philadelphia, June 30, 1795, Randolph to Adet, Dept. of State, July 6, 1795, *ASP FR,* I, 594-596; Randolph's "Memorandum" of July 14, 1795, for Washington, in Fitzpatrick, *Washington's Writings,* XXXIV, 245 n., 246 n. On July 27, from Mount Vernon, Washington asked Randolph: "What says Mr. Adet upon the subject of the treaty, and the movements thereupon?" Randolph replied that Adet had been ill and that he did not recollect any of his opinions, although he had bolted into objections "zealously" and retreated "suddenly" (July 31). *Ibid.,* pp. 249-250, 250 n.
[14] Mangourit to ———, Dec. 23, 1795, AAE CP EU, Vol. XLIV, f. 554.

France was in a state of war with the American government, "but only with the government." The outrages that France suffered in America, the partiality shown France's enemies, the wrong done by the Jay treaty, the infractions of treaties, all these grievances together, he said, constitute certainly a state of hostilities. During this state it was, he felt, not necessary to declare again in consultation France's connection of friendship with the American nation. If war were declared against the United States it would only draw tighter the bonds which united it to England. Together they would take the Antilles and entirely destroy French commerce in America. There would be no advantage to France in such a war. This was Delacroix's answer to war-sentiment within the Directory. Then he laid down a guide for French policy. France should try, he recommended, to influence the American people to bring about a rupture between these two natural enemies, the United States and England.

What advantage would there be to the United States in such a policy? In noting the American advantages the Minister developed an old theme. The United States might become one of the principal maritime powers; its commerce could furnish subsistence to France and to her colonies, in return receiving French manufactures. The United States allied to France in war against England, could force England to divide her maritime forces. Even though the Washington government was opposed to antagonizing England, the discontent of the people might force Washington to take a strong stand against England. The American people must be incited to popular agitation. The French Minister Plenipotentiary had been playing the dangerous role of inciter; Citizen Adet, Delacroix believed, had the qualities for continuing the task.[15]

Yet, for a while, the Directory went ahead with plans to replace Adet and to entrust his successor with responsibility for carrying out Delacroix's policy. That the Jay treaty violated "the alliance which binds the two peoples" stood out as the foremost French grievance in the new set of instructions.[16]

[15] "Rapport au Directoire Exécutif par le Ministre des Rélations Extérieures," [Paris], Jan. 16, 1796, *ibid.*, Vol. XLV, ff. 41-53.

[16] "Mémoire pour servir d'instruction politique au Citoyen Vincent, envoyé comme Ministre plénipotentiare de la Republique auprès des Etats-unis," [Paris], March 6, 1796 (signed by the President of the Directory), *ibid.*, XLV, ff. 182-191.

Despite France's anger the House of Representatives at the end of April, 1796, voted funds to implement the Jay treaty. To Adet as to other Frenchmen this was tragedy, another triumph of England and English gold.[17] In analyzing this defeat he asked bitterly: Who committed the American government to make the English treaty? Who persuaded Washington to ratify it? Who agitated to get it through the House of Representatives? *"Le parti Anglois,"* he informed his superiors. Who comprised this English party? Old tories, merchants with British connections and other men of finance, particularly officers of the Bank of the United States.[18] The audacity of this English faction, he believed, had to be curbed if a desirable state of relations of France and Great Britain with the United States were to be re-established. This could be done, he suggested, only by means of the 1778 commercial treaty. Without taking an openly hostile attitude France could declare that the free-ships-free-goods clause in the commercial treaty was inapplicable because Americans allowed the English the special favor of seizing French goods on neutral American ships without allowing similar privileges to the French. France might then retaliate against the Jay treaty by seizing American ships loaded with English goods.

These measures would hit hardest pro-English Federalist merchants, who profited from trade with England and who were committed to the Hamiltonian policy. The administration would bear the blame for the consequences of such a disastrous policy, a policy which could be traced to the administration's Jay treaty.

[17] Even elements of the anti-Revolution press of French refugees in the United States had protested against the iniquitous Jay treaty. As if admonishing a wayward friend forgetful of obligations the press asked of Americans: "Allies of France what became of you?" Childs, "French Opinion of Anglo-American Relations. . . ," *French-American Review,* I, 27.

[18] Delacroix already had analyzed the so-called English party. "The rich merchants in the United States form the English party," he had told the Directory. "Hamilton is its head; Hamilton is audacious and courageous, but the people do not like him; he does not find partisans in this numerous class which alone brings about revolution." On this alleged weakness Delacroix had based his hopes for overthrowing the Federalists and reversing American foreign policy. "Rapport au Directoire Exécutif par le Ministre des Rélations Extérieures," [Paris], Jan. 16, 1796, AAE CP EU, Vol. XLV, f. 46; for details on Delacroix, see Raymond Guyot, *Le Directoire et la paix de l'Europe* (Paris, 1911), pp. 68-70; Masson, *Le Département des affaires etrangéres. . . ,* pp. 361-362.

As a corollary of this retaliatory policy, Adet saw the possibility of electing a pro-French president and of assuring the ascendancy of France in the councils of the American government. In this way, he concluded, France could offset disadvantages growing out of the union between the United States and Great Britain. Honor and national interest would not allow France to observe in silence the conduct of the American government.[19] Regardless of Adet's views to the contrary, such a policy, if persisted in, and if a pro-French government did not succeed Washington's, meant hostilities on the seas between Frenchmen and Americans. It meant the end of the Franco-American alliance.[20]

* * * * *

In addition to developing his suggestions on policy for his home government, Adet, of course, carried on his other duties. He pressed Randolph to begin negotiations on a new commercial treaty and new consular convention.[21] He protested, as violations of French treaty rights, the seizure by American authorities of the French armed vessels *La Vengeance* and *Le Cassius*. The cases of these ships illustrate some of the difficulties faced by the Washington administration in trying to reconcile French treaty rights with its policy of neutrality.

In the sea war against the British, as we have seen, the French had to depend upon American assistance. France was able to some extent to use her Caribbean islands as bases from which to attack British commerce; she had, however, to rely upon American aid for armaments. Such aid was prohibited by the neutrality legisla-

[19] Adet to Minister of Foreign Relations, Philadelphia, May 3, 1796, in Turner, *CFM*, pp. 900-906.

[20] Sir Robert Liston, the new British minister, saw the implications of the Directory's harsh policy as advocated by Adet. "I am glad to observe," he told Hammond, "that the French, by illegal captures of American Ships, & other insolent behavior, are likely to spread ill humour against themselves in this country, & turn the publick attention, which the opposition papers are constantly endeavouring to fix on trifling irregularities on our part, into a different channel." Philadelphia, June 20, 1796, Sir Robert Liston Papers, The National Library of Scotland, microfilm copies in the Library of Congress. Within the Directory such reaction did not mean too much as there was a militant group which wanted war with the United States, but was restrained by the moderates. *Mémoires de Larevellière-Lépaux*, II, 258; Lyon, "The Directory and the United States," *AHR*, XLIII, 515.

[21] The correspondence exchanged on the new commercial treaty is in *ASP FR*, I, 640-641.

tion. Yet, the pro-French fervor of Americans—and the desire for profit—made it possible for unarmed French vessels to come into American ports as traders, secretly or otherwise obtain armaments, and go out to sea to prey on British commerce. The next time the vessel appeared in an American port she would be armed as a ship of the French navy, and, if accepted as such, under the 1778 treaty entitled to freedom of American ports. American authorities then faced the question: Was this truly a vessel of the French navy entitled to special treaty privileges or was she a ship which had violated the neutrality laws and hence subject to seizure? One interpretation would offend France and the other would offend Britain. Usually, France suffered.

The case of the French privateer *La Vengeance* fitted this pattern. When she entered New York harbor in July, 1795, with a Spanish prize, New York authorities seized her on the grounds that previously she had been armed in an American port in violation of the neutrality laws. Adet protested that her seizure was based on "mere suspicions" and vitiated article 17 of the 1778 commercial treaty. Adet's protest did little good.

According to the federal authorities in New York a libel could be filed against a ship without an affidavit or other evidence to substantiate the allegations upon which the suit was based. Failure to establish his case meant that the libelant would have to stand the costs and damages. This usually acted as sufficient deterrent to prevent abuse of the process. When a war vessel was involved, however, merely by meeting costs of litigation those who would, could put the ship out of action as effectively as if she had been sunk. While involved in the ensuing litigation, *La Vengeance* was kept from harassing British commerce.

La Vengeance was condemned under dubious circumstances. All officers of the district court, Adet charged, were interested in her condemnation. Finally, upon appeal, the sentence was reversed, and the case ultimately decided in her favor. The proceedings had lasted over a year, the vessel being sold meanwhile, according to Adet, for a "tenth part of the cost of her armament." A French war vessel was thus put out of action permanently by American neutrality laws and red tape.[22]

[22] For pertinent documents on the case, see *ibid.*, 621-629; see also Adet to

Similar to the case of *La Vengeance* was that of the corvette *Le Cassius*. In this instance American authorities not only seized the vessel, they also arrested the captain, a former American citizen. The arrest, Adet protested, was "a violation of principles and our treaty," as was the detention of the corvette. He questioned the motives of the person who brought suit against the *Cassius* by implying that he sought to aid England by immobilizing the vessel. While not denying the libelant's English connections, Secretary of State Pickering noted that the person in question had also a personal motive; he was part owner of the prize taken by the *Cassius,* and if the corvette and her equipments were confiscated he stood to gain half their value.

Even if the *Cassius* had been armed in the United States, Adet said, her seizure was invalid. She was at the time of seizure a vessel of the French government "and the nineteenth article of our treaty expressly states, that vessels may freely enter and sail from ports of the United States without receiving the least hindrance." Then he expressed the hope that "the Government of the United States will take proper measures to prevent the force of the republic from being paralyzed in its ports, and evil minded people from abusing the laws in order to arrest every French vessel coming into the United States. For if a single information be sufficient to stop one vessel," he pointed out acidly, "there is no reason why the first frigate which shall arrive from Europe should not be seized as having armed in the United States."

Over a year after the initial seizure, the charges against the corvette were dismissed. In the meantime, Adet had abandoned the ship to the United States, reserving the right to reparation "for the injuries and damages" arising from the long drawn out proceedings.[23] Such treatment at the hands of American authorities tended to confirm French views as to the pro-English orientation of the

---

Minister of Foreign Relations, Philadelphia, March 21, 1796, in Turner, *CFM,* p. 862; for a general discussion, see Ford, "Pickering," in Bemis, ed., *The American Secretaries of State. . .* , II, 192-194.

[23] For pertinent documents on the *Cassius* case, see *ASP FR,* I, 629-639. Adet's reasons for abandoning the *Cassius* are in Adet to Commission on Foreign Relations, Philadelphia, Sept. 3, 1795, and Adet to Minister of Foreign Relations, Philadelphia, March 21, 1796, in Turner, *CFM,* pp. 780-781, 861-862.

American government; the French became convinced that under the Federalist regime the alliance was meaningless.

Adet also protested that in not defending its neutrality and in allowing the British to seize American provision ships bound for France, the United States "presented to England a poniard to cut the throat of its faithful ally."[24] In other instances he complained that the United States did not behave like an ally and that it did not act even as a neutral toward France. The British at this time were preparing an attack on French Caribbean possessions, particularly against Saint Domingue. In preparation they purchased quantities of flour, other supplies, and horses in the United States and recruited the services of Americans. With the expectation that the French, under the terms of commercial treaty of 1778, would allow the ships to pass unmolested, they chartered American bottoms to carry many of the purchases to their Caribbean destinations.

"If your fellow-citizens are prohibited from serving in the cause of France," Adet told Pickering, "neither should they be permitted to range themselves under the British flag; otherwise neutrality would only be a vain term, and a certain mean[s] of assisting secretly, and without running any risk, a power which no one would dare to aid openly." Horses, he continued, were contraband of war. If the American government did not stop their export it would be tolerating trade in contraband. The British were enrolling American grooms. They recruited the crews of their ships blockading French Caribbean ports from mariners they took from American ships. If the American government did not take steps to enforce its neutrality, he concluded, France would blame the United States for loss of her Caribbean islands.[25]

For the American government to stop the sale of flour as a "courtesy" to France as Adet asked, Pickering countered, would have been unneutral. While admitting that horses were contraband, and hence subject to confiscation if captured at sea, he maintained that the American government was not obligated to prevent their sale or shipment. In fact, when the governor of Virginia took steps in Norfolk to stop the sailing of a sloop loaded with horses for the British, he was ordered to release the vessel.

[24] Adet to Pickering, Philadelphia, Sept. 28, 1795, *ASP FR,* I, 643.
[25] Adet to Pickering, Philadelphia, Jan. 12, 1796, and March 29, 1796, *ibid.,* pp. 644-645.

Backed by an opinion of the Attorney General and by the President, Pickering contended, in effect, that there was nothing in the sales to the British of which France had any right to complain, that an "impartial neutrality" forbade the United States to place restraints on that trade.[26]

This made Republicans bristle. From Portsmouth, Virginia, for example, a Republican reported that the "recruiting business goes on briskly here—I am told about 1500 cavalry will be shipped in a few days—great numbers cross from hence daily. Ask a republican what he thinks of this business, he hangs his head. Sighs and says—If I say a word, I shall be the 'partizan of war and confusion.' "[27] Echoing these sentiments, Senator Stevens Thomson Mason of Virginia said, "the French must be certainly very good natured to bear patiently all this marked partiality to their Enemies yet I hope they will for tho' I love the French People I am not a *partisan of war and confusion.*"[28] Adet despaired. What good, he wrote to his superiors, does the friendship of the American people do us when the Secretary of State is pro-English and the government is against us?[29]

This feeling had been strengthened by an unfortunate occurrence early in Adet's mission. The French National Convention had decreed that the Republic's colors should be presented to the United States and had entrusted Adet with the presentation, in which he was to deliver a warm salutation from the Committee of Public Safety. After coming to the United States and discerning the Executive's anti-French orientation, he delayed the ceremony. Fearing that the flag might be slighted and hoping to use the ceremony as

[26] See Pickering to Adet, Philadelphia, Jan. 20 and March 25, 1796, and Adet to Pickering, Philadelphia, March 11, 1796, *ibid.*, pp. 645-650. Richard Hildreth, *The History of the United States of North America* (6 vols., New York, 1849), IV, 680; for the Virginia embargo on horses, see John Steele to James McHenry, Richmond, March 27, 1796, with enclosures of Jan. 29, in Bernard C. Steiner, ed., "Correspondence of James McHenry," *WMQ*, 1st Series, XIII, 102-104.

[27] The extract is dated Jan. 20, 1796, in the *Federal Gazette and Baltimore Daily Advertiser*, Feb. 15, 1796.

[28] Mason to Joseph Jones, Philadelphia, Feb. 29, 1796, Joseph Jones Papers, Duke University.

[29] Adet to Commission of Foreign Affairs, Philadelphia, Jan. 30, 1796, in Turner, *CFM*, pp. 824-825.

a forum from which to appeal for Franco-American unity, he waited until Congress convened.

In December when Adet indicated that he wished to present the flag, President Washington set aside January 1, 1796, "a day of general joy and congratulation" for the ceremony. In delivering the colors to the President, Adet said France was "long accustomed to regard the American people as her most faithful allies" and that she wanted to draw the two countries closer. He pointed out that the American colors were displayed in the hall of the National Convention. The message from the Committee of Public Safety had the same warm glow; it spoke of the "sacred ties" and the "indissoluble" bonds between France and the United States.

Washington's response, though complimentary to "our magnanimous allies," disappointed Adet. He had expected the French flag to be displayed prominently in the House of Representatives; instead, the President announced he would deposit it in the archives of the United States. The French minister expressed his disappointment to Pickering. Shutting up the flag in the archives, he protested, would be looked upon by the French Republic "as a mark of contempt. Would it not be convenient," he enquired, "to fix this flag in a similar place to that which yours occupies in France, and where the national honor expected to see it?" Pickering replied with a relatively tactful but admonitory rebuff. Personally he considered Adet's presenting of the colors absurd, an act designed to inflame public passions.[30]

Adet reported in disgust that the flag "will be hidden away in an attic and destined to become the fodder of the rodents and insects that live there." He suggested that the American flag be removed from the hall of France's legislative body. In his view, French overtures of friendship had been met with indifference and scorn.[31]

[30] Pickering's comments were made to Phineas Bond, British *chargé d'affaires* in Philadelphia. Bond to Grenville, [Philadelphia], Jan. 2, 1796, No. 1, Henry Adams Transcripts.

[31] For the flag episode, see the documents in *ASP FR*, I, 527-528. These include the message of the Committee of Public Safety of Oct. 21, 1794, and Adet's message to Washington and the response of Jan. 1, 1796. For Adet's protest to Pickering, Philadelphia, Jan. 9, 1796, and Pickering's response of Jan. 15, 1796, see pp. 656-657. For Adet's report of the episode, see Adet to Committee of Public Safety, Philadelphia, Jan. 16, 1796, in Turner, *CFM*, pp. 811-814. For a description of the flag, see Bernard Faÿ, *The Two Franklins*, p. 293.

The distrust between the two countries increased, even minor irritants being magnified into major insults. Adet made an issue, for example, of the fact that a Philadelphia publication in its listing of diplomatic precedence had placed Great Britain in first place, a position France previously had occupied. He asked the American government to suppress the publication. This, of course, could not be done. Pickering pointed out that pulications were private and not subject to government regulation.[32]

* * * * *

As antagonism between the two nominal allies deepened, their differing interpretations of treaty obligations also contributed to the growing rupture. Prior to 1796 the United States had allowed the French to sell prizes their privateers brought into American ports. To France, maritime underdog in the struggle with Great Britain, this was a valuable privilege. Early in 1796 the Jay treaty went into effect with its article 24 which prohibited "privateers" in the service of England's enemies from selling their prizes in American ports. Soon after this British officials in the United States asked the American government to stop the sale of French prize goods in American ports. The United States then took steps to comply with the request.[33]

Early in May the House of Representatives passed a resolution—reputedly written by Hamilton—forbidding the sale of prizes in the United States by all belligerents. Adet entered an immediate protest against this resolution. It contravened the commercial treaty, he said, and was the opposite of impartial neutrality; it favored England to the disadvantage of France. "But if," he said, "it be the duty of a neutral neither to grant nor refuse more to one of the belligerent powers than to another, when there do not exist particular stipulations provided for by treaties previous to the war, it follows that the law in question being in favor of Great Britain

[32] Adet to Pickering, Philadelphia, March 3, 1796, and Pickering to Adet, Dept. of State, March 14, 1796, *ASP FR*, I, 657-658.
[33] Only British prizes taken by French privateers were not allowed to be sold in American ports. France was the only belligerent who sold prizes in American ports. For details, see Hyneman, *The First American Neutrality*, pp. 123-125; for Alexander Hamilton's instructions to collectors of customs governing the sale of prizes, see *ASP FR*, III, 339; for the instructions of Aug. 4, 1793, see I, 140-141.

cannot be conformable to the rules of neutrality." Pickering replied
that France had no right to sell prizes in American ports. As to the
charge of favoring Britain, he disposed of it with the argument that
"a neutral nation can be responsible only for the *equality* of its *rules
of conduct* towards the belligerent Powers, and not for the *effects*
of an exact observance of those rules, which must depend on the
situation and circumstances of the warring Powers themselves."[34]

By the end of June, 1796, administration policy on the sale of
prizes in American ports was clear. France did not have treaty
rights allowing such sales; the administration interpreted the Jay
treaty as forbidding sale of British prizes taken by French privateers.
The Treasury Department, therefore, instructed customs collectors
to forbid entry to such prize property. To the Directory this action
gave proof to its view that as a result of the Jay treaty France had
lost an advantage of her alliance with the United States.[35]

Adet now officially gave the American government a copy of the
Executive Directory's decree of July 2, 1796, which was issued after
the House of Representatives had implemented the Jay treaty. It
declared that France "will treat neutral vessels, either as to confiscation, or as to searches, or capture, in the same manner as they shall
suffer the English to treat them." This policy, amounting to repudiation of the 1778 commercial treaty and hence of the alliance, the
decree claimed to be justified on the ground that the commercial
advantages secured by the 1778 treaty now benefited enemies of
France. As Adet pointed out, France, in effect, expected the United
States to force the English to respect American neutrality. France

[34] For the House resolution on sale of prizes, see *Annals of the Congress. . . ,* 4th Cong., 1st sess., May 7, 1796, p. 1329. After the bill was
amended the House postponed action on it at this time. There was opposition to it "on the ground that the measure . . . approached very nearly to an
encroachment upon existing treaties" and that "it might give offence to some
of the belligerent powers with whom they desired to be on good terms," May
3, 1796, p. 1489. For House debate on the bill, see May 11, 1796, pp.
1340-1347. See also Adet to Pickering, Philadelphia, May 18, 1796, and
Pickering to Adet, Dept. of State, May 24, 1796, *ASP FR,* I, 650-652; Adet
to Minister of Foreign Relations, Philadelphia, June 3, 1796, in Turner, *CFM,*
pp. 911-913.
[35] Oliver Wolcott, Jr., to Collectors of Customs, Treasury Dept., June 30,
1796, *ASP FR,* I, 340; Executive Directory to Minister of Foreign Relations,
Oct., 1796, AAE CP EU, Vol. XLVI, f. 392; the Directory directed the
Minister of Foreign Relations to inform the American government that
France still claimed the right to sell prizes in American ports.

followed England's lead, he said, only because she was forced to do so. "France, bound by treaty with the United States, could find only a real disadvantage in the articles of that treaty which caused to be respected as American property, English property found on board American vessels. They had a right, under this consideration, to expect that America would take steps in favor of her violated neutrality."[36] These actions and arguments were, in substance, in accord with the policy Adet had urged upon the French government in May.

Pickering responded that the Directory's decree did not distinguish between ordinary neutrals and the United States, which by virtue of the commercial treaty of 1778 stood on ground different than that of other neutrals. British seizures of French goods on American ships had the sanction of international law, he pointed out, but France was restrained by the free-ships-free-goods clause of the 1778 commercial treaty from following the British example. Hence he asked Adet for clarification of the French action. Was American commerce liable to suffer new restrictions at the hands of France? Were the restrictions placed on American commerce considered to be of a nature "to justify a denial of those rights which are pledged to us by our treaty with your nation?"[37]

Adet's ultimate answer had almost the character of a nullification of the Franco-American alliance. In a long note with appended documents, in which he reviewed the whole quarrel between France and the United States over neutrality, he "traced the catalogue of grievances of the French republic" against the United States. He demanded "the execution of that contract which assured to the United States their existence, and which France regarded as the pledge of the most sacred union between two people, the freest upon earth." He pointed out that "the American Government

[36] Decree of the Executive Directory of July 2, 1796, and Adet to Pickering, Philadelphia, [Oct. 27, 1796], *ASP FR,* I, 576-577. The French decree was not a sudden departure in French practice; it authorized openly what had been practiced covertly. Bassett, *The Federalist System. . . ,* pp. 220-221.

[37] Pickering to Adet, Dept. of State, Nov. 1, 1796, *ASP FR,* I, 578. Hamilton did not like Pickering's answer. "There was something of hardness and epigrammatic sharpness in it," he said. In his opinion, "our communications should be calm, reasoning, and serious, showing steady resolution more than feeling, have force in the idea, rather than in the expression." Hamilton to Wolcott, Jr., Nov. 22, 1796, in Gibbs, ed., *Wolcott Papers,* I, 398.

cannot pretend to impartiality; it cannot say that it has maintained an equal neutrality between France and England, since it has granted to Great Britain advantages denied to France. But every one of these advantages granted to England was a real injury to the republic; and if it is not maintained, without sporting with all principles, that a government may consider itself as neutral, in granting to a belligerent Power advantages which it refuses to another, it is clear that the Government of the United States, after having made its treaty with Great Britain ceased to be neutral, when it opposed itself to the participation by France, in the favors granted to the English."

Then Adet went on to announce "that the executive directory regards the treaty of commerce concluded with Great Britain as a violation of the treaty made with France in 1778, and equivalent to a treaty of alliance with Great Britain; and that, justly offended at the conduct which the American Government has held in this case, they have given him orders to suspend, from this moment, his ministerial functions with the Federal Government." He hastened to add that "the American people, are not to regard the suspension of his functions as a rupture between France and the United States, but as a mark of just discontent, which is to last until the Government of the United States returns to sentiments, and to measures, more conformable to the interests of the alliance, and the sworn friendship between the two nations."[38] At the same time he stressed that "this alliance was always dear to Frenchmen; they have done every thing to tighten its bands. The Government of the United States, on the contrary, has sought to break them." Then the French minister concluded with a listing of French grievances and a high-flown propaganda appeal to the American people. "Let your Government return to itself," he advised, "and you will still find in Frenchmen faithful friends and generous allies."[39]

[38] Despite the portentous developments in Franco-American relations John Quincy Adams, at this time in Europe in close touch with political developments there, did not believe that France wished "to be at positive variance with the United States." Later he reported that the Directory did not wish "an absolute rupture" with the United States. John Quincy Adams to Secretary of State, Nov. 16, 1796, and to John Adams, The Hague, Feb. 23, 1797, in Ford, *The Writings of John Quincy Adams*, II, 43 n., 131.

[39] Adet to Pickering, Philadelphia, Nov. 15, 1796, *ASP FR*, I, 579-583, appended documents follow; "Mémoire pour servir d'instructions au Citoyen

This bold appeal to the people against the government and President Washington, according to the Federalist view, not only nullified the French alliance, but also marked a declaration of war on the Washington administration.[40]   In the manner of Genet, Adet had bypassed the American government and used the note as a manifesto with which to appeal directly to the American people; at the same time that he forwarded it to the State Department he sent a copy for publication to Bache's *Aurora*.   A summary of the note's contents with extracts from the appended documents appeared in print before a full translation had been made in the State Department.   Adet's manifesto, in short, was designed to compel the Federalist government to change its tone and "to enlighten the people."[41]

Federalists were furious.   "Nothing can be more insolent than Adet's appeal to the people of the United States against their Government," raged a North Carolina Federalist, "and nothing more extraordinary than the conclusion, where he informs them, though the Directory have determined to act in direct violation of an express article of the Treaty, that no *rupture* is contemplated with the United States."[42]   Other Hamiltonians centered their fire on the alliance, maintaining that it was the means by which Genet and Adet had sought to draw the United States into war against England.[43]

In the same vein another defender of Federalist policy denounced

Adet, Ministre plenipotentiare de la republique Francaise, auprès des etats-unis" (from the Executive Directory), [Paris], Aug. 23, 1796, AAE CP EU, Vol. XLVI, ff. 137-140.   In this memoir the Directory gave its reasons for recalling Adet, mainly that the recall expressed its view of the conduct of the American government.   Delacroix to Adet, Paris, Aug. 24, 1796.   In accord with the memoir Delacroix ordered Adet to suspend his functions. *Ibid.*

[40] William Vans Murray Papers, Commonplace Book, Dec. 10, 1796 (Princeton).   Murray claimed that the note revealed French designs to use the United States not as a friend but as an instrument against Great Britain.

[41] Adet to Minister of Foreign Relations, [Nov., 1796], in Turner, *CFM,* 970; Ford, "Pickering," in Bemis, ed., *The American Secretaries of State. . . ,* II, 204; Hildreth, *The History of the United States. . . ,* IV, 682-683.

[42] Samuel Johnston to James Iredell, Dec. 25, [1796], in McRee, *Life and Correspondence of James Iredell,* 483.

[43] *Columbian Centinel* (Boston), Jan. 11, 1797; also William Willcocks to Adet in the *New York Gazette,* Dec. 8, 1796, reprinted in the *Federal Gazette and Baltimore Daily Advertiser,* Dec. 5, 1796.

Adet's note as "a mere *in terrorem business*. Do the Directory expect," he asked, "the President will [go] down on his knees and ask pardon of the French government, *for struggling to preserve peace?* Or do they expect the United States will purchase peace with a few million dollars?" Then he prophesied that "the tide of affection for the French will change—it is now turning to keen resentment." Requesting "one word more," he counseled that "if the French consider the treaty as violated, it is presumed the United States will take them at their word and consider it as violated on the part of the French. We are then in a situation to take the President's advice, *never to ferm* [*sic*] *another treaty of commerce* with any nation. The commercial part of the British treaty will end in two years after the war. *Never let another be formed.*"[44]

While admitting that it angered the pro-British faction and aroused the anti-French press, Adet reported to his superiors that the note's publication had gained favor with friends of France and that it received a good press among the anti-English papers.[45] To Pickering, Adet's communications were unsatisfactory explanations for French policy. "If the publication of these notes," he said, "addressed in reality to the *people* of the United States, was expected to promote the interests of France, the minister and his government will find themselves egregiously mistaken. I have heard of but one sentiment concerning them, and that of indignation." What, he wondered, did France want of the United States short of war with Great Britain? Adet's appeal marked the end of all correspondence with the French minister; Pickering made no direct reply to its allegations.[46]

Adet's flamboyant appeal had plunged him into the midst of America's domestic political battles. Federalists pointed out that the manifesto was designed to "wean us from the government and administrators of our own choice; and make us willing to be governed by such as France shall think best for us—beginning with Jeffer-

[44] *The Herald: A Gazette for the Country* (New York), Nov. 23, 1796.

[45] Adet to Minister of Foreign Relations, [Nov., 1796], in Turner, *CFM*, pp. 968-972.

[46] Pickering to Rufus King, *Philadelphia,* Nov. 26, 1796, Rufus King Papers, Huntington Library; Pickering to C. C. Pinckney, Philadelphia, Nov. 26, 1796, National Archives, Dept. of State, Diplomatic and Consular Instructions.

son."[47]   But the declaration was said to have been "received by the middle and southern states with satisfaction, and with a determination to gratify France with an administration which will accord with its wishes."   Adet had begun his open campaign to influence the election of 1796.[48]

Washington's second term was coming to a close; he had already delivered his Farewell Address and had indicated his intention to retire from public office.   The time seemed ripe to advance the cause of France by helping to defeat the pro-English Federalists and so bring to power the pro-French Republicans.

*   *   *   *   *

Despite the initial conciliatory efforts of Fauchet and Adet to win the American government to a favorable French policy, American foreign policy in the French view had continued pro-British. Each French government had therefore resorted finally to the same policy: that of intervention in American politics.   In such intervention they were encouraged, as we have seen, by the Jeffersonians, who contrived to use French diplomatists and French policy for their own ends.   Ultimately each minister of the French Republic turned from the government to the opposition party for support of the alliance, each attempted to turn the people against the government, and each fell from grace by becoming unacceptable to the administration and to Federalist leaders.

While over-all American foreign policy was of minor significance to French statesmen, who in these years were occupied with weightier problems in Europe, they were concerned over any Anglo-American *rapprochement*.   They knew that British policy toward the United States was directed to destruction of the Franco-American alliance and to alienating the United States from France. Logically, the French viewed with alarm any evidence of success in British policy, minor though it be.   To thwart enemy policy they were willing to go to almost any lengths.

[47] *Gazette and Daily Advertiser* (Charleston), Jan. 2, 1797, from the *Connecticut Courant* signed SENTINEL.   Sentinel declared that "as Bulls for the dethroning of Princes used to begin and end with grace; so does this denunciation of wrath, with *love to the people*—though coupled by the way, with *hatred to the government.*"

[48] Oliver Wolcott, Sr., to Oliver Wolcott, Jr., Litchfield, Nov. 21, 1796, in Gibbs, ed., *Wolcott Papers,* I, 397.

The United States, caught in the middle of the great Anglo-French conflict, was not entirely a free agent.[49] Whatever it did in foreign policy was bound to affect its position relative to one of the struggling powers. American politics reflected this dilemma. Basically then, to the French the real enemy was not the American government, and certainly not the American people, but Great Britain.

In keeping with this view, successive French governments from 1793 to 1797, with variations, made a distinction between the attitude of the American people and that of the Federalist government toward France and the alliance. They saw the Washington administration as a captive of British policy, dominated by the pro-British mercantile governing minority, whereas the masses were ardently pro-French and pro-alliance.

In attacking Federalists and their government, French statesmen held that they were attacking England, aiding the American people to free themselves from a minority government controlled by the British, at the same time that they were advancing French policy. This view of the welfare of the American people as bound to that of France was held also by Republican leaders and was propagated in their political activities.[50]

French statesmen were supported in their conviction that most Americans wanted French friendship, that Americans looked upon France as a partner in revolution, and that Americans were grateful for the life-giving 1778 alliance, by the reports of their ministers in the United States, by those of returned *emigrés,* and by assurances of Republican politicians.

Not all French officials or *emigrés* from America shared this

[49] See, for example, Childs, "French Opinion of Anglo-American Relations. . . ," *FAR,* I, 21-22.

[50] *Ibid.,* p. 22. The *Gazette Nationale ou Moniteur Universel* in these years reflected official French policy; nonofficial journals also shared its views. *La Décade Philosophique,* for example, attacked Washington as one who had "forgotten who were and still are the enemies of his nation," and who had always had "a striking predilection for the English," quoted in Childs, "French Opinion of Anglo-American Relations. . . ," *FAR,* I, 25-26. William Vans Murray, on the other hand, said that Washington's vigilance had prevented an explosion by the French party and that this was why the "anti-federal party" took incessant pains to impress on the minds of the French that the government was British. Therefore, concluded Murray, the French supposed that in ruining the country they injured the British. William Vans Murray Papers, Commonplace Book, Dec. 8, 1795 (Princeton).

view of American friendship for France. Charles Maurice Talley-
rand, for example, discounted American gratitude as a basis for
Franco-American relations. Discerningly, he observed that, as
Americans were concerned with earning wealth, their ties with
Great Britain would increase. In the pursuit of gold, he held,
passions and emotional connections of the past would vanish. The
Jay treaty came merely as the *coup de grâce*.[51]

In the spring of 1797, soon after his return to France from exile
in America, Talleyrand addressed the National Institute on the
commercial relations between the United States and England.
Again he stressed that in spite of superficial and emotional sympathy for France by Americans, economically and socially the
United States was bound to England, that "she remains altogether
English in the greater part of her habits." Clearly, France had
failed to exploit her favorable relationship with the United States
in the immediate post-Revolution years. Great Britain, consequently, had regained the favored trade connection. Indeed, her trade
with the United States was at the time far greater than it had ever
been. The population of the United States was increasing, and
with it American needs, which Britain was capable of supplying.

Franco-American amity had a great obstacle to overcome in that
Britain and the United States shared a common language and institutions based on the common law. "In every part of America
through which I travelled," he pointed out, "I have not found a single Englishman who did not feel himself to be an American, not a
single Frenchman who did not find himself a stranger." Obviously,
Talleyrand held no sanguine view on the strength of the 1778
alliance. It was to him a marriage of convenience, little else.[52] In
the closing months of 1796, as the American presidential elections
approached, the 1778 alliance still appeared desirable to the Directory
if it could be revived and supported by a pro-French government
in America.

* * * * *

[51] Georges Pallain, ed., *Correspondance Diplomatique de Talleyrand, La
Mission de Talleyrand à Londres en 1792. Ses Lettres de l'Amérique à Lord
Landsdowne* (Paris, 1889), pp. 421 ff., and cited in Childs, "French Opinion
of Anglo-American Relations. . . ," *FAR*, I, 28.

[52] Charles Maurice Talleyrand, *Memoir Concerning the Commercial Relations of the United States with England* (Boston, 1809); the quotations are
from pp. 5, 6.

Talleyrand in his memoir had pointed out that to overcome English advantages in the United States France would undoubtedly have to resort to political action, "that it would, perhaps, require a French establishment in America to counteract their [English] ascendancy with any hopes of success."[53] The Directory had launched just such a policy, and Adet, like Genet before him, engaged in Western intrigues to implement it. It was not difficult to stir up seccessionist sentiment among frontiersmen of the Western settlements, where such sentiment had never died out.

Although Spaniards had long attempted to foment Western secession, Adet, as did other Frenchmen, thought that a secessionist movement would receive greater support if sponsored by France. With an eye to future French repossession of Louisiana, he believed that secession would help the future French military position there. Such a movement would also weaken the Washington government and the Federalist party and would aid his efforts to bring the pro-French Jeffersonians to power. These activities would be consonant with the policy of the Directory and of the Minister of Foreign Affairs, Delacroix, who saw in Louisiana a means to implement French plans toward the United States, a means with which to influence American foreign policy.[54]

In March, 1796, Adet commissioned General Victor Collot, former governor of Guadaloupe then on parole from English capture, to make a military, economic, and political reconnaissance of the Ohio and Mississippi valleys. Foremost among the general's objectives was to ascertain the strength of secessionist sentiment in the West and to assess the possibilities of terrain for military defense.

[53] *Ibid.*, p. 13.
[54] For Adet's views, see Adet to Minister of Foreign Relations, Philadelphia, Feb. 9, 1796, and June 21, 1796, in Turner, *CFM*, pp. 826-831, 928-930. The French foreign ministry received a number of memoirs in this period suggesting repossessing of Louisiana; this was stressed among other things in "Memoire sur les États unis d'Amérique—La Florida—et Louisiane" and "Analysis of Memoir on Our Situation with the United States," by C. Derehé, Dec. 2, 1795 and [Feb., 1797], AAE CP EU, Vols. XLIV, ff. 407-417, and XLVII, ff. 177-178; Turner, "The Policy of France toward the Mississippi Valley," *AHR*, X, 271; for continuing Spanish interest in Western secession, see Whitaker, *The Mississippi Question, 1795-1803*, pp. 157-158; Durand Echeverria, trans., "General Collot's Plan for a Reconnaissance of the Ohio and Mississippi Valleys, 1796," *WMQ*, 3rd Series, IX (Oct., 1952), 513-514.

French statesmen hoped that the West, and perhaps the South also, could be induced to secede from the United States, form a new confederation, and make a new alliance with France, one subordinate to French policy.[55] As part of their design French strategists kept in touch with Americans who had been in French service at the time of Genet's projected attack on Louisiana several years earlier. General George Rogers Clark and his aide, "Colonel" Samuel Fulton, were among those who supplied the French with intelligence on affairs in the West. Fulton, in particular, worked closely with Adet; in April, 1796, after he had taken a trip West to intrigue with Indians and had consulted with Clark, Adet sent him to Paris with despatches.[56] At this time Fulton assured Clark that "Citizen Adet is Desposed to Do eavery thing in his power for our benifit."[57]

The plan for his "reconnaissance" which Collot submitted to Adet emphasized that France lacked sound information on the existing political situation in the United States. Then he added that the threat to France's navy, colonies, and foreign trade, "the hostility of the Federal government towards the French Republic openly manifested by the formation, in the midst of a bloody war, of ties of friendship and mutual advantage with our cruelist enemies; the impossibility of being able any longer to delude ourselves concerning the prodigious influence exercised by the English over the American government and the major portion of the Eastern states," and the necessity for countering that influence "by some other powerful opposing force" were reason enough for plotting against the government of an ally.[58]

[55] John Quincy Adams, for example, believed that French plans for a new alliance with a western republic had been formed as early as the time of Genet's instructions. To John Adams, The Hague, April 3, 1797, in Ford, *The Writings of John Quincy Adams*, II, 156.

[56] See Adet to Minister of Foreign Relations, Philadelphia, Feb. 9, 1796, in Turner, *CFM*, p. 828; Murdoch, *Georgia-Florida Frontier 1793-1796*, pp. 95-96.

[57] Fulton Clark, Philadelphia, April 4, 1796, in Turner, "Selections from the Draper Collection," *American Historical Association Annual Report for the Year 1896*, I, 1098; Turner, "Policy of France toward the Mississippi Valley," *AHR*, X, 270-272; Echeverria, "General Collot's Plan. . . ," *WMQ*, 3rd Series, IX, 514; George W. Kyte, "A Spy on the Western Waters: The Military Intelligence Mission of General Collot in 1796," *Mississippi Valley Historical Review*, XXXIV (Dec., 1947), 429.

[58] See Echeverria, "General Collot's Plan. . . ," *WMQ*, 3rd Series, IX, 516.

With Adet's blessing, Collot left Philadelphia in March, 1796, proceeded to Pittsburgh, St. Louis, and New Orleans, and returned by sea to Philadelphia in December. Along the way, to those he trusted, he stressed the advantages of French control over the heart of the North American continent. A force of two thousand to three thousand determined frontiersmen, Collot concluded, was all that was necessary to take the Spanish lands. His maps and his observations outlined a thorough preparation for a possible defense of French-held Louisiana against Americans at the line of the Alleghenies; the Louisiana envisioned by Collot stretched from the Alleghenies to the Rockies, and hence included both Spanish and American territory.[59]

During the reconnaissance Collot learned also of a plot for an attack against Louisiana under English auspices, the so-called Blount Conspiracy. The conspirators, among whom were Senator William Blount of Tennessee, and a number of prominent frontiersmen as well as one or more British agents, had planned to seize the poorly defended Spanish dependencies of Louisiana and the Floridas with an army of frontiersmen and Indians. Included in the strategy was a combined land and sea assault on New Orleans across American territory, with the British supplying the attacking fleet as well as additional troops from Canada. Although the English government later denied responsibility for the plot, it was known to Robert Liston, the British minister to the United States, and received his circumspect support.[60]

When he returned to Philadelphia, Collot reported the results of his mission to Adet and informed him of the Blount Conspiracy.

[59] Turner, "Policy of France toward the Mississippi Valley," *AHR*, X, 273; Kyte, "A Spy on the Western Waters," *MVHR*, XXXIV, 431-441.

[60] For details on this aspect of the Blount Conspiracy, see Whitaker, *The Mississippi Question, 1795-1803*, pp. 104-114; Francois Barbé-Marbois, *The History of Louisiana*, pp. 163-164; Turner, "Policy of France toward the Mississippi Valley," *AHR*, X, 273-274; Robert Liston to Lord Grenville, Philadelphia, Jan. 25 and March 16, 1797, in Frederick Jackson Turner, ed., "Documents on the Blount Conspiracy, 1795-1797," *AHR*, X (April, 1903), 582-583; Perkins, *The First Rapprochement*, pp. 99-100; for Adet's comments on the conspiracy, see Adet to Minister of Foreign Relations, Philadelphia, Feb. 24, 1797, in Turner, *CFM*, pp. 989-993; see also William H. Masterson, *William Blount* (Baton Rouge, 1954), pp. 303-310; Heloise H. Cruzat, "General Collot's Reconnoitering Trip down the Mississippi and his Arrest in New Orleans in 1796, by order of the Baron De Carondelet, Governor of Louisiana," *Louisiana Historical Quarterly*, I (April, 1918), 305-307.

Details of the British frontier plot were forwarded to the Spanish minister in the United States, who promptly expressed his fears of a British *"coup-de-main"* to the Secretary of State. Such intelligence displeased Pickering. Western intrigue, he was convinced, did not implicate the British, but rather resulted from pernicious French influence among the frontiersmen.[61]

Since the spring of 1796 Federalist leaders had suspected that France had launched preparations to alienate the Western lands, taking advantage of the uneasily dormant Western discontent. Pickering, Wolcott, Jr., and others believed that in a secret clause of the Franco-Spanish treaty of Basel of July, 1795, France had been promised repossession of Louisiana. "We have often heard," Pickering said, "that the French government contemplated repossession of Louisiana; and it has been conjectured that in their negociations with Spain the cession of Louisiana & the Floridas may have been agreed on. You will see all the mischief to be apprehended from such an event. The Spaniards will certainly be more safe, quiet and useful neighbors. For her own sake Spain should absolutely refuse to make these cessions."[62]

Mere rumor of a negotiation for transfer to Louisiana raised Federalist temperatures. Federalist reasoning on Louisiana and France was simple and logical. They were convinced that France had never abandoned her North American aspirations. If France should obtain Louisiana from Spain and, in a peace with Great Britain, regain Canada, obviously "the consequences would be very important to the United States." Among other things, the acquisition would lead to a separation of the trans-Allegheny West from the Union, attempts at which had already been incited by French agents.[63]

[61] See Yrujo to Pickering, Philadelphia, March 2, 1797, *ASP FR*, II, 68; Robert Liston to Lord Grenville, Philadelphia, June 24, 1797, in Turner, "Documents on the Blount Conspiracy. . . ," *AHR*, X, 589-590; Whitaker, *The Mississippi Question, 1795-1803*, p. 104.

[62] Pickering to Rufus King, Dept. of State, Feb. 15, 1797, Pickering Papers, Mass. Hist. Soc., Boston. Although France did not get Louisiana at Basel, Pickering's suspicions were justified, as has been indicated, in that France had tried hard to get it. See Le comité de salut public a Barthélemy (Instructions), Paris, May 12, 1795, in Kaulec, *Papiers de Barthélemy*, VI, 17-27.

[63] The British suspected that Adet had recommended that recovery of Louisiana be joined with repossession of Canada. Liston to Grenville, Philadelphia, Nov. 18, 1796, Henry Adams Transcripts.

Looking to future national development, Federalists reasoned that if French designs reached fruition "the United States would be encircled by an artful, insinuating, active nation, and must forever renounce the hope of obtaining by purchase or amicable means, the territory west of the Mississippi, to the ocean. If the French get footing there, nothing short of conquest will ever enable the Americans to secure the property and jurisdiction of that vast country, which would otherwise naturally and easily fall into their range of settlements." On the basis of such manifest destiny, "whether the French, Spaniards or English will make the best neighbors, is left for every one to determine."[64] Oliver Wolcott, Jr., for one, did not mince words. If the French succeeded in getting a footing on the continent he was convinced that "they will be the worst and most dangerous neighbours we could have." Unlike the English, the French will "be like ants and weasels in our barns and granaries."[65]

These were not the only dangers. French possession of Louisiana might lead to French domination of Mexico and Spanish lands to the South. "In the hands of the plodding Spaniards they do no harm and little good to the world at large," said a New England newspaper; "but in the hands of an active nation, Mexico would be a dangerous engine of power." French entrenchment in Louisiana, furthermore, would endanger the possessions of all other powers in the West Indies.

Even though grandoise, seemingly far-fetched, and "liable to errors," such speculations, reasoned Federalists, were valid. Americans needed to be vigilant. "The Americans possess the best regions of the North Continent[,] that is, that portion which unites the best climates, and a soil to make a bold hardy race of freemen. No doubt can exist that it is our interest to keep ourselves detached from European contests, and if possible prevent any powerful nation from making establishments in our neighborhood, which will be likely to excite jealousies, and controversies hereafter on this side of the Atlantick."[66]

[64] The *New York Herald*, reprinted in the *New Hampshire and Vermont Journal: Or The Farmer's Weekly Museum* (Walpole, N. H.), Sept. 6, 1796.

[65] Oliver Wolcott, Jr., to Oliver Wolcott, Sr., Philadelphia, Oct. 17, 1796, in Gibbs, ed., *Wolcott Papers*, I, 387-388.

[66] The *New Hampshire and Vermont Journal: Or The Farmer's Weekly Museum* (Walpole, N. H.), Sept. 6, 1796.

Many thinking Federalists in these years echoed this refrain, which in 1796 was not directed against all of Europe, but specifically at France. Such ideas, of course, received their classic statement in Washington's farewell to public office, and later in the Monroe Doctrine. Even Jefferson, in later years, adopted such reasoning as his own.

It followed logically, then, that when Adet sent Collot on his reconnaissance the deed struck Federalist leaders as confirmation of their deep suspicions of French designs. General Collot, moreover, talked too much. He indiscreetly showed his "plan" to a "gentle-man" who forwarded the information to Oliver Wolcott, Jr., who in turn brought the damning evidence of the validity of Federalist suspicions to the attention of President Washington. Among other things, Wolcott's informant stressed that he had seen Collot's "in-structions in writing from M. Adet," and that the Frenchmen "were moreover instructed to use all means in their power to pro-mote the election of Mr. Jefferson as President of the United States." He implied, too, that Albert Gallatin was in collusion with Adet. Even before his departure, Collot's objective and the existence of a French plot were known to the American government.[67]

As a countermeasure, the Washington administration appropri-ated a secret service fund of five hundred dollars in hopes of dis-covering Adet's accomplices. Secretary of War James McHenry took immediate steps to head off Collot's expedition. To General Arthur St. Clair, governor of the Northwest territory, he sent a warning to watch for the French spy who was out to encourage Westerners "to secede from the Union, and form a separate connec-tion with a foreign power." Collot and his party, McHenry be-lieved, had important papers; he asked that St. Clair seize them and forward them to President Washington.[68]

The Federalist officials also hired an undercover agent to follow Collot and to report on his activities. The agent reported to Oliver

[67] See memoranda of May 19 and 21, 1796, Philadelphia, in Gibbs, ed., *Wolcott Papers*, I, 350-352; Whitaker, *The Mississippi Question, 1795-1803*, p. 120. Adet had informed American and Spanish officials of Collot's planned trip, obtaining—not without misgivings—their permission. He did not reveal the real intent of the trip. Kyte, "A Spy on the Western Waters," *MVHR*, XXXIV, 431.

[68] See McHenry to St. Clair, War Office, May, 1796, in Smith, *The St. Clair Papers*, II, 395-396.

Wolcott, Jr., that Collot attacked the Jay treaty and indicated that severe French reprisals would result. "We shall see, said he [Collot], how the mass of the people of this country will like the British alliance, and how they will treat those characters who have given it support; the energy and resources of France are not known in this country, for if they were, they should have been a sufficient motive to defeat British influence." Then he added that "France has no footing on this continent, but who knows how soon they may get possession of Louisiana and both Floridas from the Spaniards in exchange for some other property? If such be the case, as there is great probability, what will become of the produce of your Kentucké, your western territory, indeed of all the country this side of the Alleghany mountains? You will be reduced to the necessity of throwing yourself into the arms of the French, and abandon the Union which cannot give you a market. . . ."[69]

Several years later Judge Hugh Henry Brackenridge revealed that Collot, while on his "reconnaissance," had called on him "frequently" and "without common prudence" had tried to win his support in gaining the Western country for France. Federalist Senator James Ross of Pennsylvania was at that time attempting to convert Brackenridge to support of the Jay treaty. He warned the judge about French intrigues, that "there was a party in the U. S. who wanted to overturn the govmt, who were in league with France, that France, by a secret article of treaty with Spain was to have Louisiana." This, coupled with Collot's indiscretions, convinced Brackenridge that "there was a conspiracy to deliver our country or some part of it at least to the French." He reported his conversations with Collot to Ross, who gave the information to the President.[70]

Despite the continuing rumors—Monroe even reported from Paris rumors of French designs on Western territory, which the French denied—substantial evidence of French intrigue could not be uncovered. Pickering and other Federalists continued to believe that France threatened the existence of the Union and that Westerners supported her seditious plots. Where there was intrigue, they were convinced, there were Frenchmen and Republicans. This was

[69] Report of the undercover agent, Pittsburgh, June 15, 1796, in Gibbs, ed., *Wolcott Papers*, I, 353-354.
[70] The Anas, March 27, 1800, in Ford, *Writings of Jefferson*, I, 287.

good political propaganda; ancient fears and prejudices could be aroused easily. Americans read that "the efforts of the French to obtain territory on the Mississippi, are only a revival of that deep policy which led Louis XVth to establish a chain of posts on the frontiers of our settlements from the Ohio to the Lakes."[71] How seriously the administration took the intelligence of French plotting in the West was shown by the fact that Washington in his farewell entered a specific warning to the West against "an apostate and unnatural connection with any foreign power. . . ."[72]

So much did evidences of French designs alarm the administration that Washington's caveat to the American people was buttressed by a blunt warning from Pickering intended for the French government. Taking official cognizance of the rumors which had "for some time been current that Louisiana and the Floridas were or would be ceded to France," he informed Charles Cotesworth Pinckney that the French government "should know how much the cession would displease the United States." French-American friendship would be endangered by the French "becoming our Continental neighbors." He declared that "the energy and activity of the two nations would infallibly produce competitions and quarrels mutually injurious and afflicting." So long as France restricted her American holdings to the Caribbean and South America "our reciprocal wants demanding reciprocal supplies, will promote our respective interests, and form a strong tie to render permanent the friendly relations subsisting between us. If on the contrary, a rupture should be occasioned in the manner just hinted, the United States could not fail to associate themselves with Great Britain, and make common cause against France. But the same policy which dictated to France the importance and necessity of our separation from Britain, should induce her to avoid every measure which would again throw us into the arms of her rival."[73]

[71] *The Minerva*, reprinted in *The Herald: A Gazette for the Country* (New York), Feb. 22, 1797.

[72] Farewell Address, Sept. 19, 1796, in Fitzpatrick, *Washington's Writings*, XXV, 221; Gibbs, ed., *Wolcott Papers*, I, 355; Whitaker, *The Mississippi Question, 1795-1803*, p. 120.

[73] "Another very interesting reason for excluding the French from any possessions north of the Gulph of Mexico," Pickering added, "cannot fail to occur to you—the danger of communicating their principles of unqualified and premature liberation of the negroes; which if brought into operation in

From the viewpoint of American national self-interest, Pickering was right, but this was strong language to be directed to an ally. His warning did demonstrate that French policy toward Louisiana was having the opposite effect from that intended. Instead of intimidating the American government and reviving the alliance, it was destroying the alliance and driving the United States into Britain's embrace. France nonetheless coveted Louisiana and continued to put pressure on Spain to cede it.[74]

Pickering's threat of making common cause with Great Britain was sound diplomacy; he used effectively the most important diplomatic weapon in the hand of his relatively weak country against a powerful probable enemy. He appealed to French self-interest by stressing that it had been French policy since before the American Revolution to keep Americans and Great Britain apart. Yet his strictures, coupled with persistent French designs on the American continent, pointed up the incompatibility of the interests of France and of the United States on the North American continent and the futility of the Franco-American alliance as long as that basis for antagonism existed.

How contradictory French and American policies were at this time can be seen by comparing Pickering's ideas, which represented administration thinking on foreign policy, with those then current in the French foreign office concerning the future of Louisiana. One report prepared for the French Minister of Foreign Affairs stressed the danger of an Anglo-American coalition in the Caribbean. Prompted by this fear, the French writer urged acquisition of Louisiana to thwart this potential Anglo-American combination. Without weighing properly the might of British sea power, he rationalized that if France regained Louisiana she would be actually more powerful in the New World than in Europe. Since Americans would be welded to the French political system, they would be forced to observe strictly their alliance with France.[75] In addi-

the Southern States, especially South Carolina and Georgia, would be their total ruin. Although the original enslaving of the blacks is deeply to be deplored, their hasty emancipation would produce greater evils than their continuance in a state which may be gradually ameliorated." Pickering to Pinckney, Philadelphia, Feb. 25, 1797, National Archives, Dept. of State, Diplomatic and Consular Instructions.

[74] For details, see Lyon, *Louisiana in French Diplomacy*. . . , pp. 87-98.
[75] Report of Sept., 1796, AAE CP EU, Vol. XLVII, f. 180, quoted in

tion to regaining Louisiana by cession or by exchange for eastern Saint Domingue, other proposals considered by the Directory and known to Americans at this time included plans for taking Canada by conquest and the sending of a powerful armed expedition to New Orleans.[76]

As Washington's administration drew to a close, it is clear that France considered the American government to be in the enemy's camp, despite the existence on paper of an alliance purportedly effective "forever." Adet, who had come to the United States on what was to be a mission of conciliation had, after the Jay treaty, turned to a policy of intrigue and coercion similar to that of his two predecessors.[77] With the backing of his superiors he plotted French reconquest of Louisiana. The plan, which called for secession of the trans-Allegheny West from the United States and for subsequent French control of the heart of the North American continent, was inspired by French disappointment in the 1778 alliance and by reaction to the Jay treaty, and represented an effort to control American foreign policy through threat and encirclement. Yet the plan was only one aspect of French policy toward the United States. Just as disturbing to the administration and to Federalists in general were collateral French efforts to influence domestic politics.[78] These efforts, given the nature of American politics at this time, added discord to the last years of Washington's Presidency.

James, "French Opinion as a Factor in Preventing War between France and the United States," *AHR*, XXX, 47; also "Instructions données au Général Pérignon par le Directoire," [July 8, 1796], quoted in Lyon, *Louisiana In French Diplomacy. . .* , pp. 89-90.

[76] See John Quincy Adams to John Adams, The Hague, Aug. 13, 1796, to the Secretary of State, Oct. 16, 1796, and to John Adams, Feb. 23, 1797, in Ford, *The Writings of John Quincy Adams,* II, 20, 31 n., 128; James, "French Opinion as a Factor in Preventing War between France and the United States," *AHR*, XXX, 48.

[77] It should be remembered that Adet believed that the majority of the American people were favorable to France and her Revolution; he intrigued against the government, not the people—a distinction which he maintained but which is at times difficult to see. See, for example, Adet to Minister of Foreign Relations, Philadelphia, June 4, 1796, in Turner, *CFM*, p. 915.

[78] Two major grievances harbored by Federalists against Adet were his efforts "to promote a separation of the western territory from the government of the United States" and his interfering "in our most sacred rights of election for President and Vice-President." William Willcocks in *The Minerva,* reprinted in *The Herald: A Gazette for the Country* (New York), Dec. 28, 1796.

CHAPTER FOURTEEN

DIPLOMACY IN POLITICS

THE ELECTION OF 1796

We must raise up the people and at the same time conceal the lever by which we do so.... I propose to the Executive Directory to authorize me to send orders and instructions to our minister plentipotentiary at Philadelphia to use all means in his power in the United States to bring about a successful revolution [l'heureuse Révolution] *and Washington's replacement, which assuring to the Americans their independence, will break off treaties* [sic] *made with England and maintain those which unite them to the French Republic.*—Charles Delacroix, Minister of Foreign Relations, to the Directory, Paris, January 16, 1796.

The alliance in its future operation must be against our interest. The door to escape from it is opened. Though we ought to maintain with good faith our engagements, if the conduct of the other party releases us, we should not refuse the release, so far as we may accept without compromitting our peace. This idea is very important.—Alexander Hamilton to Oliver Wolcott, Jr., November 22, 1796.

* * * * *

IN HIS initial efforts to defeat the Jay treaty Adet had tampered with American politics; after the House of Representatives had voted funds to implement the treaty, he began seriously to work toward the overthrow of the Washington administration. At the time he did not know Washington already had decided to retire, eschewing a third term. Meantime politics had wrought decisive changes in Paris. In October, 1795, the bourgeois Directory had come to power. Unlike previous governments of the Republic, the Directory, as an adjunct to its war policy against England, took an interest in American affairs. Aroused by the Jay treaty and looking upon Washington's Federalist government as captive of English policy, it even considered declaring war against the United States.

The Directory entrusted Charles Delacroix with conduct of foreign affairs.[1] In assessing relations with the United States, Delacroix concluded that France was in a state of war with the Washington government but not with the American people, who still remained constant in their attachment to France. He recommended, therefore, that the Directory adopt firm measures to call the American allies to their real interests and make them denounce England as their real enemy. "We must raise up the people and at the same time conceal the lever by which we do so," he said. At the same time he suggested directing the French minister in Philadelphia "to use all the means in his power in the United States to bring about a successful revolution (*l'heureuse Révolution*) and Washington's replacement."

This policy, Delacroix said, would break the Jay treaty and invigorate the 1778 alliance. Jefferson would replace Washington and France would enjoy the influence in the United States which she deserved. The likelihood of success with the policy, he observed, was good. Washington had fallen in public esteem; journals now openly attacked him. Former friends were now critics.[2]

Having thus taken into account what it conceived to be the temper of American popular opinion, the French government intervened in the presidential election of 1796, placing its weight behind the Republican party. It embodied that policy of intervention in instructions to a new minister scheduled to succeed Adet. The Directory looked upon Jefferson as favorable to French policy and urged his support. While working for Jefferson's election, the

---

[1] "The Minister Delacroix," John Quincy Adams said, "means not well to the harmony of the two countries, and there are prejudices and passions of other individuals which will labor to interrupt the good understanding, which the interest of both requires." To Joseph Pitcairn, The Hague, Nov. 13, 1796, in Ford, *The Writings of John Quincy Adams*, II, 41-42.

[2] "Rapport au Directoire Exécutif par le Ministre des Relations Extérieures," [Paris], Jan. 16, 1796, AAE CP EU, Vol. XLV, ff. 41, 45, 49-51; a part of the document is printed in Bemis, "Washington's Farewell Address. . . ," *American Historical Review*, XXXIX, 257-258. Some French officials expected a popular revolution in the United States to overthrow the Federalists, such revolutions having occurred in Europe—in Holland for example. Earlier, Genet had called Washington "the living idol which the Americans have set up for themselves," Minnigerode, *Genet*, p. 348.

French representative in the United States was to take whatever measures were necessary to draw every possible advantage from the election crisis.[3] The Directory did not send the new minister; instead it decided to retain Adet. It fell to him to carry out the intervention policy, one which fitted his own ideas and recommendations.[4] He succeeded in making French intervention a main issue in the campaign of 1796. The fate of the alliance hinged on the outcome of the election.

* * * * *

The Directory's decision to intervene was only one element, though an important one, in the complex politics of the election of 1796. Domestic issues and the Jay treaty itself contributed others. Final acceptance of the Jay treaty plunged Franco-American relations to their lowest depth since independence and marked a great political triumph for Federalists. For Republicans the Jay treaty was a political as well as a foreign policy defeat. Yet to Republicans all hope of ultimately defeating the treaty did not appear lost. Seeing the extent of the treaty's unpopularity, Republican leaders believed that it would make an excellent campaign issue in the election of 1796 as an unrivaled rallying point for national sentiment. Thomas Jefferson, James Madison, and other party leaders believed that popular opinion still remained largely pro-French and anti-British. Being politicians they reacted logically. Their party had ready-made national issues; they felt that they had only to exploit them properly for victory. In the election of 1796 their campaign was to be against the Jay treaty and the pro-British "system" of Alexander Hamilton.[5]

[3] "Mémoire pour servir d'instructions politique au Citoyen Vincent, envoyé comme Ministre plénipotentiare de la République auprès des États-unis," [Paris], March 6, 1796 (signed by the President of the Executive Directory), AAE CP EU, vol. XLV, f. 188; "Mémoire sur les effets du dernier traité des États-Unis est des l'Angleterre, et les remèdes a employer," (for the Executive Directory, no author), [May, 1796], *ibid.*, ff. 323-351.

[4] See Adet to Minister of Foreign Relations, Philadelphia, May 3, 1796, in Turner, *CFM*, pp. 900-906; Faÿ, *The Revolutionary Spirit in France and America*, p. 396.

[5] Phineas Bond said that it was understood that Republican opposition to the Jay treaty was planned by Jefferson "for the double purpose of promoting the interests of France and of advancing his candidacy for President." To Grenville, Philadelphia, May 4, 1796, No. 30, Henry Adams Transcripts.

One towering obstacle stood in the way of success: George Washington. So deep was the impression he had made on fellow-Americans that to attack him would be to injure the attacker. Twice he had been chosen President without a dissenting vote. If he so desired, undoubtedly he could have held the office for the third time. For, as a foreign observer remarked, "there is a Magic in his name more powerful in this Country than the Abilities of any other man. . . ."[6] No one was better aware of this than Jefferson. "Republicanism," he advised, "must lie on it's [sic] oars, resign the vessel to it's pilot [Washington], and themselves to the course he thinks best for them."[7]

The political situation in 1796, however, was different from that of 1789 or 1792; Washington probably could not have had a third term as the result of unanimous choice. In the battles over neutrality, the Jay treaty, and other issues, he had revealed his partisanship. To Republicans and Francophiles the guise of being above party appeared hypocritical. The French, too, had changed their view of Washington; they placed him in partnership with Hamilton at the head of what they called the English party.[8] Some now spat at the mention of his name, denounced him as a monocrat, as an Anglomaniac, and prayed for his removal from office. Washington in 1796 had become a central figure in emerging party politics. He was a prime target for violent, personal attacks. Seemingly there was no crime that opponents would not accuse him of perpetrating.[9]

[6] Robert Liston to Grenville, Philadelphia, Oct. 13, 1796, No. 14, *ibid.;* the quotation is from Henrietta Liston to James Jackson, German Town, Oct. 16, 1796, in Perkins, ed., "A Diplomat's Wife in Philadelphia," *William and Mary Quarterly,* 3rd Series, XI, p. 604.

[7] Jefferson to James Monroe, June 12, 1796, in Ford, *Writings of Jefferson,* VII, 80. Madison, too, complained of Washington's prestige. Madison to Jefferson, May 22, 1796, Madison Papers, Library of Congress, XIX, 68, cited in Schachner, *Thomas Jefferson. . . ,* II, 581.

[8] See the observations of John Quincy Adams to Joseph Pitcairn, The Hague, March 9, 1797, in Ford, *The Writings of John Quincy Adams,* II, 140.

[9] See, for example, McMaster, *A History of the People of the United States. . . ,* II, 289. While opposing him, many of Washington's critics still recognized his virtues. One, for instance, remarked that "the best man that ever lived possessing the influence of the P[resident], is a dangerous man; the more so if guided in any of his measures by others who may not be so virtuous. God grant we may never have cause to say 'curse on his

Although not representative of a universal American feeling, the following sentiments expressed in *"The Political* Creed *of a* Western American"* do give an indication of the change that had taken place in the political reaction to Washington. "I believe," declared the writer, "that the treaty formed by Jay and the British king, is the offspring of a vile aristocratic few who have too long governed America, and who are enemies to the equality of man, friends to no government but that whose funds they can convert to their private emolument. . . . I believe the period is at hand when the inhabitants of America will cease to admire and approve the conduct of the Federal executive, because they esteem the man who fills the chair of state. . . . I believe the political dotage of our good old American chief, has arrived; and that while we record his virtues in letters of gold, we should consign his person to the tender offices due to virtuous age, and transfer him from the chair of state to the chair of domestic ease."[10]

At the same time so bitter had become feeling between English and French partisans among Americans that domestic issues were subordinated to those of foreign policy. In their conviction that the Federalist administration did not truly represent the American people, that the people were pro-French, the French were encouraged by pro-French partisans who indicated that the Federalist government would topple if only France were to take a strong stand.[11]

As 1796 opened, Republicans intensified their attacks against the Federalist administration. In the House of Representatives, under the leadership of Albert Gallatin, they renewed their assaults

virtues; they have undone his country.'" Joseph Jones to James Madison, Fredericksburg, Feb. 17, 1796, in Worthington C. Ford, ed., "Letters from Joseph Jones to Madison, 1788-1802," *Proceedings of the Massachusetts Historical Society, 1901, 1902,* Second Series, XV (Boston, 1902), 155.

[10] *Kentucky Gazette* (Lexington), Sept. 26, 1795.

[11] At this time La Rochefoucauld-Liancourt, for example, reported that the common people in the United States were overwhelmingly pro-French and anti-British. Such sentiments prevailed especially "among the country-people and persons of second rank," those who "form the bulk of the nation; who, as I have already frequently observed, being less influenced by political views, and less swayed by the spirit of party, than the higher classes of society, are more strenuously attached to France, their interests not being interwoven with the successes of Great Britain." *Travels. . . ,* II, 139, see also pp. 64-65.

on the economics of Hamilton's system. In addition to its political effect, the Republican attack in this case had another result. By increasing the power of the House over financial matters, it cut down a source of power for the over-all Hamiltonian system.[12]

With Hamilton's system under fire on both domestic and foreign policy and with himself the target of abuse, Washington found the demands of his office increasingly difficult to endure. Publicly he maintained a dignified silence, but privately he revealed the strain. Midway in the year he confessed that "until within the last year or two ago, I had no conception that Parties would, or even could go, the length I have been witness to; nor did I believe until lately, that it was within the bounds of probability; hardly within those of possibility, that, while I was using my utmost exertions to establish a national character of our own, independent as far as our obligations, and justice would permit, of every nation of the earth; and wished, by steering a steady course, to preserve this Country from the horrors of a desolating war, that I should be accused of being the enemy of one Nation and subject to the influence of another; and to prove it, that every act of my administration would be tortured, and the grossest, and most insidious misrepresentations of them be made." These misrepresentations, he claimed, gave "one side *only* of a subject, and that too in such exaggerated and indecent terms as could scarcely be applied to a Nero; a notorious defaulter; or even to a common pick-pocket."[13] When, a few days later, he offered the Paris legation to Charles Cotesworth Pinckney, he expressed similar sentiments. The "greatest embarrassments" to the administration, he emphasized, emanated from Americans who were disposed to promote the views of another nation, France, rather than their own.[14]

Even Washington had come to see that the myth of nonpartisanship was shattered. The foreign policy questions dealing with the French alliance had become an issue capable of transforming the

[12] Treasury and hence Executive control over finance was cut down through the creation of the Ways and Means Committee to check all appropriations and expenditures; Gallatin became its first chairman. Adams, *The Life of Albert Gallatin*, p. 157; Schachner, *The Founding Fathers*, p. 387; Bassett, *Federalist System...*, pp. 138-141.

[13] Washington to Jefferson, Mount Vernon, July 6, 1796, in Fitzpatrick, *Washington's Writings*, XXXV, 120.

[14] Washington to Pinckney, Mount Vernon, July 8, 1796, *ibid.*, p. 130.

opposing local alliances of Federalist and anti-Federalist into inte-
grated national parties. This was an issue capable of capturing
public imagination in a way which abstruse problems of finance
could not.[15]

Despite his increasing distaste for the office and the increasing
speculation about his declining a third term, the President remained
silent as to future plans.[16] Upon him the start of the official campaign depended; Republicans hesitated to propose a rival candidate
until Washington's intentions were known. Leaders of both political parties, however, believed that he would not run. "He gave
me intimations enough," John Adams said, "that his reign would
be very short." Early in 1796, and even before, both parties had
laid tentative plans which did not include Washington as a candidate.[17]

If Washington had desired a third term, the desire was withered
by the criticism to which he had been subjected from the end of
his first term. When he decided against a third term he did so
primarily because he was disgusted with the abuse of political opponents. "The true cause of the general's retiring," one of his staunchest supporters said, "was . . . the *loss of popularity* which he had
experienced, and the further loss he apprehended from the rupture
with France, which he looked upon as inevitable."[18]

Opponents charged Washington with betraying a solemn pledge
to France by destroying the French alliance. Personal attacks
accused him of taking more salary than was allotted him. His
mail was tampered with and forged letters of 1777 were refurbished

[15] Binkley, *American Political Parties. . . ,* pp. 45-46.

[16] Over a year earlier, following the resignation of Hamilton and Knox
from the Cabinet, Hammond had heard rumors, for example, that Washington had indicated he would retire in 1797. Hammond to Grenville,
Philadelphia, Jan. 5, 1796, No. 1, Henry Adams Transcripts.

[17] The quotation is from John Adams to wife, Philadelphia, March 25,
1796, Adams, *Letters of John Adams Addressed to His Wife,* II, 214. Earlier
(Philadelphia, Jan. 7, 1796), Adams had told his wife that he believed
Washington would retire. *Ibid.,* p. 189. Republicans shared the same ru-
mors. "It is pretty certain that the President will not serve beyond his
present term," reported Madison to Monroe. Philadelphia, Feb. 26, 1796,
Letters and Other Writings of James Madison (Cong. ed.), II, 83; see also
Madison to Monroe, Philadelphia, May 14, 1796, in Hunt, *The Writings of
James Madison,* VI, 301 n.

[18] Cobbett, *Porcupine's Works,* IV, 444 n. The italics are in the original.

and printed as genuine. He was particularly upset by Thomas Paine's bitter attack from Paris.[19] Republicans were convinced that Paris was the source of the anti-Washington campaign. "The pamphlet war against the character of the President," wrote John Quincy Adams, "was begun under the auspices of the French government the last summer." He warned that it was to be renewed.[20]

Jefferson, too, had lost patience with Washington. Disgusted by the administration's pro-British policy, particularly by Washington's support of the Jay treaty, he wrote in a private letter to his Italian friend Philip Mazzei that American politics had changed. He said that "an Anglican, monarchical & aristocratical party has sprung up, whose avowed object is to draw over us the substance as they have already done the forms of the British government. The main body of our citizens however remain true to their republican principles." Then he explained that "against us are the Executive, the Judiciary, two out of three branches of the legislature, all the officers of the government, all who want to be officers, all timid men who prefer the calm despotism to the boisterous sea of liberty, British merchants & Americans trading on British capitals, speculators & holders in the banks & public funds, a contrivance invented for the purposes of corruption, & for assimilating us in all things, to the rotten as well as the sound parts of the British model." Next Jefferson's pen cut into Washington personally. ". . . it would give you a fever," he said, "were I to name to you the apostates who have gone over to these heresies, men who were Samsons in the field & Solomons in the council, but who have had their heads shorn by the harlot England."[21]

Given the tensions of politics and foreign policy, the criticisms were no more than Washington could have expected. Yet they

[19] For details, see Stephenson and Dunn, *George Washington*, II, 409; McMaster, *A History of the People of the United States. . . ,* II, 249-250; Paine to Washington, Paris, July 6, 1796, in Foner, *The Complete Works of Thomas Paine*, II, 691-723.

[20] John Quincy Adams to John Adams, The Hague, Aug. 13, 1796, in Ford, *The Writings of John Quincy Adams*, II, 21.

[21] The quotation follows the text in Howard R. Marraro, "The Four Versions of Jefferson's Letter to Mazzei, *WMQ*, 2nd Series, XXII (Jan., 1942), 24-25; the letter is dated Monticello, April 24, 1796. Ultimately the letter was published in the Paris *Moniteur* (Jan. 25, 1797) and republished in the United States, causing Jefferson considerable embarrassment. Schachner, *Thomas Jefferson. . . ,* II, 578-579.

upset him. Not unreasonably, Federalists concluded that the attacks were designed to induce his resignation and remove him from the 1796 election.[22] They succeeded. Despite pressures to stay and ride out the storm, Washington in May, 1796, disclosed that he intended definitely to retire.[23]

As usual, he turned to Hamilton for advice. No longer did he wish to be "buffited in the public prints by a set of infamous scribblers." He regretted that he had not announced earlier and *"publicly,* what seems to be very well understood, and is industriously propagated *privately.* It would have removed from the mind of *all* and left the field clear for *all:* It would, by having preceded any unfavorable change in our foreign relations (if any should happen) render my retreat less difficult and embarrassing. And it might have prevented the remarks which, more than probable will follow a late annunciation, namely, that I delayed it long enough to see, that the current was turned against me, before I declared by intention to decline." Then he asked, when would be "the *next* best time" for the publication of his farewell to the nation?[24]

With his eye on the coming election Hamilton advised Washington to hold off his public announcement as long as possible. "I do not think it is in the power of party to throw any slur upon the lateness of your declaration," Hamilton said. "And you have a justification in the state of things. If a storm gathers, how can you retreat? . . . The proper period now for your declaration seems to be *Two months* before the time for the Meeting of the Electors. This will be sufficient. The parties will in the meantime electioneer conditionally, that is to say, *if you decline;* for a serious opposition to you will I think hardly be risked."[25]

[22] John Quincy Adams to Sylvanus Bourne, London, Dec. 16, 1795, in Ford, *The Writings of John Quincy Adams,* I, 453.

[23] See Washington to Jay, Philadelphia, May 8, 1796, in Fitzpatrick, *Washington's Writings,* XXXV, 36-37. Earlier than this, as has been seen, Washington had given definite indications of retirement. The French knew early that Washington planned to retire and to issue a state paper to the nation. See Adet to Minister of Foreign Relations, Philadelphia, June 9, 1796, in Turner, *CFM,* p. 920.

[24] See Washington to Hamilton, Mount Vernon, June 26, 1796, in Fitzpatrick, *Washington's Writings,* XXXV, 103-104; see also Washington's letter to Hamilton of May 15, 1796 (Philadelphia), *ibid.,* p. 50.

[25] Hamilton to Washington, July 5, 1796, *ibid.,* p. 104 n. and in Lodge, *The Works of Alexander Hamilton,* VIII, 408-409. Republicans recognized

Hamilton's reasoning appeared sound. Three months before the gathering of electors Washington announced his intention to retire. First he submitted his Farewell Address to the Cabinet, on September 15, 1796, and four days later gave it to the people in the columns of David C. Claypoole's *American Daily Advertiser* (Philadelphia). He had planned a valedictory in 1792, and James Madison had then drafted one; the 1796 version, in which Hamilton's hand was prominent, was a piece of partisan politics directed at a specific situation. At the time it was recognized for what it was, a campaign document. The 1792 version had not stressed politics nor had it touched on foreign affairs. In the 1796 version these elements were central.[26]

The specific target in foreign affairs was the alliance with France. The President struck at Adet's activities, at French meddling in American politics (while passing over British meddling) and at the allegedly dangerous implications of the French alliance. Washington told Hamilton that had it not been for the status of "party disputes" and of foreign affairs, he would not have considered it necessary to revise his valedictory. To combat foreign (French) intrigue "in the internal concerns of our country," he was convinced that a caveat to the nation was necessary. It is indeed easy "to foresee," he warned, "that it may involve us in disputes and finally in War, to fulfill political alliances." This was the crux of the matter; the alliance was no longer an asset.[27]

---

that Washington's delayed announcement of retirement was a political scheme emanating from Hamilton, "designed to prevent a fair election, and the consequent choice of Mr. Jefferson." John Beckley to William Irvine, Sept. 15, 1796, Irvine Papers, cited in Cunningham, "The Jeffersonian Party to 1801," p. 142.

[26] The 1792 version of the Farewell Address is in Fitzpatrick, *Washington's Writings*, XXXV, 51-61; the Sept. 19, 1796, version is on pp. 214-218; for a detailed analysis of the address and its various contributors, see Victor Hugh Paltsits, ed., *Washington's Farewell Address* (New York, 1935). Usually Washington's advice on foreign policy is taken as the substance of the Farewell; see Albert K. Weinberg, "Washington's 'Great Rule' in its Historical Evolution," in *Historiography and Urbanization*, Eric F. Goldman, ed. (Baltimore, 1941), p. 113. Marshall Smelser in "George Washington and the Alien and Sedition Acts," *AHR*, LIX, 326, and in "The Jacobin Phrenzy," *The Review of Politics*, XIII (Oct., 1951), 476, places the Farewell Address in its context as a political document, as does Joseph Charles, "Hamilton and Washington: The Origins of the American Party System," *WMQ*, 3rd Series, XII, 262.

[27] Bemis, "Washington's Farewell Address. . . ," *AHR*, XXXIX, 262-263.

Washington's valedictory gave the Federalist answer to Republican accusations that the administration had sold the country to the British. It trumped the outcry over the Jay treaty and was a justification and defense of administration policies. As such it was designed and as such it became the opening blast in the campaign to prevent the election to the presidency of Thomas Jefferson. The Farewell laid the basis for Federalist strategy of using Washington's great prestige to appeal to patriotism, as against the evil of foreign machinations, to make "Federalist" and "patriot" synonyms in the minds of the electorate.[28]

Washington opened the address with the announcement that he would not be a candidate for a third term and then stressed the advantage of union and the evils of political parties. He warned "in the most solemn manner against the baneful effects of the Spirit of Party, generally." Party spirit, he said, "opens the door to foreign influence and corruption, which find a facilitated access to the government itself through the channels of party passions. Thus the policy and and [sic] the will of one country, are subjected to the policy and will of another." With the French Republic in mind, he advised against "a passionate attachment of one Nation for another." Such "sympathy for the favourite nation," he warned, leads to wars and quarrels "without adequate inducement and justification."

A free people, he said, ought to be *"constantly* awake" to "the insidious wiles of foreign influence," and then he elaborated upon

---

Washington understood that basic in any nation's foreign policy was self-interest, and that at this stage of American development it was to the nation's advantage, particularly from his Federalist viewpoint, not to be bound by the French alliance. Sound though this view may be in perspective, in 1796 it appeared to opponents a partisan political view. To Republicans loyalty to the alliance and hostility to England appeared the best means of promoting national self-interest. See the first draft of the Farewell enclosed in Washington to Hamilton, Philadelphia, May 15, 1796, in Fitzpatrick, *Washington's Writings*, XXXV, 56-67; Roland G. Usher, "Washington and Entangling Alliances," *North American Review*, CCIV (July, 1916), 29-38.

[28] Binkley, *American Political Parties. . .*, p. 51. For a stimulating discussion of the Farewell Address which attacks the myth that Washington's words constituted an inspired charter for a permanent foreign policy based on isolationism, see Louis B. Wright, "The Founding Fathers and 'Splendid Isolation,'" *Huntington Library Quarterly*, VI (Feb., 1943), pp. 173-178; sounding the same theme, James G. Randall, "George Washington and 'Entangling Alliances,'" *South Atlantic Quarterly*, XXX (July, 1931), 221-229, stressed that the phrase "entangling alliances" came from Jefferson, not Washington.

his "Great rule of conduct," avoidance of such influence. In oft-quoted words he advised that Europe go its way and that America follow her own interests. In extending commercial relations with European nations he recommended "as little *political* connection as possible." Alluding to the bitter experience of the French alliance and stressing fidelity to "already formed engagements," he said that "'tis our true policy to steer clear of permanent Alliances with any portion of the foreign world."

Washington hoped that his departing words might "now and then recur to moderate the fury of party spirit, to warn against the mischiefs of foreign Intriegue [*sic*], to guard against the Impostures of pretended patriotism." He attacked political opposition, chastised the public for its attachment to France, and concluded with a defense of his foreign policy, particularly his policy of neutrality based upon the Proclamation of Neutrality of April 22, 1793, which he called the "index" to his plan.[29]

* * * * *

The ideas and foreign policy principles of the Farewell were not unique to either Hamilton or Washington. They were prevalent Federalist ideas on foreign policy and politics and can be found in much of the polemical political literature of the time. The concept of nonentanglement with Europe was common among others than the Federalists. Often it was a reaction to a specific annoyance—the French alliance. When stated in terms of nonentanglement with Europe in general, an attack against the alliance had great psychological appeal; in time the specific intent was lost and only the generalization remained.[30]

The Federalist press coupled the general idea of nonentanglement in European politics with the evils of the French alliance and used the whole against Republicans. "Among the various motives which have been urged by our Jacobins," one Federalist gazette said eight months before Washington announced his retirement,

[29] The quotations follow the text printed in Fitzpatrick, *Washington's Writings,* XXXV, 214-238.

[30] For a discussion of this point, see Weinberg, "Washington's 'Great Rule,'" in Goldman, *Historiography and Urbanization,* pp. 109-138. Earlier expressions of the idea of nonentanglement relative to the congressional resolution of June 12, 1783, are discussed in Bemis, *Diplomacy of the American Revolution,* pp. 166-167.

"to entangle the United States, in the politics of Europe, and render them subservient to the views of France, none have been more successfully applied than those of gratitude to that nation, for the supposed disinterestedness, with which she took part in our late revolution. . . . a regard of her own interest, and a gratification of her passions solely directed the subtle politics of *France*, in her conduct toward this country."[31]

The foreign policy ideas reflected in the Farewell Address were not uniquely American principles; like most things in America they had crossed the Atlantic. In the writings of the eighteenth-century *philosophe*, Condorcet, the ideas of the Farewell seem to find echo. Condorcet warned against diplomatic agreements involving automatic obligations which would bind a nation's freedom of action. "Alliance treaties seem to me so dangerous and so little useful that I think it is better to abolish them entirely in time of peace," he said. "They are only means by which rulers of states precipitate the people into wars from which they benefit either by their mistakes or by carrying out their plots against freedom, and for which the emergency serves as a pretext."[32]

Other *philosophes*, such as Guillaume-François le Trosne and Gabriel Bonnot de Mably, whose works were read in America, also warned against formal treaties and emphasized that political alliances should be avoided.[33]. Concerned with political morality in practice as well as in theory, the *philosophes* pointed out that two successful modern republics, Venice and the Netherlands, owed their success to the policy of avoiding political alliances and of following exclusively their commercial interests. These republics had placed their faith in the bonds of trade which would strengthen their connections with other nations. Such foreign policy ideas, logical in theory and successful in practice, appeared worthy of emulation by a New World republic unhampered by the despotic traditions and political jealousies of European diplomacy. In America significant

[31] "A Correspondent" in the *Columbian Centinel* (Boston), Jan. 6, 1796.
[32] Quoted in Gilbert, "The 'New Diplomacy' of the Eighteenth Century," *World Politics*, IV, 13-14.
[33] For an analysis of a contemporary American critique of Mably, see Alexander DeConde, "William Vans Murray's *Political Sketches*: A Defense of the American Experiment," *Mississippi Valley Historical Review*, XLI (March, 1955), 623-640; Murray's isolationist ideas and the idea of nonentanglement are discussed on pp. 637-638.

efforts were made to put into practice the radical foreign policy principles of eighteenth-century political thought.[34]

In the domestic political battles at hand, the ideological context of Washington's valedictory mattered little. His words stoked an already hot political situation. "It will serve as a signal," exclaimed Fisher Ames, "like dropping a hat, for the party racers to start, and I expect a great deal of noise, whipping, and spurring; money, it is very probable will be spent, some virtue and more tranquillity lost; but I hope public order will be saved." If "the sentiments in the President's address" were adopted by the electorate, he said, then better men—Federalists—would be elected and the business of government would not be obstructed.[35]

Madison had feared that under Hamilton's influence the address would be a campaign document. The valedictory confirmed his assumptions; it was almost completely political. Under the influence of the British faction, Washington obviously sought to destroy the French alliance, Madison informed Monroe in Paris. "It has been known that every channel," he wrote, "has been latterly opened that could convey to his mind a rancor against that country [France] and suspicion of all who are thought to sympathize with its revolution and who support the policy of extending our commerce and in general of standing well with it. But it was not easy to suppose his mind wrought up to the tone that could dictate or rather adopt some parts of the performance."[36] Federalist circles, on the other hand, were convinced that French animosity against Washington had been created by Republicans for political purposes. In Washington's Farewell they found considerable comfort; it was reprinted and widely circulated.[37]

[34] Eighteenth-century ideas of a reform diplomacy had strong influence on the beginnings of American diplomacy, Gilbert, "The 'New Diplomacy' of the Eighteenth Century," *WP*, IV, 28.

[35] Ames to Oliver Wolcott, Jr., Dedham, Sept. 26, 1796, Gibbs, ed., *Wolcott Papers*, I, 384-385.

[36] Madison to Monroe, Sept. 29, 1796, quoted in Brant, *James Madison: Father of the Constitution. . .* , p. 442; as Washington had anticipated, opponents claimed that the motive behind the Farewell was Washington's knowledge that he would not be re-elected if he ran. McMaster, *A History of the People of the United States. . .* , II, 290-291.

[37] Pickering to John Quincy Adams, Dept. of State, Dec. 9, 1796, Pickering Papers, Mass. Hist. Society, Boston; also, John Quincy Adams to John Adams, London, April 4, 1796, in Ford, *The Writings of John Quincy Adams,*

Men often attempt to rationalize their partisan views in timeless or patriotic appeals; so it was with Washington and Hamilton. The valedictory bore directly on the coming election, on the French alliance, and on the general status of Franco-American relations. Washington's advice for the future, taunted a critic, "is but a defence for the past." The address warned against "permanent alliances," he said; "this extraordinary advice if fully exemplified in your departure from the spirit and principle of the treaty with France, which was declared to be permanent, and exhibits this very infidelity you reprobate in a most striking and lamentable light." Washington had not, the critic continued, "adhered to that rigid and neutral justice which you profess—every concession to Britain in prejudice of France was a deviation from neutrality."[38] Much of the evil Washington attributed to faction, he claimed, came from the Federalist party. "Your examples of party influence are uniformly drawn from occasions wherein your personal opinions, your pride and passions, have been involved. . . ."[39]

Washington's aim was true; he damaged the French alliance and gave vigor to the Federalist political effort. Why, critics asked, was it unwise to extend the nation's political engagements? Was not the Jay treaty a political connection, practically an alliance with

I, 484. John Quincy Adams praised the address. He wrote Washington that he hoped "it may serve as the foundation stone" for future American policy and "that it may control the fury of domestic factions and check the encroachments of foreign influence." The Hague, Feb. 11, 1797, *ibid.*, II, 119-120. Samuel F. Bemis in "John Quincy Adams and George Washington," *Proceedings of the Massachusetts Historical Society, 1941-1944,* LXVII (Boston, 1945), 365-384, maintained that young Adams's ideas had an influence on Washington's mind as the Farewell Address was being prepared. To support his contention he placed in three parallel columns Washington's words in the two drafts of the address and John Quincy Adams's pertinent expressions.

[38] [William Duane], *A Letter to George Washington, President of the United States: Containing Strictures on His Address of the Seventeenth of September, 1796, Notifying His Relinquishment of the Presidential office,* by Jasper Dwight of Vermont [pseud.] (Philadelphia, Dec., 1796), pp. 40-45; Weinberg, "Washington's 'Great Rule,'" in Goldman, ed., *Historiography and Urbanization,* p. 115. Yet in later years politicians and others referred to Washington's advice as an enduring guide to policy; see, for example, Henry Cabot Lodge's address of Feb. 16, 1916, at Morristown, New Jersey, entitled, "Washington's Policies of Neutrality and National Defence," in his *War Addresses* (Boston, 1917), pp. 117-136.

[39] Duane, *A Letter to George Washington. . . ,* p. 31.

England?[40] Could the Republic of France be more harmful to the United States than the monarchy of England?

Realizing the political implications of the address, Adet sent a copy home, commenting that "it would be useless to speak to you about it. You will have noticed the lies it contains, the insolent tone that governs it, the immorality which characterizes it. You will have no difficulty in recognizing the author of a piece extolling ingratitude, showing it as a virtue necessary to the happiness of States, representing interest as the only counsel which governments ought to follow in the course of their negotiations, putting aside honor and glory."

Adet believed that these were Hamilton's principles. Feeling that the address deserved the contempt of honest men, that it would arouse the indignation of "patriots," and that it would not have the effect on the people that the British faction had hoped it would, Adet pitched into the campaign battle to insure that the address would not have its intended effect.[41]

* * * * *

The lines of political battle became clear. Although Hamilton hoped to bring Thomas Pinckney to the presidency, the leading Federalist candidate was John Adams; on the Republican side Jefferson towered above other possibilities.[42] In June, not long after

[40] Hamilton, *History of the Republic. . .* , VI, 536-537. Although Americans viewed the Farewell, in many instances, as purely a political document, that is not to deny that some men, as reflected in the Farewell, wanted a genuine neutrality which would save the United States "from the exactions and insolence of both" England and France. See, for example, James Kent to Moss Kent, Sept. 19, 1796, in William Kent, *Memoirs and Letters of James Kent. . .* (Boston, 1898), p. 174.

[41] Adet to Minister of Foreign Relations, Philadelphia, Oct. 12, 1796, Turner, *CFM*, p. 954: Bemis, "Washington's Farewell Address. . . ," *AHR*, XXXIX, 263. For the British reaction to the Farewell, see Perkins, *The First Rapprochement*, p. 57.

[42] Washington early had looked upon Vice-President Adams as his successor. Dauer, *The Adams Federalists*, p. 92. For a discussion of the 1796 election with emphasis on Adams and domestic politics, see pp. 92-111. For Hamilton's plot to replace Adams with Pinckney, see Rufus King to Hamilton, May 2, 1796, and Hamilton to King, May 4, 1796, in Hamilton, ed., *Hamilton's Works*, VI, 113-114; for French opinion on Washington's successor, see François V. A. Aulard, ed., *Paris pendant la réaction Thermidorienne et sous le Directoire*, III, 595, Report of the Central Bureau, Paris, Nov. 27, 1796.

Washington's contemplated departure was known, Adet was aware of this party line-up. At that time he believed, and so informed his superiors, that French intervention would be decisive in the choice of the next administration, that friends of France would be elected if the Directory made known its views on the conduct of the federal government.[43] Upon the proper choice of the next President depended not only the maintenance of friendship with Great Britain, but also perhaps continuance of the Union; the British, too, had a vital stake in its outcome.[44]

Adet considered Adams an enemy of France and a friend of England, and electioneered for Jefferson.[45] A trip to New England gave him the opportunity to sample public sentiment along the way. His impressions supported his conviction that the American people were still attached to France and that all that was needed to invigorate the American alliance was a new, Republican administration. In Massachusetts he bolstered sagging morale of pro-French Americans by indicating that France would not allow the election to go by default, that she would not abandon them to the mercy of England.[46]

While it may have boosted Francophile morale, Adet's Boston appearance evoked Federalist alarm. Noting that Adet associated with "Jacobins only," one prominent Federalist was nonetheless "extremely mortified" at the reception given him by some of the "best citizens," especially "when it is known that the undue influence of that nation [France] among the people already endangers the union and government of the U. S." He considered "Ox Feasts," at which Adet was entertained, "as acts of supererrogation

---

[43] See Adet to Minister of Foreign Relations, Philadelphia, June 9, 1796, in Turner, *CFM,* pp. 920-921.

[44] Bond to Grenville, Philadelphia, May 4, 1796, No. 30, Henry Adams Transcripts. Washington assured Robert Liston that his government strongly desired to cultivate a strict and friendly good understanding with Great Britain. Philadelphia, May 28, 1796, No. 2, *ibid.*

[45] The Directory approved of Adet's meddling and counted on Jefferson's election. Delacroix wrote to Adet that his despatches confirmed what the Directory had expected would result from its measures directed against Washington's government. [Paris], Nov. 2, 1796, AAE CP EU, Vol. XLVI, ff. 355-357.

[46] Adet to Minister of Foreign Relations, Boston, Sept. 24, 1796, in Turner, *CFM,* pp. 947-949.

[*sic*] and as tending to confirm in the minds of the people erroneous opinions, which are extremely mischievious."[47]

On his return from New England, Adet made himself a main issue in the campaign. At this time he filled his despatches with information on the unsettled American political situation and attempted to assess the temper of public opinion, particularly toward France.[48] The future conduct of France toward America, he made clear, would be governed by the election's outcome. Choosing what he considered to be the opportune moment, he published on October 27 the first of a series of manifestoes. He conjured up the prospect of war with France and then stressed that Jefferson's election would eliminate such a possibility. With the Quakers of Pennsylvania, Federalists lamented, Adet's strategy of fear worked. Fearing a Federalist-sponsored war against France, Quakers cast their votes for Republicans.[49] "French influence never appeared so open and unmasked as at this city [Philadelphia] election," cried William Loughton Smith, Alexander Hamilton's congressional mouthpiece. "French flags, french cockades were displayed by the Jefferson party and there is no doubt that french money was not spared. . . . In short there never was so barefaced and disgraceful an interference of a foreign power in any free country."[50]

Adet's procedure was to write an official note to the Secretary of State and then send a copy for publication to Bache's *Aurora*. In his note of October 27 he protested against American foreign policy and appealed to the people to renew their friendship with France by dissavowing the Jay treaty and honoring the French alliance.[51]

Referring to Adet's note and to his own acidulous response,

[47] George Cabot to Rufus King, Brookline, Sept. 24, 1796, in King, *Rufus King Correspondence*, II, 91.

[48] Adet to Minister of Foreign Relations, Philadelphia, Oct. 27, 1796, in Turner, *CFM*, p. 958.

[49] Fisher Ames to Christopher Gore, Philadelphia, Dec. 3, 1796, in Seth Ames, *Works of Fisher Ames*, II, 206; John Adams to wife, Philadelphia, Dec. 4, 1796, in C. F. Adams, ed., *Letters of John Adams Addressed to His Wife*, II, 231; Oliver Wolcott, Jr., to Oliver Wolcott, Sr., Philadelphia, Nov. 27, 1796, in Gibbs, ed., *Wolcott Papers*, I, 400-401.

[50] William Loughton Smith to Ralph Izard, Philadelphia, Nov., 1796, in Ulrich B. Phillips, ed., "South Carolina Federalist Correspondence, 1789-1797," *AHR*, XIV (July, 1909), 785.

[51] Adet to Pickering, Philadelphia, Oct. 27, 1796, *ASP FR*, I, 576-577.

Pickering labeled the transaction "very unpleasant," maintaining that he sent his reply to Adet's note to the press "with great reluctance." He believed that the representations of the French Minister "were of a nature to render it extremely desirable that the conduct of the American Government should be as publicly vindicated." Pickering also timed his note to influence the election. Adet's manifesto was published on Monday, October 31; Pickering answered on the following day, and two days later, on Friday, November 3, presidential electors were chosen in Pennsylvania.[52] Adet's note was "altogether designed as an electioneering manoeuvre," Federalists complained, "the govern^t. and every respectable character views it in that light."[53] Federalists had responded accordingly.

A few days later (November 5) the *Aurora* carried Adet's second manifesto, dubbed by Federalists the "cockade proclamation." In the name of the Directory, it called upon all Frenchmen in the United States—in the land of an ally—to wear the tricolored cockade, "the symbol of a liberty, which is the fruit of eight years toils and privations, and of five years victories." Those who did not thus give public evidence of their support of the French Republic were to be denied the services of French consuls and the protection of the French flag. Immediately the tricolored cockade blossomed in the streets. Americans as well as Frenchmen mounted it as a badge of devotion to the French cause. It became a symbol of republicanism.[54]

Ten days later Adet followed the "cockade proclamation" with a final note which he again sent simultaneously to the Secretary of State and to Bache's *Aurora*. This was the note in which he announced that because of the Jay treaty his functions as minister had been suspended and he was returning to France.[55] Again Adet

[52] For the text of Pickering's note of Nov. 1, 1796, see *ibid.*, 578; see also Pickering to Rufus King, Dept. of State, Nov. 14, 1796, in King, *Rufus King Correspondence*, II, 108-109.

[53] William Loughton Smith to Ralph Izard, Philadelphia, Nov. 3, 1796, in Phillips, "South Carolina Federalist Correspondence. . . ," *AHR*, XIV, 781.

[54] The proclamation is in AAE CP EU, Vol. XLVI, f. 352, and is reprinted in Cobbett, *Porcupine's Works*, IV, 154-155. Adet's promulgation of the "cockade proclamation" was under orders from his home government. Adet to Minister of Foreign Relations, Philadelphia, Nov. 12, 1796, in Turner, *CFM*, p. 967.

[55] Adet to Pickering, Philadelphia, Nov. 15, 1796, *ASP FR*, I, 579-583.

had timed his announcement so that it might have a maximum political influence, particularly upon the electors who were soon to choose Washington's successor.[56] He had, in fact, received instructions from the Directors early in autumn, as soon as they had learned that the House of Representatives had voted funds for the Jay treaty, to end his official mission and to stay a few months longer as an observer. Adet had held these instructions and then used them as a last minute maneuver in the campaign.

Federalists were furious. John Adams, against whom the manifesto was directed, found "it an instrument well calculated to reconcile me to private life. It will purify me from all envy of Mr. Jefferson, or Mr. Pinckney, or Mr. Burr, or Mr. any body who may be chosen President or Vice President."[57] Republican leaders, although eager to use the issue of the French alliance to gain votes, were not happy with Adet's interference. Madison said Adet's note worked "all the evil with which it is pregnant." Its indiscretions, he added, gave comfort to Federalists, who had the "impudence" to point out that it was "an electioneering maneuver" and that "the French government have been led into it by the opponents of the British treaty."[58]

Denouncing Adet's pronouncements as brazen electioneering maneuvers by a foreign agent, Federalists demanded to know how Bache had obtained the last manifesto before it had been translated in the Department of State. The manifesto touched off a pamphlet war; both sides used Adet's notes and Pickering's replies as campaign ammunition. William Cobbett, violent Francophobe and anti-Jeffersonian, published Adet's notes and an adverse commentary under the title of *The Gros Mousqueton Diplomatique; or Diplo-*

[56] "I have had it published," Adet reported, "in order to arouse public sentiment when presidential electors were about to be chosen and in order to determine what effect it would produce upon the government and to judge what I might expect from the next session of Congress." Adet to Minister of Foreign Relations [Nov., 1796], in Turner, *CFM,* pp. 969-970.
[57] Adams to wife, Stratford, Conn., Nov. 27, 1796, in C. F. Adams, ed., *Letters of John Adams Addressed to His Wife,* II, 229.
[58] Madison to Jefferson, Dec. 5, 1796, Madison Papers, Library of Congress, quoted in Brant, *James Madison: Father of the Constitution. . . ,* p. 445; see also Fisher Ames to Christopher Gore, Dec. 13, 1796, cited in Tinkcom, *The Republicans and Federalists in Pennsylvania, 1790-1801,* p. 173. Ames despaired over French influence in the United States.

matic Blunderbuss.[59]   Labeling Adet an "unprincipled shameless bully," Cobbett explained that he denominated the manifestoes a blunderbuss because in "all the long list of fire arms, none is so difficult to adjust, or makes so much noise and smoke, with so little execution, as a *Blunderbuss.*"

Adet may have influenced the election; but like Genet, he injured the cause he tried to aid.   French popularity, according to competent observers, decreased as a result.[60]   Washington drew even closer to the British.   One New England writer declared that since Adet's electioneering on behalf of Jefferson "there is not an elector on this side of the Delaware that would not be sooner shot than vote for him."[61]   Another observer maintained that Adet's meddling "irretrievably diminished that good will felt for his Government and the people of France by most people here."[62]

Unaware of this adverse reaction, Adet believed that his actions

[59] *The Diplomatic Blunderbuss* is reprinted in Cobbett, *Porcupine's Works,* IV, 137-206; see also McMaster, *A History of the People of the United States. . . ,* II, 301.

[60] Liston to Grenville, Philadelphia, Nov. 15 and Dec. 9, 1796, Nos. 24 and 31, Henry Adams Transcripts.   Liston complained that Republicans charged British gold was being used in the election and confessed "that a persevering repetition of such accusations has at last the effect of procuring them a degree of credit."   A Republican clergyman was surprised at how the people cursed the French at this time.   Bentley, *Diary of William Bentley, D. D.* (entry of Nov. 8, 1796), II, 207.

[61] For the observation on Washington, see Henrietta Liston to James Jackson, [Philadelphia], 1796, in Perkins, ed., "A Diplomat's Wife in Philadelphia. . . ," *WMQ,* 3rd Series, XI, 605; "The People," *Connecticut Courant,* reprinted in the *New Hampshire and Vermont Journal: Or, The Farmer's Weekly Museum* (Walpole, N. H.), Nov. 22, 1796.   Robert Goodloe Harper wrote to his constituents that if there had been no other objection to Jefferson than French exertions on his behalf it would have been sufficient for opposing him.   Philadelphia, Jan. 5, 1797, in Elizabeth Donnan, ed., "Papers of James A. Bayard, 1796-1815," *Annual Report of the American Historical Association, 1913* (2 vols., Washington, 1915), II, 25.

[62] Philip Key to James McHenry, Annapolis, Nov. 28, 1796, in Steiner, *Correspondence of James McHenry,* p. 202.   Later, certain French officials came to believe that the activity of Adet coupled with that of his predecessors plus the seeming duplicity of the French government brought victory to the Federalists in 1796.   Even Jefferson, it was pointed out, came to believe that the French sought to destroy the American constitution.   Louis-Guillaume Otto, "Considerations on the Conduct of the Government of the United States Toward France, 1789-1797," [Paris, June 17, 1797], AAE CP EU, Vol. XLVII, ff. 401-418, cited in James, "French Opinion as a Factor in Preventing a War Between France and the United States, 1795-1800," *AHR,* XXX, 46.

and the Directory's measures would influence the electors in favor of Jefferson.[63] What Adet and the Directory had not taken into account was that invariably when a foreign diplomat takes sides openly in the politics of the nation to which he is accredited he places the party leader in the position of being considered a pawn of a foreign government. Whether true or not, this gives the opposition an opportunity to denounce foreign interference and to pose as the defender of national honor. So it was with Adet. His activities seemed to confirm the warnings in Washington's Farewell Address.

How long, Noah Webster asked, would "the *delicacy* of our government . . . suffer every species of indignity from the agents of the French nation in this country?" Webster was convinced that "the *French strength* in our country rests principally on a general ignorance" of French views. Such ignorance, he contended, could be corrected.[64] Developing this theme, Federalists attacked the French alliance, denounced French domestic interference, and pitted the patriotism of Washington and Adams against the Jacobin-tainted Republican campaign. Voters were warned to beware of foreign influence, to "decide between the address of the President and the [French]"; Adet and the Directory wished, Federalists claimed, to draw the nation into war and to sever the Western from the Atlantic states.[65]

To true Federalists such admonitions were not mere campaign propaganda. The acquisition of the Floridas and Louisiana in the Southwest, Newfoundland and the British fisheries in the Northern seas, and other British settlements bordering the United States to the North and Northwest were French objectives. Federalists claimed that the French had timed their plots to coincide with the presidential elections and had tried to split the nation geographically and divide it internally. Adet was then to deliver his masterstroke; he was to proclaim his manifesto of grievances and "appeal to the

[63] Adet to Minister of Foreign Relations, [Nov. 22, 1792], in Turner, *CFM*, p. 972.
[64] Webster to Pickering, New York, Nov. 24 and Dec. 8, 1796, in Warfel, *Letters of Noah Webster*, pp. 142, 144.
[65] "Americanus" in the *Gazette of the United States,* reprinted in *The Herald: A Gazette for the Country* (New York), Dec. 3, 1796.

people." No doubt clouded the Federalist mind; the union was in danger. "We must *unite* or die as an independent people!"[66]

In Paris, Charles Cotesworth Pinckney responded to the news of Adet's "disorganizing manoeuvres" in much the same vein. Linking party differences to French influence, he wished "that we would banish all party distinctions and foreign influence; and think and act only as Americans—for all parties in this country [France] unite in thinking that we ought to act as if we were altogether their dependents, and indebted to them solely, and not to our own exertions for our liberty and independence. Hence, our treaty with Great Britain is here generally execrated, and our having any kind of commercial connexion with that country, even if the treaty had not been made, would, I believe, have been disliked. They wish to destroy the trade of Great Britain, and they look upon us as one of her best customers; and to obtain their object, they care not what we suffer."[67] Pinckney's observations were sound but they did not cover all sources of Franco-American friction.

Some Americans, probably for political reasons, and some Frenchmen who had been resident in America or who knew the United States, had in part inspired Adet's electioneering and the general policy of the Directory toward the United States. The reports of Revolutionary *emigrés* who in 1796 and 1797 were returning to France undoubtedly had an effect on France's view of the alliance.[68] La Rochefoucauld-Liancourt, for example, spoke bitterly of the Jay treaty as "a monument of the weakness of America," maintaining that it violated the "ancient treaties with France" and attempted to destroy the alliance. "It is the general voice," he observed in his American travels, "that America ought to form an offensive and defensive league with France, and to declare war against England.

[66] Comment of William Vans Murray on a letter on this subject from James McHenry, Philadelphia, Nov. 19, 1796, William Vans Murray Papers, Library of Congress.

[67] Pinckney to Secretary of State, Paris, Feb. 1, 1797, *ASP FR,* II, 18; Faÿ, *Revolutionary Spirit,* pp. 395, 401-403. French policies were influenced more by the reports of French ministers in America; yet French statesmen were aware of the views of French observers in America. See Talleyrand to Moreau de Saint-Méry, Paris, Sept. 8, 1798, which notes that La Rochefoucauld-Liancourt's account is in press. Moreau de Saint-Méry, *Voyage. . . ,* p. 395.

[68] Childs, "French Opinion of Anglo-American Relations. . . ," *FAR,* I, 32.

But, on the other hand, I have been assured that the richer class of the people are, for the greater part, of opinion, that a treaty of commerce and political amity with England is indispensibly necessary to the welfare of America."[69]

Federalist leaders were aware, or suspected, that Americans were giving the French a slanted view of American opinion.[70] Young John Quincy Adams, then in Europe, observed that "there is a great ignorance of the character and sentiments of the American people in France among those who imagine that any manoeuvre of *theirs* could turn an election against the President of the United States." Then he touched on the faith of Federalists in Washington. "France," he prophesied, "will find it more easy to go through five and twenty revolutions at home, than to root out that man's merits and services from the memory of Americans, or a proper sense of them from their hearts."[71]

Some Federalists also looked upon the successes or failures of French arms as a barometer of French and Republican attitudes toward the American government. If French arms had been victorious against the Austrians in 1796, one Hamiltonian said, "the nation would have been so imperious, that war or something very troublesome and humiliating would have succeeded, considering the powerful party of Americans who would have more than kept pace with their French friends in haughtiness." Referring undoubtedly to John Quincy Adams as his "indisputable" channel, he disclosed that "the French Directory were governed entirely by advice of Americans who were in Paris, and by information received there

[69] See La Rochefoucauld-Liancourt, *Travels. . . ,* I, 381-382, 408, 484-485.

[70] Federalist gazettes exploited the situation. See, for example, the *New Hampshire and Vermont Journal: Or, The Farmer's Weekly Museum* (Walpole, N. H.), Jan. 10, 1797. In lashing out sarcastically at the Directory and pro-French Americans the writer declared that "some have thought it would soothe the offended spirit of the Directory, if all persons in office should be required to take an oath of allegiance and fidelity to the French Republic, one, *universal* and indivisible; the certificate of the oath being dated the *first* year of American liberty."

[71] Adams to Joseph Pitcairn, The Hague, Nov. 13, 1796, in Ford, *The Writings of John Quincy Adams,* II, 42. In defending Washington, Mrs. Abigail Adams viewed the opposition as the "offspring of faction, and nursed by sedition." Referring to Washington personally, she remarked that "we shall not look upon his like again." To Thomas B. Adams, Quincy, Nov. 8, 1796, in Charles Francis Adams, ed., *Letters of Mrs. Adams, the Wife of John Adams* (3rd ed.; 2 vols., Boston, 1841), II, 231-234.

from Americans on this side of the water, in all their movements respecting America."[72]

* * * * *

Federalist alarms over collusion between Republicans and the French did not stop French interference in American politics, nor did the interference end with the choosing of electors in November. As few of the electors were pledged to a specific candidate, the campaign continued until December 7, when the electors cast their ballots. Although Adet's diplomatic functions had been suspended, he remained in Philadelphia in the interval between the November elections and the meeting of electors to continue his antiadministration campaign. Adet and the Republicans hammered at similar themes, stressing that if Adams were elected the errors of the Washington administration would be continued. Adams was committed to Washington's policies, which would lead to war with France. "Whether the French Directory have only been drawn in to favor the election of a favorite, or whether in their trances and delirium of victory they think to terrify America, or whether in their sallies they may not venture on hostilities, time will discover. Americans must be cool and steady," Adams advised, "if they can."[73] Adet meanwhile continued to report to the Directory on political developments, planning to remain in Philadelphia until the end of the next session of Congress.[74]

With the election still undecided, Congress met on December 5. In his opening speech to this second session of the fourth Congress, President Washington spoke as an angry man when he drew attention to the seriousness of the crisis in Franco-American relations. He emphasized that American trade was suffering serious injury in the West Indies "from the cruisers and agents of the French repub-

[72] Uriah Tracy to Wolcott, Jr., Philadelphia, Jan. 7, 1797, in Gibbs, ed., *Wolcott Papers*, I, 415-416, Ford, *The Writings of John Quincy Adams*, I, 481. Young Adams contended that French dissatisfaction with the Jay treaty actually was inspired and fostered by Americans in Paris.

[73] John Adams to wife, Philadelphia, Dec. 4, 1796, in C. F. Adams, ed., *Letters of John Adams Addressed to His Wife*, II, 231. One of the basic charges directed against Adams was that he was too closely connected to the British party. "Cassius," in the *New World* (Philadelphia), cited in Woodbury, *Public Opinion in Philadelphia. . .* , p. 126.

[74] Adet to Minister of Foreign Relations, Philadelphia, Nov. 22, 1796, in Turner, *CFM*, pp. 974-975.

lic," and that communications from Adet portended further trouble. Yet, he claimed, it had been his constant desire "to maintain cordial harmony and a perfectly friendly understanding with" the French republic. Further information on this "interesting subject," he told Congress, would come in a special message.[75]

Like kerosene poured on hot coals, Washington's last words to Congress inflamed opponents of his foreign policy. In the Virginia legislature men argued that they should not by any declaration commit themselves to support the President's measures as they respected France.[76] Washington's speech, other opponents claimed, offered additional evidence of his hostility to the French Republic. Since Congress last met, they said, fifty American ships had been seized by the British to every one taken by the French. American seamen have been impressed and mistreated at the hands of the British. Yet Washington's address contained not one word about the British depredations. All self-respect, concluded one critic, is forgotten when British wrongs are concerned; with the French only do we talk of self-respect and dignity. Another critic demanded an examination of the President's conduct. It was the peoples' right, he pointed out, to know how far he deserved the censure of "their great and good allies, the French."[77]

As usual, both the Senate and House of Representatives responded to the President's opening address. Before the House could agree on the response, a bitter party quarrel culminated in an attack on Washington and his pro-English foreign policy. The Federalist committee in the House charged with drafting the reply, headed by Fisher Ames, brought in a document endorsing administration policies. Aroused Republicans turned thumbs down on the proposed

[75] Speech of Dec. 7, 1796, *ASP FR,* I, 31; for Washington's agitation during the speech, see Henrietta Liston to James Jackson, Philadelphia, Dec. 9, 1796, in Perkins, ed., "A Diplomat's Wife in Philadelphia. . . ," *WMQ,* 3rd Series XI, 606. Mrs. Liston, wife of the British Minister, sat next to Washington as he read the speech.

[76] John Marshall to James Iredell, Richmond, Dec. 15, 1796, James Iredell Papers, Duke University. Marshall commented: "To what has America Fallen!" See also Adams, *An Autobiographical Sketch by John Marshall,* pp. 20-21.

[77] Newspaper comment cited in McMaster, *A History of the People of the United States. . . ,* II, 305. For Adet, of course, the speech had little appeal; see Adet to Minister of Foreign Relations, Philadelphia, Dec. 15, 1796, in Turner, *CFM,* p. 978.

draft. Finally, a compromise reply was drawn, which pleased neither ardent Federalist nor dedicated Republican.

Twelve Republicans went on record as opposed to the modified version; they were glad to see Washington go and said so. The House message, moreover, reflected the Republican sentiment toward France and expressed "anxiety and deep regret" over existing relations. "Instead of blame on our government," Fisher Ames said in keeping with Federalist doctrine, "it was our own base Americans at Paris, and a base party here, who fomented, encouraged, and now openly abetted, the injury and the insult."[78]

As he had indicated he would do in his opening speech, Washington on January 16 sent a special message to Congress on the critical state of relations with France. Since Adet's complaints covered Franco-American relations from almost the beginning of the European war, the President considered it necessary to review those relations and to accompany his message with supplementary papers covering much of the correspondence with Fauchet and Adet. The first documents, dated January 16 and written by Pickering as instructions for the guidance of Pinckney in Paris, reviewed relations with France from the beginning. This was the Federalist answer to Adet's complaints, to French charges that the American government had destroyed the alliance of 1778. "Will the ministers of the French republic never cease to reproach us with 'ingratitude'?" It is time, Pickering said, "that these claims to our gratitude were investigated, and their extent ascertained."

The alliance and French aid during the war of independence, Pickering argued, benefited France as much as they did the United States. At first France refused an offensive alliance. Finally, to gain assistance against a probable English attack, France signed an *"eventual* and *purely defensive"* alliance. "Thus it is manifest that the United States were to be left still to fight their own battles, *unless Great Britain should choose to increase the number of her enemies by attacking France,* in which it would be as truly the interest of France as of the United States to make it a common

<hr/>

[78] For the House's message (Dec. 16, 1796), see *ASP FR,* I, 33-34; for the quotation, Fisher Ames to Christopher Gore, Philadelphia, Dec. 17, 1796, in Seth Ames, *Works of Fisher Ames,* I, 211. For the debate over the response, see Bassett, *The Federalist System. . . ,* pp. 147-148; Hildreth, *The History of the United States. . . ,* IV, 694-696.

cause." France's objective in allying herself with the United States, he said, "was to diminish the British power, and thereby promote the safety and interest of her own people," hence the "modern claims of boundless and perpetual gratitude" are groundless. Clearly, French aid and the alliance resulted from France's "exertions to advance *her own interest* and *secure her own safety."*

In reviewing Franco-American frictions after independence Pickering took up the French complaints presented by Genet, Fauchet, and Adet, and then presented evidence to destroy them by showing that the United States was not at fault. In a tone of aroused patriotism the Secretary of State concluded "that there has been no attempt in the Government of the United States to violate our treaty, or weaken our engagements with France: that whatever resistance it has opposed to the measures of her agents, the maintenance of the laws and sovereignty of the United States, and their neutral obligations, have rendered indispensable."[79]

These ideas, along with those in Washington's Farewell, played on a much reiterated Federalist theme, a theme echoed in the gazettes. To look upon the French as friends and allies, went the refrain, was nonsense. "Interest is the pole star of their conduct," warned a variation of the theme; "such it has proved in every stage of their connections with us. Have they not told us themselves, that they will not regard their treaties if they afterwards discover them to be disadvantageous?" Americans had more to fear from the French than from the English. The French had had, and had endeavored to have, "and are determined *to have,* a ruling influence, and controul, over the councils of our nation, and over the good people of the United States. . . ." To combat this, *"the first words our children should see in the primer, after,* WORSHIP *thy* CREATOR, ought to be NO FOREIGN INFLUENCE."[80]

[79] Washington's message of Jan. 19, 1797, is in *ASP FR,* I, 559; Pickering to Pinckney, Dept. of State, Jan. 16, 1797, is on pp. 559-576.

[80] William Willcocks, "To the People of the United States," the *Minerva,* reprinted in the *Herald: A Gazette for the Country* (New York), Dec. 28, 1796, Jan. 18, 1797, italics in the original. In his articles Willcocks maintained that he proved that France from the beginning had sought to involve the United States in the war and to bring Anglo-American commerce to an end. In the *New Hampshire and Vermont Journal: Or, The Farmer's Weekly Museum* (Walpole, N. H.), March 17, 1797, "A Free American" stressed the same theme. Among other things he advised: "Americans,

Although a diplomatic document embodying views of the American government which, ostensibly, Pickering intended for the government and the French Republic, Pickering did not compose his note for purposes of diplomatic exchange. Pinckney was not able to present Pickering's views to the French government. Pickering's note was as much a political manifesto as were Adet's notes; it was, as Pickering admitted, the administration's answer to Adet's meddling and his appeals to the American electorate—the administration's "vindication."[81]

After Washington laid the document before Congress, it was released immediately to the press and, by order of Congress, was printed and bound into a pamphlet of a hundred pages. Pitched on a high level of patriotic appeal, like Washington's Farewell, the note portrayed the administration as defending the nation against unjustified foreign pressures and gave additional support to the Federalist campaign to depict Republicanism as the tool of foreign interests and Federalism as synonymous with patriotism.[82] "Mr. Adet," Pickering said in justifying the note, "having published both his notes containing so many erroneous statements and so many aspersions on the Government, in all its branches, its vindication became a work of necessity; and the prompt publication of the letter was as proper for the information of our Citizens at large as for the use of the members of Congress; seeing it was intended

---

for ye are neither French nor British, be ye no longer deceived by professions of friendship from *any foreign* nation. Depend upon it, they only wish to promote *their interest,* at the *expense of yours."*

[81] Pickering to John Quincy Adams, Dept. of State, Jan. 17, 1797, Pickering Papers, Mass. Hist. Soc., Boston.

[82] Pickering to Charles Cotesworth Pinckney, Philadelphia, Jan. 21, 1797, National Archives, Dept. of State, Diplomatic and Consular Instructions; Ford, "Pickering," in Bemis, ed., *American Secretaries of State. . . ,* II, 206; Bemis, "Washington's Farewell Address," *AHR,* XXXIX, 266. Between Jan. 24 and Feb. 3, 1797, the *Aurora* carried installments of the Pickering note. For reactions of various Federalist leaders to the note see Pickering, *The Life of Timothy Pickering,* III, 360-364; for the favorable British reaction, see Grenville to Liston, Downing Street, April 8, 1797, Mayo, *Instructions to British Ministers. . . , AHA Ann. Rep.* (1936), III, 134. In Virginia, Federalists printed a thousand copies of the note in pamphlet form, paying for them by popular subscription. They distributed the pamphlets to counteract the activities of Republican congressmen. Edward Carrington to Pickering, Richmond, Feb. 14, 1797, Pickering Papers, Mass. Hist. Soc., Boston.

to exhibit to your view a clear statement of all the points in dispute and the reasoning of the Government upon them."[83]

The note attempted to justify the dissolution of the French alliance. Federalists were "fully satisfied that it must do infinite service to our country."[84] Republicans, attacking Pickering's "insulting manifesto" as a partisan document, would accept no such justification for scuttling the alliance. Administration policy as exemplified by Pickering's note, they contended, was a "system of hypocrisy and treachery."[85]

Behind the note, as behind the Farewell Address, lay the penetrating mind of Alexander Hamilton. The Franco-American crisis, he believed, was "as critical a situation as our government has been in; requiring all its prudence, all its wisdom, all its moderation, all its firmness." In this state of mind, through Oliver Wolcott, Jr., he had relayed his ideas on how to meet the crisis to Pickering, who embodied them in his note. Hamilton, though no longer in the government, still dominated the Cabinet; it looked to him for guidance. He had suggested that Adet not be answered directly, that the note should be addressed to Pinckney. The French alliance, he had stressed, "in its future operation must be against our interest." Adet and the Directory had provided the opportunity for escape from this alliance, which had always been embarrassing to Federalists; the opportunity must not be lost. "This idea," he concluded, "is very important."[86]

Reflecting Hamilton's concerns, Washington, too, had considered the idea important, taking a deep interest in the note and making suggestions while Pickering composed it.[87] Not long after he had

[83] Pickering to Charles Cotesworth Pinckney, Philadelphia, Feb. 11, 1797, National Archives, Dept. of State, Diplomatic and Consular Instructions.

[84] George Cabot to Pickering, Brookline, Feb. 2, 1797, Pickering Papers, Mass. Hist. Soc., Boston; John Jay to Pickering, Albany, Jan. 31, 1797, *ibid.*

[85] See Woodbury, *Public Opinion in Philadelphia. . .* , pp. 90-91; McMaster, *A History of the People of the United States. . .* , II, 313-314.

[86] Hamilton to Oliver Wolcott, Jr., Nov. 22, 1796, in Gibbs, ed., *Wolcott Papers,* I, 398-400. In this letter Hamilton presented a detailed outline for the reply to Adet; see also Wolcott, Jr., to Hamilton, Dec. 8, 1796, p. 407. Some people believed that Hamilton actually wrote the note; this Pickering denied, maintaining that the note was the result of "tedious research & laborious application." Pickering to Dr. John Clarke, Philadelphia, March 13, 1797, Pickering Papers, Mass. Hist. Soc., Boston.

[87] Washington to Secretary of State (Private), Jan. 9, 1797, in Fitzpatrick,

indicated to his intimates that he intended to retire, he had suggested that Pickering prepare a paper on Franco-American relations for Congress. Sensitive to "the continual attacks which have been made and are still making on the administration," Washington wanted the paper composed as a refutation of the charges that his administration was antialliance and anti-French.[88] Later, incensed by Adet's manifestoes, he had asked Hamilton, "Would it be proper do you conceive, at the ensuing Session, which will close the political scene with me, to bring the French Affairs, since the controversy with Genet fully before Congress?" Hamilton had advised that "it is all important to us first, if possible, to avoid rupture with France; secondly, if that cannot be, to evince to the People, that there has been an unequivocal disposition to avoid it."[89] Washington, as usual, had followed Hamilton's advice.

* * * * *

Already alarmed by what he discerned to be a growing Federalist sentiment for war against France, Adet quickly grasped the significance of Pickering's words and of Hamilton's ideas for the future of Franco-American relations.[90] None of his charges against the American government, he believed, had been refuted by Pickering. The Pickering note, he was convinced, evolved from an administration plan to break the alliance with France. It was calculated to irritate the French government, to drive it to take hostile measures against the United States. Such measures would inflame the people against France and would create the impression that all justice lay on the American side and that France sought to use the United States for her own purposes. Adet ascribed this scheme to the machinations of the English party. Wanting no outright break

Washington's Writings, XXXV, 360-361; Pickering, *The Life of Timothy Pickering,* III, 358.

[88] Washington to Secretary of State (Private), Mount Vernon, July 18, 1796, in Fitzpatrick, *Washington's Writings,* XXXV, 143-145.

[89] Washington to Hamilton, Philadelphia, Nov. 2, 3, 1796, *ibid.,* pp. 251-256; Hamilton to Washington, Nov. 4, 5, 1796, in Lodge, *The Works of Alexander Hamilton,* VIII, 421-424. For Washington's disgust with Adet and his hopes for the effectiveness of Pickering's note, see Washington to David Stuart, Philadelphia, Jan. 8, 1797, in Fitzpatrick, *Washington's Writings,* XXXV, 357-360.

[90] For Adet's reaction to Federalist talk of war, see Adet to Minister of Foreign Relations, Philadelphia, Jan. 20, 1797, in Turner, *CFM,* pp. 983-986.

with the United States, he stressed the disadvantages to France in a rupture.[91]

Other Frenchmen, too, were alarmed by the increasingly anti-French actions of the federal government. One of these, a fiery and little-known refugee editor from Saint Domingue, Tanguy de la Boissière, was employed by Adet to publish a pamphlet in refutation of Pickering's political despatch. With discernment and moderation he analyzed the "great and serious quarrel" which was destroying the Franco-American alliance. Unlike most of his compatriots, he did not look upon American neutrality as distinctly anti-French. Seeing logic in American neutrality, he accepted the contention that the United States was not strong enough to withstand British depredations at sea; "to suffer what it does not approve and cannot prevent," he said, "is the common lot of weakness." Yet, like most Frenchmen, he could see no good in the Jay treaty; it was undeniably anti-French. Why, he asked, could not the American government offer to France the same terms given to Great Britain?[92] Although less desirable than those in the 1778 treaties, the terms at least were fair. In explaining the Franco-American dilemma he touched on the familiar theme of Britain's efforts to separate the United States from France.[93]

[91] Adet to Minister of Foreign Relations, Philadelphia, Feb. 3, 1797, *ibid.*, pp. 986-988.

[92] This view was known to Americans. See Joseph Jones to James Madison, Fredericksburg, Dec. 9, 1796, in Ford, "Letters from Joseph Jones to Madison, 1788-1802," *Proc. Mass. Hist. Soc.,* XV, 158. Jones remarked: ". . . I should suppose the French would be reconciled if the new administration should by a commercial treaty place France on the same footing as we have G[reat] B[ritain]."

[93] C. C. Tanguy de la Boissière, *Observations sur la dépêche écrite à le Janvier 1797, par M. Pickering, Secrétaire d'État de l'Amérique à M. Pinckney, Ministre Plénipotentiare près de la République Française* (Philadelphia, 1797), and cited in Childs, "French Opinion of Anglo-American Relations. . . ," *French-American Review,* I, 27-29. Moreau de Saint-Méry published an English translation of Tanguy's pamphlet by Samuel Chandler (Philadelphia, 1797). Adet held Tanguy in high regard. In 1796 (Philadelphia) Tanguy wrote *Mémoire sur la situation commercial de la France avec les États-Unis de l'Amérique depuis l'anneé 1775 jusques et y compris 1795,* followed by *Sommaire d'observations sur les États-Unis de l'Amérique.* In this work Tanguy sought to prove that the 1778 treaty was not to France's advantage, asserting that Americans obtained from France a trade balance in money with which they supported English industry. Buron, "Statistics in Franco-American Trade," *Journal of Economic and Business History,* IV, 571. The memoir was printed under Adet's orders and paid for by French govern-

Tanguy's and Adet's concerns were not without foundation. Hamilton and other Federalists now talked of war with France. "Our merchants," Hamilton informed Washington, "are becoming very uneasy on the subject of the French captures and seizures." The seizures presented an "evil of a magnitude to be intolerable, if not shortly remedied." Although protesting that he desired peace with France, he warned that "this country cannot see its trade an absolute prey to France, without resistance." Appraising the situation as similar to that with Great Britain prior to the Jay treaty, he recommended a similar course of action. If nothing were to come of negotiation he advised "measures of self-defence." "Anything is better than absolute humiliation. France has already gone much further than Great Britain ever did."[94]

Washington, too, was disturbed. "The conduct of France towards the United States," he replied, "is, according to my ideas of it, outrageous beyond conception; not to be warranted by her treaties with us; by the Law of Nations; by any principle of justice; or even by a regard to decent appearances. From considerations such as these something might have been expected; but on her professions of friendship and loving kindness toward us I built no hope; but rather supposed they would last as long, and no longer, than it would accord with their interest to bestow them; or found it would not divert us from the observance of that strict neutrality, which we had adopted, and was [sic] persevering in." What, he asked, should the United States do to preserve peace, "consistently with the respect which is due to ourselves?" With war considered to be in the offing by the President and his advisers, clearly the French alliance was dying.[95]

---

mental funds. Adet considered the work important; he restricted the number of copies and took pains to keep it from Americans. Adet to Minister of Foreign Relations, Philadelphia, March 20, 1796, in Turner, *CFM*, pp. 843-845. See also McMaster, *A History of the People of the United States. . . ,* II, 313-314.

[94] Hamilton to Washington, Jan. 19, 1797, in Ford, *The Writings of George Washington,* XIII, 370-371. John Jay, while approving Pickering's note, did not regard Franco-American animosity "as a misfortune," though he neither desired nor expected a war with France. To Pickering, Albany, Jan. 31, 1797. Pickering Papers, Mass. Hist. Soc., Boston.

[95] Washington to Hamilton, Philadelphia, Jan. 22, 1797, in Fitzpatrick, *Washington's Writings,* XXXV, 372-373. Some Federalists saw in the difficulties with France the virtue that the nation might be cured "of extraneous

In France feeling against the American government ran strong; Washington was said to be in total contempt. Antiadministration Americans in Paris fanned French resentment, while Federalists in America encouraged mounting anti-French sentiment.[96] French policy, like that of England, was motivated by the European war; to France America's attitude was important basically in its relation to the war. France, in the words of John Quincy Adams, considered the United States "a weight in the balance of Europe" and shaped her policy accordingly.[97]

Among all Americans French relations now aroused serious concern.[98] One Republican congressman wrote a circular to his Virginia constituents stressing the value of the French alliance and that "every consideration of our own national interest as well as of national safety, strongly recommend a continuance of friendship and good understanding with [France]." Continuing, he warned that "it is apparent that endeavors are made to foment a prejudice in the public mind against the French nation. These must be the efforts of a party in favor of Britain, with a view to reconcile the idea of a rupture with France, and foster that of a *closer* union with Britain. . . ." Anyone who really preferred peace would hope that every honorable means would be taken to bring about an amicable adjustment of Franco-American difficulties.[99]

In newspapers and elsewhere men debated the alliance, the mounting crisis with France, and the possibility of war. As was his practice in time of crisis Hamilton once again took to the press to defend administration foreign policy and to attack the French

---

attachments," that the embarrassing French alliance would be destroyed. Chauncey Goodrich, to Oliver Wolcott, Jr., in Gibbs, ed., *Wolcott Papers*, I, 417.

[96] John Adams to Wife, Philadelphia, Jan. 14, 1797, C. F. Adams, ed., *Letters of John Adams Addressed to His Wife*, II, 240; John Quincy Adams to Joseph Pitcairn, The Hague, March 3, 1797, in Ford, *The Writings of John Quincy Adams*, II, 134.

[97] John Quincy Adams to John Adams, The Hague, Jan. 14, 1797, *ibid.*, II, 88.

[98] For an example of how Franco-American relations affected even local governing bodies, see the reaction of the Pennsylvania House of Representatives in Tinkcom, *Republicans and Federalists in Pennsylvania, 1790-1801*, pp. 203-204.

[99] John Clopton to Isaac Youngblood, Philadelphia, Jan. 24, 1797, John Clopton Papers, Duke University.

alliance.[100]   Another prominent Federalist, Noah Webster, editor of the *American Minerva,* wrote a series of eleven articles in which he attacked the alliance; his articles were reprinted and circulated widely, and in the Federalist press such attacks now became common.[101]   Webster in his articles said France had equated the term "ally" with that of "vassal"; "an open enemy," he declared in echo of French sentiment toward America, "is less dangerous than an *insidious friend.*"[102]   Genet, he pointed out, was supported by those who from the first had opposed establishment of the Federal government.   They hoped to strengthen their party and Genet "was encouraged to hope, from the popularity of the French cause, to gain partizans enough to *divide the people from the government,* and thus drag the United States into the war.   Thus began an alliance between antifederalism and gallicism, or Frenchism which *has* and *still does* threaten the tranquillity of our country, and even the permanence of our government."[103]

Although the British had also injured the United States, Webster maintained that the American connection with Great Britain was stronger than the French alliance because "our connection with her is solely *an alliance of interest.*   This is the true basis of all national connections.   We are therefore in no danger from Great Britain."   Referring to the French ministers from Genet to Adet, he explained that no agent of the British government had attempted to divide the American people from the government, "or dared to foment sedition in our peaceful land.   Such bold insults are practiced only by our *generous allies.*   It is right; it is necessary that the insidious designs of such *sly, intriguing,* but *ambitious* and *domineering allies,* should be unmasked.   They are more dangerous

[100] Under the signature "Americanus" Hamilton on Dec. 6, 1796, published "The Answer," his reply to Adet, printed in Lodge, *The Works of Alexander Hamilton,* V, 348-362; under the signature "Americus," he published a series of articles, beginning Jan. 27, 1797, entitled "The Warning," in which he warned against French influence and the alliance. *Ibid.,* pp. 363-392.

[101] Webster's articles were titled "To the People of the United States" and ran from Dec., 1796, through Feb., 1797. Warfel, *Noah Webster,* p. 229.

[102] No. 1, *Minerva,* reprinted in the *Herald: A Gazette for the Country* (New York), Dec. 17, 1796. The texts of the articles consulted were all in the *Herald.*

[103] No. II, *ibid.,* Dec. 21, 1796.

than armies of foes."[104] In a burst of national selfrighteousness he said in his final essay that "the history of all treaties of alliance will show that France never had an ally that was so useful to her in her wars; that cost so little, assisted her so much, or humbled her foe so effectually."[105]

Upon the administration's deeds hung the issue of war or peace. The nation's loyalties were divided; might not the nation split North and South if the Federalist government went to war with France? One writer in a Charleston paper observed that "from the favorable bias towards the French manifested by the people of the southern states, it appears not improbable, that they will be averse to such a measure [war]; and thus, by opposing the wishes of the northern and great commercial states, hasten that separation which has so often been looked forward to with dread by every American patriot.[106] In New England, too, men spoke of splitting the Union, believing that for New England separation was necessary to prevent corruption by French influence.[107]

With talk of war and dismemberment filling the air, Republicans sought some means of saving the peace, of salvaging the French alliance. Some proposed a special mission comparable to Jay's last-minute effort to save the peace with England; others insisted that such a mission was the only means by which the Franco-American breach could be healed.[108] While he had certain objections to the

[104] No. III, *ibid.*, Dec. 28, 1796.

[105] No. XI, *ibid.*, Feb. 25, 1797.

[106] *City Gazette and Daily Advertiser* (Charleston), Feb. 4, 1797.

[107] This sectional animosity and its effect on foreign policy was a theme long discussed, North and South. New Englanders at the time of the Jay treaty furor had feared that they would be dragged into a war by the South, a war they did not want. See Fisher Ames to ————, Philadelphia, May 6, 1794, in Fisher Ames, *Works of Fisher Ames,* p. 478; see also John Quincy Adams to Charles Adams, The Hague, June 9, 1796, in Ford, *The Writings of John Quincy Adams,* I, 493-494; Dauer, *The Adams Federalists,* p. 102; John Adams to wife, Philadelphia, April 5, 1794, in C. F. Adams, ed., *Letters of John Adams Addressed to His Wife,* II, 151-152.

[108] When the rumor of Pinckney's mission became current the *Aurora,* for example, predicted that Pinckney would not be received. It maintained that only a special envoy or special powers for Pinckney could heal the breach with France. *Aurora,* Jan. 24, 1797, reprinted in the *Kentucky Gazette* (Lexington), March 11, 1797; for a French speculation on a possible new mission, see Jean Marchand, ed., "Une lettre du Duc de Liancourt a Talleyrand (1797)," *Revue d'histoire diplomatique,* XLIII (1929), 469; the letter is dated [Philadelphia], March [4?], 1797.

idea, Hamilton, seeing in it some political benefits, reluctantly supported "an extraordinary mission to France," and suggested a three-man commission. It was, he confessed, "an unavoidable concession to the pressure of public exigency and the state of internal parties."[109] Convinced that French conduct was "outrageous beyond conception," Washington saw no virtue in such a mission. On what basis, he asked, could a special emissary be sent to France when Pinckney already had gone there to explain America's situation and to remove "inquietudes"?[110]

* * * * *

Several weeks later, on February 8, 1797, with war likely, with French hopes for a revived alliance dashed, and with a Federalist victory already known, the electoral votes for President were-counted. By three votes John Adams, who wisely perceived that he was "not enough of an Englishman, nor little enough of a Frenchman for some people," was elected second President of the United States.[111] Federalists continued in control of foreign policy. Jefferson, however, captured the second highest electoral total and became Vice-President.[112] America's first contested presidential election, although a Federalist victory, gave comfort to Republicans and struck some fear into Federalist ranks. But Republican strength had not been quite sufficient to overturn the government and hence to reverse the course of Franco-American relations; to staunch Hamiltonian Federalists this aspect of the election indeed tasted sweet. In various election post-mortems, in New England in particular,

[109] Hamilton to Washington, Jan. 22, 1797, in Lodge, *The Works of Alexander Hamilton*, VIII, 444-446.

[110] Washington to Hamilton, Philadelphia, Jan. 22, 1797, in Fitzpatrick, *Washington's Writings*, XXXV, 373.

[111] John Adams to wife, Dec. 12, 1796, in C. F. Adams, ed., *Letters of John Adams Addressed to His Wife*, II, 208. The electors' ballots had been announced on the first Wednesday in January, but were not counted formally until the first Wednesday in February.

[112] Adet realized before the meeting of electors that Jefferson, "in spite of the intrigues against him," would become Vice-President. Although he rejoiced in Jefferson's election he understood that the Virginian was drawn to France primarily because he feared England. Even Jefferson, declared the French minister, "is an American, and as such, he cannot sincerely be our friend. An American is the born enemy of all the peoples of Europe." Adet to Minister of Foreign Relations, Philadelphia, Dec. 31, 1796, in Turner, *CFM*, pp. 982-983.

such Federalists rejoiced that the "French party is fallen" and that the French alliance was at last valueless. Even Adet, one of them pointed out, "avows, and it is rather a tough point to avow, that our treaty is disadvantageous." Now he may inform the Directory that it has "been deceived by the revolutionary Americans in Paris; that we (at least the Yankees) have not been traitors, and have ceased to be dupes."[113]

Aware of the cleavage in the Federalist hierarchy, particularly as revealed by Hamilton's efforts to maneuver Adams out of the Presidency, the French did not accept Adams' victory as the end of the all-but-dead alliance. Despite their efforts to elect Jefferson, the French could and did take some comfort in Adams's elevation to the Presidency. On the positive side, Adams's victory excluded Hamilton and Washington from immediate control of American foreign policy and so removed the two dominant figures in the government's anti-French, pro-British policy.[114]

Knowledgeable opinion in Paris anticipated that Adams would be disposed more favorably toward France and the alliance than had been Washington and the Hamiltonian Federalists.[115] Interpretations of the election by astute French observers and others in America substantiated such a view. Adams, they pointed out, would

[113] *New Hampshire and Vermont Journal: Or, The Farmer's Weekly Museum* (Walpole, N. H.), March 7, 1797.

[114] The election results "mortified" the French, as John Quincy Adams put it, but they did not end French efforts to influence the United States. John Quincy Adams to John Adams, The Hague, Feb. 3, 1797, in Ford, *The Writings of John Quincy Adams,* II, 104; to Abigail Adams, The Hague, Feb. 8, 1797, *ibid.,* pp. 110-111. Jefferson maintained that John Adams "is perhaps the only sure barrier against Hamilton's getting in." He believed that Adams "is detached from Hamilton, and there is a possibility he may swerve from his politics in a greater or less degree." Jefferson to Madison, Jan. 1, 1797, and to Archibald Stuart, Monticello, Jan. 4, 1797, in Ford, *Writings of Jefferson,* VII, 99, 103.

[115] See "Rapport du bureau central du 30 nivose," 29 nivose, an V (Jan. 18, 1797), in Aulard, *Paris pendant la réaction thermidorienne,* III, 700. The British, however, could take considerably more comfort in the election results. Adams's election, Robert Liston said, "may be considered as favourable to the interests of His Majesty; not because I perceive in Mr. Adams any partiality of sentiment towards Great Britain, but because he detests the principle and dreads the predominance of our enemies, and because the firmness of his character removes all danger of his being *bullied* into measures which he does not approve." To Grenville, Philadelphia, 13, 1797, No. 5, Henry Adams Transcripts.

act independently, he saw advantage in the alliance, and he hated England. He would reverse the anti-French policy of Hamilton and Washington. If Washington's administration had continued, French reasoning went, the inevitable result would have been a final rupture with France. With Adams things were different; undoubtedly he would move to straighten out the foreign-policy mess he had inherited.[116]

Yet the son of the new President expressed opposite views on the future of American foreign policy. The failure of the French in their attacks against Washington and in the election of 1796, he wrote, should reveal to them the "temper" of the American people. "Can France possibly believe," he asked rhetorically, "that Mr. Jefferson, or any other man, would dare to start away from that system which Washington has thus sanctioned, not only by his example, but by his retirement?"[117]

* * * * *

In the few weeks remaining of the Washington era relations with France continued to deteriorate. Several days before Washington left the government, Pickering presented Congress with evidence of French injuries to American commerce. He reported on French attacks against American shipping and atrocities committed against American seamen, and listed American grievances and claims against France since the start of the European war. The documents he submitted revealed that American ships, cargoes, and seamen had suffered and were suffering grievously at the hands of French nationals.[118]

Particularly distressing were the activities of French agents in

[116] Liancourt to Talleyrand, [Philadelphia], March [4?], 1797, in Marchand, "Une lettre du Duc de Liancourt. . . ," RHD, XLII, 468-472; Adet to Minister of Foreign Relations, Philadelphia, Dec. 15, 1796, March 10, 1797, in Turner, CFM, pp. 978-980, 993-994.

[117] John Quincy Adams to Joseph Pitcairn, U. S. Consul in Paris, The Hague, Jan. 31, 1797, in Ford, The Writings of John Quincy Adams, II, 95-96.

[118] Earlier Pickering had complained to Great Britain through Thomas Pinckney (Oct. 22, 1795) of British depredations in the Caribbean. "At Bermuda," he wrote, "the conduct is scandalous"; and the "nest of plunderers," he said, should be broken up. Rufus King Papers, Huntington Library.

the Caribbean, such as Victor Hugues, governor of Guadaloupe.[119] Hugues had issued a number of decrees on his own authority which struck at American shipping. Several of them were directed specifically against American commerce in the Caribbean. In one decree, which he attempted to enforce to the limit of his resources in retaliation against American policy on the sale of contraband goods to the English, he declared that all vessels loaded with contraband articles of any kind regardless of destination were liable to seizure and confiscation. In another decree he declared that all neutral vessels bound to or from British ports would place their cargoes in jeopardy of confiscation. In a third decree he prescribed like treatment of ships bound for any French or Dutch Caribbean islands held by the British. Also subject to confiscation were vessels "which shall have cleared out under the vague denomination of *West Indies.*" This drastic action, Hugues announced, was justified because the United States had not lived up to the 1778 alliance.[120]

The activities of men such as Hugues, as distinguished from those of the French ministers in the United States, were not sanctioned by the French government.[121] Motivated more by desire for personal enrichment than by patriotism, the men who swooped down upon American shipping under the dubious authority of Hugues's

[119] An interesting and favorable sketch of Hugues by an American who had resided in Guadaloupe is in the *New Hampshire and Vermont Journal: Or, The Farmer's Weekly Museum* (Walpole, N. H.), Oct. 6, 1795.

[120] The decree of the French government of the Windward Islands at Aux Cayes in St. Domingue, of Sept. 27, 1796, which violated the principle of free-ships-free-goods is in *ibid.,* Oct. 18, 1796; for details see Pickering's message to Congress of Feb. 28, 1797, plus appended documents in *ASP FR,* I, 748-766; Hugues's decrees of Aug. 1, 1796, and of Feb. 1, 1797, are on pp. 759-760.

[121] Pickering ascribed the activities of French privateers in the Caribbean to Adet. He had learned that Adet "wrote the [French] commissioners that they could not treat the American vessels too badly," Pickering to Charles Cotesworth Pinckney, Philadelphia, Jan. 21, 1797, National Archives, Dept. of State, Diplomatic and Consular Instructions. For interesting gossip as to the connection between Adet and French plunder in the Caribbean, see Captain Samuel Morison to ————, Cap François, Feb. 28, 1797, in Samuel E. Morison, ed., "A Yankee Skipper in San Domingo, 1797," *Massachusetts Historical Society Proceedings, 1915-1916* (Boston, 1916), XLIX, pp. 270-271. See also Isaac McKim, Baltimore merchant to James McHenry, Jan. 25, 1797, and Pickering to McHenry, Feb. 2, 1797, in Steiner, *The Life and Correspondence of James McHenry,* pp. 191-192.

decrees and those of other French agents in the Caribbean who adopted similar tactics were little better than pirates.[122]

"We can account for such conduct," Pickering wrote, "only on the principle of plunder; and were not the privateers acting under the protection of Commissioners from the French Government, they would be pronounced pirates. Britain has furnished no precedents of such abominable rapine." In an obvious observation he concluded that "these proceedings are rapidly rendering the name of frenchmen as detestable as once it was dear to americans and if suffered by their Government to be continued, total alienation will be inevitable."[123]

*   *   *   *   *

To Federalists a source of particular bitterness and a symbol of Francophilism at its worst was Joshua Barney, veteran and hero of the American Revolution. In September, 1794, he had presented the American flag to the National Convention and, like Monroe, he had at that time been contaminated by the "fraternal embrace." Later, this English-hating American sea captain accepted the rank of commodore from the French, and under him privateers roamed the Caribbean flying the tricolor and hunting British ships. In December, 1796, he brought two of his privateers to Norfolk, and from there he went on to Baltimore.[124]

Barney's presence in the United States aroused Federalist scorn; almost immediately he became an issue in the political campaign. The Federalist press accused him of maltreating American and British prisoners captured in the Caribbean and of raiding Amer-

[122] Phillips and Reede, *Neutrality.* . . , II, 81. There were few captures of American ships by the French in European waters; the Caribbean was the hotbed of such activity. Pickering recognized that the indiscriminate plundering of American ships might be the result of arbitrary orders of French colonial administrators. Pickering to Rufus King, Philadelphia, Jan. 17, 1797, Rufus King Papers, Huntington Library.

[123] Pickering to Charles Cotesworth Pinckney, Philadelphia, Feb. 11, 1797, National Archives, Dept. of State, Diplomatic and Consular Instructions. Pickering believed that the French depredations in the Caribbean would not cease until the home government took a hand, if then. Pickering to John Quincy Adams, Dept. of State, Jan. 17, 1797, Pickering Papers, Mass. Hist. Soc., Boston.

[124] For an account of Barney's career at this time see Hurlbert Footner, *Sailor of Fortune: The Life and Adventures of Commodore Barney, U. S. N.* (New York, 1940), pp. 193-225.

ican commerce. Even worse, a Federalist paper condemned him for desecrating the American flag. By design, it said, he had suffered the flag to be "ignominiously reversed on board the French frigate Medusa." These allegations, later shown to be little more than rumor, made good campaign propaganda. A defender of Barney maintained that the "many lies" were circulated by the British party in an attempt to injure him, and through him, relations with France. Refuting the flag accusation, "A Friend of Truth" pointed out that the flag had been profaned by mere accident, and that once Barney heard of it, he had immediately rectified the situation.[125]

Barney's conduct in the United States alarmed the Federalists. Americans wined and dined him, and Republicans greeted him as a hero fighting in the cause of liberty. Lacking prudence, he boasted, apparently, that he had orders from the Directory to capture American shipping. With such pronouncements, as had Adet in his electioneering, he coupled the threat of war, declaring that if Jefferson were not chosen President France would declare war within three months. His words and the Republican response appalled Federalists. They condemned "the wise-acres of Baltimore for complimenting Barney, an avowed agent of the Directory."[126] "Ours," one of them said bitterly, "is the only country where such insults would be tolerated from a native citizen."[127]

* * * * *

While American politics frothed, two days before Washington was to turn over the government to John Adams, another blow, the

[125] *City Gazette and Daily Advertiser* (Charleston), Feb. 1, 4, 1797; Hildreth, *The History of the United States.* . . , IV, 703-704

[126] For an attack on Barney as well as a defense of the Baltimore citizens, see the *Federal Gazette and Baltimore Daily Advertiser,* Jan. 7, 1797.

[127] Chauncey Goodrich to Wolcott, Sr., Philadelphia, Jan. 9, 1797, in Gibbs, ed., *Wolcott Papers,* I, 417. In New England, Federalist scorn was also summarized in these words: "Is there any country, where even the base, the cowards, and the hirelings presume to publish their traitorous preferences of a hostile cause to its own? Is there any other country, which would allow itself to be insulted by the emigrant BARNEY with the publick newspaper threat of levying war, in our very harbours and bays? Is there any where else a nest of miscreants who would feast such a man? In France, that land of equal liberty, Barney would have been guillotined, in half an hour." *New Hampshire and Vermont Journal: Or, The Farmer's Weekly Museum* (Walpole, N. H.), March 7, 1797.

full impact of which would not be felt until Adams had taken office, was struck in Paris at the dying alliance of 1778. As Adet had recommended almost a year earlier, the Directory on March 2, 1797, published a decree abandoning the free-ships-free-goods principle.[128] With the decree the Directory retaliated for the Jay treaty, punished the Federalist government, and tried to force American foreign policy to conform to French policy. The decree violated the commercial treaty. The French rationalized their action by saying they were merely "reconciling" the commercial treaty with the later Jay treaty. The free-ships-free-goods clause no longer applied, they pointed out, not because of their unilateral action, but as the result of the Jay treaty provision which first modified it.

According to the French interpretation, the second article of the commercial treaty bound the United States to grant no favor to other nations which should not accrue immediately to France also. Yet by the Jay treaty, the Directory pointed out, the United States had allowed the English to seize French goods on neutral American ships without allowing France the same privileges in respect to English goods carried in American bottoms. With British seapower dominant, the reciprocal privilege would have done the French little actual good. The Directory nonetheless insisted that the 1778 treaty had been modified and violated by the Jay treaty to the disadvantage of France.

After placing the burden of treaty violation upon the United States, the Directory declared that henceforth, in accord with article 17 of the Jay treaty, enemy goods on neutral ships were subject to seizure and confiscation, that, in accord with article 18 of the treaty, the contraband list of the 1778 commercial treaty was enlarged, and that, in accord with article 21 of the treaty, every American serving under an enemy flag, "without being allowed in any case to allege that he was forced to it by violence, menaces, or otherwise," shall be treated as a pirate. In conformity with articles 25 and 27 of the 1778 commercial treaty, moreover, American ships which did not

---

[128] The text of the decree is in *ASP FR*, II, 30-31. Compare Adet's proposals in his despatch to Minister of Foreign Relations, Philadelphia, May 3, 1796, in Turner, *CFM*, pp. 900-906. John Quincy Adams said the objectives of the decree were to plunder American commerce, to attack Anglo-American trade, and to throw the odium for such depredations upon the American government and the Jay treaty. To John Adams, The Hague, March 30, 1797, in Ford, *The Writings of John Quincy Adams*, II, 149.

"have on board a list of the crew [*rôle d'equipage*] in proper form" were declared lawful prize.

Even though the *rôle d'equipage* was called for in the 1778 treaty, and France technically was within her treaty rights in demanding that American ships carry one, by the demand she violated the spirit of the treaty of amity and commerce and of the alliance. In one sense, strict application of the decree was equivalent to a declaration of maritime war against American commerce. American vessels normally did not carry such papers, and the French knew it; never before had France sought to enforce this treaty stipulation.[129] By insisting on technicalities, the Directory, as Adet had recommended, gave the Federalist government a taste of its own medicine. Labeling the decree a "cool and informal act of barbarous vengeance," one Federalist editor said "the man who attempts to justify it merits the reward of traitor."[130] In consummating the Jay treaty the Washington government had not violated the letter of the alliance, only its spirit. Neither country had, in its own view, violated the 1778 treaties, but in a real sense both had done so. With war in the offing, it was foolish to speak of an alliance binding two enemies, an alliance which each now ignored, and which the men in control of American government despised.

* * * * *

As Washington left office, no doubt he could look back with justifiable pride on the many accomplishments of his administration. He had launched a nation; he had set in motion a noble experiment in the government of men which given God's grace was to endure. To few men has there fallen opportunity for such an accomplishment. Yet he could not help realizing that his ideal of a unified nation without political parties and free of European political attachments had been shattered. Politically, the country was deeply divided; its foreign relations were such that it was on the verge of war with its wartime ally.[131] While unjust in their implications,

---

[129] James Brown Scott, ed., *The Controversy over Neutral Rights between the United States and France, 1797-1800* (New York, 1917), p. 15; E. Wilson Lyon, "The Directory and the United States," *AHR* (April, 1938), XLIII, 517-518.

[130] Noah Webster, quoted in Warfel, *Noah Webster*, p. 230. The Directory's decree gave certain Federalists the needed excuse to urge war.

[131] "Americus," writing in the *Gazette of the United States*, observed that

Benjamin Bache's words on Washington's departure had a ring of truth, and undoubtedly they were painful to the first ex-president. Washington's legacy to John Adams in foreign policy was a ship of state caught between "rocks and shoals," an administration that had started with France as a friend and had ended with her as an enemy. The official bond between the two nations, the alliance of 1778 which had been drawn to last "forever" and which had been the cornerstone of American foreign policy at the beginning of Washington's administration, was practically dead.

"already in certain circles is heard the debasing doctrine, that *France* is determined to reduce us to the alternative of war with her enemies or war with herself, and that it is our interest and safety to elect the former." Reprinted in the *Columbian Centinel* (Boston), March 18, 1797. "A True Hearted American" blamed all the difficulties on "the influence created by a party here, in favor of France, a pestilent influence which ought to be hunted out of the country." He warned that the "political connection with France *is bad*" and might be ruinous. *New Hampshire and Vermont Journal: Or, The Farmer's Weekly Museum* (Walpole, N. H.), March 21, 1797. See also Oliver Wolcott, Jr., to George Cabot, Philadelphia, March 27, 1797, in Lodge, *Life and Letters of George Cabot*, p. 118. Wolcott, a few weeks after Washington left office, predicted a continuing crisis and urged preparations for war with France.

CHAPTER FIFTEEN

EPILOGUE

THE SIGNIFICANCE OF THE WASHINGTON
YEARS IN AMERICAN DIPLOMACY

Our remote situation from other nations promises long peace; they will not be fond of contending with an empire so fast increasing, so firmly established, and having such powerful resources at command. The causes which create war among European powers, do not here exist; and we have nothing to fear to disturb the public tranquility unless it be the petty depredations of the Indians on our frontiers, which a small exertion of the military power will entirely quell.—"Observations on the Prospects of America," *National Gazette* (Philadelphia), November 3, 1791.

Proud with reason of having thrown off the oppressive yoke of England, the United States were too ready to play a part among the nations of Europe; and to involve themselves in the interests of foreign powers, from which nature had most happily separated them.—La Rochefoucauld-Liancourt, *Travels Through the United States.*

* * * * *

IN THE opening pages we asked: What, in eight years of the Washington administrations, destroyed the French alliance?[1] In seeking answers, in searching out causes and motives, we exploited the theme of the interaction of domestic politics and foreign policy, stressing significant implications. Yet there remains another ques-

[1] A few months after Washington had left office, the French, in taking stock of the defunct alliance of 1778 and the low state of American relations, asked the same question. What, in eight years, had alienated their principle ally? What were the remedies? Louis-Guillaume Otto, "Considerations sur la Conduite du gouvernement des États unis envers la France, depuis 1789 jusqu'en 1797," [Paris, June 17, 1797], AAE CP EU, Vol. XLVII, ff. 401-418.

tion which, while suggested in the foregoing pages, should be examined in the broader context of American history. What significance do the crucial Washington years have in American political and diplomatic history?

If these pages shed any light on the question, they show that the traditional picture of the beginnings of our national history which has heretofore been painted in bold strokes remains firm in the main outline but that some major details should be modified. These first years under the federal government have been depicted as "our Golden Age," as "the classic age of American statecraft," an era which produced men of "heroic stature," particularly among the statesmen who molded foreign policy.[2] While the founding fathers were undeniably men of rare ability, above the average of succeeding generations of politicians, they do not emerge in this study "men of talents and genius on a scale perhaps unexampled in the history of the world."[3] Instead, like all men, they appear mortal, with human strengths and weaknesses, with petty faults, at times with heroic virtues.

The statesmen of the Washington era, to some extent, played their politics and diplomacy by ear. They were marked too often in their attitudes by selfish, irrational behavior; too often they placed political advantage above national welfare. Jefferson, and, to a greater degree, Hamilton, in their political pursuits and in their connivance with agents of foreign powers committed acts which in the mid-twentieth century would appear treasonable.

While recognizing that the Washington administrations were distinguished at times by remarkable foresight and brilliant statesmanship, we should not overlook the political opportunism and partisan strife over foreign policy of the time, seldom if ever equaled in our history. Statesmen of our generation are often compared to the founding fathers of the Washington years as pygmies to

[2] The quotations are from Becker, "What Is Still Living in the Political Philosophy of Thomas Jefferson," *American Historical Review*, XLVIII, 692, and Hans J. Morgenthau, *In Defense of the National Interest: A Critical Examination of American Foreign Policy* (New York, 1951), p. 3.

[3] The quotation is from Schachner, *The Founding Fathers*, p. vii. For a pro-Jefferson interpretation of the foreign policy of the period which challenges the traditional interpretations, see Albert H. Bowman, "Jefferson, Hamilton, and American Foreign Policy," *Political Science Quarterly*, LXXXI (March, 1956), 18-41.

giants. Such comparisons are unfair and unjust; recent statesmen in their own context have blundered as badly, but have at times performed just as brilliantly.[4]

Being men, the founding fathers were not infallible. Yet succeeding generations of Americans have, in worship of the past and in seeking guidance for their own pressing problems, glorified them and have accepted them as infallible guides in foreign policy. To assume that Washington's Farewell Address, basically a statement of the partisan political philosophy of Alexander Hamilton, established long-enduring principles to guide the nation in foreign policy for generations to come is to endow Washington with powers reserved for the gods of Olympus. It is to assume that the United States for over a century and a half was capable of pursuing a foreign policy of its own choosing, free from the caprices of party and the foibles of other more powerful nations. Actually, in the 1790's the United States was relatively so insignificant in the scale of international power that in any struggle in which the major maritime powers took a real interest it could be little more than a pawn. In relations with the great powers Federalist statesmen were fortunate; they were able to use the opportunities that fell their way. The nation was then led by men who showed real ability in capitalizing on the misfortunes of Europe.

Chance, then as now, played a vital role in the course of our foreign policy. Even though England had most of the advantages in the Washington years, relations with France and England might have gone either way. A stroke of fortune, aided by the vital tie of blood, of culture, and of similar institutions, perhaps more than anything else, thrust us on England's side to the abandonment of the French alliance. Without the support and prestige of Washington and under a more democratic electorate, might not Americans have overthrown the Hamiltonian system and cast America's

[4] George F. Kennan, an astute interpreter of recent foreign policy, for example, has remarked that "early American statesmen had a better idea than our generation has—a clearer idea, at any rate—of what they were trying to do in the conduct of governmental affairs generally." *Realities of American Foreign Policy* (Princeton, 1954), pp. 3-4. See also Morgenthau, *In Defense of the National Interest*, p. 3. Morgenthau maintained that the United States "owed its existence and survival as an independent nation to those extraordinary qualities of political insight, historical perspective, and common sense which the first generation of Americans applied to the affairs of state."

lot with the French alliance and Republican France?[5] As it was, Federalists and Republicans in their struggle over foreign policy were motivated by self-interest. Each party was convinced that its program, its foreign policy, was in the national interest. The founding fathers were divided on almost every important issue, on the basic philosophies of politics and foreign policy. Who could say, in the context of the times, which side was wrong?

* * * * *

Many students of American foreign policy accept the view that under the American democratic system the orientation and conduct of foreign policy reflects domestic political patterns. To succeed, they say, foreign policy must have the support of the Executive, of the Congress, and of the public. In the Washington years foreign policy conformed to no such criterion. In this period, in relation to the French alliance, we have an example of foreign policy being con-ducted despite a hostile public opinion until that opinion changed or partially changed. Washington's foreign policy in relation to Great Britain and France was a partisan foreign policy, a foreign policy of one political party, perhaps a minority party.

In assuming that foreign policy reflected the public sentiment of the time, men have often interpreted the Washington era as spawn-ing principles of isolationism. Yet the period was far from isola-tionist. While it was true that many, regardless of party, nourished the illusion that the United States could isolate and immunize itself from the politics of Europe, other Americans took the opposite view. They tried to thrust the United States into European affairs. Bas-ically, American attitudes toward Europe and toward isolation were, as they have always been, mixed. Some men believed that "the causes which create war among European powers, do not here exist," while others "were too ready to play a part among the na-tions of Europe; and to involve themselves in the interests of foreign powers, from which nature had most happily separated them."[6]

[5] Timothy Pickering, although a staunch and unyielding Federalist, bore testimony to how chance might well have fallen the other way under Wash-ington. He maintained that had Hamilton not succeeded, Jefferson would have been the dominant influence in the Washington government; his pro-French foreign policy therefore would have prevailed. Charles, "Hamilton and Washington. . . ," *William and Mary Quarterly,* 3rd Series, XII, 265.
[6] The quotations are from "Observations on the Prospects of America"

To quote selected passages from the founding fathers giving voice to hopes and unrealized sentiments without analyzing the actions of the same men, which often were in direct opposition to their isolationist phrases, gives an inaccurate picture of these men and their time. Which best reflects a man's attitudes, his words written to influence other men, or his deeds committed to realize definite objectives?

Although the era of Washington did not in practice set the precedent for a foreign policy of isolationism, there is no denying that it was an age of precedent making in politics and foreign policy. It was not, however, an era in which precedents were established with majority agreement and approval; Washington (even though he may have thought he did) never had a nonpartisan foreign policy. The precedents he left in foreign policy and politics are not clear-cut, having evolved often from political expediency or *ad hoc* diplomatic expediency rather than from exalted principle. As in most periods of stress and storm and as a result of their practical origins, the precedents are mixed and contradictory. What has come to be accepted as binding precedent has gained acceptance because of the authority of time and of the reverence which has blanketed the figure of Washington and also the sacred group denominated founding fathers.

The principle of avoidance of entangling alliances, like most else in Washington's administration, was based on partisan politics, the child of Hamilton's fecund brain. Since the Hamiltonians were anti-French, in their view the French alliance was entangling. Ironically, they saw no evil in close connections with Great Britain; under the circumstances, in Federalist eyes there could be no "entanglement," with its evil connotations, with Great Britain. If cooperation with Great Britain was just and proper, the French alliance alone, as has been maintained, could not have shown by example the danger of entanglement in European international politics.[7]

in the *National Gazette* (Philadelphia), Nov. 3, 1791, and La Rochefoucauld-Liancourt, *Travels. . .* , II, 546.

[7] See Samuel F. Bemis, "The Background of Washington's Foreign Policy," *Yale Review*, XVI (Jan., 1927), 318. The epitome of Washington's foreign policy, according to popular understanding, was the principle of avoiding "entangling alliances." See Henry M. Wriston, "Washington and the Foundations of American Foreign Policy," *Minnesota History: A Quarterly Magazine*, VIII (March, 1927), 26.

Fears of French entanglement reflected Federalist rationalization, universalized for political consumption.

Whether or not it be entangling has little to do with the real value of an alliance. By definition, an alliance entangles. To have value to both parties, to survive stresses and strains, an alliance should be based on mutual interests; paper bonds alone do not tie effectively. If an alliance is to prove reliable, both parties should continue to fear the contingency or party against whom the alliance was originally directed. There must be, moreover, reasonable hope or assurance that together the allies are capable of meeting the contingency with success. Above all, the alliance should serve the interests of both parties.

After the peace of 1783 the French alliance met none of these conditions. With the exception of the brief war scare of 1793-94 which preceded the Jay treaty, the strength of American animosity toward Great Britain (notably on the part of the Washington administration) was not sufficient to demonstrate the mutual interests of France and the United States under the alliance. The alliance, in fact, became a major source of Franco-American friction. As has often been the case, the stronger party in an alliance usually incites suspicion and jealousy in the weaker country, particularly if the government of the weaker country is antagonistic to it and believes that the alliance entails acceptance of domination by the stronger power. In the Washington period this fear of the French connection was present from the beginning; but more important, Federalists exploited it for political purposes in support of the Hamiltonian system.

Since French statesmen wished to manipulate their ally, they spoke often of gratitude being the binding cement of the alliance. Yet they recognized that mutual benefits gave real adhesion; they understood the partisan source of American opposition to the alliance. Reflecting eighteenth-century concepts, they believed that an alliance cannot be permanent except among natural allies. The Franco-American alliance, they maintained before consummation of the Jay treaty, was natural because of the position of the two countries; it could do neither country harm. Realizing that the proper measure of an alliance is the importance of its advantages to either party, they came to recognize that to Americans, notably to the

Federalists, the alliance had lost its advantages; that Americans under the alliance would defend their own interests, but that they
would not make war to succor an ally, particularly one distrusted
by the powerful political and financial elements in the community.

When a people take such a stand, the French concluded, it is useless to cultivate their friendship as an ally in time of war. This was
one reason why the French never implemented the alliance.[8]   In
spite of these obstacles, certain French officials believed up to the
end of the Washington years that the alliance would triumph in
the United States because it had the support of the masses who
they believed were still pro-French.

*   *   *   *   *

Within the sweep of history, the quarrel with France and the
party bitterness in the Washington years had in them the same elements found in similar situations in later years. Undoubtedly, as
some have seen it, the conflict with France had in it elements of
friction between rival nationalisms.[9]   Yet Federalists and Republicans successfully suppressed their national feelings—if they had any
independently of their politics—when dealing with the foreign
power they preferred. The political struggle over foreign policy
had in it elements which later became important factors in our
political history: sectionalism, antiforeignism, appeal to the past,
and defense of the *status quo* by those in power.

Particularly in the Northeast, stronghold of Federalism, sectionalism and nativism had strong roots. Praising the wisdom of New
England's intolerance of foreigners and deprecating the mongrelism
of Pennsylvania, which received foreigners with open arms, "asking
no questions who, or what they were," one New England Federalist
pointed out that seven-eighths of the Whiskey rebels and over half
the malcontents who opposed Washington were foreigners. "A very
great proportion" of Washington's slanderers and opponents of the
Jay treaty were newcomers. "If our government," he warned,
"should be shaken to the center and broken to pieces by the power

[8] "The Alliance between France and the United States," Létombe to
Commission of Foreign Relations, [1794], AAE CP EU, Vol. XLI, ff. 241-
247.
[9] See, for example, Frances S. Childs, "A Secret Agent's Advice on America, 1797," in *Nationalism and Internationalism,* ed. Edward Mead Earle
(New York, 1950), p. 22.

of faction, it will receive its death blow from the hands of southern strangers. The multitudes, whom every ship brings over, foaming with rage, and half mad with the spirit of fanaticism, call the restraints of law the chains of despotism."

There was no such foreign opposition to good Federalist government in New England; it had no Whiskey rebels or turbulent frontiersmen as had Tennessee and Kentucky. The people of New England, he said, "are fitted for government by long and tranquil experience, and disposed by character and education to respect and to aid, instead of opposing the persons, who are called by themselves to administer the government." As to foreign policy, "if foreigners had been excluded from Congress, the [Jay] Treaty clamour would have been far less formidable, than it was. The danger of disorganizing and rushing into revolutionary confusion arises from the same quarter—Take away strangers, and our *native* mobocrats would be few, and might be kept within some bound of safety, if not reason." Then he identified Federalism with Americanism, and Republicanism with foreign anarchy. "The Demogogues tell you that they speak the voice of the people; it is the voice of these noisy factions and turbulent foreigners they speak, and not that of the true American people."

Coupling antiforeignism with sectionalism, he clinched his case for the administration. "Take away the Representatives for the southern Negroes," he said, "which amount to ten or eleven, the anti treaty majority in the House of Representatives of Congress, and probably every anti government majority shrinks instantly into a minority—But when to these you add the *Foreigner Representatives* the minority is still more diminished and the sense of our nation, if these were excluded, would appear to be, as it really is, for supporting our government, the President, and the leading measures of his administration."[10]

Rational though such a theory might have appeared to confirmed New England Federalists, it did not comport with the facts. From the beginning, Washington's foreign policy was a partisan policy in keeping with the Hamiltonian system; in sum, it was Hamilton's foreign policy. No important foreign policy decision

[10] *New Hampshire and Vermont Journal: Or, The Farmer's Weekly Museum* (Walpole, N. H.), March 7, 1797.

was made without Hamilton having a part in it. Almost all the important ideas, almost all the significant measures under Washington originated with Hamilton. The Hamilton "engine of government" was all pervasive, touching all aspects of administration and policy. But Washington was essential to the system. Without his unquestioning support, without the backing of his awesome prestige and opposition-smothering popularity, it could never have been carried into effect. Washington the popular hero was far more potent politically than his party or the all-encompassing ideas of Hamilton.

Used as a tool by Hamiltonians and convinced that opposition to Federalism was personal opposition and "faction," Washington in his last years became intensely partisan without knowing it. As Jefferson remarked just before the General retired, "his mind has so long been used to unlimited applause that it could not brook contradiction, or even advice offered unasked." Under the circumstances and in view of Hamilton's *de facto* dominance in the government, Jefferson "long thought therefore it was best for the republican interest to soothe him [Washington] by flattering where they could approve of his measures, & be silent where they disapprove. . . in short to lie on their oars while he remains at the helm, and let the bark of state drift as his will and a superintending providence shall direct."[11]

Since it has long been known that Hamilton, perhaps aided by "a superintending providence," guided the helm of the bark of state during most of the Washington era, it is difficult to account for the efforts of posterity equipped with critical methodology to conjure Washington into a statesman of far-seeing vision and ability. Much easier to understand, but perhaps just as difficult to explain, is the veneration he won from his own people as a statesman.[12]

---

[11] Jefferson to Archibald Stuart, Monticello, Jan. 4, 1797, in Ford, *Writings of Jefferson*, VII, 101-102. John Adams, apparently, never forgot that Hamilton in implementing his system had made a "tool" of Washington. Adams to Benjamin Waterhouse, Quincy, July 12, 1811, in Worthington C. Ford, ed., *Statesman and Friend: Correspondence of John Adams with Benjamin Waterhouse, 1784-1822* (Boston, 1927), p. 65. Within the Federalist party, moreover, Hamilton possessed a greater influence "than the President himself." William H. Trescot, *The Diplomatic History of the Administrations of Washington and Adams, 1789-1801* (Boston, 1857), p. 181.

[12] Even foreigners spoke of Washington in superlatives. See Nathan

Far from being a statesman of wide grasp, Washington lacked the broad intellectual qualities capable of constructing the all-embracing Hamiltonian program with its sweeping domestic and foreign policy objectives. Slow of mind, he took his ideas and theories, without much question, from Hamilton. Grounded though it was in the broad principles of Hamilton's system, Washington's foreign policy in implementation was *ad hoc* and often governed by political expediency; each policy, while conforming to the over-all philosophy of Alexander Hamilton, was a specific response to a specific situation.

Given the politics, the Hamiltonian theory, and the context of the Washington era, we can see that it was not a period when government on the basis of lofty principle sought to follow a policy of isolation and nonentanglement. It was, instead, a period wherein one party took control of the new national government, supported by men of wealth and position, and successfully attempted to change the foreign policy orientation of the nation. At the end of eight years the government had reversed the basic foreign policy alignment of the nation so that a former enemy was an ally and an ally-in-name was in a state of open hostility, almost of undeclared war. Under the circumstances, the French alliance was doomed from the beginning of the new national government, because of its capture by Washington and Hamilton.

This era of Washington was a crucial time, and Hamiltonians knew it; they knew that in implementing Hamilton's system what they did would form precedents for the future. In giving Hamilton dominance in his government, in accepting the Hamiltonian system as the philosophical foundation of his government, Washington had made his government incompatible with the French alliance. By so doing, from the viewpoint of American responsibility, he planted the seeds of war with France; the roots of the Quasi-War (1797-1800) with France gained nourishment in the Washington administrations.

Great though Washington's accomplishments as a soldier had been, as President in his declining years he is not seen at his best.[13]

Marchant to Mrs. Henrietta Liston, [Edinburgh?], Jan. 11, 1797, Liston Papers, National Library of Scotland (microfilm copy).

[13] Charles, "Hamilton and Washington. . . ," *WMQ*, 3rd Series, XII, 260; for a generous appraisal of Washington by Jefferson in later years when, re-

Not able to comprehend the political implications of his office, looking upon opposition to his measures as disloyalty, he seems at times a bewildered figure, overshadowed by politicians and manipulated by Hamiltonians to their own political advantage. In the words of Thomas Jefferson, he was "fortunate to get off just as the bubble is bursting, leaving others to hold the bag."[14] Washington left to his successor the legacy of the entangling alliance of 1778, which in its death throes brought on the undeclared war with France, an entanglement in its implications more dangerous than the alliance.

moved from the heat of political strife, Washington's virtues as a statesman and a man might be highlighted without obscuring his faults, see Jefferson to Dr. Walter Jones, Monticello, Jan. 2, 1814, in Ford, *Writings of Jefferson*, IX, 447-450.

[14] Jefferson to Madison, Jan. 8, 1797, *ibid.*, VII, 104.

INDEX

Adams, Charles F., ed.: *Letters of John Adams to His Wife,* cited, 98 n.; *Letters of Mrs. Adams,* cited, 479 n.; *Memoirs of John Quincy Adams,* cited, 197 n.; *Works of John Adams,* cited, 6 n.

Adams, Henry, *Life of Albert Gallatin,* cited, 65 n.

Adams, Herbert B., *Life and Writings of Jared Sparks,* cited, 305 n.

Adams, James Truslow, "Jefferson and Hamilton Today," cited, 54 n.

Adams, John: appointed minister to Great Britain, 67; appraised by Adet, 472; attacks French Revolution, 174-175; and commercial treaty with France, 6-7; *Defence of the Constitutions,* cited, 174 n.; diplomatic skill, 11; elected President, 3, 492; and election of 1796, 471-472; and European entanglements, 5-6; French reaction to election of, 493-494; and Genet's influence, 306; and nonintercourse bill of May, 1794, 97; and Nootka Sound Crisis, 70 n.; and peace of 1783, 10; quoted, 342; quoted on Anglo-French rivalry, 13-14; re-elected Vice President, 61

Adams, John Quincy: attacks Genet, 291; attacks Thomas Paine, 176; on French alliance, 370; on Jay treaty, 136, 412-413; quoted, 423

Adams, John Stokes, ed., *Autobiographical Sketch by John Marshall,* cited, 132 n.

Adet, Pierre Auguste: adverse effect on 1796 election, 476; appraisal of his mission, 455; appraisal of Washington's Farewell, 471; biographical sketch, 424; and British violations of U. S. neutrality, 434-435; and domestic politics, 456; end of correspondence with Washington government, 442; estimate of Jefferson, 492 n.; and French flag episode, 435-436; instructions of, 425; and Jay treaty, 425-428; manifestoes, 439-441, 473-475; notes of, 365; opposes complete rupture with U. S., 486; opposes John Adams in 1796, 472; proposes retaliation against U. S., 430-431; recalled, 379; surprised by Monroe's recall, 387; trip to New England, 472

Agar, Herbert, *Price of Union,* cited, 48 n.

Albany Argus, cited, 296 n.

Albion, Robert G., *Forests and Sea Power,* cited, 205 n.

Albion, Robert G. and Jennie B. Pope, *Sea Lanes in Wartime,* cited, 92 n.

Alexandria Gazette, cited, 115 n.

Allen, Gardner W., *Our Naval War with France,* cited, 207 n.

Alliance, concept of in transition, 7

Amacher, Richard E., *Franklin's Wit & Folly,* cited, 28

Ambler, Charles H., *Sectionalism in Virginia,* cited, 239 n.

American Daily Advertiser (Philadelphia), cited, 114 n.

American Minerva (New York), cited, 257 n.

American Revolution and Franco-American friendship, 5, 30

American State Papers, Foreign Rela-

82; and John Quincy Adams, 370; and Louisiana, 410; main bulwark of, 308; meaningless, 499; no defenders in Washington's government, 63; and Northwest posts, 13; not invoked by Genet, 202; opposition to, 150-151; pleases Washington, 7; and possibility of war, 489-490; and proclamation of neutrality, 90, 227-231; proposal to revise, 162; and protective tariff, 73-74; and Robespierre, 395; source of Franco-American friction, 506; spirit violated in 1783, 9; status of, 191-195; supported by Jefferson, 51; Talleyrand's view of, 445; target of Farewell Address, 465, 467; touched off a world war, 8; and U. S. obligations, 419; value to France, 170; and Washington's policy, 510-511

French benevolent and patriotic societies, and democratic societies, 254

French Revolution: American reaction to, 173-174; and American Revolution, 176-178; attacked by John Adams, 174-175; Federalist opposition to, 181; and Franco-American commerce, 145, 154; and Franco-American relations, 30; Gouverneur Morris's antipathy toward, 314; impact on U. S., 85-86; influence on Jefferson, 55, 55 n.-56 n.; and Jefferson, 29; problems from wars of, 32; reports of Gouverneur Morris on, 331-334; and Saint Domingue, 172

French ships, and American neutrality, 431-434

Freneau, Philip, founds *National Gazette,* 58-59

Frontiersmen, U. S., and France, 239

Fulton, Samuel, and French in the West, 447

Funding plan, Hamilton's, 40

Galbaud, Thomas Francis: governor-general of Saint Domingue, 272; and Genet, 278-280

Gallatin, Albert: attacks Hamilton's system, 460-461; leads attacks on

Hamilton's financial policies, 64-65; quoted, 275

Gardoqui, Diego de: and Monroe, 356; negotiations with Jay, 243-244

Gazette and Daily Advertiser (Charleston, S. C.), cited, 443 n.

Gazette Nationale ou Moniteur Universel, cited, 360 n.

Gazette of the United States (Philadelphia): cited, 58 n.; founded, 59

Genet, Edmond C.: abandoned by Jefferson and Madison, 289; alarms Washington, 89; and American merchants, 281; appeal to Congress, 302-303; appeal to the people, 218, 261, 285-289; appraisal of, 284, 306-310; arrives in U. S., 173; biographical sketch, 183-185; blundered in *Little Sarah* affair, 222; and Canada, 247-248; and commercial treaty of 1778, 210; and debt payment, 212; demands prosecution of Jay and King, 292-294; and democratic societies, 252-253; desperate need for money, 250, 280; did not invoke French alliance, 197; Federalist efforts to destroy, 260; and French fleet, 275-276; and French refugees, 277, 281-282; and Gouverneur Morris, 336-338; and Henfield case, 214-216; injures French alliance, 290, 297, 308, 309; instructions of, 198-200; and Jay-King certificate, 287-289; landing at Charleston, 200; and mutinous sailors, 278-279; and new commercial treaty, 162; origins of his mission, 182-183; Papers, Library of Congress, cited, 142 n.; and political parties, 283-284; protests British violations of neutrality, 232; publication of correspondence, 302-303; reaction to his recall, 300-301; recall, 298-299, 304; shocked by neutrality proclamation, 202; struggle with Federalist government, 211, 213; and tonnage duties, 282-283; and Western plots, 235-236

Genet, George Clinton, *Washington,*

15; quoted on Louisiana, 25-26; signs consular convention, 22

Vermont, secessionist sentiment in, 67

Vessels, act for the registering and clearing of, 40

Virginia Gazette and General Advertiser (Richmond), cited, 230 n.

Virginia Herald and Fredericksburg Advertiser, cited, 94 n.

Vossler, Otto, *Die amerikanischen Revolutionsideale in ihrem verhältnis zu den europäischen,* cited, 29 n.

Walters, Raymond, Jr., *Alexander James Dallas,* cited, 45 n.

Walther, Daniel, *Gouverneur Morris,* cited, 305 n.

War: alternative to Jay treaty, 138; Anglo-French and influence on U. S., 86-87, 180, 186; crisis of 1794 with Great Britain, 94, 98-99; crisis with Spain, 241-247; Federalist talk of, 486, 488-491; possibilities with France, 140, 428-429; talk of in Directory, 380; threat of between U. S. and Great Britain, 85

Ward, Adolphus W., and G. P. Gooch, eds., *Cambridge History of British Foreign Policy,* cited, 153 n.

Warfel, Harry R.: (ed.) *Letters of Noah Webster,* cited, 86 n.; *Noah Webster,* cited, 181 n.

Warren, Charles: *Jacobin and Junto,* cited, 118 n.; *Supreme Court in United States History,* cited, 129 n.

Washington administration: and Adet's first manifesto, 439-441; loses nonpartisanism, 62; modified interpretation of, 502-503

Washington, George: Adet's reaction to, 426; alarmed by French seizures of American ships, 488; alarmed by reaction to proclamation of neutrality, 89; appraisal of his foreign policy, 510-511; approves of Gouverneur Morris's mission, 340; approves Hamilton's policies, 48; attacked for signing Jay treaty, 118; and Bank of the United States, 44; circular on French war to Cabinet,

186-187; cool to Genet, 202; decides French treaties are binding, 195-196; decision to retire, 464; disapproves of Monroe's conduct, 351; favored improved commercial relations with France, 145; Farewell Address of analyzed, 465-471; and French flag, 435-436; and French ultimatum, 373; friend of Gouverneur Morris, 316; greatest political crisis, 111; Hamilton's tool, 509; hastened death of democratic societies, 266; headed a partisan foreign policy, 504; impressed by Fauchet, 398; and Jay-King certificate episode, 295; launches new government, 33; leaves Presidency, 3, 65; messages to Congress on Franco-American crisis, 480-481, 482; modified interpretation of his Presidency, 502-503; and Monroe's recall, 383-384; and Morris's reports on French Revolution, 332; and neutrality regulations, 224-226; and Nootka Sound Crisis, 69; planned retirement after one term, 60; pleads for peace within administration, 59; pleased with French alliance, 7; political ideal, failure of, 4, 499-500; and political parties, 34-35; political target in 1796, 459-460; prevents Genet's arrest, 305; quoted on Franco-American relations, 17; reasons for retiring, 462-463; retirement of, 443; revokes Duplaine's exequatur, 291; sees political parties grow, 461-462; signs revised consular convention, 24; and special mission to France, 492; used by Federalists against democratic societies, 261-264; and Western intrigue, 453

Washington, Henry A., ed., *Writings of Thomas Jefferson,* cited, 29 n.

Wayne, Anthony: and Battle of Fallen Timbers, 110; commander of frontier forces, 85

Webster, Noah: attacks French alliance, 490; on French interference

I

DI